Que's 1995 CD-ROM Buyer's Guide

David D. Busch

que

Que's 1995 CD-ROM Buyer's Guide

ISBN: 1-56529-883-7

97 96 95 94   6 5 4 3 2 1

Interpretation of the printing code: the rightmost double-digit number is the year of the book's printing; the rightmost single-digit number, the number of the book's printing. For example, a printing code of 94-1 shows that the first printing of the book occurred in 1994.

Publisher: David P. Ewing

Associate Publisher: Corinne Walls

Publishing Director: Brad R. Koch

Managing Editor: Anne Owen

Product Marketing Manager: Greg Wiegand

For Jonathan and Teryn, my Junior Reviewers.

Credits

Publishing Manager
Thomas H. Bennett

Acquisitions Editor
Nancy Stevenson

Product Director
Jim Minatel

Production Editor
Heather Kaufman

Technical Editors
Aaron Branham
Randall G. Bryant
David Collar
LouAnn Gilkey
William Hartman
Paul McIntyre
David Taffett

Senior Reviewers
William Brown, Jr.
Paul H. Hermann
John Husvar
Gloria George O'Neal
Brian Rock
Catherine Rock

Figure Specialist
Cari Ohm

Acquisition Assistant
Ruth Slates

Editorial Assistant
Theresa Mathias

Book Designer
Amy Peppler-Adams

Cover Designer
Tim Amrhein

Production Team
Stephen Adams
Angela Bannan
Stephen Carlin
Maxine Dillingham
Karen Dodson
Theresa Forrester
Joelynn Gifford
Dennis Clay Hager
Aren Howell
Bob LaRoche
Elizabeth Lewis
Steph Mineart
Tim Montgomery
G. Alan Palmore
Nanci Sears Perry
Linda Quigley
Dennis Sheehan
Kris Simmons
Clair Schweinler
Sue VandeWalle
Mary Beth Wakefield

Indexers
Rebecca Mayfield
Johnna VanHoose

Composed in *Adobe Garamond* and
MCPdigital by Que Corporation

About the Author

David D. Busch has been demystifying computer technology through his no-nonsense approach (tempered with light humor) since 1980, through 45 books and more than 2,000 magazine articles in leading publications, from *Computer Shopper* to *Home PC*. He is the first person to win "Best Book" honors twice from the Computer Press Association—for both Macintosh and IBM PC-oriented books. Busch shuffled some 300 discs in and out of five different Mac and PC CD-ROM drives while researching this book.

Acknowledgments

Authors often try to be falsely modest by crediting the success of their efforts to hordes of hangers-on who contributed in some small way. However, in the case of this book, my efforts genuinely *were* modest compared to the dedicated souls who spent long hours putting all the CD-ROMs reviewed here through their paces.

I'm especially grateful to my six Senior Reviewers, who not only evaluated a dozen or two discs each, but who really buckled down when the deadline was moved up to churn out even more excellent reviews on short notice. Special thanks go to William Brown, Jr., Paul H. Hermann, John Husvar, Gloria George O'Neal, Brian Rock, and Catherine Rock. John also posts reviews regularly over the Internet (jhusvar@nimitz.mcs.kent.edu), so you can read his comments between editions of this book.

Nine other reviewers handled discs within their own specialized areas of expertise in a prompt and professional manner. They were Catherine Busch, Mark Boarman, Kristina Downs, Norman Jennings, Tony Phillips, Steve Simonis, Elke Warnick, Skyler Wood, and Deanne Zeman. If I hadn't found these experts in things like OS/2, Ham Radio, Sports Trivia, and Arcade Games, I don't know what I would have done.

My Junior Reviewers, Jonathan and Teryn, aged 6 and 4, spent about four hours a day wringing every last drop of functionality out of a broad selection of children's and educational CDs. Jon was especially patient in explaining how individual features worked to his slow-to-comprehend father. They're already veteran computer users since the age of three, and Jon recently handed down the 386 system that's been in his bedroom the last couple years to his sister, and moved up to a 486-40 of his own, complete with CD-ROM drive. If you want some guarantees that the preschool and primary school discs reviewed in this book were genuinely appreciated by youngsters in the proper age range, these two, along with five or six other neighborhood "test kids," made the primary evaluations.

As always, a great deal of behind-the-scenes work at Que helped turn a rough idea (which was *theirs*, not mine) into a mountain of fresh discs, and a loose collection of disjointed reviews into polished chapter collections. Que books are always as much the work of their staff as of the author(s), but this one took some extra work.

Trademarks

All terms mentioned in this book that are known to be trademarks or service marks have been appropriately capitalized. Que Corporation cannot attest to the accuracy of this information. Use of a term in this book should not be regarded as affecting the validity of any trademark or service mark.

Contents at a Glance

Contents

Introduction

The growth in popularity of CD-ROM and multimedia technology is an amazing story, even in an industry in which unexpected and unprecedented waves of change have become commonplace. As recently as four years ago, CD-ROMs were a joke—literally. I once complained before a Computer Press Association group that the critically acclaimed book it was presenting with an award was nevertheless a poor seller. "It's moving off the shelves faster than CD-ROMs," I said, wryly. Today, the same comparison would be a compliment. They're not laughing at CD-ROMs anymore.

And why not? CD-ROM drives have become the most-desired add-on peripheral since the laser printer. We can expect more than 4 million CD-ROM drives to be installed in IBM PC-compatible computers *alone* by the end of 1995, according to CI InfoCorp, a market research company. They have become a standard component in a huge percentage of the Macintosh and Power Macintosh systems sold, and may totally supplant the 5.25-inch floppy disk drive in new PCs before the year is out.

The CD-ROM explosion has created a need for a book like *Que's 1995 CD-ROM Buyer's Guide.* Faster and cheaper CD-ROM drives have led to an increased demand for CD-ROM discs, and it's so cheap to produce a CD these days (70 cents a disc or much, much less) that disc publishers are filling the market faster than Yankee Stadium on Bat Day. The choices you face are bewildering. It's impossible for you to test every CD-ROM on the market so that you know which discs are worth buying and which are worthless. What can you do?

This book can help. Que, the largest and most successful computer book publisher in the world, asked me to assemble a team of reviewers to work with me and the Que technical staff to screen CD-ROMs *for* you. We spent months collecting multiple copies of virtually every important CD-ROM on the market, and a great proportion of the lesser discs for careful, individual review. We tested each disc and gave them a real workout, examining their interface and navigational tools, quality of the information, application, or database included, and relative weaknesses and strengths. We were able to compare the discs with all the similar discs on the market and choose only the very best for our recommendations. Then, we turned the whole thing around at top speed so that this book could be published while the data we assembled was current.

You should find this screening helpful, because we found that many top-selling discs weren't quite as stellar as their sales figures indicated. If we thought a leading game program was simplistic and not very challenging (even though visually stunning), we told you so. When expensive and flashy discs were worth every penny asked for them, we told you that, too.

What's in This Book— And What's Not

The reviews make up the bulk of the book, and rightly so. This is a guide to purchasing CD-ROMs above all else. Each of the discs reviewed has been assigned a rating. The very best CDs, which rated three-and-one-half to four stars,

are profiled in longer reviews. A second tier of important and worthwhile discs, earning two-and-one-half to three stars, merited slightly shorter reviews. Although only about half the reviews in this book were entirely written by me (with judicious editing by the Que experts, who had their own copies of these discs), I rewrote or edited all the others and checked out virtually all the discs myself to ensure consistency in our ratings and reviews.

You can trust what you read here. However, I should caution you that all criticism should be taken with at least a small grain of salt. The chief value of a reviewer comes when the reader understands the critic's biases, preferences, and rating system, best obtained by reading some of the reviews themselves. For example, many years of viewing have told me that if Gene Siskel doesn't like a movie, but Roger Ebert *does*, I probably will like the film. Ebert's views on films coincide with my own more closely: he's a little more tolerant of mindless action films that deliver nothing more than excitement (as I am). I also know enough about my preferences and Ebert's that I know when I will enjoy a film even if he doesn't. (I still don't know why I am the only person in the United States who loved *Ishtar.*)

As recently as four years ago, CD-ROMs were a joke— literally.

So, as you read the reviews in this book, you'll glean a sense of not only what discs are good and what discs are bad, but why we pegged them so. That will help you to read between the lines, so to speak. Because we used many different reviewers, the viewpoints change somewhat from review to

review, but I think you'll find a remarkable consistency in this book.

The number of discs reviewed in each category varies by the depth of the offerings in each genre. There are many more discs devoted to games, education, and children than to movies or music (so far!), so we've proportionately loaded up on the former three categories.

We've also steered away from reviewing discs of major applications that are available on floppies and in a CD-ROM format (such as CorelDRAW! or Adobe Photoshop), even if the CD-ROM component added extra value and functionality. That's because such reviews really concentrate on the non-CD-ROM aspects of the software. The fact that it's available on disc is a peripheral benefit, at best.

The Fine Print: Guarantees and Disclaimers

No, I'm not going to weigh you down with legalese. The only ironclad guarantee I'm offering is that this entire book was typeset using fine print—the best typefaces money could buy. However, I do want to include one urgent disclaimer: The suggested list prices shown in this book are (fortunately for you) subject to rapid and repeated change. Vendors have been constantly lowering prices to meet competitive pressures and to make allowances for reduced costs as sales increase. So the prices shown may represent the *maximum* you can expect to pay for a disc, but very likely you'll actually pay much less.

You can also consider the list price indicated in the reviews and listings as a yardstick for gauging whether a disc is inexpensive, moderately priced, or

expensive. But don't write to tell me you've discovered an incorrect price. By the time the Second Edition of this book is published, it is likely that the majority of the prices will have changed.

Prices on CD-ROMs have never been simple to establish. At one point, most of the discs in Microsoft's line were priced at $79.95, except for *Encarta*. Now, the Redmond, Washington software giant has abolished suggested retail prices on all its products, saying that they have little relationship to the price discs are actually sold for.

You need only look at the prices asked for encyclopedia discs to see what I mean. When research on this book started, most of them had an official list price of around $395.00. I don't know anybody who ever paid that much for one of these. I paid $129.00 for my copy of *Compton's Interactive Encyclopedia* at a time when it was listed at three or four times that. Before this book was finished, *Encarta*, *Comptons*, or *Groliers* encyclopedias could be purchased from discount software houses for $99.00 or less.

When I started researching prices for this book, I knew I was in trouble when I looked up *Rebel Assault*, the LucasArts game, in three different, reliable sources, and discovered three different list prices. Before long, I had compiled multiple prices for most of the discs in this book.

The final prices used in the reviews and listings were established using a two-stage process. Wherever possible, a recent copy of the vendors actual catalog was used to determine the price. Alternatively, I used the prices shown in ads placed by that vendor in leading multimedia magazines. Then, prices were checked against recent mail order catalogs issued by high-turnaround resellers, like Microwarehouse/CD-ROM Warehouse. Where serious discrepancies were noted (e.g., a $395 disc was available virtually everywhere for $79.95), I used the lower price. Finally, where vendors suggested retail prices for discs were not available, we used the street prices for those discs.

What does all this mean for you, the CD-ROM buyer? If you see a disc selling for $79.95, you can probably count on paying $50 to $75 for it early in the life of this book, then $30 to $60 in six to 12 months when it becomes heavily discounted—or even discontinued by the publisher. Those estimates apply only to regular retail packages. Discs that have been bundled with hardware typically sell for much less. For example, if you buy a CD-ROM drive, you may be able to purchase three $79.95 disks for $99.00 total.

Discs that are supposed to be bundled are often unbundled and sold individually against the vendors wishes, too. I've purchased discs that list for $59.95 for as little as $20.00 at computer flea markets. I didn't get the original packaging, or, sometimes, a manual, but I saved a great deal of money. (I'm not condoning illegal unbundling, but it's not always possible for the consumer to tell when a disc is a gray market product or not, and it's certainly not illegal for you to purchase such discs.)

Also, keep in mind that discs that are updated (like *TIME Almanac*) can be purchased in last years version for much less than the list price of this years edition. You may even get a discount or free upgrade to the latest disc.

In summary, we'll always try to keep the prices in future editions of this book updated, but you shouldn't take any of the price listings as absolutes. The content of most discs changes infrequently, so the reviews will remain valid for a long time. But, prices in the computer industry change rapidly, and, in the case of CD-ROMs, generally go down over time. Think how pleased you'll be to find that $99.95 game you discovered through this book can be had for only $40.

Why Us?

The popularity of CD-ROMs will undoubtedly generate several guides like this one (or that *should* be like this one) during the second half of this decade. Ours is a winner because it was assembled by a team that has already delivered the kind of solid information multimedia CD-ROM purchasers are looking for.

You already know about Que. It's the company that's sold 30 million copies of its *Using...* series of books, and already produced best-selling titles like *Discover Windows 3.1 Multimedia*. That cachet alone is enough, and is the main reason why you won't find my name on the cover of this book.

However, I'm no newcomer either. Since 1983, I've written some 45 books, including a clutch of volumes for Que, and won "Best Book" honors from the Computer Press Association the first two times it passed out the awards. I'm relentlessly cybernetically ambidextrous, trading disks and CD-ROMs back and forth all day long between my side-by-side 486DX2-66 and Macintosh Quadra computers (named Click and Clack).

I'm best known for injecting a bit of humor into the otherwise dry, staid computer publishing industry, and you'll find a touch or two in this book. There are very few outright gags within these pages, but I think you'll find I don't take things too seriously—unless they deserve it. (Check out my review of *The History of Blues* in Chapter 8 if you want to see what happens when I get overly passionate about something.)

The team of reviewers I assembled were chosen for their affinity for the discs that needed to be evaluated. It was almost always practical to assign a review to someone with at least a modicum of expertise in the genre being examined. Movie and music CD-ROMs were reviewed by movie buffs and a (former) semi-professional rock/blues musician. (Okay, me. You dragged it out of me.) Some technical and computer training CD-ROMs were reviewed by a systems integrator/trainer (not me), and all the children's games and educational programs were exhaustively tested by real, live 4- and 6-year-old children, even though the reviews themselves were written by their father.

Our review of The Family Doctor was crafted by a multiple sclerosis patient who has seen more doctors in the past several years than he cares to admit. Business CDs were looked at by business people, educational CDs by reviewers with some teaching experience, and games by those who love games (I'll admit to receiving a lot of help in this arena).

They're not laughing at CD-ROM anymore.

How This Book Is Organized

The structure of this book is simpler than most computer volumes. We haven't padded it out with useless background information, how-to tutorials, or other extraneous material. The bulk of this guide consists of the reviews themselves and listings of CD-ROMs that weren't reviewed. You'll find everything you need in one of these three sections.

Part I: A New World of CD-ROM Multimedia

This section provides information on CD-ROM software and hardware. Chapter 1, "Purchasing CD-ROM Software," offers some insights on how and why the CD-ROM revolution happened, and explains the key differences between the different types of discs on the market. Chapter 2, "Hardware Requirements," details hardware requirements for both PC and Macintosh platforms. You learn exactly what you need in terms of RAM, hard disk space, video, and sound capabilities. Chapter 3, "Untangling CD-ROM Confusion," untangles some of the CD-ROM confusion involving the drives themselves. You learn about double, triple, and quadruple-speed drives, operating system and software requirements, and other important issues for today and tomorrow.

Part II: Multimedia CD-ROM Software

The second section offers ten chapters of reviews and listings of different categories of CD-ROMs. You find detailed evaluations of nearly 300 discs in categories like Business, Reference, Education, Children's, Movies and Music, Games, General Interest, Graphics, and Shareware. Each review includes information about the publisher, format, and suggested list price. Chapters end with pages of listings of virtually all the other CD-ROMs available in that category.

Part III: Resource Listing

This part includes the names, addresses, and phone numbers of all the CD-ROM publishers featured in this book. You can use this information to request catalogs, find local distributors for products you are interested in, or make direct purchases.

Part I

A New World of CD-ROM Multimedia

Chapter 1

Purchasing CD-ROM Software

The beauty of the CD-ROM is its simplicity. After you've successfully installed a CD-ROM drive in your computer (and many systems come with these drives already installed and configured), all you need to do to enjoy a CD is pop the disc in the drive and follow the included installation instructions.

There's no need to swap multiple floppy disks in and out, or even to create complex directories on your hard disk. Frequently, CD-ROM software runs directly off the CD-ROM, with only a few files stored permanently on your computer to speed operations a little. And often, the exact same CD-ROM can be used with both IBM PC and Macintosh compatible systems, so you may not even need to know what kind of computer you own to buy the right disc!

Even so, you can benefit from a little background information on CD-ROM software, if only to understand the direction of the CD-ROM revolution we're currently in the midst of. This chapter looks at the reasons behind the pending explosion in CD-ROM software and explains the standards you need to be aware of to purchase and use these discs.

The CD-ROM Explosion's Long, Long Fuse

CD-ROMs have been with us in one form or another for nearly a decade, and other formats of optical disc (which is what a CD-ROM actually is) have been sold since the first laser discs became available in 1974.

You probably don't care to know the technology behind the CD-ROM, so

I'll boil it all down to a single sentence: CD-ROMs are circular, 4.75-inch, write-once, read-many times (WORM) discs on which digital information is represented very compactly by tiny holes that can be read with lasers attached to high resolution sensors (see fig. 1.1). That's enough techno-babble: *Car & Driver* doesn't spend much time explaining internal combustion, does it?

Capable of storing up to 680M of information on a single disc, CD-ROMs were at first almost exclusively devoted to distributing large databases of information. Telephone directories, massive computer reports, census data, huge operations manuals, scientific bibliographies, and other text-oriented material were efficiently stored on these laser discs.

The advantage of using CD-ROMs for data distribution was obvious: The discs could be mass-duplicated with the same manufacturing techniques used for the higher-volume CD audio disc, and could be read by anyone equipped with a CD-ROM player, which was a modified version of consumer audio CD players. So, information providers could distribute massive amounts of information, which could be read by anyone with a $500–$800 CD player. The cost to the originator of the disk could be a few dollars per disc, or more, depending on the quantity ordered and, if necessary, could be recouped by charging those who used the

A typical CD-ROM disc.

in System 7 and, on the PC side, Microsoft Windows. A full screen of text in ASCII format at 80 columns × 25 lines (2,000 characters) requires a paltry 2K of RAM to display and 2K of hard disk space (or *less*, with compression) to store. Today, 1024 × 768-pixel graphical displays of 16.7 million different colors are common, so that same screenful of information may require 2.5 megabytes—1,000 times as much RAM and hard disk space!

Manipulating that information is no problem for today's 486, 68040, and PowerPC computers and their video components, but how do you *store* all that graphical data? Even though you don't really need 2M to store every screen you view, the amount of permanent storage required by today's games, applications, and visually oriented databases is enormous. The capacious storage offered by CD-ROMs is a perfect match for software that truly takes advantage of the processing power of modern computer systems. You may rarely need 340,000 individual pages of text on a single disc, which is how database providers of old saw CD-ROMs, but you can certainly use 500 1M bitmapped clip-art images on one disc.

The advent of sound, particularly in business-oriented applications. Macintoshes have had sophisticated sound capabilities since the first 128K Mac was introduced. However, PCs were limited to an anemic internal speaker until the original Adlib and Sound Blaster sound cards were introduced half a decade ago. PC sound was at first used only to add life to games, but many sound cards found their way into computers that were also used for business.

When the installed base of sound-capable computers became large enough, we began to see more serious applications that took advantage of

information $150 to $2,000 for the privilege of accessing the data.

Still, the market for CD-ROMs was limited. Discs filled with scientific or business data are of interest only to scientists or business people. An $800 CD-ROM player can be easily justified by a business or educational institution, even in quantities, and the value of the information made $150 discs a bargain. However, consumers were not interested in buying $200 dictionaries or $99 full-text reproductions of books they could purchase for $19.95 in hardcover form, or other similar software, even when the price of drives dropped to the $400 level and below.

Reasons for the Growth of CD-ROM Software

So, what is behind the CD-ROM explosion we are witnessing today?

There are many reasons, all of which work together to produce the rapid growth that has swept over the industry. Those reasons, listed in what I feel is the order of importance, are as follows.

The huge growth of powerful, image-capable personal computers. It's a close call, but I rank the advent of low-cost 486-based PCs and 68040- and PowerPC-based Macintoshes ahead of the sound revolution. Certainly, we needed sound capability to arrive at the multimedia workstations we have today, but CD-ROMs would have succeeded even without sound on today's beefier computer systems.

Indeed, the future of CD-ROM technology was assured when the first Apple Macintosh was introduced in 1984. Macs took us from character-based software and interfaces to the graphical environments we have today music and voice. At first, these were only options, because, after all, not every non-Macintosh was capable of reproducing quality sound. Eventually, it became practical to build games and applications that virtually required a sound card because there were enough sound machines around to justify them.

That was the birth of computer multimedia: sound plus graphics equaled computers that could do everything that videotape players or sound/slide or filmstrip projectors could do—and much more, thanks to computer interactivity. There was suddenly a vast new market for software that took advantage of the sound capabilities of Macintoshes and PCs, and the storage facilities of the CD-ROM. While sound files themselves aren't nearly as huge as image files, high quality sound does benefit from the luxury 680M of storage can provide.

On the PC side, the incorporation of sound capabilities into Windows 3 provided an additional boost, since Windows offered a standard graphical interface developers could write to (like the Macintosh has had all along). Programming tools such as C++ and Visual Basic could use the standard facilities of Windows to speed development of sound-capable CD-ROM products.

Lower-cost CD-ROM drives and interfaces. CD-ROMs could have become a success even if drives remained at the $400–500 price point we saw before 1994. Given the advantages of CD-ROM software, a $500 player was a bargain. But prices didn't stop their plunge at $400. The drop has been as dramatic as the rise in disc sales.

At the beginning of 1994, I purchased a state-of-the-art external CD-ROM drive for my Quadra 650 for $289.00, and an internal unit for my 486DX2-66 PC for $299.00. As I write this book, I see advertisements in mail order catalogs for equivalent units for $199, including one listed at $139.00 (or $79 if you purchase it with a $99 Grolier Multimedia Encyclopedia). CD-ROM drives today cost what floppy disk drives cost last year. I could predict that prices will stabilize at the $125–$199 level, and still be proved perilously pessimistic before the next update of this book is due.

CD-ROM drives are so low in cost today that they will be included as a standard component of every computer sold in 1995 and beyond.

Lower-cost CD-ROM discs. The final major market-driving factor behind the CD-ROM revolution is the plummeting cost of the discs themselves. The price-performance ratio is becoming more attractive in two ways: you're getting much, much better discs at a much, much lower cost.

Look at the typical CD-ROM encyclopedia to see what I mean. They were originally developed as a lower-cost alternative to a hardbound encyclopedia, with some fancy retrieval options thrown in. You might pay $500 or more for a set of encyclopedia books that strain your bookshelf and force you to page through several volumes and a dozen articles to find all the information you need on a topic (*see also:* was the original version of hypertext!).

A text-based encyclopedia, often converted directly from the hardbound original and priced at $150-$200, saved the consumer some money and fattened the publisher's profits, since, even a few years ago, a CD-ROM could be produced for the cost of *shipping* a multi-volume hardbound encyclopedia. Develop a keyword index and throw in a modest searching engine that could display all the articles meeting the keyword parameters the user typed in,

and you had a useful, cost-effective product. Everybody was happy.

Today, if you still want that text encyclopedia, you can probably pick one up for $25 or so. They have been largely supplanted by $395 multimedia encyclopedias (which never really sold for much more than $149 and which now have $89-$99 street prices—or less) with the same text you got before, supplemented by hours of video clips, tons of sound bites, thousands of still photographs, animations, and other things. The product you get today is hundreds of times better than the one you purchased a year or two ago, and costs much less.

Most CD-ROM discs reviewed in this book cost $29.95 to $79.95, with a large group of them clustered in the $39.95–$49.95 range. Those are suggested list prices. You may pay half that for discs bought from discount outlets or bundled with computer or CD-ROM systems. Even so, expect prices to go even lower during 1995 and beyond.

That's because CD-ROMs are so cheap to produce. If you, Joe or Jane Average, collected 500M of information you wanted to convert to CD-ROM format, you could have 1,000 discs produced from any number of suppliers for $1,500. That's $1.50 per disc. A 21-year-old entrepreneur I know just had a set of discs produced for 70 cents each, quantity unspecified, but it doesn't take a genius to figure that the Microsofts and Broderbunds of the world must pay about a quarter for each of these things.

Add in development costs (which drop as vendors begin sharing standardized interfaces among discs), packaging, and advertising (the last two being the real bulk of the cost of the CD), and you see how discs sold *in large quantities* to this vast new market can be peddled profitably for $19.95—or a lot less.

Certainly, mega-efforts with huge costs behind them can and will bring higher prices. But there are many CD-ROMs that can and should be sold at bargain basement prices. Some of the best discs reviewed in this book—such as *Video Movie Guide* (Chapter 8) or *Sound Choice* (Chapter 8)—come in cheesy cardboard packaging with no manual. They probably didn't cost a lot to develop. Yet, they're great discs. When computer owners can accumulate huge libraries of good CDs for $10-$25, the sales of discs at all price points will increase. When the average cost is low, you can afford to splurge on a $99 disc now and then.

CD-ROMs are good for vendors, too. This factor is not a real market-driver like the others, and consumers of CDs may not be aware of it, but it is important nevertheless. Vendors love CD-ROMs. CD-ROMs discourage piracy because it isn't practical to copy them: it doesn't make sense to spend $400 on magnetic media to pirate a $40 CD-ROM.

CD-ROMs are also cheaper to produce than the equivalent floppy disks. Corel charges $200 less for the CD-ROM version of CorelDRAW! compared to the version that comes on floppy disks. Care to guess why? Vendors can pack CD-ROMs with tons of stuff that has a high perceived value among consumers—clip art, for example—yet which costs the supplier almost nothing. They can price the disc at $49.95, make a ton of money, and the consumer still feels he or she is getting a bargain. Is this a win/win situation, or what?

CD-ROM Standards

We must delve back into CD-ROM technology for a moment to explain about the different standards you should understand when purchasing a disc. But don't worry, we're only going to get one toe wet. I'm going to tell you what the standards are, but nothing at all of how they work.

All CD-ROMs are not alike. The digital data on them can be written by using one of several different standards. These have names like Red Book, Yellow Book, Green Book, and Orange Book, after the color-coded covers the manuals overseen by the Dutch manufacturer, Philips N.V. (which developed the technology and serves as a guardian and clearinghouse for many of the standards) applied to these discs. I refer to the common names of each of these standards because odds are slim that you'll ever have the need or desire to actually peruse a Red, Yellow, Green, or Orange book itself.

■ **CD-Audio**. This standard defines the familiar audio CDs that you've probably been enjoying on your home CD player for years. Digital audio data is stored in bits and bits just like computer programs, and then it is read and converted to music through a device called a digital-to-analog converter (DAC) in your audio system.

Computer CD-ROM drives can also read audio CDs. You may, however, need a special driver program to start the audio CD playing and to change from track to track. To hear the sound, you can plug a set of headphones into the headphone jack on your CD-ROM drive, connect its output to your amplifier or speakers, or use a special cable to connect the drive to your sound card (if you're using a PC).

■ **ISO-9660/High Sierra**. This International Standards Organization (ISO) standard defines a type of data structure that can be read by DOS/Windows, Macintosh, or Commodore Amiga computers, when those platforms are equipped with appropriate driver software (more on that in Chapter 3). Many CD-ROMs are furnished in this format and include both Mac and PC access software, which can, in turn, read the same data files or a special set created for each type of computer. Since CD-ROMs have so much storage space, it's often possible to develop ISO-9660 discs that provide virtually the same functions and features on both types of computers. Many discs of this sort are noted in the reviews.

However, you should be aware that many other discs can be used only on the platform for which they were designed. You may be able to insert a DOS-oriented CD-ROM in your Macintosh CD-ROM drive, open the disc, and view all the files contained on it, but if the access software wasn't specifically written to run on the Mac, you won't be able to run the programs. The reverse is also true: Mac CD-ROMs may not be happy in a PC environment. Always check a CD-ROM before purchasing it to make sure it is compatible with the computer system you want to run it on. We look at the differences between DOS, MPC1, MPC2, and Windows-compatible discs in Chapter 3.

■ **CD-ROM Interactive**. This CD-ROM format, often called CD-I, is most often used in stand-alone players that are connected to a television set and keyboard/keypad. You won't use CD-I discs in your computer CD-ROM drive.

■ **CD-ROM XA**. This CD-ROM format is an extension of the ISO-9660 standard, adding support for discs that are erasable and updatable. All other types of discs have their data written to them at one time, in a so-called single session. Most of the discs you use in your CD-ROM drive were actually pressed, like waffles coming out of a waffle iron, exactly as audio CDs are produced.

However, we now have a new kind of disc that can be written to by a laser/magnetic device (generally costing $4,000 and up, and used only by companies rather than individuals). Since these discs can be written to more than once (and some types can be erased and rewritten), they are called multi-session discs. Kodak Photo CDs, which

incorporate photographs scanned by your photofinisher, are a type of multi-session disc. Others are written as part of a database updating process.

Nearly all CD-ROM drives now sold are XA compatible. The only XA-format discs you are likely to encounter will be Photo CDs you create from your own photos with the help of your finisher, or Photo CDs compiled by others for sale as high resolution clip art.

What's Ahead

The CD-ROM formats discussed in the previous section are all well-established, and you probably don't have to worry about any new ones being introduced for the next few years (although Kodak continues to enhance its Photo CD format).

What you can expect are CD-ROMs that take advantage of new software and hardware technologies built into your computer system. These include the following:

■ **Video**. Microsoft's Video for Windows on the PC, QuickTime for the Macintosh, and QuickTime for Windows will see extensive application in CD-ROMs during 1995 and beyond. Each technology makes it possible to display small video images on your screen, bringing CDs to vivid life. Since none of these technologies is pervasive as yet, the CD-ROMs that require them include run-time versions, and you must install them on your hard disk as required. Additional video technologies have been announced that will bring full-screen, more realistic video to CD-ROMs during the coming years.

■ **New Operating Systems**. In the Macintosh world, System 7.5 and QuickDraw GX (if any vendors decide to support it), will offer software developers some new tools for bringing you faster, more realistic on-screen graphics. 1995 should see the rapid

adoption of Windows 4.0 in the IBM PC world. The new Windows will have more efficient use of memory and higher performance, which should boost the speed of most CD-ROM software. It also has a completely revamped user interface, which may require some significant rewriting of applications now on CD-ROM.

■ **Faster Hardware**. The Power Macintosh 6100, 7100, and 8100 models have all proved to be from four to ten times faster than equivalent Quadra models when running native software, and 1995 will be the year when all major applications—including those that depend on CD-ROM—convert to that mode. Apple's "fat binary" format lets a single application run in an optimized mode on either Power Macs or 680x0-based Macintoshes, so those of us who choose to remain with our older systems will still be able to run the same applications (albeit at lower speeds).

In the PC world, the 486DX2-66 chip seems destined to become the low-end, entry level microprocessor, with DX4, Pentium, and even IBM's new PowerPC systems bringing even higher levels of performance to Windows and OS/2-based computers.

These faster Mac and PC systems, coupled with triple and quadruple speed CD-ROM drives should make CD-ROM software even more practical and popular in the coming years. We may be in the middle of a revolution, but the changes are only beginning.

In this chapter, we looked at the reasons behind the pending explosion in CD-ROM software and explained the standards you need to be aware of to purchase and use these discs. We also looked at the factors behind the current CD-ROM explosion's long, long fuse, and why you can expect rapid growth in this technology in the coming years.

Chapter 2

Hardware Requirements for Your Multimedia PC or Macintosh

Virtually all the discs reviewed in this book are multimedia discs, which, in the broadest terms, means they contain something more than just text. To qualify as "multi" media, a CD-ROM may contain pictures, video, sound, animations, plain text, linked text (hypertext), and other features in various combinations. Any computer equipped with the cheapest CD-ROM drive can view text; to access multimedia features, you need something more in the way of hardware.

This chapter explains the key hardware requirements for multimedia CD-ROMs on both IBM PC and Macintosh platforms. You'll see that equipping your system to handle multimedia need not be expensive, but that, at the same time, the "minimum" requirements may not be sufficient for many of the high-powered discs that nominally call for them.

What Is Multimedia?

The term *multimedia* predates desktop computer technology by many years. Educational tools using filmstrip or slide projectors linked to synchronized cassette recorder soundtracks have been classroom workhorses for decades. Business conferences and seminars are spiced up by motion picture or slide-show/sound extravaganzas that often feature dozens of projectors, massive screens, and thundering speakers. You even find this brand of multimedia at amusement parks.

Desktop multimedia was initially a way to harness the power of the personal computer to manage all the sound and visual elements of these presentations in a new way. However, the sheer size of image and sound files used in these shows restricted desktop presentations to relatively simple productions, such as those generated by Microsoft PowerPoint or Aldus Persuasion.

CD-ROMs, which can easily store 70 minutes or more of music or up to 680MB of image files, freed developers from most storage constraints. For the first time, it became possible to produce multimedia programs that could be stored on and run from a single compact disc.

Standards Needed

Macintosh systems were the first to see real multimedia applications in any quantity. Indeed, the first CD-ROM I ever owned was the Apple Developer Helper CD (also known as Phil and Dave's Excellent CD), issued in April of 1989, when I was still a member of the Apple Certified Developer program. A year later, I received the Apple Information Source Sampler, which had even more goodies on it. PC CD-ROMs were only a gleam in most users' eyes at that time.

Why did Apple have a head start (which it squandered, since PC CD-ROM installations have since jumped far ahead)?

It was because the Mac, manufactured and marketed by a single company, has always been fairly well standardized. Until the last few years, when the Macintosh line grew into separate Performa, LC, Quadra, PowerBook, DuoDock, and Power Macintosh lines (have I forgotten a couple?), there wasn't the bewildering variety of Mac models we have today to confuse the issue. A Mac was basically a Mac.

For example, every Macintosh sold in the last six or seven years has a built-in SCSI (Small Computer Systems Interface) port, so anyone who wanted to use a CD-ROM drive could buy a SCSI model and plug it in, and then drag a few extensions to the System folder so that the Mac could recognize the new drive. Then, restart the Mac and you were in business.

All Macs since 1984 have had a graphical interface and quality sound, too. Basic Mac sound is much superior to the tinny speaker most IBM PC users find in their stock machines. The 256-color displays required to view multimedia CD-ROMs are the only feature needed for multimedia that is actually optional. So, a "standard" color Macintosh is pretty much CD-ROM ready,

Two SCSI ports on the back of a Macintosh device. The two ports are used to chain multiple devices.

and many of these machines are being sold with a CD-ROM drive built in.

PC users needed a lot more guidance before multimedia could catch on in the IBM world. There are more IBM PC-compatibles in use today with no graphical user interface at all (that is, non-Windows PCs) than there are Macintoshes. Certainly, a PC that doesn't have Windows available can successfully run many CD ROMs, including those that have their own graphical environments. However, without a standard graphical interface, CD-ROM developers had to reinvent the wheel each time they created a graphical disc, or recycle a lowest common denominator tool that could be used with many different CDs.

Of course, PCs didn't have quality sound capabilities, and there were enough color video standards to make your head spin, with acronyms like CGA, EGA, VGA, SVGA, XGA, and MCGA.

Luckily, Microsoft, busily on the road to Total World Domination, got the ball rolling by incorporating multimedia extensions into Microsoft Windows 3.0, and creating the Multimedia PC logo you see on many of the CD-ROMs you purchase. The logo itself, and the role of setting the actual standards for multimedia PCs, was taken over by the Multimedia PC Marketing

The SCSI port on the back of a Macintosh.

Council—a subsidiary of the independent Software Publishers Association.

This group has established two sets of standards (so far), defining what are known as MPC Level 1 and MPC Level 2. (MPC Level 3 is pending as this is being written.) These are nothing more than lists of minimum PC hardware requirements. Any PC meeting MPC Level 1 compliance should be able to run a CD-ROM calling for MPC-1 successfully. At this time, all the discs reviewed for this book that are available in PC format require no more than MPC-1 equipment. However, all of them run much better on an MPC-2 machine.

The following sections outline the MPC-1 and MPC-2 requirements. You see that both are fairly easy to meet with virtually any PC-compatible sold in the last year or two. If you find that, even with the relatively relaxed standards for MPC-1, your machine fails to qualify, don't despair. Upgrading to MPC-1 can be inexpensive, and even non-MPC-1 machines can use quite a few excellent CD-ROM discs.

MPC Level 1 Requirements

I'm going to list each minimum requirement for MPC Level 1 compliance, and take some time to explain what they mean and how likely your machine is to meet this requirement.

386SX or compatible microprocessor. That means 286 and 8088-based (original IBM PCs and XTs) are left out. These earlier machines are probably too slow to work with CD-ROMs successfully, and can't run the latest versions of Microsoft Windows (either at all, in the case of 8088 machines, or in the most efficient Enhanced mode for 286 computers).

Any 386SX-based computer is likely to have a processor speed (measured in megahertz) of 16MHz to 33MHz, fast enough for both CD-ROMs and Windows, and with the 386 chip's special internal memory management features needed for the more powerful Windows Enhanced mode.

If your computer is less than three or four years old, you probably have a 386 or higher (486 or Pentium chip). If not, you may be able to upgrade with a kit available from Cyrix and others.

The original MPC-1 specification of November, 1990 called for a 12MHz 286-based computer, but this was subsequently revised to the current levels, because the earlier chip really wasn't practical for multimedia applications.

2MB of random access memory (RAM). This is the minimum required to run Microsoft Windows. Your system probably has more, and, at $45 or so per megabyte, this is the single least expensive performance booster you can invest in. If you're serious about multimedia CDs, consider adding more.

3.5-inch, 1.44MB floppy disk drive. First available on computers introduced in 1987, this type of floppy disk drive has been installed on most computers sold in the last seven years. You may not actually need a 1.44MB drive to run multimedia CDs, but if a vendor supplies a floppy disk with the CD-ROM, it may offer only the 3.5-inch variety. If your system has only a 1.2MB 5.25-inch drive, you can add a 3.5-inch drive or replace your larger floppy drive with one that fits in the same bay, but has slots and mechanisms to accommodate both.

30MB hard drive. Many CD-ROM discs require at least a little hard disk space for some of their own software. These may be special drivers, video, or sound extensions that become part of Windows (such as QuickTime for Windows), or files that improve performance when run from your hard disk rather than the CD-ROM itself.

With Microsoft Windows, a few applications, and the software required by some CD-ROMs, you'll find that 30MB is barely adequate. Fortunately, most CD-ROM users will have an 80-150MB hard drive or larger. Upgrading is fairly easy and economical for newer computers. They are as easy to install as a CD-ROM drive itself:

just slide the unit into a vacant bay and connect to the cable used for your first hard disk (you may have to purchase a two-drive cable). Then, run FDISK (a DOS program that partitions, or defines, areas of your hard disk for use) following the instructions that come with the drive to prepare it.

Two-button mouse. If you have a PC mouse, it has two or more buttons. There are no one-button mouses for the IBM PC, and any three-button-mouse user can emulate a two-button model by the simple expedient of not expecting anything to happen when the middle mouse button is pressed.

101-key keyboard. This is the standard keyboard used with all computers after the 1985 PC-AT. Unless you have an 8088 machine, your keyboard will meet this standard.

Serial, parallel, MIDI I/O, and joystick ports. You find the serial and parallel ports on virtually every machine, but, oddly enough, most multimedia CD-ROMs don't really require either one unless you want/need to print something, use a modem with the CD-ROM, or must attach your mouse to one of the parallel ports.

Slightly less common (but still prevalent) are MIDI I/O ports (you'll find one on your sound card doing double-duty as a joystick port), and

joystick (aka "game") ports (also found on a special game card, or the same I/O interface that contains your serial and parallel ports; indeed, you may have more than one joystick port and will need to disable one).

Microsoft Windows 3.0 with Multimedia Extensions, or Windows 3.1 or later. Very few people are still using Windows 3.0. If so, they must obtain the Multimedia Extensions from Microsoft or another source. Windows 3.1 or later users have all the multimedia support files they need on their installation disks. These are usually copied to your hard disk and activated when you install a CD-ROM drive, sound card, or other multimedia peripheral.

MSCDEX driver, version 2.2 or later. This is the Microsoft CD Extension driver required to enable DOS and Windows to recognize your CD-ROM drive. It's supplied with later versions of DOS, Windows and Windows for Workgroups, and most CD-ROM drives. The key thing to watch out for here is to make sure that an old installation program doesn't install an outdated version of MSCDEX. DOS 6.2 comes with MSCDEX Version 2.23, for example.

CD-ROM drive capable of transferring data at a sustained rate of 150KB per second, taking up no more than 40 percent of your computer's CPU time, with an average seek time of 1000 milliseconds or less, audio CD (Red Book) outputs (can be nothing more than headphones), and a front-panel volume control.

Whew. What's all this stuff mean? It's obviously pretty critical, because it defines the CD-ROM drive itself. Luckily, virtually every CD-ROM drive on the market today meets or exceeds the standards outlined in the preceding paragraph.

150KB-per-second transfer rate means that the drive must be able to read from the disc and supply information to your computer at a rate not less than 150,000 bytes per second. That's the same speed required to read audio CDs, so there are no

CD-ROM drives that are actually slower than that.

Moreover, most 386SX and higher computers can easily handle that much data with less than 40 percent of their CPU resources, so this should be no problem to meet either.

The 1000 millisecond seek time (the time needed to find a particular track on the disc) is not very stringent, either. Of the five CD-ROM drives I own, the slowest is a 150KBps, 700 ms unit that is several years old. Most drives sold today have access times of 450–200 ms. This one is not likely to trip you up.

Nor should you worry much about having CD audio capabilities and outputs or front panel volume controls; I've never seen a drive without them.

Sound Blaster-equivalent sound capabilities. The MPC specification doesn't mention Sound Blaster, of course, but that's what it is calling for: 8-bit digital audio, with MIDI-in, MIDI-out (MIDI is musical instrument digital interface—a sound specification), and on-board analog sound mixing capabilities. If you have a Sound Blaster or card that claims Sound Blaster

A Sound Blaster sound card.

compatibility, you have all this.

The actual specifications are more detailed and look like these: 8-bit wave audio (digitized sound) at 22.05 kilohertz and 11.02 KHz sampling rates, using no more than 10 percent of your computer's

A CD-ROM drive.

CPU time. 8-bit 11.025 KHz wave audio recording capability with microphone level input. MIDI (music synthesizer) with ability to play back multi-voice, multi-timbral sounds, 6 melody notes simultaneously, and 2 percussive notes simultaneously (8 "voices"). On-board ability to mix audio CD, synthesizer, and wave sounds (three channels) into one stereo line source out of the computer's back panel.

Unless you're prepared to delve more deeply into sound capabilities, just look for Sound Blaster compatibility in setting up your minimal MPC machine; that will do just fine.

VGA-compatible display adapter and monitor with 640 × 480 pixel resolution, and 16 colors. My four-year-old daughter's 1987-vintage IBM PS/2 386 machine meets this spec, easily. However, you'll find that the minimum standard is not the one used in practice by many CD-ROM developers. There are discs that claim MPC-1 compatibility that require 256-color displays. The loophole is that while MPC-1 requires only 16 colors, the same specification strongly recommends 256-color capabilities. (It also recommends that your CD-ROM drive have 64KB of on-board buffer memory.)

MPC Level 2 Specifications

MPC Level 2 was adopted in May, 1993 to allow vendors to specify a level of equipment with more performance. Even these MPC-2 standards aren't too difficult to meet; most new computers easily exceed all of them except, possibly, for video (MPC-2 calls for 65,536 colors). Even so, few CD-ROM discs actually require MPC-2 compliance, although all perform better on MPC-2 machines.

Let's look at the MPC Level 2 specifications in some detail, so you can see what I mean.

All Level 1 specifications, including mouse, keyboard, floppy drive, Windows,

MSCDEX driver, and so forth, are required as minimums for MPC-2. The other requirements are additions to that list.

486SX or compatible microprocessor running at 25 MHz or faster. I'm not aware of any 386 machines still being marketed (there may be a few laptops with that chip), and there are certainly no 286 or 8088 machines being manufactured new anymore. Indeed, in 1995 you can expect the 486DX2-66 chip to become the new entry level microprocessor as DX4, Pentium, PowerPC, and chips from Cyrix duke it out for high-end supremacy. (I am not making this up!)

4MB of RAM (8MB recommended). This is still a conservative figure, because anyone running Windows with only 4MB of RAM probably won't be happy if they run more than one application at a time. My six-year-old son gets by just fine with 4MB on his 486-40, but he runs one game or one CD-ROM at a time, never more.

160MB hard disk drive. Drives of this size are very common now, and the larger capacity will serve you well with many CD-ROM applications. That's because most disc installations offer the option of installing many of their files on your hard disk to improve performance. The average seems to be about 2 to 5MB worth, but I recently installed a game that wanted to copy 20MB worth of files to my hard disc! If you have 20 or 30 CD-ROMs that you use frequently, it's easy to fill up 40–50MB with CD-ROM files.

CD-ROM drive with a sustained data rate of 300KB per second, using no more than 60 percent of your computer's CPU time, with an average seek time of 400 milliseconds or less and XA/multisession capable.

Whew. Here we go again. A 300KBps drive is also known as a dual-speed CD-ROM drive, because, even though it may transfer data at 300KBps most of the time, it must be able to slow down to the 150KBps audio specification to play audio discs and

audio tracks included as part of your computer CD-ROM disc. However, such drives are most commonly known as double speed drives today, because they operate at double the speed of the original 150KBps units.

Any 150KBps drives remaining in manufacturer's stocks were closed out early in 1994 at $79–$99 price levels. Virtually every new drive sold today is 300KBps or faster. There are many triple speed drives (450KBps) and a few quad speed units (600KBps), but these are still somewhat rare, and not even MPC-2 software requires them.

You are more likely to encounter a drive with 400 ms or slower average seek times, but the common "minimum" today is around 350 ms. Many drives offer 280–200 ms access—or faster. When you consider that hard disk drives that have 28 ms access times (ten times faster) are considered hopelessly out-of-date in the era of 8–12 ms drives, you can appreciate just how slow CD-ROM drives still are in comparison.

I discussed XA and multisession compatibility in Chapter 1. Your CD-ROM drive must have this capability to access discs that use XA recording techniques for data, audio, and graphics, or that have been written in more than one session, such as Kodak Photo CDs and recordable CDs.

16-bit digital audio. This more advanced audio is available from newer sound cards, such as the ProAudio Spectrum and Sound Blaster 16, which you can readily discern from their 16-bit adapter cards.

The actual specification calls for a faster 44.1 KHz sampling rate, in both mono and stereo (providing potentially more accurate sounds), and requires that no more than 10 percent of your computer's CPU time should be taken up playing 22.05 KHz and 11.02 KHz sounds. Up to 15 percent can be expended with 44.1 KHz audio.

Most sound cards actually have four stereo inputs, for digitized audio (WAV), synthesizer (e.g., MIDI), CD-audio, and stereo line in, plus a monaural mixer input for the microphone.

VGA-compatible display adapter and monitor with 640 × 480 pixel resolution and 64,536 colors. In practice, you'll find very few CD-ROMs that require more than 256 colors. Indeed, some won't work properly with more colors, and are too stupid to recognize that you have more, not fewer. (The previous version of Compton's encyclopedia disc was like this; it kept chiding me for having only 16 colors available, when I actually had 16.7 million.)

Most discs that expect 640 × 480 and 256 colors still work fine with higher resolutions and more colors, though. They may create a 640 × 480 window in the center of your larger screen, or automatically resize their panes to accommodate the extra real estate. Some produce weird color effects at higher color levels, but you can learn to live with these as I did. (The drivers for my Thunder/24 video card don't offer an option for using anything other than 16.7 million, 24-bit color!)

Recommendations. The MPC-2 specification also includes strong recommendations (but not minimum requirements) for several other features. These include support for CD-ROM XA audio capabilities, the International MIDI Association-adopted ADPCM (adaptive differential pulse code modulation) algorithms, a 64KB on-board buffer, and the full-motion video capability to deliver 1.2 million pixels per second using no more than 40 percent of the CPU's capacity.

Beyond MPC

The MPC Marketing Council doesn't actually certify PC systems; it just charges vendors a fee for the right to use the MPC logo on software and hardware that meets the specifications. MPC can be applied only to software or complete multimedia PC systems or upgrade kits, not individual components like CD-ROM drives or sound boards.

Vendors decide for themselves that their systems are compliant, although with Level 2 systems, the Council does provide tests that the vendors can administer themselves to assure that the standards are being met.

The projected MPC-3 standard being considered by the Council will call for even more powerful hardware, but don't worry about being left in the dust. It's likely the specifications will just call for equipment more in line with what's being commonly sold today: 200-plus megabyte hard disks, 800 × 600 display, and 8MB of RAM.

Macintosh Multimedia Hardware Requirements

Unfortunately, there are no MPC-style standards for the Macintosh that can tell you instantly whether or not your particular machine can run a given disc. Some are quite undemanding and will run happily on an old Mac SE with 4MB of RAM. Others require at least a 68030 microprocessor to take advantage of all the multimedia features. If you do have an ancient Macintosh, you should check out the individual requirements of each disc,

printed on the packaging, before purchasing that CD-ROM.

Otherwise, though, Macintoshes are quite a bit more multimedia and CD-ROM friendly than PCs, which I noticed when I installed a drive for use with my Quadra 650. The first friendly thing I figured out became apparent before the unit even arrived from the mail order house: it cost a lot less. I didn't need to purchase a separate SCSI interface or a sound card compatible with the drive. I just bought the external drive, paying about $250 at a time when internal PC SCSI drives were selling for at least $50 more. (Prices for both have come down since; you can buy a double speed Macintosh drive at this writing for $150 and up).

Because there was no interface card to install, I didn't need to open my Mac. Indeed, all I had to do was plug in the power cable, unplug a daisy-chain cable going from an external hard disk to an external Bernoulli drive (the last device in my particular SCSI chain), and plug it into the new CD-ROM drive instead. I then connected the CD-ROM drive to the

An external Apple CD-ROM drive.

external Bernoulli with a second daisy-chain cable, and made sure it had a different SCSI ID from the other devices (all can be set externally). Then I powered up the Mac, dragged a few files from the supplied installation disk to my System file, and restarted. Presto! There was my CD-ROM drive.

External drives are very easy to add to a Macintosh system (CD-ROM drives are even available as battery-powered units for PowerBooks), but they may also be mounted internally in some models. Your drive supplier can sell you a replacement faceplate, if required, to accommodate the internal drive. Macs with a built-in CD-ROM drive can even start up from a CD, if it's one made especially for that Mac (that is, it has compatible system software and appropriate enabler). That's a slow option, of course, but a valuable one if you someday find your start-up hard disk has died.

Like me, you'll need to add a few extensions to your System folder to make your Mac recognize your CD-ROM drive, provide audio CD capabilities, and use all your software. The High Sierra Access, ISO-9660 Access, and Audio CD Access extensions should be furnished with your drive. You'll also need Foreign File Access to be able to recognize files on PC-oriented CD-ROMs. Other multimedia oriented extensions will be installed by software requiring them: you may need to update your QuickTime or Sound Manager extensions to use the latest CD-ROMs, for example.

My own CD-ROM drive came with a Control Panel that could be used to enable or disable the supplied caching software with any drive on my system—not just with the CD-ROM drive. You may also want accessories like Voyager's CD Audio Toolkit, which lets you access audio CDs from within HyperCard stacks.

Sound Considerations

As I noted, all Macs have good quality sound built in, which can be made better by plugging external speakers into the jack on the back of the unit. That may be all you need for multimedia use; indeed, my Quadra's internal speaker gives me all the sound quality I want, most of the time. You can, however, purchase add-on sound cards for NuBus-equipped Macs if you need more sophisticated sound capabilities. Most of us don't need that much quality unless we're doing high-end audio production.

Later Macs also have sound recording capabilities built in, and some are even furnished with a microphone. I purchased a cheap mic for my Quadra, and get good enough quality. Some models, such as the lamented AV Macs and the new Power Macintoshes in AV dress, can record CD-quality sound with no additional hardware by using the Sound control panel.

The Future

In the section "Beyond MPC" earlier in this chapter, I mentioned some of the things we can expect to see in the PC world in the coming years, such as an MPC-3 specification. Both Mac and PC users can expect a convergence of multimedia CD-ROM systems that will benefit both platforms.

Specifically, we're already seeing a trend toward production of combined CD-ROMs that work equally well with either platform. Mounted on a PC, it's seen as a PC CD-ROM, and the installation setup program installs the appropriate software for that type of system. Place the same CD-ROM in a Macintosh drive, and the Mac sees only the Macintosh software and features. That's a boon for everyone involved, since the vendor doesn't have to produce and market dual versions, retailers don't have to stock them,

and computer users don't need to worry about which version to buy. Those of us with both types of computers get the additional benefit of being able to use the CD-ROM with either kind of machine.

There's also a convergence of sorts in terms of the drives themselves. Many CD-ROM drives you purchase today are furnished as identical SCSI models for use with either PC or Macintosh. Only the driver software differs. Unfortunately (or fortunately, depending on how you look at it), a new type of PC drive, which uses the PC's IDE interface, is here now. Such drives won't be compatible with Macintoshes, unless an IDE interface suddenly appears for the Mac. (That's not as far-fetched as you might think; Mac owners have often drooled over the low-cost IDE hard disk drives available in the PC world. Some vendor might be moved to provide a MAC IDE interface.)

In terms of applications, the trend is definitely toward a single program in separate versions that can run on either system. Microsoft Word 6.0 uses a single manual for its PC/Windows and Macintosh incarnations. The popular Windows CD-ROMs *Encarta* and *Cinemania* have both been introduced in Macintosh versions.

It's safe to say, then, in the future you may have to choose what system you buy and what operating environment you work under, but you won't have to make that choice depending on the CD-ROMs you want to use. Both Macs and PCs should have the same multimedia capabilities, with the same associated costs, for the long-term.

Chapter 3

Untangling CD-ROM Confusion

This chapter looks at some of the sticky points you're likely to encounter. For example, what type of CD-ROM drive do you buy? What sound card is needed? How can you choose the correct interface for your system? Do you want a system that uses caddies? You'll find all the answers here, with no long-winded, technical explanations to confuse you further.

Do I Need an Internal or External CD-ROM Drive?

Both Macintosh and PC owners can purchase CD-ROM drives as internal units mounted in the same case as their CPU, video card, and disk drives, or as an external unit that is connected to the main computer with a cable. Which is best for you? There are some advantages to each type of drive:

• Internal drives are less expensive. You're not paying for a case or power supply with an internal drive—just the bare drive itself and an inexpensive ribbon cable to connect it to the interface. An external drive will cost $60–$100 more.

• Internal drives are "cleaner." That is, you don't have extra power, data, and audio cables trailing around. Everything is inside your computer.

• Internal drives don't take up any additional desktop space.

• Internal drives move with your computer—and don't move without it.

Having an internal drive means you have one less thing to unplug and move when you relocate your system, which can be quite often for those who cart their computers

A PC with an internal CD-ROM drive.

around to perform demos. It also means it's more difficult for an unethical person to run off with your CD-ROM drive without taking the whole computer. A compact drive may fit inside a briefcase, but an entire system won't.

• External drives are easier to install. If you already have an interface card installed, you don't even have to open your computer. That might occur if you're using a Macintosh, or have a PC with another SCSI device connected to an interface with an external port. Just plug, and play.

• External drives don't use up a precious drive bay in your computer, which may be important if you have multiple peripherals installed already—such as a couple of floppies, a tape drive, or perhaps a Syquest

or Bernoulli removable mass storage subsystem. It can also be important if you have one of those slim, "space saver" cases used in some Macs and PCs. And, of course, laptops and notebook computers such as the Mac PowerBook don't have a drive bay at all!

• External drives can be used with more than one computer, if each has its own interface. Just unplug the drive, plug into the new system, and then restart or reboot. A single CD-ROM drive can be used with multiple computers in a pinch—or regularly if you must save money.

You'll want to consider these factors when you decide which type of drive to purchase next.

Sound Card Considerations

It might be a good idea to take some time to clear up some potential confusion that often results over the role of sound cards in multimedia PCs. These cards actually are multifunction cards that do many different things. I'll enumerate each of them, so that you can decide which features you need when choosing a sound card of your own. This next section is going

to be heavy with discussions of sound technology like FM synthesis versus wave tables. I'm just going to discuss the basic features, which can be confusing enough. The things to look for in a sound card are as follows.

Sound Capabilities

Simple enough, right? Nope, you have more options available than you might think. Virtually every sound card available today has what is called Sound Blaster compatibility, which means it is able to mimic a Sound Blaster card when used with DOS programs (including those supplied with some CD-ROM discs) that use the hardware capabilities of the Sound Blaster.

You may not need Sound Blaster compatibility, or choose to use it, especially if you don't use sound programs from DOS. If you need sound only within Windows, that is supplied by your sound card's *Windows* driver, and is entirely separate from the Sound Blaster capabilities.

For example, my main computer is packed full of interface cards, but I rarely run DOS programs needing Sound Blaster

compatibility. So, I have disabled that function on my Pro Audio Spectrum sound card, thereby freeing up a hardware interrupt request needed for other interface cards in my system.

I still have Windows sound, which uses hardware resources, of course (a direct memory access (DMA) channel and an upper IRQ (11), for you techno-nerds). I venture into this territory so you'll be aware that while Sound Blaster capability is an indicator of a sound card's MPC-1 compliance, in and of itself it is not required to use CD-ROMs under Windows. All you need is a sound card that otherwise meets the specs (CD audio, number of voices, and so on), and its Windows driver.

Sound cards have special features that make them more or less flexible or accurate when it comes time to record or reproduce specific types of music or sound, but I'm not going to get into those in this chapter. We're concerned here solely with how well such cards work with multimedia CD-ROMs.

CD Audio Connectibility

Any MPC-1 compliant sound card can play CD audio, which isn't surprising because audio CD players and CD-ROM players share many of the same components. However, the way in which the card connects to your CD-ROM drive can be important.

If you have an internal CD-ROM drive, ideally you want a sound card with a connector on the board that accepts an audio cable that plugs into the back of the internal CD-ROM drive. CD audio sound flows directly from the disc drive to the sound card, and then out to your speakers in all its high resolution digital glory. Alternatively, the CD audio cable can run from the CD-ROM drive to the drive's proprietary interface card, and then from a pair of connectors on the back of the interface card to the external input jack on the back of your sound card.

Attaching the cable to an external CD-ROM drive.

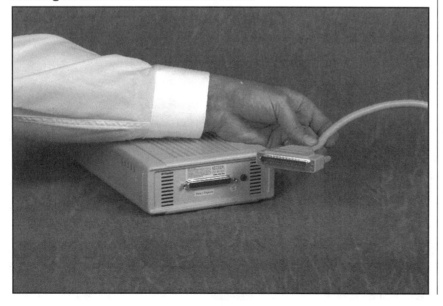

If you have an external CD-ROM drive, you should be able to connect the audio output jacks on the drive to a cable that plugs into the input jack on your sound card.

With none of these options in place, you'll still be able to hear sound from your CD-ROMs through your sound card, but it will be strictly the *synthesized* sound produced by your application—not the direct, CD-quality audio from the drive itself. This might be easier to understand if you stop to realize that some Windows programs offer an alternative of producing sound through your sound card's driver, or using CD audio, while other programs use *both*.

Without the CD audio capability, you may not be able to use all the features a program offers. *Howie's Tuneland* (reviewed in Chapter 7) is an example: the characters talk to you through the Windows driver, but if you don't have CD audio connected, you can't hear them sing and play instruments.

An internal drive with connecting cable directly to the sound card is the "cleanest" way to ensure CD audio capabilities. Make sure a cable is available for your drive, and that it can be connected to your particular sound card. Original Sound Blaster cards didn't have an on-board connector, but Sound Blaster Pro and later models do. You can still achieve CD audio with other cord options, but it is more complicated to do so. If this is important to you, consider buying a sound card and CD-ROM together as a kit (which will include the correct cable). There's no standard for this cable and almost every sound card and CD-ROM have different connectors, therefore requiring a special cable, depending on the card and drive.

CD-ROM Drive Connectability

Some sound cards have a proprietary interface built in that is compatible with a

The audio cable (a) connects the output from the interface card (b) to the sound card input (c).

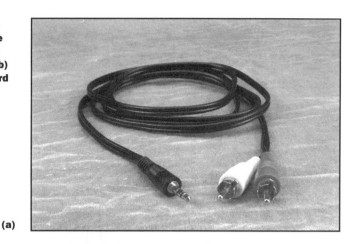

(a)

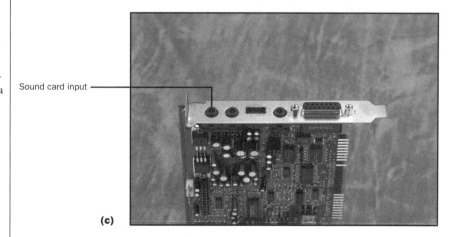

Interface output

(b)

Sound card input

(c)

particular kind of CD-ROM drive. Others have a standard SCSI interface. Whether you'll want either capability depends on

other factors, such as the type of CD-ROM drive you want to use and other components in your system. The important factors to

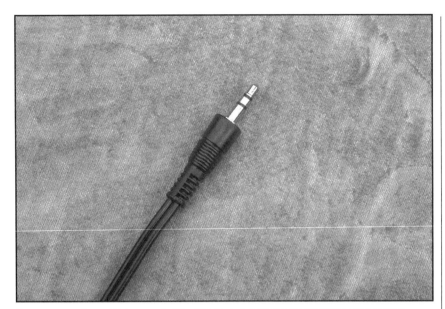

Use a connector with two ends like this to connect the headphone plug on the drive to the input on the sound card.

consider are as follows.

Sound cards with a proprietary interface save a slot: you don't need a separate interface card for your CD-ROM drive. However, the interface may limit the type of CD-ROM drive you can use with that card (although you can use *any* CD-ROM drive with the sound card installed if you have a free slot to install a separate interface card).

Some sound cards can be used with specific Sony, Panasonic, or Mitsumi CD-ROM drives; the vendor can tell you which ones are compatible with a particular card. The Sound Blaster MultiCD has three separate interfaces on the card, so that it can be used with certain models of any of those three brands or even with one of each (that is, up to three different CD-ROM drives controlled by the same card).

Generally, sound cards with a particular proprietary interface must be used with the exact CD-ROM drives they were designed for. You can't use just *any* Sony or Panasonic drive, for example. Find out ahead of time which drives are compatible, or consider buying the drive and sound card as part of a kit. You may pay less for such a

bundle.

As noted above, just because a sound card interfaces with a particular CD ROM doesn't mean you can't use a different CD-ROM drive with that card. You'll just have to supply your own interface card and use another slot.

Other sound cards, like the Pro Audio Spectrum 16 and Sound Blaster SCSI-2, have a standard SCSI interface that can be used to drive a SCSI CD-ROM unit. SCSI drives are usually more expensive, but may be your only choice.

Keep in mind that, at least at this writing, the SCSI interface found in most sound cards is a slow, 700KBps interface that is not fast enough for use with hard disk drives. You can't use the sound card as a catch-all interface for your CD-ROM drive, hard disk, and other peripherals, such as a scanner or a Bernoulli drive.

In addition, not all sound cards have a SCSI port that can be used with external SCSI devices. You may have to purchase a special connector and bracket to provide a "door" to the outside world for your sound card.

You can "ignore" the SCSI interface built into your sound card and use a separate SCSI adapter for your CD-ROM drive and hard disk, or do like I do and use both. More than one SCSI adapter can be plugged into the same computer if you have enough free slots. The best reason to use the one on your sound card is to save a slot.

You might find the single-slot solution you're looking for in a new line of SCSI interface cards from Adaptec, which also include sound capabilities. They are primarily SCSI interfaces, and therefore are fast enough for any hard disk or other peripheral. They feature "business sound," which is another way of saying they'll work with Windows applications, including your CD-ROMs, but may not include all the high fidelity sound and recording options of full-fledged sound cards.

Double-, Triple-, Quad-Speed Drives, Changers, and Towers

As I noted in the last chapter, your choices of CD-ROM drives have grown significantly in the past year. Nobody should really consider a single-speed drive. But can you safely purchase a double-speed unit with the triple- and quad-speed drives coming on the market? And what about these multi-CD units you see advertised?

For most people, a double-speed drive will be the prudent choice through 1995, unless the prices on the faster units drop sharply. I paid $169 for the last double-speed drive I purchased: would it have been worthwhile to spend twice as much for a triple-speed unit?

No. In fact, it might have made more sense to buy two double-speed drives for the price of one triple-speed unit, and thereby have twice as many discs online at one time. If I used both discs equally, I could probably make up for the slower transfer rate by the time I'd save not swapping CD-ROM discs constantly.

If you really want to use more than one disc frequently, investigate the six-disc changers from Pioneer and others. These units still have only one CD-ROM reader inside, but can switch internally from one disc to another very quickly. Each phantom drive is addressed by a different drive letter, so that you can access multiple discs quickly and easily. Because the $1000 changers are often quad-speed units, once the disc you want is mounted, access is that much faster.

There are also CD-ROM "towers" containing four to eight or more CD-ROM drives. Each drive is accessed by a different drive letter, so you can quickly run out of alphabet if you have several connected to your computer. They are most often required by network users and electronic bulletin board systems (BBSs) that must make different CD-ROMs available to multiple users, simultaneously.

CD-ROM drives mounted in individual computers can also be shared over a network. My home office systems are all linked over a Windows for Workgroups network, and the CD-ROM drive in each is shared over that network by the other workstations. It's like having three or four CD-ROM drives in one computer.

Caddies or No Caddies?

You often see reviews of CD-ROM drives mention the "inconvenience" of using *caddies*, which are special cartridges that hold the CD-ROM as it is inserted in the drive. Inconvenient? For whom? If your CD-ROM drive uses caddies, you'll want to buy a separate caddy for each CD you own. Then, you'll find it more convenient to use these CDs: instead of opening the jewel box, sliding open a drawer, dropping in the disc, closing the door (and using the reverse process to unmount the disc), you just grab the caddy you want and slip it in the drive. I love caddies. People with children or clumsy coworkers love caddies: they protect the disc from fumble-fingers. In truth, CD-ROM

caddies are only inconvenient for four groups of people:

- Computer magazine writers who get hundreds of CD-ROMs free for review (all received without caddies), and must then manually insert the disc into one of the few caddies they own in order to use it. If you fall into that category, or happen to own a few hundred CD-ROMs for some other reason, you may find caddies inconvenient to use.

- People who pay too much for their caddies. I've seen them in computer superstores priced at $9.95 each. I buy my caddies in quantities of 20, and pay only $3.50 each for them. It's an excellent investment for protecting a $29.95 to $49.95 CD-ROM. At that price, you can afford one for every CD-ROM you have.

- Folks who are on a real tight budget. Drives that use caddies cost more, and the caddies themselves are an extra expense. If you're using CD-ROMs on a shoestring, you won't want to use them.

- Those who share CD-ROMs among several different computers, several of which use caddies and several of which don't. That's what you get for mixing drive types.

The moral: buy the same type of drive (with or without caddies) and use them (or not) depending on what your budget allows.

How Do I Install and Troubleshoot a CD-ROM drive or Sound Card?

For PC users, I highly recommend Que's companion volume to this one, *Discover Windows 3.1 Multimedia*. This fat volume goes into a lot more detail about multimedia, CD-ROM, and sound card concepts, and includes comprehensive instructions for choosing, installing, and enhancing everything from joysticks to disc jukeboxes. Another good book is Que's *The CD-ROM Book*, which is even more recent and includes lots of helpful detail about hardware.

Now, it's time to take a close look at some of those great CD-ROMs I've been telling you about.

A CD caddy.

Part II

Multimedia CD-ROM Software

Chapter 4

Business and Productivity

Business and personal productivity CD-ROMs are those you can use to improve the quality of your work or assist you in other ways, such as for personal finance. I'm not including applications like CorelDRAW! or Adobe Photoshop that happen to be available on CD-ROMs, because they must be evaluated using a whole different set of criteria. Instead, this category is made up of things like business reference works that are packed with data that can be used for marketing. Others can improve your business skills, or help you operate your computer more efficiently.

Y ou'll find that the discs reviewed in this chapter include a broad range of useful programs and databases. CD phone directories, like *PhoneDisc USA* and *Direct Phone*, give you immediate access to dozens of prospects, associates, and businesses. If you need information, *Business Library* or *PC Library* can put a hefty bookshelf of technical and business information at your fingertips. There are also discs that can help you optimize your computer, like the best-selling *ROMaterial* series, or improve the appearance of your word processing documents (*Font Axcess* or *Fantastic Fonts*).

If you're a business owner, you'll want to check out discs like *Clinton Health Care Plan*, or perhaps get some training from the Wilson Learning series of CDs, with titles like *Keep Your Cool* and *Sell to Needs*. If a little laughter will spice up your next presentation, there's a disc for you, too: *Great Business Jokes*.

The reviews and listings in this chapter don't cover every single business-oriented disc. You can also find good information that applies to business needs in the reference and education chapters that follow.

Font Axcess

Rating:

Publisher Name:
Quantum Axcess

Software Requirements: **MPC**

Suggested Retail Price: **$19.95**

If you look up "value-added" in an unabridged dictionary, there ought to be an entry about Quantum Axcess. This company has built a fine inventory of slick CD-ROM products with great interfaces using, essentially, public domain, shareware, and freeware products. You'd never know from looking at the full-color packaging for *Font Axcess* that its 1,000+ TrueType fonts were created by dozens of individual type designers, and offered to you at no charge or for a small registration fee.

I've included *Font Axcess* in this chapter, rather than the one dealing strictly with shareware, because its contents are more closely aligned with the interests of business owners and individuals looking for personal productivity enhancements than with those of the typical shareware scrounger. If you need great-quality fonts for desktop publications, presentations, word processing documents, advertising material, or other applications, you're bound to find the one you need on this disc.

Included with the disc is a great utility called ViewType, which lets you browse through all 1,000 fonts, either through large samples displayed in a default text passage and size, or by using text and point size that you specify. (When you type in your own text, ViewType offers helpful ABC, abc, and 123 buttons you can click to add a full alphabet or set of numbers to your type sample, without you needing to enter the characters manually.)

The displayed text can be left or right justified or centered, as you prefer. Handy buttons in a ribbon at the top of the screen let you change these attributes, switch to bold, italic, or underlined versions of a font, or increase the point size display with a click of the mouse button.

Here's a nice touch: Instead of showing each font using standard text, you can ask ViewType to use the embedded information about the font that the font designer included within the font itself. For commercial fonts, that may include the vendor name and specifications of the font, while shareware fonts often include registration information right in the font file. This text may be more interesting and

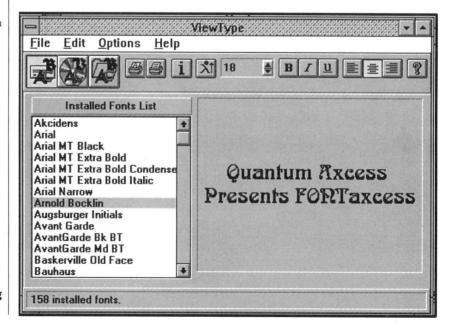

Quantum Axcess's *Font Axcess* CD-ROM has a great browser/installer that you can use to preview fonts before copying them to your hard disk.

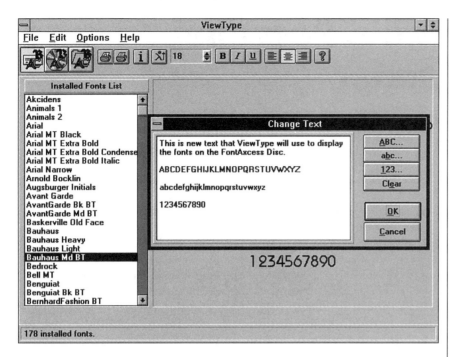

You can change the text displayed in the font preview box to anything you want.

useful than just stock phrases that are the same for every font you view.

When you see a font you'd like to use, click the Install button and the utility installs the font for you. If you like to use a lot of different fonts, you can also use Windows own Font Control Panel to install the fonts, and tell Windows not to copy the fonts to your System directory when setting up the typestyle. You could then use the font directly from your *Font Axcess* CD-ROM, and save a few hundred megabytes of hard disk space. Of course, this disc would have to be in your CD-ROM drive anytime you wanted to use those particular fonts.

ViewType can also display samples of fonts already installed on your system, and can selectively show only fonts from a particular folder. The program can print out a complete listing of fonts, using a single line sample from each, or create a full-page type sample of individual fonts.

For most business users, **Font Axcess** *provides try-out versions of all the fonts you'll ever need (many require a small registration fee), with an easy-to-use installer/viewer.*

There are many shareware and commercial font utilities on the market, and ViewType (which requires no additional fee: it's not shareware) is one of the better ones. If Quantum Axcess would add a facility for

uninstalling fonts, it would be perfect.

I won't list all the available fonts on the disc here. Rest assured that with 1,000 varieties to play with, you'll find equivalent typefaces to every commercial typeface you've ever seen, in the body text, display type, and decorative type categories. There are sturdy book faces here, eye-catching headline fonts, and imaginative fonts in the shape of everything from paper clips to crackling flames. You'll find calligraphic (handwriting) fonts, classic typestyles that have proved their popularity over decades, and new novelty fonts.

The quality of the fonts varies a little, which is understandable considering the wide ranging sources for these typestyles, but *Font Axcess* will do for anything short of professional typography (where so-called "expert" sets are needed that include extended character sets, tons of kerning pairs, and other specialized features).

Jonathan Pond's Personal Financial Planner

Rating:

Publisher Name:
Vertigo Development Group

Software Requirements: MPC

Suggested Retail Price: $69.95

F inancial advisors will tell you that it's not how much you make that counts, but how much you keep. As someone who's made quite a lot over the last

Learn about insurance from this well-written interactive CD-ROM.

20 years, but kept almost none of it, I wish I'd had this CD-ROM available when I made more of my spending decisions.

Jonathan Pond has written nine books, had regular columns in *Cosmopolitan* and *Newsweek*, and appears on the radio program, "Your Money with Jonathan Pond." He has also made 300 television appearances during the last three years and addresses more than 80 groups annually. How Pond had enough time to offer input for this CD-ROM is beyond me.

However, Pond has done an excellent job in putting together an ActiveBook, Vertigo Development Group's name for its interactive reference guides. An ActiveBook

appears on-screen in a format much like a real book, but with enhancements that let you use the information in much more powerful ways. Pond himself lurks in the background to catch errors or help you solve problems. Computer algorithms streamline the process by performing complex calculations and analyses for you automatically.

Like a real book, this one has a table of contents that lists key major topic categories like Less Liquid Investments (e.g., real estate) and Retirement Basics. There's also a glossary and index for reference.

Each chapter title has a button that can be clicked to display subsections. Additional

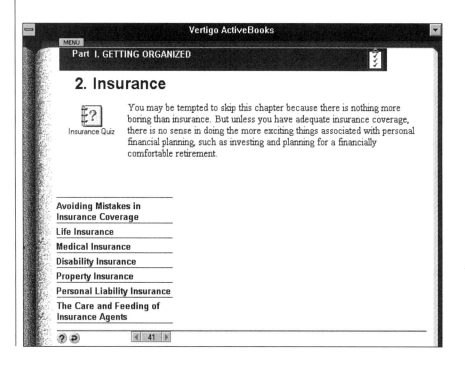

buttons can be clicked to further expand (or contract) subheadings. If you understand the hierarchy of how the information is arranged (and it's logical enough), you can quickly find a topic of interest. If you're not sure where to find what you need, the index can locate specific keywords quickly.

Each page also has a help icon and a history icon that returns you to the most recently viewed page, or any page in the history list. Other buttons return you to the table of contents at any time, and move ahead or back one page at a time.

Jonathan Pond guides you through every step in planning for a secure financial future in this clever, interactive CD-ROM.

The book metaphor keeps this Windows-based program very clean-looking and un-Windowslike. For example, all the tools are hidden behind a Tools menu tab glued to the top of the page. Tools let you add or remove notes and bookmarks to the text, look up keywords in the index, or copy or print sections of the book for permanent reference.

Headings at the top of each page (like the header on this book) show the current heading title, but are active: clicking the heading name takes you to the table of contents.

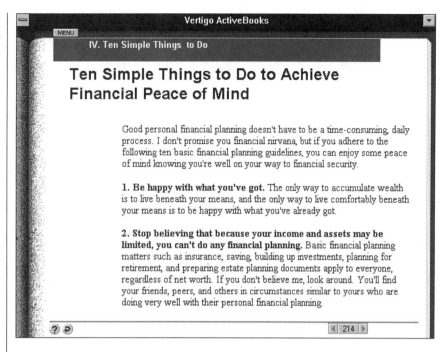

Ten things to keep your peace of mind and offer valuable advice.

An "idea" icon appears on many pages. Click the idea and a quick top pops up right on the page. Click anywhere else to close it.

Solution Pages let you calculate important financial values, such as home prices you can afford, down payments, interest rates, and other values. The Putting The Kids Through College section, for example, produces a table that lets you input your current loans and figure out how much is required to pay for a college education.

While working with any Solution Page, you can select the Author Menu to get the author's tips and suggestions for that page. A box pops up with tips like, "Your monthly housing payments are too high. Most lenders do not want you spending more than 28 percent of your monthly income on housing costs. Try increasing your down payment, finding a mortgage with a lower interest rate, or a more inexpensive house."

If you decide to follow the author's suggestion for that Solution Page, you can click a button to apply the choice.

You'll enjoy working with Jonathan through all the exercises, ranging from taking the Wealth Test to evaluate your financial knowledge, through the Smart Planner Report. If you aren't as worried about how much money you make as how much you keep, this CD-ROM will help you get the most bang for your bucks.

Keep Your Cool

Rating: 1/2

Publisher:
Wilson Learning Corporation

System Requirements:
MPC/Macintosh

Suggested Retail Price: **$49.95**

N ow this is a rather pleasant surprise. At first glance it looks like, "Ho hum, another handy-dandy self-help book; platitudes, prosperity, and pop-psych." Well, not so.

Keep Your Cool is, in fact, a self-improvement program. It is psychologically oriented, and it is aimed at teaching you something. But it's straightforward, easy to understand, and the whole thing just makes sense. There's no new-agey psycho babble and no "This-CD-will-solve-all-your-problems!" hype. What Wilson Learning Systems puts forth here is plain, solid information about how you can learn to be aware of and handle your emotional responses to your own advantage, and how to understand and evaluate emotional stress so that you can use it productively.

Using audio-visual aid clips and quite nicely laid-out programmed learning techniques, the program leads you through various stress-producing situations. Then it sets up several alternative reactions on several levels and allows you to choose one.

The ABC model is used to teach behavior modification in easy steps.

It shows the likely consequences of the choices and then presents alternative approaches that might yield other outcomes and gently leads you through explanations of how they differ.

One of Wilson Learning Systems' approaches is the A-B-C Model. A is an Activating Event, a stimulus. B is a Belief about the Activating Event that influences how you might react. C is the Consequence of the interaction of A and B. The program acknowledges that everyone has different Belief Systems and, therefore, will experience different Consequences. What's different is how effectively Wilson introduces the idea that people can alter their Beliefs with learning or reevaluating them and how effectively they can take control of the

emotional response and redirect it advanta-geously using their next approach.

Stop, Challenge, and Focus is Wilson's technique for taking control. It's possible to experience any of several stress responses. One can immediately react with Anxiety or Worry, Anger, Fear, Jealousy, Guilt, or other panic responses. Wilson recommends you first Stop and examine just what Underlying Assumptions drive that panicky feeling. Then, Challenge those assumptions, evaluate them and, especially, try some alternatives. Lastly, break the initial panic response and focus on putting that energy to work so that you get the response you want and start working the situation around to your advantage and working your response around toward the most advantageous

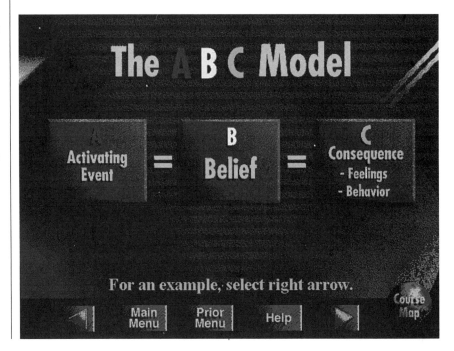

action for your situation. The basic unspoken message seems to be, "You don't win battles by fighting yourself."

Keep Your Cool is about managing emotions. Events happen, regardless of our desires. Negative events, according to this program, are never best handled with negative emotions. That tends to trap you in a Survival Mode, fight-or-flight, that tends to circle upon itself paralyzingly. Using the Stop-Challenge-Focus technique, they claim, enables you to move from Survival to Connection Mode, where helpful action becomes possible because knowledge, skills, and strengths are freed for use.

A pleasant surprise, a self-help tool that really does help without heavy-handed psycho babble or guilt-tripping.

A mere review can't fully represent this product, there's more, much more. Wilson Learning Systems takes you through numerous simulations and training events. They test your progress with game-like simulations, some of which are quite humorous. Their final exam, if you will, is a time machine trip through history, helping great figures accomplish their goals. The presentations are downright fun. For example: Michelangelo's reactions to getting "the Sistine Chapel Project dumped on him" is hilarious. This section, Mastery Simulation, would, itself, be worth the admission.

Finally, *Keep Your Cool* helps you apply the techniques to your personal situation in

Wilson Learning's sophisticated approach to personal development is easy to learn by using this disc.

the Personal Opportunity section, taking the training into application. By helping recall past occasions when the negative emotions exacerbated problems and applying these techniques to see how effectively managing emotions might have produced different results, the program reinforces its lessons. Then, using a mild form of guided imagery, *Keep Your Cool* helps you build in the techniques so they tend to become an automatic response whenever negative emotions occur. The idea is to break the survival cycle, enter the Connections Center where productive techniques reside, and manage your emotions to manage the crisis.

For PC-compatible machines, *Keep Your Cool* installs in two versions, Keep Your Cool and Keep Your Cool Lite. If your system is on the lower margin of the system requirements, the Lite version varies only in having slightly lower quality graphic backgrounds. Everything else seemed to run cleanly, even on the test system, a 486-25 with only a single-speed CD-ROM drive. You won't dash through this CD. For one reason, it's absorbing and tends to keep nudging you to the next step. For another, it's a big and powerful learning tool. Fortunately, the authors make navigating it

easy.

You can stop at any point and even drop out entirely. To go back, choose Main Menu and just click where you left off. Alternatively, there's the Course Map that will highlight your position. Clicking any course selection takes you right there with a minimum of fuss. Regrettably, the Course Map video is mildly glitched on this review copy, having some double-imaging problems. It doesn't prevent using it, but it's a flaw that probably cost it a rating star or so. Selecting any section for review works quite as easily. You'll probably find yourself reusing *Keep Your Cool* often.

Keep Your Cool isn't exceptionally fast operating; there's too much going on for that. Its powerful interactive sessions, though, tend to make things worth waiting for. Possibly its best feature is that it doesn't beat the user over the head trying to convince. Practical, real-world examples and equally practical, real-life techniques lead you to consider your own stress-management practices and adopt any, all, or none Wilson recommends. It's a mirror, not a spotlight. Quite a nice addition to your mental tool kit.

PhoneDisc USA Residential

Rating:

Publisher Name:
Directory Digital Assistance, Inc.

Software Requirements:
MPC/Macintosh

Suggested Retail Price: **$83.00**

Why let your fingers do the walking when your computer does the job much better? Certainly, it takes quite a few directory assistance calls at 25 or 50 cents a pop to equal the $83.00 suggested retail price of this disc set. But is that Information operator so helpful when you're looking for Fred Q. Schwartzmiller, who moved somewhere out West—but you're not sure where? Or when you need to find a specific Manuel Rodriguez in Southern California. Or if all you need are some addresses and you don't even *care* about the phone number?

PhoneDisc USA Residential is a set of two CD-ROMs (one for the Eastern United States, one for the Western United States) containing 80 million residential names and addresses. You can also purchase a two-disc Business set, or a four-disc Reverse reference (which lets you search even if you know only the phone number or address).

With any of these discs, you can quickly search for any given name (or business, in the Business set) in any region, limiting your search by state, city, ZIP code, or telephone area code. There's no "meter" clocking your retrievals against a preset limitation, and you're free to print out hard copies of the listings you collect. As a bonus, you can even dial a number directly from the CD-ROM listing!

PhoneDisc USA's character-based, DOS interface (which runs just fine under Windows) is *fast*. It doesn't wait for you to finish typing in a name; as you key in the first few letters, the program races ahead to list the first name meeting the parameters entered so far. Start typing the name BUSCH, DAVID, for example, and you'll see members of the Bu family, some folks named Bus, and a few Buscas before the first Busches show up on-screen. In effect, search time is nil: by the time you've finished typing your entry, the listings are there waiting for you.

PhoneDisc USA squeezes 80 million published home telephone numbers onto two CD-ROMs and retrieves them for you using a variety of selectable parameters, with amazing speed.

Okay, so it's nice to know there are 109 different Busch, D. listings in the Eastern United States. How do you zero in on the one you want? When you press tab, a dialog box pops up with space to type in a city, state abbreviation, street name, ZIP code, or area code. If that isn't enough, you can type a name fragment, and PhoneDisc will search for those characters *anywhere* in a name (e.g., use *therine* to locate both Katherine and Catherine). Multiple parameters can be entered on a line, separated by commas (e.g., OH, IN, IL). House numbers can also be specified, and prefacing an entry with a minus sign excludes it from the search. That is, -ALBANY would search for all entries except those in towns named Albany.

This flexibility lends itself to some fairly weird searches. I located all the Eastern residents of the U.S. whose names begin with B and who live at 100 Main Street in their respective towns. Unfortunately, *PhoneDisc* can be led astray because of faulty error checking. Use CA (California) as a parameter when using the Eastern USA disc, and it happily goes off into the never-neverland of endless searches (at least, we gave up before *PhoneDisc* did).

Another weakness is some inexplicably missing names. We were unable to locate our favorite computer author's listed home phone number, although others in the same city (including said author's mother) turned up on request. Despite 80 million names and phone numbers, not all published listings are included.

I particularly liked the interchangeability offered between the residential, commercial, and reverse discs. The same search engine is used for all three sets, and you can install and run it for any of them. Just make sure you have the disc you want to use in the drive when you launch the program.

PhoneDisc is updated quarterly, and a

substantial number of Americans do move each year (an estimated one in seven), so theoretically about 3.5 percent of the listings on the disc you buy today will be different in three months. In practice, many homeowners move within the same town and keep the same phone number, and when the number does change, the phone company installs one of those forwarding recordings to supply you with the new number. So, unless up-to-date numbers are a life-and-death matter for you, don't worry about updating more often than once a year, if that.

The biggest challenge you face is justifying the purchase of this disc. Do you really make that many calls without knowing the correct number? If you go beyond the mundane personal phone call, you'll find dozens of ways you can use *PhoneDisc USA* for fun and profit. Consider these:

• Compile a list of your high school, college, or armed services comrades for a reunion. *PhoneDisc* helps you track them down wherever they may have moved.

• Look up old friends or distant relatives, even if you're not sure where they might be.

• Need to pull some strings? Want to check out the job market without alarming your present employer? Use the business version of *PhoneDisc* to discover the home telephone numbers of key business contacts, then give them an informal call without the pressures of the office or nosy secretaries.

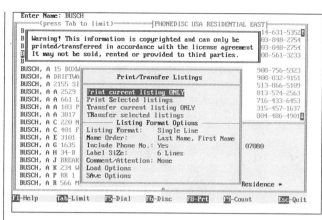

PhoneDisc Residential, Business, and Reverse let you print out listings to labels or other report formats.

• Wonder how many people share your surname in the United States? Or have the exact name as you? *PhoneDisc* may help you find out that you're not as unique as you thought!

• Receive a telephone message at home with only a last name that doesn't ring a bell? Avoid embarrassing yourself by checking out that name, using the area code as a delimiter. You'll probably easily find the caller's first name and address, too. If you still don't know who you're talking to, at least you'll be on a first name basis.

• Want some addresses? Directory assistance is now allowed to provide you with three listings per call (at up to 50 cents each call!), and addresses as well, but if you have 20 or 30 addresses to collect, all that phoning and jotting can get tedious.

PhoneDisc can direct the information you compile to your printer, or save it as an ASCII file compatible with your word

processor. The procedure required is a little confusing, but can be quickly learned. To either print or save, you must press the F8-Prt key, and then select from Print current listing ONLY, Print Selected listings, Transfer current listing ONLY, or Transfer selected listings.

After you've figured out that Transfer means Save to disk, you may still be confused because you haven't really selected any names. Just press Enter, and *PhoneDisc* shows you how to mark the first and last names in your list. It saves all the names in between (up to a maximum of 50 listings per save).

When printing the names and addresses, you can specify a mailing label format, enter comments, or recycle a previously-saved file with these and other options from the disc. *PhoneDisc*'s strengths are its speed, low price, and flexibility. In addition to the weaknesses noted above, it's clumsy to load both East and West discs to perform a search of the entire country. Perhaps future data squeezing technology will allow the publisher to compress both databases onto a single disc. That's a nit-pick to be sure, on the order of noting that the Encyclopedia Britannica would be a lot more portable if they could publish it in a single volume. *PhoneDisc USA* is a useful home and business tool for anyone who deals with names, addresses, or phone numbers, or the interminably curious or nosy.

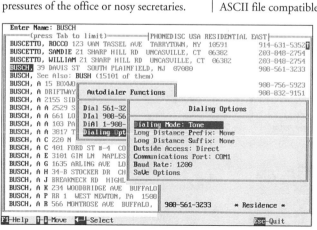

PhoneDisc Residential, Business, and Reverse can dial a number for you if your computer has an attached modem.

ROMaterial Again

Rating: 🔘 🔘 🔘 1/2

Publisher Name:
Moon Valley Software

Software Requirements: **MPC**

Suggested Retail Price: **$69.95**

There's no arguing with success. Moon Valley Software's *ROMaterial* has consistently been on the CD-ROM best-seller lists over many months, residing at the top of the charts with other megabest-sellers like *Rebel Assault* and *The 7th Guest*. You have been buying this disc by the zillions, even though advertising for a modest offering like this one is obviously at much lower levels than for products backed by, say George Lucas or British billionaire Richard Branson. You folks love *ROMaterial*, and have created the demand for *ROMaterial Again*—the sequel.

I hate it. I know I said there's no arguing with success—but this is *my* book. I'll pick a fight with anybody I want. You don't really need any of the features it provides, and some of them can even be harmful to your productivity. At the same time, you may not be able to resist playing with all the cool stuff on this CD-ROM. I'm honor-bound by the fictitious Reviewer's Code to tell you about all the irresistable features in *ROMaterial Again*, and then follow that up with some caveats. As you read this review, you can temper my comments with the knowledge that they were written by someone who *hates* this disc.

Basically, *ROMaterial* gives you the tools and gadgets (including the utility program Icon Hear It) you need to mess around with your Windows system. You can change any icon in your system to one of the supplied goofy icons. These icons can be animated, and emit unlikely sounds when clicked. If you want your painting program's icon to paint itself, or you need a Windows icon with actual lightning behind the window, you can have that. The animated icons provided cover virtually every popular program, from Quicken to ProComm, WordPerfect to Word for Windows. The icon animations are lively and professional-looking.

Half a gigabyte of irresistible but largely useless animated and sound-filled icons, cursors, and other gadgets make this a lightweight best-selling disc.

The CD-ROM includes seemingly thousands of sounds you can associate with icons (or other Windows events), ranging from garden variety sound effects (crashing,

With *ROMaterial*, you can change your cursor to any of hundreds of different types supplied.

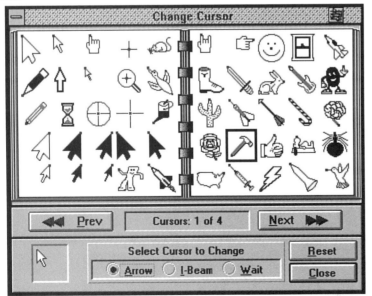

sneezing, gas station air hose, etc.) to human voices. I should note that the sound effects are among the best I've heard. These are not your lousy public domain .WAV files you may have downloaded from a BBS system. There are several different sampling rates: 11kHz, 22kHz in both 8-bit mono and stereo, as well as 16-bit, 22kHz stereo sounds.

The categories are all shrewdly arranged so that you can find people sounds, animal sounds, system messages, and other noises quickly. Normal English phrases, as well as those by French, Spanish, German, Italian, Swedish, and Japanese males and/or females are included, along with an astonishing set of "sexy female" responses that don't, for a change, sound like they were uttered by a bored receptionist. (I will admit that my OK responses in dialog boxes now are met with a sigh, Oooo-kay.)

Sounds can be attached to a wide variety of system events, designated to play at random, or chained in sequence so you can cascade a virtual mini-presentation of noises that are activated at the click of your mouse. What possibilities there must be for the truly evil mind! You can tell Icon Hear It to pronounce the current time on the quarter-, half-, or full hour (or never) and play Solitaire or Minesweeper with speech enhancements (if that's important to you).

If you're dissatisfied with your cursor, you can change that, too. You can modify the standard arrow, I-beam inserting point cursor, or the infamous "waiting" hourglass to something else, including a hypodermic needle, Gumby, a lightning bolt, a hummingbird, or the always-useful Fender Jazz bass guitar.

Your cursor can be animated, too; changed into a heavenward-rising angel, bomb, blimp, or climber. There's also a sports car and toucan for those who demand entertainment from even a lowly cursor. Among the other meddling you can do with your system is set up video screen savers (watch Mt. Rushmore transform itself

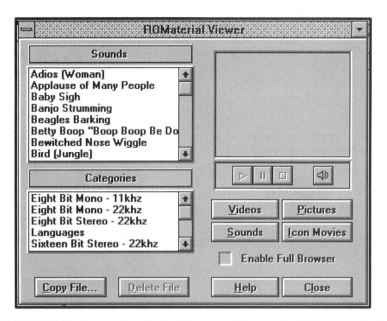

ROMaterial Again gives you hundreds of sounds, videos, animated icons, and other enhancements for your Windows desktop.

through a morphing process you never anticipated!) and randomizing wallpaper schemes.

There are other gimmicky programs that can do most of these things for you, but the reason why *ROMaterial* is a best-seller is clear. First, Moon Valley gives you 500MB or more of files. There aren't just a few .WAV sounds here; there are hundreds. You get hundreds of cursors and icons, lots of animations, music, and much more. Second, they've made this nonsense remarkably easy to access. Most commands and options are available from your Program Manager's menu bar or the ROMaterial Browser. There should be a law against making Windows vandalism this easy.

Now, it's time for the warnings. Keep in mind that this reminder is coming from someone who once had his computer scream "Gooood morning, Viet Nam!" everytime it was turned on, and "Th, th, th, thaat's all folks!" every time it was shut off. For about a week, closing a window evoked the sound of shattering glass, and drag-and-drop motions were accompanied by horrid scraping

sounds.

Most of the gimmicks provided by *ROMaterial* grow old real fast. You'll soon find animated icons distracting, and the constant sounds annoying. Every animation provides a tiny delay, and each weird icon you choose to put to work consumes your limited system resources. Lots of .WAV files can eat up your hard disk space in a hurry. You don't really need a screen saver, because modern VGA screens don't need saving (the VGA monitor on the otherwise idle network server in my home office sits transfixed for 12 hours a day, and in three years has never "burned in").

Still, you may be unable to resist trying out these effects on your own system, if only to relieve the boredom. However, even if your system can stand the performance penalties all these gadgets entail, don't expect to be interested in keeping any of them active for very long. Now, please excuse me. There's a sultry female voice reminding me to save this file.

Sell To Needs

Rating:  1/2

Publisher Name: **Wilson Learning Corporation**

Software Requirements: **MPC/Macintosh**

Suggested Retail Price: **$49.95**

*S*ell to Needs is an interactive multimedia program for business people. It was designed for either a novice salesperson or a seasoned one. Quoting them directly: "The program provides strategies for discovering your customers' needs and presenting solutions in ways that bridge the gap between what they have and what they really want." This is not the run-of-the-mill hotshot sales magic. This is a new approach in that it really goes into depth concerning communication and having the potential customer tell you what you need to know in order to sell your product.

As I began this two-hour course, it occurred to me that just about anyone could benefit from it. I don't think I have ever met anyone who is perfectly adept at communicating, and in the sales field, it is of paramount importance. The booklet points this out by saying "Learning is most effective when it improves your personal life as well as your professional life."

In a QuickTime, Max Barrows says: "Hey, I love to talk, and I'm good at it! I can make a crackerjack presentation at the drop of a hat. But this loving to talk has been the single greatest obstacle to my success. I had to learn this the hard way because when you're talking, you're not listening. When you don't listen to your customer, you don't have a prayer of ever understanding their problems. How you going to solve a problem that you don't understand? Learn to ask questions."

It is easy to install, and you must reboot to activate the movie player (if you don't already have QuickTime for Windows installed on your system). Screen interaction is simple, using your mouse, with a nice "review" feature built right in. It begins with the main menu, which has help, a "play" forward arrow, and a globe icon entitled Course Map. I really liked the Course Map. It shows users where they are, and allows them to go anywhere else. In the beginning there are two salespeople and you hear their pitching style, then you are asked to choose the one you would most likely buy from. The point is well made that none of us really like to be sold to. The question is "Do you buy stuff because some yahoo with a pinkie ring ran a bunch of sales techniques on you?" I had to chuckle at that! You buy, Barrows explains, because on some level you have a gap between what you have and what you want...and therein is the *need*.

Sell to Needs *can help veteran and new salespeople alike—or anyone who wants to get across an idea or sell a concept.*

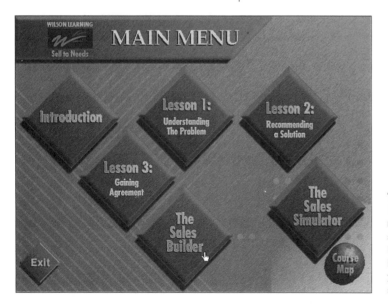

The *Sell to Needs* main menu offers several lessons for improving your selling skills.

There are three main lessons:

1. Understanding the Problems
2. Recommending a Solution
3. Gaining Agreement

Within the lessons, there is a presentation, explanation, samples, and text on-screen. You can go backward, forward, or jump ahead. This makes it very nice for review or for looking something up quickly if you are in a bind with a customer. After the lesson, there is an easy quiz that is followed by a program generated—yet appropriate—response, depending on your answer. That amazed me!

The demeanor is that of a gentle teacher who is always ready to help re-teach and review if you don't understand. The Learn and then Apply format works very nicely. I was especially impressed with the intelligent and logical way they handled the very difficult task of alleviating the tension when it comes time to sign the dotted line. In fact, both the seller and the buyer are tense, and you see how to work with this and get beyond it all. In sales, of course, this is the place where we make it or break it. I found the methodology to be very logical, and I'll bet it works if it is executed properly.

This program really involves the user. It draws one to go on and see what happens and how you fare with your response. But, it is not intimidating in any way; it is a very comfortably done course.

After the three lessons, there are two parts.

The Sales Simulator, which provides a safe place for you to try out your skills.

The last is the Sales Builder. With the help of your own notes or computer, you can customize these applications to your own field and review the course quickly. It is *Sell to Needs* in a Nutshell, and synopsizes in an interactive manner, the entire set of theories and techniques.

Note: I liked that they have replaced the tired old sales jargon with a gentle new collection, such as "gaining agreement"—in my day, they called that "closing the guy." The approach and style is fresh and politically correct, having no tired gender faux pas; good training for all of us. I found myself being nicely reminded of my need to listen and respond appropriately. Great program!

Sell to Needs: This disc in the Wilson Learning series provides information any salesperson can use to work better and smarter.

Taxi

Rating:

Publisher Name:
News Electronic Data, Inc.

Software Requirements: **MPC**

Suggested Retail Price: **$79.95**

*T*axi is another one of those CD-ROMs that help define what multimedia is all about. Five minutes with this disc and you'll know why there are some things CDs and computers can do that books alone cannot. This single disc has virtually everything a traveler to New York, Chicago, Los Angeles, San Francisco, or Washington D.C. needs to know to book a room, locate a good restaurant, or find something to do between appointments. Whether you're visiting these cities on business or pleasure, *Taxi* helps make your trip more business-like or pleasurable.

This disc is the best preparation you can have for visting these top five locations, short of boning up on the native language of its cab drivers. And that's the only problem with *Taxi*: Just when you need it most, it may be back in your office or home, sitting in your CD-ROM drive. Luckily, you can print out maps and information ahead of time to take with you, or fax them to your destination for retrieval there.

Honest reviews of hotels and other facilities are a strong point of the *Taxi* CD-ROM.

Taxi is a Microsoft Windows-based program with a massive database of information on each of the five covered cities. Don't fault this disc for not covering more cities until you see how much data is included for the five biggies (which are, after all, the top destinations for a vast number of trips each year—and locals will find this disc priceless, too).

First, there's a comprehensive street map, continuously zoom-in-able like DeLorme's *Street Atlas*. You can click the Taxi button to create an easy-to-follow path from where you are to where you want to go, taking into account all the one-way streets and other semi-permanent obstacles in your path. For cities this large, even residents will value the advice this module provides.

Next, there's a restaurant guide based on Zagat Surveys. Capsule descriptions tell you what to expect from each eatery, including prices and dress codes. You may search the restaurant database by dozens of parameters, including type of food, ratings (not just best food, but by decor, service, or views!), special features (such as wine list, after-midnight dining, etc.), and much more. Trust me, no matter what criteria you use to select a restaurant (say, you want informal, cheap, Thai restaurants with a great view, located within two miles of your hotel), *Taxi* will accommodate you.

If that weren't enough, when you've selected your restaurant, click once with the mouse and *Taxi* provides a customized map with your bistro highlighted with a little symbol! No more hunting through the Yellow Pages in your hotel room (no more

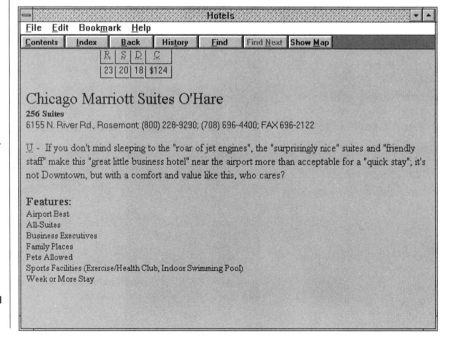

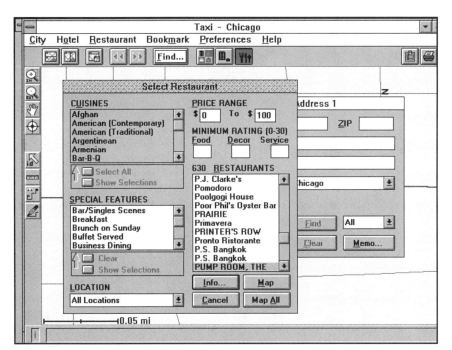

Taxi lets you select restaurants using your own special criteria, then view a map to the establishment at the click of a button.

hunting *for* the Yellow Pages in your hotel room). You can march into your target city already equipped with a list of places to eat, and lacking only enough time to visit them all.

Hotels can also be selected by using similar broad selection parameters. Choose by amenities, location, price, food, and other important—to you—measures. You can also find landmarks, museums, plan a walking tour, or retrieve other key information from this disc. The accuracy and honesty of the information is refreshing (whole chains of hotels are described as "bland but reliable"), and it's the kind of data you can count on, with very little risk.

There are several drawbacks to this disc, of course. First, there's the matter of portability. If you travel to one of these five cities, this disc may be your big incentive to get a notebook computer with a CD-ROM drive attached. Otherwise (unless you have access to a computer through a branch office), the information is not available to you while you're traveling—the exact time you may need something most, on the spur of the moment.

Taxi *is an incredible and useful database of hotel, restaurant, and route information for the five largest cities in the United States.*

Using *Taxi* effectively requires advance planning. You'll need to search through the database and print out maps, hotel guides, restaurant lists, and so forth ahead of time, and take a sheaf of paper along with you on the trip. This is not the most ideal of circumstances.

The other main drawback to *Taxi* is that once you've used it for one of these cities, you'll wish it were available for all the other, smaller destinations you frequent. Happily, the vendor plans to add other key cities,

from Atlanta and Boston to Dallas, Miami, San Diego, and St. Louis (and a dozen more in between).

Finally, *Taxi* requires a lot of your hard disk space. Our installation took up 29MB and wasn't even a full configuration. What you get in exchange for all that magnetic real estate is relatively fast access to the mapping and path information. The hotel and restaurant databases reside on your hard disk, as well. A full installation copies all the mapping data to the disk, so that you don't even need the CD-ROM to use the program. I didn't even explore this option: I only have a 1 gigabyte hard disk drive in my main computer, and 30-40MB here or there can start to add up to something substantial rather quickly.

Company travel departments, travel agents, and anyone who visits these cities a lot (or lives in one of them) will find *Taxi* an essential disc to have.

Allegro PC Library

Rating: ◉ ◉ ◉ 1/2

Publisher Name:
Allegro New Media

Software Requirements: MPC

Suggested Retail Price: $59.95

The only way Allegro's *PC Library* will be too elementary for you is if you can leap tall buildings with a single bound or if you have Kodak stamped somewhere on the inside of your cranium. Other than that, you will certainly get your money's worth out of this CD-ROM title.

Replete with some 30 titles, ranging from hardware discussions to operating systems to software and network instruction, *PC Library* provides an excellent source of informational materials at ready access to the user.

Search features include wild card, proximity, and Boolean (and, or, not) methods. Automatic page turning (cruise control) is another user-friendly feature that makes this package easy to use. That means you can search for keywords using DOS wild card specifications (e.g., IBM*), specify how close physically in the text the next two keywords should appear for a search to retrieve a passage, or search for combinations of terms (such as IBM PC AND CD-ROM, or COMPUTER OR SYSTEM NOT MACINTOSH).

Hot spots (green or gray text) are used throughout the text to denote concealed images, narrations, text, or video. The CD-ROM comes with a complete instruction manual that is well organized, easy to use, and full of descriptions of the tools available for manipulating and accessing the data on the CD-ROM.

The books on this CD-ROM include topics such as Harvard Graphics, Paradox, Microsoft Access, WordPerfect, Windows 3.1, Windows for Workgroups, LANtastic, Novell Netware, Excel, Quattro Pro, Microsoft Project, Lotus 1-2-3 Release 2.4, Lotus 1-2-3 Release 4.0 for Windows, PC parts and components, Upgrading PCs, OS/2 2.0, and even a title pertaining to children and computers.

A collection of 30 easily searchable computer manuals and 50 interactive videos with reasonably up-to-date information for the novice to old pro.

In addition to the books on *PC Library*, there are some 50 interactive videos, and many, many pictures, tables, and images. Interested in how to physically install a modem? Well, hop over to the video section and ask to see the video clip showing a modem being installed in a slot on a motherboard.

The downside, if any, is that software and hardware change so quickly that it is difficult to keep track of the most up-to-date changes and technologies. Even at that, this title has more than enough in the way of materials on it to easily justify its purchase. What we need are frequently updated versions of this disc, provided on a quarterly basis with all the latest information.

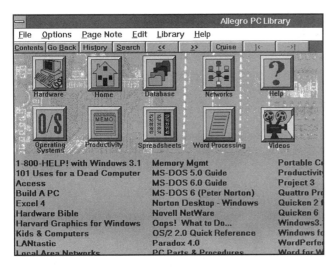

Dozens of useful books are available on the *Allegro PC Library* disc.

Business Library

A llegro's provided yet another solid hitter with its *Business Library, Volume 1.* With only the information and advice provided on a range of topics such as sales, marketing, finance, management, real estate, and career development, this CD-ROM title would merit a good hard look. However, and in addition to the above, you get roughly two hours of video in the form of three videotapes, which are also included on the CD-ROM.

A good basic business library, all on one easy-to-use disc, is included in this Allegro offering.

The book titles, twelve in all, include the *Business to Business Communications Handbook; The Feel of Success in Selling; Finance and Accounting for Nonfinancial Managers; How To Get People To Do Things Your Way; How To Make Big Money in Real Estate in the Tighter, Tougher '90s Market; International Herald Tribune Guide to Business Travel EUROPE; Joyce Lain Kennedy's Career Book; Meeting Rules and Procedures; State of the Art Marketing Research; Successful Direct Marketing Methods; Successful Telemarketing;* and *Total Global Strategy, Managing for Worldwide Competitive Advantage.*

The video titles, totaling three, are comprised of *30 Timeless Direct Marketing Principles, From Advertising to Integrated Marketing Communications,* and *New Product Development.*

Search features include wild card, proximity, and Boolean (and, or, not) methods. Automatic page turning (cruise control) is another user-friendly feature that makes this package easy to use. Hot spots (green or gray text) are used throughout the text to denote concealed images, narrations, text, or video. The CD-ROM comes with a complete instruction manual that is well organized, easy to use, and full of descriptions of the tools available for manipulating and accessing the data on the CD-ROM.

There is virtually no learning curve to using this title, everything is an easy point-and-click away. Books and videos are segmented by chapters or sections providing bite size pieces to deal with. The topical

Rating:

Publisher Name:
Allegro New Media

Software Requirements: **MPC**

Suggested Retail Price: **$59.95**

materials provided in *Business Library,* as the titles indicate, provide a broad range of subjects from which to choose.

If you are looking for a series of business titles and videos for your home or business library, you will be hard pressed to locate a nicer collection of titles under one roof than what you will find in Allegro New Media's *Business Library.*

Allegro Business Library: **Finance and Accounting for NonFinancial Managers is among the books included in this business library disc.**

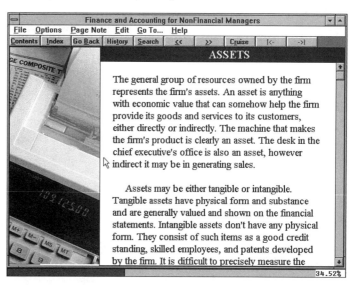

The Clinton Health Security Plan: What It Means, What It Costs

Rating:

Publisher Name:
Allegro New Media

Software Requirement: **MPC/ Macintosh**

Suggested Retail Price: **$14.95**

What could have been a dry, boring database of information has been brought alive and even made personal by this CD-ROM. For businesses and individuals seeking information on the health-care proposal at hand—particularly how it may affect their firm or family—this package should be a welcome addition to the reference library.

If you were expecting a dry, boring copy of the Clinton health-care plan, you will be pleasantly surprised by this effort from Allegro New Media. While the CD-ROM does include the plain-vanilla text of the Health Care Act (and there is a *lot* of it), it also contains a host of peripheral opinions, interviews, addresses to the public, video clips, Presidential addresses to Congress, and even addresses, telephone, and fax numbers of Congressmen in the House and Senate.

This type of resource is one area where the power of CD-ROM can be exploited to save vast amounts of research time. By opening up the section on the Health Care Act and performing a word search,

information can be located in literally the blink of an eye.

Additionally, the text and videos are surrounded by a variety of pictures in the left margin, and two control bars—one along the right-hand side to move around within a section, the other a red control bar along the bottom that allows you to roam quickly throughout the CD-ROM in general—making this title not only exceptionally easy-to-use, but also easy on the eyes.

Supplementing the CD-ROM are video clips such as Health Care Speeches and Reports, including speeches by both the President and Hillary Rodham Clinton, video question-and-answer sessions with individuals involved in the health care industry, and even the September 22, 1993 address by the President to the Joint Session of Congress in both written and video form.

In the Commentaries section are

Health Care Speeches and Reports
Speeches
President & Mrs. Clinton's Speech at Ambridge, Pa 11.3.93
President's Remarks at Kennedy Library 10.29.93
Remarks at Johns Hopkins 10.28.93
Remarks on Business & Social Responsibility 10.21.93
Remarks to The Pool Leaving Hyatt 10.21.93
President's Remarks on Health Care & Violence 10.8.93
Remarks to AFL-CIO in San Francisco 10.4.93

position papers by the American Bar Association, National Association of Health Underwriters, U.S. Chamber of Commerce, and the National Federation of Independent Businesses to name just a few.

Also included in text form on the CD-ROM is *Health Security: The President's Report to the American People.*

Providing accessible information on President Clinton's proposed health-care plan, this disc is a valuable long-term benefits planning aid for individuals and businesses.

If the Clinton plan makes it through Congress in anything resembling the form presented on this disc, savvy business owners will want to review the information herein to plan for the coming changes. Individuals, too, can glean lots of important data from the CD. If health care in the United States as implemented in the opening years of the 21st century is important to you, The Clinton Health Security Plan: *What It Means, What It Costs* is an important CD-ROM for your reference library.

Direct Phone

There are various criteria you can use to choose a CD-ROM phone directory, and the most important of all should be whether or not the number you want to find is in there, and correct. That may not be the only parameter, but it's way ahead of whatever is in second place.

By that standard, *Direct Phone* is a real winner. I'm in there. *PhoneDisc USA* couldn't find me, and I've had the same listed telephone number for more than 20 years. But, with one quick check of *Direct Phone*, there I was, big as life. Now, if I ever move and need to find out what my old phone number was, I can use this disc. You can use *Direct Phone* to find phone numbers, too, without spending the big bucks some other disc sets entail. You do give up a little in flexibility and power, however.

Direct Phone is easy to use. Just load the DOS-based shell program (which works for all the ProPhone products) and type in a name. There is one disc for residential phone numbers (I'm on that one), and another disc for business phone numbers. Some other sets have one for East Coast and one for West Coast, for each category. ProPhone publishes updates of this disc in January, April, July, and October.

All the phone disc publishers bandy about some statistics about how many phone numbers change each year, and also about how many listings are on their disc that aren't on those of their competitors. In truth, though, unless you're a fan of the Grateful Dead, most of your friends don't pack up and move that often. The kind of people whose residential phone numbers change that often aren't the folks you want to associate with anyway. Businesses tend to be even more stable.

So, the actual percentage of out-of-date numbers you encounter is likely to be very small, even if you update yours only once a year or so. I quite happily used a 1991 business CD directory until very recently, when I replaced it with one of the discs reviewed for this book. Unless you're compiling phone numbers and addresses for business purposes (and, granted, many users of this product will be), don't worry too much about accuracy of every single number you find. Overall, your hit rate will be quite good.

> **Direct Phone *is a good, inexpensive phone directory with business and residential listings for the entire U.S. on one disc each.***

(ProPhone spends around $100,000 annually to buy phone books and ship them to China, where the names are manually entered and shipped back to the United States at about 2 million names a week.)

Direct Phone lets you retrieve listings by last name. ProPhone offers other, more expensive versions of its phone database that let you find listings by address (including portions of the address), city, state, ZIP code, phone number, and type of business (including SIC code). Because the same searching engine is used for all its products, you may find that there are parameters shown that you can't access. If you'd like to look up all the attorneys in New York City, say, to mount some sort of personal vendetta (I've read that the city has 30,000 too many lawyers), you can't do it.

But, if you want a cheap, usable phone number look-up tool, *Direct Phone* is hard to beat. You can use this disc to locate long-lost relatives, college roommates, missing class members for that 20-year reunion, or just the phone number for that Lebanese pizza joint you remember in Toledo. I found 86 different David Buschs in the United States, which makes you shudder when you think about it.

Rating: ◉ ◉ ◉

Publisher Name: **Pro CD, Inc.**

Software Requirements: **MPC**

Suggested Retail Price: **$99.95**

Fantastic Fonts

Rating:

Publisher Name:
Expert Software

Software Requirements: MPC

Suggested Retail Price: $49.95

The Random House Collegiate Dictionary defines "host" as a "multitude or great number...of things." When you install Expert Software's *Fantastic Fonts*, you get exactly that—a host of fonts.

Some 365 TrueType fonts lie dormant on this CD-ROM just waiting to be unleashed in your Windows applications. From the dignified Palmer Normal to the flashy Antic to the flowing Zack Medium, you will find enough variety to suit almost any need.

The 365 available fonts offer a distinct and refreshing advantage over many standard font packages: quantity. As often as not, many packages contain only 17, 20, or 50 fonts tailored to meet a specific application. With *Fantastic Fonts'* 365 choices, it probably doesn't matter what the application is, you will find a suitable font for it.

Aside from the sheer number of fonts, the quality of those chosen by Expert Software to be included on this CD-ROM certainly makes putting together a report, school paper, newsletter, or business card much easier. In fact, you may find yourself having just too much fun with your document and being too flashy if you aren't careful.

The documentation that is supplied with the CD-ROM provides examples of all the fonts contained in the package. An especially nice feature, since Windows only allows one font at a time to be displayed in the font manager. Additionally, the documentation is very well written, with sufficient detail to help even the novice Windows user in installing fonts.

While all the fonts on this disc aren't fantastic, there is a wide enough variety of them to meet the needs of any desktop publisher using Microsoft Windows.

Expert Software has grouped these fonts into three basic categories: Serif, Sans Serif, and Decorative.

Serif fonts are text fonts, intended to meet the needs of long documents such as school papers and business reports, and are the easiest to read with hooks and curves at the ends of the characters to lead your eyes to the next character. Sans Serif fonts are intended to be used in "serious" documents, such as spreadsheets or, in large bold letters, a headline.

Decorative fonts provide an artsy twist to a word or document by drawing attention to it. You might find these used in a business card, club logo, or youth newsletter.

Installation is a snap, or perhaps a click (of the mouse). Once installed, you can access these fonts through any appropriate Windows application such as a word processor.

Also included are 50 borders for use with applications that support Windows MetaFile graphics. Examples provided with the documentation for *Fantastic Fonts* include Word for Windows 2.0, WordPerfect 5.2 for Windows, and Ami Pro 2.0. While these are not the current versions of the noted applications, the borders still seem to work with the later versions.

All in all, Expert Software's *Fantastic Fonts* will be a welcome addition to your software collection, providing enough fonts to fulfill almost any amateur desktop publisher's needs.

Great Business Jokes

Don't worry about your job: it will be around a lot longer than *you* will.

And, our product isn't really delayed—it just doesn't match the description on the packaging yet.

If neither of those are funny to you, there are bound to be some out of the 175-plus gags on this CD-ROM that you will find side-splitting. Senses of humor vary, so ClipAction has put something on this disc for everybody. You find old chestnuts sprinkled in among fresh new material, so don't complain. If just one of these jokes puts your audience at ease during your next business presentation, you'll get back the cost of this disc in extra sales, improved relations, or, just maybe, that big raise you've been dreaming about.

Great Business Jokes is a CD-ROM with a collection of business- and computer-oriented funnies. You get both Video for Windows and QuickTime versions on the same disc, so that you can pass this disc around the office and anyone can use it. Although this product is advertised as using "professional standup comedians," don't expect to see anyone you've heard of delivering gags in a comedy club setting. The clips all appear to have been taped in front of a bedsheet or something taped up on the wall, and the comics, while definitely professional, are still waiting to be discovered—somewhere. Each clip is only a few seconds long, and can be played with provided software.

The cheesy production values won't bother you if you just want to view the clips and get some sense of how the gags should be delivered, or are clueless about timing.

You can run one over and over until you get it right, or collect a bunch of them on floppy disks for review on a machine that's not equipped with a CD-ROM drive (I can just see these disks taped up on the bulletin board!).

However, you're also advised to actually incorporate the clips into presentations that accommodate these video formats, such as Microsoft PowerPoint, WordPerfect Presentations, Aldus Persuasion, or Corel Show. Uh-uh. Bad idea. You won't make any points with these cheap shots.

Unpolished performances of decent jokes make this a fun, but unessential disc of business humor for speechwriters and presenters.

Moreover, finding an appropriate joke isn't exactly easy. There's no browser or other search facility, although the complete text of all the gags is provided in a document you can load into your word processor and hunt through with global searching commands for keywords. I suppose you could search for "boss" or "accountant" or "lawyer," but you'd have to be smart enough to also look for "CEO," "CFO," and "attorney," to cover all the bases.

And wait a minute...if all the jokes are in that document, why not print out the text and just use that. Why bother with the video clips? Why bother with this disc at all—why not just buy a joke book? Well, I'll tell you why. *Great Business Jokes* is a lot more fun to play with than any stupid joke book. There really were some jokes here we hadn't heard before...a lot of them.

Maybe you need a presentation with cheap looking video clips. Or, you really wanted a CD-ROM drive so you could play Microsoft Golf, and this CD was the closest thing you could come to for an excuse to buy one. If you can find this disc at a low price, it's a lot of fun. I've already told you what to expect—and what not to expect.

Rating: ◉ ◉ 1/2

Publisher Name: **ClipAction**

Software Requirements: **MPC/Macintosh**

Suggested Retail Price: **$89.95**

Home Office Executive for Windows

Rating: ●

Publisher Name:
Quantum Axcess

Software Requirements: **MPC**

Suggested Retail Price: **$19.95**

T alk about quantity: This CD-ROM has an abundance of programs. Just about anything you need to improve your business skills is here somewhere. Although the disc gives you about 190 programs and they only occupy approximately 100MB, they are varied and very useful. The programs are a combination of shareware and freeware. They appear to be the pick of the best.

The CD-ROM installs in Windows and installation instructions are printed on the disc. The installed program is basically a well-ordered menu program from which all other programs can be run or installed. Quantum Axcess has supplied a text file that gives detailed instructions about installing in case you run into problems. Once installed, the program occupies less than 1MB of disc space. If you have used Quantum Axcess's other CD-ROMs, such as *300+ Way Cool Games for Windows,* you are already familiar with the menu interface. It's basically the same.

The menu shows a brief description of each program selected and allows you to see the different programs available by giving you several icons on the toolbar to select from, such as All Programs (183), Personal Information Manager programs (32), Financial Programs (32), and Miscellaneous Programs (9). If you want to select only programs that run under Microsoft Excel (34), Microsoft Word for Windows (41), WordPerfect for Windows (14), Quattro Pro for Windows (10), Lotus 123 for Windows (6), or Ami Pro for Windows (27), these can be selected by clicking the associated icon; the menu displays only programs for that application.

A program selected from the menu will run without installation by simply clicking the Run button. If the Run button is grayed, the program requires installation and clicking the install button will install the program.

There is lots of good business-oriented software for home office workers in this easy to access soft ware collection.

The Miscellaneous section includes Global Time, a program that displays the time on a map, Maintenance Planning & Management Development to track inventory, and preventative maintenance. There are all types of Personal Information Managers: Account Manager 1.3, Business Plan Master, Client Book, and Mini Calendar. The selections for the spreadsheets are made up mostly of template and macro files for the different applications.

There are lots of programs to choose from and this CD-ROM should have enough really good ones to make it worthwhile for anyone looking for shareware or freeware applications that will help them in business.

Among the hundreds of business oriented programs on this disc is this mortgage analyzer.

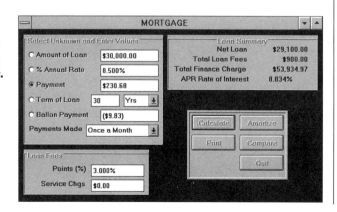

MPC Wizard

Aris Entertainment has shrewdly put together a disc with tons of multimedia oriented utilities, drivers, benchmark programs, and explanatory files, and then made it available at a price that any PC owner would find difficult to resist. If you want to test your system or update your video, CD-ROM drive, or sound board driver to the latest version, you'll want this disc. And, if it happens to include some samples of Aris' hot MediaClips multimedia sounds and images—available for purchase separately— then so much the better, for everyone concerned.

MPC Wizard *has valuable multimedia hardware tests, a truckload of video, soundboard, and CD-ROM drivers, and a preview of Aris' MediaClips product, at an unbeatable price.*

The installation program installs several modules to your system. One of these is the MediaClips viewer. The royalty-free sound, video, and graphics clips are interesting, but

probably not the main reason why you purchased this disc. The *MPC Wizard* program is the real payoff.

That utility's main menu screen has five buttons arrayed along the left side of the window, with a large text and graphics viewing window occupying the rest of your screen. You can select from What's an MPC? (a good introduction to MPC-1 and MPC-2 specifications), MPC Tests, Install Driver, Test Results, and Exit.

In the Tests section, you can give your drive a workout with the CD-ROM test to make sure it is performing up to speed. There's a color capability test to determine how many colors you can display in Windows. The Sound Tests help ensure that your PC can play standard audio tracks, .WAV files, and MIDI files. There's a Video for Windows test button to see if your system can play back digital motion video in the Microsoft Video, Intel Indeo, and SuperMatch Cinepak formats.

In the Drivers section, you can choose recent video drivers of 85 different types, 16 different makes of sound board drivers, but

only two CD-ROM drivers (Chinon and Pioneer). Because drivers change frequently, it's likely that the version of this disc that you buy will have different drivers than mine, and probably a lot more options. Having all these drivers on one disc can be a lifesaver if you manage to lose or damage a key installation disc for a video card, sound board, or CD-ROM drive. You may even find that this disc has newer drivers than the ones you are using. That's particularly important for Windows drivers for video cards, which are typically updated every couple months to add features or remove bugs.

Rating: ◉ ◉ ◉

Publisher Name:
Aris Entertainment

Software Requirements: MPC

Suggested Retail Price: $14.95

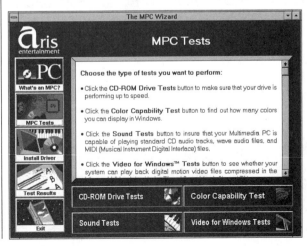

The *MPC Wizard* lets you test your MPC computer, install drivers, or review the requirements for multimedia systems.

Multimedia Business 500

Business owners, executives, salespeople, job seekers, or career advisors will love the wealth of information contained on this CD-ROM. You find essential data that can be used to choose stocks for your portfolio, create mailing lists of top companies, or search out a young growth company for employment opportunities.

More than 450 major U.S. publicly held corporations (from Kodak to Xerox) are profiled, along with 40 important privately held companies (such as Domino's Pizza). That makes 490 firms, instead of 500—but

Profiles like this one of Eastman Kodak Company give you valuable background information about a corporation.

who's counting? Everything from heavy industrial firms to biotechnology and microchips is included.

For each company in the database, you find a detailed description of the firm and its history. The names, titles, ages, and pay of key executives are also displayed, so, if you're planning to apply for a job as CEO of, say, IBM, you'll be able to tell at a glance whether it pays enough to be worth your while. There's up to 10 years of employment data if your job goals are a bit more realistic. The company reports are extracted from *Hoover's Handbook of American Business,* while the financial information was supplied by Standard & Poor's Compustat Services.

Those compiling mailing lists will find addresses, phone, and fax numbers for each company, along with important products, brand names, and competitors. The latter information can help you properly classify each company on your mailing list. Stock pickers will appreciate all the information described above, plus the financial and stock information, dating back as far as 10 years

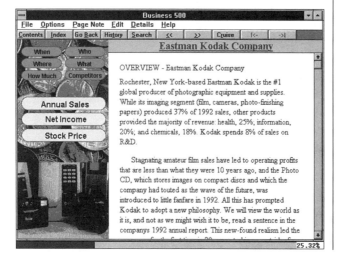

for some of the companies on the list.

This information is easy to retrieve through a standard Microsoft Windows interface that looks a lot like the one you find in any Help file. Click Contents or Index buttons to view listings of the companies and topics covered, or choose the Search button to find a company quickly by typing in the name or keywords. There are 50 different categories (size, products, sales, etc.) that can be used as search criteria. There are also forward and back buttons and a history list that can be used to retrace your steps, or jump quickly through the database.

Business 500 *includes information on nearly 500 of the top publicly and privately held corporations in the United States.*

Because you can create your own notes and annotations, print listings, and cut and paste text into your word processor, *Business 500* automates compiling mailing lists and reports based on the data on this disc.

The multimedia aspects of *Business 500* aren't overwhelming, but they're interesting, nevertheless. There are 50 PR-type videos of company product demonstrations, and executive interviews that similarly must be viewed with a grain of salt.

Multimedia PC *Maximizer*

Any business owner will love *Maximizer,* which is shopping and keeping abreast of the electrono-wonderland at its finest. In this land of "update or disintegrate," most computer users love to see what is available whether for purchase or simply to follow the wonderful offerings that are out there. Everything you want to know about products that are on the market for your PC is included on this disc.

The Main Screen is broken into two parts. One side holds the table of contents, and the other side shows the information on the product that you have highlighted. Sometimes there is audio and animation. Of course, the on-line glossary is fantastic and very nicely done. How many times have you begun to read about something new and said, "What the heck is this all about?" Just click the Gloss button and look it up.

Many phrases in this CD are cross-indexed and have help available. It is simple to navigate and is divided into groups for ease of use. There are 13 chapters, which are: CD ROM & Personal Computers, Kodak Photo CD, CD ROM & Business Software, CD ROM & Sales/marketing, CD ROM & Business Databases, CD ROM & Clip Media, CD ROM & Home Reference, CD ROM & Home Education, CD ROM & After Hours, Illustration & Animation, Simulation, Investment Protection, and Computer Media. Six appendixes include: Promotions and Coupons, Graphics & Demos, Product Index, Company Index, Multimedia Press Kits, and Multimedia Publications. Within each chapter and appendix, the contents are broken down by title. Again, just click and

read, listen, or watch what the company has to say about its product.

The top right side offers Audio, Info, Coupon, and Graphics. When applicable, the box is darkened for your selection/deselection. As you are using this CD, you may stop for a bit, which activates a Slideshow/Commercial. Clicking the mouse or any key will bring you back.

> *Anyone has time to click around and read the concise, well-presented product information on Maximizer. The only problem I had in using this CD is that my wish list has definitely grown! Try it out, you'll really be amazed.*

The *Multimedia PC Maximixer* folks offer a contest and a survey that when submitted get you a discount for your next edition. If you find yourself interested in a product but want to know more, there is an

Rating: ◉ ◉ ◉ 1/2

Publisher Name: **Takin' Care of Business, Inc.**

Software Requirements: **MPC**

Suggested Retail Price: **$59.95**

Info Card that you can fill out, print, and mail in. There is also a discount granted for this participation. At any time, there is a Print and Print Panel option so that you can print the contents of the text panel to your printer.

Takin' Care of Business does just that. The intent is clear that these folks offer a delightful way to market products. What they provide is a bonus of information and education. The interface is simple and easy to use. A novice or a seasoned pro could access its features with equal ease. The consumer of today is in no mood for extra razz-ma-tazz, we just want the facts and access to more. Plus we like a good deal. It's all here.

Of course, if you have a product to market and are looking for fresh new ways, this is a "must see!" I know folks who won't look at a resume unless it wiggles and sings to you! As a consumer, I found this format to be non-threatening, plus I was sitting down! There is nothing more difficult than trying to stand at a shelf in a store and decide on the integrity and quality of a new product.

Professor Multimedia

Rating:

Publisher Name:
Individual Software

Software Requirements: **MPC**

Suggested Retail Price: **$79.95**

*P*rofessor Multimedia can teach any businessperson how to choose and use multimedia tools through a series of lessons that use the very multimedia tools discussed to bring users up to speed faster than a quad-speed CD-ROM drive. It provides an overview of several of the leading authoring tools, from Microsoft PowerPoint to WordPerfect Presentations, as well as several lesser-known tools.

All the instructional material can be reached through a decidedly un-Windows-like interface that depends on large picture icons and buttons rather than pull-down menus. You'll need no instruction to use this interface, however, because the functions and options are readily apparent from the on-screen displays. Most screens have a menu, Return, or Exit button that takes you back to the previous screen, the main menu, or exits from the current lesson.

Professor Multimedia is a lively introduction to multimedia hardware and software, with valuable basic how-to lessons and overviews that anyone can learn from.

The main screen offers four inviting topics for exploration: Pizazz (an overview of what multimedia can do, with some stunning graphics examples); What is Multimedia? (a more thorough look at what components make up the typical multimedia presentation); Everyday Multimedia (which looks at uses for multimedia in the home, education, and for entertainment); and Multimedia in Business (a description of multimedia presentations and some of the software tools used to create them).

Separate sections explore the world of graphics, sound, animation, video, multimedia PC hardware, and tools and accessories. You can get a quick lesson on .WAV digital sound, audio CD soundtracks, or MIDI music, and then jump right into animation or a look at different graphics options.

If you still don't understand what multimedia is all about, this disc includes several demonstration programs, such as Microsoft's *Dinosaurs*, Ebook's *Impressionism and its Sources*, and Broderbund's *Arthur's Teacher Trouble*. There are lessons that lead you through creating a mini presentation with five of the top packages, ranging from Lotus Freelance to PowerPoint. The video, sounds, and graphics files on the disc can be used to experiment with multimedia, or reused in your own presentations, if you wish.

Professor Multimedia won't teach you everything you need to know about multimedia, but it will show you the broad range of things you need to learn. It makes an excellent introduction to multimedia for business people, teachers, or students, and could even be used as a demo tool to show clients the capabilities of multimedia. This is a great introduction to an important new technology.

Professor Multimedia can teach you all about multimedia for the IBM PC.

Sure!Maps

For those looking for a customizable map database, *Sure!Maps* should readily supply all your needs. As a database, editing, and retrieval utility, *Sure!Maps* (which comes with detailed full-color raster maps) provides strong planning and research tools.

What do you get with *Sure!Maps*? In and of itself, the base *Sure!Maps* package will probably not satisfy your needs. The purchaser gets a full set of USGS raster maps, including 1:22,000,000 and 1:1,000,000,000 scale world maps, 1:2,000,000 scale United States maps, sample maps (only) of portions of the Dallas metropolitan area at 1:24,000 and 1:100,00 scales; a sample SPOT satellite imagery map of portions of the Dallas metropolitan area; a sample Etak street-level map of portions of the Dallas metropolitan area; a 35,000 city database to locate U.S. cities on the maps by name or by latitude and longitude; ZIP code and area code prefix databases suitable for use in locating cities and to access demographic data such as population statistics and Metropolitan Statistical Area (MSA) information. Also provided are an Icon library of some 100 standard graphical symbols suitable for assigning titles and readily placeable anywhere on the maps, and an Icon editor that allows you to create your own symbols.

What don't you get with *Sure!Maps*? You don't get the optional map sets of more than 60 United States metropolitan areas. These map sets are available at an additional cost from Horizons Technology, Inc. A review of its catalog indicates that areas are mapped such that three to five major metropolitan areas are grouped on one CD-ROM.

For instance, the South Map Set contains USGS raster maps at 1:24,000 and 1:100,000 scale and street level vector maps of the Birmingham, Alabama area, the Atlanta, Georgia area, the Little Rock, Arkansas area, and the Memphis, Tennessee area.

Within these four metropolitan areas, some 12 of the 227 counties listed contain geo-referencing so that you can pinpoint addresses by manual entry and your address information will be linked with the corresponding address contained in the county map.

Sure!Maps *is easy to use, but the cost of the extra map databases can mount quickly.*

Depending on what you are interested in, prices vary widely. For instance, the detailed map sets (described above), which exist for a variety of metropolitan areas, cost an additional $99.00.

Regional maps, containing the raster maps in scales of 1:24,000 and 1:100,000 but do not contain the street-level vector maps, cost an additional $49.00. Spot Satellite Imagery Map Sets, which provide seamless satellite images of a major metropolitan area at a scale of 1:62,500,

Rating:

Publisher Name:
Horizon Technology, Inc.

Software Requirements: **MPC**

Suggested Retail Price: **$199.00**

cost an additional $499.00.

Also, for an additional $325.00, *Sure!Maps* offers custom maps of your choice.

Sure!Maps is a comparatively easy-to-use software. There is an excellent users manual provided with the base package. If you are not one for reading the directions before putting your child's Christmas gift together, it may take you a little longer, but even at that, Horizons Technology has made this very user friendly.

When would a purchaser need *Sure!Maps*? Horizons Technologies provides several applications/possible scenarios, including a sign company that wants to identify the location and availability of billboards for tracking purposes and also as a sales tool to show clients best locations relative to schools, businesses, residential areas, and so on.

If you are looking for detailed maps with the flexibility of an adjustable database, *Sure!Maps* should provide you with all the assistance you need.

Additional CD-ROM Titles

Title: 1000 of the World's Greatest Sound Effects
Suggested Retail Price: $49.95
Publisher: Multimedia
Platform: MPC/Macintosh
Description: Complete collection of sounds for your projects and multimedia business presentations.

Title: 1.1 Million Health & Medical Industry Reference Directory
Suggested Retail Price: $49.00
Publisher: American Business Information
Platform: MPC
Description: Complete reference work for the health care field, with names of care providers and their suppliers, phone numbers, addresses, and more.

Title: 11 Million Businesses Phone Book
Suggested Retail Price: $49.00
Publisher: American Business Information
Platform: MPC
Description: Every business phone number in the book is on this disc—or so they say.

Title: 3-D Tutor
Suggested Retail Price: $119.95
Publisher: Zelos!
Platform: Macintosh
Description: Tutorial on how to bring your graphics projects for business to life.

Title: 70 Million Households Phone Book
Suggested Retail Price: $69.00
Publisher: American Business Information
Platform: MPC

Description: Find your household, or those of your friends and enemies, through this comprehensive phone listing.

Title: 9-Digit ZIP Code Directory
Suggested Retail Price: $49.00
Publisher: American Business Information
Platform: MPC
Description: Look up ZIP codes quicker than a call to the post office.

Title: A Zillion Sounds
Suggested Retail Price: $24.95
Publisher: EBook
Platform: MPC/Macintosh
Description: Sound effects and clips for multimedia presentations in business.

Title: Accumail
Suggested Retail Price: $295.00
Publisher: Group 1 Software
Platform: MPC
Description: Database of valid U.S. addresses & ZIP codes

Title: Airworks Music Library
Suggested Retail Price: $49.95
Publisher: EBook
Platform: MPC/Macintosh
Description: Popular music for use in your multimedia presentations.

Title: America Alive Guidisc
Suggested Retail Price: $99.00
Publisher: CD Technology
Platform: MPC/Macintosh
Description: A wealth of information necessary to plan your business and

vacations trips. Photos, movies, and maps covering all 50 states, major cities, and attractions.

Title: American Business Phone Book
Suggested Retail Price: $298.00
Publisher: ABI Inc.
Platform: MPC
Description: Database of U.S. business telephone numbers, updated regularly.

Title: American Yellow Pages
Suggested Retail Price: $695.00 - 12 months
Publisher: American Business Information
Platform: MPC
Description: A regularly updated, highly accurate listing of businesses in the United States.

Title: Best Businesses
Suggested Retail Price: $39.95
Publisher: Affiliated Software Distributors
Platform: MPC
Description: Listing of top businesses in the U.S.

Title: Career Opportunities
Suggested Retail Price: $49.95
Publisher:: Quanta
Platform: MPC/Macintosh
Description: Know more before you choose your career. Includes job title, salary, future outlook, similar fields, job opportunities, and more.

Title: CD-CAD 3.7
Suggested Retail Price: $49.95

Publisher: Wizardware Multimedia
Platform: MPC
Description: Computer Assisted Drawing (CAD) software for your IBM PC.

Title: Complete Home and Office Legal Guide
Suggested Retail Price: $39.95
Publisher: Chestnut
Platform: MPC
Description: Law library and 500 legal forms from the authors of the *BBS Legal Guide.*

Title: ComputerWorks
Suggested Retail Price: $49.95
Publisher: Software Marketing
Platform: MPC
Description: Explore your computer through animated graphics. Learn the history of computers and test your computer know-how.

Title: Desktop Magic
Suggested Retail Price: $49.95
Publisher: Wizardware Multimedia
Platform: MPC
Description: Multimedia tool for business users

Title: European Update
Suggested Retail Price: $495.00
Publisher: Macmillan New Media
Platform: MPC/Macintosh
Description: Quarterly reports for anyone doing business in the European Community.

Title: Executive's Factomatic
Suggested Retail Price: $39.95
Publisher: Compton's NewMedia
Platform: MPC
Description: Facts and figures that any executive will want to know.

Title: Factomatic Business Library
Suggested Retail Price: $129.00
Publisher: Compton's NewMedia

Platform: MPC
Description: A library of information for the executive, covering key business and legal topics.

Title: Font Elegance
Suggested Retail Price: $49.99
Publisher: Fantazia Concepts
Platform: MPC
Description: Stylize your documents to capture attention. 3,000+ fonts for easy use and access.

Title: Future Test: Career Series
Suggested Retail Price: $49.95
Publisher: Future Technologies
Platform: MPC
Description: Aptitude tests for a variety of business and professional careers.

Title: Globe & Mail/Financial Times
Suggested Retail Price: $995.00
Publisher: Globe Information Services
Platform: MPC
Description: Full text of Canadian Globe & Mail and Financial Times.

Title: Government Giveaways for Entrepreneurs
Suggested Retail Price: $59.95
Publisher: Inforbusiness, Inc.
Platform: MPC
Description: Free stuff, including information, bargain merchandise, and grants for business people from the U.S. Government.

Title: Herald Tribune's Business Travel in Europe
Suggested Retail Price: $29.95
Publisher: Compton's NewMedia
Platform: MPC
Description: Everything you need to know to travel in Europe on business, pleasurable or otherwise.

Title: How Computers Work
Suggested Retail Price: $79.99

Publisher: Time Warner Interactive Group
Platform: Macintosh
Description: Graphical tour through the innards of your computer.

Title: Improving Your Job and Career Prospects
Suggested Retail Price: $49.95
Publisher: Queue
Platform: MPC/Macintosh
Description: Get a better job, or advance in the one you already have, through the tips included on this disc.

Title: Information U.S.A.
Suggested Retail Price: $69.95
Publisher: Infobusiness
Platform: MPC
Description: An almanac of business information, charts, graphs, and data for the businessperson.

Title: Interactive Business English, Parts I & II
Suggested Retail Price: $49.95
Publisher: Dyned International
Platform: MPC
Description: Disc-based lessons on English as used in business settings.

Title: Interactive Training for Directors
Suggested Retail Price: $199.00
Publisher: Media In Motion
Platform: Macintosh
Description: Learn about interactive training programs and how they can be used in business.

Title: Japan Business Travel Guide
Suggested Retail Price: $39.95
Publisher: Compton's NewMedia
Platform: MPC
Description: Avoid faux pas and get things accomplished during your travels in Japan with this helpful guide to customs and practices in the Far East.

Title: Job Power Source: Job Finding Skills for the '90s
Suggested Retail Price: $49.95
Publisher: InfoBusiness
Platform: MPC
Description: How to get a job and climb the corporate ladder.

Title: Jurassic Park: The Screen Saver
Suggested Retail Price: $34.95
Publisher: Asymetrix
Platform: MPC
Description: Movie soundtrack plus photos, animation, and sound effects.

Title: Marketplace Business with D & B Data
Suggested Retail Price: $995.00
Publisher: Marketplace Information
Platform: MPC
Description: Names, addresses, and Dun and Bradstreet Information on many U.S. businesses.

Title: Marketplace Business
Suggested Retail Price: $695.00
Publisher: Marketplace Information
Platform: Macintosh
Description: Names and addresses of many U.S. businesses.

Title: NAFTA
Suggested Retail Price: $99.95
Publisher: Young Minds, Inc.
Platform: MPC
Description: Complete North American Free Trade Agreement text.

Title: National Directory of Addresses & Telephone Numbers
Suggested Retail Price: $249.00
Publisher: Omnigraphics
Platform: MPC
Description: Yet another directory of business names, addresses, and telephone listings.

Title: National Trade Databank

Suggested Retail Price: $360.00
Publisher: U.S. Dept. of Commerce
Platform: MPC
Description: Official Commerce Department trade statistics database.

Title: Negotiators Factomatic
Suggested Retail Price: $39.95
Publisher: Compton's NewMedia
Platform: MPC
Description: Learn skills, tricks, and tips useful for negotiating contracts, orders, and other transactions.

Title: North American Facsimile Book
Suggested Retail Price: $299.95
Publisher: Quanta Press Inc.
Platform: MPC
Description: Fax & mail addresses of 150,000+ businesses in U.S., Canada, and Mexico.

Title: OSHA Regulations
Suggested Retail Price: $88.00
Publisher: U.S. Government Printing Office
Platform: MPC/Macintosh
Description: Database of information on Occupational Safety and Health Administration rules.

Title: People Who Lead People
Suggested Retail Price: $95.00
Publisher: Positive Employee Relations Council
Platform: MPC/Macintosh
Description: For managers to help handle difficult personnel through role-playing games.

Title: Personal Daily PlanIt: Earth, Paradise, or Adrenaline
Suggested Retail Price: $9.95 each
Publisher: Media Vision
Platform: MPC/Macintosh
Description: Keep track of your days through voice command. Choose wildlife, swimsuit models, or sport scenes as

backgrounds.

Title: PowerTalk!
Suggested Retail Price: $49.95
Publisher: ZCI Publishing
Platform: MPC/Macintosh
Description: Complete text of the following best-sellers: *Unlimited Power*, *Awaken the Giant Within*, *Other People's Money*, and *Unlimited Wealth*, plus info on authors and reviews of the books.

Title: ProPhone Business database
Suggested Retail Price: $349.00
Publisher: ProCD, Inc.
Platform: MPC
Description: Business telephone listings, updated regularly.

Title: Public Relations Handbook
Suggested Retail Price: $49.95
Publisher: Compton's NewMedia
Platform: MPC
Description: A public communications primer for businesses.

Title: Sales Managers Factomatic
Suggested Retail Price: $39.95
Publisher: Compton's NewMedia
Platform: MPC
Description: All the tips and tricks a sales manager needs to sell, sell, sell.

Title: Secrets of Executive Success
Suggested Retail Price: $39.95
Publisher: Compton's NewMedia
Platform: MPC
Description: Learn how to succeed in business by really trying.

Title: Secrets of Power Negotiating
Suggested Retail Price: $49.95
Publisher: IBM Corp.
Platform: MPC
Description: Learn the secrets of striking a deal.

Title: Selling In the 90's

Suggested Retail Price: $59.95
Publisher: Compton's NewMedia
Platform: MPC
Description: New tips for selling effectively.

Title: SpeedDial
Suggested Retail Price: $395.00
Publisher: Bureau Development
Platform: MPC
Description: Phone numbers and more in a massive telephone database.

Title: Standards Search
Suggested Retail Price: $300.00
Publisher: Society of Automotive Engineers
Platform: MPC
Description: All the SAE standards needed by automotive designers, engineers, and their suppliers.

Title: Stockwatch Canada
Suggested Retail Price: $395.00
Publisher: OSS Inc.
Platform: MPC
Description: Information about companies on the Toronto, Montreal, and Vancouver Stock Exchanges.

Title: Supervisors Factomatic
Suggested Retail Price: $39.95
Publisher: Compton's NewMedia
Platform: MPC
Description: Tips and tricks of the master supervisors, revealed for your edification.

Title: Take Five
Suggested Retail Price: $49.95
Publisher: Voyager Company
Platform: Macintosh
Description: Activities to unwind without leaving your desk.

Title: Tax Info '93
Suggested Retail Price: $39.95
Publisher: Walnut Creek
Platform: MPC

Description: Lots of government tax information. Presumably '94 and '95 updates will be available for later tax years.

Title: Technotools
Suggested Retail Price: $39.95
Publisher: Chestnut
Platform: MPC
Description: Tools you can use to bend computer technology to your will.

Title: Telephone Talk Volumes 1/2
Suggested Retail Price: $299.00
Publisher: Libra Multimedia
Platform: Macintosh
Description: Multi-lingual telephone speaking exercises. Learn how to communicate by phone more effectively.

Title: Training for Business Success
Suggested Retail Price: $49.95
Publisher: IBM Corp.
Platform: MPC
Description: Learn how to advance on the corporate ladder.

Title: The Vest Pocket MBA
Suggested Retail Price: $29.95
Publisher: Compton's NewMedia
Platform: MPC
Description: Cash-flow, revenue, and other business procedures streamlined.

Title: The Windows Collection
Suggested Retail Price: $59.00
Publisher: American Databankers
Platform: MPC
Description: Windows programs for business, home, and education.

Title: Too Many Typefonts
Suggested Retail Price: $29.95
Publisher: Chestnut
Platform: MPC
Description: Large collection of shareware and freeware fonts.

Title: Trade Opportunities Vol. 1

Suggested Retail Price: $299.00
Publisher: Wayzata Technology
Platform: MPC/Macintosh
Description: Information on thousands of companies, their products, and customers.

Title: Trade Opportunities Vol. 2
Suggested Retail Price: $149.00
Publisher: Wayzata Technologies
Platform: MPC/Macintosh
Description: Listings covering more than 40,000 companies not covered in the first edition.

Title: Type Fest
Suggested Retail Price: $69.95
Publisher: EBook
Platform: MPC/Macintosh
Description: Hundreds of fonts for your business documents.

Title: Type Treasury
Suggested Retail Price: $69.00
Publisher: Bitstream Inc.
Platform: Macintosh
Description: More fonts for your Macintosh business documents.

Title: Type Treats
Suggested Retail Price: $90.00
Publisher: Raynbow Software
Platform: MPC/Macintosh
Description: Yet more fonts for your business documents.

Title: TypeCase
Suggested Retail Price: $49.95
Publisher: SWFTE International Ltd.
Platform: MPC
Description: A collection of fonts with a great font browser utility.

Title: U.S. Postal Exam Pre-Release
Suggested Retail Price: $99.95
Publisher: Future Technologies
Platform: MPC
Description: Study for a post office job.

Chapter 5

Reference

Reference works are what CD-ROMs are all about: one compact disc containing everything you need to know, with all the facts, figures, maps, and other data, for a specific area of knowledge. Encyclopedias are very popular, especially since Microsoft raised the ante by porting its popular *Encarta* offering over to the Macintosh.

Amidst all the multimedia offerings, you still find a few text-heavy works. The reference category is a little more forgiving of multimedia weakness than others, because all we really need are the facts. Some top discs to look for in this category include *Microsoft Bookshelf*—if you can only find room for one reference CD-ROM among your collection of games or personal interest discs, this is the one you should have. The same company also brings you Microsoft *Encarta*, a dazzling new multimedia encyclopedia.

Other reference works in this chapter include atlases, including *Street Atlas USA*, which lets you zoom in to incredible levels of magnification to find virtually any street in the United States. There's also *CNN Global View*, an atlas that spices up its maps with Cable News Network video clips from the recent past. *Expert Astronomer* is your planetarium-on-disc when you need a reference work to the heavens.

Most of these reference works have videos, sound bites, pictures, and hypertext laced with links that lead you from cross-reference to cross-reference, until you're finally lost amidst a sea of information. But never fear! One click on the main menu icon and you're back at home base and ready for another research project. Read on to see the richness available in CD-ROM reference works.

Barron's Complete Book Notes

Rating: ◉ ◉ ◉ ◉

Publisher Name:
World Library Inc.

Software Requirements: **MPC**

Suggested Retail Price: **$99.95**

*B*arron's Complete Book Notes is the complete, unabridged text of 101 of Barron's most frequently used literary guides on one CD-ROM. The majority of writers have only one entry, although recognized "heavy hitters" in the

English language have more (William Shakespeare has 14, Charles Dickens has 5, and Ernest Hemmingway has 4). Barron's Guides, of course, are what you buy when you don't have time to read the book, but want to do a better job than picking up a "Classics Illustrated" comic book, right? Well, not really. The intent behind the Barron's Guides is to provide a student with a wide variety of information that will help him more readily understand a work that he has read. You can use them to shortcut, but they are a much more powerful resource when used properly.

Barron's Complete Book Notes installs itself in its own program group, World Libraries CD-ROM. If you buy any other products of this series (such as 171 Great

Mystery Classics or one of the Library of the Future CD-ROM products), they will install themselves in this program group, too. Installation is easy; you switch to the drive letter of your CD-ROM and type IN-STALL. You can choose an easy installation, or answer a few questions to customize the installation. The questions are very straightforward; there's almost no way to have a problem. You can install for either DOS or Windows.

After you double-click the Barron's Book Notes icon, you enter the program. A main menu comes up, allowing you to search by titles, authors, words, or strategy. Clicking the Titles button gives you a list of titles available. The first is "How to Use Barron's", followed by *Adventures of*

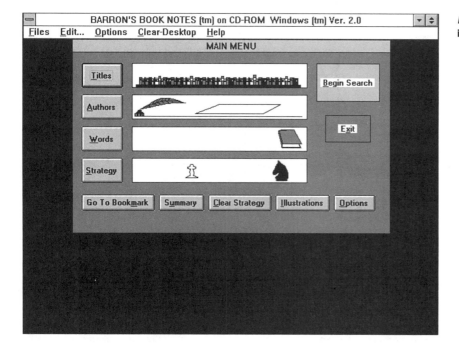

Barron's Book Notes provide insights into 101 classics of literature.

Huckleberry Finn by Mark Twain. If you have any doubts about what Barron's Guides are meant to do, click the first entry. There are also some brief interface details in this document, so it's worth scanning the first time you use the guide.

For a test case, Eric Maria Remarque's *All Quiet on the Western Front* was chosen, because this book was recently read by the author of this review. The title screen was selected, and the entry for *All Quiet on the Western Front* was selected by double-clicking the left mouse button. After a 1-2 second delay, the first page of the review comes up on-screen. It contains the date of the book's publication, followed by the author's name and book title. The name of the author of this particular Barron's Notes and the series editor's name and acknowledgments are next. This is followed by the table of contents.

The first significant information comes next: the biography of the author and the times he lived in. This is followed by sections detailing the plot, characters, setting, theme, style and structure, point of view, and form of the book. Then comes the story section, which is a chapter-by-chapter account of the book. Next is a "tests and answers" section that gives sample multiple choice and essay questions that might be asked of a student studying this book. Potential term paper topics, a glossary, and a critical reviews section follow. Credit is then given to the advisory board for Barron's Guides. The guide ends with a bibliography of Eric Maria Remarque, including a short description of his other works and those books written about him. In the table of contents, each of these sections is given a keyword, which can be highlighted. A hypertext button can then be clicked, and the program will skip to that section. There are a relatively small number of illustrations that are available in some of the guides; if the book you are reading contains an illustration, a small red block with an "IL" shows up in the upper right corner of the

page in which it is referenced. The Illustration button is unghosted on that screen and it can be viewed. The illustrations can also be viewed outside a guide; they have their own table of contents.

101 of Barron's most used Book Notes, available in one easily used software product, offers much to those who need such literary references, or who are just fond of great literature.

This CD-ROM offers a number of possibilities. The most obvious is, of course, for a student who will have to read a number of these works as part of an English course. English professors may want to have it on hand for reference. Some of the less obvious uses of this disk might be as a trivia buff's literature companion or a reader's preview guide, to help prioritize his/her reading. It is a good buy for those interested in literature; they will come up with their own ways to exploit the large amount of information available within it. The CD-ROM is much cheaper than the total price of all the individual guides.

You can't mark up a CD-ROM, but you can print part of the text, or the whole guide, and mark it up. The implementation is relatively fast; no lengthy delays like some CD-ROM-based data compilations, and the interface is clean and functional. There were

some glitches that occurred; moving some screens by a single line occasionally clipped the tops off one or more rows of letters. This seemed only to occur after resizing the screen to maximum size. It's almost full screen as configured: resizing it gets you a few lines at the price of such glitches. At times, a navigation command seemed to send the program to the wrong place; a request to go to screen 37 of one book might put you at the top of a different book.

These problems might also be those of a novice user, misunderstanding the interface slightly. Don't let these minor problems scare you. If you like literature, or need a reference like *Barron's Complete Book Notes*, this product is meant for you!

Compton's Interactive Encyclopedia for Windows

Rating:

Publisher Name:
Compton's New Media

Software Requirements: **MPC**

Suggested Retail Price: **$99.95**

Compton's and I go way back. I used a *Compton's Encyclopedia* all through high school and college at home (this 35-year-old set is still on the shelves at my Mom's house). I strayed for awhile in the mid-1970s with a tempting $1.99-a-volume deal for a Funk & Wagnalls edition (now augmented with 17 year-books). I returned to the fold last year when I purchased *Compton's Multimedia Encyclopedia* (the predecessor to this one) for $129.00. It seemed like a bargain at the time.

But, if you want to talk about bargains, look at what you can get today. For a $99.95 street price, you can purchase the latest Compton's on disc (renamed from Multimedia to Interactive to reflect its richer user interface). I bit. I even called up Compton's New Media and for $99.00 more (plus $30 shipping), I ordered the print version of this very same encyclopedia.

InfoPilot is your gateway to all the information in *Compton's Interactive Encyclopedia*

I'm planning to replace that old Funk & Wagnalls.

Just because I like it doesn't make *Compton's* the best CD-ROM encyclopedia on the market. I've had the chance to review all of them for this book, and found a lot to like in each. *Encarta* is flashy and fun to use, like a new toy. *Grolier's* has a depth to its articles that you won't find elsewhere. But *Compton's* combines the best of each of its rivals, with solid data and some multimedia gimmicks that will warm the heart of the sternest computer nerd.

For example, if you have a special ReelMagic add-on video board, you can get a version of *Compton's Encyclopedia* that uses the ReelMagic hardware capabilities to present all the video on the disc in high resolution, full-screen, full-motion splendor. That knocks the video-in-tiny-postage-stamp-windows offered by every other encyclopedia (including Compton's regular version) right out of the water.

This latest edition has improved pictures, which can be accessed from a variety of articles by clicking a camera icon. Sounds, maps, an atlas, sidebar articles (tables, lists, or related documents), slide shows, videos, animations, tables, charts, flags, and other multimedia add-ons can be accessed by clicking their own special embedded icons. A See-Also icon takes you to related articles.

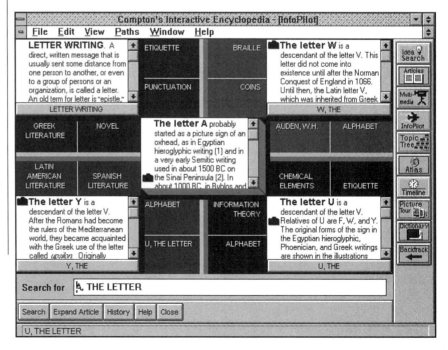

Compton's Interactive Encyclopedia includes dozens of great videos that you'll enjoy, despite the relatively small display window.

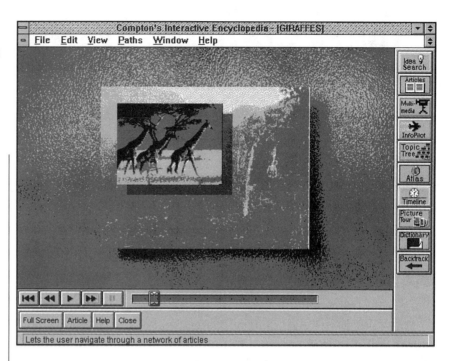

The More About icon explains additional information, and the Take Another Look icon opens a window that explains difficult concepts in even more detail.

There are a pair of timelines, one for the United States and one for the world at large. You can use these to view all world or U.S. events that happened simultaneously during a selected time period. This is a great tool for studying historical events and putting them in their proper perspective. You can jump directly from events noted on the timeline to their respective encyclopedia entries, or just click the Detail button to see what other articles, videos, or sounds are availble on that topic.

Solid, fact-filled, and brimming over with multimedia additions, **Compton's Interactive Encyclopedia** *makes researching ideas and information fun and exciting.*

Although this encyclopedia uses a standard Windows interface with pull-down menus, button bars for commands at the side of windows, and scrolling lists, Compton's has put a lot of thought and energy into using Windows features to streamline your searches.

InfoPilot is one of Compton's searching engines, which has five individual windows that can display a group of related articles simultaneously. It makes an excellent tool for browsing through a group of articles. You can type in keywords in order of their relevance to the topic at hand so that the resulting articles will always be arranged in a list you can look through from the top down, without wasting any time reading peripheral material. There's a Topic Tree that is used to narrow down searches by subject matter.

The Idea Search window helps you find text and pictures about any topic, using a word or phrase that describes your topic or question. You can use this facility when you have a question about a subject, but don't know exactly where to look. You may want to know about Moslems in Spain, or just see a few pictures related to the architecture they left behind. There are many different phrases and words you can type in that will lead you to the articles, pictures, and videos you want.

Virtually any word you see in one of the articles can be looked up quickly using a built-in Merriam-Webster online dictionary just by clicking the word with your mouse. Best of all, *Compton's* uses a "virtual workspace" that can remember what articles you had open and restore the desktop to that arrangement when you're ready to resume your research.

Compton's is an excellent CD-ROM encyclopedia, with a rich heritage, solid information, and lots of multimedia add-ons. If you can buy only one CD encyclopedia, this one won't disappoint you.

Expert CD-ROM Astronomer

Rating: ●

Publisher Name:
Expert Software, Inc.

Software Requirements: **MPC**

Suggested Retail Price: **$49.95**

*E*xpert CD-ROM Astronomer claims to be the #1 Personal Planetarium program. This is probably on the basis of sales; it is quite easy to find, as are most Expert software products. As far as quality goes, that is a very difficult claim to justify. It is not outclassed by other astronomy/planetarium programs, but each

In-depth information like this makes *Expert Astronomer* a find disc for the star-gazer and serious astronomer alike.

program offers differences in features and interfaces. To argue about the best planetarium program is much like arguing about the best car. Each of us will have a personal answer, depending on price, features, convenience, beauty, etc. *Expert CD-ROM Astronomer* has a set of features somewhat different from other planetarium programs; this, its relatively low price, and wide availability will attract many customers.

Expert CD-ROM Astronomer is actually a pair of programs that work together. Expert Astronomer is the planetarium program; Expert Astronomer Multimedia is a multimedia presentation program that can either work alone or in conjunction with Expert Astronomer.

For instance, you might be using Expert Astronomer, looking at the brightest star in

our sky (apart from the sun), Sirius. You can click it and get some basic facts. On the window that gives you those facts, you see an icon of a slide under the three controls on the left. If you click it, Expert Astronomer Multimedia is launched. A text description comes up, describing Sirius.

For some objects, there are photos and even videos; there are over 40 minutes of narrated videos on the CD-ROM. Once you're in the multimedia program, you can follow related threads that have a hypertext link to Sirius, like the Sun. Or you could click the Contents icon and go to the contents screen. You can click various regions of the screen and go on a multimedia tour of the subject. On this screen, you can also look at lists of all the photographs and videos present on the CD-ROM. There

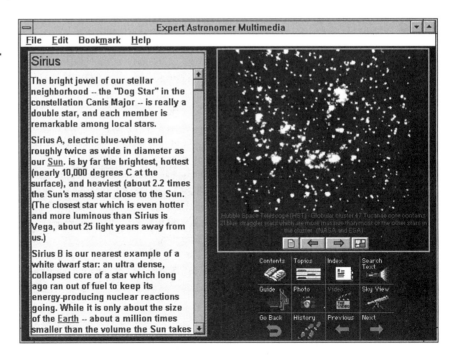

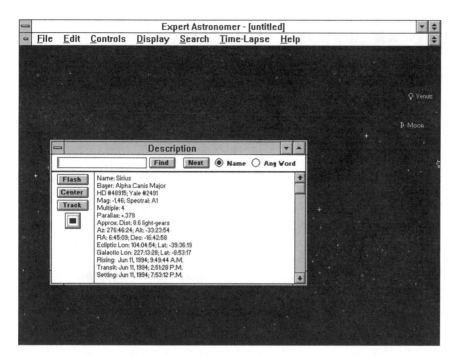

Expert Astronomer **is a good reference guide to the heavens, with complete listings on major stars and planetary bodies.**

are many ways to move through the multimedia presentations; navigation controls are fairly obvious. This type of multimedia presentation isn't commonly seen among astronomy programs. It is both well done and useful.

A powerful multimedia astronomy program, combned with a quite adequate planetarium program in a low-cost package that's rightfully a bestseller.

Expert Astronomer, the planetarium program, has a fairly full set of features. There are over 12,000 celestial objects it can display. The display can be customized in a number of ways: you can have the constellations displayed and named or suppressed. You can display or suppress various deep sky objects like nebula, clusters, and galaxies. You can have the star names displayed. You can set the program up to view the sky from any place on Earth, other planets, or the space shuttle.

You can display or suppress the horizon. You can add sky glare to better simulate viewing conditions at your location. You can suppress stars below a certain magnitude (apparent brightness). There are a lot of other things you can do, too. These are all pretty standard for such programs. There isn't much unique about the planetarium program, but because the package is considerably cheaper than other astronomy programs, this can certainly be understood. It does have a fairly full complement of capabilities and would be very suitable for

beginners and intermediate level stargazers. These programs often go into the field with stargazers; it would be nice to have it while observing. However, it requires quite a PC to run it; few laptops could handle it. It is a bit slow even with a double-speed CD-ROM; it is getting a lot of data from the disk. For the price, however, it's a real buy. It would make a good first astronomy/planetarium program for an interested stargazer.

Global Explorer

Rating:

Publisher Name: **DeLorme**

Software Requirements: **MPC**

Suggested Retail Price: **$125.00**

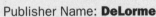

DeLorme Mapping's *Global Explorer* is the armchair adventurer's passport with plane tickets included. (It has a "fly" function where you set up a destination and the display shows the distance and routing, choice of two routes, with intermediate stops). You don't get frequent-flyer miles, though.

Complex as it is, *Global Explorer* was surprisingly easy to learn. You can probably learn to use it without even consulting the complete and concise manual.

It works very much like DeLorme's *Street Atlas*. Use magnification buttons to navigate in and out from world view to close up, moving from world or region view, map centering by mouse click, and so on. Some of its functions are appropriate to a world atlas' broader requirements, though.

The Gazetteer function lets you type in a country, region, "province," point of interest, or other name and go directly there

on the map. It also displays a list of similar names that you can select by point and click if you're unsure of the exact spelling. Each selection is accompanied with a listing of what kind of object the name represents and where it's located.

One thing jumped out at me about those listings: the United States is made up of states not provinces. DeLorme seems to have used "province" as a generic name for political subdivisions but, to me, calling the USA's states provinces just grates a bit. The Gazetteer is also the starting point for most of the CD's text information. Enable the Country box and then click the country desired and then the Info button. A Windows Help-style box appears with profile information for that country. Within

that is an index of Country and Dependencies Information.

The Fly function is intriguing. You can select any place as "here" and any other (via the Gazetteer) as "destination." Click the Fly button and *Global Explorer* tells the distance (miles and kilometers) the trip covers and shows the route on the map, complete with stops enroute and airport codes. It also produces an alternate route. The Direct Fly function shows destinations with direct flights available from the departure point.

Global Explorer's Street Find function is limited compared to *Street Atlas USA* but, after all, there are a lot more cities to cover world-wide. The really big cities are fairly complete. The function only works at magnification level 12 or higher and most of

The road maps in *Global Explorer* can show you the best way to get from hither to yon.

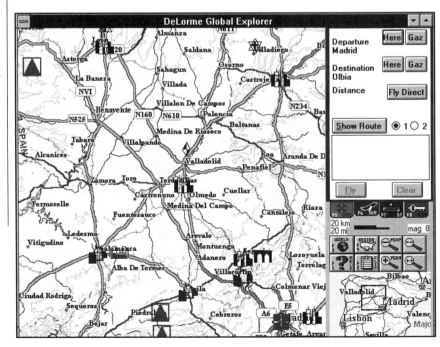

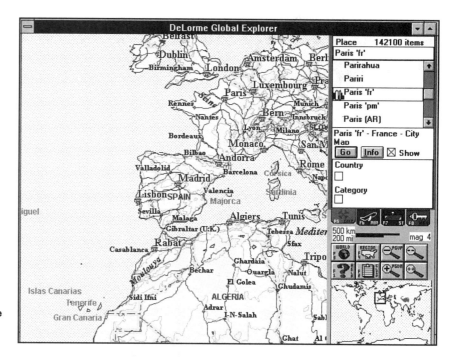

Global Explorer shows large maps of the world, and lets you zoom in to amazing levels of detail.

the smaller cities just aren't mapped at that level, effectively disabling Street Find. Where it does work, though, it's the same as in *Street Atlas USA*. You enter the street name, click Search or Locate, and the street is highlighted on the map display.

Global Explorer *is aptly named, with seamless zooming in and out and a unique fly function that lets you plan air routes between any two cities.*

If you leave the Gazetteer's Show selection box enabled, points-of-interest are shown by various iconic markers on the maps. Passing the mouse cursor over these pops up an identifier flag, and a mouse click invokes either a short description or a selection dialog that presents several such points to select by highlighting and clicking.

Just for the fun of it, I tested *Global Explorer* by trying to follow the so-called Pilgrim Trail religious pilgrims travelled in the Middle Ages—the Way of St. James. Starting at Santiago de Compostella in Spain, I was able to trace the route, cathedral by basilica by cathedral, all the way to St.Denis, near Paris. Probably no one but a wannabee Art Historian like me would do that, but it showed me the program is pretty comprehensive, at least in Europe. It seems all the other major medieval sites are there. By the time I finished playing around that way, I had my latest term paper subject: CD-ROM Technology as Textbook.

A few places seemed to be either shifted

or misplaced from the locations I remember them being but I'm not geographer enough to be sure. It's also possible I'm confusing their locations on medieval maps I've had to use with their contemporary political placement.

I did repeatedly try to locate Aix-au-Chappelle, France before remembering it is now Aachen, Germany again. Throughout history many places changed names and countries depending on who won the previous spring's war. Some have criticized *Global Explorer* for misplacements, so it might be well to check another reference if there is doubt. I, myself, wasn't quite certain of a couple of locations. Because I had no chance to trek to a library, this is maybe, maybe not.

Overall, the program is impressive in appearance, runs well and quickly for its size and complexity, and seems like it would make a good quick reference for geography studies or travel planning, not to mention just armchair adventuring.

Great Literature Plus for Windows

*G*reat Literature Plus for Windows is a great move forward for the Bureau of Electronic Publishing. This veteran vendor of CD-ROM titles is successfully making the transition from bland, text-heavy discs to more innovative CDs. This one presents the usual megadose of classic literature wrapped inside a more powerful searching and reading interface. This disk and *Library of the Future* belong in the collection of any serious reader.

Back in the Dark Ages of CD-ROM technology (two years ago), you could put together a fairly useful (and popular) title by collecting 100MB or so of public domain text. CD-ROM pioneers ate these things up at $49-$100 simply because there were so few discs available, and it was sort of nice to have a whole library of 500 to 1,000 books all on one silvery disc. In these multimedia times, publishers are finding that massive collections of ASCII text won't fly anymore. The public is demanding more.

You get a lot more with *Great Literature Plus for Windows*. Start with sheer text volume. There are some 1,800 titles on this disc, ranging from *The Aenid* to *Wuthering Heights*. Everything the Bureau could get its hands on that has been converted from hard copy to ASCII has been included, which is one of the great things about CD-ROM: there's room for everything, and therefore likely to be something for everybody.

> **Great Literature Plus for Windows *combines almost 1,900 classic books, plays, and poetry collections with music, narrations, and artwork with a hokey but usable Windows interface.***

In addition to the great public domain literature you'd expect to find (the index lists Shakespeare, Steinbeck, Shelley, and Robert Louis Stevenson just in the "S" section alone), there's a generous amount of trivia, rarities, and obscurities as well. You probably don't have a copy of Louis Pasteur's Physiological Theory of Fermentation on your bookshelf, nor Thomas Carlyle's inaugural address on being installed as Rector at Edinburgh University at your fingertips. But if you were doing a paper on either man, you'd find this information handy and convenient.

This Microsoft Windows program has been enhanced from the Bureau's original text-only version (still available as a Macintosh and DOS-based Great Literature disc) with a grafted-on graphical front end that does make accessing the information more comfortable. The opening screen shows a drawing room/home library with cute labels: the door is marked Exit; a magnifying glass on a credenza labeled Find, a painting on the wall as Gallery, and a bookshelf as Works By Subject. However, the same commands are available from a row of command buttons at the top of the window, immediately underneath a menu bar with additional commands. This mixture of Windows conventions works once you get used to it.

Find lets you search by words, either in all topic groups (author bios, complete works, music gallery, or narration gallery) or in any combination of these. You can search the topic titles only for the keywords, the complete text, or only through a list of previous topics found. A list of multiple keywords will be found if located "near" one another, which is within eight words by default, but can be reset to another value you type in. A pop-up Hints box gives examples of typical search phrases and the topics that will be found (e.g. bee* will locate both bees and beehive).

You can browse through lists of all works by a given author, if you like. This type of search can reveal some surprises. Daniel Defoe is represented by *On the Education of Women* and *Shortest-Way with the Dissenters*, but not by *Robinson Crusoe* (!). You'll find 41 works by William Shakespeare, but only one by the prolific Charles Dickens (*The Ivy Green*, heard of it?). Obviously, there are some holes here, even though *Great Literature* does have some prize books and plays.

You may also search works by subjects, ranging from Criticism of the Arts, through Religion and Mythology, Drama, Travel, Fiction, and Science.

Anyone using this disc to research school papers will welcome the addition of new Galleries, which hold caches of still artwork, animations, music, narrations, and mini-bios of the authors. The latter are brief but include all the high points of the author's life, including where and when born, death, and an interesting FYI box, which presents interesting notes, such as that Washington Irving (author of *The Legend of Sleepy Hollow*) was buried in Sleepy Hollow Cemetery, not far from the site of his tale.

There are roughly 500 pictures from the works on the disk, arranged in alphabetical order by topic. The 30 musical selections have only a tenuous connection to the printed works, at best (e.g., Wagner's "Die Walkirie" is paired with the Icelandic Volsunga saga). The primitive animations are outright stupid, unless we've missed the point. They last only a few seconds and depict things like Alice chasing after the White Rabbit and Sir Walter Raleigh's ship landing ashore and throwing him up on the sand. (I'm not making this up.)

The narrations are more fun, with readings from about 60 interesting works, assuming you appreciate having almost the entire cast of Full House as narrators (well, just Bob Saget and Dave Coulier, joined by George Kennedy—who's come a long way from Cool Hand Luke to this.)

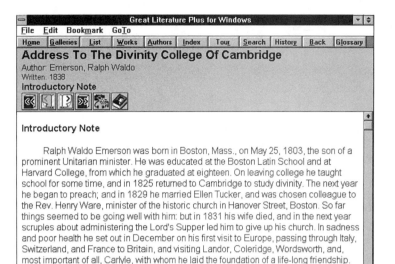

Introductory notes spice up the literary works on the disc *Great Literature Plus for Windows*.

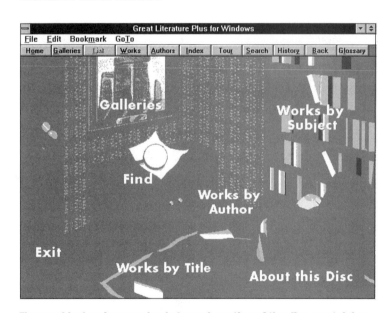

The graphical main menu leads to each section of the disc, containing pictures, music, and sound galleries and text works.

Great Literature Plus for Windows is light years ahead of the text-only classics collections of only a few years ago. If you're a student, educator, or just like the old writings best, you'll want to add this to your collection. Many of the holes in coverage are plugged by other discs, such as Library of the Future, and, besides, 1,900 different books don't take up much room on your shelves if you have them in CD-ROM format.

Grolier Prehistoria

Rating:  1/2

Publisher Name:
Grolier Electronic Publishing

Software Requirements: **MPC**

Suggested Retail Price: **$69.95**

While everyone else is struggling to come up with yet another way to market dinosaurs, Grolier has developed a richer, more comprehensive reference guide to prehistoric life that doesn't limit itself to the most famous branch of the reptile family. *Grolier Prehistoria* ventures far afield to look at 500 different prehistoric animals, including some that predated dinosaurs by 250 million years. You'll also find those giant mammals, like Megatherium—a ground sloth the size of an elephant! If dinosaurs are starting to seem pretty ho-hum to you or your child, this disc may add new life to extinct animals.

Prehistoria is made for browsing through its 500 million years of natural history. Its articles, videos, sounds, and slide shows are divided into Time Tracker, Search, Grolier Museum, Gallery, Classifications, and Creature Show modules. In each section, you can search for specific animals, view pictures or videos, read text, and hear the name of the animal pronounced. Text and pictures can be printed or exported to files you can use in your reports or term papers.

Time Tracker is a graphic timeline that lets you view the configuration of the continents for 11 different geological eras. You can click one or more icons representing classifications such as fish, amphibians, reptiles, birds, mammal-like reptiles, or mammals, and then start a search that sweeps in all the creatures in that era that meet your description. You can learn a lot from this section. Did you know that mammals inhabited Jurassic Park? Even that far back—well before the Cretaceous Period with its famous T. Rex and other dinosaur monsters—there were tiny, mouselike mammals making pests of themselves.

The Search module lets you type in keywords, like "giant" and "mammal" and view a scrolling list containing the results of your query. Then, just click the name of the animal to see a picture and text about that creature. You can use AND, OR, and NOT operators to include or exclude specific animals and characteristics.

The Grolier Museum has exhibits, like a real museum, with topics like "What is a dinosaur?" and "Calculating dinosaur speed." There are also videos you can view, grouped together by subject, such as "Dinosaur Battles." Many of these are identical to the videos included in *Microsoft's Dinosaurs*, but with different names. Here, "T-Rex Attack" is the same video as "The Hunt" on the Microsoft offering, but with added narration. Because you probably won't purchase two prehistoric animal CDs, this duplication isn't much of a problem.

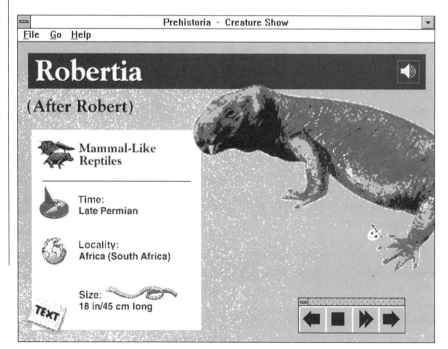

Study mammal-like reptiles in *Grolier Prehistoria*.

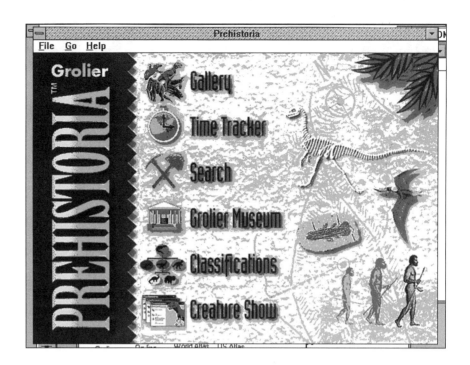

Grolier Prehistoria has six fascinating gateways into its information about more than 500 prehistoric creatures.

You also find a Fossil Lab in the Grolier Museum, and some recommendations of places you can go to see actual fossils.

Grolier Prehistoria *is a comprehensive multimedia reference to 500 million years of prehistoric life, with museum exhibits, videos, and sound clips*

Gallery is another tool for roaming through prehistoric times at leisure. It arranges animals by families, so that you can browse through groups of prehistoric creatures looking for animals you'd like to know more about.

Classifications lets you explore prehistoric life from the perspective of the scientific hierarchy that arranges living things into classes, subclasses, orders, genus, and species so that related animals can be grouped together in logical ways. Creature Show is an encyclopedia of 500 prehistoric animals, with full-color illustrations and detailed text. Descriptions of appearance, behavior, and favored habitat are included.

Elsewhere, in Knowledge Explorer, you find animations, sound, and video with essays that discuss key issues in paleontology. The narrated videos star fossil explorers who explain how they discovered and analyzed important prehistoric finds.

Grolier Prehistoria is more of a reference work than the "dinosaur" discs, because it has viewer hypertext links to lead you astray, and more comprehensive coverage of non-dinosaurs of the ancient past. The lack of a web of criss-crossing references is fortunate, because this disc doesn't have a simple means of backtracking through multiple screens. You can always pull down the Go menu to return to your most recent Search result lists, but moving back and forth between recent screens isn't automatic.

I like *Grolier Prehistoria* because it covers a lot more than dinosaurs. Those big swimming lizards, giant flying reptiles, and funny-looking early mammals are just as interesting and the equal to Jurassic Park's residents in fun.

Library of the Future, 3rd Edition

Rating:

Publisher Name:
World Library, Inc.

Software Requirements: **MPC**

Suggested Retail Price: **$149.95**

The future ain't what it used to be. In fact, if you've followed *Library of the Future* through its last three incarnations, you'll agree it just keeps getting better. In the past two years, this disc has expanded from a simple DOS interface and roughly 500 literary works to a slick DOS and Windows interface (on a single CD-ROM) and 1,750 complete, unabridged titles. Video clips from movies based on the books on the disc, as well as other illustrations, are also crammed into World Library's flagship disc.

All the best-loved classics are included on this disc, along with all those books you had to read to get through your English or World Lit classes. For kids, there are dozens of *Aesop's Fables*, all of Hans Christian

Andersen's favorites, along with *Peter Pan*, the *Wizard of Oz*, and scores of Brothers Grimm stories. Mystery and horror fans will find all of Conan Doyle's Sherlock Holmes adventures, the best of Poe, and classics like *Dracula* and *Frankenstein*.

The more serious reader will appreciate masterworks like *War and Peace*, Boswell's *Life of Johnson*, *Don Quixote*, Chaucer's *Canterbury Tales*, *Robinson Crusoe*, Charles Dickens' greatest novels, or, perhaps philosophical works of Immanual Kant.

But, do you really want to read a major novel perched in front of a computer screen? World Library makes this task as easy as possible, with user-selectable typefaces and point sizes for text, and a convenient autoscrolling screen that can be set to page

through at your own reading pace.

If you'd rather rely on *Library of the Future* as a research tool, the improved Windows interface helps there, too. You can read up to eight works at a time (two in the DOS-only version), in side-by-side read/compare windows. Bookmarks and user notes can be created to mark and annotate a particular volume.

The retrieval engine lets you search entries by keyword, subject, phrase, and date, or look for matches that fall within a century, era, country, or category you specify. Browsing is easy, too, because you can view lists of all of an author's included works, or scroll through sets of books and documents that match any of the other parameters.

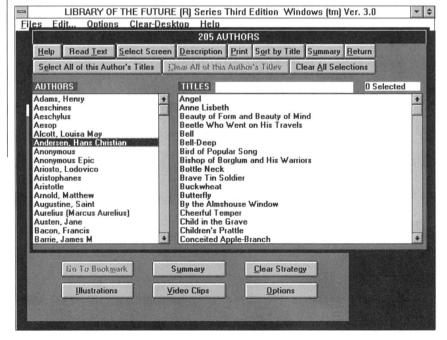

Some 200 authors and thousands of works are represented on *Library of the Future*.

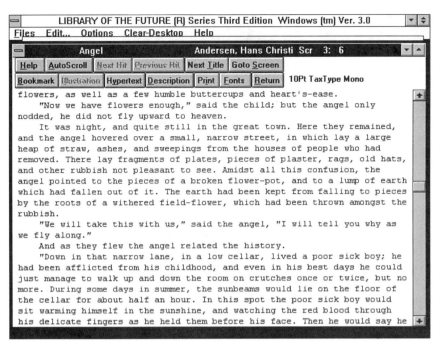

Library of the Future, *3rd Edition now includes virtually every major classic you've ever heard of, and quite a few that may be new to you, among the 1,750 works that are easily accessible through an improved Windows and DOS interfaces.*

Once you've begun reading or reviewing a work, *Library of the Future* encourages you to cross reference what you're looking at with other titles in the database. Suppose you're reading *Don Quixote*, and wonder what other authors may have written about windmills. Click once on the "hypertext" button, type in "windmill," and a few seconds later you'll find a passage highlighted from Thomas Bulfinch's *Age of Chivalry* and another from Thomas Paine's *Age of Reason*.

Because these are all works in the public domain, there are no built-in restrictions against copying or printing out the full text of any of them. You might not want to generate a hardcopy of *War and Peace* in this way, but the Code of Hammurabi could make a nice conversation piece at your next discussion group.

Library of the Future may indeed represent how we'll store, research, and review our books in the future. You may still want a bound copy of *The Three Musketeers* for pleasure reading, but you'll pass it along to someone else after you've finished and rely on this disc for reference. It's also fun to read a few pages or chapters of a book you've heard a lot about before deciding to invest in a "real" copy.

The 12 video clips (all from old, old movies) and nearly 300 illustrations copied from ancient books are interesting, but nonessential to the enjoyment of this CD-ROM. Among the classic literature collections available on disc, this one ranks as one of the most comprehensive and easy to use. Consider adding it first to your collection.

Lovejoy's College Counselor

Rating:

Publisher Name:
Media Interactive Software

Software Requirements: **MPC**

Suggested Retail Price: **$99.95**

*L*ovejoy's College Counselor is a guide to the main aspects of selecting a college. The main focal points are: Select a College, which has comprehensive information about 1,600 colleges; Find Financial Aid, 2,500 sources including government and hard-to-find private sources; Identify Employment Prospects, a look at 120 of the fastest growing jobs currently in the market; Choose a Major, in which majors are described as an aid for matching interests.

This CD is the nice counselor we all would have loved to have back in our day! No way is this CD going to wreck our future by telling us we cannot become a rocket scientist, nor will it tell all the girls to become nurses and marry doctors. This is a wonderful way to be guided without any real input other than the information that is needed for this all-important task.

As soon as you launch *Lovejoy's*, a nice lady comes in and offers to hold your hand throughout, helping you only when you need her, by clicking her picture. She also knows how to stay out of your way when you don't need her help.

The install was easy, but be sure to have your serial number handy (it's inside the cover of the manual). At the main screen, there are the familiar choices of File, for Print, Print Setup, or Exit; Edit for Copy, Annotate and Bookmark, Navigate; and Help, which is a well-done companion to the on-line guide. Radio buttons offering Main Menu, Index, Go Back, Search, Rewind, and Forward are also available.

> *This disc is a must for high school juniors and seniors, as well as undecided college freshmen who want to plan their careers, choose a major, or find financial aid.*

In the College Profiles module, you can choose from Overview, Admissions, Student Body, Financial, Academic, Activities, and Campus Life. The guide made a point of saying that we must remember that the source of information included is from the college or university. Phone, fax, and addresses are given on the first page. If a person really wanted to utilize the Windows capability, they could just copy and paste into a Word Processor and compose letters or faxes as they go along.

Under Financial Aid you can select Athletic Aid, Club/Corporate Affiliation, Ethnic-Specific Aid, Government Aid, Majors/Interests, National Merit, Special Needs, Religious Affiliation, Residence/Location, Union Affiliation, and Vocational/Technical Aid.

I have always heard the money is out there, if you can just find it! I think Lovejoy has conquered this problem! Let's look at Ethnic-Specific Aid. I chose American Indian Science & Engineering Society. The details provided include the name of the grant or scholarship; name and address of the sponsoring organization; contact, criteria, majors, and dollar amount of the average award; and the college level and deadline for application. At this point, I clicked the Guide Icon just to see what she had to say. She explained it all very well and reminded me to double-check the all-important deadline. Just like Mom!

Under Majors, you can choose listings by Category and an Alphabetical Listing. Then, in the Careers section, your choices include an Overview, Alphabetical List, List by % Change, and List by # of Jobs.

I was curious about the List by % Change. The explanation was easily found at the top of the list. The list categorizes career options by the percent change in job availability that the career was projected to reach by the year 2005. I wonder how they do that! I still wasn't satisfied, so I selected More Info... and a pop-out provided me with another resource. It says that a company named Takeoff/Multimedia has a video available entitled Careers for the 21st Century, they also included the 800 number.

The Career button showed me a list, I selected education, because I know so many teachers who are having problems finding jobs. Looks like they expect growth as school enrollments increase, but warns that competition for principal, assistant principal, etc. will be present because many teachers now meet the requirements. Of course I was really curious to know the single largest growth area. Are you ready to hear this? The first one in the list, with a projection of 6,135,000 jobs by 2005 is, drum roll...retail sales workers!

Secondary school teachers fall in at 1,717,000. Well, I figured it would be fun to see the least projected jobs of the future. If you know anyone who is planning on going to college to become a mining engineer, tell them that by the year 2005, it is predicted that it will be the least out of a list of 120 careers to get jobs, a mere 4,368 available positions. I guess I'll discourage my kids from becoming gold mine engineers in that case!

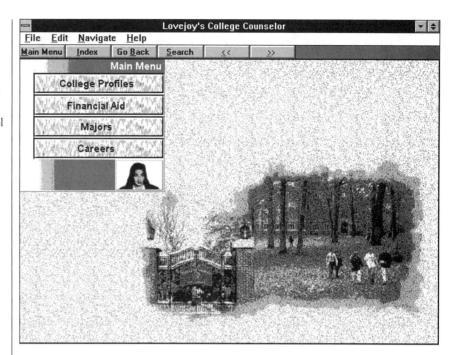

Find a college, locate financial aid, and decide on a major or career using the information in *LoveJoy's College Guide*.

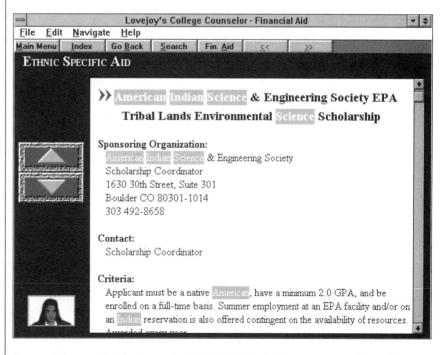

A powerful search engine turned up this scholarship in the financial aid section.

Microsoft Bookshelf for Windows

Rating: ● ● ● ●

Publisher Name: **Microsoft**

Software Requirements: **MPC**

Suggested Retail Price: **$79.95**

If you can only find room for one reference CD-ROM among your collection of games or personal interest discs, this is the one you should have. There are better encyclopedias and dictionaries than those included with *Microsoft Bookshelf* (Microsoft's own *Encarta* and Random House's *Unabridged* come to mind), more comprehensive collections of quotes, better almanacs, and more detailed atlases. But when you want to pop in one disc and find information that may relate to any of these categories, *Bookshelf* is still your best choice. Although updated annually, this disc remains useful for several years after its issue date: the changes made are minor.

The updated 1994 edition has 80,000 word pronunciations, dozens of audio clips, animations, video clips of historical events, packed in with 160 national anthems, 230 national flags, and a new QuickShelf information retrieval button bar.

You can choose whether to search through all seven reference works in *Microsoft Bookshelf*, or confine your quest to a single volume.

Seven printed volumes have been converted to CD-ROM format for this disc.:

- *The American Heritage Dictionary,* Second College Edition, contains 200,000 definitions for 60,000 words, plus brief biographies, photos, and useful audio clips of correct pronunciation (try *that* with a conventional dictionary!).
- *Bartlett's Familar Quotations,* Fifteenth Edition has 22,000 classic quotations with images and more audio clips.
- *The Concise Columbia Dictionary of Quotations* has 6,000 additional quotes of more recent derivation.
- *The Concise Columbia Encyclopedia,* Second Edition, covers 15,000 topics with text, images, and animation. Although you'll often find scarcely more than a few paragraphs on each topic, the information is accurate and may be sufficient for casual inquiries.
- *The Hammond Atlas* has low-detail, but still useful maps of continents, countries, and the United States, accompanied by flag images, audio clips of national anthems, and pronunciations of key geographic names.
- *Roget's II Electronic Thesaurus* contains brief synonyms and antonym lists for a collection of key terms.
- *The World Almanac* and *Book of Facts* include statistics, facts, zip codes, and trivia.

Unless you're preparing a major research paper, the information in these seven books may be all that you need. The real strength of Bookshelf is the ability to search through one reference or all of them.

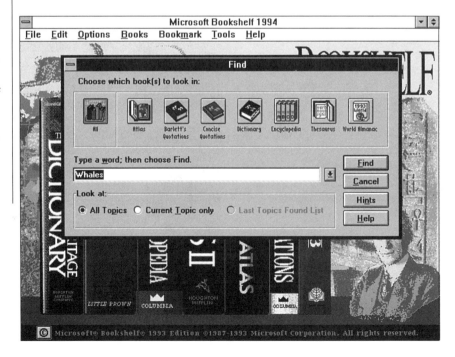

Microsoft Bookshelf 1994 features seven complete reference works in one package.

Searching for Benjamin Franklin, for example, turns up 148 references spanning both quotation references, articles in the encyclopedia (from lightning to Franklin stoves), and citations in the almanac.

Microsoft Bookshelf *is a useful all-in-one reference book that provides fast answers to quick questions, with plentiful cross references, audio clips, and visual add-ons.*

As you might expect from a Microsoft product, the Windows interface is silky-smooth. You can access any book by clicking a graphical image of its spine in the opening screen, or through a pull-down menu. A toolbox of icons at the bottom of the screen lets you search, consult the index, move from article to article, or retrace your steps (through a list of the 40 most-recently viewed topics). There are options for annotating articles with your own comments, inserting a bookmark to help you return to a given place later, and quick searching of both new topics and a backlist of earlier retrievals.

Microsoft gives you QuicKeys access to Bookshelf from other Windows applications: select a word in the other application and then press a previously-defined key combination. If you're able to keep *Bookshelf* in your CD-ROM drive all the time, this capability can prove handy.

The chief weakness of *Microsoft Bookshelf* is the lack of depth and sparseness of its coverage. You'll find many topics and words not included at all, or represented by minimalist entries (Jean-Paul Sartre's "biography" is 64 words long, and most of that is a list of major works). Clearly, this CD-ROM is designed to provide fast answers to quick questions.

A major strength is the bountiful cross-references between works, and the ability to search through a variety of texts to find all references to a single keyword or phrase. Microsoft Bookshelf may not be the last word in online reference works, but it's probably the first place you should start.

Microsoft Encarta

Rating:

Publisher Name: **Microsoft**

Software Requirements:
MPC/Macintosh

Suggested Retail Price: **$99.95**

Personally, I hope the anti-trust wonks turn up nothing sinister in their investigation of Microsoft. If *Microsoft Encarta* is any indicator of the byproducts we can expect from Bill Gates' quest for Total World Domination, Chairman Bill can dominate my world anytime. Simply put, *Encarta* is nothing like any encyclopedia you've ever worked with—electronic or otherwise—starting with its name.

It may not be the best encyclopedia (Grolier's may have more thorough articles) or even the fastest to use (our old text-based, non-multimedia encyclopedia can find 20 references in less time than *Encarta* takes to load its introductory splash screen). But *Encarta* takes the prize for pure impressiveness.

In the old days, a set of encyclopedias stood on your shelves with fancy bindings, ready to impress your friends and neighbors with at least an air of erudition. *Encarta* is the modern-day equivalent. Everything about *Encarta* seems specifically included to dazzle you, from the moment you open the slick packaging and view the lush full-color manuals to that first moment when the

impressive splash screen explodes on your screen. Sure, it's manipulative, but *Encarta* makes you love being toyed with.

This is not all style and no substance. *Encarta* includes eight hours of audio (that in itself is pretty impressive on a CD-ROM that could hold only 75 minutes of digital audio). In addition to the pervasive narration, there's 200 natural animal and bird sounds, words and phrases in 60 foreign languages, and 1,500 pronunciations of geographic place names alone. More than 65 percent of the photographs on this disc are in full color, which would be costly to implement in a print encyclopedia, but a natural for one stored in electronic form.

The 1994 edition was made particularly faster, and Microsoft expanded into Macintosh territory for the first time. There are new articles in areas of topical interest, such as Hillary Rodham Clinton. The text entries tend to be on the brief side: if you're looking for depth, Grolier's is a better choice.

Encarta is based on the 29-volume Funk & Wagnall's Encyclopedia, a sturdy and serviceable work that has been a mainstay on our bookshelf in my home office since 1975. In fact, you'd be amazed to know that many of the entries in *Encarta*, the epitome of 90s information technology, are verbatim from that earlier work. Just out of curiosity, I looked up Achilles in both *Encarta* and my 1975 encyclopedia. The entries were identical. For topics that haven't changed much in a thousand years, *Encarta* actually has little to offer over the book set we purchased at the supermarket for 99 cents a volume almost 20 years ago. (In college, I was shocked to discover that the main

mythology reference books in the University library were all published in the late 1800s, when the school was founded.)

Encarta *is a dazzling production with lots of flash and enough substance to please anyone looking for a good encyclopedia that takes advantage of computer technology.*

However, everything that does change has been updated. More than 25 percent of the topics were revised, and there are new articles on such new groundbreakers as Eric Clapton (okay, so they're 32 years too late).

The opening screen offers five choices, Contents, Category Browser, Gallery Wizard, Find Wizard, and Encarta Highlights—or you can just enter the encyclopedia and start using the tools. The Browser and Wizards use intelligent searching methods to track down all possible articles of interest based on sketchy information you type in. These are great when it's term paper time—or you just want to explore a topic thoroughly.

Browsers will want to check out the Highlights section, which lists 20 "editor's choice" selections that give you a quick glimpse at the broad scope of *Encarta*. Topics you can preview include Changing Our World, Languages of the World, Notable Women, Atlas, Sports, Orbital Simulator, Visual Arts, Jazz, Videos, Illustrated Timeline, Writers and Poets, Animations, United States, Animals of the World, Historical Maps, Anatomy, World and Folk Music, Wonders of Nature, and Slide Show.

These are all special features you can explore to discover things like what happens if you change the moon's orbit, or need to know some detailed information about jazz or its leading artists. These make a good starting point for getting to know *Encarta* quickly.

Like its Funk & Wagnall's source, *Encarta* is sometimes a little lightweight for serious research, but it should have all the information an elementary, middle school, or high school student would need for most study.

Despite all the technological hoopla, *Encarta* does fall down in several places. Somehow, the installation program failed to detect my state-of-the-art multimedia setup, which includes a 1024 x 1024 (that's not a typo), 24-bit video card, a 16-bit sound card, and double-speed CD-ROM drive. It told me that my equipment does not meet MPC standards (no, it exceeds them) and that the videos and sound would not play properly. They did anyway.

The second failing is in the sizing of the screen. *Encarta* uses a 640 x 480 display area, even if you have an 800 x 600 or 1024 x 768 (or higher resolution) Windows display. I didn't check out the new Macintosh version, but don't assume it has the same difficulty, because Macs generally have better links between screen size and video. On a high-res screen, the tiny display area is difficult to read. Luckily, my video

card has built-in zooming, so I could zero in on the portions I wanted to view. But if other encyclopedia makers didn't have this trouble with Windows, why should Microsoft, which invented Windows, for heaven's sake?

Encyclopedias are such an important part of your reference library that I recommend that serious students try to get at least two of them. No one set covers everything

completely, and at $89 or less, it's not hard to afford several different editions. I'd propose getting *Encarta* or *Compton*'s for the multimedia flash, add Grolier's for depth of coverage, or maybe picking up a copy of Grolier's old text-based encyclopedia for $20 or so when you want to look something up without spending five minutes loading the darn thing and accessing the search engine.

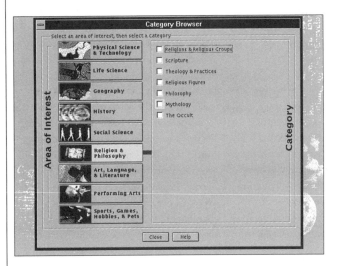

Encarta has a category browser that lets you choose from topics of interest for informal study.

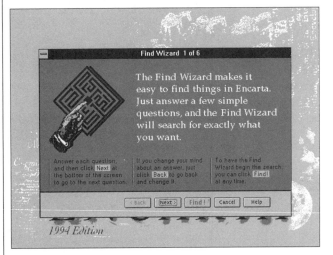

Encarta's Find Wizard can locate all the articles of interest using input you provide, including keywords, subject matter, and related ideas.

Monarch Notes on CD-ROM

Rating:

Publisher Name:
Bureau Development, Inc.

Software Requirements:
MPC/Macintosh

Suggested Retail Price: **$79.95**

*M*onarch Notes on CD-ROM is a must-have disc for students, teachers, or anyone who loves literature. In one compact package you find exhaustive commentary and concise summaries of more than 500 major literary works by 165 different authors, all adapted

Author biographies help you become better acquainted with the creators of important literary works.

from the comprehensive Monarch Notes series.

Photographs and audio readings spice up the disc, but the emphasis is on fast, powerful searches of well-researched text commentary. *Monarch Notes* is one multimedia CD-ROM that can be just as valuable for those still living in the unimedia age.

As a worthy rival to the better known Cliff's Notes, the Monarch series lends itself to adaptation to CD-ROM format through its rich coverage of both classics and newer works. This disc isn't filled to the brim with dusty examinations of masterworks by George Eliot or William Butler Yates. Alice Walker (*The Color Purple*) and Ray Bradbury (*The Martian Chronicles*) are in here, too, along with Sylvia Plath, Ursula K.

LeGuin, and J.R.R. Tolkien. In its breadth and depth of coverage, *Monarch Notes* is unsurpassed.

The minimalist Discpassage retrieval engine (both Macintosh and PC versions are included on a single CD-ROM) lets you quickly find the information you need to study a specific work, or swarms of related data and references to useful for researching compare/contrast literary explorations. The more recent Windows version of this disc that came out while this book was being prepared has the same controls and features.

The interface relies on pull-down menus to active searches or browsing sessions by words, authors, titles, or subjects. The key difference between searching and browsing is that the searching dialog box lets you enter up to seven different specific names

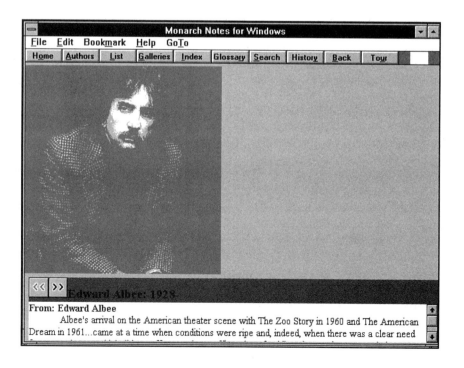

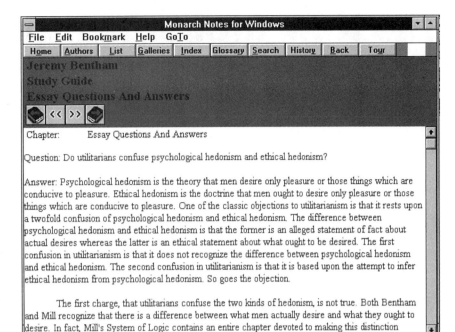

You can locate specific topics, authors, or works quickly, and then read the exhaustive Monarch Notes about your area of interest.

and phrases, coupling each set of them with AND, OR, and NOT parameters (so you could look for "Shakespeare" OR "Sir Francis Bacon" NOT "Comedy" to look for commentaries that mention either author, but not in reference to comedies).

The Browse dialog box, in contrast, presents you with an alphabetical list of topics that you can scroll through and a space to type in a single keyword for searching. This mode is ideal for looking for information when you're not quite sure exactly what you want—or for a leisurely dip into the informational pool.

There aren't many navigational options, nor will you need many. In the non-Windows version, there are no hypertext links or cross references, but many articles have figures or audio readings associated with them. Mac users will find these in the Document menu in the main menu bar, while PC owners will know additional material is available when the "F9 Figures" notation appears at the bottom of the screen.

The Mac and PC versions (included on the same disc) differ in two other ways. Mac

users can specify the font, style, and size of the text used to display the commentaries, and can also cut, copy, and paste parts of the document. This capability is useful if you want a hard copy of an article for highlighting or further study.

Monarch Notes on CD-ROM isn't fancy, nor does it use the multimedia capabilities of your computer to their fullest extent. It ranks as a top CD-ROM for scholars and literature lovers simply because it offers some of the best critiques of major literary works available, and lets you access that information faster and easier than the original printed format.

Monarch Notes on CD-ROM *is a must-have study aid for lovers of great literature, with insightful and exhaustive studies of hundreds of important works in an easily-accessible format.*

The New Grolier Multimedia Encyclopedia

Rating: **1/2**

Publisher Name:
Grolier Electronic Publishing

Software Requirements:
MPC/Macintosh

Suggested Retail Price: **$99.95**

The Encyclopedia Wars continue—and you're going to be the winner! *Compton's Interactive Encyclopedia* and *Microsoft Encarta* continue to ladle features on their multimedia reference libraries like syrup over pancakes, and each time the ante is raised, prices seem to come down. We've gone from $395 text-only encyclopedias to $99 audiovisual extravaganzas like this latest *New Grolier Multimedia Encyclopedia.*

This disc is like an old friend dressed up in new clothes. It contains the complete text of Grolier's 21-volume Academic American Encyclopedia, which will be quite familiar to many computer users, because it's essentially the same as the reference supplied online through CompuServe for several years. But that's old news; CD-ROM users have had high-powered searching of an encyclopedia database available for several years.

Nor is Grolier a new name to CD-ROM owners: the original *New Grolier Electronic Encyclopedia* is one of the most frequently-bundled discs available in the past several

years. This multimedia version also has the complete text of the AAE, comprising nearly 33,000 articles. However, where the old edition had a few pictures as its sole nod to the increased capacity of CD-ROM, this multimedia renovation adds pictures, maps, animations, videos, essays, and sound.

You'll also find 8,000 new or updated articles that reflect the latest developments in the world of politics, entertainment, and other arenas.

The Microsoft Windows-based program has 12 key sections, each letting you access the available database of information in different ways. You'll find a title list if you care to search through article titles in alphabetical order (much like a conventional encyclopedia). There's a word search function, too, which rapidly scans through the built-in index to locate all articles that meet criteria you type in.

A timeline section arranges information chronologically, so that you can view all related events that occurred concurrently, spanning a variety of disciplines. Events happening at the same time aren't listed in parallel fashion, though, but as a continuous list that's not easy to study.

There are also individual lists of still photos, maps, multimedia maps, videos, animations, and sounds that you can scroll through.

So far, this all sounds interesting, but fairly standard. Is there anything to make Grolier's stand out from, say, *Compton's* or *Encarta*? You'll probably find many of the articles have greater depth than those in the two chief competitors, but a preference for

one or the other will depend on the academic level of the user. Younger students may actually prefer *Encarta*'s simpler approach. However, Grolier's real claim to fame is its Knowledge Explorer and Knowledge Tree modules, which provide innovative ways to search for information—through canned presentations and a hierarchical arrangement of articles by subject area, respectively. These functions can be accessed from any screen through a clever toolbar.

When you access any of the 11 main sections, the toolbar, with 19 icons in a single row, appears above the window (the toolbar can also be configured as a vertical, two-column display). The buttons on the toolbar provide access to other sections, such as the timeline, maps, pictures, videos, or sounds. Others access the Knowledge Tree or Knowledge Explorers, or activate specific searching features, such as browsing, word search, or word index (finding every occurrence of a word in the encyclopedia. Each is listed in alphabetical order, along with the number of times that word appears in the entire encyclopedia!). Still more buttons move the display to the next link (any term can be linked to another in the encyclopedia, hypertext fashion), or establish a bookmark to "save" your current place for later return.

The word index itself is an interesting way to browse through the encyclopedia, because you can rapidly see how "popular" a specific word is. If you see that the word "octopus" appears in 18 different articles, you might be interested in following up to see that the mollusk is written up in articles you might expect: invertebrate, octopus, squid, but also some you might not expect: American literature, Antarctica, and eye.

The Knowledge Tree gives you access to information in a logical, hierarchical structure. That's an excellent method to use when you may not know enough about your topic to ask the right questions.

You work your way down from six top level topics: arts, geography, history, science, society, and technology. If you wanted to know about Jupiter, you'd start with Science, and then discover you can explore both scientific topics themselves, or the history of science. You'd work your way down the tree through Astronomy, to the Solar System, then Planets and Planetary Systems, Planets, and finally individual planets like Jupiter. Because of the hierarchical structure, it's easy to see related topics on the same level. While you're exploring Jupiter, you might want to also check in with Saturn or one of the other planets.

The Picture Index is your gateway to all the pictures in the encyclopedia, organized by subject: animals, fine arts, history, media, medicine, military, politics, religions, and leaders. Pictures with sounds associated with them have asterisks after the picture title.

The maps are copyrighted 1993 by Electromap, Inc., and so should reflect most of the changes the turmoil in Europe has wrought. In addition to the conventional maps, you can access six categories of multimedia maps: early american history, exploration and expansion, ideas and beliefs, modern wars and conflicts, prehistoric and

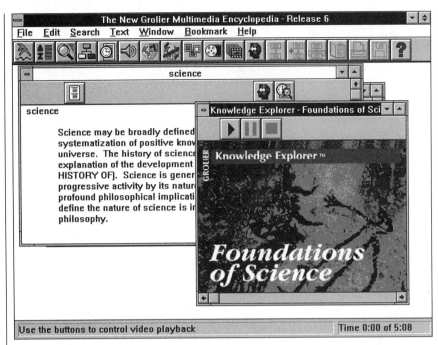

Grolier's Knowledge Explorer helps you come up to speed quickly on important topics through audiovisual presentations.

ancient peoples, and transportation.

The animations cover the human body, simple machines, mechanical processes and natural processes. Sounds fall into animal and bird sounds, famous speeches (snippets from JFK's Inaugural Address and FDR's "fireside chats" for example), musical instruments, and musical selections. Don't expect much imagination in the music department: every CD-ROM musical overview ever produced provides "Eine Kleine Nachtmusik," Beethoven's Fifth Symphony, and other old warhorses. Videos cover animal life, historical events and personalities, plants and fungi, science and technology, space exploration, and U.S. presidents.

Knowledge Explorer is a collection of audiovisual essays on general topics, such as areas of the world (Asia, Europe, etc.) and major subjects (Music, Human Body, Foundations of Science). You can view the essays and then jump to related articles through the embedded links. This is an

excellent way of getting up to speed on a topic through a concise and informative presentation.

One disconcerting trait of Grolier's Encyclopedia (actually, it's a feature if you stop to think about it), is the tendency to clutter up the screen with dozens of child windows containing previously-accessed articles, sounds, videos, or pictures. If you're researching a topic, you'll welcome the chance to return to any window you've already opened, but if you're wandering around aimlessly you'll have to clean up from time to time by closing a few panes.

Grolier's New Multimedia Encyclopedia is a worthy successor to its less audiovisually-oriented predecessor, and a powerful contender for battle with Compton's and Encarta. The multimedia glitz is less showy than Encarta's, and Compton's interface is a little easier to navigate. Grolier's Knowledge Tree and Knowledge Explorer make it an excellent research tool that will please high school and college students.

Time Almanac

Rating:

Publisher Name:
Compact Publishing

Software Requirements: **MPC**

Suggested Retail Price: **$79.95**

Think of the *Time Almanac* as a yearbook for your electronic encyclopedia. While *Grolier's*, *Compton's*, and *Encarta* are all updated more-or-less annually, the emphasis in each of them is on important factual information that doesn't change much from year to year. With the *Time Almanac*, on the other hand, the focus is on the opposite aspect of news and the world around us: what's new, different, changing, experiencing a transition?

That's not to say that *Time Almanac* isn't chock full of important historical data. It just happens to be top heavy with late-breaking news as only *Time* magazine can cover it. On this disc, you find 20,000 different articles. The largest number of those entries are concentrated between 1989 and 1993, in the complete text of every issue of *Time* magazine during that span. You have the most concentrated document of

recent history ever created by humans, all on a single compact disc.

The rest of the articles dip into important periods during *Time's* entire 70-year publishing history. You also find more than an hour of video clips from CNN Newsroom's major stories on 50 key events between 1989 and 1993: the Gulf War, the second Russian Revolution, Clarence Thomas hearings, the LA riots. They're all here.

Everything is accessible through a Windows interface with six different sections that may be selected from the main menu page: weekly issues, highlights, United States, the World, video portraits, and NewsQuest, a trivia game. Within each section, a ribbon containing command buttons is displayed along the top of the

screen. Click various buttons to select videos, charts, photographs, maps, or other media related to the topic you are browsing through. There's also a pop-up search window you may use to hunt for articles and other materials with key words you supply.

If you need to research "ancient" history, there's a lot of that on this disc, too. Time magazine coverage of each of the last 18 presidential elections is documented with more articles and an additional 31 film clips, plus photos and voting data. There are historical photos, charts, and magazine covers dealing with key events from the 20s through the early 90s. Multimedia portraits bring major figures of our time to life.

This is an almanac, right? So you'd expect to find lots of figures and statistics. You won't be dissappointed. There are 400

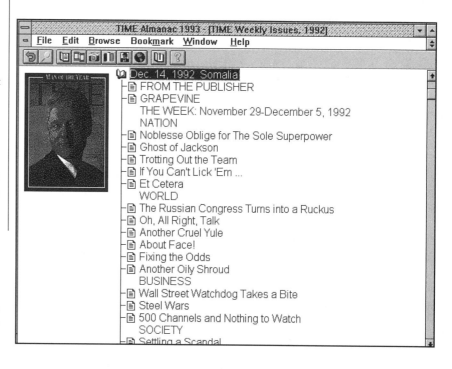

You can browse through articles in *Time* magazine, issue by issue, with the *Time Almanac* CD-ROM.

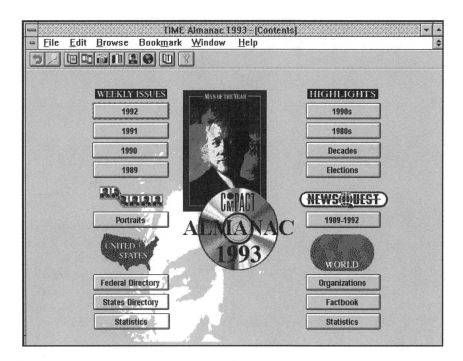

You'll be astounded at how much information is packed onto the _Time Almanac_—including the full text of every _Time_ magazine from 1989 through 1992!

tables from the U.S. Statistical Abstract covering people, government, industry, sports, the environment, and other topics. The entire 1992 declassified CIA World Factbook, augmented with U.S. State department information, is included. American history buffs will find famous documents from American history, a directory of the members of the 103rd Congress, and information such as area codes, postal rates, and census data.

The Newsquest game has 1,500 trivia questions, taken exclusively from _Time_ magazine issues from 1989–1992. The object is to identify the author of a Time quotation by answering questions and revealing portions of the quote, letter by letter. Can you buy a vowel? Sorry, no, but the game will provide hints from time to time in exchange for a slight penalty.

Also included with this disc is an excellent Teacher's Guide, with 32 suggested study activities on topics like Urban Unrest, Somalia, and McCarthyism. These all span a wide historical period, and so make excellent exercises for any 20th Century American History class.

The **Time Almanac** _includes the complete text of_ **Time** _magazine from 1989-1993, CNN video, statistics, maps, and a lot more._

For example, you can study Elvis Presley's effects on popular culture (which isn't as outrageous as the USC class on "Films of Keanu Reeves"). From the 1950s menu, in the Decades section, you can review articles like "Elvis and Rock and Roll" from the May 14, 1954 issue of TIME. Then, browse through later articles in 1956 and 1958, and then click on the Link icon to jump to updates written in 1963 and 1965, comparing Elvis's music to

that of folk artists and the Beatles.

Other activities in the teacher's guide offer suggestions for studying LBJ and the Great Society (not the rock group with Grace Slick), or researching how the war in Vietnam divided our country.

There may be better almanacs available on CD-ROM, but you won't find one that combines the depth of recent news coverage as this one. If you own an electronic encyclopedia, you'll want to buy the _Time Almanac_ to preserve your investment at a reasonable cost.

U.S. Atlas

Rating: ⊙

Publisher Name:
Software Toolworks

Software Requirements: **MPC**

Suggested Retail Price: **$79.95**

D on't throw away that coffee-table U.S. Atlas or your glove-box nationwide roadmap, either. Software Toolworks' *U.S. Atlas* isn't a street-level (or even *county*-level) compendium of all the geographical information about the 50 states. But the maps, which are probably not detailed enough for most tastes, aren't the real story.

This Microsoft Windows-based disc is actually a rich, multimedia introduction to thousands of interesting facts about each of our states, with topographic maps, statistical maps, and do-it yourself graphs that can form a firm foundation for any grade 6-12 term paper or report. Entertaining videos show the natural and human-made wonders of each state. If you think of *U.S. Atlas* as the appendix portion of a regular atlas, enriched with videos and sound, you'll have a good idea of what this disc is all about.

The Windows interface is intuitive and easy to use, with most functions available from a button bar, and the rest stacked on pull-down menus at the top of the 640 x 480 screen. (It's not sizable, so users of 800 x 600 super-VGA and beyond must view the contents as a small pane on their large screen.)

Let's get the political boundary maps out of the way first. They're not bad, but have nowhere near the level of detail you'd need to find anything on, say, your hometown—unless you come from a city of 100,000 population or more (and there are only about 200 of those in the U.S.). You get just two levels of maps: an overall map of the entire U.S. with nothing shown but state boundaries and state names, and a state map, which is accessed by clicking the state name in the master map. The state map shows major interstate and state highways and 30 or so key cities. Additional information is available for four or five of these cities, which are highlighted in red. The roadway map can be changed to a county map for each state; information about a particular county or city pops up in a viewing window when you double-click the county or city name.

U.S. Atlas *offers simple maps and some tools for exploring the United States through statistics, graphs, video, still photos, and sound.*

Click on Cedar Rapids, Iowa, for example, and you're shown a viewing window listing population, growth rate from 1980-1986, birth rate per 1,000 population, and percentage of population that is over 65, black, Hispanic, or college educated. Per capita income, poverty level, unemployment, and crime rates, along with concentration of police protection, are also shown. You can find out a time zone, area code,

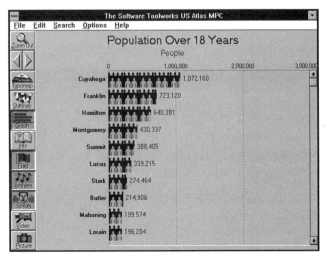

Population figures and other information can be graphed easily.

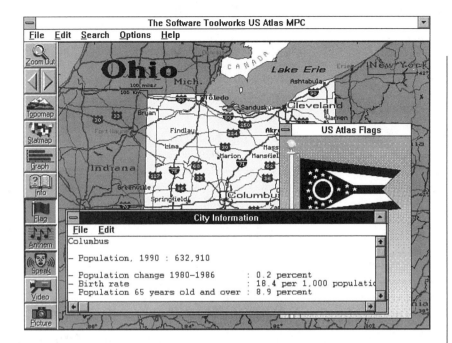

latitude, longitude, mean temperature, and annual precipitation, too. All this information can be copied to the Windows Clipboard and pasted into another application—making it a perfect resource for term papers prepared on a computer.

The real good stuff is available from a button bar arrayed on the left side of the main display window. These buttons control zooming in and out (not much of a challenge given only two levels of maps), access to topographic maps, statistical maps, graphs, information windows, state and national anthems, speech, videos, and still pictures.

The graphs you can create with this disc are astonishing. You can choose to generate a graph representing statistical information about the entire United States, just one state, or any combination of counties within a state that you specify. You could choose to graph information about leading metropolitan counties in your state, just the counties surrounding your city, or selected agricultural counties in the state.

What can you graph? There are 20 comprehensive topics available, ranging from Asian/Pacific Islander Population to Wholesale Sales. If you're interested in population statistics, you can graph black, Hispanic, Native American, Asian, or white populations, population density, or population over 18 years of age. You can also look at number of farms, receipts in retail sales or service businesses, and how many physicians are available. Housing units, crime rates, new housing starts, and other categories can also be selected.

Once you've selected your state and the counties you want graphed, you can generate the graph, or choose to see only the top or bottom 15 counties for that category. For example, I discovered a sparsely populated rural farming county in Ohio, my home state, in which Asian and Pacific Islander inhabitants make up only .03 percent of the population. You could spend hours playing with the graphing functions of this disc.

The statistical map functions are similar, providing a color-coded county map of a selected state, displaying relative information within any of the categories listed above.

Thanks to the magic of the Windows Clipboard, any map or graph you create can be copied and pasted into another Windows document, such as a school report being prepared with a word processing program such as Windows Write or Word for Windows.

The multimedia portions of the disc are entertaining and effective. You can listen to any state's anthem, although not all are available (including, alas, Beautiful Ohio), but each flag will hoist itself on an animated flagpole when you select the state for further study. Videos and good full-color still photos are available for many states and larger cities. Major cities merit entire slide shows (Cleveland has six different pictures, Chicago 16, and, inexplicably, Los Angeles only 4).

As noted in the review of Software Toolworks' *World Atlas*, the audio Help and voice announcements built into this reference are great helps to those not yet able to read, or those with visual impairments. You can turn the speech feature on and off, as well as state anthems and routine flag-raising.

U.S. Atlas lets you create your own maps with markers of your choosing to highlight things like boat marinas, diamond mines, nuclear power plants, airports, and other features of your choosing.

This disc is one of those that must be explored to be appreciated. If you loaded the disc and gave the maps a quick look-over, you'd be disappointed. But playing with the statistical features and multimedia for awhile reveals Software Toolworks' *U.S. Atlas* for what it is: a learning tool about our country, rather than a simple reference work. If you want streets, get DeLorme's *Street Atlas USA*. If you want raw information, check out one of the excellent encyclopedias reviewed in this book. But if you'd like to ease your youngster into an appreciation of the many facets of the U.S., add this disc to your collection.

World Atlas

Rating: 1/2

Publisher Name:
Software Toolworks

Software Requirements: **MPC**

Suggested Retail Price: **$79.95**

The latest version of the venerable Software Toolworks *World Atlas* has been beefed up with videos, optional display of flags of each nation, and some interesting national anthems. The maps still aren't as detailed as you might like, but, taken with the new multimedia material, this overall package is a good general-purpose geographic reference.

While the ubiquitous *World Atlas* (one of the most-bundled discs on the market) isn't the be-all and end-all of geographical information programs, Software Toolworks does not present it as such. It is a solid package that would serve well for students up through middle school and into the earlier high school years.

The information is current to the publication date, so the latest boundaries in countries like Bosnia-Herzegovina and Serbia are as accurate as possible given the state of flux in those countries. However, no matter who publishes a disc, it's always a good idea to check the information against other sources. The whole world may be on this CD, but all the available information about it isn't.

This is quite a nice little CD, and more informative than you might think at first.

It's nowhere near as complex as DeLorme's *Global Explorer*, but it doesn't present itself as such a large reference, either.

Installation is typical Windows: run SETUP, tell it where to put the hard disk files, and then get out of the way. The program creates a group and icons. Open the group, double-click the World Atlas icon, and your plane is departing on time. So far, it's ahead of the new Denver International Airport by a mile.

The interface is Windows-simple. A coarse map of the world is flanked on the left by a stack of eleven 3D buttons. These page between maps, select the statistical map or graphing options of the program, activate help, and trigger a display of national flags and anthems. Other buttons turn speech on and off or select video clips of the currently highlighted country.

Move the mouse cursor to the name of any region on the map (usually continents or portions of continents, such as Northern Africa, Southern Africa, North America, and so on) and click. A digitized voice pronounces the name of the region. As you zoom in to select an individual country, the national banner rises on a flag pole and the national anthem is played. The anthems themselves make a fascinating exploratory side trip; some Asian countries, for example, have anthems that have very Western classical sounds. Other themes turn up over and over—it's surprising how many countries share the same national song! Speech, flags, and anthem music can be toggled on or off with a click of the appropriate button.

Those with visual impairments will want to leave the speech setting on, however, and will find *World Atlas*' Audio Help a real

boon. This is a feature that other CD-ROM publishers would do well to imitate. Help files seem traditionally to be set up in the smallest possible type. It's nice to click Help and have an audio option ready to use. Now if Software Toolworks had offered that option for all the information files, they'd really have something!

> *A good basic world atlas with not too much mapping detail, but with some fascinating multimedia add-ons, including 45 videos, flags, and national anthems.*

The CD offers 45 videos linked to certain cities. Each selection, for places like Amsterdam, Kathmandu, or Los Angeles, features a mini-travelogue with background sound effects and text captions, but, thankfully, no annoying voice narration. The minimalist approach is clean and fun to watch. Many selections have associated still pictures of some landmarks.

Informationally, there's a good quick-reference type overview of each country's geography, land and people, agricultural and manufacturing numbers, health statistics, political structure, languages, religions, and even crime statistics where available. This is one of those places where you might have liked either a sound option or larger type.

Unfortunately, only a few major cities in each country have associated information files, videos, or the other additions. The U.S. is more than Chicago, Los Angeles, New York, and Washington, D.C., and countries like Spain have much more to offer visually than Madrid (one of the newer and least historic capital cities in Europe). We would have liked a little more data and larger screens overall.

Back on the plus side, topographical maps add a nice touch but are limited to the region level. There is a graphing function that allows comparison of countries' various statistics, and there's a nice flag picture for each nation.

Bottom line? It's nice, it's quick, it's a well put together package, and it's a handy quick reference. It's not, and doesn't seem intended to be, the complete geography of the world. Besides, the kids will probably love it. No need to read 50 pages of a manual to start playing with it. They'll probably even learn something before the idea creeps up on them that that's what they're supposed to do. For adults, it's a useful quick reference. There are bigger and, presumably, better atlas CDs, but this one covers the basics solidly enough for general use.

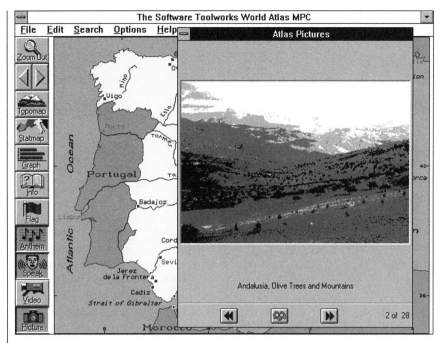

The 28 pictures available for Spain make *World Atlas* a good tool for studying this country, and many others.

The map on the opening screen is your gateway to exploration.

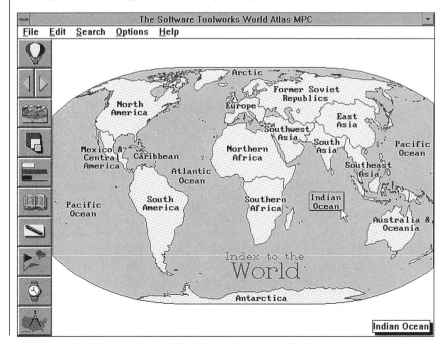

CNN Newsroom Global View

I f you're looking for a nice video atlas with some bonuses included, then you should be pleased with *CNN Newsroom Global View*. Compact Publishing has combined a world atlas (including full-color maps) with a variety of news videos on world events and world clock (a screen saver, calendar, and world time display utility) into an entertaining and useful CD-ROM package.

As you might expect from the CNN connection, there's also a large amount of useful geographical, demographic, and other information available, along with a selection of news videos you'll find interesting and educational.

The World Atlas feature provides detailed maps of every country (including their respective flags), databases about the countries such as military and economic resources, and people group descriptions, of which the data can be manipulated into such formats as pie charts, line charts, and scatter charts. Of particular interest will be the human rights fact sheets available on countries. If you are looking, for instance, for the background on the Rwanda civil war and the estimated 200,000 deaths that have occurred as a result, *CNN Newsroom Global View* provides you with the background conflict involving the government Hutus and the minority Tutsis so that you can follow the news reports coming out of the country.

World Clock feature displays local time and sunrise and sunset across the earth (based upon your computer's clock).

Distances can be measured between two points on the earth, and if you are planning a trip, this utility can be used to determine, for instance, when sunrise will occur at your destination. There is a fun screen saver that will capture your attention in the form of a large, rotating earth moving around your monitor's screen. Also, a handy tool is provided in the form of a date appointment book.

A good world atlas with the Cable News Network stamp of approval on its news videos and other informational components.

The news videos are a series of "video essays" on a host of topics, including Earth Matters, Collapse of Communism, Cultures in Conflict, African Politics and Poverty, Waging Peace, and Small World. Under these "global" topics, there are subdivisions of topics that can be viewed. Under Cultures in Conflict, for example, we find topics such as Northern Ireland, Balkans, Drug Wars, and several others.

Overall with its detail on countries and peoples, world clocks, and host of utilities, this DOS-based package is a good tool to have in your collection.

In addition to an atlas, *CNN Global View* includes video clips of major news events for the past year.

Countries of the World

Although the format is not particularly spectacular, if you are looking for a database with lots of information on some 190 countries and territories, you may find Bureau Development, Inc.'s *Countries of the World* a good CD-ROM title to have on your shelf.

Included as a part of the database of *Countries of the World* are some 5000 pictures, illustrations, and tables. Also found in the package is the CIA World Fact Book. To get a flavor for the types of items found on the CD-ROM, located text titles under Czechoslovakia to include a business guide, important addresses, Czechoslovakia's private enterprise law, and a business guide on the move.

The discussions under China include, in part, Pre-communist Chinese History (and subtitles concerning Historical Setting, The Chinese Regain Power, and the Rise of Communism). The People's Republic of China section includes the CIA World Factbook, a world study of China, "What's new in China" and "National Negotiating Styles".

The various countries databases include country maps, sound exerpts of the country's national anthem, illustrations of the country's flag, and a text study of the country.

The format includes search and browse features by word, author, title, and subject.

Countries of the World is not as flashy as other databases. There is no auto-scrolling features that permit the text to roll up the screen automatically, nor are there any multimedia presentations.

However, there is a lot of information in *Countries of the World*, and as long as your expectations do not include fancy graphics, sophisticated sound tracks, and motion picture multimedia, you should find this title to be a useful addition to your library.

Rating: ◉ ◉ 1/2

Publisher Name:
Bureau Development, Inc.

Software Requirements:
MPC/Macintosh

Suggested Retail Price: **$79.95**

No flashy multimedia, but this disc has lots of good information about all the major countries of the world—and quite a few you've never heard of.

DeLorme MapExpert

Rating: 💿 💿 💿 1/2

Publisher Name:
DeLorme Software

Requirements: **MPC**

Suggested Retail Price: **$295.00**

If you like *Street Atlas USA*, reviewed later in this chapter, you'll love DeLorme's *MapExpert*. It's basically the same product, at least as far as the map database goes, with greatly enhanced features and functions that let you prepare your own custom, annotated maps with ease. Are these new features worth double the price of *Street Atlas*? If you work with maps a lot, you'll probably think so.

I rated this program higher than *Street Atlas* because it has all the tools that the less expensive program should have had in the first place. While *Street Atlas* is an interesting product, *MapExpert* is genuinely *useful*. Unless you just want to find a few streets and, perhaps, print out a simple map, this disc is a much better choice.

As with *Street Atlas*, you can zoom in and out continuously throughout the United States, locating any street just by placing the mouse on the approximate position where the avenue is located. If you're just browsing through, you can center the cross-hair on a city or locale, click the left mouse button to center the map on that spot, and just zoom in until you find the street you want.

You also can search for streets by place name (city and state), ZIP code, and phone number (area code and exchange). From there, you can use the Streets Find function to pin down any particular address block. Or you can zoom to the maximum level and then use Streets Find to go the rest of the way. You can mark locations and save them to a file. These functions can all be accessed by clicking an icon in the handy floating tool palette that you can move anywhere on-screen.

So, what are the extras you get with *MapExpert*? One of the best features is the MapPrinter module. This lets you preview and print high quality maps—in color if you have a color printer.

While you can't change the base map with notes like those above, you can add layers that overlay on top, much like a sheet of clear acetate that has been marked up. *MapExpert*'s MapMarker tool lets you draw with a virtual highlighter pen to mark routes and personalize your maps. You can create your own symbols or use the cartographic symbols the program provides. Line width, patterns, and other attributes are customizable and editable later on. There's even a tool for automatically calculating distances between two points on the map.

Maps can be exported in Windows Metafile or BMP (bitmap) format for use in other graphics applications.

MapExpert has simple pull-down menus (center) plus a tool palette (right) so all functions are available with a few mouse clicks.

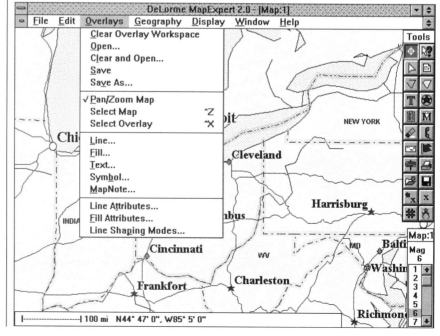

DeLorme Street Atlas USA 2.0

DeLorme Mapping is onto something here. It's not absolutely perfect—but it's not far off. Virtually every named or designated street and road, highway, and byway in the entire United States is contained in this CD-ROM set, along with a few detours and dead-ends. We managed to find the little central Ohio crossroads village that was the site of many weeks climbing the tailings piles of the abandoned coal mines, along with some nearly-forgotten back roads and even a few of the legendary tiny dead-ends where late teens used to park the old Edsel and discuss the meaning of Life.

That adds up to a pretty good map book in any book. Because you get the whole USA in a single package, it adds up even better. Coupled with a CD-ROM interface for laptop computers, this set would be a salesman's or truck driver's dream.

The Microsoft Windows-based navigational program that accompanies the CD works right out of the box, installs easily, and doesn't argue with anything else that may clutter Program Manager. Once we learned the buttons' functions and got used to the magnification feature (it should take less than 20 minutes), *Street Atlas* found everything we looked for, without exception.

You can search by place name (city and state), ZIP code, and phone number (area code + exchange). Once you get that close, Streets Find can identify the street down to the address block. At that level, the status bar at the bottom of the screen even tells which addresses are on which side of the street. If you're just browsing through, you can center the cross-hair on a city or locale, click the left mouse button to center the map on that spot, and just zoom in until you find the street you want. Or you can zoom to the maximum level and then use Streets Find to go the rest of the way home.

DeLorme Street Atlas USA *is a comprehensive collection of highly-detailed maps of virtually every street in the United States.*

We tried both methods in New York City, Baltimore, Los Angeles, Hilo, HI, Anchorage and Fairbanks, and a slew of small and medium-sized cities and towns. So far *Street Atlas* hasn't failed. Some of the real out-back rural roads we looked at just for curiosity aren't marked often enough, and there should be county identification for those places where a street name changes at the county line. Some roads, of course, have only local names. They appear on official maps only as being there, unnamed, if they aren't dedicated to a political subdivision.

A particularly nice feature is the Overview Map. It provides a "quick move" capability for those times you find yourself in high magnification but a little way to one side of the suburb you're really seeking.

Rating:

Publisher Name:
DeLorme Software

Requirements: **MPC**

Suggested Retail Price: **$125.00**

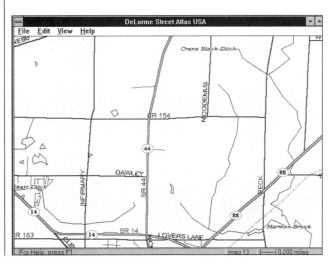

You can zoom in continuously from an overall view of the United States to a detailed look like this one with DeLorme's *Street Atlas*.

InfoMagic "Usenet"

Rating: 1/2

Publisher Name: **InfoMagic**

Software Requirements: **UNIX**

Suggested Retail Price: **$29.95**

Wheee-Whew! I didn't know they grew 'em that big! InfoMagic produces CD-ROMs for the UNIX (TM) and LINUX (TM) freaks among us and for most everyone else, such as those who are interested in the Internet. I don't know where these folks get their energy but I want a share.

626,547,450 bytes. That's huge in anybody's book. *InfoMagic "Usenet"* includes a large collection of FAQ (Frequently Asked Questions) files from the UseNet News, masses of scripts and source files from those news groups that cater to programmers and/or system administrators, game sources, and on and on and on. All the files I looked at viewed easily using DOS' "edit" program.

This would be the disc for a BBS operator wanting to decide which newsgroups to subscribe to or for the UNIX system administrator looking for handy items to compile and stash in the usr/bin directory or for the PC user looking for a lot of reading material.

This isn't any pansy, point-and-click pushover. It runs straight out of DOS. You treat it like any other drive. The directory structure is well laid-out and not at all difficult to use. Files are arranged in logical groupings and you can find what you want with a little effort. There's an index to more or less help you find your way around the source files, but you are the search program.

Complete listings of Usenet newsgroups, plus a horde of MS-DOS versions of UNIX-type tools for those who must handle both UNIX and DOS platforms.

There's a directory of tools for handling UNIX-style files in DOS called, appropriately enough, DOSTOOLS, which allows you to untar, unshar, UUdecode, and convert files from UNIX format to DOS format for printing, or just for extracting the compressed ones. I didn't find any compressed files on this disc, but there might be some, so it's nice to have the tools at hand.

What do I think of it? Well, there's a lot here, a big lot! It's a data junkie's dream for $29.95, list. Just for fun: Take a look at \sources\misc\volume2\c_puns. It reads fine with DOS' edit program and it's good for a chuckle or two.

I'm going to try to hang on to this disc for a few weeks and really delve into it. This CD is so big there's got to be a lot more interesting stuff hiding among the branches of the directory tree. Who knows what lurks in the heart of InfoMagic? I'm willing to bet The Shadow works for 'em.

Shakespeare: The Complete Works of William Shakespeare

If you think of Shakespeare as some dead guy they *tried* to forced you to read in 11th grade Literature class, you'll probably want to skip this review. We're not passing judgement here; the old Bard is tough going for some, and reading things you like (instead of Shakespeare) is infinitely better than not reading at all.

But, if you love great literature, drama, or history, you'll be interested in *Shakespeare: The Complete Works of William Shakespeare*, whether or not you happen to be a serious student of Stratford-On-Avon's most famous dramatist. Everything is here: all the plays and sonnets, presented in two versions—American English and Queen's English (the Queen, of course, being Elizabeth I).

You can get all this in paperback at about the same price, of course. What makes the CD-ROM version of Shakespeare so valuable is the remarkable access you have to his words, using the DiscPassage character-based interface. You can search by phrase, subject, or title to find a specific passage you're interested in. Or, you can browse through all the works at leisure by using the same parameters, looking for something

interesting that you might not have known was there.

The automated searching capabilities of CD-ROM make a perfect tool for studying the words and themes Shakespeare used. These can be used effectively by scholars as well as the interested, but easily-befuddled, fan of Shakespeare.

Unfortunately, DiscPassage is not our favorite CD-ROM interface. Shakespeare is definitely another disc in which the content overcomes the presentation. The archaic character-based DiscPassage interface offers not much more than a window into the original text (reformatted for the longer lines provided by computer video displays), and a simple searching engine that is quick, but not loaded with options.

True, stage directions are separated from the dialog itself, and the reformatting provided the opportunity to clearly indicate lines that are spoken by two (or more) characters simultaneously. But, there's no multimedia pizazz, video clips, sound bites, or other add-ons to spice up the purely text presentation.

You can search or browse by word, subject, or title (author is listed in the menu,

but not really available, because Shakespeare is the only author on this disc). You may also switch between American and Queen's English databases and view a title page, glossary, and list of plays and poetry. The closest thing to multimedia available are two (count 'em) portraits of Shakespeare.

A few function keys can be used to zip you from one passage to another during searches, and text can be directed to your printer. The best thing you can say about DiscPassage is that once you've installed it, you can use the same limited interface with a variety of other reference works (such as Audubon's Birds).

One caution: Though distributed in an ISO-9660 format that should be usable with both PC and Macintosh systems (similar discs from this publisher include separate Mac and PC versions of DiscPassage), we were unable to read this CD-ROM on our Macintosh computer. We might have had a defective disc, but at least one other user reported the same problem to us. If you're a Mac owner, or hope to use the disc on both platforms, check your copy before signing the check.

Rating: 💿💿 1/2

Publisher Name:
Creative Multimedia

Software Requirements:
MPC/Macintosh

Suggested Retail Price: **$29.99**

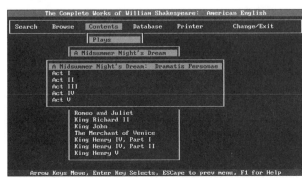

You can navigate through the menus of *Shakespeare* quickly to find a play or poem you want to review, or use the searching or browsing functions to find specific topics or words.

Small Blue Planet

Rating: 🔵 🔵 🔵

Publisher Name:
Now What Software

Software Requirements:
MPC/Macintosh

Suggested Retail Price: **$79.95**

Small Blue Planet has the unexpected features you'd expect from a company that uses an interrobang (combination question mark and exclamation point) as its logo. This disc is a space age world atlas, combining traditional maps with satellite imagery that bring our planet, small and blue, to life.

The standard world and political maps you'd expect in an almanac are here, updated through March of 1993 in the version we reviewed. There are also global and U.S. relief maps, produced through spectacular satellite photographs. You can actually see the hole in the ozone layer above Antarctica, smoke from the burning rainforests in the Amazon basin, and swathes of trees clearcut from the Pacific Northwest.

These stunning images are the results of your tax dollars at work, so you might as well enjoy the fruits of U.S. spy plane overflights, NASA and military space craft, and a variety of images captured by satellites.

The program's graphical interface is easy to use. All features can be explored using nothing but your PC or Mac's mouse. The main menu presents you with five different panels picturing four different types of maps (geopolitical, relief, satellite imagery, and Chronosphere) and a Satellite Gallery of images. The Chronosphere is a unique feature, providing both a "flat" map and spinning globe that show the movement of daylight from one point to another on the surface of the Earth as the day progresses.

You can click icons next to each image to view information about the area you are viewing. Pop-up windows display information about natural resources, population, and other aspects.

You can zoom in on any of the maps to view portions of the planet in detail. Text explanations of what you're seeing, as well as the images themselves, can be exported and reused in your own documents and publications, provided you give proper credit to the government agencies or other originators of the material. (The process is eased by a ? icon within each picture display that can be clicked to view detailed information about the image, how it was captured, and instructions on contacting the organization or company that captured the image.)

The Gallery has a wide range of images, including NASA high altitude aircraft photography, LANDSAT imagery, U.S. Geological Service aerial photographs, and satellite images captured using only narrow, specialized portions of the spectrum (e.g., infrared).

You find pictures of many large cities and natural landmarks shown in both overhead and oblique views. I found the Niagara Falls photos especially interesting, because my own favorite look at this tourist attraction came from a helicopter ride above the Falls several years ago. However, you'll find New York City, Athens, Greece, and other popular sites covered, as well. You find the USA at night, Oahu and Pearl Harbor, the plateau of Tibet, and the fault lines around Los Angeles all clearly pictured. Von Daniken's "ancient astronauts" are also represented with examples of "vortices" that some believe mark space ship landing sites.

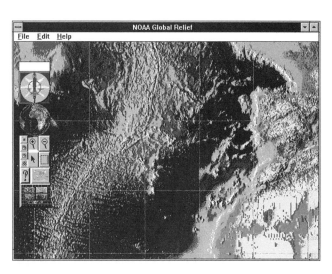

Relief maps like this one help you understand the texture and complexity of the Earth's surface.

TIME Man of the Year

*T*IME *Man of the Year* CD is just what you'd expect from one of the leaders in news journalism. Time has collected massive quantities of news, articles, videos, etc., in a format that is a pleasure to use. At first I just browsed around and played a bit to see what it was about: this disc is a browser's paradise. I found a movie of Hitler speaking about the future of the German people. There were clips with Kennedy, King, Henry Ford's pioneering assembly line, Albert Einstein, and several others. The program is set up in a relational database format, so looking for linked subjects is fast and easy.

The program is easy to navigate, too. In the main screen, and elsewhere in the program, there are eight icons, including a U shaped arrow—a Return icon—that backtracks through your most recent searches through the database. There is also a magnifying glass. Clicking it will bring up the keyword search menu. You can examine different subjects by scrolling through the

type of information (usually text), the date of publication, or title of article.

To test the searching capabilities, I highlighted an article written on November 16, 1992 entitled "What will he do?" The article pops up for you to read and the word Aaron is highlighted, but surprisingly enough, it is an article about Clinton and the election. Next I ran a search on the whole name Henry Aaron. His name is found on the CD six more times. Imagine the research and report-writing a person could do with this!

One of the Aaron sightings is found in the 1963 Man of the Year article about Martin Luther King, Jr. We find that Mr. Aaron was once Mississippi's NAACP President. If this sparks interest, you can just keep going on and on, and look up, say, NAACP, or even Mississippi. I had to ask myself if I would ever have read this much if it hadn't been so easy and, in fact, intriguing to see how easily I could navigate.

At this point, I clicked the U shaped

arrow to get back. When I was at the beginning, the arrow was "grayed out," indicating that it was no longer an option. The next icon looks like an open book and is called Return to the Contents Screen. Selecting that, the offerings were Man of the Year, 1992, or Portraits. Let us say that I didn't recognize the Man of the Year, I simply clicked that icon and was led to many other years of TIME Man of the Year covers, until I landed on 1927's choice, Charles Lindbergh (the very first Man of the Year).

The next icon appeared to be a magazine, which brought up a menu that listed Man of the Year, Woman of the Year, and People of the Year from 1927 to 1992. After that there were listings for Portrait of the Year Publications.

All in all, I enjoyed Time Man of the Year and developed even more respect for their tradition of quality and progressive format.

Rating: ● ● ●

Publisher Name:
Compact Publishing, Inc.

Software Requirements: **MPC**

Suggested Retail Price: **$69.95**

Time Man of the Year has articles and photos of every Man, Woman, Person, and Machine of the Year selected by the news weekly.

U.S. History on CD-ROM

Rating: ◉ ◉ 1/2

Publisher Name:
Bureau Development, Inc.

Software Requirements:
MPC/Macintosh

Suggested Retail Price: **$99.95**

U. *S. History on CD-ROM* is just that: A compilation of titles on the history of the United States. Although this title certainly does not qualify as "flashy," nor does it contain many bells and whistles, there is a good deal of information contained within it.

The format uses drop-down menus with contents such as American People, The Armed Forces: Structure and History, War and Conflicts, and Science and Its Effect on Society. Each of these menu entries provides a gateway to a wide range of materials for a student (or interested onlooker) to delve into.

The sub-topics available are grouped in a logical order—under War and Conflicts, you find The Revolutionary War, The Civil War, The World Wars, and Post-World War Conflicts: 1950-present.

Further division occurs under each of the sub-topics. The Civil War, for instance, is grouped according to Fort Sumter, Appomattox Court House, John Brown's Raid, and Vicksburg, with an orderly structure for locating each event. The articles, done by a variety of authors across a broad range of time, are well written and contain a good deal of information.

There are some other interesting topics within the CD-ROM. For instance, if you are looking for a definition of Aeromedical Evacuation Unit, replete with standard government jargon, you can find it in the Department of Defense Dictionary of Military and Associated Terms.

It should be noted that this CD-ROM is not as fully-featured as are many of them out today. There are no special multimedia effects and the text is just text—sort of like looking at a typewritten sheet of paper on-screen. Also, the "install" directions on the CD-ROM itself seem to have an error. The instructions tell you to install from the CD-ROM drive to the CD-ROM drive—a bit of a nuisance.

Overlooking these items, however, and giving credit where credit is due, there is a lot of information within the confines of *U.S. History on CD-ROM*. All in all it is a title worth keeping on the shelf, especially if you have more than a passing interest in American History.

> ## U.S. History on CD-ROM *is a text-based compilation of American history facts, figures, anecdotes, and information.*

Browse through the chapter headings to find the information you want, or search by keywords.

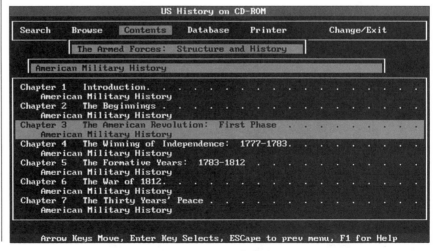

World Vista

Not another world atlas! We groaned when we saw this one, until we saw the Applied Optical logo on the back of the disc. This vendor's offerings have been some of the most pleasant surprises among relatively unknown discs we reviewed for this book. But not this time. *World Vista* promises a lot, and the interface is colorful and attractive, but when you start exploring the CD, you find out it comes up short. The two-star rating we gave it is probably stretching things a bit, awarded more for Applied Optical's efforts at preparing a slick disc than for the results they came up with.

If you want to know what I am complaining about, look no further than this disc's maps. You expect a lot from the maps in an atlas disc, right? The source here is the renowned Rand McNally database. But, many of the maps in *World Vista* look a little out of focus, as if somebody used a 35mm camera to photograph the map directly out of a printed book. The detail is scarcely impressive, either. Street maps may show the city itself and a couple of main drags and landmarks, but little else. The first map you see when you explore Spain shows the country as a vast expanse of white with a dot in the middle labeled "Madrid." After 10 trips to that country, I know there's a lot more to it than that!

The opening screen presents you with five gateways into the disc: Countries, Bookshelf, World Topics, and Maps. Unfortunately, many pathways lead to the same information. You can access the maps by choosing the Countries, Bookshelf, and Maps pathways, or locate flags of individual countries through several different ways. When you do find interesting information,

it's often sparse. In the Spain section, under Music, you'll find exactly one representative composition. There were only 10 pictures of Spain, and none of them displayed correctly: they were all squeezed vertically as if projected through a "wide-screen" anamorphic lens. Many countries have language samples, too, largely spoken passages that translate simple phrases like, "My name is..." or "How are you?"

There's useful information about culture, politics, economy, and geography but not in any detail. If you have one of the three leading multimedia encyclopedias, you certainly already have everything on *World Vista*—and more.

The worst thing about the lack of content is that the multiple pathways keep leading you back to the same things. As you explore a new area of the disk, an interesting

topic may turn up. Click it, and you find the same limited information you already encountered previously.

If you can find this disc at a computer swap meet for a very low price, it does have good, basic information. But don't make *World Vista* your only CD-ROM atlas, and don't judge the rest of Applied Optical's wonderful product line by this turkey.

Rating: ◉ ◉

Publisher Name:
Applied Optical

Software Requirements: **MPC**

Suggested Retail Price: **$59.95**

World Vista has a nice-looking interface, but the available information is rather sparse.

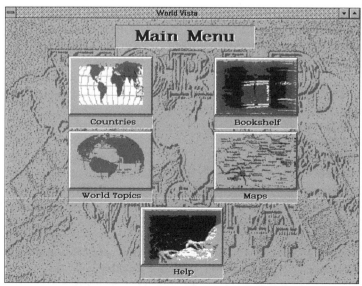

Additional CD-ROM Titles

Title: 20th Century Video Almanac: People
Suggested Retail Price: $199.00
Publisher: Software Toolworks
Platform: MPC
Description: A five disc set covering the people who made the news in the 20th century. Includes text, photos, and film.

Title: 20th Century Video Almanac: Science & Technology
Suggested Retail Price: $199.00
Publisher: Software Toolworks
Platform: MPC
Description: Five outstanding discs using film, images, and text for a study on scientific and technological subjects.

Title: 20th Century Video Almanac: Sports
Suggested Retail Price: $199.00
Publisher: Software Toolworks
Platform: MPC
Description: A five disc set of newsworthy events of the past and present sports world.

Title: 20th Century Video Almanac: The Best of our Century
Suggested Retail Price: $199.00
Publisher: Software Toolworks
Platform: MPC
Description: A compilation of the finest moments of the 20th Century.

Title: 20th Century Video Almanac, Politics, War & Disasters
Suggested Retail Price: $199.00
Publisher: Software Toolworks

Platform: MPC
Description: Set of five discs encompassing recent and past happenings of the 20th Century.

Title: 800 College Boards
Suggested Retail Price: $49.95
Publisher: Queue
Platform: MPC/Macintosh
Description: Studying for the most common college admissions tests.

Title: Advanced Maps
Suggested Retail Price: $49.95
Publisher: Expert
Platform: MPC
Description: Detailed maps of the U.S.

Title: Agriculture and Life Sciences
Suggested Retail Price: $199.00
Publisher: Interactive Design & Development
Platform: MPC
Description: Farm and biological data and statistics from the census bureau.

Title: Aidsline
Suggested Retail Price: $495.00
Publisher: Aries Systems
Platform: MPC/Macintosh
Description: Database of articles, abstracts, and references to AIDS material.

Title: Aircraft Encyclopedia
Suggested Retail Price: $69.95
Publisher: Quanta

Platform: MPC
Description: Everything you wanted to know about nonliving things that fly.

Title: American Heritage Illustrated Encyclopedic Dictionary
Suggested Retail Price: $39.95
Publisher: Xiphias
Platform: MPC
Description: Dictionary with illustrated encyclopedia of facts and figures.

Title: American Journey 1896-1945
Suggested Retail Price: $59.95
Publisher: Ibis Communications, Inc.
Platform: MPC
Description: American history from after the Spanish American War to the end of World War II.

Title: American Vista Atlas
Suggested Retail Price: $59.95
Publisher: Applied Optical Media Corp.
Platform: MPC
Description: U.S. Atlas, similar to World Vista reviewed in this chapter.

Title: Ammunition Handbook, 3rd Edition
Suggested Retail Price: $795.00
Publisher: Jane's Information Group
Platform: MPC/Macintosh
Description: Learn how to blast stuff apart.

Title: Anatomist
Suggested Retail Price: $295.00

Publisher: Folkstone Design
Platform: Macintosh
Description: A human anatomy CD-ROM for Macintosh.

Title: Armor & Artillery, 15th Edition
Suggested Retail Price: $795.00
Publisher: Jane's Information Group
Platform: MPC/Macintosh
Description: More fighting stuff for war buffs, military, veterans, and history fans.

Title: Atlas of U.S. Presidents
Suggested Retail Price: $39.95
Publisher: Applied Optical Media Corp.
Platform: MPC
Description: Washington to Clinton with key dates, accomplishments, and personal notes.

Title: Bible Lands, Bible Stories
Suggested Retail Price: $59.95
Publisher: Context
Platform: MPC
Description: Learn about Old and New Testament events and background.

Title: Bible Reference Library
Suggested Retail Price: $69.00
Publisher: ISSC
Platform: MPC
Description: Search the Bible for favorite verses and stories using keywords.

Title: Bibliodisc—The Canadian Encyclopedia
Suggested Retail Price: $895
Publisher: Canadian Telebook Agency
Platform: MPC
Description: 500+ books published or distributed in Canada, eh!

Title: Bibliography of Canadian Politics and Society
Suggested Retail Price: $200.00
Publisher: Apak Systems
Platform: MPC

Description: Bibliography of Canadian politics and social events.

Title: Canadian Government Profiles
Suggested Retail Price: $149.00
Publisher: BetaCorp Technologies
Platform: MPC
Description: Telephone and fax numbers and addresses of Canadian government offices.

Title: Career Opportunities
Suggested Retail Price: $69.95
Publisher: Quanta
Platform: MPC/Macintosh
Description: Learn about careers, before it's too late.

Title: CD-1/CD-2, Army Publications
Suggested Retail Price: $241.00
Publisher: US Army Publishing and Printing Command
Platform: MPC
Description: Database of Army publications. Valuable for government contractors.

Title: Clinton: Portrait of Victory
Suggested Retail Price: $39.99
Publisher: Time Warner Interactive Group
Platform: MPC/Macintosh
Description: If you're still wondering how Clinton got elected, you can check out this interactive CD-ROM and see for yourself.

Title: Compton's Family Encyclopedia
Suggested Retail Price: $295.00
Publisher: Compton's NewMedia
Platform: MPC
Description: An easy-to-use encyclopedia for the whole family.

Title: Computer Reference Library
Suggested Retail Price: $39.95
Publisher: Chestnut
Platform: MPC
Description: All you need to know about computer applications, utilities, and systems.

Title: Congressional Record on CD-ROM
Suggested Retail Price: $785.00
Publisher: FD Inc.
Platform: MPC
Description: Record of congressional proceedings, for those nights when you have insomnia.

Title: Congressional, Federal and Judicial Directory
Suggested Retail Price: $395.00
Publisher: Staff Directories Ltd.
Platform: MPC
Description: Telephone and fax numbers with addresses of Congress, Federal agencies, and the Judiciary.

Title: Consumers Reference Disc
Suggested Retail Price: $695.00
Publisher: NISC
Platform: MPC
Description: Reference data for the consumer, sort of like Consumer Reports for the incurably curious.

Title: Countries Encyclopedia
Suggested Retail Price: $395.00
Publisher: Bureau Development Inc.
Platform: Macintosh
Description: Includes over 1000 illustrations, maps, and photos, on every country in the world.

Title: County & City Data Book
Suggested Retail Price: $150.00
Publisher: U.S. Bureau of Census
Platform: MPC
Description: Census data on U.S. counties, along with other key information.

Title: County Business Patterns
Suggested Retail Price: $150.00
Publisher: Census Bureau
Platform: MPC
Description: Census data on buying and selling habits of U.S. counties.

Title: Creation Stories
Suggested Retail Price: $49.99
Publisher: Time Warner Interactive Group
Platform: MPC
Description: A study of different cultures' beliefs on how the world began.

Title: Desert Storm: The War in the Persian Gulf
Suggested Retail Price: $49.99
Publisher: Time Warner Interactive Group
Platform: MPC/Macintosh
Description: Relive President Bush's shining moments as Saddam is beaten into submission.

Title: Dictionaries & Languages
Suggested Retail Price: $39.95
Publisher: Chestnut
Platform: MPC
Description: Foreign language dictionaries

Title: Dictionary of the Living World
Suggested Retail Price: $149.95
Publisher: Media Design Interactive
Platform: MPC/Macintosh
Description: Dictionary of life science information.

Title: Economic Censuses Report Series Vol. 1
Suggested Retail Price: $475.00
Publisher: Census Bureau
Platform: MPC
Description: Includes data from all seven economic censuses conducted to date.

Title: Economic Censuses Zip Code Statistics Vol. 2
Suggested Retail Price: $475.00
Publisher: Census Bureau
Platform: MPC
Description: Economic Census data sorted by ZIP code.

Title: Emergency Medicine Medline
Suggested Retail Price: $395.00
Publisher: Macmillan New Media
Platform: MPC
Description: Database of emergency medical information—poisons, trauma, etc.

Title: Encyclopedia of Associations
Suggested Retail Price: $995.00
Publisher: Gale Research
Platform: MPC/Macintosh
Description: Database of associations, professional groups, lobbies, etc.

Title: Encyclopedia of 20th Century Murder
Suggested Retail Price: $29.95
Publisher: ZCI
Platform: MPC
Description: Lots of information on murders of this century.

Title: Encyclopedia of Organized Crime
Suggested Retail Price: $29.95
Publisher: ZCI
Platform: MPC
Description: Lurid database of information about the mob.

Title: Encyclopedia of the JFK Assassination
Suggested Retail Price: $29.95
Publisher: ZCI
Platform: MPC
Description: Database of information about the shooting of John F. Kennedy.

Title: Encyclopedia of US Endangered Species
Suggested Retail Price: $29.95
Publisher: ZCI
Platform: MPC
Description: Read about endangered species, before it's too late.

Title: Encyclopedia of Western Lawmen & Outlaws
Suggested Retail Price: $29.95
Publisher: ZCI
Platform: MPC
Description: Lots of data about white hats, black hats, gunfights, shoot-outs, and other lore of the Old West.

Title: Endangered Species
Suggested Retail Price: $49.95
Publisher: Quanta
Platform: MPC/Macintosh
Description: Vanishing wildlife live on through this disc.

Title: European Monarchs
Suggested Retail Price: $79.95
Publisher: Quanta
Platform: MPC/Macintosh
Description: Kings and Queens, and Dukes of Earl in this database of royalty.

Title: Fabs Reference Bible
Suggested Retail Price: $395.00
Publisher: FABS International
Platform: MPC
Description: Look up Bible references by keywords or names.

Title: Federal Grants/Funding Locator
Suggested Retail Price: $495.00
Publisher: Staff Directories Ltd.
Platform: MPC
Description: Explore Uncle Sam's pockets through this funding and grant database.

Title: Fedstat
Suggested Retail Price: $195.00
Publisher: U.S. Statistics Inc.
Platform: MPC
Description: Database of statistics compiled, researched, and maintained by the Federal government.

Title: Fighting Ships, 97th Edition
Suggested Retail Price: $795.00
Publisher: Jane's Information Group
Platform: MPC/Macintosh
Description: All the good stuff about boats and ships with teeth.

Title: GAIA/Environmental Resources
Suggested Retail Price: $99.00
Publisher: Wayzata Technology
Platform: Macintosh
Description: Database of areas of environmental concern.

Title: Golden Book Encyclopedia
Suggested Retail Price: $295.00
Publisher: Jostens
Platform: Macintosh
Description: Children's encyclopedia.

Title: Government Giveaways for Entrepreneurs
Suggested Retail Price: $59.95
Publisher: InfoBusiness Inc.
Platform: MPC
Description: MPC Database of government grants and funding.

Title: Great Mystery Classics
Suggested Retail Price: $49.95
Publisher: World Library, Inc.
Platform: MPC/Macintosh
Description: Wonderful mystery stories on disc.

Title: Health Today
Suggested Retail Price: $195.00
Publisher: Queue
Platform: MPC/Macintosh
Description: Health information for the 90s.

Title: Heart, The Engine of Life
Suggested Retail Price: $99.00
Publisher: UpData
Platform: MPC
Description: Illustrated reference about the heart and circulatory system.

Title: Historical Congress Committees 1789-1991
Suggested Retail Price: $395.00
Publisher: Staff Directories Inc.
Platform: MPC
Description: Database of congressional committees from the beginnings of our country to the gridlock of modern times.

Title: Hollywood Encyclopedia
Suggested Retail Price: $69.95
Publisher: ScanRom publications
Platform: MPC
Description: Encyclopedia of movie and video trivia and information.

Title: Illustrated Facts: How the World Works
Suggested Retail Price: $39.95
Publisher: Xiphias
Platform: MPC/Macintosh
Description: Exploration of how the world around us operates.

Title: Illustrated Facts: How Things Work
Suggested Retail Price: $39.95
Publisher: Xiphias
Platform: MPC/Macintosh
Description: How mechanical things operate.

Title: Improving Your Job & Career Prospects
Suggested Retail Price: $49.95
Publisher: Queue
Platform: MPC/Macintosh
Description: Get a better job, or know the reasons why you can't.

Title: International Defense Directory
Suggested Retail Price: $795.00
Publisher: Jane's Information Group
Platform: MPC/Macintosh
Description: Lots of information about defense agencies, contractors, and their products.

Title: Isaac Asimov's The Ultimate Robot
Suggested Retail Price: $79.95
Publisher: Byron Preiss Multimedia
Platform: MPC/Mac
Description: The late scientist's study of cybernetics.

Title: Library of the Future, First Edition
Suggested Retail Price: $149.00
Publisher: World Library, Inc.
Platform: MPC/Macintosh
Description: More than 500 great books in ASCII format.

Title: Library of the Future, Second Edition
Suggested Retail Price: $299.00
Publisher: World Library, Inc.
Platform: MPC/Macintosh
Description: Includes the contents of the First Edition, plus 500 more books.

Title: Middle East Diary
Suggested Retail Price: $99.95
Publisher: Quanta
Platform: MPC/Macintosh
Description: A study of the history, people, and problems of the Middle East.

Title: Modern Congressional Committees 1947-1991
Suggested Retail Price: $195.00
Publisher: Staff Directories
Platform: MPC
Description: Find out what really happens behind closed doors in Congress, from Post WWII onward.

Title: Multimedia Birds of America
Suggested Retail Price: $49.95
Publisher: CMC Research, Inc.
Platform: MPC/Macintosh
Description: Pictures, sounds, and videos of birds of the USA.

Title: Multimedia Encyclopedia of Mammalian Biology
Suggested Retail Price: $195.00
Publisher: McGraw-Hill Europe
Platform: MPC
Description: Multimedia database of mammals and their innards.

Title: Multimedia Space Encyclopedia
Suggested Retail Price: $116.00
Publisher: BetaCorp Technologies

Platform: MPC
Description: Encyclopedia of space exploration.

Title: North American Facsimile Book
Suggested Retail Price: $299.95
Publisher: Quanta
Platform: MPC/Macintosh
Description: Fax phone numbers for the USA.

Title: North American Indians
Suggested Retail Price: $69.95
Publisher: Quanta
Platform: MPC/Macintosh
Description: History of the lives and times of the native American Indians.

Title: Officer's Bookcase, Military Terms and Acronyms
Suggested Retail Price: $79.00
Publisher: Quanta
Platform: MPC
Description: Military terms and acronyms in dictionary format.

Title: OSHA Regulations
Suggested Retail Price: $88.00
Publisher: U.S. Government Printing Audience
Platform: MPC/Macintosh
Description: Database of Occupational Health and Safety Administration rules.

Title: Oxford English Reference Library
Suggested Retail Price: $149.94
Publisher: ISSC - IBM
Platform: MPC
Description: Oxford Dictionary, Thesaurus, and other Oxford reference books.

Title: Physician's Desk Reference
Suggested Retail Price: $595.00
Publisher: Medical Economics Data
Platform: MPC
Description: The classic, invaluable reference on prescription drugs.

Title: Picture Atlas of the World
Suggested Retail Price: $99.95
Publisher: National Geographic
Platform: MPC
Description: The world as seen by National Geographic Society photographers.

Title: Prescription Drugs
Suggested Retail Price: $79.95
Publisher: Quanta
Platform: MPC/Macintosh
Description: Information about thousands of prescription drugs.

Title: Publications of the US Geological Survey
Suggested Retail Price: $350.00
Publisher: American Geological Institute
Platform: MPC
Description: Key documents, pamphlets, and other publications of the USGS.

Title: Scouting Report
Suggested Retail Price: $79.95
Publisher: Quanta
Platform: MPC
Description: Report on major league baseball statistics.

Title: Seals in the Government
Suggested Retail Price: $79.00
Publisher: Quanta
Platform: MPC
Description: All the seals and logos of the U.S. government. Somebody must have a need for this.

Title: Software Toolworks Reference Library
Suggested Retail Price: $99.94
Publisher: Software Toolworks
Platform: MPC
Description: World Atlas and Encyclopedia, with other reference works.

Title: Space Series: Apollo
Suggested Retail Price: $69.95
Publisher: Quanta

Platform: MPC/Macintosh
Description: A study of man's journey to the moon.

Title: Terrorist Group Profiles
Suggested Retail Price: $79.95
Publisher: Quanta
Platform: MPC/Macintosh
Description: Learn more about the politically motivated groups that terrorize our world.

Title: The Aircraft Encyclopedia
Suggested Retail Price: $69.00
Publisher: Quanta Press
Platform: MPC
Description: Hundreds of black-and-white and color VGA pictures of aircraft.

Title: The Book of Lists #3
Suggested Retail Price: $39.95
Publisher: VT Productions
Platform: MPC/Macintosh
Description: Lots of trivial information, arranged in handy list form.

Title: The Canadian Encyclopedia
Suggested Retail Price: $395.00
Publisher: McClelland and Stewart
Platform: MPC
Description: Multimedia encyclopedia with emphasis on Canadian topics.

Title: The CIA World Factbook
Suggested Retail Price: $49.95
Publisher: Quanta Press
Platform: MPC/Macintosh
Description: All the information the spies collected for their own use that has been declassified and made available to us ordinary folks.

Title: The College Handbook
Suggested Retail Price: $69.95
Publisher: Macmillan New Media
Platform: MPC
Description: Information on Colleges and Universities in the United States.

Title: The Dictionary of Crime
Suggested Retail Price: $49.95
Publisher: ZCI Publishing
Platform: MPC/Macintosh
Description: More lurid stuff about crime and chicanery.

Title: The KGB World Factbook
Suggested Retail Price: $49.95
Publisher: Quanta
Platform: MPC/Macintosh
Description: Declassified KGB information about the world and its countries.

Title: The Life Skills CD
Suggested Retail Price: $495.00
Publisher: Queue
Platform: MPC/Macintosh
Description: Getting through life better and more effectively.

Title: The Multimedia Family Bible
Suggested Retail Price: $79.95
Publisher: Candlelight
Platform: MPC
Description: Includes study guide for the King James text, along with Bible stories and maps of the Holy Land.

Title: The New Family Bible
Suggested Retail Price: $49.99
Publisher: Time Warner Interactive Group
Platform: MPC
Description: Modern version of the Bible in easy-to-understand language.

Title: The Oxford English Dictionary
Suggested Retail Price: $895.00
Publisher: Oxford Press
Platform: MPC
Description: A multimedia version of the famous, definitive dictionary of the English language.

Title: The Oxford English Reference Library
Suggested Retail Price: $149.95

Publisher: ISSC
Platform: MPC
Description: Reference works on English and literature.

Title: The Random House Unabridged Dictionary, Second Edition
Suggested Retail Price: $100.00
Publisher: Random House
Platform: MPC/Macintosh
Description: Probably the best dictionary you can get on CD-ROM this side of the OED.

Title: The U.S.A. State Fact Book 1993-1994
Suggested Retail Price: $49.95
Publisher: Quanta
Platform: MPC/Macintosh
Description: A registry of the states including data and statistics.

Title: U.S. Presidents
Suggested Retail Price: $69.95
Publisher: Quanta
Platform: MPC/Macintosh
Description: Compilation of interesting facts about our presidents.

Title: U.S. Navy Climactic Atlas
Suggested Retail Price: $61.00
Publisher: U.S. Navy
Platform: MPC
Description: Worldwide marine climactic atlas.

Title: USA TODAY, The '90s Volume One
Suggested Retail Price: $69.95
Publisher: Con*text Systems, Inc.
Platform: MPC
Description: Articles and more from the national newspaper, USA Today.

Title: U.S.A. Wars: Civil War
Suggested Retail Price: $39.95
Publisher: Quanta

Platform: MPC
Description: Information about the War Between the States.

Title: U.S.A. Wars: Desert Storm With Coalition Command
Suggested Retail Price: $49.95
Publisher: Quanta
Platform: MPC
Description: Stuff about the Desert Storm conflict in the Middle East.

Title: U.S.A. Wars: Korea
Suggested Retail Price: $69.95
Publisher: Quanta
Platform: MPC/Macintosh
Description: Complete coverage of the Korean conflict.

Title: U.S.A. Wars: Vietnam
Suggested Retail Price: $69.95
Publisher: Quanta
Platform: MPC/Macintosh
Description: Details of a war that divided our country.

Title: U.S.A. Wars: World War II
Suggested Retail Price: $79.95
Publisher: Quanta
Platform: Mac
Description: Complete coverage of the war against Germany, Italy, and Japan.

Title: Webster's Ninth New Collegiate
Suggested Retail Price: $199.95
Publisher: Highlighted Data
Platform: Macintosh
Description: Comprehensive dictionary for students and business.

Title: World Encyclopedia of 20th Century Crime
Suggested Retail Price: $49.95
Publisher: ZCI Publishing
Platform: MPC/Macintosh
Description: World-wide crime in all its glory.

Chapter 6
Education

I've lumped into the Education category a vast range of discs that cover every subject taught in primary and secondary school, as well as college. These range from language study courses like Applied Optical's *Language Discovery* to Queue's *Origins of the Constitution*. Nearly every discipline is well-represented on the Macintosh because of the popularity of this platform in schools, and PCs are not far behind.

You can study the land of EuroDisney in *Let's Visit France*, or visit other lands through companion CDs that cover Mexico, South America, and Spain. Or, visit the animal kingdom with *San Diego Zoo Presents...The Animals*.

Many discs can help teach you a foreign language. In addition to *Language Discovery*, we look at HyperGlot's *Learn to Speak Spanish*, and a series of discs from Syracuse Language Systems that includes *Goldilocks & the Three Bears in Spanish!* If French, Italian, or some other language is more to your liking, all these discs are available in most popular tongues. I evaluated the Spanish versions because I am most familiar with that language. I read French fairly well, and tried out French versions of discs every chance I got. All the foreign language discs have a lot going for them: CD-ROM technology really lends itself to this area of study.

There are quite a few natural history CDs in this chapter, too. Most of them try to find a new angle to look at dinosaurs, from *Microsoft's Dinosaur* disc to *Dinosaur Safari*. There's even a 3D dino disc.

U.S. history, Shakespeare, and civics are also well represented. If you want to learn what it's like to be a member of the House of Representatives in Washington, D.C., or how it feels to live in space, there are CD-ROMs that can duplicate the experience fairly accurately. Education has suddenly gotten a lot more fun. I just wish they'd had discs like these available back when it was possible to teach *me* anything!

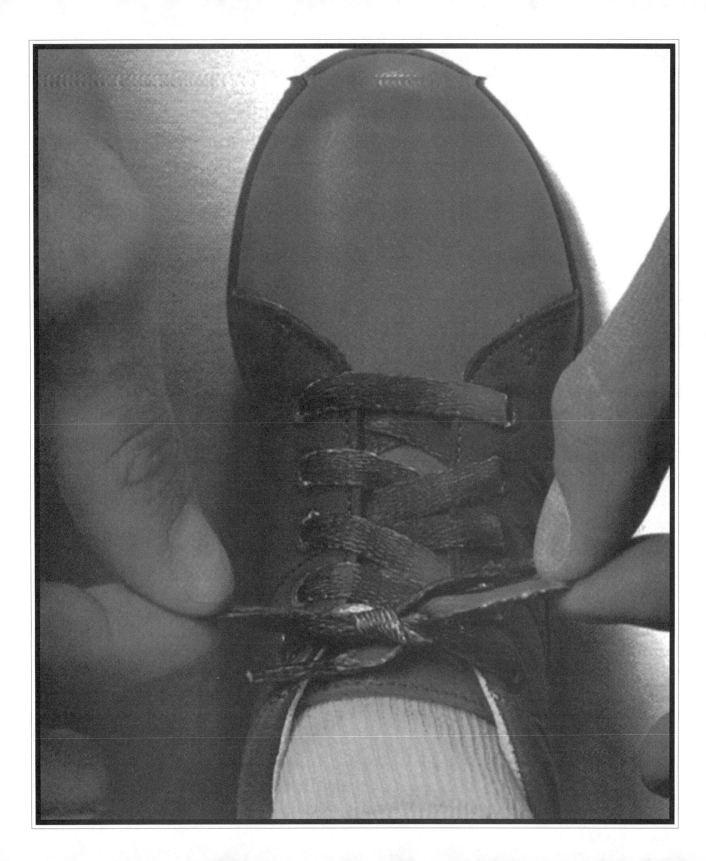

Electronic Library of Art: Renaissance Masters I

Rating: ●●● 1/2

Publisher Name: E Book, Inc.

Software Requirements: MPC

Suggested Retail Price: $49.95

To the strains of "Pictures at an Exhibition," the main screen of Ebook's *Electronic Library of Art: Renaissance Masters I* opens as a gateway to the world of painting, sculpture, stained glass, and other fine art. Although the opening theme isn't especially appropriate music (Moussorgsky did *not* have Renaissance paintings in mind when he wrote the Russian masterpiece), it does get you in the proper mood for this multimedia exploration.

Once you've gotten to the main menu of this program, you can select from four different Italian Rennaissance pieces to play in the background continuously as you browse through your own masterwork gallery. There are hundreds of works here, not limited to paintings. You'll find wood carvings, chalk works, bronze, charcoal, frescoes, terracotta, oil, tempera, and pen and ink drawings here. More than 150 artists are represented with hundreds of works. If you love art but have never studied it seriously, you'll find stunning works by masters you may not be familiar with.

Unlike many printed art books, this disc doesn't rely on old war horses and classic favorites exclusively.

Each piece is accessed through Ebook's Windows Viewer program, which is also used for many of its other CD-ROMs, including *Sleeping Beauty* and *A Christmas Carol*, reviewed elsewhere in this book. A small browsing window lets you look at thumbnail images of artworks that meet your specifications. At a click you can produce a larger view for closer study.

Browsing is quite easy, because you can select artworks based on six different parameters. You can choose to search for works by a specific artist, those created in one medium, works of a certain type (architecture, painting, sculpture), or search by date, school, or exact title. In all cases, *Electronic Library of Art* doesn't leave you hanging like a classic painting in deserted gallery. Each category features a pull-down list you can search through if you'd rather not type in specifications unaided.

There is also The Art Game on this disc, a multiple-choice quiz where you answer questions about randomly selected works of art. A portion of the selected work of art is displayed. If that section is not enough to let you identify the whole piece, you can click a gray section of the display window to reveal another portion. Once you have selected a correct answer, your score is determined by the number of sections of the

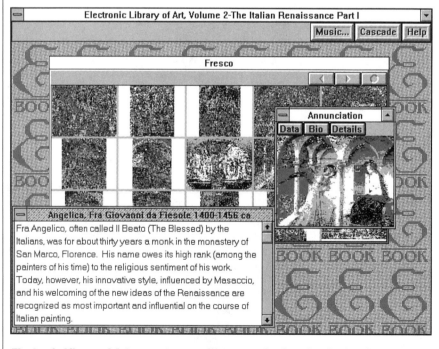

Electronic Library of Art **presents you with an amazing bounty of artworks.**

picture that you did not have to see to guess correctly. If you needed to uncover the whole picture to select a correct answer, you receive just one point. In the Easy mode, the entire picture is presented at once, and there is a more difficult Scrambled mode that mixes up the pieces, making it more difficult to identify the work.

Electronic Library of Art *is a comprehensive look at one period of art, using hundreds of colorful images and some stirring background music to set the mood.*

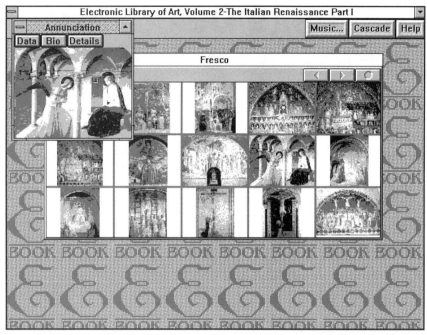

Background information on the artist can be summoned by clicking the Bio button.

We had a little trouble with the game, as the picture opened up on top of the question dialog box, and we had to close it to enter an answer. However, the weird video setup on our main machine (1024 x 1024 resolution) sometimes confuses Windows programs, so this probably isn't a fatal flaw.

You probably won't buy this disc for the game anyway, even though it makes a nice tool for checking your knowledge of Renaissance Art. You'll find the rich vein of wonderful paintings and other pieces more of an incentive to come back to the *Electronic Library of Art* over and over to explore these works. Ebook plans a whole series of discs for this library. We also received *Impressionism and It's (sic) Sources*, which appears equally interesting if your tastes run to more modern art.

Language Discovery

Rating: ◎ ◎ ◎

Publisher Name:
Applied Optical Media

Software Requirements: **MPC**

Suggested Retail Price: **$49.95**

I f you're looking for a demonstration of what CD-ROMs are "good for," look no farther than this disc. Language study and multimedia technology were made for each other, as anyone who's been penned in a study carrel with headset and cassette recorder will tell you. *Language Discovery* gives you, on a single CD, a comprehensive and entertaining introductory course in French, English, German, and Spanish, with sound, graphics, and a rich vein of words and phrases that only a CD-ROM can provide.

Think of what you'd want to see in a basic language program: It's all in this unassuming Windows-based application. CD-ROM discs are rugged enough for students to handle, and can't become entangled in the player like a tape. Native speakers (well, the narrators listed in the credits all have suitably ethnic last names) clearly pronounce each word or phrase, offering valuable "reference" sounds for conversational practice. The graphics are imaginative and engaging for primary and secondary students.

Although adapted from a Prentice Hall textbook for younger students, you'd never know it from the interface. *Language Discovery* looks like a program developed especially for multimedia, from its colorful main menu to its lively games.

There are no pull-down menus or scrolling list boxes in this program (other than in the Help file). Every action is performed by clicking three-dimensional buttons and bars embedded in the various screens. When a list is too long to display on a single screen, the student can click book icons showing turning pages (for page up and page down) or arrow buttons that change the list one line at a time. Younger students may find this easier to handle than Windows' default interface.

The main screen, for example, has four buttons, which lead to each of the language study sections of the disc. From this screen you can choose Learn Words, Find Words, Dictionary, and Word King (a game). There's also a Help button that takes you to a standard Windows Help file of text instructions. Click an underlined word in any of the Help screens and a pop-up box provides further instructions.

The Learn Words module is the basic learning tool of this disc. Study is not arranged in typical chapter/lesson format. Instead, you can choose from 40 different "scenes" or settings that encompass all the material normally learned in traditional language courses. The scenes range from "at school," "camping," and "food," to "minibeasts" (small animals and bugs) and "world of stories." The imaginative categories will keep youngsters interested and working hard.

Within each scene, the student is shown 12 small pictures in two rows. The student can click any of these icons to see the word in the currently selected language, its

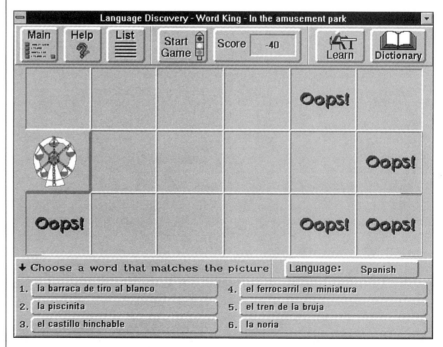

The Word King game in *Language Discovery* tests student knowledge.

translation, and to hear the pronounciation. Arrow buttons are available to move to additional pictures (30 to 40 per scene).

Students can click a button to change the direction of the translation (for example, from English to French to French to English). Another button can be clicked to change from English to Spanish, French, or German. This is one disc that can be shared by several language classes, used to compare one language with another, or used to study English as a second language.

This introductory language course for younger students concentrates on be-ginner vocabulary studies in Spanish, French, German, and English, with lively graphics and native-speaker nar-rators as incentives.

To use the Find Words module, the student selects one of the same 40 scenes used for Learn Words. This time, though, he or she is presented with a drawing of the scene itself. Then the student moves a magnifying glass-shaped cursor around to find selected objects, as requested by the program. The word or phrase is shown in a window and a voice pronounces it. If the student clicks the matching object, the result is a resounding "correcto!" (in Spanish;

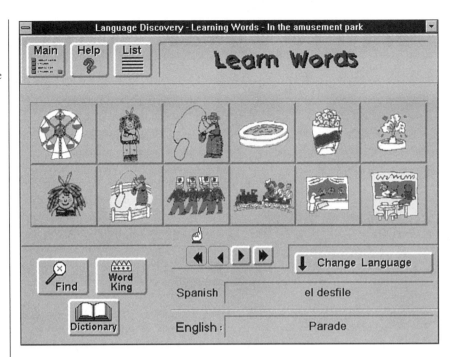

Students can learn words by matching them with colorful pictures in *Language Discovery.*

other terms in French, and German, of course).

The Dictionary module has several thousand words (every word on the disc), their translations, and pronunciations available for study. The student can page through the list ten words at a time, or click a button representing a letter of the alphabet and jump directly to alphabetized groups.

Word King is a game that can be used to test the student's knowledge of the words in the program. In the first three levels of the game, the student is shown one icon at a time, using a screen similar to the Learn Word module. A limited amount of time is available to choose a word that matches the picture from a list of six. The student is allowed up to 18 wrong answers in level one before the game is over. In level two, 12 wrong answers are permitted, but level three allows only six.

The game gets even harder in levels four through six. A full display of 18 icons is

shown. The computer pronounces a word, and the student must try to match it with its icon. Each time you get a wrong answer, you lose a "life," represented by a dwarf. The number of lives provided in these more difficult levels ranges from 12 to six.

Language Discovery doesn't make you wend back through hierarchical screens to move from one function to the next. Buttons for the scene list, main menu, and all four programs in the course are all available from most screens.

This disc is aimed squarely at first-time language students in the late elementary or junior high categories. There's no grammar, conjugation, or rules to learn; everything is centered around word study as a basis for graduating to conversational classes. As you should surmise from its name, this disc will help students discover language. It's an entertaining introduction, indeed.

Learn to Speak Spanish

Rating: ◎ ◎ ◎ 1/2

Publisher Name:
Hyperglot Software Company

Software Requirements: **MPC/ Macintosh**

Suggested Retail Price: **$149.00**

Using Hyperglot's disc can have you speaking Spanish faster than you can spell S-O-C-K-S. (Hyperglot offers other CD-ROMs in Chinese, Japanese, German, French, Italian, Russian, and English.) This dual-format CD-ROM provides everything you need—including a 350-page study guide—except a microphone and a stern taskmaster.

Learning a foreign language thoroughly involves equal parts of vocabulary study, memorizing grammar rules, and practice in conversation. Hyperglot's *Learn To Speak Spanish* provides a smattering of all three. There's a fun-to-use vocabulary module that will help you build an impressive Spanish vocabulary in no time.

The conversational portion of the program lets you listen and learn from self-paced sessions with native (Latin American) Spanish speakers. You can even practice pronunciation by recording your own voice through your Mac or PC's sound card and comparing the results with the correct pronunciation. (Here, a real Spanish teacher would be more reliable.)

The grammar stuff (all those irregular verbs, pronouns, adjectives, and other annoyances) are relegated to a fat 360-page text and workbook filled with drills, exercises, and explanatory material.

I thought I'd seen every possible way to learn a foreign language, but this is new and fun. After four years of Spanish, two years of French and Latin in high school, a couple more in college, and even a few months studying Vietnamese in the mid-60s before it became rather unpopular with my generation, I've been something of a language junkie.

I never became fluent in any of those languages, mind you, so I approached *Learn to Speak Spanish* with skepticism. Surprise! You can learn something from a CD-ROM.

Your study begins from the main screen, which shows the first 15 of the 30 available lessons/chapters. These all center around the conversational situations that occur during the typical business or pleasure trip to a Spanish-speaking country. You can choose from Arrival, Changing Money, Getting A Taxi, Arriving at the Hotel, and other traditional scenes.

If you prefer, you can view the lessons not in chapter order but by the grammar lessons covered in each.

Each chapter starts with an introduction screen and a short video clip that was actually shot in Mexico City. You can move from scene to scene by clicking navigational arrows at the top of the screen, or click the title bar to bring up a toolbar of buttons that lead to chapter sections such as vocabulary drill, communications skills, or a word jumble game.

The Vocabulary screen lets you listen and learn new vocabulary words, and

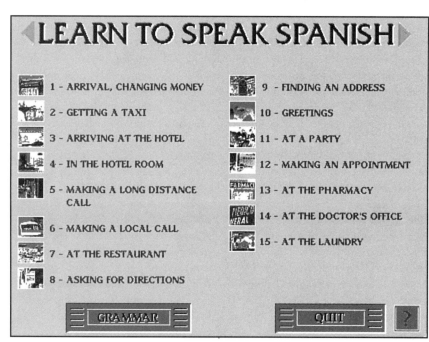

◀ LEARN TO SPEAK SPANISH ▶

1 - ARRIVAL, CHANGING MONEY
2 - GETTING A TAXI
3 - ARRIVING AT THE HOTEL
4 - IN THE HOTEL ROOM
5 - MAKING A LONG DISTANCE CALL
6 - MAKING A LOCAL CALL
7 - AT THE RESTAURANT
8 - ASKING FOR DIRECTIONS
9 - FINDING AN ADDRESS
10 - GREETINGS
11 - AT A PARTY
12 - MAKING AN APPOINTMENT
13 - AT THE PHARMACY
14 - AT THE DOCTOR'S OFFICE
15 - AT THE LAUNDRY

GRAMMAR   QUIT   ?

Learn to Speak Spanish **provides 15 different chapters you can explore in any order.**

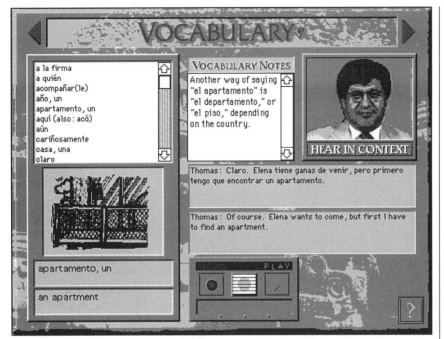

VOCABULARY

a la firma
a quién
acompañar(le)
año, un
apartamento, un
aquí (also: acá)
aún
cariñosamente
casa, una
claro

VOCABULARY NOTES
Another way of saying "el apartamento" is "el departamento," or "el piso," depending on the country.

HEAR IN CONTEXT

Thomas: Claro. Elena tiene ganas de venir, pero primero tengo que encontrar un apartamento.

Thomas: Of course. Elena wants to come, but first I have to find an apartment.

RECORD   PLAY

apartamento, un

an apartment

You may hear a word used in context, then record it with a microphone plugged into your sound card to compare pronunciations.

practice recording them in your own voice. You learn words by selecting one of the chapter's new words from a scrolling list. A definition of the word appears in a window, and vocabulary notes about the word appear in another. For example, if you select tiene (he/she has), you see that it is a form of the word tener, and that you learn to conjugate that verb in Chapter 6.

If you click the Hear in Context window, a short video clip taken from that chapter's movie plays with a native speaker using the word in context. You may repeat the clip as many times as you want, which will probably be necessary: unlike Spanish students and, sometimes, their teachers, actual speakers of the language tend to ellide words together and otherwise make them sound differently in full sentences than when you pronounce them alone.

At the bottom of the vocabulary window is a recorder pane. If your Mac or PC has a microphone attached, you can click the

Record button. The word will be pronounced and then recording starts. You can record the word yourself by speaking into the microphone. Then, click Play and both your version that you just recorded and the actual pronunciation are played back as many times as you wish.

Anyone who has sat in a study carrel with headphones repeating words over and over will appreciate this self-paced method. As I noted earlier, you have to be your own judge as to how accurate your pronunciation is. Subtle nuances can be difficult for beginners to hear.

Luckily, though, you can re-record your pronunciation of the word until it sounds exactly like that of the native speaker. You'd better want to sound Mexican, however, since that is the dialect used for this disc. My Castillian is supposed to sound more elegant (somewhat like British English does to Americans), but there is still a big difference between the Latin version of cinco

(five)—seenk-o—and the Continental—theen-co. Either version is understood anywhere, so learning Mexicano is not a bad idea.

The Vocabulary Drill module lets you practice your new vocabulary, either in Spanish-to-English or English-to-Spanish mode. You can record your own pronunciation, here, too.

The Story Screen lets you see and hear the native speaker using everyday Spanish at normal speeds. You can practice saying longer Spanish sentences, and deciphering them as they are spoken. You can watch the chapter's full movie clip or work through it sentence by sentence.

There's also an Action Screen that provides a continuation of the story, with several native speakers engaging in a dialog. This more advanced mode will really give your comprehension a workout.

The Listening Skills screen repeats sections of the chapter's movie, but with blanks that you must fill in with the correct word. This tests how well you've mastered the vocabulary of the chapter.

Exercise Screens test your grammar skills by asking you to change articles from singular to plural, or provide the correct verb tense. If you get stumped, click the Show Answers or Show Grammar buttons for help.

The text and workbook is a good one, oriented like the CD-ROM to conversational Spanish in travel settings. It can give you all the grammar you need to get by if you work through its exercises religiously. Unlike *Language Discovery*, also reviewed in this chapter, *Learn to Speak Spanish* is aimed at an older audience—high school to adult beginners.

I still think that a formal class with a proficient teacher is the second best way to learn a language. This CD-ROM is a close third, however, and is even more useful if used in conjunction with either of the first two choices.

Learning Windows 3.1

Rating:  1/2

Publisher Name:
Paragon Consultants

Software Requirements: **MPC**

Suggested Retail Price: **$39.95**

The only downside to Paragon's *Learning Windows 3.1* is that it is not bundled with every Microsoft Windows package sold. Anyone who learned to use the Windows operating system the hard way will wish they'd had access to this disc. It's a comprehensive, carefully structured introduction to using Windows that assumes you're neither an idiot nor a dummy, but simply in search of some extra help. This program would rate four stars if it weren't for some minor, but still troublesome, errors in its presentation that could cause problems for the beginners the program is intended for.

Windows isn't quite the intuitive operating system that it's made out to be. There are menus to master, drag-and-drop features that don't work quite like you (or a Macintosh convert) might expect them to, non-mnemonic keyboard shortcuts to learn, and mysterious functions hidden deep inside File Manager. This may all change when the next version of Windows appears, but, for now, new Windows users really need a CD-ROM like this one.

Learning Windows 3.1 presents exactly the right information essential for getting started by using Windows itself as a learning tool. As you launch the program and the training begins on how the mouse works in a Windows environment, you get the feeling that the folks who developed this software really understand the trials and tribulations of the Windows neophyte. This interactive, multimedia trainer leaves the student with a new (or renewed) confidence in his or her ability to work inside Windows 3.1.

The CD-ROM software interacts with the student via the mouse and keyboard. Typically, the training ground is either a simulated Windows environment like that which appears when Windows is first loaded, or, in some cases, the student actually works within his own computer's Windows 3.1 operating system software.

Either way, *Learning Windows 3.1*'s environment is a perfect setting for the lessons, because it mimics the "real" Windows that the student is studying. Those who are using Windows for Workgroups will also find this disc useful, even though it doesn't cover networking functions in detail, because both versions of Windows share an interface that is identical at the levels explored by this tutorial.

"Follow me!" mouse action and keystrokes are used to help the student participate in the training. First the program performs an action, and then you're urged to do likewise, as both practice and confirmation that you understand the concept being explained. You learn scrolling by scrolling, and master sizing, minimizing, or maximizing windows by actually doing it. If you make a mistake, the program lets you know where you went wrong.

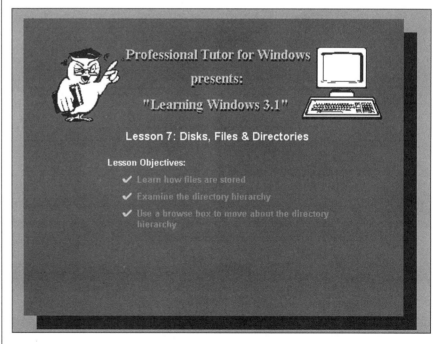

Learning Windows 3.1 uses Windows itself to teach novice users how to navigate this popular graphical user interface.

Indeed, friendly pop-up messages accompany the trainer's voice, which leads the student step-by-step through the 10 lessons. The narration is available in digitized form through your Windows sound driver, or in a higher-quality CD-audio format if your sound card has an audio cable connecting it to the CD-ROM drive (CD-audio can also be heard through headphones plugged into the "phone" jack on the drive).

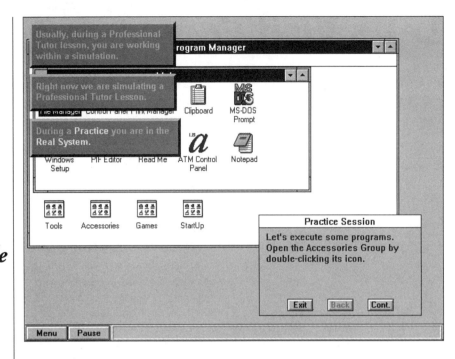

The 10 easy lessons in this training guide to Windows 3.1 make the best argument yet that a CD-ROM drive and sound card belong in every Windows computer.

The exercises can be studied in any order, either to review information already learned, or to address a student's pressing need for immediate knowledge about a particular area. Each lesson is accompanied by a review of the information covered and a short multiple choice and true/false quiz (there's no condemnation—and resulting embarrassment—for wrong answers, so even easily-intimidated workers won't be discouraged by the self-test sessions).

Separate sections cover using the mouse and menus, accessing, copying, and deleting files with File Manager, customizing your Windows environment, using Help, and printing.

Occasional humor and satirical comment help keep the training lively and entertaining, but the underlying effort is to help the student learn the basics (and a little beyond). The voice used as the audio instructor in the training is exceptionally clear and professional. A "Practice Window" appears on-screen to provide detailed, step-by-step instruction when the student is told to perform an action. The CD-ROM software occasionally takes over the mouse cursor on-screen to show the student the steps required to accomplish the desired end.

The lessons are divided into small enough bites that the student feels neither overwhelmed nor burned-out after

completing a session. Because the lessons are structured in these concise segments, it affords the student the opportunity to quit the lesson and practice within his or her own computer's Windows environment.

If you or someone you know feel like your knuckles drag the ground in a Windows environment, *Learning Windows 3.1* will most likely help you evolve into proficient Windows user. This is a handy disc to have around when a new user is ready to be trained.

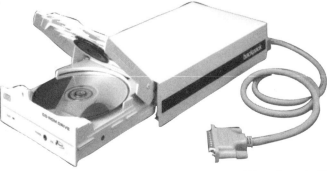

Let's Visit France

Rating:

Publisher Name:
Queue

Software Requirements:
Macintosh

Suggested Retail Price: **$49.95**

On the surface, *Let's Visit France* (and companion CDs that cover Mexico, South America, and Spain) bears a striking resemblance to one of those film strips you sat through in French II while your teacher sneaked off to the lounge for a quick break. A pleasant voice provides interesting commentary as a parade of postcard-perfect still color photos march across the screen. There are four different slide shows to choose from. If that's all there were to this CD-ROM, you'd be better off with a video tape: at least the images on tapes *move*.

Dig a little deeper, and you'll find that this disc has significant advantages over either videotapes or film strips. *Let's Visit France* can be used by a single student or a group, without the need for a teacher to supervise operation of a VCR or film strip projector. The student can select English or French narration, add helpful on-screen subtitles, and stop the show at any time to review a scene, jump to another part of the presentation, or get additional information from the index.

Although the four presentations on this disc (Let's Visit France; Paris, Je T'aime, France: Region by Region; and The Cuisine of Provence) were undoubtedly taken

directly from existing AV shows on other media, the publisher has made good use of multimedia tools to add flexibility to the package. That makes *Let's Visit France* an excellent teaching tool.

Make no mistake: this disc is aimed squarely at high school French students. It's not much of an armchair travelogue but, rather, is a good introduction to French geography, culture, and customs for young French scholars. In addition to the slide shows, there's a step-by-step cooking demonstration and three French reading comprehension quizzes packed into the 267MB on this disc. A teacher's guide and transcripts of the slide programs are also included.

Each of the presentations are roughly 20-30 minutes in length. The first, "Let's Visit France," is a quick tour of the entire country, beginning with a generous segment on Paris. The slides are presented in a window on-screen, with nine to ten button controls (depending on whether French or English narration is selected) available to activate various functions and options (the buttons can be made invisible by pressing the space bar if you find them obtrusive).

The student can choose to have the sound played through the computer's speaker or through a headset plugged into the CD-ROM drive. The show can also be viewed silently by using the optional subtitles that can be superimposed on-screen by clicking a text icon at lower right. While the show advances from scene to scene automatically, the student can manually advance or go back to any slide in the series by clicking an arrow button.

Visiting France was never easier than with this narrated CD guidebook, in both French and English.

A magnifying glass icon also appears that is a gateway to the index. Students can jump directly to any slide in the series, going from Paris to Provence with a few clicks. This is an easy way to conduct research or review material for a test.

When French narration is selected, the student can choose from either English or French subtitles. Beginners will find the English translations of the dialog helpful in understanding what is said, while switching to the French subtitles makes it easier to follow along with unfamiliar French pronounciation.

The second presentation, "Paris Je T'Aime (Paris, I Love You)," concentrates on the City of Light through the discoveries of a new student who has transferred to the city. The navigation and soundtrack options are the same as for "Let's Visit France."

The third show, "France: Region By Region" is a set of 12 silent (no narration or music) slide presentations, each with roughly a dozen images of a different important region of Spain. The accompanying captions can be read (in English only) with a scrolling text box. The modules are informative, but provide little advantage over reading the same material in an illustrated text book. Students might be moved by the novel technology to browse a little longer, but otherwise don't gain much from having this material on CD-ROM.

"The Cuisine of Provence," the fourth presentation on the CD, seems a bit out of place until you realize that experimenting with the cooking of a foreign land can be an interesting way to augment language studies. This module, which provides an overview of many different dishes, offers step-by-step instructions for cooking a simple mid-day meal, starting with spinach-stuffed mushrooms and finishing with a tasty desert. It's probably the only portion of this disc of interest to adults or non-French students.

The least useful section of the disc are the three reading comprehension tests,

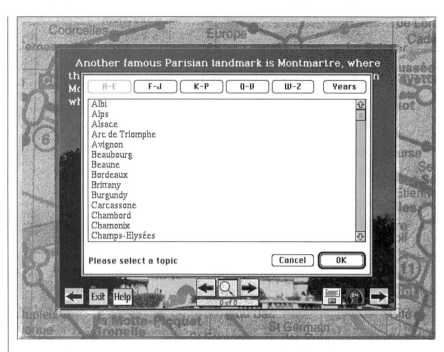

Any presentation can be interrupted for a quick tour though the index.

which offer a series of text quizzes identical to those you find in any French textbook or reader. Some educators will want to use them as a supplement, but there are better and more comprehensive computer-aided instruction programs for French available. In the Macintosh version, this module insisted on telling us two or three times that there was no printer attached to our computer—which might well be the case for Macs set up in a language lab.

Let's Visit France makes a good tool for enriching French language study, although live action video and other multimedia enhancements would give this disc more of an edge over the slide show media it was derived from. Even so, expect CD-ROMs like this to replace simpler formats in the near future: they're easier to use, need not be any more expensive, and can leverage the flexibility of the computer to provide the teacher and student with many more options.

Based on narrated slide shows, this disc adds a choice of French or English narration and subtitles, a searchable index, and ease of use to high school French language study.

Microsoft Art Gallery

Rating: 3 1/2

Publisher Name:
Microsoft

Software Requirements: **MPC**

Suggested Retail Price: **$79.95**

You know a disc has to be something special when *Byte* magazine runs an entire article explaining the special technology used to make the images look good. That's the case for *Microsoft Art Gallery,* which, according to the *Byte* article, uses a new kind of palette of colors to optimize the appearance of each work of art shown, even on monitors that can display only 256 different tones.

That certainly seems to be the case here. If you have only 256 colors to work with, you can be sure they are the right 256 colors to show these paintings from London's National Gallery of Art in full-screen 640 x 480 pixel resolution. We compared the images of several works with the same painting as reproduced in Time-Life's National Gallery/London book in its Great Museums series. The colors did seem quite accurate, but the detail, even in full screen mode, was severely lacking. Nevertheless, this is bound to be one of the finest CD-ROM treatments of these works you are going to see for quite awhile. Microsoft worked directly with the National Gallery to produce a loving and cultured look at some fine artworks.

Indeed, this multimedia presentation was in fact originally created for the benefit of visitors to the museum, and underwritten by a lavish grant from American Express. Microsoft—and we CD-ROM owners—are the beneficiaries of this largess. This disc has representative works from the National Gallery's 2000 Western European paintings, covering 800 years of art. Perhaps not in the same league as Paris' Louvre or Madrid's Prado, London's National Gallery is a fine collection with an excellent cross-section of works by major artists.

The main menu gives you four entries to the information on the disc, plus a General Reference that serves as a glossary for the terms used to describe the works of art and their creators. You'll wander through choices like Artists' Lives, which presents the lives of the artists and their paintings in the collection.

Or, you might prefer the historical atlas, which presents the pieces organized by place and time. You'll find all Spanish masters grouped together, for example. Or, you can select all paintings created in Amsterdam around 1600 to view other works painted contemporaneously with Rembrandt's own. I'm a fan of El Greco, and a frequent visitor to his adopted hometown of Toledo, so I was interested in seeing what other works of art were being created in Spain while the master from Crete dominated his own private world. I found some interesting works by Luis de Morales, who died shortly after El Greco moved to Toledo, and three early works by Velázquez. Exploring Spanish art in this way was almost as much fun as wandering through back streets of Toledo.

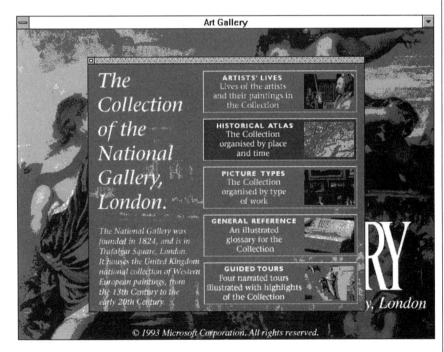

Microsoft Art Gallery concentrates on the wonderful collection of the National Gallery in London.

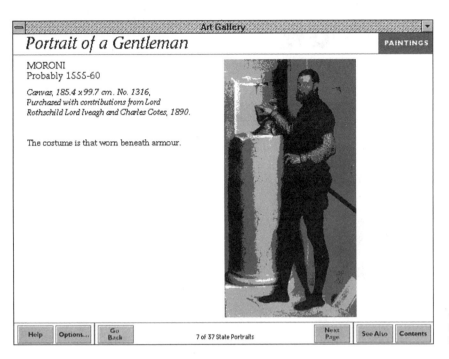

Portrait of a Gentleman | PAINTINGS

MORONI
Probably 1555-60

Canvas, 185.4 x 99.7 cm. No. 1316,
Purchased with contributions from Lord
Rothschild Lord Iveagh and Charles Cotes, 1890.

The costume is that worn beneath armour.

| Help | Options... | Go Back | | 7 of 37 State Portraits | | Next Page | See Also | Contents |

As you view a painting, you can read about its background, or browse to the next painting in the collection.

The Picture Types section groups works of art by their type, and there are four Guided Tours that take you on a walk through the great museum much as an in-person tour would. Each of the pictures shown in all the sections of this disc is backed with abundant information about the artist and the particular work of art. As with all Microsoft discs, there are many hypertext links you can click on to march off on a quest for related or (eventually) unrelated information.

For example, when you're viewing a wonderful painting by Velázquez, you can click the See Also button and wander off to a section explaining about the master's life in the court of Felipe IV, or perhaps a discussion of religious images of saints. On viewing his painting of the Immaculate Conception, you might end up exploring how other artists of that or other eras portrayed the same subject.

Microsoft Art Gallery *wisely concentrates on the works in a single museum, with excellent images and background information about art in London's National Gallery.*

This disc would be better if there were more details presented of individual paintings—that is, closeup looks at small sections in high resolution, so that you can appreciate the color, brush-strokes, and technique of the artist. But, *Microsoft Art Gallery* is good enough that we can look forward to other discs exploring different great museums of the world. How about it, Microsoft? Can you bring us, say, the Rijksmusem in Amsterdam or the Uffizi in Florence—soon?

Microsoft Dinosaurs

Rating: ◉ ◉ ◉ ◉ ◉

Publisher Name:
Microsoft

Software Requirements: **MPC**

Suggested Retail Price: **$79.95**

Microsoft Dinosaurs **provides an exciting exploration into the lives and habits of these prehistoric reptiles.**

Don't blame the current mania over dinosaurs on Steven Spielberg or Michael Crichton. Their collaboration *Jurassic Park* became the top money making movie of all time not simply because Spielberg is a great director or Crichton writes exciting books. Human beings are plain fascinated with dinosaurs of all shapes, sizes, and dispositions, in part because, even removed by 70 million years or so, they're the closest brush you can have with alien lifeforms without leaving Earth.

So, the half dozen or so CD-ROMs devoted to dinosaurs like this one satisfy more than curiosity about the latest craze. They provide us with essential information that will fascinate every child from four to ninety-four.

Microsoft's CD-ROMs are so uniformly good that you come to expect nothing less than dazzling graphics, great sound, and impeccably-researched information from their offerings. *Microsoft Dinosaurs* won't dissappoint you. There are 1,000 high-quality full-color illustrations and photographs, 200 articles, and 800 pop-up windows. There is a selection of Guided Tours narrated by "Dino Don" Lessem, author and dinosaur expert. Best of all,

you'll find live-action movies, which are actually animations, but look as if they were filmed on location during the Cretaceous Period.

My kids have a ritual they follow when they use this disc. First, they load the program and venture past the main screen to launch a video sequence called The Hunt. Then, they watch in rapt attention until the giant carnivore springs out from behind a leafy hiding place. At this point, both youngsters, as well as any friends they have have invited over for the show, scream at the top of their lungs in mock fright. For about 60 seconds. Or, at least until I come out of my office expecting to see a visitor wearing a hockey mask in our dining room.

Yes, this disc is *that* engaging and *that* much fun.

From the main Contents screen, you have seven choices. Select Atlas to view a map of the ancient worlds, complete with habitats and dominant creatures of each area. Choose Timeline to track the rise and fall of major species and learn why some beasts you see pictured in the movies never could have encountered each other in real life. The Families module teaches you about related groups of dinosaurs, while the Index can be used to search for specific keywords. Guided Tours take you on a narrated vist through Mesozoic Park, while the Dinosaur Movies provide amazingly realistic animations that are much better (and safer) than actually being there.

Every choice leads you on a tempting path to other subjects. For example, clicking Jurrassic Period in the Timeline brings up a screen of different life forms, with topics like Reptiles of the Sea, Reptiles of the Air, and What is Paleontology? I clicked Theropods, which looked promising. Another screen popped up with some inviting looking creatures, such as Allosaurus and Piatnitzkysaurus. Up in the corner of the screen was an icon that read Meat-Eaters, so I clicked that next.

In a few seconds, there was yet another screen picturing a carnivore as big as a house munching on an ex-dinosaur of some species, accompanied by realistic slurping and chewing noises. Eight more subtopics were highlighted. I clicked Meat-Eating Teeth and was treated to still another screen with information about dinosaur teeth. The word serrated was highlighted, so I clicked that and got another window, which included a speaker icon. Click that and you get the correct pronunciation (sur-RATEd, not SER-ated). Argh! Another icon, labeled Teeth of Meat Eaters. That led to a completely different screen with more subtopics and highlighted words. This could take all night!

All during my journey, icons were available at the bottom of the screen to summon help, backtrack along my wayward path, or jump directly to one of the other areas. Microsoft not only makes dinosaur hunting fun, it makes it easy.

The information is as accurate as possible considering the type of data that scientists have to work with. Using nothing more than bones or bone fragments, they're able to piece together an idea of what these creatures looked like. But keep in mind that it's impossible, based on studies of bones

only, to do more than conjecture about skin textures and coloration, or the purpose and use of bony plates, spikes, and other accoutrements.

When you watch the accompanying movies, you have to stop and think that most of what you see is just guesswork.

Microsoft Dinosaurs is richly endowed with extra features that you might not expect, but will love to have. For example, you can export dinosaur images from the disc to your desktop published documents, Windows desktop background, or screen saver. You can print out Fact Cards about individual dinosaurs. Collect 'em all, or trade 'em with your friends!

There are lots of dinosaur discs on the market, but this one ought to be your first stop, if only for its gorgeous images and chilling repertoire of growls and ambient noises from the age of reptiles.

This graphics, sound, and video-rich CD-ROM may not be the only dinosaur disc on the market, but it's way ahead of whoever is in second place.

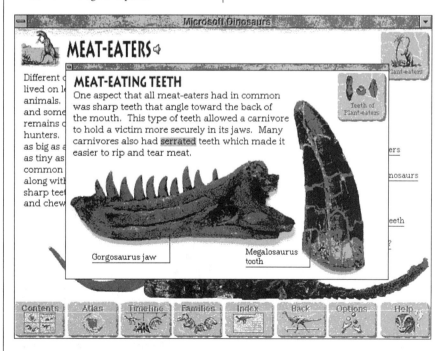

One thing leads to another as you follow fascinating hypertext links in *Microsoft Dinosaurs*.

MindQuest: Medieval France

Rating: ◉ ◉ ◉ ◉

Publisher Name:
Blue Mountain Software, Inc.

Software Requirements: **MPC**

Suggested Retail Price: **$79.95**

*M*indQuest: Medieval France is a fascinating tool for the armchair tourist or student with eclectic tastes. With this program you can take multimedia jaunts through history, touring sites mainly in medieval France, but stretching as far away as Stonehenge and the Western U.S., learning a bit about the architecture, history, food, personages, geography, and climate of the areas involved.

When you start the program, you are asked to type a name for your journal. You can save your journal at any time and come back later to where you were, bookmark fashion, or you can add a journal, or split a journal. This last option allows you to clone your journal and take each version in a different direction simultaneously by using a split screen. You can then discard one and save the other as your journal. You can have a total of sixteen journals in any one session. After choosing your journal name, pull down the "mode" menu on the main menu screen and choose either Slide Show or Time Explorer. The Slide Show gives you full-screen views of the 600+ color photographs on the CD-ROM, many of which are superb and accompanied by music. Above the picture a caption bar names the site and

tells its location, so that you can go into Time Explorer at your leisure and find out more about the site.

Time Explorer is where the fun begins. The table of contents has both icons at the bottom and navigation buttons at the top, both sets of which perform the same functions. You can click your mouse on Europe to see how France is situated geographically within Europe. Several cities and regions appear on the map, including Koln, Granada, Venice, Viking, and England. Clicking a name takes you to a picture and text showing something of interest in that area, for example, Cologne Cathedral (in Koln), or Stave church (under Viking).

You can see that the program is limited neither to medieval sites nor to France, although the accompanying booklet says

that it concentrates on the period from 1066 to 1307: from the Battle of Hastings to the disbanding of the Knights Templar by Philip the Fair. When your first picture and explanatory text appear on-screen, there is also a set of navigation buttons. Click one of these to continue your exploration. Typically, you can choose the region, the century, a time tour or a site tour, or any number of other parameters.

From the table of contents, the Timeline option gives you a choice of six eras, from Romanesque (1050-1100) to Demise of Gothic (1300-1350). Clicking one of these gives you a brief text overview of the era, along with a chart listing several sites. Clicking one of the names takes you to that site, and you can take a tour from there. Clicking the Contents item Mandala gives you a geometric figure showing the cycle of

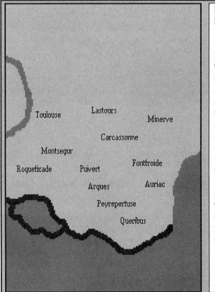

Languedoc
Languedoc Map
The name "Languedoc" comes from the ancient language of the south of France, where the word "yes" was "oc," rather than the French "oui." Here the tragedy of the crusade against the Cathar heretics was played out against the dry rocky terrain to which they fled. We can still see many of their fortresses on steep precipices, between which it is said they communicated at night with signal fires. Like the Civil War in the American south this crusade of almost 800 years ago is still remembered in this region, and stone "Cathar crosses" are found in some of the small, out-of-the-way villages. Languedoc produces very good red table wines such as Minervois, Corbieres and Rousillon. They are the perfect accompaniment to a hearty dish of Cassoulet, for which the region is famous.

Medieval France **offers extensive background about early France and its regions.**

The interior photographs of cathedrals in *Medieval France* are gorgeous.

Eiffel Tower - River Seine
If you travel to France, there is little doubt that your journey will include a nighttime walk along the River Seine.

Chapelle
St Chapelle - Exterior
St Chapelle was never designed for a large gathering; consequently there are no side aisles or accompanying buttresses. This meant that the walls were really a ring of columns with great curtains of stained glass inserted between them.

SiteTour
St Chapelle - Apse windows
St Louis (IX) had the chapel built to house the relics of the Crown of Thorns, which he had purchased from the Venetians. It was placed in a gold reliquary on this dais, surrounded by over 6000 square feet of stained glass.

seasons and the moon, the four Evangelists, the four elements (earth, air, water, fire), and four holy women (Virgin Mary, Eve, Magdalene, and Isis, the goddess of death). Four pop-up windows offer a few words of explanation.

The most useful Contents items are Narrator and Librarian. Clicking Narrator gives you a choice between Grand Tour and Time Tours. The Librarian offers seven choices of handy, though sparse, reference materials.

MindQuest: Medieval France can appear imposing at first. The best way to start is to choose Time Explorer, and then Narrator. Then click GrandTour. A map of France appears on the left side of the screen on which the various regions are listed. The narrator tells you a little about France and the tour, and this text appears on the right half of the screen. Clicking the right mouse button eliminates the text and centers the picture. Clicking again returns the text and picture to their previous positions.

When the narrator stops speaking, click the Grand Tour navigation button on the

top and the tour starts. Maps of each of the regions of France appear, with accompanying narration and text telling what the area is famous for: its history, landscape, and cuisine, for example. Each of these maps has names of several sites highlighted. Clicking one of the names shows a photograph of the site with accompanying description and music instead of narration. The first time through, however, it's best to go through the whole tour to get the big picture.

After the narrator finishes, or after you've read the text, you have to click a navigation button to continue. Just keep choosing Grand Tour until you get back to the beginning. The problem with this tour is that, without the map of France, you don't have a good idea of where the region is located in the country. To find out, click the France navigation button, study the map for a minute, and then click the Prior button to go back to the previous screen. Click Grand Tour" to continue. (If you click Grand Tour while on the map of France, you go back to the beginning of the tour, so beware!) If you like to see where you've been, Prior can take

you back as many as 12 screens, but with a shorter text and no narration.

As you can see, the possibilities of this program are great. It centers on the cathedrals of medieval France, but ranges rather far afield at times. The narrator's pronunciation of French is passable overall, sometimes excellent and sometimes lacking. The 20 minutes of "medieval musical score" sounds more Renaissance, but is pleasant background music played by solo acoustic guitar. You can turn off the sound, if you choose. The text is useful and well researched, but there are a number of misspellings that really are inexcusable in a program that is otherwise outstanding. The ability to cross-reference so much information across so much area and time is wonderful for time explorers. Unfortunately, if you want to look up one specific site, you have to do some digging. A simple alphabetical index of sites would be a tremendous help to those who know where they want to go, but can't figure out how to get there. Some of the images lack detail because they are too small, especially those in the VideoTours. This is a great pity, as some of them would be striking if they were larger and had good resolution.

MindQuest: Medieval France is a wonderful program for anyone wanting to increase his knowledge of the cathedrals of medieval France, and to learn a little about that era and France in general. People expecting castles and knights in armor will be disappointed, although there are some castles, almost invariably in ruins. This is basically an adult program, although a bright junior high student undismayed by the vocabulary may enjoy it. The slide show has a wider audience. All in all, if the topic appeals to you, buy this program—you'll love it. In its niche, it's excellent.

Multimedia Animals Encyclopedia

Rating: ◉ ◉ ◉ ◉ ◉

Publisher Name:
Applied Optical Media Corporation

Software Requirements: **MPC**

Suggested Retail Price: **$59.95**

Virtually everything you ever wanted to know about birds, fish, mammals, reptiles, and amphibians is now at your fingertips in this multimedia CD-ROM title. This is another one of those unassuming little discs from Applied Optical. Inside that plain-looking jewel box is a disc worthy of the big-bucks packages that come backed with six inches of foam to fill out the box. You'll be pleasantly surprised when you run *Multimedia Animals Encyclopedia*.

Billed as a "multimedia 'who's-who' of the world's creatures," this disc is based on the *Illustrated Animal Encyclopedia*, published by Marshall Editions, Ltd., of London, and is enhanced with video images, habitat illustrations, sounds, and other multimedia add-ons.

With some 2,000 of Earth's creatures parked on this CD-ROM, my guess is it will be a while before you will want for information on an animal not found on your computer. The CD-ROM comes complete with pronunciations of the animal names, including the vernacular and scientific names, range maps that depict locations of the animals, the sounds made by the animals themselves, behavioral and physical descriptions of the animals, and relative comparisons of the animals' sizes.

A great learning tool for the budding young forest ranger or the trivia fanatic, this CD-ROM title can keep you occupied for hours on end. Virtually any way that you desire you can search for information on an animal. Searching by name is a no brainer. But some of the neat research criteria include searching for animals by region and searching (comparing) animals by diet comparison.

The menu selections provide, at a touch, habitats, range maps, classifications (including class, order, and family), conservation status, a general description with nice detail, and diet (with diet comparison).

Let's say, for instance, you want to sort animals by size. For the *Multimedia Animals Encyclopedia*, that's no problem. The Bookshelf provides easy access to that information. Wonder what animals eat birds? Wonder no longer. At the click of a button, you find a listing of bird hungry animals. Selecting animals by habitat, such as deserts, forests, lakes, and rivers, is equally

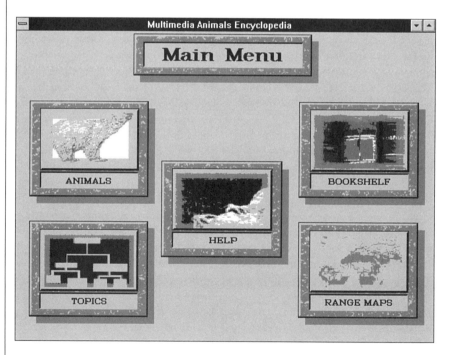

Start your tour of the animal kingdom from this main menu.

as easy. If you get stuck, extensive on-line help is available.

And of course, for the true biologist, there are those marvelous classifications. Animals are sorted by class, order, and family. Also included on the CD-ROM is a handy glossary of terms.

The CD-ROM requires 256 color capability, but works at higher color settings, as well. The illustrations are clear and detailed. Animal sounds are provided for some 220 of the animals.

In-depth look at the habits and habitats of 2,000 creatures, with sound and vivid color pictures.

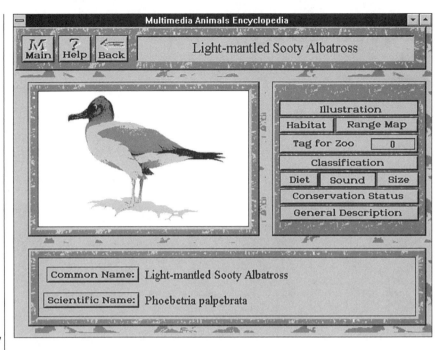

Detailed illustrations of each animal is accompanied by a database of information on habitat, range, classification, diet, and other features.

What makes this CD-ROM an exceptionally useful tool is the capability to switch from animal to animal with minimal effort. If, for instance, you sort the animals that live in the desert, you then can click any of the animals listed and jump to the detailed information and illustration associated with that animal. With *Multimedia Animals Encyclopedia*, there is no need to back out of one screen or menu to access further information in another menu. The information can be attained by simply clicking the animal(s) listed. This CD-ROM

has made information on animals truly user-friendly.

There is very little waiting on the information that you request. Its illustrations and supporting information are generated almost at the blink of an eye. Also of note, the on-line help, which is available at virtually every screen, is exceptionally well done.

The only downside, if there is any, is that you have to listen very carefully to the some of the pronunciations to get the nuances of the words. But this is a minor issue in comparison to the pluses this CD-ROM has

to offer. The accompanying booklet is somewhat skimpy, too, but all you really need, once you've gotten past the installation program, is right on the disc itself.

If you like learning about animals for education or just for fun, *Multimedia Animals Encyclopedia* is sure to be a hit around the house. It's one of those rare discs that is suitable and of interest to all ages.

Normandy

Rating: ◉◉◉ 1/2

Publisher Name:
Quanta Press, Inc.

Software Requirements: **MPC**

Suggested Retail Price: **$39.95**

June 6, 1944: Allied Expeditionary Force soldiers, sailors, and marines landed on the beaches of Normandy, France and World War II began to end. From those corpse-littered beaches to the fortress at Cherbourg, on through the hedgerow's bitter battles of attrition to the town of St. Lo, they fought, and died, in their thousands, in their tens of thousands.

On both sides, the opposition was demonized. German soldiers were characterized as "Huns," barbarous demons lacking the smallest shred of humanity. Allied soldiers were "soft yanks, decadent Britishers, Jew-loving dogs." Fifty years later, the insults are being forgotten, the wounds are healing. Even some of the reasons for the war are being lost to the comforting distance of years. This CD-ROM book serves to help assure that what those fighting men did is not forgotten. Nor should it be.

Built around Microsoft's Multimedia Viewer, *Normandy* is as much an experience as a text. It includes newsreel footage, recorded radio announcements, more than 650 photographs of the battles and the men and women who fought them, and numerous full-text copies of official reports. There are interviews with American and German soldiers and reports of many of the battles and unusual incidents that happen in war. One, a report on a returning group of captured German nurses, seems to point up the professionalism of some of the German forces.

Normandy installs easily, creating its directories and transferring its files effortlessly. Navigating through the CD's 668MB is easy, point and click.

The opening screen shows Gary Sheahan's painting, "Omaha Beach," accompanied by a sound clip of the radio announcement of the landing. Clicking the hypertext brings up a choice screen with Media Clips, Photographs, Monographs, Reference, and Interviews options.

Media Clips consists of two selections of newsreel footage of the landings and several audio clips of radio announcements and programs related to the invasion. Monographs is a collection of reports and writings about the invasion, its consequences, and militarily practical lessons learned. Reference is a collection of documents from the time. Interviews contain transcriptions of interviews with soldiers and officers at and shortly after the assault.

The Media Clips collection lends a sense of immediacy to this historical document. The two newsreel clips comprise about 18 minutes of Video for Windows clips divided into "From the Beaches to Cherbourg" and "From the Hedgerows to St. Lo." They have all the grainy, gritty quality of 40s newsreels. The five audio clips range from the first radio reading of Eisenhower's SHAEF

With the 50th anniversary of the Normandy Invasion commemorated in 1994, this disc is particularly timely.

```
    The U.S. Army at Normandy        12:04:52 PM

File  Edit  Bookmark  Help
Contents  Go Back  History  Search    <<     >>
```

```
Date: 6/17/44
Description:
190392S
17 June 1944
A French Peasant says a Prayer as he places flowers
on the body of an American soldier killed in the
front of his home in France.
```

Each photograph is provided with a descriptive caption.

Communiqué Number One at 3:32am to Roosevelt's leading the Nation in Prayer at 10pm on June 6, 1944. You can imagine being huddled around the family radio, thinking of "our boys hitting the beaches" on that grim day.

The Photographs collection is riveting. There are more than 650 official and news photos chronicling D-Day and the fighting that followed. Many are humorous. Many are heart-rending. You can see the people who did the real fighting; how they lived and how they died; how they managed the daily grind; and how their sense of humor crept out, even in the midst of war. All the photos are good quality and you can opt to enlarge any of them for clearer viewing. They range in subject from official War Dept. pictures of equipment to battlefield shots to feature shots of the American GI's irrepressible good nature and German prisoners' underlying humanity. It takes some time to view all these pictures but it's worth the effort.

Among the References is the story of the transfer of a group of German nurses near Sept Vents, France during the fighting. The story is a mildly humorous recounting of how the opposing forces made contact and effected the transfer. Some of the by-play between the American and German soldiers is illuminating in how traditional soldiers' complaints transcended their being on opposite sides.

Interviews contain several transcribed interviews conducted by G-2 (Intelligence) of soldiers and officers who fought through the invasion. Their comments present the line officers' and soldiers' perceptions of the battle. Also, Medal of Honor winner listings are presented here along with listings of other medal awards, particularly Distinguished Service Cross.

Overall, this CD is more than just a memorial, more than just a nice multimedia reference. It is a historical document as valuable for the serious student as for those casually curious about "D-Day."

A fine production on a serious subject, June 6, 1944, "D-Day, the Invasion of Normandy." It provides ready access to important data about the beginning of the end of World War II.

The San Diego Zoo Presents... The Animals!

Rating: ◉ ◉ ◉ ◉

Publisher Name:
The Software Toolworks

Software Requirements:
MPC/ Macintosh

Suggested Retail Price: **$39.95**

What a great disc! Although it's been available for several years, San Diego Zoo's *The Animals!* is still as fresh and interesting as the latest multimedia extravaganza on the market. A live-action tour through the exhibits of one of the world's premier zoos, this disc has everything you expect from a first rate CD-ROM: stunning video clips on an amazing range of topics, thousands of photographs and pages of information on animals and their habitats, and hours of audio narration.

This is one CD-ROM that has been *deservedly* overexposed, wrapped up in uncountable CD-ROM bundles and offered at rock-bottom prices from mail order houses. Don't be put off by the hype—grab yourself a bargain.

The core of this disc centers around the animal "exhibits," which can be accessed from a graphical main menu that resembles a three-dimensional map of the zoo itself. Your mouse can wander up and down paths leading to habitat types (tropical rain forest, savanna, grasslands, mountains, and so on) or other zoo centers of interest (research center, library, nursery, tours, stories, or kid's area). Click that portion of the main map and you're instantly transported to a new area to explore.

Selecting Grasslands, for example, takes you to a scene of grazing bison, accompanied by natural sound effects of the insects and birds that inhabit this area. A scrollable box of text tells you about grasslands in general. You can click camera, loudspeaker, or filmclip icons at the bottom of the screen to see additional still photos, hear more sounds, or view narrated videos about the current scene. A quick click of an arrow icon takes you to the next exhibit within the grasslands area.

You can go back to the main menu map at any time, retrace your steps through the zoo, or access particular animal exhibits

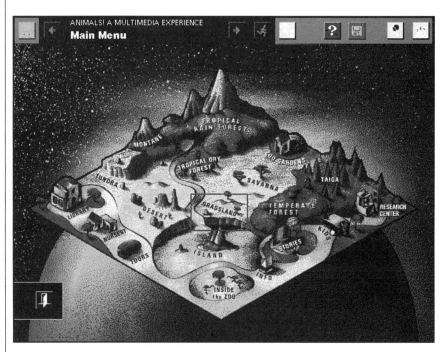

The Animals! uses a three-dimensional map, representing the San Diego Zoo itself, to provide easy access to its exhibits.

directly. More than 200 exotic animals, birds, and reptiles are shown in 350 different exhibits.

But that's only the start. The Kid's Corner lets even the youngest child enjoy the zoo through mini-videos that tell stories, present fun activities, show and explain about baby animals, offer amazing animal facts, or test knowledge through a "name that animal sound" quiz.

The Research Center has fascinating information on the Zoo's Center for Reproduction of Endangered Species' various research projects. The Library offers a list of maps, movies, sounds, videos, and text you can browse through. The Nursery concentrates on baby animals, while Tours gives you the choice of customized guided tours of exhibits, with themes like Animals in Disguise, Primates, or Jaws, Claws & Creature Features.

You'll spend hours exploring the 82 award-winning video clips, 1,300 color photographs, 2,500 pages of text, and more than 180 minutes of audio on this disc. It's amazing that so much information can be packed on a single CD-ROM, yet still be easily accessible. While its user interface bares no

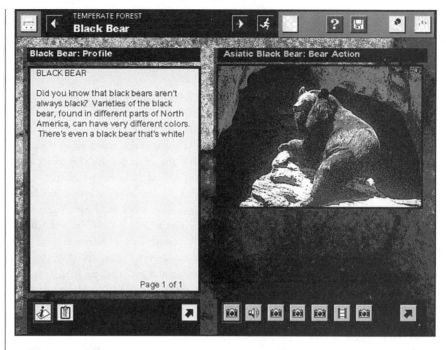

Individual exhibits include videos, still photos, and sound.

resemblance to the Windows or Macintosh interface you're used to, you won't care—this one is better for zoos!

With no obvious weaknesses, *San Diego Zoo Presents...The Animals!* has to be the one CD-ROM by which all other nature discs are judged. This one belongs in your library.

This rich treasure-trove of animal lore bristles with exciting video clips, informative audio, and thousands photographs and text pages, all easily accessible for hours of enjoyable browsing.

Seven Days in August

Rating: ◉ ◉ ◉ 1/2

Publisher Name:
Time Warner Interactive

Software Requirements:
Macintosh

Suggested Retail Price: $79.95

Time magazine's *Seven Days in August* recounts the single momentous week in 1961 when the Berlin Wall was constructed, providing a chilling apex to the Cold War that would lead the world to the brink of nuclear war in October of the following year. The events are made that much more poignant by the followup material, also on this disc, that describes through the eyes of some of the survivors the tumbling of the Wall 28 years later, in November, 1989.

This disc is solid history, presented in a new and exciting way that is possible only with the multimedia capabilities of CD-ROM. This program is an eight-part, day-by-day reconstruction of the events of that week with nearly three hours of photographic montages, music, and narration. There are also games to test your knowledge, and glimpses back at popular culture of the day, which help to recapture the mood and spirit of the times.

The main menu of *Seven Days in August* is a graphical matrix, with chronological milestones running down the left side of the screen: each row represents a single day,

such as Thursday, August 10, through Wednesday, August 16. The last row is labeled November, 1989.

The columns that march across the width of the screen delineate key topics for each of those days. Berliners include eyewitness accounts of the events. Profiles provides biographical information about the key players, such as JFK, Nikita Krushchev, and Germany's Conrad Adenauer. The Roundtable section offers discussions by journalists and policy makers from both sides of the conflict, such as McGeorge Bundy, JFK's national security advisor, who recall the events from their perspective of years later.

The Wall chronicles the events in Germany step by step, while Home Front shows what was going on in the United States in terms of civil rights and the "space race" during this period. There's even a section called "Berlin, Wisconsin," that contrasts the differences between small-town America and Soviet-dominated Eastern Europe. You can access any of these events in the visual menu grid by clicking that section with the mouse.

If these world-shaking events seem too grim, the disc also provides "Souvenirs of 1961," which presents sample comic strips (Popeye, Blondie, Beetle Bailey, Dick Tracy, etc.), popular tunes ("The Lion Sleeps

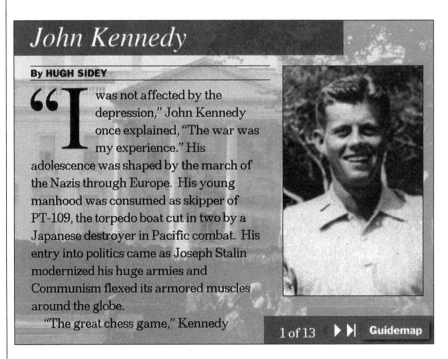

John Kennedy

By HUGH SIDEY

"I was not affected by the depression," John Kennedy once explained, "The war was my experience." His adolescence was shaped by the march of the Nazis through Europe. His young manhood was consumed as skipper of PT-109, the torpedo boat cut in two by a Japanese destroyer in Pacific combat. His entry into politics came as Joseph Stalin modernized his huge armies and Communism flexed its armored muscles around the globe.

"The great chess game," Kennedy

1 of 13 ▶ ▶| Guidemap

You'll gain insights about the important players in the Cold War in *Seven Days in August*.

Tonight"), and the latest automobiles from Detroit and, oddly enough, West Germany. This section gives you a real look at what proved to be one of the closing years of the 50s. (Most of us who lived through the era agree that the 60s didn't start until 1964 and lasted through Nixon's resignation in 1974. The 70s was an abbreviated decade, chiefly because of disco music.)

Can it be possible that *The Tropic of Cancer, Catch-22, The Agony and the Ecstasy, To Kill a Mockingbird,* and *The Rise and Fall of the Third Reich* were all on the best-seller lists at the *same time*, during this week? It truly was an incredible week all around, and *Seven Days in August* brings it to life.

The interactive games are a nice, but frivolous, addition. You'll act as fashion adviser to the late Jacqueline Kennedy and challenge your knowledge of baseball trivia. (Quick! How many home runs did Mickey Mantle hit during the 1961 season that was in progress during these events? 54?)

Seven Days in August *is a classic* Time *magazine look at an important week in world history, when the building of the Berlin Wall raised the Cold War to new heights of tension.*

Seven Days in August provides looks at events in Berlin, the US, and elsewhere during the week the Berlin Wall was built.

You can search through topics by using an index that provides a written listing of all key features in the archives. There is an atlas, recently declassified historical documents such as State Department position papers and cables (telegrams) between leaders, old *Time* magazine articles, and a "Who's Who" of the era. The only defect with this disc, if you can call it that, is the lack of any video coverage.

Everything is presented in still photo and sound narration format, although some exciting film, television speeches, and other full motion material is available. There's a trade-off, however: instead of an hour of video, you get four-hours of still material and sound.

Serious history students will love this disc, as well as we old-timers who just want to recall a momentous time in our lives.

20th Century Video Almanac

Rating:

Publisher Name:
The Software Toolworks

Software Requirements: **MPC**

Suggested Retail Price: **$79.95**

Obviously, personal computers have a long way to go before they'll display full motion video as well as, say, those little pocket LCD-screen color portables you can get at the electronics store for $119.00. Software Toolworks at least is brave enough to try and overcome the limitations of our hardware with *20th Century Video Almanac*, a series of five different CD-ROMs with 350 different video clips totalling four hours of footage. We tested an overview disc, sold separately, that has 100 historic clips and one hour of video.

The good news is that The Software Toolworks doesn't limit its video to the tiny, postage-stamp images you get with any of the Microsoft Windows video products. You can see larger, more detailed animations and less jerky motion with this product. The bad news is that its quirky, non-MPC requirements may make it difficult for you to run this disc as a DOS session inside of Windows, or even to use it outside of Windows if you have many drivers loaded into memory.

But let's look at the good parts, first. You find 2,000 photos, hundreds of pages of stories about historical events of the 20th century, and a timeline that can help you select events to study from the vast sweep of

world history we've seen in the 20th century. You can explore each era by choosing a day or decade, and then selecting one of four categories. These include Arts & Entertainment; Science & Technology; Sports; and War, Politics, & Disasters (all pretty much the same thing, anyway).

All the big events that were captured on film or video are included, from Woodstock to JFK's inauguration. You can watch clips from the 1916 World Series, or witness key events of World War II first-hand. If Nixon's resignation was a big point in your life, you can relive that moment over and over through the video clips on this disc.

I really enjoyed this trip down memory lane, because I seem to have a habit of being present at major news events. I was about 100 yards away from the student shootings at Kent State University in 1970, visiting Detroit when Jimmy Hoffa vanished, in Washington, D.C. on business when the jet crashed into the bridge, and staying in a hotel in Madrid, Spain when Bing Crosby collapsed on a golf course there and died in 1977. I don't consider any of these things my fault, not even for the resignation of one of our Presidents during a family vacation near San Clemente, California. Yet most of these high points of my life are right here on this disc.

It's easy to find the event you want, either by looking for all "on this day" entries for the current (or any other day you choose), or by searching for keywords, categories, or subject lists. If you enjoy this disc, The Software Toolworks offers others that are dedicated to individual topics, such as People or Sports.

However, be prepared to struggle a bit to get this program running. *Video Almanac* requires 580K of RAM, and a VESA-

compatible Super VGA graphics card *with the VESA driver installed*. If you generally run Windows and are accustomed to having all your applications running under Windows (even DOS programs), you may run into problems, like I did. First, it's likely you may not have 580K of RAM available to your DOS sessions, even if you use an advanced memory manager program to load drivers into upper memory. Second, this may be the first program you've ever run that requires loading a DOS VESA driver, so you may not know what that is, or even where your copy is. I have four 486 computers here with a few gigabytes of programs running on them, and this is the first time I've had to load a special DOS video driver to get a program running.

The payoff, of course, is better video than you'll probably get from unadorned Microsoft Windows. So, if your hardware and drivers are up to the task, you'll enjoy *20th Century Video Almanac*.

Extra hardware demands pay off with better quality video from this recent history treasure-chest of video images and news reports.

3D Dinosaur Adventure

Knowledge Adventure should get extra points for originality. *3D Dinosaur Adventure* enters an already-crowded dino-disc arena ready to scrap for supremacy. What does it bring to the party that hasn't been done before? How about stupefyingly realistic 3D graphics that will terrorize you and your kids. There are also some amazingly stupid antics tucked away in this disc that will either have you shaking your head in disbelief, or rolling in the aisle. This is one educational disc that doesn't take itself too seriously.

Let's start with the 3D stuff first. There are three kinds of 3D images in *Dinosaur Adventure*, all fairly spectacular. The sparsest kind of 3D is the real thing: you need to put on red/blue 3D glasses to see the effect. The opening screen lets you know what you're in for, as a ferocious Allosaurus rambles toward you at full speed, seemingly leaping out of the screen to take a bite. There's more of this realistic brand of 3D image inside the Dinosaur Museum which is, sadly, limited to only four rooms, and in the Dinosaur encyclopedia. After you view these images, you'll wish there were a lot more in *Dinosaur Adventure*.

The second kind of 3D is also pretty thrilling. Many scenes use virtual-reality-type "fly throughs," in which you're transported as if on a magic carpet through the gates of an amusement park, Jurassic Jungle, over the treetops, and down onto a plain filled with living, breathing dinosaurs. You don't need the 3D glasses for these sequences, because this is only simulated 3D. The effect is still pretty good. You also find similar virtual reality movement in the world of Zoomscape, a game in which you attempt to save various dinosaurs from an impending comet collision, wandering

through hallways that resemble those in the popular games Doom or Castle Wolfenstein.

The third variety of 3D images on this disc are 3D models of various dinosaurs, shown first in wire-frame mode, and then with textures that you choose, ranging from checkered tablecloths to wood tones to metallic gold. Kids love this "Create-A-Saurus" game. You're able to rotate the 3D models on-screen to view them from several angles.

> *With 3D graphics, virtual reality fly-throughs, and 3D modeling, this disc is an adventure that kids and adults will explore for hours.*

The disc also has 30 movie sequences in which dinosaurs move and perform in other ways, although primarily in simple, short scenarios with no plot. The clips are more visual studies of the dinos in motion, as opposed to the elaborate mini-movies provided in *Microsoft Dinosaurs*. However, the lighting and texturing is flawless, so you'll enjoy these movies thoroughly.

3D Dinosaur Adventure includes quizzes and games and other fun activities. Some involve some incredibly silly commentary from the dinosaurs themselves. "What's for

dinner? YOU!" one of them growls in a voice straight out of a Saturday cartoon. Others pull off imitations of Clint Eastwood or Arnold Schwarzenegger as they disparage your choice of texture in the Create-A-Saurus game. Again, kids seem to love this inanity, although adults will tire of it quickly.

There are supposedly sections in this program for children of all ages. A few will insult the intelligence of even prevocal children. In the storybook module, for example, there's some solemn prose about dinosaurs noting that "some are big, some are small, some are wet, some are dry, some fly though the sky, some walk on the ground." Whew! At least Dr. Seuss's One-Fish-Two-Fish rhymed!

The biggest weakness of this disc is the dino encyclopedia, which has illustrations that are not up to the quality of the rest of the CD. Some quizzes ask you to identify a dinosaur, and then present you with four choices that are too small to let you make out many details of the creature.

However, if you want a dinosaur encyclopedia, you can buy *Microsoft Dinosaurs*. This disc nicely complements that one with more games and silliness, and some great 3D graphics.

Rating: ◉ ◉ ◉

Publisher Name:
Knowledge Adventure

Software Requirements: **MPC**

Suggested Retail Price: **$79.95**

Audubon's Birds/Audubon's Mammals

Rating:  1/2

Publisher Name:
Creative Multimedia

Software Requirements:
MPC/Macintosh

Suggested Retail Price:
$49.99 each/$79.99 for both

These two CDs, currently sold as separate products, are really a single treasure-trove of images and information for nature-lovers. They include illustrations and text from John James Audubon's landmark works on the wildlife of North America.

A gifted artist who painted portraits of his subjects in their natural habitats, Audubon published *Birds of America,* a collection of 500 full-color lithographs, in 1840–44. Later, he collaborated with Rev. Bachman to produce his 150-lithograph work, *Quadrupeds of North America.*

Audubon kept copious notes and diaries of his travels. The text on these CDs is fully as intriguing as the illustrations, maybe more so. His writings detail the appearance and habits, the anatomy, and the habitats of the birds and mammals he studied and his experiences discovering and studying them. They often read like an old adventure novel, though the 19th-century style may a bit stilted for many tastes. More than 150 years later, Audubon's penchant for detail and vivid description still captures the imagination and holds your interest.

Both CDs contain the complete text and illustrations of the "Octavo" editions (reduced-sized editions published in seven volumes between 1840 and 1844). The digital versions of his illustrations are as adequate to reproducing Audubon's magnificent paintings as 640 x 480 resolution can be. The real lithographs are gorgeous, even in print reproductions; the digital reproduction successfully conveys most of that quality.

Bird calls and animal sounds accompany the text and pictures, recordings provided courtesy of Cornell University's Library of Natural Sounds. These add a certain cachet to the illustrations and a lot of interest to the experience. Unfortunately, only 116 of the bird and 47 of the animal plates are accompanied by sound clips. It's particularly nice to view a color plate and listen to the sound clip simultaneously.

These CDs suffer from their interface, which is provided in versions for both IBM PC and Macintosh systems. It would be nice to see them reissued with a more attractive, snappier, modern front end. The proprietary DiscPassage interface is powerful, with a search engine that can report any occurrence of any word on the disc; maybe too many occurrences if your criterion is too broad. But the DOS-based interface is also less than compelling because even shareware catalogs now have game-like interfaces, hyper-linked text, and point-and-click selection. CD technology has advanced a lot in the past year. Audubon's works deserve an interface that will draw to them their due and proper attention.

Audubon's Birds and *Audubon's Mammals* may lack some of the multimedia polish of the latest educational offerings, but the contents rank as a scientific, artistic, and historical treasure that nature lovers will treasure.

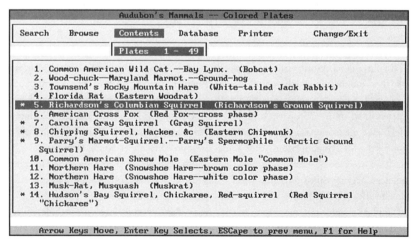

You can search through and view Audubon's original color plates through the DiscPassage search engine.

Black American History: Slavery to Civil Rights

*B*lack American History is more than a CD-ROM presentation on the history of African-Americans: it's a complete course of study that can be used in middle schools, junior high, and high schools. In addition to a variety of illustrated, narrated programs covering everything from the Colonial Period to Protest Movements, there are tests that measure student comprehension, a teacher's guide, answer key, and historical documents for further study.

Black American History *is a comprehensive course of study in an important segment of our country's history, featuring narrated presentations highlighted with the actual voices of important African American leaders.*

Actual voices of leading figures involved in the events, including the Reverend Dr. Martin Luther King, Jr., bring this aspect of our history to vivid life. Dramatic presentations representing more than 75 African-American personalities, from Sojourner Truth and Harriet Tubman to Thurgood Marshall and Ralph Bunche, add strength and reality to the program.

Your course starts from a main menu screen with nine choices, such as The Abolistionists, Reconstruction, The Harlem Renaissance, and The Depression. Clicking one of these sections leads to a 15-minute narrated presentation, illustrated with historical photos, drawings, and charts.

While viewing a section, the student can access an Index at the click of a magnifying glass icon to view related topics, or page through faster than the normal display by clicking left and right arrow buttons. Text display can accompany the spoken narration, or sound can be turned off if a "silent" mode is desired in the classroom.

At the end of each section, the student can be quizzed with multiple choice questions to see how well the material was understood. Scores can be printed or stored to your hard disk. The program is clever enough to store scores in a "miscellaneous" section if the student enters an invalid name or ID number by mistake. Most teachers will prefer to sort out stray scores later rather than have the student denied the opportunity to take the test through an error.

The narrated texts include important written materials accompanied by speech and sound effects on topics like The Quest for Freedom, Supreme Court Cases, and Black Voices.

Rating: ●●1/2

Publisher Name:
Queue

Software Requirements:
Macintosh

Suggested Retail Price: **$39.95**

Under the latter section, for example, you can hear talks by James Baldwin, Martin Luther King, Langston Hughes, and others. The Quest for Freedom has narrations on African-American business leaders, achievers in literary arts and sports, and pieces on their roles as patriots and soldiers, scientists, and inventors.

Supreme Court Cases covers four key court decisions that have had profound effects on our history, including Brown vs. the Board of Education and the historic Dred Scott decision.

Although the programs on this disc are basic slide-show audiovisual material enhanced by additional spoken word segments, it's convenient to have all this information on a single CD instead of a dozen audiotapes, film strips, videotapes, or other media. Black American History is a CD-ROM that belongs in every classroom where history is studied, examined, and cherished.

Capitol Hill

Rating:

Publisher Name:
The Software Toolworks

Software Requirements: **MPC**

Suggested Retail Price: **$79.95**

C*apitol Hill* is a pretty good disc once you get past the brain-damaged installation routine. It's a civics-lesson/simulation that lets you pretend you're a representative to the United States House of Representatives from your home state. You can work your way through swearing in, freshman orientation, juggling for committee appointments and, finally, answer some tough trivia questions and be elected Speaker of the House.

There's really more simulation than game here, with 45 minutes of video clips, 500 photos, stirring original music, and narration by someone who just has to be Alec Baldwin's only unsuccessful brother. It's really a lot of fun, and bound to be educational for anyone who's never served a prison term (or otherwise come in contact with public officials).

Your first obstacle is to get past the installation program for this Microsoft Windows-based program. It kept wanting to install QuickTime for Windows (which had been installed about four times previously on this computer), and kept chiding us about the dire results of not following its recommendations. Then, INSTALL flipped because we wouldn't let it mess with our PATH statement in AUTOEXEC.BAT.

Receive some advice from a fellow member of Congress early in your visit to Capitol Hill.

(Sorry, Mr. Programmer, but you might not be aware that under DOS 6, paths can also be set in CONFIG.SYS, where they don't have to deal with that nasty 128-character limitation or likelihood of being tampered with by brain-damaged install programs.)

The actual fun part started thereafter. We signed in with name and home state, received the good news of our election, and then watched as a plane took us to Washington, D.C. for our January 3 swearing-in ceremony. It was pretty cool. Then Alec Baldwin's husky-voiced brother (or someone who sounds just like him) handed us our Personal Digital Assistant, with all the controls we need to move smoothly through the halls of Congress.

Capitol Hill *is a legislation simulator for students and adults who want to know how Congress works.*

YOUR OFFICE

U.S. Representative Lynn Woolsey
D-California, 6th District, Santa Rosa

CAPITOL HILL

Next, we moved through Orientation, learning all about the legislature and how it came to be (a little late for that, but probably a good idea, nonetheless), and moved on to our office. *Capitol Hill* lets you browse through budget folders, pending legislation, and other materials in a very realistic manner. From time to time we were called to the floor of the House to vote on a measure. When we were all done learning, there was a board game we had to master (by answering multiple-choice trivia questions) to move from deputy whip up to Speaker of the House.

It actually took a couple tries to scale to a significant rung in the line of Presidential succession, but I managed it. High school students who need to pass their civics exams to graduate or adults with a morbid curiosity about how our country works (one tip: it's worse than how hot dogs are made) will love this disc. It's an entertaining simulation of life on *Capitol Hill*, with great video and some fascinating insights.

Dinosaur Discovery

Who are these Applied Optical Media guys, anyway? I keep stumbling on discs from this group that don't look like much from the packaging, and that haven't been written up much in the magazines. But when I load the program to check it out—wow! *Dinosaur Discovery* is another one of those finds. Plain white booklet in a jewel box, with a single full-color picture on the front and a lot of text on the back of the case. You're expecting, maybe, just another dinosaur CD?

Wrong again! If you can believe it, *Dinosaur Discovery* actually includes lots of information you won't even find in the other prehistoric CDs. There's lots of in-depth data about classication, location, and behavior. Indeed, if anything, this disc is too detailed and designed at a level a bit higher than the average junior dinosaur lover. Kids start to be fascinated with these creatures in first grade or earlier, and their passion tends to run out of steam before the end of primary school.

Indeed, *Dinosaur Discovery*'s coverage of more than 150 dinosaurs and prehistoric animals may be too much for these youngsters, without a little guidance from a parent or older sibling. On the other hand, everyone from junior high school student to adult can re-discover their love for denizens of the Mesozoic Era through this classy, information-rich disc.

Like all the other Applied Optical CDs we've found, this one boasts a gorgeous interface that's both inviting and easy to use. The main menu offers five choices: Dinosaurs, Topics, Bookshelf, and Activities. Dinosaurs lets you investigate a specific animal by selecting it by genus name. Use this section to find a particular dinosaur quickly.

The Topics section provides sub-sections like Museum, Chronicles, and Glossary, along with a helpful introduction. Museum details individual species, Chronicles includes icons you can click to study fossils, appearance, behavior, evolution, and other topics through more than 30 narrated slide shows. Under Glossary, you find definitions of all the terms used on the disc.

Bookshelf is a gateway you can use to browse through characteristics like classification, period, and size to locate similar groups of dinosaur families. You may print out information about each dinosaur along with a picture, and use the output in school reports and term papers, if you like. That will be a great help for students using the disc for research.

The Activities module has games that help you learn the names of all the beasts profiled on this disc. Just learning to pronounce the names of some of these creatures is a feat in and of itself.

The scientific credentials behind this disc are impeccable. Peter Dodson, associate professor of anatomy at the School of Veterinary Medicine of the University of Pennsylvania, and George Olshevsky, editor of *Mesozoic Meanderings* and skilled translator of technical terminology into layperson's terms, are listed as consultants. Some text and illustrations came from the *Encyclopedia of Dinosaurs*, published by Publications International, Ltd.

Rating: ◉◉◉

Publisher Name:
Applied Optical Media Corporation

Software Requirements:
MPC/Macintosh

Suggested Retail Price: **$39.95**

Dinosaur Discovery includes a dino encyclopedia with picture and pronunciation available at the click of the mouse.

Dinosaur Discovery includes information about dinos you won't find in competing discs.

Dinosaur Safari

Rating:

Publisher Name:
Creative Multimedia Corp.

Software Requirements:
MPC/Macintosh

Suggested Retail Price: $39.95

Kids and adults are gobbling up anything with dinosaur pictures on it. There are already other dino CD-ROMs on the market and, let's face it, the raw material is somewhat limited. Everybody wants to see the old warhorses—even Jurassic Park wouldn't dare open without a T. Rex—and there's just so much you can do with the creatures that are available. After all, these beasts have been dead for millions of years. What do you do?

If you're Creative Multimedia Corp, you do something creative. Turn dinosaur hunting into a game, throw in a few aliens (without otherwise compromising the scientific accuracy), and unleash the whole thing on an unsuspecting world. The result, *Dinosaur Safari*, is an unrelenting success. Kids and grown-ups alike can have fun learning about prehistoric animals by using a camera, notebook, and camcorder to "capture" them on travels through time.

That's the delightful premise behind this disc. You're a dinosaur hunter sponsored by the National Chronographic Society (established 2319), which publishes the Universe-famous multimedia datazine, National Chronographic. You're charged with collecting pictures, sound, and video of dinosaurs for an upcoming issue, "Dinosaurs of the Mesozoic."

Your journey starts in the Clanagram room, where you select a target animal—dinosaur and non-dinosaur reptiles, such as pterosaurs, protosaurs, and thecodonts. If you don't have the foggiest notion of what these are and why they are not dinosaurs, take heart. You learn everything as you hunt them down on your safari.

Dinosaurs are worth the most money, while closely related creatures are worth slightly less. Distant relatives are worth least of all. After you've chosen your beast, it's down the hall to the chronosphere room; inside the Krono Sphere you set off for your travels through time. Inside the room there is a view screen and pockets for five data crystals. There are also controls for traveling through time, for moving around the world, for accessing information, for identifying plants and animals, and for taking snapshots.

You can collect more than one picture of a dinosaur if you haven't used up all five of your crystals on each visit. Better pictures earn more money. The best capture the whole dinosaur (not partially obscured by a plant or other formation) in dramatic action—caught in the act of being itself, so to speak. (Are you listening, Allen Funt?)

You pay for all the energy you use. You must return to your starting point before you run out of energy. So, your trek is a race against time, too.

As you roam around, you hope to see the dinosaur you've chosen to hunt. There are 62 different locations in each time period, only one-third of which are on land. To find your animal, you must learn about the plants and animals of the era and how they relate to each other and your chosen dinosaur. When you finally see the animal, snap a picture. When you return from your safari, go back to the clanagram room and trade your best data crystals for energy credits and other rewards, such as better tools for your dinosaur hunts (such as a radar device or dinosaur lure). It's quite a challenge to track down the creatures through the various time periods and habitats. Although this is clearly a game, you'll learn quite a bit along the way.

Smile, Mr. Dino! You're on *Dinosaur Safari's* picture list, and worth extra credits in this game/learning program.

Goldilocks and the Three Bears in Spanish

Although we reviewed the Spanish version of this disc, French and English (as a second language) versions are also available, for kids 4-12. Syracuse Language Systems believes that you can learn Spanish the same way you learned English—by hearing it spoken and used in common, everyday situations. *Goldilocks & the Three Bears in Spanish* is a great tool in a comprehensive Spanish conversation course. Young students—or their parents—can pick up a surprising amount of knowledge just by listening to the delightful story on this disc and playing the games associated with each of its 21 pages.

Total immersion language study is nothing new, of course. The idea is to avoid studying grammar and simply start using the language in conversation, learning the meanings of words and the proper way to use them from context alone. It works, as I can attest. I've learned more Spanish from ten trips to Europe since 1973 than I did from three years of the language in high school and another two in college.

Goldilocks is simply the classic children's story told entirely in Spanish. There are no translations available, no "grammar" icons to press, nothing that tells you how to conjugate a verb. Just listen to the story, advancing a page at a time by clicking page icons. After each page is read, you can click Goldilocks herself to hear some comment from her.

There are also game icons on each page. Every page has an associated game or quiz, also in Spanish, in which the student is asked to answer a question, play Tic-Tac-Toe, name colors or objects, choose the biggest or smallest, or play Bingo. Many of the games have different levels so that you can change the degree of difficulty to match the abilities of the student. Syracuse Language Systems has done a wonderful job of filling this disc with a variety of games and activities; they really help reinforce the lessons.

Rating:

Publisher Name: **Syracuse Language System**

Software Requirements: **MPC**

Suggested Retail Price: **$89.95**

But does *Goldilocks* teach your child Spanish? This disc can certainly help. The narrator speaks relatively slowly and clearly, at least she was easier to understand than I found the average Spaniard. The Latin American pronunciations will be most useful to students in this country. Listen to the disc a few times and you'll be able to decipher the conversation quite well.

However, actually learning conversational Spanish (forget about formal grammar for the moment) requires a lot more practice and many other exercises. *Goldilocks* should just be one part of an overall Spanish study program. (Syracuse offers many other discs that can be used in conjunction with this one.) Very young students may require some help in understanding what is going on, as the sentences, while not complex, are not in the "See Spot run" category. But that's what total immersion is all about: you understand little at first, then more and more as you're exposed to a language used in context.

Goldilocks & The Three Bears in Spanish offers the opportunity to learn Spanish by hearing it spoken during this interactive story.

Introductory Games in Spanish

Rating:

Publisher Name:
Syracuse Language Systems

Software Requirements: **MPC**

Suggested Retail Price: **$79.95**

We reviewed the Spanish version of this disc, but other versions, for kids 4-12, are available in French, German, Japanese, and English.

The 27 games on this disc teach more than 200 words and phrases through the time-honored total-immersion method. There's no English spoken at all: all the instructions, questions, and responses are in Spanish. You don't even see written Spanish. There's nothing standing between you and your understanding of what's being said but your ears and a few inches of brain.

Hearing these words spoken correctly and then repeating them can help Spanish students achieve perfect pronunciation. I can't overestimate how important conversational practice is in the mastery of language. I've been able to *read* Spanish fairly well for many years, but still recently found myself at a business lunch in Madrid where my new associates asked me to pronounce this word, or that word. Then they'd giggle. I asked what was going on. "You Americans! No matter how hard you try, you just can't pronounce words with "rr" in them," she said, rolling the letter like a Shakespearean actor.

With a little practice and this disc, you may be able to reclaim our country's honor. Just play one of the games, arranged in three

groups of nine on successive screens. The child (or adult) can learn colors, shapes, common clothing items, or parts of the face in entertaining games.

A total of 27 games that help students of all ages learn to pronounce, understand, and use Spanish.

Other activities teach modes of transportation, common items found in the bathroom, foods, and time-telling. There's also a set of jigsaw puzzles, a BINGO game, and a Concentration-type pair-matching game. There's enough variety here to keep any child occupied for hours. Kids also find

the total immersion method natural and fun; if they can figure out what's going on from the context, they're happy.

The BINGO game is a kind of review, drilling the student in all the nouns previously learned. Like many of the activities, there are various levels of difficulty. At level one, the player always wins, as there is no penalty for an incorrect guess. Starting at level two, incorrect answers result in a penalty: the student gets an X instead of a marker, so the chances of getting a straight line are reduced.

The booklet accompanying the disc provides hints for expanding the activities, changing the rules of the games, and taking the lessons outside the CD as games played without the computer. You'll want to augment this disc with other Spanish lessons for real proficiency, but *Introductory Games in Spanish* makes a great study aid for primary students to adults who want to learn the language by listening and speaking.

Each of these buttons leads to a different game in Spanish.

Languages of the World

Languages of the World is a multi-language translating program that can convert words and simple phrases from one language to another by using 17 built-in bilingual and multilingual dictionaries covering 12 different languages. You won't find it a panacea for complex translating needs. If you need a business letter translated from English into Russian, you'd really better explore one of the specialized translation programs on the market. But if you're a student of language and just want to compare the structure and vocabulary of any of these tongues, *Languages of the World* is a great tool.

It boasts a mundane Microsoft Windows interface, with pull-down menus for Dictionary, Options, Window display, and other choices, along with a set of buttons labeled with function key commands. You can click the button with the mouse or press the associated function key to carry out commands like Translation (F3), Related Words (F4), or Show Characters (F5). Most of the time, you'll be working with the Search dialog box, which allows entering words, selecting languages, and specifying other options.

The languages covered include Chinese, Danish, Dutch, English, Finnish, French, German, Italian, Japanese, Norwegian, Spanish, and Swedish. There is also a dictionary of American idioms, which we used to look up terms like John Denver's favorite phrase, "far out."

Chinese and Japanese words can be displayed or entered using Roman characters, or in kanji and kana characters. We took advantage of this facility to look up the true meaning of the word "Toyota," but the closest we could come was "toyu," meaning kerosene. The only famous car manufacturer we were able to find was

"Subaru," which means Pleiades (a constellation) and makes a lot more sense when you think about the group of stars that makes up that company's logo.

Some languages offer several dictionaries (there may be a technical dictionary as well as one for everyday words, for example), and you can choose both the source and destination language for any translation. The program can copy dictionary entries and graphic characters to the Clipboard for pasting into other Windows applications, and you may print dictionary entries and graphic characters for permanent reference.

This program did a good job of translating words and simple phrases, catching common idioms in all the supported languages. For example, the Spanish "de vez en quando" was properly translated as "from time to time" rather than literally as "from time in when." As with most dictionaries, none of the naughty

Rating: ●●●

Publisher Name:
NTC Publishing Group

Software Requirements: **MPC**

Suggested Retail Price: **$59.95**

words we looked up could be found in any language.

There are many options with this program. You can choose to translate a word into all the supported languages for comparison, and search for related words. If a typed entry is not found, *Languages of the World* shows you the closest match. This disc is easier to use than a multilingual dictionary, and a lot more fun for the casual language browser.

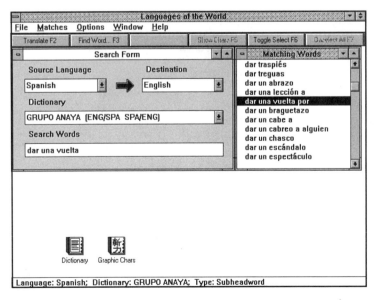

***Languages of the World* can translate between a variety of languages very rapidly.**

Shakespeare Study Guide

Rating: 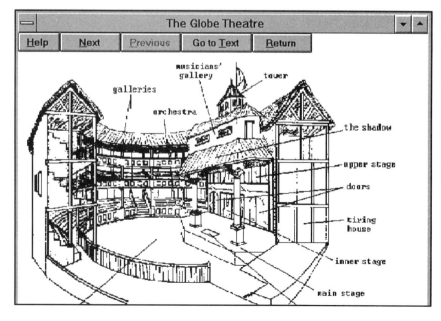 1/2

Publisher Name:
World Library, Inc.

Software Requirements: MPC

Suggested Retail Price: $79.95

A rose by any other name would smell as sweet. Indeed, this CD-ROM title, comprised of all of Shakespeare's works along with some of Barron's Book Notes, is provided with user-friendly interfaces making it a nice addition to your CD-ROM text collection.

World Library, Inc. provides a host of features to support the text documents. Searches can be performed by word, phrase, subject, date, country, era, century, and category. Works can be paralleled (side by side) for comparison purposes, text can be easily printed, and there are some illustrations to supplement the documentation. Bookmarking features and user notes are also provided with the *Shakespeare Study Guide*.

This CD-ROM contains both a Windows and a DOS version. The Windows version has a few extra features such as selectable font typefaces and point sizes and cutting and pasting features for insertion into other documents. A very handy auto-scrolling feature is available, with adjustable speed, which allows hands-free reading of text. (This tool alone makes this CD-ROM much easier to read than most titles.) Compared to *Shakespeare on Disc*, this one is much friendlier to Windows users, with a more modern interface than the DiscPassage provided for the other title.

The Barron's Book Notes are a nice addition to the CD-ROM and are provided for most of the major titles. Barron's is structured with information categorized by plot, the characters, the author and his time, and other elements. You can use Barron's to gain a deeper understanding of Shakespeare's words. (Note: Barron's Book Notes are available on disc, too; see the review elsewhere in this book.)

The only noticeable improvements that would really make this title stand out would be the addition of some multimedia features. There are some illustrations to supplement the text, however, it is primarily a text document.

One other very nice feature if you need technical support (which isn't very likely), World Library, Inc. provides a toll-free technical support number.

All in all, this title with its handy search features, Barron's Book Notes, and convenient auto-scrolling makes the *Shakespeare Study Guide* a useful tool for Shakespeare aficionados.

All of Shakespeare on a single disc, with accompanying Barron's Book Notes, in both DOS and Windows versions.

The Globe Theatre

Help | Next | Previous | Go to Text | Return

musicians' gallery
tower
galleries
orchestra
the shadow
upper stage
doors
tiring house
inner stage
main stage

This diagram of the Globe Theatre shows how the venue appeared in Shakespeare's time.

Sherlock Holmes on Disc!

Sherlock Holmes students and enthusiasts will be pleasantly surprised with the Creative Multimedia Corporation release of *Sherlock Holmes on Disc!*, a complete package of Sir Arthur Conan Doyle's works supplemented by a biography and poetry. Holmes fans are notorious for their zeal at studying these works, which were published over a 30-year span from 1887 to 1917. This disc gives them the tools they need to study every word, phrase, and character in the Holmes legacy.

Comprised of three main text parts, the CD-ROM contains *The Complete Works of Sherlock Holmes* (every Sherlock Holmes story written by Sir Arthur Conan Doyle), *The Medical Casebook of Arthur Conan Doyle*, a biography of Sir Arthur Conan Doyle written by Alvin Rodin and Jack Key, and *Late Asters*, poetry by Dr. George S. Bascom, focusing on perspectives from the viewpoint of a physician.

Although the format of the CD-ROM is not particularly flashy, it provides easy access to all the titles and nice searching features.

The Complete Works of Sherlock Holmes also comes with the linoleum block prints made by Dr. George Wells in the 1960s. The prints, which add a nice touch to the text, can be accessed from within a story by hitting the F9 function key and then choosing the image.

For those who want to know all the jots and tittles of the Doyle biography, *The Medical Casebook of Arthur Conan Doyle* provides that same type of access to associated reference material with the same keystroke.

The explanation for the inclusion of the *Late Aster* poetry, although apparently not directly related to the Sherlock Holmes material, is cryptically explained with the statement "Ask the great detective himself." A couple of images have also been included with the *Late Aster* poetry. Can we spell "padding" boys and girls? Or, is it that we don't really understand the thinking of Holmes' Irregulars—are they really interested in every scrap of information available? If so, someone should gain the rights to some of the many books of criticism and examination of Holmesiana, or the latter-day "new" Holmes stories, like "The Seven Per Cent Solution."

This disc is far from complete, although it does include every Sherlock Holmes story, but will be welcomed by Holmes fans looking for an easy way to search through the immortal words of Arthur Conan Doyle.

Rating:

Publisher Name:
Creative Multimedia Corporation

Software Requirements:
MPC/ Macintosh

Suggested Retail Price: **$29.95**

An interesting footnote can be found in the CD-ROM notes concerning perhaps the phrase most widely associated with Sherlock Holmes ("Elementary, my dear Watson"). However, in the interest of suspense we leave you to seek out that bit of information.

With the complete works, biography, poetry, prints, and search capabilities, *Sherlock Holmes on Disc!* proves to be an enjoyable title that will complement every Holmes student's library.

Space Shuttle

Rating:

Publisher Name:
The Software Toolworks

Software Requirements: **MPC**

Suggested Retail Price: **$79.95**

I f you can't make it to Space Camp in Huntsville, Alabama, this *Space Shuttle* CD-ROM is the next best thing! It's a simulator/ adventure along the lines of *Capitol Hill*, another offering from the same The Software Toolworks/Amazing Media/ Follett Software team. Both *Capitol Hill* and *Space Shuttle* use lively video clips presented on a Personal Digital Assistant (PDA) and other small screens in the display area. The PDA is used as a remote control to move from orientation to training, and then on to actual mission launch. You end up playing a trivia game that measures how much you learned during the project.

There's a definite educational angle to this disc, but it's so much fun that adults will end up playing along with their kids. The genuine NASA video, photographs, authentic schematic diagrams, renderings, and other touches add realism to this simulation. This may be your only chance to experience the thrill of preparing for space flight.

Your mission starts at Johnson Space Center, where you receive an overview of the Space Shuttle program during your orientation. Then you visit the flight simulator facilities to learn and practice skills needed to travel to outer space. The training program is rigorous, but nothing you can't handle with a quick mouse and steady eye. When it's Mission Launch time, you go back to the Control Room and get ready for the launch.

You can choose from one of 53 actual NASA missions. You might handle the

Space Shuttle is better than Space Camp for those who want a glimpse at astronaut training.

delivery or maintenance of a multi-million-dollar satellite, or chance a risky, untethered space walk. If scientific experiments are more your cup of tea, you can supervise a weightlessness experiment.

After you've practiced living and working in space, you can test your knowledge with the Lift-Off game, which is a simple board

game (it's like *Uncle Wiggly Goes To Space*) in which you roll the dice and then advance that many squares every time you get a correct answer. Choose the wrong multiple-choice answer, and you bounce backwards. The questions are hard, so this game really gives your memory a workout.

Like *Capitol Hill*, this program is saddled with a mindless installation program that can't believe you may already have QuickTime for Windows installed. It didn't handle the display on our main test machine properly, so we had to install it on a more basic 486DX-50 with the required 256-color 640 x 480 resolution display. It's a bit ridiculous to find programs that can't run on anything other than basic hardware these days, but The Software Toolworks is far from the only offender.

I had only one problem with the disc: the discussion of the ill-fated shuttle Challenger was oddly muffled, although the video clips before and after it played properly. It's a pity that information about the one space craft likely to be of most interest to users of this disc is defective.

This disc is a great learning tool, and provides everything you need to know about U.S. Space Shuttles. The simulated training mission makes absorbing this knowledge painless—or even fun.

Touring Indian Country

What a close call! This great CD-ROM just missed the cut as one of the top discs in the rich Education category. A fascinating guide to the living heritage of native Americans, *Touring Indian Country* combines valuable historical references with a unique look at contemporary Indian culture. Think of it as a travel guide that includes information you can use to tour modern reservations and attend current cultural events around the country.

Yes, in one sense the tour is presented on-disc, so you can visit with native Americans from an armchair perspective. You find 140 high-resolution images and 60 video clips that take you right to the front row. There is also an audio soundtrack that features traditional southwestern sounds spiced with music from Litefoot, the first Native American rapper.

More exciting, though, are the opportunities presented to visit and learn about this important part of our heritage in person, through listings of tribal families and a calendar of scheduled powwows, rodeos, intertribal socials, and other public ceremonies. More than 300 Indian tribes in the United States encourage visitors to come view their ceremonies, arts, crafts, and historical sites. *Touring Indian Country* can help you become a more informed visitor, ready to learn and appreciate

the history, customs, and cultural diversity that native Americans have generously agreed to share.

The disc is based on *Indian America: A Traveler's Companion*, Third Edition, by Eagle/Walking Turtle (Gary McLain), an Irish/Choctaw artist and writer who traveled around the U.S. visiting American Indian communities for six years. The Windows interface, tempered with a rich Indian motif, provides interactive access to a wealth of information extracted from Eagle/Walking Turtle's book.

A complete listing of tribes can be accessed by clicking on a map of the United States. The database includes tribal locations, visitor contact information, notes on art forms, and ceremonies open to the public. Another section provides a listing of Indian Moons, which are vivid descriptive names applied to months of the year. The Sioux, for example, call March the "Moon when the buffalo cows drop their calves."

The native American calendar of events lists Indian markets, rodeos, and fairs, with locations, dates, and phone numbers. A population table charts the growth of Indian residents by state between 1980 and 1990. Also included on the disc is a handy glossary, which explains all the terms used in the book.

It's so easy to lose touch with our past—the author, for example, is one-eighth American Indian, but managed to learn very little of this heritage from his Blackfoot grandfather, who died in the mid-1950s. This disc provides a convenient introduction to some important insights about our country and its native people.

Rating: ◉◉◉

Publisher Name: **MPI Multimedia**

Software Requirements: **MPC**

Suggested Retail Price: **$39.98**

Information about Indian tribes, population, Indian "moons," and other exciting facts are found in *Touring Indian Country*.

TriplePlay Spanish

Rating:

Publisher Name:
Syracuse Language Systems

Software Requirements: **MPC**

Suggested Retail Price: **$89.95**

If you're avidly reading all the language reviews in this chapter, you probably noticed that I recommended Syracuse Language Systems' *Introductory Games* and *Goldilocks & The Three Bears*, all intended for kids 4-12, as excellent teaching tools for adults, too. Apparently, the vendor agrees with me, and has created this TriplePlay series for ages 9 and up (through adult) with the same fun-and-games approach as all the Playing with Language titles. In addition to *TriplePlay Spanish*, versions for French and English (as a second language) are also available.

This disc has a new set of interactive games and activities that can teach more than 1000 words and phrases, using a total immersion approach. No English instructions, no English Help, no written words in the program, anywhere. Everything is done with clearly spoken speech instructions, so that you can learn pronunciation as you gain proficiency in your chosen language.

The emphasis is on fun, and don't worry

about getting all the answers right. You can learn as much from the correction of an inappropriate response here as from getting it right. I can still remember my first trip to Cordoba, Spain, more than 20 years ago, where I proudly tried out my pitiful high school/college Spanish at a fruit stand. "Quiero uno kilo de..." I started out, only to be met with a smile and wagging finger. "*Un kilo...un* kilo," the vendor insisted. That lesson has stuck with me all along, and to this day I always handle those situations by saying, "Quiero *dos* kilos de..." even if I didn't particularly *want* four and a half pounds of sliced ham.

You'll have more fun cutting yourself a slice of Spanish from this excellent disc. The words and phrases are a little more complex than those in the two Syracuse CDs aimed at younger children, and the Windows program interface itself is more sophisticated. You'll find drag-and-drop features in some of the games, like Square Off, Jigsaw Puzzle, or Memory Mania, as well as various Conversation activities. There's even a tool

bar that lets you choose skill level and other options while you're playing.

A visual dictionary, which is a two-dimensional array of objects, helps define the words used on the disc. You're not entirely on your own, here. You may select games by categories, choosing from a vertical row of icons at the left side of the screen. Click one of them (Food, Office, Travel, Clothing, Numbers) and any of the 32 games in the Game Menu that apply to this category are highlighted. There are three levels of games, each progressively more difficult. A chart in the thorough instruction guide provided lets you see exactly which games are available at each level.

Most of the games will already be familiar to you in other contexts, so learning time for the rules will be minimal. You can play Bingo, Concentration, box off squares on a grid, assemble jigsaw puzzles, or build a family tree. At higher difficulty levels, the games all take on the ambiance of a particular everyday situation, such as going on vacation, playing tennis, in the library, or shopping for clothing.

If you or your child want to sharpen your language skills, but don't want to bother with learning grammar rules from a textbook (or even working with any sort of formalized lesson at all), *TriplePlay* is exactly the sort of disc that can help you enjoy what you're doing and learning.

TriplePlay Spanish offers games that will interest children as young as nine as well as adults.

Twain's World

There are databases that are good because they contain a lot of information, and there are multimedia packages that are good because they provide entertaining software, ease of interface, colorful menus, and a good variety of subjects. *Twain's World* is a rare combination of both.

Bureau Development has outdone themselves with this comprehensive compilation of the life and works of Mark Twain. The opening menu affords the viewer the opportunity to choose from several sections, including the two principle sections, *The Complete Works* and *Galleries*. These two principal sections of *Twain's World* contain the text of favorite Twain stories and short stories, essays, letters, and speeches as well as narratives, slide presentations, pictures, animations (which will amuse all age groups), and video clips.

In addition to these, the viewer can select a timeline of the life of Samuel Clemens, with various significant markers in his life noted along the way. The timeline is an entertaining way to follow Twain's life. The markers are bright and pictoral in nature and offer a hint behind what is happening at that moment. By clicking the marker, text appears which describes the event or occurrence.

If *Twain's World* were simply a comprehensive database of Samuel Clemens's work, it would be hard to get overly excited about it. But it isn't. Merged within the text, in *The Complete Works* are opportunities to access multimedia clips, photos and even click-on definitions of uncommon words. The text is easy to read, and controlled by minimal movement of the mouse.

The *Galleries* section allows you to select all multimedia topics on the Twain's World CD-ROM. The choices include viewing the characters from his writings, video clips and animations with sound, pictures with short descriptions, and narrative clips.

The animations, which are comparatively short and colorful are sure to entertain the young ones in the family. But this is not merely a children's entertainment device. It is obvious that the collaborators of the CD-ROM sought the advice and input of Twain scholars. Included in the multimedia section of this CD-ROM are some excellent slide presentations, supported by narrative, of Twain's life.

Twain's World *is an enchanting look into the life and works of the 19th Century's best-loved American author, with animations, slide presentations, and vivid audio enhancements.*

The audio is crisp and, where words are spoken, they are exceptionally clear. Of particular note is the slide presentation and narrative of Twain's life. Full of detail, the viewer is brought into the life of Twain and made to feel as though he knows both the author and his family. This author found the level of detail provided in this narrative to be exceptionally well done.

Perhaps the most useful of the tools used to maneuver the CD-ROM is the List button. In the click of a mouse button, you can list all of the available topics available for the area that you are in. Listening to a narrative, you simply click List and choose another selection if you so desire. If you are checking out Judge Thatcher and are curious as to the artist's conception of Becky, just click List and choose her by name.

Twain's World is exceptionally well done, comprehensive and full of detail. As a tool for the student or just for the casually curious, this title by Bureau Publishing will provide hours of entertainment. The only downside, if there is one, is that unless you have a laptop computer with color, you can't curl up in bed with *Twain's World*—and you will wish that you could!

Rating: ●●●

Publisher Name: **Bureau Development, Inc.**

Software Requirements: **MPC1**

Suggested Retail Price: **$69.95**

Where in the USA/World/Time is Carmen Sandiego?

Rating: ⊙ ⊙ ⊙

Publisher Name:
Broderbund

Software Requirements:
MPC/Macintosh

Suggested Retail Price: **$80.00**

Have your kids learned their geography? If not, *Carmen Sandiego* can help them. Today, *Where in the World is Carmen Sandiego?* and its sibling programs, *Where in the USA is Carmen Sandiego?* and *Where in Time is Carmen Sandiego,* are perhaps the classic edutainment program for the IBM PC and Mac. It's not enough that students must answer challenging geography-based questions, they must use their knowledge to find the evil criminal mastermind, Carmen Sandiego. Aimed at ages six to 12, this program is education software at its best.

Although Carmen Sandiego is available on disk, the new Deluxe Editions on CD-ROM have enhanced sound-effects, movie-like music tracks, and more vivid animations.

You can explore 30 of the world's great cities in tracking down Carmen and nine cohorts, all members of Villains International League of Evil (VILE). Using a portable videophone that provides direct personal communications and news flashes, the player picks up clues by flying around the world to interview witnesses and suspects. You can review evidence, dossiers on suspects, and information about particular countries. A World Almanac is packaged with the game to let you look up more key facts on your own.

Each stop includes snapshots of the country and city being visited, with various tidbits of information cleverly worked into the plot. For example, a tour guide may recall that the suspect asked about Spanish exploration and produced a snapshot of a Cerro Silver Mine. With those clues in hand, you're off to investigate New World mining activities in Lima, Peru. All during the game, a digital clock ticks off the remaining seconds allowed for your quest.

When enough evidence has been collected, the gumshoe can issue a warrant for the arrest of a suspect. To get a valid warrant, you must gather all the evidence identifying that particular crook. After Carmen's gang has been rounded up, you may snare Carmen herself, and then gain a conviction in court. The object of this game is to obtain warrants for as many of the crooks as possible, or track them to their hideouts before time runs out.

This educational game pits a student's knowledge of world geography against fleeing master criminals as the youngster attempts to track down Carmen Sandiego and her gang. The video and animation in *Carmen Sandiego* are first-rate, and the problems challenging. It's no wonder that this game has spawned a top-rated television show and other spin-offs. The books supplied with the various versions of the game are themselves valuable study aids. This classic deserves its ranking on the best-seller lists.

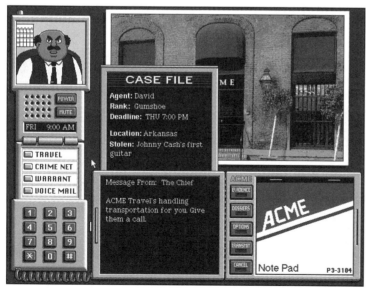

Get your instructions from The Chief, then head out in search of Carmen Sandiego.

Additional CD-ROM Titles

Title: 3-D Body Adventure
Suggested Retail Price: $69.96
Publisher: Knowledge Adventure
Platform: MPC
Description: Explore the human body, with vivid 3D graphics.

Title: 800 College Boards
Suggested Retail Price: $49.95
Publisher: Queue
Platform: MPC/Macintosh
Description: Study guide for preparing for college admission tests.

Title: African Wildlife
Suggested Retail Price: $99.95
Publisher: Gazelle
Platform: MPC/Macintosh
Description: In-depth guide to exotic animals using text and photos.

Title: A Multimedia History of American Literature
Suggested Retail Price: $495.00
Publisher: Queue
Platform: MPC/Macintosh
Description: In depth study of American Literature through the authors and their works.

Title: A Survey of Western Art
Suggested Retail Price: $49.95
Publisher: Compton's NewMedia
Platform: MPC/Macintosh
Description: Rich pictures of paintings and other artwork, with commentary.

Title: A World of Animals
Suggested Retail Price: $99.95
Publisher: National Geographic
Platform: Macintosh
Description: Animal life as seen through the cameras of National Geographic photographers.

Title: A World of Plants
Suggested Retail Price: $99.95
Publisher: National Geographic
Platform: Macintosh
Description: Botanical life as pictured by National Geographic photographers.

Title: A+ French Tutor
Suggested Retail Price: $195.00
Publisher: Queue
Platform: MPC/Macintosh
Description: Tutorial in French grammar, vocabulary, and reading skills.

Title: Advanced Math
Suggested Retail Price: $195.00
Publisher: Queue
Platform: MPC
Description: Tutorial for the advanced student with interactive lessons in Algebra, Equations, Geometry, and more.

Title: After the Fire: American Literature, 1865-1914
Suggested Retail Price: $99.95
Publisher: BookWorm
Platform: Macintosh
Description: Post-Civil War, Pre-WW I writings of leading American authors.

Title: Algebra Made Easy
Suggested Retail Price: $39.95
Publisher: Compton's NewMedia
Platform: MPC
Description: Enjoy learning algebra through graphics and interface.

Title: All About Science I/II
Suggested Retail Price: $495.00
Publisher: Queue
Platform: MPC/Macintosh
Description: Interactive programming for grades 5-9: Matter & Energy, Investigating Our World, Exploring Science II, and Science of Living Things.

Title: Amazing Universe
Suggested Retail Price: $79.95
Publisher: Hopkins Technology
Platform: MPC/Macintosh
Description: A multimedia tour of our galaxy and the universe beyond.

Title: American Journey 1896-1945
Suggested Retail Price: $59.95
Publisher: Compton's NewMedia
Platform: MPC
Description: The story of America as a superpower through sound and photos.

Title: Ancient Egypt, Middle East & Greece
Suggested Retail Price: $295.00
Publisher: Queue
Platform: MPC/Macintosh
Description: Interactive study of the culture and accomplishments of these countries.

Title: Ancient Lands
Suggested Retail Price: $79.95
Publisher: Microsoft
Platform: MPC
Description: Travel back to ancient Greece, Rome, or Egypt and learn more about the people, politics, and land. Easily accessed maps and subtopics help you explore these lands.

Title: Animals and How they Grow
Suggested Retail Price: $99.95
Publisher: National Geographic Society
Platform: MPC/Macintosh
Description: Natural history and animal lifestyles as pictured by vivid National Geographic photography.

Title: Apollo
Suggested Retail Price: $69.95
Publisher: Quanta
Platform: MPC/Macintosh
Description: A history of man's journey to the moon using text and images.

Title: Art History Illustrated
Suggested Retail Price: $495.00
Publisher: Queue
Platform: MPC/Macintosh
Description: Tutorial of art from Ancient Greece and through the ages.

Title: Atlas of U.S. Presidents
Suggested Retail Price: $39.95
Publisher: Applied Optical Media
Platform: MPC
Description: Learn more about our Presidents through this graphics and text program.

Title: Berenstain Bears: Learning at Home
Suggested Retail Price: $39.95
Publisher: Compton's NewMedia
Platform: MPC
Description: Join the Jan and Stan Berenstain's popular bear family in learning important household lessons that every child needs to know.

Title: BERLITZ Think & Talk French/German/Italian/Spanish
Suggested Retail Price: $199.00
Publisher: HyperGlot
Platform: MPC/Macintosh
Description: Learn a foreign language the way the U.S. Foreign Service Institute trains their people.

Title: Bug Adventure
Suggested Retail Price: $47.35
Publisher: Knowledge Adventure
Platform: MPC
Description: Bugs! Insects! Creepy crawly things!

Title: Building Reading Comprehension
Suggested Retail Price: $495.00
Publisher: Queue
Platform: MPC/Macintosh
Description: Collection of reading programs for elementary through college students.

Title: Building Vocabulary Skills
Suggested Retail Price: $49.95
Publisher: Queue
Platform: MPC/Macintosh
Description: Help in gaining necessary vocabulary skills to succeed on college entrance exams.

Title: Career Opportunities
Suggested Retail Price: $69.00
Publisher: Quanta
Platform: MPC
Description: Help for students and individuals in making career choices. Data from U.S. Department of Commerce.

Title: CD Calculus
Suggested Retail Price: $99.95
Publisher: John Wiley & Sons Smart Books, Inc.
Platform: MPC
Description: Learn Calculus the easy way—if there is such a thing.

Title: CellEbration
Suggested Retail Price: $289.00
Publisher: Science for Kids
Platform: MPC/Macintosh
Description: Learn about cells, mitosis, and other topics.

Title: Chaos: Fractals & Magic
Suggested Retail Price: $69.95
Publisher: Quanta
Platform: MPC
Description: Fractal images and how they are used.

Title: Chinese Writing Tutor
Suggested Retail Price: $59.95
Publisher: HyperGlot
Platform: Macintosh
Description: In-depth program on the Chinese writing system. Lessons and practice drills in the standard and simplified system. Voice reproduction in Mandarin.

Title: Coates Art Review: Impressionism
Suggested Retail Price: $79.95
Publisher: Quanta
Platform: MPC/Macintosh
Description: Complete review of the artists and their works from the Impressionist period includes Renoir, Gauguin, Monet, and their contemporaries.

Title: Columbus...Day by Day
Suggested Retail Price: $119.95
Publisher: Timebox, Inc.
Platform: MPC
Description: The epic voyage of Christopher Columbus, examined day by day.

Title: Composer Quest
Suggested Retail Price: $99.00
Publisher: Dr. T's Music Software
Platform: MPC
Description: Interactive music programs that teach about noted composers and their works.

Title: Comprehensive Review in Biology
Suggested Retail Price: $295.00
Publisher: Queue
Platform: MPC/Macintosh
Description: Outstanding programs with lessons, reviews, and practice for high school and college students.

Title: Compton's Family Choice
Suggested Retail Price: $49.95
Publisher: Compton's NewMedia
Platform: MPC
Description: In-depth programs in a variety of educational subjects for all ages.

Title: Countdown
Suggested Retail Price: $29.95
Publisher: Voyager
Platform: Macintosh
Description: Three mathematical games that let children adjust the level to always keep math fun!

Title: Coral Kingdom
Suggested Retail Price: $199.00
Publisher: Wings for Learning/Sunburst
Platform: MPC/Macintosh
Description: Students explore coral environments. High quality images and audio.

Title: Creation Stories
Suggested Retail Price: $49.99
Publisher: Time-Warner
Platform: MPC
Description: Legends from 60 cultures on how the world began.

Title: Curious George Learns the Alphabet
Suggested Retail Price: $49.95
Publisher: Queue
Platform: Macintosh
Description: Animated and narrated story, with games, involving George and the ABCs.

Title: Dandy Dinosaurs
Suggested Retail Price: $59.95
Publisher: Multicom
Platform: MPC/Macintosh
Description: Yet another dinosaur disc, with multimedia pictures and sounds.

Title: Dangerous Creatures
Suggested Retail Price: $79.95
Publisher: Microsoft
Platform: MPC
Description: A study of 100 carnivorous animals by index, region, weapons, or habitat. Text and graphics with hotspots for related information. Choose from several guided tours shown from the viewpoint of either a naturalist, photographer, or storyteller of magic.

Title: Developing Writing Skills
Suggested Retail Price: $295.00
Publisher: Queue
Platform: MPC/Macintosh
Description: An interactive program to improve your writing, making it more accurate and concise.

Title: DinoSource
Suggested Retail Price: $59.95
Publisher: Westwind Media
Platform: Macintosh
Description: More dinosaurs, none of them purple or prone to singing stupid songs.

Title: Earth Science
Suggested Retail Price: $175.00
Publisher: Queue
Platform: MPC/Macintosh
Description: Learn all about the oceans from this geology study disc.

Title: Earth Science II
Suggested Retail Price: $275.00
Publisher: Queue
Platform: MPC/Macintosh
Description: Learn all about weather and climate.

Title: EasyKana
Suggested Retail Price: $99.00
Publisher: HyperGlot
Platform: Macintosh
Description: Lessons on both the Katakana and Hiragana syllabaries. 300+ Japanese words pronounced by native speaker. Worksheets for practice in writing the characters.

Title: Electricity & Magnetism
Suggested Retail Price: $49.95
Publisher: Cambrix
Platform: MPC
Description: Interactive disc on the principles and theories of electricity and magnetism. Photos, animation, demonstrations, and games allow youngsters to play along and learn.

Title: Electronic Home Library
Suggested Retail Price: $79.95
Publisher: World Library, Inc.
Platform: MPC/Macintosh,
Description: Text on over 925 works of literature, religion, science, drama, philosophy, and much more.

Title: Elementary Grade Builder 3 Pack
Suggested Retail Price: $29.95
Publisher: Compton's NewMedia
Platform: MPC
Description: Combination of math, spelling, and memory programs in one package! Includes Math Maze, Spellicopter, and Designasaurus.

Title: Emergent Level One/Two
Suggested Retail Price: $49.95
Publisher: Discis
Platform: Macintosh
Description: Stories, poems, and songs with illustrations and photographs especially suited for young readers. Part of the early learning series.

Title: European & American Painting
Suggested Retail Price: $89.95
Publisher: Electronic Arts
Platform: MPC
Description: An evaluation of painting styles and major works by Western artists.

Title: European Monarchs
Suggested Retail Price: $79.94, Quanta
Platform: MPC/Macintosh
Description: Information on the royalty of Europe. Important data and trivia on the royal families.

Title: Exploration
Suggested Retail Price: $95.00
Publisher: Queue
Platform: MPC/Macintosh
Description: Photos and re-created graphics let the student discover, explore, and settle the American continent.

Title: Fire and Ice: London's Tales of the Yukon
Suggested Retail Price: $49.99, Queue
Platform: Macintosh
Description: Presentation of Jack London's best stories in an interactive format that enables users to clip, write, and illustrate their own stories.

Title: Forces, Motion, Work
Suggested Retail Price: $329.00
Publisher: Science for Kids
Platform: MPC/Macintosh
Description: Simple physics for elementary schoolers and up.

Title: Fraction-Oids
Suggested Retail Price: $69.99
Publisher: Mindplay
Platform: MPC
Description: Simplify fractions for the young student through games.

Title: French Reading Lab
Suggested Retail Price: $19.95
Publisher: HyperGlot
Platform: Macintosh
Description: Uses Hypertext tools for reading and comprehension lessons.

Title: Future Test: Admission Series
Suggested Retail Price: $49.95
Publisher: Compton's NewMedia
Platform: MPC
Description: Prepare for success on the college admission exams. Preparatory lessons for 25 of the most often required exams in America.

Title: Future Test: Career Series
Suggested Retail Price: $49.95
Publisher: Compton's NewMedia
Platform: MPC
Description: Study material for career exams given by businesses. Reviews for both private sector and civil service exams, with quizzes, graphics, final exams, and more.

Title: GED CD
Suggested Retail Price: $495.00
Publisher: Queue
Platform: MPC/Macintosh
Description: Outstanding collection of material to prepare for the GED.

Title: German Passive Voice Tutor
Suggested Retail Price: $59.95
Publisher: HyperGlot
Platform: Macintosh
Description: Studies in all the tenses, modals, subordinate clauses, and more. Lessons with practice programs.

Title: Great Mystery Classics
Suggested Retail Price: $49.95
Publisher: World Library, Inc.
Platform: MPC
Description: Hundreds of old mystery classics, available on CD-ROM.

Title: Great Poetry Classics
Suggested Retail Price: $49.95
Publisher: World Library, Inc.
Platform: MPC
Description: Add over 1,100 of your favorite poems to your library in this one edition. Classics from Blake to Yeats.

Title: High School Math
Suggested Retail Price: $175.00
Publisher: Queue
Platform: MPC
Description: Tutorial with lessons and drills in algebra, geometry and even an intro to trigonometry. Special review to prepare for the SATs.

Title: History of Western Civilization
Suggested Retail Price: $125.00
Publisher: Queue
Platform: MPC
Description: Gandhi called "western civilization" a good idea, but this disc has the historians' views on the topic.

Title: I Photograph to Remember
Suggested Retail Price: $39.95
Publisher: Voyager
Platform: Macintosh
Description: Pedro Meyer's acclaimed family memoir, documenting his parent's last years of life. A personal and artistic expression of love. Narrated in both English and Spanish.

Title: Illustrated Civil War
Suggested Retail Price: $49.00
Publisher: IT Makers
Platform: Macintosh
Description: Multimedia book with pictures on the War between the States.

Title: Illustrated Facts: How the World Works
Suggested Retail Price: $39.95
Publisher: Xiphias
Platform: MPC
Description: How the world around us operates.

Title: Illustrated Facts: How Things Work
Suggested Retail Price: $39.95
Publisher: Xiphias
Platform: MPC/Macintosh
Description: How mechanical devices work—or should.

Title: Impressionism and its Sources
Suggested Retail Price: $49.95
Publisher: Electronic Arts
Platform: MPC
Description: The roots of impressionistic art, with many examples of seminal works.

Title: Intermediate Math
Suggested Retail Price: $195.00
Publisher: Queue
Platform: MPC
Description: Learn key math skills through an interactive drill and practice. Complete tutorial covering all math subjects for grades 3-9.

Title: Introductory Chemistry
Suggested Retail Price: $89.00
Publisher: Falcon Software
Platform: MPC
Description: Disc-based introduction to chemistry.

Title: Isaac Asimov Science Adventure II
Suggested Retail Price: $47.35
Publisher: Knowledge Adventure
Platform: MPC
Description: Learn science from the late, great educator/scientist/writer.

Title: ITN World News 1992
Suggested Retail Price: $99.00
Publisher: Sony
Platform: MPC/Macintosh
Description: Variety of 1992 news articles from the International Television News Network.

Title: Jack Grove's Explorer Series—Vietnam
Suggested Retail Price: $69.95
Publisher: Quanta
Platform: MPC
Description: History through this famed photographer's photos. High quality photos of the colors, customs, and life of Vietnam.

Title: Journey to the Planets
Suggested Retail Price: $59.95
Publisher: Multicom
Platform: MPC/Macintosh
Description: Visit other planets in our solar system through multimedia pictures, clips.

Title: Jr. High Grade Builder 3 Pack
Suggested Retail Price: $29.95
Publisher: Compton's NewMedia
Platform: MPC
Description: Play to learn: lessons in grammar, geography, history, and a study of the human body.

Title: KanjiMaster
Suggested Retail Price: $149.95
Publisher: HyperGlot
Platform: Macintosh
Description: Learn to recognize, write, and pronounce basic Kanji through lessons and drills. Meanings and pronunciation of 352 Kanji and nearly 200 compounds.

Title: Kids in History: How Children Lived in the 20th Century
Suggested Retail Price: $39.98
Publisher: MPI Multimedia
Platform: MPC/Macintosh
Description: Interact with youngsters of this century while they work and play. Includes trivia, moments of historical importance, and some of the best early toy commercials.

Title: Last Chance to See
Suggested Retail Price: $59.95
Publisher: Sony
Platform: MPC
Description: Douglas Adams' look at endangered species.

Title: Learn By Myself: The City Mouse and the Country Mouse
Suggested Retail Price: $24.95
Publisher: InterActive
Platform: MPC/Macintosh
Description: The classic children's story in interactive book form.

Title: Learn By Myself: The Lion and the Mouse
Suggested Retail Price: $24.95
Publisher: InterActive
Platform: MPC/Macintosh
Description: Let your kid pull his own thorns and read this book on his own.

Title: Learn By Myself: The Little Red Hen
Suggested Retail Price: $24.95
Publisher: InterActive
Platform: MPC/Macintosh
Description: Another children's classic brought to life on CD-ROM.

Title: Learn By Myself: The Tortoise and the Hare
Suggested Retail Price: $24.95
Publisher: InterActive
Platform: MPC/Macintosh
Description: Broderbund's version is funnier, but this one costs less.

Title: Learn By Myself: Goldilocks and the Three Bears
Suggested Retail Price: $24.95
Publisher: InterActive
Platform: MPC/Macintosh
Description: The fairy tale makes a good introduction for beginning readers.

Title: Learn French with Asterix I, II, & III
Suggested Retail Price: $149.94, EuroTalk
Platform: Macintosh
Description: French tutor using Asterix, the popular French comic strip character.

Title: Learning about Ecological Systems
Suggested Retail Price: $125.00
Publisher: Queue
Platform: MPC/Macintosh
Description: Interactive book on ecology and how it affects lifecycles.

Title: Learning about Management Series
Suggested Retail Price: $69.00
Publisher: Guarantee Software
Platform: Macintosh
Description: Several discussions of management topics for executives.

Title: Learning About Our Environment
Suggested Retail Price: $75.00
Publisher: Queue
Platform: MPC/Macintosh
Description: Students become familiar with the ideas of growth, competition, cooperation, specialization, and succession through this multimedia program. Discussion on how industry and the urban and modern community will affect the future.

Title: Learning All About Animals
Suggested Retail Price: $125.00
Publisher: Queue
Platform: MPC/Macintosh
Description: Interactive tutorial about animals and their classifications. Includes the framework to characterize even the simplest of animals. Explains the interdependence of life forms and natural selections. Includes a strong study of American reptiles.

Title: Learning All About Cells & Biology
Suggested Retail Price: $145.00
Publisher: Queue
Platform: MPC/Macintosh

Description: An entry to learning of the life in a microscope. Basic theories and questions of modern biology in an interactive multimedia study.

Title: Learning All About Dissection
Suggested Retail Price: $145.00
Publisher: Queue
Platform: MPC/Macintosh
Description: Introduction and an overview of dissection as a scientific learning tool.

Title: Learning All About Plants
Suggested Retail Price: $195.00
Publisher: Queue
Platform: MPC/Macintosh
Description: Multimedia text on botany and other plant things.

Title: Learning All About Weather & Climate
Suggested Retail Price: $99.95
Publisher: Queue
Platform: MPC/Macintosh
Description: Experience the power of nature through graphics as you learn about the water cycle and air movements. Photos and diagrams explain meteorology.

Title: Learning to Read—Adult
Suggested Retail Price: $69.00
Publisher: Guarantee Software
Platform: Macintosh
Description: A reading primer for the adult student—not an easy thing to prepare, since adults can't stomach the typical Dick and Jane readers.

Title: Lessons from History: A Celebration of Blackness
Suggested Retail Price: $129.00
Publisher: EduQuest
Platform: MPC
Description: By Jawanza Kunjufu author of African American Images in Chicago.

Title: Lessons In American History
Suggested Retail Price: $49.95
Publisher: Queue
Platform: MPC
Description: Collection of interactive tutorials include lessons, reviews, drills, and test

Title: Lewis & Clark
Suggested Retail Price: $69.00
Publisher: TMM Inc.
Platform: MPC
Description: No, not the Superman television series—this disc deals with the two explorers who opened up the American Northwest.

Title: Library of the Future, First Edition
Suggested Retail Price: $149.00
Publisher: World Library, Inc.
Platform: MPC
Description: Comprehensive collection of over 1,100 literary works. Includes the entire works of Shakespeare, Sherlock Holmes, and more.

Title: Library of the Future, Second Edition
Suggested Retail Price: $299.00
Publisher: World Library, Inc.
Platform: MPC
Description: Complete library for the home includes literary classics for all ages.

Title: Lifemap Series
Suggested Retail Price: $39.95
Publisher: Warner New Media
Platform: Macintosh
Description: How did life begin? How did insects learn to fly? Why don't we know this already?

Title: LinguaROM III
Suggested Retail Price: $999.00
Publisher: HyperGlot
Platform: Macintosh
Description: Two discs include 38 foreign language programs for Spanish, French,

German, Italian, Russian, Japanese, and Chinese languages.

Title: Lyric Language French/Spanish
Suggested Retail Price: $59.95 each
Publisher: Compton's New Media
Platform: Macintosh
Description: Youngsters learn through video and songs, the fun way to speak a foreign language. Includes word games, graphics, images, and more!

Title: Macbeth by William Shakespeare
Suggested Retail Price: $99.95
Publisher: Voyager
Platform: Macintosh
Description: Out, out, damned spot! And take your ignorance of the bard with you!

Title: Macmillan Dictionary for Children
Suggested Retail Price: $39.95
Publisher: Macmillan
Platform: MPC/Macintosh
Description: Fun and easy use of the dictionary through an animated guide.

Title: Making The Modern: 19th Century Poetry in English
Suggested Retail Price: $99.95
Publisher: BookWorm
Platform: Macintosh
Description: Finally, poetry in a language I understand!

Title: Mammals: A Multimedia Encyclopedia
Suggested Retail Price: $149.95
Publisher: National Geographic Society
Platform: MPC
Description: National Geographic photographers look at animals, and the animals look back.

Title: Marvin Minsky: The Society of Mind
Suggested Retail Price: $49.95
Publisher: Voyager
Platform: Macintosh

Description: The scientist's work and ideas. Includes Stephen Jay Gould: *On Evolution.*

Title: Mastering English Grammar
Suggested Retail Price: $395.00
Publisher: Queue
Platform: Macintosh
Description: I done used this disc, and it ain't bad.

Title: Mastering Math
Suggested Retail Price: $195.00
Publisher: Queue
Platform: MPC/Macintosh
Description: 'Rithmatic for grades 3–9.

Title: Mathcopter
Suggested Retail Price: $39.95
Publisher: Compton's NewMedia
Platform: MPC
Description: Learn math from your aerial tutor.

Title: Mavis Beacon Teaches Typing
Suggested Retail Price: $79.95
Publisher: Software Toolworks
Platform: MPC/Macintosh
Description: The best-known typing tutor in the world comes to CD-ROM.

Title: Middle Ages
Suggested Retail Price: $195.00
Publisher: Queue
Platform: MPC/Macintosh
Description: Not entirely evil, just mid-evil doings of the pre-Renaissance.

Title: Multimedia Space Encyclopedia
Suggested Retail Price: $116.00
Publisher: BetaCorp Technologies
Platform: MPC
Description: Encyclopedia of outer space stuff, for space-age enthusiasts.

Title: Multimedia Encyclopedia of Mammalian Biology

Suggested Retail Price: $195.00
Publisher: McGraw-Hill Europe
Platform: MPC
Description: Learn about animal innards and functions from this classy disc.

Title: Nature's Way
Suggested Retail Price: $59.00
Publisher: Gazelle Technologies
Platform: Macintosh
Description: Multimedia book on Nature, which takes in an awful lot.

Title: Origins of the Constitution
Suggested Retail Price: $49.95
Publisher: Queue
Platform: MPC/Macintosh
Description: Learn the history of our country's most important document.

Title: Our Earth
Suggested Retail Price: $99.95
Publisher: National Geographic
Platform: Macintosh
Description: Gorgeous National Geographic photography of our planet and its inhabitants.

Title: Our Solar System
Suggested Retail Price: $39.95
Publisher: Chestnut
Platform: MPC
Description: Photos of the galaxies taken around the world. Programs, star locators, data, and simulations from NASA, Washington, and more.

Title: Perseus Sources and Studies on Ancient Greece
Suggested Retail Price: $150.00
Publisher: Yale Univ. Press
Platform: Macintosh
Description: Detailed study of ancient Greece, in case someone asks you "What's a Grecian urn?"

Title: Physical Science I—Learning All About Machines & Mechanics
Suggested Retail Price: $95.00
Publisher: Queue
Platform: MPC/Macintosh
Description: Gain some mechanical advantage from this disc.

Title: Physical Science II—Learning All About Heat & Sound
Suggested Retail Price: $95.00
Publisher: Queue
Platform: MPC/Macintosh
Description: Learn that physics is not all smoke and mirrors.

Title: Physical Science III—Learning All About Light & Lasers
Suggested Retail Price: $95.00
Publisher: Queue
Platform: MPC/Macintosh
Description: Phasers on stun: this disc is harmless, but educational.

Title: Physical Science IV—Learning All About Electricity & Magnetism
Suggested Retail Price: $195.00
Publisher: Queue
Platform: MPC/Macintosh
Description: I was drawn to this title, which covers simple electronics topics.

Title: Physical Science V—Learning All About Motion
Suggested Retail Price: $165.00
Publisher: Queue
Platform: MPC/Macintosh
Description: May the centrifugal force be with you as you study this disc.

Title: Physical Science VI—Learning All About Matter
Suggested Retail Price: $145.00
Publisher: Queue
Platform: MPC/Macintosh
Description: Find out what's the matter with our universe.

Title: Planetary Taxi
Suggested Retail Price: $39.95
Publisher: Voyager
Platform: MPC
Description: Program to help 8–14 year olds learn about the solar system.

Title: Playing with Language English:French:German: Japanese:Spanish
Suggested Retail Price: $69.95
Publisher: Syracuse Language
Platform: MPC
Description: More games in multiple languages.

Title: Poe's Tales of Terror
Suggested Retail Price: $49.95
Publisher: Queue
Platform: Macintosh
Description: Edgar Allen Poe really knew how to scare you, as this disc will show.

Title: Poetry in Motion
Suggested Retail Price: $29.95
Publisher: Voyager
Platform: Macintosh
Description: There's a song title in here somewhere, and also some pretty good lyrics.

Title: Practical Reading Comprehension
Suggested Retail Price: $495.00
Publisher: Queue
Platform: MPC/Macintosh
Description: Reading isn't half as important as understanding; hence, this disc.

Title: Pre GED CD
Suggested Retail Price: $495.00
Publisher: Queue
Platform: MPC/Macintosh
Description: Get ready for the high school diploma equivalency exam with this disc.

Title: Professor Gooseberry's I Can Read Club: Always Arthur

Suggested Retail Price: $49.95
Publisher: Imagination Pilots
Platform: MPC/Macintosh
Description: No, this isn't Dudley Moore's latest film, it's a children's story kids can read themselves.

Title: Professor Gooseberry's I Can Read Club: Buster's First Thunderstorm
Suggested Retail Price: $49.95
Publisher: Imagination Pilots
Platform: MPC/Macintosh
Description: Buster learns that thunder isn't what kills you, it's the lightning.

Title: Professor Gooseberry's I Can Read Club: Who Wants Arthur
Suggested Retail Price: $49.95
Publisher: Imagination Pilots
Platform: MPC/Macintosh
Description: More Arthur, for kids who want to read.

Title: Pronunciation Tutor
Suggested Retail Price: $49.95
Publisher: HyperGlot
Platform: MPC/Macintosh
Description: I found out it's TOO-tor, not Too-TORE. Lots of sound clips on this one.

Title: R' Room
Suggested Retail Price: $29.95
Publisher: Chalk
Platform: Macintosh
Description: Readin, Riting, and Rithmitic for 8–12 year olds.

Title: Reasoning Skills
Suggested Retail Price: $49.95
Publisher: Queue
Platform: Macintosh
Description: Logic and problem solving for young learners.

Title: RedShift
Suggested Retail Price: $59.95
Publisher: Maxis

Platform: MPC/Macintosh
Description: Great new astronomy disc. I wish this one had been available for review.

Title: Renaissance & Reformation
Suggested Retail Price: $245.00
Publisher: Queue
Platform: MPC/Macintosh
Description: Learn about Renaissance times, and the Protestant Reformation.

Title: Rome
Suggested Retail Price: $195.00
Publisher: Queue
Platform: MPC/Macintosh
Description: Everything about Rome, the city steeped in history and hills.

Title: Russian Noun Tutor
Suggested Retail Price: $79.95
Publisher: HyperGlot
Platform: Macintosh
Description: You'll like this one, tovarisch.

Title: Schoolware
Suggested Retail Price: $99.00
Publisher: Quality Learning Systems
Platform: MPC
Description: Elementary and secondary material on the fundamentals of reading, grammar, capitalizations, and punctuation.

Title: Science Adventure II
Suggested Retail Price: $69.95
Publisher: Knowledge Adventure
Platform: MPC
Description: More science studies in multimedia format.

Title: Scooter's Magic Castle
Suggested Retail Price: $49.95
Publisher: Electronic Arts
Platform: MPC/Macintosh
Description: Learn about science from Scooter.

Title: Sesame Street: Numbers
Suggested Retail Price: $49.95
Publisher: EA*Kids
Platform: MPC
Description: The gang from Sesame Street interacts with your children in games for the 3- to 6-year-old.

Title: Shakespeare Series
Suggested Retail Price: $24.95
Publisher: Compton's NewMedia
Platform: MPC/MacIntosh
Description: The interactive Bard of Avon.

Title: Shuttle Astronaut
Suggested Retail Price: $99.95
Publisher: AVCA
Platform: MPC
Description: Fun and educational software program on spacecraft and the skills of the shuttle astronaut.

Title: Simple Machines
Suggested Retail Price: $289.00
Publisher: Science For Kids
Platform: Macintosh
Description: Students explore how simple machines work.

Title: Smallscale
Suggested Retail Price: $50.00
Publisher: Synapse
Platform: Macintosh
Description: 75 science experiments submitted and tested by high school teachers. Complete text instructions and tips on presentation.

Title: Software Jukebox: A+ Grade Builder
Suggested Retail Price: $49.95
Publisher: SelectWare Technologies, Inc.
Platform: MPC
Description: Improve elementary kids' classroom performance with the games on this disc.

Title: Space in Motion
Suggested Retail Price: $99.95
Publisher: Jasmine Multimedia
Platform: MPC/Macintosh
Description: Multimedia video on space and astronautics.

Title: Space Series: Apollo
Suggested Retail Price: $69.95
Publisher: Quanta
Platform: MPC/Macintosh
Description: Learn about the Apollo program, which sent men to the moon.

Title: Space Shuttle Physics
Suggested Retail Price: $99.95
Publisher: Britt Communications
Platform: Macintosh
Description: You'll have a blast with this challenger.

Title: Stephen Jay Gould: On Education
Suggested Retail Price: $49.95
Publisher: Voyager
Platform: Macintosh
Description: The famous scientist offers his thoughts on teaching and learning.

Title: Super Spellicopter
Suggested Retail Price: $34.95
Publisher: Compton's NewMedia
Platform: MPC
Description: Learn to spell corectly (and many other words)!

Title: SuperStar Science CD
Suggested Retail Price: $59.00
Publisher: New Media Schoolhouse
Platform: Macintosh
Description: More science for your Mac. "Talking Schoolhouse" for science skills.

Title: Survey of English Literature
Suggested Retail Price: $495.00
Publisher: Queue
Platform: MPC/Macintosh
Description: By the best English surveyor since George Washington.

Title: Tense Tutors
Suggested Retail Price: $59.95
Publisher: HyperGlot
Platform: MPC/Macintosh

Title: The African-American Experience
Suggested Retail Price: $129.95
Publisher: Quanta
Platform: MPC
Description: A study of the history of African-Americans from their beginnings in Africa.

Title: The American Revolution
Suggested Retail Price: $79.95
Publisher: Queue
Platform: MPC/Macintosh
Description: Interactive study of the American Revolutionary War with Great Britain.

Title: The American West
Suggested Retail Price: $49.95
Publisher: Queue
Platform: MPC/Macintosh
Description: Learn important events in American history through looks at cowboys, Indians, ranchers, outlaws, and other legendary figures of the old West.

Title: The Anglo-Saxons
Suggested Retail Price: $59.95
Publisher: Cambrix
Platform: MPC
Description: England and the Anglo-Saxon history through its lifestyle and culture. British Museum collection of photos.

Title: The Best Literature Workbook Ever!
Suggested Retail Price: $195.00
Publisher: Queue
Platform: MPC/Macintosh
Description: Well, they said it, not us. But you can learn a lot of literature anyway from this disc.

Title: The Best of Herman Melville
Suggested Retail Price: $29.95
Publisher: Queue
Platform: Macintosh
Description: Thar she blows! *Moby Dick* and other classic tales from Melville.

Title: The Best of Mark Twain
Suggested Retail Price: $29.95
Publisher: Queue
Platform: Macintosh
Description: Samuel Clemens' work on compact disc.

Title: The Biology of Life
Suggested Retail Price: $299.00
Publisher: Media Design
Platform: MPC/Macintosh
Description: The facts of life through the wonder of multimedia.

Title: The Blue Whale
Suggested Retail Price: $15.90
Publisher: StarCore
Platform: MPC/Macintosh
Description: A multimedia study of the Blue Whale.

Title: The College Handbook
Suggested Retail Price: $69.95
Publisher: Macmillan New Media
Platform: MPC
Description: Everything you need to know for college.

Title: The Complete Maus
Suggested Retail Price: $59.95
Publisher: Voyager
Platform: Macintosh
Description: Pre-Fievel telling of the Holocaust from the point of view of a mouse. The Nazis are all cats. Adapted from the comic strip, this is a classic.

Title: The Constitution Papers
Suggested Retail Price: $99.00
Publisher: Johnson & Co.
Platform: MPC

Description: Magna Carta, Constitution, and other key documents from the annals of history.

Title: The Egyptian Pyramids
Suggested Retail Price: $19.90
Publisher: StarCore
Platform: MPC/Macintosh
Description: Learn about the tombs of kings.

Title: The First Emperor of China
Suggested Retail Price: $79.95
Publisher: Voyager
Platform: Macintosh
Description: That's going a long way back, but is interesting nevertheless.

Title: The French Tutor
Suggested Retail Price: $49.95
Publisher: Queue
Platform: MPC/Macintosh
Description: I can still remember my French tutor clucking, "Tres fautes!" after every sentence. You might do better with this disc.

Title: The Human Body
Suggested Retail Price: $79.95
Publisher: Discis
Platform: Macintosh
Description: Your brain, senses, bone, muscles, and other innards all covered in this disc.

Title: The Human Body
Suggested Retail Price: $99.95
Publisher: National Geographic
Platform: Macintosh
Description: National Geographic sends its photographers inside an actual human body, and here are the photos the drug store was able to print.

Title: The Human Calculator
Suggested Retail Price: $39.95
Publisher: Compton's NewMedia, Inc.
Platform: MPC

Description: Learn tricks for calculating complex problems in your head, from an expert who appears on TV a lot.

Title: The Line and Shape Eater
Suggested Retail Price: $24.95
Publisher: Compton's NewMedia
Platform: MPC
Description: Children's basic shape/geometry teaching aid.

Title: The Presidents: A Picture History of Our Nation
Suggested Retail Price: $99.00
Publisher: National Geographic
Platform: MPC
Description: US history, told through photographs and paintings of the presidents.

Title: The Presidents: It All Started with George
Suggested Retail Price: $149.95
Publisher: National Geographic Society
Platform: MPC
Description: If you're curious about George and all the men who followed him, this disc has it all.

Title: The Scavenger Hunt Series: The Congo Rainforest, The African Savannah, The Sahara Desert, and The Island of Madagascar
Suggested Retail Price: $49.95
Publisher: Davidson & Associates
Platform: Macintosh
Description: Experience the wonders of these lands through animation, music, and puzzles.

Title: The Rosetta Stone Deutsch/English/Espanol/Francais
Suggested Retail Price: $395.00
Publisher: Fairfield Language Technologies
Platform: MPC/Macintosh
Description: Full immersion program for foreign language.

Title: The Shakespeare Quartet
Suggested Retail Price: $99.95
Publisher: BookWorm
Platform: Macintosh
Description: Shakespeare and music on one disc.

Title: The Social Studies CD
Suggested Retail Price: $395.00
Publisher: Queue
Platform: MPC/Macintosh
Description: Learn civics from your multimedia PC or Macintosh. Large collection of programs in history, geography, law, government, and economics.

Title: The Spanish Tutor
Suggested Retail Price: $49.95
Publisher: Queue
Platform: MPC/Macintosh
Description: Become less annoying to native Spanish speakers by studying this disc.

Title: The Synonym Finder
Suggested Retail Price: $29.95
Publisher: Compton's NewMedia
Platform: Macintosh
Description: Over 1 million word alternates!

Title: The Ultimate Human Body
Suggested Retail Price: $79.95
Publisher: Dorling Kindersley
Platform: MPC
Description: An interactive trip through the human body. Learn with the help of animation and graphics.

Title: The View from Earth
Suggested Retail Price: $79.98
Publisher: Time Warner Interactive Group
Platform: MPC/Macintosh
Description: Photographs and multimedia showing pictures of the Earth.

Title: The Visual Almanac
Suggested Retail Price: $49.95
Publisher: Voyager
Platform: Macintosh
Description: Facts and trivia, in photographic and picture format.

Title: The Wellness Encyclopedia
Suggested Retail Price: $295.00
Publisher: Houghton Mifflin Publishers
Platform: MPC
Description: Health topic encyclopedia.

Title: The Zoo: 24 Hours
Suggested Retail Price: $69.00
Publisher: Sony
Platform: MPC/Macintosh
Description: One day in the life of a zoo isn't too bad, especially since odors haven't been added to multimedia technology yet.

Title: Three Faces of Evil: Frankenstein, Dracula, & Mr. Hyde
Suggested Retail Price: $49.95
Publisher: Queue
Platform: MPC/Macintosh
Description: Mary W. Shelley, Bram Stoker, and Robert Louis Stevenson won't collect any royalties from this disc, but it's still good.

Title: Thrinaxodon: Digital Atlas of the Skull
Suggested Retail Price: $90.00
Publisher: University of Texas Press
Platform: MPC
Description: Research this fossil through CAT scan. Full study of the skull, including all articles from last 50 years on Thrinaxodon.

Title: Time Table of History: Arts and Entertainment
Suggested Retail Price: $59.95
Publisher: Xiphias
Platform: MPC
Description: Pretty superficial, but these are bundled cheap.

Title: Time Table of History: Business, Politics and Media
Suggested Retail Price: $59.95
Publisher: Xiphias
Platform: MPC
Description: Not a great disc, but you can pick one up for a few dollars.

Title: Time Table of History: Science and Innovation
Suggested Retail Price: $59.95
Publisher: Xiphias
Platform: MPC/Macintosh
Description: My copy was a waste of money, but you might like it.

Title: Time Traveler CD
Suggested Retail Price: $159.00
Publisher: New Media Schoolhouse, Inc.
Platform: Macintosh
Description: Study history as a time traveler. 6,000 years of history through pictures, sound, and text. Control your own "time machine."

Title: Twelve Roads to Gettysburg
Suggested Retail Price: $29.95
Publisher: EBook
Platform: MPC/Macintosh
Description: Civil War buffs will love this look at the important battle.

Title: U.S. Civics
Suggested Retail Price: $49.00
Publisher: Quanta press
Platform: MPC
Description: Based on US Immigration service publications for new citizens.

Title: U.S. Postal Exam Pre-Release
Suggested Retail Price: $99.95
Publisher: Future Technologies
Platform: MPC
Description: Study for a post office job. No firearms covered, though.

Title: Undersea Adventure
Suggested Retail Price: $47.35
Publisher: Knowledge Adventure
Platform: MPC
Description: Under the sea, with fish, plantlife, and no mermaids.

Title: USA Wars : Civil War
Suggested Retail Price: $39.95
Publisher: Compton's New Media
Platform: MPC
Description: Multimedia text on the War Between The States.

Title: USA Wars: Desert Storm with Coalition Command
Suggested Retail Price: $49.95
Publisher: Compton's New Media
Platform: MPC
Description: Multimedia look at George Bush's big moment.

Title: Visualization of Natural Phenomena
Suggested Retail Price: $59.95
Publisher: Springer-Verlag
Platform: Macintosh
Description: Physics and other stuff, made visible.

Title: Vocabulearn/CE French, Level I
Suggested Retail Price: $59.95
Publisher: Compton's NewMedia
Platform: Macintosh
Description: French tutor for the beginner. If you can already speak French, you don't need this.

Title: Vocabulearn/CE Spanish, Level I
Suggested Retail Price: $59.95
Publisher: Compton's New Media
Platform: Macintosh
Description: Spanish tutor for the beginner. Not a bad introduction.

Title: Whales & Dolphins
Suggested Retail Price: $69.00
Publisher: Sony

Platform: MPC
Description: Cetacean, phone home. You're being followed.

Title: Who Built America
Suggested Retail Price: $99.95
Publisher: Voyager
Platform: Macintosh
Description: Multimedia book on the movers and shakers who moved and shook our country.

Title: Wildebeest Migration
Suggested Retail Price: $15.90
Publisher: StarCore
Platform: MPC/Macintosh
Description: Big ugly deer-like things move around, and you get to see it all.

Title: Word Torture
Suggested Retail Price: $49.95
Publisher: HyperGlot
Platform: MPC/Macintosh
Description: This language study course describes my own high school English classes.

Title: World History I
Suggested Retail Price: $295.00
Publisher: Queue
Platform: MPC/Macintosh
Description: Ancient Egypt, Middle East, & Greece.

Title: World History II
Suggested Retail Price: $395.00
Publisher: Queue
Platform: MPC/Macintosh
Description: Rome & the Celts.

Title: World History III—Middle Ages
Suggested Retail Price: $195.00
Publisher: Queue
Platform: Macintosh
Description: Multimedia book on medieval times.

Title: World History IV
Suggested Retail Price: $245.00
Publisher: Queue
Platform: MPC/Macintosh
Description: Reformation & Renaissance.

Title: World History V
Suggested Retail Price: $395.00
Publisher: Queue
Platform: MPC/Macintosh
Description: 17 & 18th Centuries.

Title: World History VI
Suggested Retail Price: $295.00
Publisher: Queue
Platform: MPC/Macintosh
Description: 18th & 19th century
England & France

Title: World History VIII—20th Century
Europe
Suggested Retail Price: $175.00
Publisher: Queue
Platform: Macintosh
Description: Multimedia book on
modern Europe.

Title: World Literary Heritage
Suggested Retail Price: $79.95
Publisher: Softbit
Platform: MPC/Macintosh
Description: Great books of the world.

Title: World of Education—Shareware
Suggested Retail Price: $99.00
Publisher: PS-SIG Inc.
Platform: MPC
Description: Shareware for use in
Education.

Title: Writing Made Easy
Suggested Retail Price: $39.95
Publisher: Compton's New Media
Platform: MPC
Description: I just wish it were!

Title: Your Personal Trainer for the
SAT 2.0
Suggested Retail Price: $59.95
Publisher: Davidson & Associates
Platform: MPC/Macintosh
Description: Help for high school
students. Take a pretest to discover where
you need help, then use the tutorial to zoom
in on these areas.

Chapter 7

Children's Discs

This is one of the largest chapters in this book, with reviews of roughly 30 CD-ROMs. There's a good reason for that: Discs in the children's category are among the very top sellers, and they're also some of the best discs of any type available. Where it's relatively easy and inexpensive to throw together a database for business, or to collect some public domain literature on disc, children's software is much more demanding.

That's because children themselves are very demanding. They've grown up watching *Where in the World is Carmen Sandiego?* on television, and expect the same lively action and challenging fun on CD-ROM. Because the stakes are high (other than games, no other category enjoys such lively interest and vigorous sales), vendors have put a lot of effort into meeting those demands.

You'll find discs like *Tuneland, Starring Howie Mandel,* that feature animation and CD audio-quality music that's as good—or better—than you see on Saturday morning television. There are interactive books like *Arthur's Teacher Trouble* that entertain while they explain important concepts. *Busytown* will keep preschoolers occupied for hours, while games like *Oregon Trail* help young children relive historical times with remarkable accuracy.

If you'd rather spend some time curled up with a good (computer) book, there are tales from well-known fables or literature in illustrated books like *The Sleeping Beauty* or *A Christmas Carol.* Whether you're looking for a simple comic book (*Goferwinkel's Adventures*) or a state-of-the-art comic adventure (*Victor Vector*), you'll find it in this category.

Best of all, children's CDs seem to be priced much lower—from $29.95 to $59.95—than discs aimed at older kids and adults (some games can cost $99.95!). So, the quality is high and prices are low for some of the best CD-ROMs you can find.

Arthur's Teacher Trouble

Rating: ●●●●

Publisher Name: **Broderbund**

Software Requirements:
MPC/Macintosh

Suggested Retail Price: **$49.95**

This is the first Broderbund Living Book review you'll read in this chapter—but it won't be the last. That's right: this company has produced a group of discs that are all first-rate. The situation reminds me of the Billboard Top 10 chart of March 31, 1964, when the Beatles had not just the #1 song in the nation, but the top *five*, all at the same time. Overall, there were seven *more* Beatles songs in the top 100. Broderbund is in much the same situation, with this disc, *Just Grandma and Me*, *The Tortoise and the Hare*, and *The New Kid on the Block* all "charting" near the top of the CD-ROM best-seller lists.

Arthur's Teacher Trouble, like all the Living Books, is a unique creature unto itself. None of the four are exactly alike, and the Arthur disc is the most educationally oriented of the quartet. In fact, much of the action takes place in a whimsical school where Arthur Aardvark and his friends have to prepare for a spelling bee.

Based on a book by Marc Brown, *ATT* takes you through Arthur's agony as he must contend with a new "evil" teacher, named, appropriately enough, Mr. Ratburn (the name is always pronounced in a derisive tone). Suspected to be "really a vampire with magical powers," Mr. Ratburn conducts his classes in Room 13 with a little more discipline than the other teachers in the building. Even so, Arthur learns a valuable lesson as he prepares for the annual spelling bee.

Like many other children's books on CD-ROM, *ATT* has special hot buttons that can be clicked to activate various actions within the page. Where this disc excels is the imagination put into the animations that result. Click Mr. Ratburn himself, and The Rat turns into a closet Elvis. Or, another time, his suit may simply change color.

The bulletin board outside the classroom

Arthur's Teacher Trouble can be played in Spanish or English versions, making it an excellent tool for language practice.

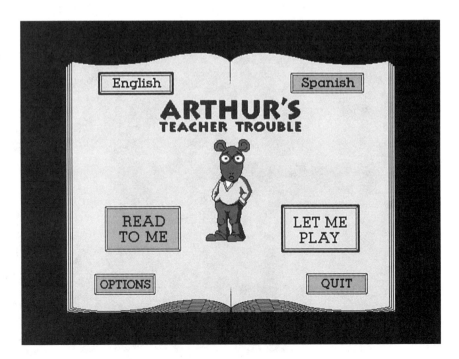

The bell rang. The first day of school was over. Kids ran out of every classroom-every one but Room 13. Here, the students filed out slowly, in alphabetical order. "See you tomorrow," said their teacher, Mr. Ratburn.

Outside Room 13, Arthur and his classmates wait for Mr. Ratburn to dismiss them.

is itself a riot of possibilities. When you click the Study Bugs poster, a bug crawls off and around the wall. The Sports Tryout flyer hits a home run, and the Dance Class notice does a spin on tip-toes. Our four-year-old spends hours clicking the Choir button to watch three cats croon a perfect chord triad.

Personally, I loved the window shades that flap wildly, the window that erupts with an automobile-style windshield wiper, and the doorknob that falls off when you touch it.

Arthur's Teacher Trouble can be played in two modes: Read to Me and Let Me Play. In Read to Me mode, the story unfolds page by page. You can still use the left and right arrow keys on the keyboard to go back a page or skip to the next one. The space bar can be used to exit the story. Or you can switch to Let Me Play mode by pressing the P key.

In Let Me Play mode, the child must click the arrow keys to go from page to page. Otherwise, the program remains on a given page, giving the kid free rein to

explore all the animations. Words can be clicked to be read to the child. You can switch back to Read to Me mode by pressing the R key at any time.

Arthur's Teacher Trouble *is a "living book" that kids can play with, or listen to, in either English or Spanish.*

Clicking the page number key at the center bottom of the screen allows the child to jump directly to a particular page. *Arthur's Teacher Trouble* can be toggled between English and Spanish, for both the written words and pronunciation. You may switch back and forth between languages, even while the story is being read, by

pressing the 1 or 2 keys on the keyboard.

That feature makes *ATT* a good tool for practicing Spanish, because you can have a page read to you in Spanish and then switch to English to receive an immediate translation. The ability to click particular words and have the correct Spanish pronunciation provided is also useful.

Kids will learn spelling as well as some valuable lessons about dealing with teachers from *Arthur's Teacher Trouble*. Marc Brown has done a good job of creating an interesting story, and Broderbund has implemented it well as a CD-ROM.

Tip: As with all the Living Books, you should be sure to watch the Credits section, which has animated sequences that are more entertaining than some of the CD-ROMs we were forced to evaluate for this book.

Fatty Bear's Birthday Surprise

Rating:  1/2

Publisher Name: **Humongous**

Software Requirements:
MPC/Macintosh

Suggested Retail Price: **$49.95**

*F*atty Bear's Birthday Surprise is a problem-solving adventure that is easy enough for kids who can't read yet, but not so simple that older kids will zip through the game in just a few minutes. Children will learn about cooking as they discover how their mind works with this first-rate game.

The goal is to build the best birthday cake ever baked, just two hours before

Kayla's birthday party. Although there's still plenty of time, Fatty and his gang must collect ingredients and actually make the cake, despite quite a few distractions, such as a bowling alley that lurks nearby. If you're familiar with the Putt-Putt series, available from the same publisher, you'll understand how this disc works.

Kids must explore the world Fatty Bear lives in, trying out different objects to solve different puzzles. They can move Fatty Bear around in the game by clicking in a direction with the mouse. Exits are pointed out with big arrows. Click one, and off he moves to the next scene.

If you remember old text-based computer adventures, you'll recall how you needed to type simple sentences like TAKE FOOD to add items to your inventory. Fatty Bear, too, collects objects that may be useful later, but kids need only to click the

object to add it to their hero's capacious pockets. There's no need to type INV, either: Fatty's objects are displayed in pockets along the bottom of the screen, so kids aren't likely to forget about a key item in their inventory. To use an object, just click it in the pocket. The cursor turns into the object, and you can then click the portion of the play area where it is to be used.

The problems are challenging but not unsolvable. Typically, the child will find a locked door and must hunt for a key, or will need a specific ingredient for the cake or to wrap up a birthday present. Two characters, Matilda Rabbit and Gretchen, appear to provide clues at one time or another. Think of them as online Help.

The big distraction in your quest for the big birthday party is the Bowling Alley. Here, Fatty Bear can take aim at pins and

Fatty Bear's Birthday Surprise is a treat for younger computer users.

Fatty Bear comes to life after Kayla goes to sleep, and plans her birthday surprise.

roll a ball in an attempt to knock them down. Just like in real bowling, there are 10 frames and two balls per frame (unless you get a strike with your first ball). Scoring is automatic.

An adventure for kids, as they help Fatty Bear prepare a cake for a friend's birthday party by using simple commands and problem-solving abilities.

There's also a piano hidden in the game, which has 10 built-in tunes, or it can be used to play music unaccompanied, using six different instruments. The notes entered appear by magic on some sheet music. The child can save up to 10 of his or her own songs on disk.

Fatty Bear was designed for children who are too young to read, so the publisher was tempted to print up a two-word manual: "Have fun!" They've packed in the set a Junior Adventurer's Handbook with pages to color (crayons are included) and things to do, instead. The handbook is intended for children aged three to seven, although some activities are too complex for the very young.

Adults never fear, however, because a complete guide to installing and using this disc is included in the jewel box, with tips on how to play the games and some troubleshooting advice if you run into driver problems or other conflicts. If you don't have a young child around to explain the games to you, or a teenager to tutor in how to operate the computer, this booklet is the next best thing. The booklet also has keyboard shortcuts adults can use to stop the game, pause, restart, or control various options such as music, text display, and type of controller (joystick or keyboard).

Your kids, however, will just use the mouse and keyboard as they solve Fatty Bear's problems and help him prepare for Kayla's birthday party.

Forever Growing Garden

Rating:

Publisher: **MediaVision**

Software Requirements:
MPC/Macintosh

Suggested Retail Price: **$59.95**

What a great idea! This is a "garden simulator" that kids can use on rainy days to plan their own garden, select seeds, and then sow them in locations ranging from a suburban front yard to a remote castle. With a little attention, food crops or flowers will spring up and grow to maturity...with a few surprises thrown in.

Virtual gardening was never easier, and there are separate versions for both PC and Macintosh, so anyone can join in the fun. The child signs up for a plot by clicking the New Garden signpost in the main screen. Saved gardens can also be restored from disk, so the "forever" part of this game's title is indeed true—as long as you remember to make timely backups.

Three different garden types are available: a flower garden in front of an inviting homesite, a vegetable patch located out in the country, or a garden located within the grounds of a medieval castle.

Your first stop is the hardware store, to pick up some seeds. Your choices will be diffrent, depending on the type of garden you've selected. If you're in the market for a flower garden, you can select from among eight different types of flowers and fantasy flowers (e.g., the snapdragons are real dragons). The vegetable patch can be filled with veggies and fantasy veggies, while the castle grounds are likely candidates for flowers and crazy hedges. An almanac is available to provide extra information on each variety.

Although *Forever Growing Garden* can be extremely realistic as a horticultural simulator, it was a stroke of genius not to limit kids to "real" plants. Even if your kids soon tire of planning carrots, they'll

Choose from suburban homesite, castle grounds, or rural field for your garden.

With a little care, your vegetable patch can be as lush as this one.

continue to have fun exploring some of the wilder creations they can sow.

An entertaining "gardening simulator" that teaches kids about plants while fulfilling their young need to putter.

In the garden, each packet of seeds (and the CD-ROM comes with some real parsley seeds for kids to grow) can be opened and seeds dragged one by one to the ready-made holes. After the seeds have been planted, it's up to your kid to grab a watering can and keep them moist. A few clicks on a special timer icon can speed up or slow down growth so that in a few minutes the garden will sprout and grow to full maturity.

When they're ready to harvest, or the flowers are ready to display, pull on some gloves, grab the snips, and reap your bounty. Trim those hedges while you're at it. Only the "real" plants can be harvested or cut. The weird fantasy plants must stay in the ground for a while longer. When you click them, they do unpredictable things.

You must dig up the old plants to make room for fresh ones, and *Forever Growing Garden* gives you a trowel to work with.

At the market, you can try to select a reasonable price for your wares. See if they sell...if not, try repricing everything. In the flower shop, you can even select a notecard and choose an appropriate vase to display your blooms. This disc is nothing if not thorough! Each garden even has its own gopher hole: try to catch all three gophers to win, while avoiding the skunk. There are many hot buttons inside the scenes, too, which you can click to activate some nonsense among the greenery.

Forever Growing Garden is one of the most original and entertaining CD-ROMs for kids we've come across. Our test kids fought over this one more than any disc they'd played with since *Busytown*.

Gus Goes to Cybertown

Rating: ◉ ◉ ◉ 1/2

Publisher Name:
Modern Media Ventures

Software Requirements:
MPC/Macintosh

Suggested Retail Price: $54.95

Gus is a pretty cool dog. He encourages your children to learn and explore while hunting for 15 different CyberBuds hidden among the 11 scenes, or "environments," available in Cybertown. Kids can learn about the environment while playing in the various shops and other areas of Gus's village.

The environmental theme pervades each of the scenes in this CD. For example, click the trash can and a little man pops out and runs over and picks up a discarded soft drink can, which he disposes of (it's sent for recycling, presumably).

There are five environments the child can visit directly from the Main Street screen. These are Addie's Market, Benny's Pet Shop, Lulu's Laundry, Cybertoys Toy Store, and the Park. There are many things to do in these initial locations.

For example, in Addie's Market, the child can look to see where each CyberBud is hiding (learning a new fact in the process), or watch as objects in the market come alive when they are clicked on. By clicking the

Today's Special's notice on the bulletin board, the youngster can activate the Shopping List Game. There are two levels; each requires the child to match items on the shelves with needs on a shopping list.

If the child chooses the correct object, it drops from the shelf into the shopping basket. In the more advanced mode, the shopping list displays text only, rather than text and picture, so the child must match the word "cookie" with the object to score a point.

The Toy Store also has CyberBuds and animated objects, but also includes a Full Motion Video bookshelf, a virtual jukebox with three original songs, a digital photo puzzle, and an Alphabet Asteroids game. The latter has letter recognition for the youngest children, and more challenging

Gus, a friendly dog, is your tour guide to *Cybertown*.

In the park of Cybertown, you can find many fun things to do

spelling with text, pictures, and sounds at the higher levels.

Gus Goes to Cybertown *teaches environmental lessons with lots of enjoyable games, songs, videos, and activities.*

In the Pet Shop, the child can play with animal morphing, changing one creature into another, or play the Bubble Count game, which asks nothing more than counting the bubbles that appear in the fishbowl. At more difficult levels, the kid may need to find the difference between two sets, or add the numbers that appear inside the bubbles.

The Laundry has a Dress for the Weather game in which Gus dons headgear, body wear, shoes, and accessories to suit various climates and weather conditions that appear outside the window of the shop.

In the Park, you and Gus can learn about 11 different eras of world history with sounds and text, or travel through time to visit those periods in person. The Park, like all the other areas, has three hidden CyberBuds. When all 15 are located, the game is over. The child can check his or her process at any time by clicking the Bud Meter icon, or receive some hints on playing the game and finding CyberBuds by selecting the Gus icon.

Gus Goes to Cybertown is a gentle and entertaining way for children to learn about the environment, while building general recognition, counting, and problem-solving skills that will help them adapt to the early primary grades in school. One of the strengths of this disc is that it doesn't rely on the same old activities most CD-ROMs aimed at young children are filled with. A great deal of imagination went into Gus, and kids will enjoy putting their own to work.

Just Grandma and Me

Rating:

Publisher Name:
Broderbund

Software Requirements:
MPC/Macintosh

Suggested Retail Price: **$39.95**

Delightful animated sequences are triggered by clicking objects shown on each page.

This entry in Broderbund's Living Book series is a perfect example of what a child's CD-ROM should contain. There's enough fun and whimsy to please any kid from age 4 to 9, a liberal sprinkling of options designed to keep interest high after repeated sessions, and solid educational content that encourages young students to think of learning as a treat rather than a chore.

Just Grandma and Me is a lively adaptation of Mercer Mayer's popular line of books about "Little Critter," a cute young mammal of indeterminate species (we vote for groundhog). Young Critter takes a bus to the beach for a day of fun with her Grandma and the other animals on holiday. Sand-filled hot dogs, going snorkeling (but not too deep!), and uncooperative beach umbrellas are all part of the low-key adventures the two enjoy.

Youngsters can choose to have the book read to them. *Just Grandma and Me* comes to life as Critter reads the story. The characters actually move around the page through lifelike animation and react to the story with giggles or short responses. The effect is more like watching a cartoon than reading a book. All the while, a pert background tune sets the lighthearted mood for the story. Mercer Mayer's stories and illustrations have already become children's' classics, so on this level alone *Just Grandma and Me* is an excellent disc.

While "read to me" mode may be the best introduction to the disc, most kids will soon be champing at the bit to review the book in its interactive mode. The child turns pages manually and clicks a special icon with the mouse to have the text on that page read aloud. Beginning readers can click individual words to have them read individually.

No child will be able to resist exploring the individual objects on each of the 12 pages in this book-disc. Delightful animated sequences are triggered by clicking almost any person or item on the page. In the opening scene, Grandma and Critter walk to the curb and wait for their bus. If you click the front door of the home they just left, a doorbell chimes. Click one of the windows, and the phone rings, Grandma's answering machine picks up, and reports that she is not home. If you "open" the mailbox by the street, a mysterious hand reaches out of it and slams the door shut.

There are lots of surprises on each page. For example, something different happens each time you go back to that mailbox. One time you may find a cat sleeping inside, or be pelted by a cascade of tumbling golf balls.

The silliness includes some visual and audio puns aimed at more astute kids. Click an ordinary rock by the roadside, and you're treated to a few bars of string-bending "rock" music. Children can easily spend hours "playing" inside the story.

Just Grandma and Me *is an interactive storybook that can be read to the student in English, Spanish, or Japanese, or used to explore both reading and the imaginative animated world of Mercer Mayer.*

This is a "mouse-only" disc with a child-friendly interface that can be used by readers and non-readers alike. In the first screen, Critter asks whether you want to play in the story or have the story read to you, and points to the button to click for each option. When it's time to leave, you're asked to confirm by clicking a Yes button (containing a nodding animated character) or a No button (with a character shaking its head).

In interactive mode, you may take as long as you like on each page, clicking a right-arrow icon to advance to the next, or a left-arrow icon to go back to the previous

page. The child may click the page number button at the bottom of each page to return to the main menu at any time.

The child may choose to have the story read in English, Spanish, or Japanese, making it accessible to children whose native language is any of those three. Those studying one of those languages can use *Just Grandma and Me* as a tool to practice foreign language conversation, too. Once you've heard the story a few times in English, the Spanish version, for example, almost translates itself in your mind.

A special options menu offers a scrolling preview of each page; the child can choose a page and jump directly to it. One tip: don't neglect to read the credits that are hidden inside this option menu. You'll be treated to a five-minute mini-cartoon featuring an inept witch and a hot five-piece jazz combo.

Just Grandma and Me is another of those discs that set the standard for all the other

"talking storybook" CD-ROMs that follow. The story is charming, the length just right for short attention spans, and the animation of Mayer's artwork is first-rate. Even the background music is catchy and varied enough to soothe parents annoyed by purple dinosaur sing-alongs.

Just Grandma and Me is recommended for households with preschoolers who like to "play" with computers, even though they can't yet read. This disc might be their head start toward early reading. Beginning readers will also enjoy the book, exploring the simple words and phrases by reading for themselves, repeating the words after Critter says them aloud, or by clicking words they are unsure of to hear the correct pronunciation.

Finally, older students will find the book an enjoyable way to practice their conversational and comprehension skills in English, Spanish, or Japanese.

Children can read the story, listen, or explore the objects in the pictures.

Lenny's MusicToons

Rating: ⊙ ⊙ ⊙ 1/2

Publisher Name:
Paramount

Software Requirements: **MPC**

Suggested Retail Price:
$49.95

Kids can learn a lot about music with five different games all launched from Lenny's Room, a penthouse pad in the heart of New York City. Kids can build their own orchestras with instruments of their choice and even create customized music videos. This disc goes quite a bit beyond most musical CDs for kids, and has great animation and sound effects to boot.

You need your sound card's MIDI (musical instrument digital interface) capabilities connected and configured properly (it's easy to overlook this step, because many Windows sound programs don't use MIDI). Detailed instructions in the accompanying guidebook provide step-by-step tips for popular sound cards, including MediaVision's Pro Audio Spectrum and the Creative Labs Sound Blaster.

Among the places kids can explore are:
Lenny's Room. This is the gateway to the other play areas, but there are things to do right here. You can click Lenny's remote control to turn the television on, or explore other objects, such as the telephone or some of the doors in the room. Don't click the toy

taxi, though, until you're ready to leave!

Lenny's Theater. Buy a ticket at the booth out front and then enter the world of musical theater. The child can put together a dream jam session, choosing specific musicians (the star/leader, a co-star, rhythm section, and backup band), venue (you can choose from amphitheaters to more intimate club locations), and props (everything except Spinal Tap's midget Stonehenge are available). After you put all the pieces together, click a button and watch your band perform. Then, as in real life, your band can break up and reassemble itself in new permutations. Because this is MIDI-based music, which is actually played rather

than just played back, you can control the tempo of the performance, from sedate to frantic.

Pitch Attack. This game helps kids develop pitch recognition and sight-reading skills. It's really an arcade game with invaders swooping in from the sky, eager to destroy Metropolis, Mars, or Toyland. But the only way to save yourself is to shoot them down by pressing the correct keys on a piano keyboard. We knew music hath charms, but this is ridiculous! Kids will love the game, and learn music in spite of themselves.

Lenny's Puzzle Book. Learning to read and understand written music is the object

Lenny's Room is your gateway to each of the fun modules.

You can choose your own band, props, and venue for your concert.

of this section. Here, Gonzo Gorilla is after some poor kittens trapped in a tree. Lenny saves his tiny friends by putting together a jigsaw puzzle made from sheet music! You can play the music and use what you hear as a clue to which pieces go where. If you can read music, that helps a lot. If not, you'll learn a little from this game in spite of yourself.

PTV (Penguin Television) is a music/video studio that can be used to create a real music video. In ToonJam Studio, you can mix performers, lighting, backgrounds, and songs to create a one-of-a-kind work of video art. You can choose from Rock & Roll, Hip, Tech, or Pop, and select one of eight different music blocks for each style. Preview segments and then add them to your video. Special effects like color, light, and motion can also be added.

Lenny's Matching Game is the ubiquitous Concentration-style pair matching game, with a musical twist. There are nine pairs of cards that must be matched, in a 6 x 3 grid. Each match reveals another

portion of the underlying cartoon. When you're all finished, Lenny provides you with a surprise.

Great musical activities make this a solid teaching tool for children who are ready to learn piano or another instrument.

Times Square. Just outside Lenny's Room there's a great view of Times Square. You'll want to check it out when you've finished playing the games. If not, the accompanying booklet includes suggestions for other fun musical activities a child can

enjoy, such as making a Humdinger Humboard Kazoo from a cardboard tube.

We found that children of about six years of age are ready to enjoy some of the activities in *Lenny's MusicToons*, although most aren't ready to begin reading music from this CD-ROM alone. However, any child of that age or older who's already started music lessons will learn in leaps and bounds from this disc. Less musically inclined kids may find themselves infected by the tune bug before they know it.

The New Kid on the Block

Rating: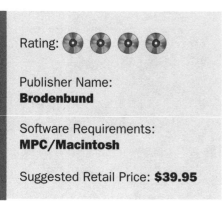

Publisher Name:
Brodenbund

Software Requirements:
MPC/Macintosh

Suggested Retail Price: $39.95

Choose a poem to hear from the pages that scroll past in this screen.

As I noted up front, if you see quite a few reviews of Broderbund Living Books in this chapter, it's not because the nice folks in Novato, CA (where the firm is based) paid us off. Quite simply, these Living Books are absolutely the best thing around. Kids love them. Parents love them. Most of the titles in this line around our house were purchased—not obtained on a complementary basis as a review freebie. Our four- and six-year-old "test kids" as well as their older brother (who's nearing 24) threaten to wear them out, if such a thing is possible.

Relax. *The New Kid on the Block* is not a solo spin-off of the bubble-gum pop group of similar name (they've grown up to NKOTB at last report, and disbanded last summer). Instead, it's a light-hearted collection of poetry by neo-folkie (to judge from the animation of him) Jack Prelutsky. Like another CD reviewed in this chapter, *Scary Poems for Rotten Kids*, this one zeroes in on the stuff that kids find fascinating, for reasons that mystify most adults. There's

nothing very scary on this disc, though, just a lot of fun.

Prelutsky is an actor, singer, and writer who looks a lot thinner in his publicity photograph in the accompanying booklet, but he puts all his skills to work in *New Kid on the Block* (albeit the acting is through an animated proxy). The core of the program is the poems, illustrated by regular *New Yorker* contributor James Stevenson.

The offerings include "When Tillie Ate the Chili," about a little girl who has some chili that may be just a little too hot. To the left of each line of individual poems is an icon (in this case, a chili pepper) that can be clicked to have that line read to the child. Or the entire poem can be read at one time.

Kids can click a Read Again arrow or one that points to the next poem to continue. Prelutsky is the narrator, but some of the actual poems are read by other appropriate voices.

There are many hidden buttons within the poems, so children can click objects and words within the page and watch them respond by jumping around or making a funny noise. Click "punches hard" in the title poem, and the character acts ferocious and mimics the off-stage "new kid" with some vigorous punching. Other words and phrases produce similar antics when clicked.

There's a variety of poems on the CD-ROM, all as clever as "Homework! Oh Homework":

Homework! Oh, homework!
I hate you! You stink!
I wish I could wash you
away in a sink,
if only a bomb
would explode you to bits.
Homework! Oh, homework!
You're giving me fits.

Our six-year-old has been having homework only for a couple months, but he already savored the sentiments more deeply than you can imagine. Other topics include, When Dracula Went to the Blood Bank, Forty Performing Bananas, and Alligators Are Unfriendly.

Sibling rivalry is addressed in poems like "My Brother's Head Should Be Replaced," "My Sister is a Sissy, and My Baby Brother," which notes:

My baby brother is so small,
he hasn't even learned to crawl.
He's only been around a week,
and all he seems to do is bawl
and wiggle, sleep...and leak.

Is Prelutsky in touch with kids, or what? If you want to encourage reading and give your child a good time, get *The New Kid on the Block*.

Quirky poetry from widely-anthologized children's writer Jack Prelutsky, which kids can listen to or play along with.

When Tillie Ate the Chili

When Tillie ate the chili,
she erupted from her seat,
she gulped a quart of water,
and fled screaming down the street,

Click the icon (in this case a chili pepper) at the beginning of each line to hear the line repeated.

Oregon Trail

Oregon Trail **lets you suffer the same hardships as the pioneers, from the comfort of your computer.**

Wagons Ho! Now boarding for a fun and educational trip along the *Oregon Trail*. For those, both young and old, interested in the early growth of our country, this CD-ROM title will provide an entertaining means to gain a flavor of what early pioneers encountered.

Now you can face the same perils as the pioneers, including disease, snakebites, and starvation! Your party sets out from Independence, Missouri, in its quest for Oregon's Willamette Valley. Choose your supplies wisely, plan the most efficient routes, and be prepared to buy or barter what you may need along the way.

Set in the 1840s, you choose your supplies, equipment, and even the departure time for the long trip from Independence, Missouri, to the Willamette Valley. As you travel, items such as your supplies, the weight of the wagon, and your health are monitored, allowing you to make decisions key to your success in arriving at your destination.

Enriched with interesting commentary by those who are travelling the same trail, and dotted with information on important landmarks and forts, this CD-ROM will provide many hours of entertaining education.

As you start the game, you can choose an occupation, and then select your supplies from Matt's General store. You want to buy enough oxen, clothing, bullets, spare wheels and axles, and food to last for your journey. Only $1680 is available for purchases, but, luckily, money went a lot farther in those days!

You can also select the month you start (planning for good weather), choosing other options along the way from a menu of activities. A map is available to check progress, along with a helpful guidebook of tips and lore. You may check your health status or rations, and choose to trade, talk, rest, or hunt. The pace of your journey can be set from steady to grueling (if you're up to it).

As you travel in pioneers' footsteps, *Oregon Trail* gives you a glimpse of what their lives were like. Death and injury coming with little warning, uncertainty in weather and traveling conditions, bad water, and so on, along with the ability to make key decisions (such as whether to rest, how to cross various rivers, how much weight to carry, what should be bartered for additional supplies, etc.) all add up to give the player some inkling of the hardships and courage that these pioneers experienced.

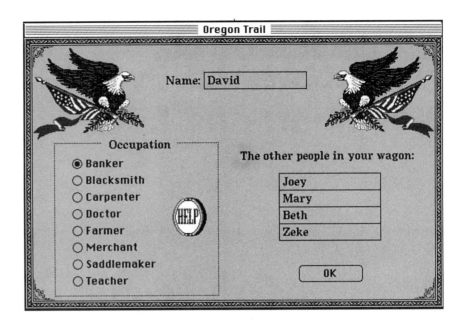

Choose your profession wisely before setting out on the trail.

The graphics supplied with this CD-ROM are more than adequate, but what really adds a dimension to it are the sound features. Complete with songs of the era and stories of pioneers spoken to you along the way, this *Oregon Trail* comes alive through your speakers. All in all, there is more than an hour of music, sound effects, and digitized speech, including some 70 guidebook entries.

MECC rates this CD-ROM title as being appropriate for ages 10 through adult. That is a fair rating. Some degree of skill is necessary for reading comprehension (they indicate a 5th grade reading level or better), however, without question *Oregon Trail* will be fun for younger ones, too, when assisted by an adult.

Oregon Trail has remained popular for a decade because of its thrilling simulation of the conditions of pioneer days. Though greatly enhanced with graphics and sound, its text and simple graphics heritage shows through. Most students will enjoy learning about the Oregon Trail from the game, but it can get repetitious with frequent playing.

This is one lesson that is best learned and then left behind. The journey is well worth the effort, however.

Travel the **Oregon Trail** *and test your ability to plan, barter, and survive hardships in this entertaining CD-ROM for ages 10 and up.*

It seems ironic that we, in this day of technology, casually use such a sophisticated device as a computer replete with CD-ROM to follow the journey of pioneers just a little over 100 years ago who went days and

perhaps weeks on end with no access to even the most basic of assistance (other than that which they could provide themselves).

MECC has combined entertainment and education in *Oregon Trail* to provide a package well worth adding to your CD-ROM collection.

Richard Scarry's Best Neighborhood Ever/Busiest Neighborhood Ever

Rating: 1/2

Publisher Name:
Activision for Kids

Software Requirements: **MPC**

Suggested Retail Price: **$49.95**

Richard Scarry wrote more than 100 wonderful children's books before he died earlier this year, and we were also lucky enough to get at least three different CD-ROM discs from his robust imagination. Earlier in this chapter, I selected Paramount's *Busytown* as positively the best children's CD-ROM I'd ever seen. That doesn't mean that these two Busytown discs from a different publisher, Activision for Kids, don't deserve serious notice. They stack up very well indeed against all the other kids' CD-ROMs I reviewed, even if the Paramount implementation is superior.

Scarry's wonderful characters—Huckle the Cat and Lowly Worm, for example—are here to take your kids through an educational playground filled with fun and learning experiences. The games are all highly original, and are suitable for children as young as three. That alone is a remarkable quality in a disc, because CD-ROMs that can truly be appreciated by the very young computer user are as scarce as empty seats at Yankee Stadium on Bat day.

Paramount's *Busytown* is based on the same Richard Scarry material, but has better animation, more interesting games, and a narrator that sounds like a friend rather than a narrator from a 1950s 16mm junior high science film. I make these points only to help you avoid confusion, not to downgrade *Best/Busiest Neighborhood*. If you really want a group of the best preschool

CD-ROMs on the market, you'll buy all three.

Busiest Neighborhood is a bustling zone of activity your child can enjoy. By moving a star-shaped cursor around each screen, he or she can explore various shops to find intriguing games and other exercises. The star flashes helpfully whenever it passes over a hot button on-screen. The child has only to press the mouse button (double-clicking is, thank goodness, not required) to activate the object. The arrow keys can also be used with computers not equipped with a mouse.

There's a lot to do in this Busytown. On Main Street alone, the child can help Shoemaker cat create some footwear, or visit awhile with Pig Soda Jerk at the Ice Cream Parlor. There's always shopping at the Toy Store, or a weather update from station ZBSY. Around the corner on Front Street, there's Betsy Bear, who needs to mail a letter to Grandma, and the Bakery, where a cake-decorating lesson awaits.

Busytown lovers rejoice: here are two more Richard Scarry delights to amuse children three and up with educational and fun activities.

Huckle the Cat can get a checkup at Doctor Bones' office while you help Mailman Cat deliver the day's mail. Children can learn music appreciation at the music store as they try out 15 different instruments.

A telephone booth or telephone is available in each screen to provide audio help, while there are Bus Stop, Exit, and Done signs scattered about to leave a particular screen. There's even a small kid mode that a parent can invoke to prevent the child from accidentally leaving Busytown. While exiting the program prematurely isn't a disaster by itself, it can turn into one if your child suddenly finds himself back at the DOS prompt or Windows program manager. A couple presses of the DEL key, and presto! no more icons!

Activision's other Busytown disc, *Best Neighborhood Ever*, is more of the same. You find Huckle and friends in the School House Playground on Market Street, while Grocer Cat and Bananas Gorilla lurk in the grocery store nearby. Kids can help the Grocer sort the fruits and vegetables, or identify colors and dress favorite characters in new clothing in the Clothing Store. At the flower shop, children can learn names of different flowers. The Busytown Library is a good place to learn about manners and special rules that apply in some environments.

My kids added these two new Busytown discs to their favorites right after they arrived, never mentioning the slightly reduced production values. They were too busy being entranced by all the things to do in these charming neighborhoods.

Richard Scarry's Busytown

Rating: ◉ ◉ ◉ ◉

Publisher Name: **Paramount**

Software Requirements:
MPC/Macintosh

Suggested Retail Price: **$39.95**

This is it. The absolute best-of-show CD-ROM in the chapter. Maybe the best in the book. I didn't want to say it, but I have to. I knew you'd be suspicious, because, after all, Paramount not only publishes this disc but owns the company that published this book. Worst of all, you're going to find out I was inordinately enthusiastic over another Paramount disc in Chapter 10—*Mega Rap, Rock and Roll.*

Did some big-wig from Hollywood come to Ohio and twist my arm to write this? No, everything is on the up-and-up. I was seduced, along with my children, by nothing more than the genius of Richard Scarry, who died while I was doing the review.

This disc has it all. Education, fun activities, great songs, wonderful animation. And Busytown is certainly an apt name for this program! *Busytown* will keep children from ages 3 to 7 occupied for hours on end with 12 different energetic activities that let kids experiment with objects, manipulate real machines, and even practice working behind the counter of a fast food restaurant. Our four-year-old tester cried when we told her it was time to stop playing in Busytown.

Although you may have seen a floppy disk version of the program, the CD-ROM version is well worth the extra money. It is spiced with lively songs and includes an extra playground, Busy Tunes, that lets the child choose from a selection of songs. The CD-ROM version is even easier on your your hard disk: you can run the program from the CD, but those with the floppy version need about 12MB of free hard disk space to hold the program files.

We received this Paramount disc shortly before author Scarry died, so the loss was even more acute when we looked at what his imagination had wrought. Busytown is populated by creatures like Bananas Gorilla, who needs to wend his way through a maze to a bunch of bananas without losing any fruit to a horde of photographers. This playground provides practice in planning, maze tracing, and simple addition and subtraction.

At Bruno's Deli, the child can help Huckle the Cat piece together complex food

orders using an animated machine, choosing from cheese, hot chocolate, soda, and other delicacies. A character comes to the counter and orders a food or drink (or sometimes both). The words and pictures representing the items also appear in boxes on-screen. Then, Huckle must push the right buttons to assemble the order by cycling among the available choices. You may not be thrilled to watch your kids prepare for a career in fast food management, but children love this module.

Youngsters from three years of age on up adore the colorful characters and exhilarating activities inside Richard Scarry's Busytown.

Other playgrounds ask kids to help build a house, deliver items from a warehouse to various locations in Busytown, or serve as an aide to Dr. Diane as she bandages hapless Norbert the Elephant. Dr. Diane's voice reminds us of an annoying fellow we knew from New Jersey, and her answer to any complaint is to put a bandage on it. Young kids can learn to identify body parts in this one.

Or, they can build and furnish Captain Salty's ship before it sets sail, or put out fires from the Firestation. Many of the activities have overt educational goals, such as the seesaw that can be balanced only by putting equal number totals on either side. Others, like the Busy Tunes Jukebox, are just fun.

The program is furnished with an amazingly complete study guide that helps parents choose activities for developing kids'

language/prereading, math, problem-solving, social, emotional, physical, motor development, art, or music skills. For example, there's a Skills Matrix with listings covering balancing, estimating, following directions, predicting outcomes, drawing conclusions, and so on keyed to each of the playgrounds on the disc. If you practice

everything outlined in the booklet, you may trim a few months off your quest for a PhD. in education.

But don't get too high-minded when you turn your kids loose with this program: they're likely to insist on playing in Busytown at their own pace.

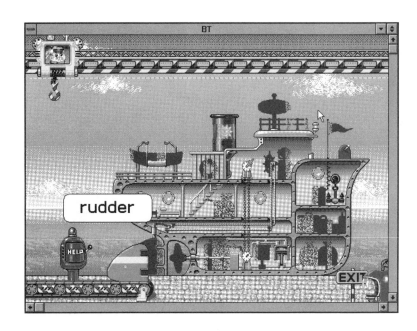

Scary Poems for Rotten Kids

Rating: 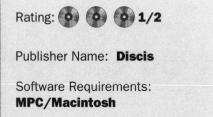 1/2

Publisher Name: **Discis**

Software Requirements:
MPC/Macintosh

Suggested Retail Price: **$49.95**

Kids can have the story read to them, or explore different portions of the pictures and text with the mouse.

Although not in the same multimedia league as Broderbund's Living Books (*Arthur's Teacher Trouble*, *Just Grandma and Me*), the Discis Kids Can Read CD-ROMs maintain the same high literary level. Award-winning poet sean o huigin (an e.e. cummings fan, perhaps?) proffers some terrifying rhymes wrapped around a gentle heart, sure to excite and please kids from age seven onward.

Kids can have the book read to them, or they can use the mouse to click individual words, phrases, and objects in the illustrations. The poems are engaging enough on their own that children don't seem to miss the eye-catching animation and underlying effects that other interactive books provide. The Discis series is so well done that disparaging its multimedia content is a little like faulting Casablanca because it wasn't filmed in color.

Scary Poems is a compilation of 14 short pieces packed into 37 illustrated pages. The poems are exactly the sort appreciated by pre-teenagers who are engrossed with things gross: always macabre, sometimes funny, spiced with a good dose of ick, but never downbeat enough to induce nightmares. These poems are "Where The Wild Things Are," with a little more bite to them.

Our test children rolled on the floor throughout "Acid Rain," in which the narrator describes a rain "that came down in heavy drops; it washed away my shoes and socks; it washed the hair off from my head, it took my ears, then I turned red." In "Midnight," a growling, scratching "thing" at the front door turns out to be the family dog, and a mean little kid gets her due in "The Day The Mosquitoes Ate Angela Jean."

Children under seven probably won't understand the "fake" horror in these poems, and while the excellent illustrations aren't grisly, they are comic-book explicit, so you'll want to steer preschoolers away from this disc.

The high quality of the content encourages children to read the book in any of a half dozen different modes. Older kids can eschew narration entirely and read the book aloud to themselves or friends, accompanied by eerie background music and sound effects. They can just click a page corner to advance to the next screen when ready, or pull a sliding arrow at the right side of the page to go directly to any screen.

Unfortunately, there's no table of contents that permits advancing to the first page of a particular story; finding the page you want is a process as mysterious as the poems themselves.

Non-readers or beginning readers can have each poem read to them. Actual children provide the voices for these mostly first-person narratives, helping to preserve the spell. Appropriate squishy and slithery sounds accompany the readings, and each page has an illustration. Most of the pictures are repeated from page to page, so a six-or seven-page poem may have only two or three different illustrations. However, there are only 10 to 20 words per page anyway, so the lack of variety isn't much of a defect. Any given poem can be read in a minute or two, and requires only a few drawings to tell the story.

The delightfully macabre poems laced with top-quality illustrations in Scary Poems for Rotten Kids encourages children aged 7 and up to explore reading.

The interactive mode will be helpful for kids learning to read. Single words are read aloud by clicking them with the mouse. A single click on a word provides the pronunciation, e.g., "spiders." Double-click the word and it is pronounced more slowly, using separate syllables, e.g., "spi-ders." Hold down the mouse button when a word is selected, and the definition of the word is provided—"spiders: small insects with eight legs that spin webs." The definitions tend to be oversimplified (for example, a spider is not an insect), and the narrators of this portion are adults seemingly kidnapped from some 1950s-era industrial training film.

Individual objects in the accompanying illustrations can also be clicked (eyes, claws, slime, etc.) to generate a pop-up word/ description and audio pronunciation of the object's name. While there are no animations or visual puns like those in some other interactive books, there's enough here to hold the interest of serious young readers (or

serious young horror fans).

Selected words are queued up in a "recall" list that can be accessed from a pull-down menu. The child can go back to any word by retrieving it from the list. While the text and narration are entirely in English, the help system, oddly enough, has a Spanish option. When Help is activated, you can learn how to operate any feature of the book by clicking it with the mouse cursor. Hispanic children who want to polish their English can use Help to learn how to interact with *Scary Poems*, and then read or listen to the English text. Though the written text itself is stuck in "English" mode, you can activate Spanish translations of individual words and phrases through a simple-to-use Customization menu.

The same menu can also be used to redefine the actions of single and double mouse-clicks, and several other parameters.

This is a dual-platform disc: the exact same CD-ROM can be used with both IBM-PC compatible and MPC-equipped systems and Apple Macintosh systems. The PC installation isn't really complicated, but

getting *Scary Poems* to work properly under Microsoft Windows proved complicated.

When the same disc was popped into a Macintosh CD-ROM drive, we were able to launch *Scary Poems* directly from the CD-ROM, with no installation at all. One dialog box warns you that Macintosh virtual memory features can degrade sound quality (we didn't have any problems). Another pops up if you've set your monitor's control panel to Thousands of Colors or Millions of Colors, and offers to change to the 256-color setting required by this disc. When you exit *Scary Poems*, the program restores your previous color setting (thank you, Discis!).

Scary Poems for Rotten Kids is a first-rate piece of literature that lends itself to a multimedia implementation of this type. Though lacking all the bells and whistles (literally) of some of the latest CD-ROMs, it's a flexible tool for encouraging reading. Because it can be used interchangeably on Macintosh and PC platforms, this disc is an excellent choice for schools or homes with mixed environments, too.

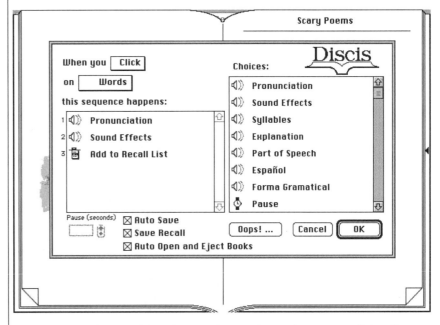

You can customize how *Scary Poems* behaves when various mouse click actions are performed.

Tuneland Starring Howie Mandel

Rating:

Publisher Name: **7th Level**

Software Requirements: **MPC**

Suggested Retail Price: **$79.95**

Forget everything you've ever read or heard about children's CD-ROMs. Tuneland takes the medium to new levels of fun with a more motion-filled, song-drenched outing that resembles a well-done Saturday morning cartoon more than a simple children's CD-ROM. Of course,

having actor/comedian Howie Mandel—who has already starred in his own weekly cartoon—as the host doesn't hurt.

Aimed at children aged 3-6 and their parents, *Tuneland*, an IBM PC-only disc for Microsoft Windows at this time, is a musical land (Old MacDonald's Farm, actually) inhabited by singing critters and your host, a bear named Lil Howie. These creatures ply you with more than 40 tunes, puzzles, jokes, and magic tricks, all arrayed in eight different scenes around the barnyard and surrounding area.

You move around in *Tuneland*, as in other CD-ROM games, by clicking hotspots scattered throughout each scene in search for Lil Howie, who turns up in the oddest places. When you find the character who has been assigned to take you to the next scene,

you're whisked off to new adventures.

The interface is the easiest one you can imagine for very young kids. If they can manipulate a mouse—or talk Mom or Dad into helping out—kids can enjoy Tuneland. Almost every object in the scenes responds to mouse clicks, and Lil Howie's hat remains in the lower right corner, a prop that returns you to the "main menu" screen in an instant.

Throughout *Tuneland*, the child encounters a barn, farmhouse, station, mountain, valley, train, pond, woods, and barnyard. They are the sites for dozens of catchy songs sung by the cartoon characters. The talking horse in the barn is the most talented equine since Mr. Ed. The child can sit entranced by these characters, or sing along.

Tuneland's barnyard is your gateway to all the musical productions on the disc.

Pick up the telephone at the train station, and you'll hear Howie Mandel himself speak to you.

The supplied booklet provides tips for getting around in the game and finding specific songs. For example, in the Farmhouse, you can click the mouse hole to produce "Three Blind Mice"; on the teakettle to activate "Polly Put the Kettle On" and "I'm A Little Teapot"; and a clock face to have "Hickory Dickory Dock" sung to you.

Impatient adults will find tips in the booklet for keyboard shortcuts, including the super-secret Shift+Esc sequence that aborts the game and returns quickly to Microsoft Windows. Other shortcuts are tied to easily remembered hotkeys, like Shift+H to go to the house, Shift+M to go to the mountain, and so on.

The songs, all folk tunes and nursery rhymes, were professionally recorded in rock, country, and even classical musical styles. The singing voices are cute, too, if a bit hard to understand at times. (Howie Mandel does the best imitation of talking on helium of anyone we've ever heard.)

The sound is full-blown CD audio—so you must have your CD-ROM drive wired

into your sound card to use this disc—and just may blow you away when you hear it. Your computer never sounded so good.

Tuneland takes CD-ROM animation and music to a new level with stunning graphics and more than 40 catchy songs.

The animation is amazing, too. The characters dance, smile, laugh, swim, and jump. The action changes each time you click an object. Click the phone at the train station, and sometimes you get Howie Mandel yourself. Repeat the action, and you may get an even bigger surprise. There's an animated blimp in the sky, pictures that transform themselves into television sets,

and more talking animals than you've ever seen outside a Walt Disney cartoon.

As each new scene is loaded, an animated character runs across the screen to entertain the child, avoiding boredom during the "slow" periods. The disc also includes a "virtual" audio CD player that can be used to play the tunes separately, outside of the game itself.

Note: All celebrity voices on this disc were reproduced by impersonators, except for the voice of Howie Mandel, which was actually him.

Wiggins in Storyland

Rating: 1/2

Publisher Name:
MediaVision

Software Requirements: MPC

Suggested Retail Price: $59.95

Think of *Wiggins in Storyland* as sort of a super-PageMaker for primary school kids. It automates the process of creating stories and poems in personalized books, complete with animated backgrounds and characters that the child creates, along with props, music, and words.

Wiggins' room is a good place to find interesting things to read.

Then the masterpiece is finished, it can be printed to any printer installed for the computer's Windows system, ready to be admired by Mom, Dad, grandparents—or jealous siblings!

Wiggins is a bookworm (what else!) who lives in a tree. His room is decked out like a library, and outside there is a "branch" limbrary where the child's own books are stored. Inside the tree are an assortment of departments that can be used to create new books with soundtracks and moving pictures.

There are eight different themes in Wiggins to choose from, a cast of 40 animated characters, a hundred different props for them to use, and an assortment of animated backgrounds. The stories can be

augmented with any of 40 pieces of background music, and if the child runs out of ideas for stories, there's an Idea Light Bulb that suggests some good scenarios.

There's lots of help along the way for young authors. Word Duck is an animated Thesaurus who can find nouns, verbs, or adjectives for the story. And Wiggins the Bookworm can pop up unexpectedly to offer his own advice. The child can also summon the friendly worm on their own for help when they get stuck.

The action starts in the Lobby of Wiggins' tree, where the child signs in. If he or she has played the game before and saved a book to disk, the youngster's name already appears on the guest list. Next, it's off to the freight elevator where the player can choose

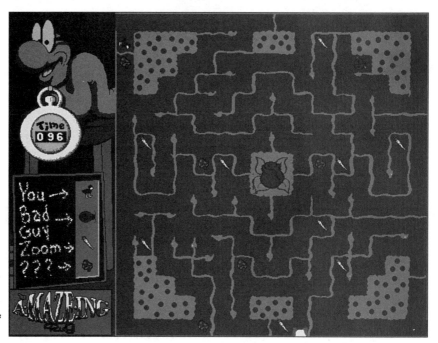

This updated version of Pac-Man is one of the games included with *Wiggins*.

to create a new book, open an existing book, or visit Wiggins' room, where some games await.

Children can create their own stories, complete with animated backgrounds and characters, as well as music and spoken sound tracks.

Books are stored in a branch limbrary, which, given the tree metaphor, really is a branch. On the Story Page, which looks like an open book with an array of icons at the top, the child selects one of the story-publishing functions.

Text entry is strictly one page at a time:

as with a real storybook, only the text that will fit on a single page can be displayed. Once the text is typed in, it's off to the Art Department, where the child can choose from among various settings. Wiggins provides a long, long landscape, any part of which can be selected as the background for the story.

Characters and props are specified by category and name, so it's simple to populate the page with interesting cartoon folks and objects for them to interact with. Word Duck is available to suggest an appropriate word to use with a particular character or prop.

In the Editing Department, the child can add magic effects, such as rotating the character in one direction or another, or cloning a miniature version of an object. Characters can change mood at the click of a mouse, with four different facial expressions available. To finish up a book, choose a Book Style to apply a cover, and select a song for each page from eight different albums with the Juke Box.

Text can be printed in any font or color.

If your sound card has a microphone attached, the child can record up to 60 seconds of commentary or narration for each page.

After a hard day of work, the child can retire to Wiggins' room, where he or she can play with almost every object in the scene. For example, the fan bounces up and down, fireplace bricks generate sounds, or he or she can make some fruit drink with the juicer. There's a paint bucket if the child is in the mood to redecorate Wiggins' room, and a quick game of Tic-Tac-Toe is available by clicking a window pane.

The floor rug hides five different mazes, all timed to keep the pressure building, and with a teleporter to move quickly from one part of the maze to another. There are just two games, but lots of other things to play with in Wiggins' room. All these are really just a bonus, because the clever story-building portion of the program makes up the meat of its appeal.

Allie's Playhouse

Rating:  1/2

Publisher Name:
Opcode Interactive

Software Requirements: **MPC**

Suggested Retail Price: **$59.95**

What a cute disc this is! There are dozens of "playroom" programs for children on the market, based on a school or home metaphor. The child clicks various objects in the room, and then plays games associated with them. *Allie's Playhouse* takes this time-honored formula and adds some wonderful new wrinkles.

The most outstanding of these is the "pick a friend" page that lets the child select a playmate to explore the playhouse with. On this screen, your youngster finds photographs of six other children—three boys and three girls—who seem to be about three to six years of age. The child can click each friend to hear the computerized companion give a little speech about himself or herself, and then choose the one who seems most compatible. During the session, this new friend pops up to explain how some of the games work. This is a great idea, and was greatly appreciated by my four-year-old daughter, who seemed to be husband-hunting the day I watched her play this.

There are a dozen or more activities, which teach math and counting, astronomy, art, spelling, geography, telling time, and many more skills. Young children can learn to identify the parts of their bodies, sing along with 16 different nursery rhymes, and identify animals and their sounds.

Allie's Playhouse adds six playmates and more than a dozen activities to your child's roster of computer-oriented pastimes.

Older children can play with Mr. Clock (an analog alarm clock) and his friend Digi (a digital clock) to learn how to tell time. They can also identify continents, or play and record their own musical selections with a color-coded piano. There's the ubiquitous coloring book module with some interesting pictures that include the equally-pervasive dinosaurs. The planets of our solar system are also shown in another section. This disc can be a lot of fun for kids ages 3 to 8 years.

Moving beyond the playroom takes the kid into the kitchen, where he or she can learn about the wonderful world of appliances (my daughter highly favors domestic automation), along with sound and object recognition.

Although there are keyboard shortcuts that parents may learn, kids can do just about anything on this disc using only the mouse. Game levels can be set by clicking buttons labeled 1, 2, or 3.

Parents can turn on a "safety" feature that prevents the child from accidentally (or on purpose) exiting this Windows-based game and messing with program groups. My own two youngest kids learned how to use the Escape key and Alt-F4 about the same time they learned to speak, so they don't need this protection. But other kids will never stumble across the key sequence (Ctrl-Alt-S) needed to bypass the safety control built into *Allie's Playhouse*. (This feature only works when your screen resolution is set to 640 x 480, since kids can easily click outside that window in other modes.)

Allie's Playhouse holds many surprises for young children and their playmates.

Annabel's Dream of Ancient Egypt

Ancient indeed! This CD-ROM is a golden-oldie, dating back to 1991, but it's still a gem thanks to its charming story, full complement of engaging activities, and the rich vein of knowledge children can mine. While it doesn't have the multimedia flash of more recent children's titles, faulting Annabel for that is a little like complaining that *Hamlet* doesn't have enough special effects.

First, there's the story. Our six- and four-year-old "test kids" usually don't like to share a new CD-ROM, and it's been getting harder to interest them in simple stories since their personal PCs have been flooded with CDs when this project started. But, a few seconds into *Annabel's Dream of Ancient Egypt*, both sat transfixed for half an hour as the epic tale unfolded. The older child read along with the words accompanying each of the 101 frames, while the younger paid rapt attention to the adorable cats. They loved the story.

Annabel is a young, nearly mature cat who lives with a human couple and several other cats, including her mother and younger sister. Annoyed by her sister's teasing, she dozes off to the opera "Aida," and discovers the land of her dreams— Ancient Egypt. There, cats are queens in a desert of sand so vast that litter boxes are entirely unnecessary. Annabel wakes, and eventually learns to apply what she dreamed to cope with anger and her sister's annoying habits.

The story is a long one, well-told, and has more than 100 separate pictures (other interactive books may have just 10 to 15 "pages"). The simple black-and-white illustrations at the beginning of the story are elegant in a minimalist sort of way, and add

contrast to the dream sequence, which is presented in full color. Most of the pictures are still drawings, with a few animations sprinkled in here and there.

> **Annabel's Dream *is* packed with tons of activities that complement its charming story of Annabel the Cat and her discovery of the land of her heart's desire.**

As with other interactive books, the story can be read to the child with or without a text display on-screen. There's a "paws" icon to freeze at a certain page, as well as a Bookmark that can remember your place in the story. Because this is a substantial tale, you might indeed find it necessary to continue reading the book at another time. An online glossary is also available that lists all the words in the text and their definitions.

Although kids will ask to hear the story again and again, there are lots of other things to do with this disc. Background information on Verdi's "Aida," exerpts from the opera, Rudyard Kipling's poem, "If," and a few

quirky additions like Timbuk 3's rollicking song "Facts About Cats," add a lot of play time to this CD. All the audio tracks can be played on a regular audio CD player, too.

There are articles about ancient Egypt and making paper, a coloring gallery where the child can colorize pictures from the book, along with a hieroglyphics translator. A nice group of games is also included. This disc is much more eclectic than you might expect, but still keeps within its cats/Egypt theme.

Because Annabel's Dream has been available for quite awhile, you should be able to find a copy at bargain prices. This precursor of all interactive books for children holds up quite well, and will charm anyone.

Rating:

Publisher Name: **Texas Caviar**

Software Requirements: **MPC/Macintosh**

Suggested Retail Price: **$59.95**

Barney Bear Goes To Space

Rating: 🔵 🔵 🔵 🔵

Publisher Name:
Free Spirit Software

Software Requirements: **MPC**

Suggested Retail Price: **$19.95**

Barney Bear Goes To Space includes a tour of Kennedy Space Center.

*B*arney Bear Goes To Space proves that you don't need the slickest interface, dozens of video clips, and mind-boggling 3D graphics to please kids. This simple, but effective, CD-ROM practically weaned one four-year-old we know from television: this is her favorite bear since Yogi.

Like its predecessor, *Barney Bear Goes To School*, this disc combines an entertaining story with games and interesting things to do. Children like to explore its nooks and crannies and will spend hours on each of the activities included. Think of *Barney Bear Goes To Space* as a software suite for youngsters.

The centerpiece of the disc is a tour of Kennedy Space Center in Florida. Barney Bear is taken on a guided walk through the mission control center, shuttle launching vehicle, and, finally, the space station Freedom. There are no heavy technical details here to confuse kids, just the kind of information about rockets and space that they eat up like candy.

Your youngster won't need heavy-duty computer skills to use this program either (our four-year-old does fine with just a mouse). A button bar at the top of the screen invokes audio help that explains how to use each function. It explains that clicking a speaker icon repeats the narration for a given page. An "eyeglasses" icon displays related photographs with additional narration. Other icons provide help with the current scene, help on how to use help (believe it or not), and exit to the next scene.

The supplementary photos are first rate, consisting of actual NASA photographs of space shuttles and other scenes of interest. All are "captioned" with audio narration—the child does not need to read to enjoy this disc.

Barney Bear's tour of Kennedy Space

Center ends with him falling asleep inside a shuttle and ending up on the Space Station. From there, the child can choose from any of five different games and activities from a picture-menu. The choices include:

- **A Simon-like color/sound memory challenge.**
- **Tour of the Solar System.**
- **Did you know?**
- **Coloring Book.**
- **Slide Show.**

Barney Bear Goes To Space is highly recommend for those looking for a good CD-ROM for their preschooler or kindergartener. After dinosaurs, outer space is one topic that all kids find interesting, and this disc is easy enough to use that the youngest child will be able to master it in no time.

A Christmas Carol

It had to happen. You just can't keep a good author down, even if he is dead. This CD-ROM version of his best-known novel might just raise Charles Dickens up all by itself.

Now *A Christmas Carol* is on CD-ROM; and it is beautifully done. Ebook, Inc. publishes multimedia versions of classic literature with all the feel of sitting with a master storyteller. If Dickens, like Jacob Marley, is wandering the Earth observing mankind, seeing this edition of his most over-produced work surely eases his passage and soothes his shade.

Ebook uses MicroSoft's Multimedia Viewer programming almost to full advantage in this effort. Text is clear and crisp, Eric Coulson's narration is magnificent, Sir Arthur Rackham's illustrations are glorious, and the music is superb. Twelve pictures, several line drawings, and eight classic Christmas songs grace the production. The graphics are interspersed throughout the text to appear as on pages of a bound book. Regrettably, the songs are not. Some background music and a few sound clips would have been a nice final polish on the production.

There are three ways to navigate the book: first is simply paging through with the arrow buttons. You can also use the index or use the automatic reader, which, regrettably, lacks indexing. You can't move to a certain page and have the automatic reader start there. Wherever you are in the book, clicking the Play/Pause button starts reading at the first page. You can use a special button to advance 10 pages at a time but, if you're 200 pages into the book, it takes quite a few keystrokes to move to where you left off. It would be nicer if the automatic reader were programmed to start at any page.

Eric Coulson's narration is a treat. He reads like a kindly grandfather, performing the novel in an endearing British accent, with excellent vocal characterizations. Reading aloud is a skill nearly everyone who has children practices, at least for a time, but few ever perfect.

The artwork in the book is very nice. Sir Arthur Rackham drew many fine line drawings and painted 12 marvelous illustrations. All are stylistically appropriate to 19th-century England. It's not possible to tell if they are watercolor or pastel drawings, but they have the flavor of fine old English watercolors with a hint of woodcut in their line structure. Sir Arthur captured the tenor of the time's costumes and the novel's moods. His illustration of Topper's pursuit of "that plump sister" is delightful with just the right hint of that good-natured bawdiness you might find at a private party among close friends.

The music selections are magnificent. Two especially stand out: "Angels We Have Heard On High," sung by Whitney Keyes with the International Children's Choir and The Bobby Clifton Orchestra, and "Good Christian Men, Rejoice," sung a cappella by The Yuletide Carolers. Keyes' voice and diction are so clear they border on painful. Rarely is listening to a singer such an experience. The Yuletide Carolers' rendition rivals Keyes' in its own province. All four of the choral voices sound clear but blend seamlessly, without overpowering each other. This is what choir directors dream of and choral music fans pray for with each purchase.

Ebook, Inc. comes right out and says this

Rating: ●

Publisher Name: **Ebook, Inc.**

Software Requirements: **MPC/Macintosh**

Suggested Retail Price: **$29.95**

CD is designed as education as much as entertainment. The Learning Guide section offers several practical approaches to using it as a teaching aid for reading, learning English as a second language, and vocabulary. The hypertext dictionary function has short definitions, or at least synonyms, for each highlighted word. The potential for reading along with the narration further enhances its educational potential. Exploring this work brings back the feeling those few really memorable teachers evoked, that sense of happy surprise that learning can be fun.

Ebook, Inc. apparently went to significant effort to make *A Christmas Carol* a useful as well as entertaining production. A few very minor missteps here and there can't significantly mar it. This is no mere electronic text, this is a performance of the novel. Closed eyes and a little imagination take you to Olde England. You follow Ebenezer and Jacob, Bob and Tiny Tim, and the Three Spirits of Christmas, an unseen (but not unaffected) participant in one of Western Literature's best tales of lost and reclaimed ideals. That it's been done so many times in so many media doesn't detract from this fine rendering.

Dr. T.'s Sing-A-Long Classics

Rating: ◉ ◉ ◉

Publisher Name:
Dr. T.'s Music Software

Software Requirements: MPC

Suggested Retail Price: $29.95

It had to happen—karaoke for kids! The next thing we know, kids will be crowding into ice cream joints after school, loosening their collars and taking turns behind the microphone singing songs from their youth. You know... "I love you...you love me...we're a happy family...."

Until that happens, there's always *Dr. T.'s Sing-A-Long Classics*, a collection of 26 kid's songs that any primary school child or parent will know by heart. This Microsoft Windows-based program has everything you need (except a microphone plugged into your sound card) to croon along with old standards like "I've Been Working on the Railroad."

Sing-A-Long Classics displays the lyrics underneath a score with the actual notes (for those who read music). The ability to read music isn't required, obviously, with such familiar songs. Most of the tunes have been transposed into the key of F (one flat for you technical musician-types), which is an easy key for young voices.

In Sing-A-Long mode, animations are displayed on a musical stage in front of you, so the kids have something to look at besides the words if they are too young to read. Four large buttons arrayed at the left side of

the screen present the most likely functions: New Song, Rewind (which lets you restart the song from any point), Stop!, and Play!. All four options have picture icons (such as a Stoplight) so even young children know which button to press with the mouse. More complex options are available from pull-down Windows menus (you can change the sound parameters, for example), best left to Mom or Dad.

There's also a Juke Box mode that lets you play the songs in any order you like, and a Little Kids mode that is, if anything, even easier to use than Sing-A-Long. All 26 songs are represented by icons at the left and right sides of the screen (flanking the animation/stage area). The youngest child can select a song by clicking the appropriate icon. If they don't know instantly that the Spider (a Black Widow, no less) produces "Itsy Bitsy Spider or the Teapot," "I'm A Little Teapot," they'll learn it quickly enough.

Songs are presented in CD audio and

MIDI file formats. With the latter, you can vary the tempo, because the songs are not recordings but, rather, actual musical scores that are "played" at the speed you specify.

The package is as complete as you could hope for. A full-color songbook with all the songs and many clever pictures is included. There's even an MPC "troubleshooting" guide that can help you pin down obvious problems if you have difficulty getting the CD-ROM to work correctly. If this is your first multimedia CD, or first that uses CD audio, you may not be aware that your CD-ROM drive isn't correctly connected to the sound card. Dr. T. even provides a diagram that shows how to wire your computer and home stereo/tape player for a karaoke recording studio! As a realistic touch, the vendor passes the ball to the real culprits in many hardware conflicts—the video card manufacturers—by listing the phone numbers for technical support for ten different peripheral companies.

Kids can sing along with simple and familiar songs using this CD.

European Racers

European Racers is a most interesting CD-ROM based software program. It contains both a car model kit with excellent multimedia instructions and a game. The game is an average road racing game, although it does have some appealing multimedia additions. The model kit, however, is superb! What Revell has done is put together a CD-ROM that teaches you how to build model kits. In the past, you bought a kit containing some instructions that weren't always very good, and went at it. Revell, in releasing *European Racers*, has changed that.

The program runs only from DOS, and has some hefty memory requirements, including a few megabytes of expanded memory (EMS). You'll almost certainly have to disable most of your other programs and/or create a special boot disk to run this program. A title screen comes up with some good video footage of the high performance cars you will soon be learning more about. A click of the mouse button takes you to the main screen of the program. The picture changes to a small automobile showroom. A sliding door on the right of the showroom rises, and four of Europe's dream machines roll into the room; each takes its place on a pedestal, which rises as each car comes to a stop. Then a female voice begins speaking, introducing the cars to you.

When you've chosen the car you want to build, a new screen comes up—the garage. As in the showroom, some items are selectable. When you pan across the room, your mouse touches the bookshelf and a Modeling Tips caption appears. If you touch the car body, a Full Assembly' caption pops up. You also have Tools (tool chest), Fun

Facts (picture), and Instructions (wall chart) hot spots, as well as a help button and a Return to Showroom icon.

Hit the return button, go back to the garage, and click the car body. This takes you to the Full Assembly screen. This screen is really impressive! Here you can call up an exploded view animation of your car by clicking the traffic light icon.

The Tools screen shows you what you need to build the kit. It lets you choose either basic tools or pro tools and customizes each list if you specify that you will not be painting the model. If you plan on painting the model, it shows you what your model will look like if you use one of eight different colors.

The most important screen to the model builder is the Instructions screen, accessed

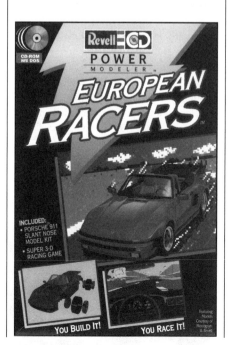

by a click on the wall chart. This screen is composed of a window and a step menu, which is a series of buttons. For the Porsche model, there are 16, numbered one to 15 and one with a > symbol. Clicking the > button leads you to the next set of sequentially numbered buttons.

Besides the modeling aspect of this product, there is also a road racing game. A real fan of race games might be happy with this game, but most people won't spend much time with it.

A very strong model kit tutorial and a weak game combine to yield a product that is still very strong. The merit of this package is in the model kit and the excellent use it makes of multimedia to aid the kit builder. Besides the kit that comes with the CD, the user can buy the other three European Racers in kit-only form, and use this CD to build them, too.

Rating: ◉ ◉ ◉ 1/2

Publisher Name:
Revell-Monogram, Inc.

Software Requirements: **MPC**

Suggested Retail Price: **$69.95**

Fatty Bear's Fun Pack

Rating:

Publisher Name: **Humongous**

Software Requirements: **MPC**

Suggested Retail Price: **$49.95**

*F*atty Bear's Fun Pack contains five different fun and challenging games for younger kids. The activities include Reversi, Tangrams, Go Fish, Lines and Boxes, and Fatty Bear's Paint Set. While many of these are available in other children's packages, this CD-ROM has just about the best implementation of each that we've seen. If your kids liked *Putt-Putt Goes to the Moon* or *Fatty Bear's Birthday Surprise*, they'll love this modest, but satisfying, disc.

Actually, some of the games will test the skills of grown-ups, too. The best example is the ancient Chinese game of Tangrams. Legend has it that a man dropped a piece of tile, which broke into 7 pieces. Trying to put them back together again, he created a number of new shapes.

In this game, you're presented with an odd shape outline, which can be filled with various combinations of colored cut-outs arrayed below it. You may choose from triangles, squares, rectangles, and parallelograms. These shapes will almost fit into the puzzle in many different ways—but only one right way. Pieces may be rotated various ways to try out different configurations. We discovered that kids just love to watch parents goof up the puzzle by attempting solutions that the children can obviously see

are wrong. Overall, there are four levels, each with 20 different shapes, getting progressively more difficult with each level.

Fatty Bear's Fun Pack *has a variety of activities that introduce young children to the joys of computing and educational games.*

The Reversi game is like most Othello versions you've seen, except that colored frogs are used instead of discs, and Fatty Bear stands in front of the 3D playing board, carefully weighing his options before making a move. This adds a realistic dimension to the game. You really feel as if you're playing against a live opponent.

Lines and Boxes is the old pencil-and-paper game brought to the computer. The object is to complete a square on a grid

without setting up the other player to complete a square instead. In the easiest mode, Fatty Bear is really, really stupid, missing quite a few obvious opportunities, so even fairly young children have a chance to win this game. Older kids won't be fooled and will resent being allowed to win, so don't let them use the lowest level. At the Hard level, Fatty Bear knows how to win, but still makes a mistake now and then. At the Hardest level, he never, ever makes a mistake. There are four skill levels in all for each of the games in *Fatty Bear's Fun Pack*.

Go Fish is a great starter card game for kids. It's a little more challenging than War, and doesn't start the fights that Old Maid does (we've seen younger kids eat the Old Maid rather than get stuck with it). Our four- and six-year old test kids had never seen Go Fish before, and learned the rules simply by playing with Fatty Bear. He talks to you, asking if you have any fours? If not, he says, "Go Fish!" It's easy to pick up strategy by trial and error with this game.

Finally, *Fatty Bear's Fun Pack* includes a Paint Set game with 35 pictures and thousands of colors, a rich palette, and special tools like an eye-dropper. Kids can mix colors to create their own hues, too.

Play Go Fish with Fatty Bear, and learn how to use the mouse at the same time.

Four Footed Friends

The animation alone is worth the price for this T/Maker entry for children. The 3D modeling is incredibly realistic, with more in common with Roger Rabbit than Bugs Bunny. One look at the interface, an animated "interactivator," will show you what I'm talking about. The next page arrow button doesn't sit there idly waiting for you to click it—it jumps, twirls, and twists to catch the child's attention! This program makes the best use of QuickTime we've seen in a children's program.

Great 3D animation accompanies 10 short poems that kids will love, and associated learning activities.

As with other animated storybooks, you can listen to the story (told with a delightful English accent), click phrases to hear them repeated, or select individual objects in the illustration to bring them to life. Mrs. Cow's blouse changes from red to a flowered pattern, and an ever-growing pile of hay is produced on her dinner plate when you click it a few times. Other four-footed friends include General Rinoceros, Kangaroo, Nanny Goat, and Madame Elephant. Each is accompanied by a silly poem that will make kids grin.

Your guides include Pablo, who lets you color your own pictures; Wendy the bookworm, who helps kids learn to read and spell by defining a word from the poem, and then asking the child to click on the chalk animal to see an activity. Albert, the number worm, provides facts and figures, and then quizzes you on what you've learned. You can access a Storybook Library, complete with Card Catalog previews, to choose a page.

There are ten main pages in this book, each featuring one animal. Select a page, and your friend reads the poem to you. After that, you can click a line of the poem to have it repeated, select the globe icon to hear and read the poem in a different language (a different language on each page—the cow speaks in French, while the Kitten is fluent in Spanish). The child can also search in the picture for hidden sounds and effects, or select the gold sparkle to see a video about the animal.

Both the Mac and Windows versions of this disc use QuickTime for the video, with a 256-color display. The disc is also furnished with a set of bookmarks and a printed version of the "book" that kids can use to read the poems on their own—without a computer involved. (What a novel concept!)

The only real failing of this disc is that there are only 10 poems, each just one four-line stanza. Although there are many different activities for each page (which serves as only a springboard), some children will be disappointed to find the book end so quickly. How about a 20-page version of this, T/Maker?

Rating:

Publisher Name: **T/Maker**

Software Requirements: **MPC/Macintosh**

Suggested Retail Price: **$59.95**

Said Mrs. Cow: "When I say 'Moo,' I do not mean to frighten you; But that is quite the only way I have, to ask you for more hay."

Mrs. Cow's plate gets extra hay when you click on it while reading this interactive book.

Goferwinkel's Adventures

Rating: 1/2

Publisher Name: **Ebook, Inc.**

Software Requirements: **MPC**

Suggested Retail Price: **$29.95**

*G*oferwinkel's Adventures in the Lavender Land is nothing more than a multimedia comic book with few options for the player, and static panels that parade across the screen one at a time as you click the mouse. So why does this ancient disc still rate two-and-a-half stars? It's a pretty good comic book, it is available at a bargain price, and it is an entertaining disc for younger children who may not be able to handle a full-fledged CD-ROM program yet. All they need to do to play along with Goferwinkel is click the mouse button.

The plot revolves around a young video game addict named William, who finds himself transported by a new game into Lavender Land, where he is magically transformed into a bird named Goferwinkel (he looks a little like a buzzard having a bad feathers day). Goferwinkel's adventure unfolds in traditional comic book panels, usually three to four to a page. Each panel is revealed when the child clicks with the mouse button.

Goferwinkel and other characters speak, and there is some lively music. The cartoon artwork is very good, and the storyline simple enough for young children to follow. Goferwinkel must save the princess that is imprisoned in the castle.

There's not really much to do, though, except click the mouse to set your own pace through the adventure. A few animations break up the still panels—generally simple sequences of Goferwinkel being chased by something. From time to time, you are asked to make a decision by clicking Yes or No. Your choice really makes no difference in how the adventure unfolds.

Goferwinkel's Adventures in the Lavender Land is a multimedia comic book with a rigid plot and few extras, but still entertaining for young children.

For example, once inside the castle, Goferwinkel finds himself in a hall with a mysterious door. You're asked if he should try his key on the door or continue down the hall. If you elect to go down the hall, a guard comes and chases you back to the door, and you flee inside it. The only real way you can affect the outcome is at the very end, when you're asked whether you'd like to give the magic crown to the princess, thereby restoring rightful rule to Lavender Land, or to the evil villain, allowing him to rule in her place. Hmmm...tough choice. The villain offers to share power with you, but if the player ends up awarding him the crown, he or she, in effect, loses the game. This is what we call a no-brainer decision, folks.

Still, we've seen Goferwinkel bundled with inexpensive CD-ROM drives, or available for purchase separately for very little. Our test kids loved the music (which can be played separately, juke box style) and memorized all the dialog. This disc is well worth the money you may pay for it, and won't disappoint if you understand going in the modest goals.

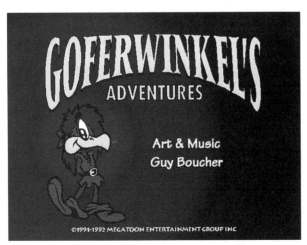

The opening screen of Goferwinkel's Adventures sets the tone for this animated comic book.

Kid Fun

id Fun is a Windows Karaoke Sing-A-Long program for kids ages two to adult, with 11 fun songs. The installation is very smooth, and takes about 1MB on the hard drive. The program uses the Video for Windows Run Time module for the animation. If you don't already have the Video for Windows, or its run time package, *Kid Fun* will install a limited version for you. A sound card is a must to be able to hear the music and voices.

The first screen you see when you start the program is a list of 11 songs, a help button, and a Quit button. The Help button displays aid in an unusual way: It guides children with pictures and a soft voice on how to use the buttons and the song list. For the Song List, just pick out what song you want to play and you are taken to another screen.

In the next screen, the song title is at the top, in the middle is a picture screen and a CD player. You have a few choices at this point. If you choose play, you not only hear the music for the song, you also see the words and the pictures for the song. If you choose Vocal, the song is sung for you with

the music and animation. If you look right in the middle of the song words' there are two arrows, one points up and one points down, this keeps your place so that you can sing with the music.

Strictly a sing-a-long package, Kid Fun lacks only interaction to make it a serious contender in the crowded children's CD-ROM arena.

The colorful cartoon pictures and the sound effects keep up with the different parts of the song, for instance with the song "If you're happy and you know it," you can hear and see a picture of the hands clapping. You can look, listen, and sing. All 11 songs

© 1993 Mindplay, Methods & Solutions, Inc. Cindy Karubian

Kids can sing along with the computer with Kid Fun.

Rating: ◉ ◉ 1/2

Publisher Name: **Mind Play**

Software Requirements: **MPC**

Suggested Retail Price: **$69.95**

have this same format. The disc provides music videos for kids to sing along with.

The CD player also has a stop button that stops where you leave off and plays from that same spot. You can also choose to rewind the song and play it again from the start. The volume control is nice, but it will only let you change the volume before or after the song, not while the song is playing. The help button has the same speech and animation as on the main menu of song titles, but the help is for the CD player. You can use the return button to go back and choose a different song to play, or you can use the quit button to quit.

All the songs in *Kid Fun* are songs about being a kid and doing the fun things kids like to do. They can pretend that cats bark and dogs meow, or that they are driving a bus, or in a castle. There are also songs about how to be good, paying attention, and following the rules in school. Kids can learn how their attitudes affect other people. The lyrics are done in a cheerful catchy way, and the music is upbeat. Some of the songs the kids know and some of the songs they will learn. The product comes with a coloring book, poster, stickers, and a trading card.

Kid Fun is a nice program but it is not as interactive as other children's programs. They can play, sing, and listen to the songs, but they really cannot do much else.

Putt-Putt's Fun Pack

Rating:

Publisher Name: **Humongous**

Software Requirements:
MPC/Macintosh

Suggested Retail Price: **$49.95**

Humongous has a humongous star on their hands. Putt-Putt, the little car with the child's voice and an amazing backlog of adventures, is back from the parade and the moon in this fun pack of games and activities.

There are six fun adventures for your child of four and up, who can learn pattern matching and recognition, develop letter and spelling skills, sharpen logic and spatial relationship abilities, all while having a ball. The six activities on this disc include Cheese King (a spelling game), Circus Puzzle Blocks, Tic-Tac-Toe, Remember!, Checkers, and Pinball. You've seen some of these in other CDs and programs for kids, but

Humongous' implementation tops them all.

Cheese King lets Putt-Putt challenge a friendly rodent by putting together simple words to match a picture, such as Hamburger. By clicking an alphabet panel until all the letters are guessed, the child can learn his or her letters or how to spell the word. Wrong answers add to the slices of cheese in the cheese wheel, so the kid must complete a word before the wheel is complete.

Checkers is an easy game for 6 year-olds and older, and Putt-Putt makes a good teacher, one who can play with the child for hours and hours. As with all the games on this disc, there are four skill levels. Beginners can beat Putt-Putt quite easily until their own prowess increases. Then, their computer opponent can be "smartened up" to provide more of a challenge.

What would a children's game pack be like without a Concentration-style matching game? Putt-Putt adds his encouragement as children attempt to match pictures of ladybugs, ice cream cones, balloons, pencils, and other objects in a 4 x 8 grid at the hardest level.

The first computerized Tic-Tac-Toe game we ever saw was at Chicago's famous

Museum of Science and Industry in the early 1960s. Although this simple game is a trivial exercise for a computer, kids like the challenge, and Putt-Putt is nice enough to offer an "easy" level, at which he makes mistakes (same as the kid!) and so can be beaten. He's impossible to beat at the hardest level, but still is a good sport about the game.

Six great games for the 4- to 7-year-old (and up), including Tic-Tac-Toe and Checkers.

Kids can solve one of six different circus puzzles with a few clicks of the mouse, or create their own pinball machine and then play it, in other activities included on this CD-ROM. Any of them will keep the child occupied for hours. While the other Putt-Putt discs can be played by children as young as three, most of these are better suited for the 4- to 7-year-old set. Adults will even enjoy playing Checkers (if they don't mind using pieces with eyes on them), and the do-it-yourself pinball game can be fun for older folks, too.

Putt-Putt makes a challenging opponent for a game of checkers in *Putt-Putt's Fun Pack.*

Putt-Putt Goes to the Moon

Here comes another glowing review about a Humongous Junior Adventure! Can this publisher do anything except put out some of the best CD-ROMs on the market for younger children?

The scenario begins as Putt-Putt visits a Fireworks Factory owned by his friend Mr. Firebird. The child can use the mouse to click various items in the factory with a puffy, over-sized arrow cursor. Clicking a window pane opens the window, allowing a butterfly to flutter in. Soon, Putt-Putt's puppy (which he adopted in his previous adventure, *Putt-Putt Joins the Parade*) leaps at the butterfly, instead pressing a forbidden lever that launches Putt-Putt on a skyrocket to the Moon. To return home, Putt-Putt has to find missing rocket parts and 10 Moon Crystals through various adventures on Luna.

Putt-Putt Goes to the Moon is available in both floppy disk and CD-ROM versions, but there are some advantages to buying the CD-ROM: the game can run directly from the disc, requiring only a little hard disk space. Both require an IBM PC with multimedia capabilities (*Putt-Putt* runs from DOS, but functions just fine under Microsoft Windows), or Macintosh LC III or later system with 256 color video display, and 2MB of RAM. The version that comes on floppies requires 13MB of free hard disk space for program files.

Only one mode is available in the PC version, but *Putt-Putt* can run using one of several different screen sizes on a Macintosh, depending on the speed of the system. "Small" and "medium" are best for slow systems, those with small monitors, or with only 256KB of video memory. The "large"

and "smoothing" modes use as much of your screen as possible, but can reduce the speed at which the program runs if you don't have a fast Quadra, LC III, Performa, or (dare we say it) Power Macintosh model. Sometimes, turning off INITs and extensions can speed up the animation of the program a little.

Another Putt-Putt adventure for young children, with a voyage to the Moon and back with a new friend.

On the Moon, Putt-Putt soon lands in trouble, as a bridge collapses and throws him into a puddle of moon goo. When the child clicks the horn button on Putt-Putt's dashboard, Rover, a lonely lunar terrain vehicle, comes to the rescue. Abandoned by one of the Apollo moon missions, Rover, like Putt-Putt, just wants to go home. Together they perform good deeds for the Moon People while assembling the pieces of the rocket needed to return to Earth.

As with *Putt-Putt Joins the Parade*, even the youngest child will be able to complete the story-adventure by randomly moving Putt-Putt from scene to scene and clicking various objects found in each. As he moves around the Moon, Putt-Putt encounters a host of other extraterrestrial characters, who help him along with advice, refreshments,

Rating: ◎ ◎ ◎ ◎

Publisher Name: **Humongous**

Software Requirements: **MPC/Macintosh**

Suggested Retail Price: **$49.95**

and the odd jobs he needs to earn his rocket pieces. (The plot may be familiar, but kids don't notice; in fact, they may be happier that this disc bears more than a passing resemblance to the first version.)

Putt-Putt's "user interface" was obviously designed for curious preschoolers who have mastered the mouse or joystick. No keyboard commands are required (except Command+Q to exit). Parents can access the remaining keyboard commands to turn sound on/off (Command+M and Command+D for music and dialog, respectively) pause or restart the game (space bar or Command+P), or change the sound volume (square bracket keys). Games in progress can be saved to disk and resumed later.

Although a child can perform the various deeds required to assemble the rocket in a different order each time, the game doesn't vary much each time it is played, and kids like it better that way.

Among the discs that very young children can enjoy, *Putt-Putt Goes To the Moon* is one of the best.

Putt-Putt Joins the Parade

Rating:

Publisher Name:
Humongous Entertainment, Inc.

Software Requirements:
MPC-1/Macintosh

Suggested Retail Price: **$44.95**

Children aged three and up are entranced by Putt-Putt, the little purple convertible with a real child's voice and the appetites and inclinations of a humanized automobile. The adventures of Putt-Putt, who likes motor oil on his Tire-O's cereal, form the basis of this easy—but involved—preschoolers' game.

The story unfolds one bright morning in Putt-Putt's garage-home, populated by animated objects and filled with sounds. The child can use the mouse to click various items in the garage with a puffy, over-sized arrow cursor. Clicking a curtain pull-cord reveals a lively frog perched on a shelf, which can then be made to snake out a long tongue to snare an annoying fly. Putt-Putt will grab and eat his bowl of Tire-Os when you've doused them with oil. Click the button of Putt-Putt's radio, and you'll hear a radio news report about a big pet parade in town.

That launches Putt-Putt on his quest to find a pet to display, earn the entry fee and enough funds for a car wash, and, finally, join the parade. Even the youngest child will be able to complete the story-adventure by randomly moving Putt-Putt from scene to scene and clicking various objects found in each.

As he moves through the town, Putt-Putt encounters a host of other characters, who help him along by loaning a lawnmower, employing Putt-Putt to perform chores, and giving him a spiffy car wash.

Putt-Putt's "user interface" was obviously designed for curious preschoolers who have mastered the mouse or a joystick. No keyboard commands at all are required (except Alt+Q or Command+Q to exit), but the game can be played with the numeric keypad's cursor keys in a pinch. Parents can access the remaining keyboard commands to turn sound on/off, pause or restart the game, or change the sound volume.

Although a child can perform the various deeds required to join the parade in a different order each time, the game doesn't vary much from play to play. Those with young children will know that this is a definite plus! The same preschoolers who want to hear a story repeated over and over love to work their way through Putt-Putt's universe again and again, seeking out familiar situations they find entertaining.

Adults may find the repetitive music and sound effects in *Putt-Putt Joins the Parade* annoying, but, again, kids are oblivious as they play along.

Available in both Macintosh and DOS versions, this disc was the first in a series from Humongous that now includes *Putt-Putt Goes to the Moon* and *Fatty Bear* (for older kids). The DOS version runs just fine under Microsoft Windows, although it's sometimes tripped up by a Windows bug that reports the sound card is already in use when it's not. You may have to relaunch Putt-Putt, or even exit Windows and try again. Your kids won't mind.

It's tough finding CD-ROMs that young children can enjoy, and *Putt-Putt Joins the Parade* is one of the best available. The graphics are more cartoon-like than photorealistic, but that's exactly what kids want and expect.

Putt-Putt is an adorable purple convertible who leads your child through an adventure.

Race the Clock for Windows

*R*ace The Clock CD for Windows is a Concentration-type game with a clever use of full-motion video instead of static pictures for matching pairs. Children can work with increasingly complex grids, match sets of videos, videos and words, or just pairs of words.

Race the Clock *is a Concentration-type matching pairs game that uses full-motion videos and sound to spice up the old favorite.*

The player uncovers squares one at a time and tries to match them up before the time runs out. The program tries to increase matching, word, and memory skills for children 3 to 12 years old.

This game can be played alone or with a friend. There are nine levels of play, and three different types of puzzles. Uncover a square and see an animated action word, like "melt", with a mini-movie picture showing an ice cube melting. Uncover another square to try and find another ice cube melting. Each of the many animated verbs is a mini movie of real people and/or real objects. Along with the animation of the word "melt," it is also pronounced with voices so that small children that can't read yet can also play.

The second type of matching puzzle is Picture/Word, in which you try to match a word, such as "wink," with the video showing the actual action. In the Word/Word version all the words are spoken for you. All of these puzzles can be played with English words or Spanish words. When the Spanish option is on, everything is in Spanish, all of the button labels and the words are spoken in Spanish. Even the help files are in Spanish. This is a very nice option to teach young and old a little Spanish.

You can choose grids of 12, 20, or 30 squares, depending on the child's skill level.

Rating: ◉ ◉ ◉ 1/2

Publisher Name:
Mind Play

Software Requirements: **MPC**

Suggested Retail Price: **$59.95**

The hard part is to remember where you've seen the other half of the match. To win, you must uncover all the squares before "Ticker the Clock" runs out of time. The amount of time you get is generous (seven to eight minutes) until you get to the more difficult levels, then your time may be only a few minutes. As the matches are made, a cartoon is revealed little by little. Finish the puzzle and you have revealed the whole cartoon.

With the two-player option, each person takes turns trying to make a match. If one gets a match, he or she may continue until he can not find another. There is no provision to personalize the two-player mode with names. In addition, the program doesn't keep score to see how many matches each player has made. In a weird stroke, the last player to make a match wins the game, no matter how many matches the other player has made.

The help option is an animated and spoken help file so that children do not have to read it. *Race the Clock* can keep even the smallest child's attention for a long time, even adults will be amazed, and will want to try their skill. The animation in the mini movies is fascinating to watch and very well presented. A sound card is a must. All and all it is a very good program.

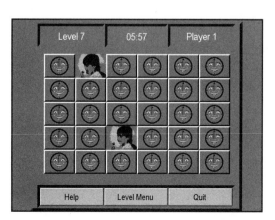

Animated movies—not still images—must be matched to win *Race the Clock*.

Rick Ribbit: Adventures in Early Learning

Rating: 🔘 🔘 🔘 1/2

Publisher Name:
Tadpole Productions

Software Requirements: **MPC**

Suggested Retail Price: **$49.95**

My kids didn't really get proficient with computers until they were about three years old—but then, they didn't have Rick Ribbit to play with. This disc is one of the few in this book that can be used and enjoyed by children as young as two. Even the Putt-Putt series, beloved of the pre-preschool set, demands more highly developed motor skills. I'd hazard a guess that children who can't talk very well will still be able to have fun with Rick Ribbit.

Rick Ribbit is a colorful frog who leads the child through various adventures in early learning. They can explore ideas like "over," "under," and "through" with simple graphics and pacing that remind you of a slow-moving Sesame Street. Although a mouse can be used, most functions can be carried out by pressing the cursor arrow keys and Enter. So, just about any kid will be able to maneuver Rick Ribbit throughout his world. Since Rick talks to you, there's no mandatory reading involved. All the controls are designed for young users: even when using the mouse, the cursor can only be moved to a limited number of places, each representing a valid move. There's no hunting around for the "hot" spots with this disc.

At the beginning of the program, Rick appears at the door of his home, and three arrow icons show the directions the child can choose to explore. To the right is a tricky water obstacle course that Rick can swim through. From time to time he encounters things like giant clams, submerged autos, and fishermen's nets. Rick pauses while the child selects an up or down arrow icon (go over or beneath the object) or a straight-ahead arrow that means full steam ahead. Happily, whichever choice the child makes, Rick manages to get past the obstacle with no trouble. (Although we were hesitant to send him through the water treatment plant. He made it okay, if a bit frazzled.)

Children as young as two can enjoy playing with Rick Ribbit as they learn counting, reading, and other skills

Inside Rick's house, the child can play with shapes, numbers, letters, and other learning games found in the pantry, or toddle off to the bedroom for a nap—actually a counting game disguised as a dream—or explore the dresser for some quick costume changes. Older kids can visit the nearby swamp, where Rick hops from rock to rock to spell out simple words. The number of rocks in the swamp indicate the number of letters in the words, so several difficulty levels are available.

The sprightly rag-time style music makes this disc a joy to play with. Don't be put off by the coarse graphics in *Rick Ribbit*. They actually are better for very young kids than complex, more realistic images that can be difficult to interpret and more distracting. The pictures are on a par with the Sticky Bear programs I use to teach kindergarteners and first graders at my son's elementary school (one day a week, only! My nerves aren't that strong!). In fact, I wish we had programs of this quality available for the ancient Apple IIes used at the school.

Although various levels make *Rick Ribbit* challenging for slightly older kids, I wouldn't recommend this disc for those much older than five or six, except as a language study tool. You see, Rick Ribbit can speak to you in English, French, Italian, or Spanish. Outside these multilingual capabilities, even the reading exercises are pitched at a level suitable for kindergarteners or below.

Shelley Duvall's It's A Bird's Life

Shelley Duvall first burst on the public consciousness as the gangly, platform-shoed groupie in Robert Altman's mid-1970s classic film, *Nashville*. Since then, she's starred as Olive Oyl in *Popeye*, and performed in other films. However, Duvall's most sterling accomplishment has been a series of wonderful fairy tail programs she's produced for children, all featuring top Hollywood stars in leading or cameo performances. Now she's produced, written, and narrated this entertaining and educational disc for kids.

In 60 colorful interactive pages, Duvall helps kids improve reading skills as they play with colorful animations. Kids can read along, learning the pronunciation and definition of words, and watch digital movies about geography, weather, birds, and the rain forest.

There are 11 original songs in all, 400 word definitions, and 26 puzzles, games, and other activities. Shelley is accompanied by a band of lovable parrots as they roam from Los Angeles to the Amazon Forest and back. The story unfolds when a fire destroys the home of Shelley and the birds, which immediately "fly south" for safety. Each of the birds, with names like Pearlie, Humpty, Mowgli, Scarlet, and Gorby(!), have personalities of their own.

Kids can listen to the narration or play on each page by clicking objects and icons. Click a butterfly, and it might flutter away.

Rating: ◉ ◉ ◉

Publisher Name:
Sanctuary Woods

Software Requirements:
MPC/Macintosh

Suggested Retail Price: $39.95

Click flowers and they bloom. Nudge a toucan, and it munches away on some berries. You can always return to the main menu by clicking the bird cage icon.

The games include jigsaw puzzles and other adventures. *It's a Bird's Life* is the sort of disc that children will want to play again and again. Aimed at ages 3 and up, it's a disc that will appeal to preschoolers and primary students alike.

Shelley Duvall takes your kids on an exciting tour to the Amazon Rain Forest in this educational and fun disc that teaches reading and other skills.

Humpty
Humpty is a male yellow-naped Amazon parrot, the ever-busy class clown. He's funny and smart, but he sometimes makes mistakes. He is young, but a gifted talker and comic singer. He enjoys clowning around, but there is a gentler, shyer side to him that makes us all love him.

Meet Shelley Duvall's animated parrots as you journey from Los Angeles to the Amazon Rain Forest.

Sitting on the Farm

Rating:

Publisher Name:
Sanctuary Woods

Software Requirements:
MPC/Macintosh

Suggested Retail Price: **$59.95**

Believe me, this disc is much better than its title. Somehow, if I were going to create an interactive story about some pretty amazing things around a barnyard, I'd give it a more animated title than *Sitting on the Farm*. Because this disc was adapted from an original story in French, I can only conclude that the title loses something in translation.

Actually, *Sitting on the Farm* is the topic of this amusing tale, a story told in rhyme and spiced by excellent illustrations. A little girl sits down to eat, finds a spider on her knee, and continually relocates her repast around the farm, only to find larger and larger animals on her lap. We can't "bear" to tell you what she ends up with!

With interactive books, a lot of the charm comes from how good the story is, so it's fortunate that this one has an entertaining storyline. However, the multimedia implementation is pretty good, too. The child can play in Listen-Along mode: the story is read a line at a time, with the pages and pictures turning automatically. There's also a Read-Along mode, which allows the boy or girl to read the story from the screen and, if they like, record their narration on the hard disk with a microphone plugged into the sound card.

In Read-Along mode, the child can click a page map button to go directly to any page of the 14 pages in the story, or click a movie camera to see an animation. There are hidden hotspots on-screen that can be clicked to get various amusing responses. The cursor turns into a word balloon whenever the child discovers an active area of the page. Young children don't have to hunt to find the fun parts.

There's also a sing-a-long version that allows listening to an instrumental track (various instruments can be turned on or off so that you can play along), or the kid can sing along using the microphone. In Write-Along mode, the child can choose from six settings for a new story of their own. Kids only have to fill in blanks, so they can be introduced to writing in small, manageable steps.

Sitting on the Farm has some hidden benefits, too. It comes in English, Spanish, and French versions on the same disc, so, coupled with the recording feature and ability to click individual words to have them spoken, it becomes an excellent tool for practicing foreign language study.

A charming story, told in English, French, and Spanish, filled with good humor and multimedia options for the young reader and writer.

Given the modest list price of this disc, the excellent story, and its triple-threat English/Spanish/French implementations, it would make an excellent choice for any young student who needs to polish up his or her writing or reading skills in any of the three languages.

First a bug appears on the little girl's knee—and that's only the beginning of her troubles!

The Sleeping Beauty

Few things match the feeling of listening to a storyteller practice that ancient art. *The Sleeping Beauty*, by Ebook, Inc., is the next best thing. It's a combination of text, imagery, a little animation, and sound that carries the fairy tale genre into a new realm. That feeling of listening to a familiar story, told by a pleasant-voiced narrator, never quite loses its appeal. There's a little childhood left in the oldest person and this CD catches and holds his attention.

The Sleeping Beauty is an old tale, beloved for centuries. This CD-ROM brings it forth yet again in a form designed to attract today's computer-literate young reader/viewer. The story is ancient, the presentation contemporary. The concept is delightful, the execution well done. There are a few flaws but none are fatal.

Using MicroSoft's Multimedia Viewer, *The Sleeping Beauty* lets you page through the text with mouse clicks. Icons on the pages invoke sound files or audibly read the whole page. The typical Windows green-highlighted and underlined words invoke a dictionary to help readers with unfamiliar words. Pastel illustrations, some animated to a small degree, by Judith K. Jones, who also retold and narrated the text, appear on certain pages, greatly enhancing the experience. The table of contents permits viewing the pictures or hearing the sound files independent of reading the text.

The color-enhanced line-art and pastel illustrations are lovely. The princess is suitably beautiful, the King and Queen suitably dignified, and the evil fairy, Nightshade, quite suitably ominous (without being too frightening). It can't be easy to illustrate a story, stay faithful to the text, and avoid overdoing it, crowding out imagination. Judith Jones manages nicely under all three constraints.

The theme music is pleasant but repetitious, most of its examples simply being instrumental variations on Sleeping Beauty's Song. Only Rosealba's and Nightshade's Songs vary significantly from the basic theme. Although it is pretty music, the same progression of notes, over and over, even for the heralds' trumpets, doesn't wear well. Nearly every included sound icon calls the base theme. It probably won't bother younger users, but an adult helper or involuntary listener might soon feel a small grating upon the ears. That irritation is certainly not exclusive to this medium or this CD. It is endemic in games, but another release would benefit from more musical variety.

The dictionary is, well, skeletal. Some of the definitions seem to suit a high-school level readership more than the younger folks for whom fairy tales exist. Longer definitions using simpler words would be better. Young beginning readers might benefit from having the dictionary pronounce each word, too. There is plenty of space left on the disc for such additions. Ebook has a potentially marvelous educational tool here, especially for beginning or handicapped readers. If they are aiming at an educational market, targeting their help functions more closely would certainly help.

Overall, *The Sleeping Beauty* adds a dimension to story telling. It's a fun CD to run, with beautiful illustrations, good narration, and nice music. The younger set will hardly notice the story sneaks a little education into the mix.

Rating: 💿 💿 💿

Publisher: **Ebook, Inc.**

Software Requirements: **MPC/Macintosh**

Suggested Retail Price: **$29.95**

Sleeping Beauty is a well-told tale with excellent graphics.

"Not so beautiful as you, my treasure," said the King.

Sound It Out Land 2

Rating:

Publisher: **Conexus**

Software Requirements: **MPC**

Suggested Retail Price: **$49.95**

There's a little more style than substance in *Sound It Out Land 2*, but that just means it will be easier to get your kids to use this subversive reading readiness tool. Like Sesame Street and Electric Company, this disc uses eye-catching graphics and fast-moving activities that beg your child to participate.

The individual discs in the Sound It Out Land *series take kids from letter recognition to reading entire sentences in easy steps.*

The lessons aren't complex, nor are they very long. There's just enough learning here to help the youngsters read a little better before a new song breaks out to liven things up a little.

Sound It Out Land uses phonics to help young readers work out words for themselves. The disc we reviewed is one of three available. *Sound it Out Land 1* introduces readers to letter sounds and simple three-letter words. This disc explores vowel sounds and consonant blends (th, sh, and so on) that are used to make four- and five-letter words and complete sentences. The final disc in the series, *Sound It Out Land 3*, tackles more complex sounds and words in whole sentences.

The game is configured like an amusement park, complete with a tram to take players from area to area. Four characters await with their own exercises and games. There's Reading Robot, Vowel Owl, Sing Along Sam, the magician, and Toucan Read. A light bulb "help" button, and options to turn songs or games on and off are also available from the main menu screen.

In each area, the child is asked to match up words and sounds, or sing along with one of six original songs on the disc. The CD audio sound is very impressive: the swooping jet sound that ping pongs from the right speaker to the left when the tram takes off for a new area is worth the price of admission to this park.

All six songs can also be played in an ordinary audio CD player (be sure and skip track one unless you enjoy the screech of digital programming "noise").

The graphics are first-rate, too. *Sound It Out Land 2* really does closely resemble a television show in its appearance and pacing. Because that's exactly what your kids are used to, they will take to this CD-ROM naturally, making it that much easier for the disc to do its job.

Sound It Out Land is an amusement park of reading activities.

The Tortoise and the Hare

What's the formula for creating the perfect children's CD-ROM program? Start with a familiar story, say a fairy tale or fable that kids have loved for generations. (You can also substitute new tales that children *will* love for the next 100 years or so.) Illustrate the story with vivid, full-color graphics, and hide some multimedia animated surprises on every page. Add lots of humor, and make it possible for kids to explore at their own speed. To keep parents happy, sneak in some learning exercises that will actually teach the kids something in a painless way.

Now, price this CD-ROM at $39.95 or less so that everyone can afford a copy. Make it available on both PC and Macintosh platforms. That should do it—but wait! There's more! Throw in a real, printed book of the story so kids can enjoy the tale at bedtime without venturing down to the home computer. If you want to be certain everything's perfect, put the name Broderbund Living Book on the box.

The Tortoise and the Hare is the fourth Broderbund entry reviewed in this chapter. This one has the same level of excellent artwork found in *Arthur's Teacher Trouble* or *The New Kid on the Block*. There are interactive pages that contain the text of the story with many active "hot spots" that can be clicked to trigger humorous animations.

It's amazing how much fun Broderbund has packed into 12 pages. Each page is a mini-story in its own right, and the developers have gone far beyond Aesop's 2,500-year-old fable to modernize it. That's quite a challenge considering the thousands of times this story has been retold in print and animation.

One new feature is the narrator, a bird named Simon, who flits from page to page to read the text associated with each screen. The child can click an icon or individual words to repeat the narration. However, individual characters on the page can also be selected to activate their own additions to the story. For example, as the Tortoise sits along the edge of a stream listening to the song of the birds, you can click each of the birds and other creatures to hear them make some comment and play their own instrumental part individually. When you're finished with the page and click the "next page" arrow, all the animals play a little tune in unison.

On other pages, you find belly-flopping frogs (who exclaim "ouch!" on landing), an adventuresome dragonfly, and other interesting characters Aesop never dreamed of. Kids can jump to any page by clicking the number icon at the bottom of the screen, and then accessing the Options page.

The Tortoise and the Hare can be played in either English or Spanish. This isn't just a dual-soundtrack treatment, either: there are

Rating: ◉ ◉ ◉ ◉

Publisher Name: Broderbund

Software Requirements: MPC/Macintosh

Suggested Retail Price: $39.95

two separate versions. In the Spanish edition, the Welcome mat in front of the Tortoise's home is replaced by a Bienvenidos mat, and the voices of the title characters are replaced by two humorous native Spanish speakers with distinct personalities.

You can't go wrong with any of the Broderbund Living Books, and this is one of the best. The series is varied enough that comparing them is a little like gauging apples against oranges, but there's a bushel of fun in this one no matter what kind of fruit it may be.

The Tortoise and the Hare do battle on the racetrack of life in this interactive book.

● This is the story of the Tortoise and the Hare. The Tortoise was a friendly fellow who moved at his own slow pace. The Hare was a busy person who was always on the move.

Victor Vector & Yondo: The Cyberplasm Formula

Rating:

Publisher Name:
Sanctuary Woods

Software Requirements:
MPC/Macintosh

Suggested Retail Price: **$39.95**

*T*he Cyberplasm Formula is the fourth adventure of flat-coiffed Victor Vector and his awesome dog companion, Yondo. In this episode, the duo is charged with saving the life of their boss, the cybernetic Curator of the Museum of Fantastic Phenomena. The head man's supply of cyberplasm has run out, and apparently not even the pharmacists of the future can read his doctor's handwriting well enough to refill his prescription. (I made that part up.)

Victor and Yondo travel through time to discover the formula for this life-giving substance, searching through ruined city streets of the technologically starved era just prior to the Great Crash. Talk about back to the future: Victor and Yondo go from their own time period back to the 21st century for this adventure! The superheroes outwit RoboCorp guards, invade the secret laboratory, and return to the present (his present, our future) to save the Curator, and defeat their arch enemy Ram Axis.

Note that Victor outwits, rather than outfights, his opponents. There is action,

but no actual killing of any creature or intelligent machine. This is a non-violent, glorified comic book that both parents and kids will love. It has 80 interactive pages, a stirring soundtrack, and graphics drawn by a former Spider Man comics illustrator. Inside the pages are skill testing games and activities.

Kids move through the pages by placing the mouse on a "hot spot" in the individual screens. They can go from building to building, find and consume food, explore inside apartments, and perform other actions. Some games must be played to move on. They include a simple Simon-type game, in which the child must remember a sequence of colors and then reenter the code by clicking a control panel. There are also rooms that must be visited in a particular order, and a secret combination lock to be deciphered.

The controls are all easy to use, involving nothing more than clicking icons at the side of the screen. Yondo and the Curator provide tips that help children solve the puzzles. Parents will enjoy this game, too, and may pick up some information in spite of themselves, as topics like the history of robotics are woven seamlessly into the storyline.

Victor's other adventures include *The Vampire's Coffin*, *The Hypnotic Harp*, and *The Last Dinosaur Egg* (also reviewed in this chapter). If your kids like this game, you'll want to pick up the others in the series. Don't be surprised to see a cartoon show and a conventional comic book built around this best-selling CD-ROM character. A single disc works on both PCs and Macintoshes, so, at $39.95 (or less) this game is a dual-platform bargain.

Victor Vector is the nonviolent superhero of this animated comic book.

Victor Vector and Yondo: The Last Dinosaur Egg

This sequel to the original Sanctuary Woods comic book/ game disc represents a change of direction for Victor Vector (sorry about that pun!). This latest adventure takes Victor and his dog Yondo on a wild chase through the Precambrian Era to the Cretaceous Period, searching for an egg from the biggest, meanest, and most publicized of all saurians: T. Rex. This interactive story uses animation and a wealth of on-screen controls to let you manage Victor's actions throughout.

Victor Vector and Yondo: The Last Dinosaur Egg *is the second edition of a series of adventures for this interactive comic-book-style hero.*

You play the role of Archivist for the 22nd-century Museum of Fantastic Pheonomena, and send agents Victor and Yondo back in time. You must help them counter malfunctioning equipment, teeming jungles, and hungry dinosaurs, along with a more futuristic villain: Ram Axis, who has designs of his own on the Tyrannosaurus.

Aimed at children aged 8 and up, this game uses comic book-style artwork, but allows the player to choose the direction the characters take through the storyline. In effect, the child becomes a movie director, more or less following the script, but choosing the order in which scenes play out and affecting some decisions. If this were a movie, though, it would be rated G, despite all the action and excitement. Nothing excessively scary happens to Victor or his faithful dog.

Movement throughout the game is carried out simply by clicking the areas of the screen you want to move to. As in any adventure game, Victor can pick up objects he finds along the way, and then use (or eat) them when the time is appropriate. On-

Rating: ◉ ◉ ◉

Publisher Name:
Sanctuary Woods

Software Requirements:
MPC/Macintosh

Suggested Retail Price: $39.95

screen controls let you access Yondo's data-collar for some helpful background information. Kids enjoy this game, and its gentle nature (Sanctuary Woods deliberately choose a non-technological name for its company) is a pleasure for parents.

Victor Vector and his digital dog Yondo start their adventure by deciding whether to attend a briefing, or skip right ahead to the action.

Additional CD-ROM Titles

Title: 20,000 Leagues Under the Sea
Suggested Retail Price: $69.00
Publisher: New Media Schoolhouse, Inc
Platform: Macintosh
Description: Jules Verne's classic tale, for kids.

Title: A Long Hard Day on the Ranch
Suggested Retail Price: $59.95
Publisher: Discis
Platform: Macintosh
Description: A story about what happens to little boys who exaggerate.

Title: A Silly Noisy House
Suggested Retail Price: $59.95
Publisher: Voyager
Platform: Macintosh
Description: A children's story about a raucous home.

Title: A World of Animals
Suggested Retail Price: $79.95
Publisher: Discis
Platform: Macintosh
Description: Butterlies, spiders, farm animals, whales, other animals.

Title: A World of Fun
Suggested Retail Price: $49.95
Publisher: Queue
Platform: MPC/Macintosh
Description: Fun games for kids.

Title: A World of Plants
Suggested Retail Price: $79.95
Publisher: Discis

Platform: Macintosh
Description: What is a seed, parts of a plant, why are plants important?

Title: ABC Songbook
Suggested Retail Price: $39.95
Publisher: Gazelle
Platform: Macintosh
Description: Accompany charming characters in song and story to learn the alphabet and basic reading skills. For ages 3–8.

Title: Adventures in Fern Hollow
Suggested Retail Price: $49.95
Publisher: Queue
Platform: MPC/Macintosh
Description: Kid adventures in learning.

Title: Adventures of Pinocchio
Suggested Retail Price: $69.00
Publisher: New Media Schoolhouse
Platform: Macintosh
Description: Narrated fairy tale, with quiz and games.

Title: Adventures of Willy Beamish
Suggested Retail Price: $69.95
Publisher: Sierra Online
Platform: MPC
Description: Adventures of a foul-mouthed little kid. Not for younger children.

Title: Aesop's Fables
Suggested Retail Price: $29.95
Publisher: Discis

Platform: MPC/Macintosh
Description: The 2500-year-old fables, retold in interactive form.

Title: Aesop's Fables
Suggested Retail Price: $29.95
Publisher: EBook
Platform: MPC
Description: Hey, after 2500 years, they have to be in the public domain, right?

Title: Aladdin and the Wonderful Lamp
Suggested Retail Price: $39.95
Publisher: Electronic Arts
Platform: MPC/Macintosh
Description: If Disney can make a buck off this old story, why not Electronic Arts?

Title: Alice: An Interactive Museum
Suggested Retail Price: $99.00
Publisher: East-West
Platform: MPC/Macintosh
Description: An off-beat tour through an interactive museum. Animation used to bring the exhibits to life.

Title: Amanda Stories CD-ROM
Suggested Retail Price: $59.00
Publisher: Voyager
Platform: Macintosh
Description: Charming stories for young children. One of the best discs we didn't get a chance to review.

Title: Animal Alphabet
Suggested Retail Price: $59.00
Publisher: Sony

Platform: MPC
Description: Youngsters learn their letters through animated cartoons and spoken text.

Title: Animal Fun
Suggested Retail Price: $49.95
Publisher: Queue
Platform: MPC/Macintosh
Description: Learn about animals from this disc through games.

Title: Animal Tales
Suggested Retail Price: $49.95
Publisher: Spectrum HoloByte
Platform: MPC/Macintosh
Description: Animal stories for young children.

Title: Animals & How They Grow
Suggested Retail Price: $79.95
Publisher: Discis Knowledge Research
Platform: Macintosh
Description: How mammals, reptiles, and birds reach maturity.

Title: Barbie and Her Magical House
Suggested Retail Price: $44.95
Publisher: Hi Tech Expressions
Platform: MPC/Macintosh
Description: This interactive adventure welcomes you to Barbie's home to visit with her and her friends. Different puzzles and educational activities in each room.

Title: Barney Bear Goes to School
Suggested Retail Price: $39.00
Publisher: Free Spirit Software
Platform: MPC
Description: An oldie but goodie as Barney Bear goes off to class and plays some great games. Not sophisticated, but preschoolers love this disc.

Title: Beauty and the Beast
Suggested Retail Price: $39.00
Publisher: EBook
Platform: MPC

Description: Famous fairy tale with animation. We miss Linda Hamilton.

Title: Beauty and the Beast
Suggested Retail Price: $69.00
Publisher: New Media Schoolhouse, Inc.
Platform: Macintosh
Description: Still no Linda Hamilton, but a good retelling of this tale.

Title: Berenstain Bears: Learning at Home
Suggested Retail Price: $39.95
Publisher: Compton's NewMedia
Platform: MPC
Description: Join the Bear Family in learning the important household lessons that every child needs to know.

Title: Betty Boop
Suggested Retail Price: $29.95
Publisher: Chestnut
Platform: MPC
Description: Classic public domain cartoons of this saucy character.

Title: Bible Lands, Bible Stories
Suggested Retail Price: $49.95
Publisher: Con*text Systems, Inc.
Platform: MPC
Description: Old and New Testament stories and background.

Title: Big Anthony's Mixed-Up Magic
Suggested Retail Price: $39.95
Publisher: Magnum Design
Platform: MPC/Macintosh
Description: Ages 5 to 10 will enjoy the music, games and magic tricks of this interactive story. Another great disc we wish we'd had a chance to review.

Title: Bugs Bunny
Suggested Retail Price: $29.95
Publisher: Chestnut
Platform: MPC
Description: More public domain cartoons from the Warner Brothers hare.

Title:. Caricaturas Classicas
Suggested Retail Price: $49.95
Publisher: Chestnut
Platform: MPC
Description: Cartoon favorites with a Spanish soundtrack. Great enjoyment for the child learning or wanting to learn Spanish.

Title: Children's Treasury of Stories, Nursery Rhymes and Songs
Suggested Retail Price: $49.95
Publisher: Queue
Platform: MPC/Macintosh
Description: Dozens of favorite stories, none of them Grimm.

Title: Cinderella
Suggested Retail Price: $29.95
Publisher: Discis
Platform: MPC/Macintosh
Description: Old story with a modern twist (not Oliver).

Title: ColoringBook
Suggested Retail Price: $39.95
Publisher: Softbit
Platform: MPC/Macintosh
Description: Lots of pictures to color.

Title: Countdown
Suggested Retail Price: $29.95
Publisher: Voyager
Platform: Macintosh
Description: Three mathematical games that let children adjust the level to always keep math fun!

Title: Creation Stories
Suggested Retail Price: $49.99
Publisher: Time Warner
Platform: MPC
Description: Legends from 60 cultures on how the world began, for young children.

Title: Creepy Crawlies
Suggested Retail Price: $69.00
Publisher: Sony

Platform: MPC/Macintosh
Description: Scary stories for scary kids.

Title: Curious George Learns the Alphabet
Suggested Retail Price: $49.95
Publisher: Queue
Platform: Macintosh
Description: Animated and narrated story, with games, involving George and the ABCs.

Title: Cute n'Cuddlies
Suggested Retail Price: $69.00
Publisher: Sony
Platform: MPC/Macintosh
Description: Cute animals and stuff in fun stories and activities.

Title: Designasaurus II
Suggested Retail Price: $39.95
Publisher: Compton's NewMedia
Platform: MPC
Description: Make your own dinosaur!

Title: Don Quixote
Suggested Retail Price: $39.95
Publisher: EBook
Platform: MPC/Macintosh
Description: Interactive story of Cervantes' classic tale of knighthood in Spain.

Title: Eagle Eye Mysteries: Jake and Jennifer in London
Suggested Retail Price: $49.95
Publisher: Electronic Arts
Platform: MPC/Macintosh
Description: Hardy Boys updated to an eagle-eyed brother and sister.

Title: Educational Games for Young Children
Suggested Retail Price: $49.95
Publisher: Queue
Platform: Macintosh
Description: Education programs for the early learner.

Title: Favorite Fairy Tales
Suggested Retail Price: $49.95
Publisher: Queue
Platform: MPC/Macintosh
Description: More classic fairy tales in multimedia format.

Title: Flash Cards on Video
Suggested Retail Price: $29.95
Publisher: Chestnut
Platform: MPC
Description: Your kids will learn in a flash.

Title: Fun Around the House
Suggested Retail Price: $49.95
Publisher: Queue
Platform: MPC/Macintosh
Description: Fun things to do using only household items.

Title: Fun Around Town
Suggested Retail Price: $49.95
Publisher: Queue
Platform: MPC/Macintosh
Description: Having fun around your city.

Title: Fun At Work
Suggested Retail Price: $49.95
Publisher: Queue
Platform: MPC/Macintosh
Description: Fun at the workplace.

Title: Greatest Children's Stories Ever Told
Suggested Retail Price: $49.95
Publisher: Queue
Platform: MPC
Description: Another Queue collection of stories on disc.

Title: Hawaii High: The Mystery of the Tiki
Suggested Retail Price: $39.95
Publisher: Sanctuary Woods
Platform: MPC/Macintosh
Description: Young detectives solve crimes in exotic settings.

Title: Heather Hits Her First Home Run
Suggested Retail Price: $29.95
Publisher: Discis
Platform: MPC/Macintosh
Description: Heather slams one out of the park in this tale.

Title: Hugo's House of Horrors
Suggested Retail Price: $39.95
Publisher: Chestnut
Platform: MPC
Description: Non-violent fun in adventures and mystery with little Hugo.

Title: Interactive Storytime Vol 1/2/3
Suggested Retail Price: $49.95
Publisher: Multimedia Corp.
Platform: MPC
Description: Children's stories in interactive format.

Title: Kaa's Hunting
Suggested Retail Price: $39.95
Publisher: EBook
Platform: MPC/Macintosh
Descrpton: Great version of a tale from Rudyard Kipling's Jungle Book.

Title: Karaoke Kids
Suggested Retail Price: $49.95
Publisher: Sirius
Platform: MPC
Description: Twelve popular children's songs for your youngster to sing. Better them than me.

Title: Kid's Zoo
Suggested Retail Price: $79.95
Publisher: Knowledge Adventures
Platform: MPC
Description: An interactive encyclopedia for ages 3 and up. Introduces youngsters to animals through their babies.

Title: Kid Works 2
Suggested Retail Price: $59.95
Publisher: Davidson
Platform: MPC/Macintosh

Description: More kid's activities for learning.

Title: Kids' Studio
Suggested Retail Price: $59.95
Publisher: CyberPuppy
Platform: Macintosh
Description: Kids' art studio for drawing original works.

Title: Kids in History: How Children Lived in the 20th Century
Suggested Retail Price: $39.98, MPI Multimedia
Platform: MPC/Macintosh
Description: Interact with youngsters of that century while they work and play. Includes trivia, moments of historical importance, and some of the best early toy commercials.

Title: Kids' Library I & I
Suggested Retail Price: $49.95
Publisher: Queue
Platform: MPC/Macintosh
Description: Stories for kids, elementary school and older.

Title: King Arthur's Magic Castle
Suggested Retail Price: $59.00
Publisher: New Media schoolhouse
Platform: Macintosh
Description: King Arthur and Merlin show kids some neat things.

Title: Learn By Myself: The City Mouse and the Country Mouse
Suggested Retail Price: $24.95
Publisher: InterActive
Platform: MPC/Macintosh
Description: Updated story of the urban contemporary mouse and the country swing mouse.

Title: Learn By Myself: The Lion and the Mouse
Suggested Retail Price: $24.95
Publisher: InterActive

Platform: MPC/Macintosh
Description: Lion, thorn, mouse, friends. Need we say more?

Title: Learn By Myself: The Little Red Hen
Suggested Retail Price: $24.95
Publisher: InterActive
Platform: MPC/Macintosh
Description: The sky is falling! Kids can read!

Title: Learn By Myself: The Tortoise and the Hare
Suggested Retail Price: $24.95
Publisher: InterActive
Platform: MPC/Macintosh
Description: Broderbund's version is funnier, but this disc costs less.

Title: Learn By Myself: Goldilocks and the Three Bears
Suggested Retail Price: $24.95
Publisher: InterActive
Platform: MPC/Macintosh
Description: Goldilocks discovers exactly what porridge is, to her dismay.

Title: Legends of Oz
Suggested Retail Price: $59.95
Publisher: Multicom
Platform: MPC/Macintosh
Description: Frank Baum's classic tale on CD-ROM.

Title: Lost & Found I, II, III
Suggested Retail Price: $39.99
Publisher: Time Warner Interactive Group
Platform: MPC/Macintosh
Description: Riddles clue the discoveries in these collages.

Title: Math Blaster
Suggested Retail Price: $59.95
Publisher: Davidson
Platform: MPC
Description: Simple math exercises for elementary students.

Title: Mixed-up Mother Goose
Suggested Retail Price: $69.95
Publisher: Macmillan New Media
Platform: MPC
Description: Fractured fairy tales for the young.

Title: Morgan's Trivia Machine
Suggested Retail Price: $35.00
Publisher: Morgan Interactive
Platform: MPC/Macintosh
Description: Sneaky facts and figures that nobody needs to know, but will learn anyway.

Title: Moving Gives Me A Stomach Ache
Suggested Retail Price: $49.95
Publisher: Discis
Platform: Macintosh
Description: A story about calming the fears of a little boy whose family is moving.

Title: Mud Puddle
Suggested Retail Price: $29.95
Publisher: Discis
Platform: MPC/Macintosh
Description: Kids love muddle puddles, and they'll love this disc.

Title: My Favorite Monster
Suggested Retail Price: $49.99
Publisher: Queue
Platform: Macintosh
Description: This little fellow will charm your little ones while teaching early reading skills through interactive stories.

Title: My Silly Book of Colors/Counting/Opposites
Suggested Retail Price: $29.95
Publisher: Discis
Platform: MPC/Macintosh
Description: A new book in the little kids can read series, exploring colors, counting and opposites.

Title: My Silly CD of ABC's
Suggested Retail Price: $29.95

Publisher: Discis
Platform: MPC/Macintosh
Description: Learn the alphabet as quickly as ABC.

Title: My Silly CD of Counting
Suggested Retail Price: $29.95
Publisher: Discis
Platform: MPC/Macintosh
Description: Testing, 1, 2, 3, testing.... You can count on this disc.

Title: Ninja High School
Suggested Retail Price: $25.95
Publisher: CD-Comix, Inc.
Platform: Macintosh
Description: Sound, color, and graphics bring life to the Ninja High School Comic Book.

Title: Once Upon a Forest
Suggested Retail Price: $39.95
Publisher: Sanctuary Woods Multimedia Corp.
Platform: MPC
Description: Share an adventure with the mouse, mole, and hedgehog from the animated movie and learn about the environment.

Title: Operation Neptune
Suggested Retail Price: $59.95
Publisher: The Learning Co.
Platform: MPC
Description: King Neptune or the planet? Only the Learning Company knows.

Title: Oscar Wilde's The Selfish Giant
Suggested Retail Price: $39.95
Publisher: Sanctuary Woods
Platform: MPC/Macintosh
Description: Oscar wrote great plays, but this story is a classic, too.

Title: Our House Featuring the Family Circus
Suggested Retail Price: $49.95
Publisher: Con*text Systems, Inc.

Platform: MPC
Description: Children's activities that are better than you'd expect from this comic strip.

Title: Peak Performance
Suggested Retail Price: $59.95
Publisher: Media Vision
Platform: MPC/Macintosh
Description: Race across the states playing trivia.

Title: Peter and the Wolf: A Multimedia Storybook
Suggested Retail Price: $34.95
Publisher: EBook Inc.
Platform: MPC/Macintosh
Description: The classic Russian story.

Title: Peter Pan: A Story Painting Adventure
Suggested Retail Price: $49.95
Publisher: Electronic Arts
Platform: MPC/Macintosh
Description: Paint your own pictures to accompany J.M. Barrie's classic tale.

Title: Ping and Kooky's Cuckoo Zoo
Suggested Retail Price: $49.95
Publisher: Electronic Arts
Platform: MPC/Macintosh
Description: Learn about animals from Kooky's Zoo.

Title: Planetary Taxi
Suggested Retail Price: $39.95
Publisher: Voyager
Platform: MPC
Description: Program to help 8–14 year olds to learn about the solar system.

Title: Porky Pig
Suggested Retail Price: $39.95
Publisher: Chestnut
Platform: MPC
Description: Six of Porky's best!

Title: Professor Gooseberry's I Can Read Club: Always Arthur
Suggested Retail Price: $49.95
Publisher: Imagination Pilots
Platform: MPC/Macintosh
Description: Usually Arthur, but not always, in this interactive book children can read.

Title: Professor Gooseberry's I Can Read Club: Buster's First Thunderstorm
Suggested Retail Price: $49.95
Publisher: Imagination Pilots
Platform: MPC/Macintosh
Description: Buster and your kids can learn about thunder and lightning.

Title: Professor Gooseberry's I Can Read Club: Who Wants Arthur?
Suggested Retail Price: $49.95
Publisher: Imagination Pilots
Platform: MPC/Macintosh
Description: Somebody must want Arthur, because this is his second disc.

Title: Rodney's Funscreen
Suggested Retail Price: $39.97
Publisher: Activision
Platform: MPC
Description: A pretty good playhouse disc for kids.

Title: Rodney's Wonder Window
Suggested Retail Price: $39.00
Publisher: Voyager Company
Platform: Macintosh
Description: More play with Rodney.

Title: Scooter's Magic Castle
Suggested Retail Price: $49.95
Publisher: Electronic Arts
Platform: MPC/Macintosh
Description: Learn along with Scooter with this interactive disc.

Title: Sesame Street: Numbers
Suggested Retail Price: $49.95
Publisher: EA*Kids

Platform: MPC
Description: The gang from Sesame Street interacts with your children in games for the 3 to 6 year old.

Title: Shelley Duvall's It's a Dog's Life
Suggested Retail Price: $39.95
Publisher: Sanctuary Woods
Platform: MPC/Macintosh
Description: Charming tale told by the actress who seems to be specializing in great children's material.

Title: Silly Noisy House
Suggested Retail Price: $59.95
Publisher: Sony
Platform: MPC
Description: Learning isn't difficult despite the din in this house set up especially for children.

Title: Swiss Family Robinson
Suggested Retail Price: $69.00
Publisher: New Media Schoolhouse
Platform: MPC/Macintosh
Description: Danger, Will Robinson! You won't soon get lost in this space, a retelling of the classic children's story of a family marooned on a desert island.

Title: Tales of the Wild Zeep
Suggested Retail Price: $59.00
Publisher: Westwind Media
Platform: MPC/Macintosh
Description: This eggplant-like creature captures your youngsters' hearts. Basic reading skills.

Title: Talking Classic Tales
Suggested Retail Price: $89.00
Publisher: New Media Schoolhouse
Platform: Macintosh
Description: Narrated fairy tales for kids.

Title: Talking Jungle Safari
Suggested Retail Price: $79.00
Publisher: New Media Schoolhouse, Inc.
Platform: MPC/Macintosh

Description: Your child takes a narrated trip through the jungle.

Title: Talking Schoolhouse CD
Suggested Retail Price: $99.00
Publisher: New media Schoolhouse
Platform: MPC
Description: Kids can learn to tell time, read, and spell through the exercises on this disc.

Title: The Adventures of Nikko
Suggested Retail Price: $39.95
Publisher: Software Toolworks
Platform: MPC
Description: Stories about Nikko for preschoolers.

Title: The Berenstain Bears Fun with Colors
Suggested Retail Price: $39.95
Publisher: Compton's NewMedia
Platform: MPC
Description: Stan and Jan Berenstain's bears learn about colors.

Title: The Berenstain Bears Junior Jigsaw
Suggested Retail Price: $24.95
Publisher: Compton's NewMedia
Platform: MPC
Description: Brother and Sister Bear help you assemble the puzzle.

Title: The Berenstain Bears Learn About Counting
Suggested Retail Price: $24.95
Publisher: Compton's NewMedia
Platform: MPC
Description: Preschoolers can master numbers with this disc.

Title: The Berenstain Bears Learn About Letters
Suggested Retail Price: $39.95
Publisher: Compton's NewMedia
Platform: MPC
Description: Ages 3 to 5 can learn all the

letters of the alphabet with the Berenstain Bears.

Title: The Berenstain Bears Learning at Home
Suggested Retail Price: $59.95
Publisher: Compton's NewMedia
Platform: MPC
Description: Learning can be fun, even at home, in this Berenstain Bears edition.

Title: The Berenstain Bears Learning Essentials
Suggested Retail Price: $29.95
Publisher: Compton's NewMedia
Platform: MPC
Description: Basic learning skills for preschoolers.

Title: The Big Bug Alphabet Book
Suggested Retail Price: $39.95
Publisher: Spectrum HoloByte
Platform: MPC/Macintosh
Description: The alphabet is a lot more fun to learn when bugs are involved.

Title: The Bingi Burra Stone
Suggested Retail Price: $29.95
Publisher: Main Street
Platform: MPC
Description: Follow Wallobee Jack through the Australian outback and join in an animated search for the legendary stone.

Title: The Cat Came Back
Suggested Retail Price: $59.95
Publisher: Sanctuary Woods
Platform: Macintosh
Description: Not the Dr. Seuss story— but just as good, for young children.

Title: The Christmas CD
Suggested Retail Price: $49.95
Publisher: Queue
Platform: MPC/Macintosh
Description: Stories about Christmas.

Title: The Human Body
Suggested Retail Price: $79.95
Publisher: Discis
Platform: Macintosh
Description: Your brain, senses, bones, muscles, etc.

Title: The Manhole
Suggested Retail Price: $39.95
Publisher: Activision
Platform: MPC
Description: What goes on inside a manhole? Your kid may be surprised.

Title: The Night Before Christmas
Suggested Retail Price: $39.95
Publisher: Discus
Platform: Macintosh
Description: Arthur Rackham's illustration of old classic tale of Saint Nick.

Title: The Paper Bag Princess
Suggested Retail Price: $29.95
Publisher: Discis
Platform: MPC/Macintosh
Description: Fairy tale with childlike visions.

Title: The Reading Carnival
Suggested Retail Price: $49.95
Publisher: Digital Theater
Platform: MPC
Description: Learning to read can be fun.

Title: The Selfish Giant
Suggested Retail Price: $49.95
Publisher: Sanctuary Woods
Platform: Macintosh
Description: Another version of the Oscar Wilde fairy tale.

Title: The Star Child
Suggested Retail Price: $49.00
Publisher: EBook
Platform: MPC/Macintosh
Description: Another classic children's story on disc.

Title: The Tale of Benjamin Bunny
Suggested Retail Price: $59.95
Publisher: Discis
Platform: MPC/Macintosh
Description: Benjamin Bunny and his cousin Peter Rabbit.

Title: The Tale of Peter Rabbit
Suggested Retail Price: $59.95
Publisher: Discis
Platform: MPC/Macintosh
Description: Mr. McGregor chases Peter around the garden in this Beatrix Potter classic.

Title: The Thai Sun Adventure
Suggested Retail Price: $29.95
Publisher: Main Street
Platform: MPC
Description: Explore exotic lands as Wallobee Jack and Francesca search for the sacred golden elephant.

Title: The Ugly Duckling
Suggested Retail Price: $29.95
Publisher: Morgan Interactive
Platform: MPC/Macintosh
Description: The duckling turns out to be a swan, and children love the story.

Title: The Ultimate Dinosaur Kit
Suggested Retail Price: $59.95
Publisher: Byron Preiss Multimedia Company, Inc. MPC/Macintosh
Description: Interactive program makes you a paleontologist. Work at dig site, and lab. Learn and experience...fun.

Title: The Velveteen Rabbit
Suggested Retail Price: $49.95
Publisher: Queue
Platform: Macintosh
Description: A children's classic story on CD-ROM.

Title: The White Horse Child
Suggested Retail Price: $49.00
Publisher: EBook

Platform: MPC/Macintosh
Description: Fantasy of a young boy by Greg Bear.

Title: Thomas' Snowsuit
Suggested Retail Price: $29.95
Publisher: Discis
Platform: MPC/Macintosh
Description: Snowsuits and kids don't mix—or do they?

Title: Three Faces of Evil: Frankenstein, Dracula, & Mr. Hyde
Suggested Retail Price: $49.95
Publisher: Queue
Platform: MPC/Macintosh
Description: Classic works by Shelley, Stoker, and Stevenson, told in multimedia format.

Title: Treasure Cove!
Suggested Retail Price: $59.95
Publisher: The Learning Co.
Platform: MPC
Description: Great undersea adventure, solving math problems as you go.

Title: Treasure MathStorm
Suggested Retail Price: $59.95
Publisher: The Learning Co.
Platform: MPC/Macintosh
Description: Explore the ice mountain and solve those math problems.

Title: Victor Vector & Yondo: The Hypnotic Harp
Suggested Retail Price: $39.95
Publisher: Sanctuary Woods
Platform: MPC/Macintosh
Description: More adventures of Victor Vector, the nonviolent hero (see reviews in this chapter).

Title: Victor Vector & Yondo: The Vampire's Coffin
Suggested Retail Price: $39.95
Publisher: Sanctuary Woods
Platform: MPC/Macintosh

Description: Not as scary as you might think, as Victor Vector uses his wits.

Title: Vitsie Visits Dinosaurs
Suggested Retail Price: $39.99
Publisher: Time Warner Interactive Group
Platform: MPC/Macintosh
Description: Learn about dinosaurs from Vitsie, who visits the beasts in person.

Title: Vitsie Visits Outer Space
Suggested Retail Price: $39.99
Publisher: Time Warner Interactive Group
Platform: MPC/Macintosh
Description: Vitsie goes to outer space, but comes back.

Title: Vitsie Visits the Ocean
Suggested Retail Price: $39.99
Publisher: Time Warner Interactive Group
Platform: MPC/Macintosh
Description: Vitsie learns about the creatures in the ocean.

Title: What Would You Do At Home?
Suggested Retail Price: $39.95
Publisher: Digital Theater
Platform: MPC
Description: Great Nickelodeon series asks what you'd do in various situations. Now you can play the TV game at home.

Title: Whale of a Tale
Suggested Retail Price: $89.95
Publisher: Texas Caviar, Inc.
Platform: MPC/Macintosh
Description: Narrated illustrated story with learning exercises

Title: Wild Learning Safari
Suggested Retail Price: $34.95
Publisher: Compton's NewMedia
Platform: MPC
Description: Learn about wild beasts and wildebeests from this disc.

Title: Wind in the Willows
Suggested Retail Price: $69.00
Publisher: New Media Schoolhouse
Platform: Macintosh
Description: Mr. Toad of Toad Hall goes on a wild ride.

Title: Word Tales
Suggested Retail Price: $59.99
Publisher: Warner New Media
Platform: Macintosh
Description: Word games with animations

Chapter 8

Movies, Music, and Television

Television didn't really kill off motion pictures, as everyone predicted in the early 50s. And phonograph records (or, audio CDs today) didn't kill off radio programming. Instead, TV created vast new markets for movie productions, while giving us something to escape from when we did venture back to theaters. And radio and the recording industry complement each other nicely, encouraging consumers to enjoy both.

Today, many kinds of media happily co-exist. *Jurassic Park* raked in $900 million in revenues at the box office worldwide on its way to becoming the most profitable movie ever. Yet, it's expected to reap another $1 billion after its October 4, 1994 release on home video. Can you imagine what a CD-ROM based on this hit would collect?

Movies are as much a part of our lives today as music has been for centuries. Obviously, we love to watch films and videos, and welcomed the change from small home screens with their fuzzy pictures in the 50s to the large "home theater" television sets of today. So, would you really be interested in taking a step back to watch a film like *It's a Wonderful Life* on your computer monitor? Or, could you watch the Beatles' classic *A Hard Day's Night* in a tiny window taking up only a couple inches of a Macintosh's screen? The answer is, yes—if something more were provided.

That's what CD-ROM technology gives you movie buffs: the capability to combine full-motion video with immediate access to scripts, biographies, cast lists, and other goodies. You get that with Voyager's version of *A Hard Day's Night*. You get a great deal more with other movie-oriented discs, like *Microsoft Cinemania '94* or *Movie Select*. These discs combine video clips with music, movie reviews, trivia, and other bonuses that tell you everything you wanted to know about a particular movie, star, director, or studio.

Some movie-oriented CD-ROMs are quirky, such as *Gilbert Gottfried's Midnight Movie Mania*. Others are downright hilarious. If you can watch *The Honeymooner's Funniest Moments* and not break a smile, you need to get out more. But, if you can't get out more, check out some of the great discs reviewed in this chapter. We wish there were more movie discs available (and there will be), but these are the best we could find.

Music CDs were once fairly rare, but now they are becoming more numerous. On a good multimedia PC or Macintosh, these can sound great! You'll find a mixture of discs devoted to classical music (with in-depth discussions of various pieces) to more pop-oriented CDs.

For example, Microsoft has produced a lush series focusing on Stravinsky, Mozart, and Beethoven, with close-up looks at one work by each composer. You'll find CD-ROMs devoted to jazz, blues, specific performers like Billie Holiday, Count Basie, or Louis Armstrong, and discs of music clips for your multimedia presentations.

Or, if singing is your only talent, you can sing along with *PC Karaoke*. All these discs sound better with good quality speakers, or even with your sound card's output piped through your home stereo system. I have a Sound Blaster Pro running through a boom box, and the sound is awesome.

You'll find that the discs reviewed in this chapter only scratch the surface (and you thought scratchy surfaces went out with vinyl records!), because more music- and movie-oriented CD-ROMs come out every week. But, you can start your musical and film journey here.

All-Music Guide

Rating:  1/2

Publisher Name:
Paragon Consultants

Software Requirements: **MPC**

Suggested Retail Price: **$39.95**

W ell kids, here it is! Once and for all, the best recordings of the best artists in just about every category, all in one place. This database is very flexible, and I think they thought of everything! There are over 200,000 albums, 30,000 artists and groups, 190,000 sidemen and instruments, 70,000 in-print classical albums, 120,000 separate classical compositions, 7,000 music books and magazines, 600 essays, instrumental maps, articles, resources, mail order numbers, and so on. Included also are reviews by the best reviewers. The Search functions are fantastic!

All Music Guide has data broken down into three main categories, which can all be accessed from the main menu. The first is Artist/Group, which has a rather detailed, no-nonsense breakdown of information. The whole point of this database format is that you need not know an artist's name, the title, or even the recording company.

All you need to know is a little bit; the Search function does all the shopping and looking for you. Choosing Search brings up a pop-up menu that requests your search string. I began mine with Stev (looking for Stevie Wonder) and did not notice at first that I should have gone by last name first, so I got a bunch of Stev.. choices. I simply clicked the Search button again and typed Wonder.

The first find was a group called Wonder Stuff. All I had to do was use the down arrow one time and there he was. The information was so detailed, I was really delighted. On the top half of the screen his name is shown, under which a classification is given as Vocal, piano. Let me tell you a few facts about Stevie from my search. His real name was Steveland Morris, he was

blind at birth. Born in Saginaw, Michigan in 1950. His first audition was for Berry Gordy, at which time he played every instrument in the studio. His first stage name was "Little Stevie Wonder" and they billed him as a 12-year-old genius. In 1963, his hit song was "Fingertips." He had to fight for independence to "do his own thing" and the rest, as they say, is history. Under Music style—another info area—his style is listed as Motown, Dance, 70 Pop, Soul, etc. There is a section entitled Similar Artists, for him, it was Ron Miller, Ronnie White, and others. Of course, in the Influences box, they list Ray Charles. (As an amazing side note, Stevie Wonder once noted that he wasn't aware that Ray Charles was blind until they worked together for the first time a few years ago. Apparently it had

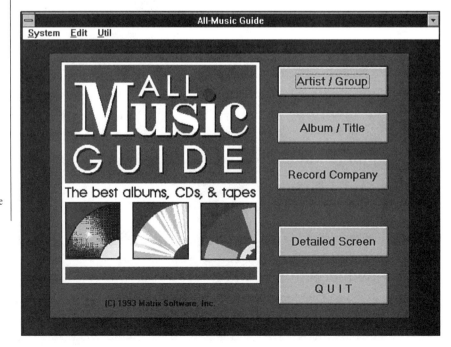

All Music Guide has information about the best albums, CDs and tapes, all in one package.

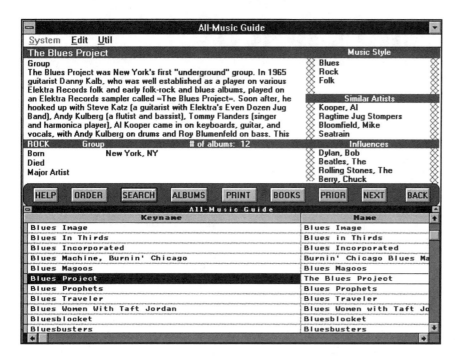

never come up—and, of course, Stevie had never had the chance to see one of Ray's album covers!)

A great reference guide to music and musicians, in an easy-to-access form. A great addition to any fan's collection.

The function choices are in the middle of the screen on radio buttons, they are Help, Order, Search, Albums, Print, Books, Prior, Next, and Back. I always like it when a program is thoughtful enough to help me go back to where I began! But, before going on, I decided to check out the Books. I found that in 1977 Audrey Edwards wrote a

book about him titled *The Picture Life of Stevie Wonder.*

A rating appears, filled in with red, very near the end. The order of searching is customizable, although I was very pleased to use the default settings. The second choice at the main menu is Album Title, and the third is Record Company. Throughout, there are ratings, and many choices to do a very thorough search/research. The entire program can be run from a Detailed Screen, which is broken down into logical sections and can be customized to suit the user's needs.

One feature I especially enjoyed was the Essay collection. I read one by Kip Lornell titled "The Blues," in which he said "... if you never had them I hope you never will."

Music is a magical force in our world; it always has been, and I am sure it always will be. There is so much of it, and there has been some that I shall never forget. Of course, there is some I wish I'd never heard, but that's another story. The very idea of having it all put together so nicely is a

comfort to me. *All Music Guide* has a "no-fluff" display and it is very common sense oriented, and the work that has gone into it must have been phenomenal. This will make a great addition to my reference collection.

Cambium Sound Choice

Rating: 💿 💿 💿

Publisher Name:
Cambium Development

Software Requirements: **MPC**

Suggested Retail Price: **$89.95**

The minute you pop this disc into your CD-ROM drive, you'll dump your haphazard methods of selecting music for the multimedia presentations you create. Cambium has distilled this exercise down to the essentials. You'll find everything you need on this disc to search and audition 841 different music files in a variety of categories, moods, formats, and lengths. If you can't find an appropriate music clip using *Cambium*

Sound Choice, there's something wrong with your ears.

The Windows-based music search/player program installs easily. It can play the selections through your Windows sound driver as .WAV files, or, for higher quality, use direct CD-Audio (through headphones, or your speakers if an audio cable connects your CD-ROM drive and sound card). The program can also play MIDI (musical instrument digital interface) files.

There are three ways to search for sound clips. Click the Pick button in the main window, and you are shown the titles, category, and tempo of all 29 pieces on the disc. Categories include Jazz, Contemporary, Rock, Latin, New Age, Orchestral, Exotic, and Classical. Other discs in the series add Broadway and Country/Folk music to the pot. You'll find original compositions as well as familar classical favorites (Mahler to Mozart). All can be used and distributed

royalty-free, under most circumstances. (The main restriction is that you can't include these music clips in your own collection of music clip "art.")

You can click a single selection, Shift+click to choose multiple consecutive selections, or Ctrl+click to pick out individual tunes from the list. Then choose Audition to listen to the pieces you've highlighted, one by one.

The Screen button brings up a dialog box that you can use to enter appropriate parameters for your search. You may click boxes to specify one or more categories, slow, moderate, or upbeat tempos, choose from predefined "moods" (active, assertive, breezy, energetic, funky, sweeping, or wistful, for example), or type in keywords of your own. Cambium describes each of the pieces using phrases like "A bass, drums, sax with a smokey ambiance," or "A jumpin' blues shuffle featuring a saxophone melody and a driving piano solo," so that you can use keywords like "sax" or "blues" to retrieve choice tunes.

Keyword searches can also focus on keywords that you enter into the database yourself, or comment lines you may type ("This tune is perfect for sales presentations!") Again, all pieces selected by your programmed search can then be auditioned individually.

A third, manual searching method can be employed just by browsing through the songs one at a time, using arrow buttons to advance or backtrack through the song list.

Search through *Sound Choice*'s database to locate the music you need for your presentation.

This disc is a music-packed resource with 841 .WAV and MIDI files in a variety of tempos and moods, which you can incorporate into your desktop presentations.

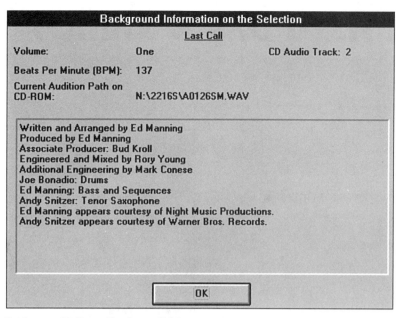

Background information is available on each selection you listen to.

Okay, what can you do with a piece once you've located it? *Sound Choice* offers 11 different versions of most selections. The Main theme is a roughly one-minute cut. As a .WAV file sampled at 22 kilohertz (roughly half the sampling rate used by full-fledged digital audio devices), each of these takes up about 5MB of disk space. They can consume as little as 250K at the coarser 11 kilohertz sample rate with optional compression.

The MIDI version of each piece is smaller yet: only 25–50K, but you must have MIDI drivers and a compatible sound card installed on the system that will be used to play them back. You can copy the .WAV or MIDI files to your hard disk and incorporate them into your presentation by using your authoring software's provision for importing sound files.

Also included are four "bumpers," which are shorter clips ranging from about two to six seconds, and make excellent transitional, introductory, or finale music in presentations. These, too, are available as .WAV and MIDI files that may be copied to your hard disk by clicking the hard disk icon. The main theme and bumpers all are designed as stand-alone snippets that are musically

complete in themselves. You won't have to fade any of these in and out to use them.

The eleventh version of each piece is the original CD-quality audio track (the full piece; no bumpers are included separately), which you can't copy to your hard disk, of course. You may play it through your sound card and record the music by using any digital audio tape (DAT) or analog tape system you may have connected. This provision lets you incorporate the music into presentations that use special sound devices and systems.

A truly exhaustive Help file eliminates the need for printed documentation. A Quick Tour program gets you started with the program quickly. Cambium says it takes some of the money it saves not printing manuals and donates it to nonprofit organizations that support the arts and the environment. The disc also comes in a mostly non-plastic eco-pack instead of the traditional jewel box.

The package includes an Uninstall program (a welcome addition should you want to remove the software without leaving

behind unwanted clutter in your Windows subdirectories (as if there were such a thing as *wanted* clutter), and a data compressor, which squeezes down database files created by *Sound Choice* on your hard disk.

While the variety of musical styles, tempos, and moods on *Sound Choice* is impressive, it's far from comprehensive. You'll definitely want more sounds to choose from, but then, this is only Volume 1.

Microsoft Windows, your CD-ROM drive, and sound card make music a viable resource for your multimedia presentations. *Sound Choice* makes music useful and easily accessible.

A Hard Day's Night

Rating: ⦿⦿⦿⦿⦿

Publisher Name: **Voyager**

Software Requirements:
Macintosh

Suggested Retail Price: **$39.95**

The Beatles star in this Macintosh version of *A Hard Day's Night*.

This disc is nothing more, or less, than The Beatles in their first movie, *A Hard Day's Night*, along with still photos, the original script, and a ton of priceless background information and commentary. What could be controversial about that?

Well, one of the two leading Macintosh monthly magazines selected this disc as the best disc of all time in their Top 50 list, while a reviewer in the other magazine chose it as "one of the worst." Is there really that much room for opinion? The answer lies in the fact that the second unnamed reviewer said the disc itself wasn't that bad, but he didn't care for the movie itself, nor did he feel it should be given the attention due to other, more deserving films.

That about sums it up. If you liked The Beatles, you'll go nuts over *A Hard Day's Night*. If your musical tastes run more to, say, Stone Temple Pilots, you may wonder what all the fuss is about. This particular review was written by someone who had the incredibly good luck to be 16 years old in 1964, when The Beatles kicked off the British Invasion. If you're 36 years old, take my word for it: Bay City Rollers and the

BeeGees were nothing like this. If you're 26 years old, there was more excitement over The Beatles than KISS and Michael Jackson combined. And you 16-year-olds—Guns and Roses were small potatoes compared to the Fab Four.

This CD-ROM puts the whole thing in perspective. First, you get the entire movie in its uncut, 90-minute, black-and-white glory, which can be viewed in several different screen formats, ranging from small and clear to large and grainy. The resolution may be less than stellar, but the movements are smooth and the music crystal-clear.

As you watch, you can read along with a cogent essay by Bruce Eder on The Beatles,

their music, and various aspects of the film you're viewing. If you like, you can mark your place in the film, and then come back and resume viewing at that exact spot. There is also the theatrical trailer for the film and clips from several of director Richard Lester's early works. You can jump directly to essays about individual songs in the movie and view them in what have to rank as some of the very first music videos ever produced.

You can read the original script, which contains scenes that were cut and dialog improvised by the irrepressible Beatles. Search for particular words in the text, or check to see action and dialogue that was ignored or cut (it's marked in square

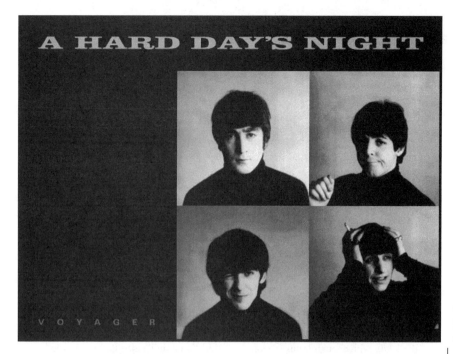

A HARD DAY'S NIGHT

VOYAGER

brackets). Improvised lines are marked with parentheses.

The Beatles, in their classic first film, are in fine form and musically precocious on this disc, augmented by scripts, commentary, and background information.

This program is actually a HyperCard 2.1 stack, so you must have that version of HyperCard or HyperCard Player to run it (a copy is included on the CD-ROM). You should also increase the amount of memory allocated to HyperCard from 1MB to 3 or 4MB, if you have enough RAM. (Highlight the program, and then click the File>Get Info menu item, and type in a new value under Memory Requirements.)

The film is included on the CD-ROM in ten different sections displayed with the included Movie Player, so if you know the one you want to view, you can run it individually without loading the full program. If you want to play with the still photos, you can load them into Adobe Photoshop or another image editor.

The amazing thing about this film is that it was begun *before* The Beatles had come to America and transformed from the rage of Europe into a worldwide phenomenon. It's a chance to see legendary figures still in relatively raw and joyous form, and to recapture the spirit of an age that is ancient history for many of you, but which lives on inside your parents or older friends.

Heart: 20 Years of Rock and Roll

Rating:

Publisher Name: **The New CD Music Show**

Software Requirements: **MPC-2**

Suggested Retail Price: **$79.95**

Someday, every major pop group will release a CD-ROM like this one: their fans will expect and demand it from them. Today, if you want an in-depth look at the music of an individual artist or group, you'd better be a fan of one of the few pioneers in this new field, like Peter Gabriel, or, in this case, Heart.

Just in case your radio has been broken for the last two decades, Heart are sisters Ann and Nancy, from the most musically-talented Wilson family to cut a record since the Beach Boys headed off to Surf City, USA. They grew up in an age when their goal—to be just like Led Zeppelin—was considered impossible for a group led by two strong-minded women. Nevertheless, Ann and Nancy managed a string of hits that rocked with the best of them in the 1970s, staged a comeback in the mid-1980s that hit the MTV generation hard, and continue into the 1990s with enough industry clout to command an innovative CD-ROM entry like this one.

Make no mistake, *Heart: 20 Years of Rock and Roll* is no nostalgic retro-documentary about a has-been group that retains a following among older baby-boomers. This disc profiles a lively group that continues as a major force on the charts. Not bad for a pair of over-40 musicians, eh?

This disc is packed with more memorabilia than Roy Rogers' museum, priceless old film and sound clips from earlier in the women's careers, interviews with Ann and Nancy, their parents, and other key players. You'll find an interactive biography, 60-second audio clips from 125 songs on 13 Heart albums, and a wealth of other material of interest to fans. *Tiger Beat* was never like this! You'll find Video Pages, a Music Room, The Stage, and other modules devoted to particular aspects of the group and its career.

Fans of the band Heart will find everything they wanted to know about the group, along with five hours of interviews and sound clips, on this CD-ROM.

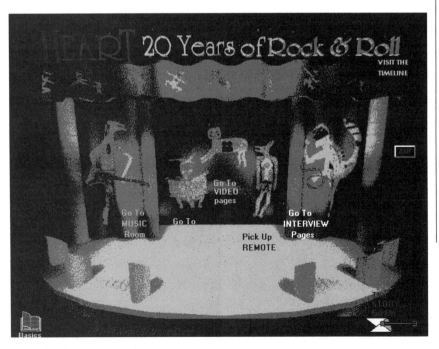

If your PC can handle the hardware demands, *Heart: 20 Years of Rock & Roll* is a fabulous disc for fans of the group.

Learn about the Wilson sisters in *Heart: 20 Years of Rock & Roll.*

It's all information that fans will treasure, but nonfans will find pointless. Whereas *Peter Gabriel's Xplora 1* can be approached by those wishing to learn more about the man and his music, Heart is oriented more toward those who want more details about the group, spiced with inside information and trivia. I wish every group I enjoyed had a disc like this—it's something to play with during those interminable waits between albums.

Beware, however, of the hardware requirements this disc imposes. This is one of the few discs reviewed in this book that truly demands MPC-2—or better— equipment. You'll want a 16-bit sound card to do justice to the music, at least 8MB of RAM—16MB is even better to smooth out the sound and visuals—and forget about trying to get by with any 256-color video card. You'll need 15- or 16-bit color (32K or 65K colors) or even 24-bit color and an appropriate Windows driver to see all this disc has to offer.

My own main computer has a Pro Audio Spectrum 16, 32MB of RAM, a double-speed CD-ROM drive, and a 24-bit color card, and I still had to close three or four Windows applications to run this disc successfully. It's great to see a CD-ROM that doesn't cater to the lowest common equipment denominator.

There are some very nice touches added to the CD. For example, because it's aimed at true fans, it's safe to say you probably own at least a few of their albums on audio CD. You can click the icon representing an album's cover, and then, at the program's prompting, remove the CD-ROM and replace it with the actual audio CD you've selected. From there, you can choose any of the songs on the album, play them, and read along with the lyrics and check out some background information on the tune at the same time. That's a wonderful addition.

But, even without the audio CDs, you'll find five hours of interviews with band members, and lots of other sounds and

sights to keep you busy. If you're only a casual admirer of the band, or perhaps have a few of their biggest hits among your favorites, there is probably too much detail here to interest you. Heart fans, however, will love this disc.

The Honeymooners' Funniest Moments

Rating:

Publisher Name: **MPI Multimedia**

Software Requirements:
MPC/Macintosh (double-speed CD-ROM drive required)

Suggested Retail Price: **$29.98**

R alph Kramden tries to get a handwriting specimen from a neighbor he suspects of sending a gift to his wife, Alice.

"Would you mind writing down your address for me?" Ralph asks.

"Why do you need my address?" the man replies, suspiciously. "I live across the hall from you right here in your own building!"

"Well," Ralph explains, "someday I might move."

Priceless moments like that one help explain why virtually every situation comedy on television today owes a debt of gratitude to Jackie Gleason and his ground-breaking television show of the 1950s. Though Gleason's Joe the Bartender and Reggie Van Gleason III remain memorable characters from that era, "The Honeymooners" skits (eventually expanded to half-hour "telefilms") are most fondly remembered.

Some 48 classic scenes from 70 "lost" episodes are brought to life on this great CD-ROM, available in a combined PC/Macintosh format.

Also packed into the 400+ MB disc are text articles on "The Honeymooners" series that include a comprehensive history of the show and helpful comments about the scenes, along with the title and original air date of each clip.

All the so-called "lost episodes" are available on videotape, so why do we need a CD-ROM that presents only snippets of each? A few minutes browing through *The Honeymooners' Funniest Moments* will quickly answer that question. The disc's producer has extracted only the most hilarious scenes from selected episodes, providing just enough build up and lead-in gags to make the climax of each that much funnier—or poignant. This CD is like a "greatest hits" compilation of 50s comedy, from a Jackie Gleason/Art Carney/Audrey Meadows perspective.

The CD-ROM format gives you the power to review favorite clips over and over again, for pure enjoyment or study (watch Gleason's eyes bug out when he notices the burglar in his apartment—it's a classic "take"). The format also makes it possible to group like scenes together so that you can compare and contrast comedy techniques without spending hours rewinding and advancing videotapes.

Exploring this disc is a joy. After a clip of the opening credits of the original show, the main screen appears. Four still photos at the right side of the screen depict the four major

themes of the show (and all situation comedies that followed): marriage, schtick, the mismatched buddies Ralph and Ed, and schemes.

Some 48 of the best classic comedy bits from 70 "lost" "Honeymooners" episodes of the early 1950s are presented along with fascinating historical information and commentary on this PC/Macintosh CD-ROM.

Click one of these to highlight the theme and 12 thumbnail freeze-frames appear, which represent the opening of a particular scene. Click the thumbnail while holding down the Command (Mac) or Control (PC) keys, and a small box pops up with comments on the scene you are about to see. A single click displays the scene in a small

The more recent popularity of kinescopes of old shows like this one proves that we'd rather look at poor quality images of really great shows than not have them available at all. As you'll see from this disc, the quality is entirely good enough for computer multimedia applications.

Accompanying the film clips are three important text articles about the show, "Ten Men in One," by Joe McCarthy, originally published in the November, 1953 issue of *Cosmopolitan*; "The Jackie Gleason Show" review, from September 29, 1959 *Variety*, and a modern look back, "Ralph and Alice and Ed and Trixie," from the October, 1985 issue of *Film Comment*. An interesting history of how the lost episodes were found and restored, and a listing of the episodes currently available on videotape is also provided.

This disc proves that nostalgia is more than just old people remembering long-gone things as much better than they really were. It's ironic that the Honeymooners' classic comedy, preserved for 40 years using a primitive combination of pre-VCR technologies, is finally reaching the masses through the latest digitized imaging.

window in the center of the screen (befitting the relatively low resolution of QuickTime movies on the PC and Macintosh—and the kinescope originals these were taken from).

The clips are only a few minutes long, but represent some outrageous moments from the show. Ralph suspects that Alice is trying to poison him with fake vitamin pills, so she tries to commit suicide by taking the pills herself. The frantic busdriver mistakes her hysterical laughter at his overreaction for death throes.

In another clip, Ralph and Ed try to extract a bad tooth by attaching it to a string tied to a doorknob. Of course, the doorknob flies off, instead. Ed suggests trying the same thing with the tooth tied to the bumper of his car instead. "You are an idiot!" Ralph shouts. "I may be an idiot, but I don't have a doorknob hanging out of my mouth!" retorts Ed.

The original "Honeymooners" sketches were a regular part of the original "Jackie Gleason Show," and not intentionally preserved in archival form for posterity. The reputation of these episodes has grown through the years primarily through the constant rerunning of a scant 39 full-fledged productions filmed for broadcast during the 1955-56 television season. In the mid-1980s, Jackie Gleason revealed that he had

some 120 hours of his old show, containing more than 70 "Honeymooners" sketches, cached at home. Recorded by filming the display on a television screen (this was before the invention of videotape), these "inferior" kinescopes were produced solely as a way to provide "live" television broadcasts to viewers in Western time zones. (They were actually broadcast a week or more after the original run, to allow time for film processing.)

Ralph has one of his usual calm discussions with Alice.

Jazz Portraits:
Count Basie/Louis Armstrong

Rating: 3 1/2

Publisher Name: **EBook**

Software Requirements: **MPC**

Suggested Retail Price: **$39.95**

lthough these two discs are sold as separate products, I'm reviewing them as a single entity because Count Basie and Louis Armstrong are so closely aligned in the pantheon of jazz greats. The interfaces of the discs are also virtually identical, so I can avoid quite a bit of duplication by looking at these loving tributes to both artists in one review.

William "Count" Basie was an influential pianist and bandleader who developed a big-band style that featured strong, rhythmic interplay among the players, and plenty of room for star soloists to kick back with long, extended instrumentals. Dr. Herb Wong, noted jazz expert and compiler of this disc, calls the Basie orchestra "the definition of jazz...with its parade of extraordinary soloists a dynamic force in jazz." Basie's unique swing piano style is still imitated today.

Louis "Satchmo" Armstrong, on the other hand, is much more than an influence on this musical style. He virtually invented many of the aspects of jazz that we take for granted today, including the style of improvisation that formed the foundation for all jazz from the 1920s onward. Armstrong was the first musician to take

improvisation beyond simple ornamentation to whole new melodies built on the foundation of chords and rhythms of the original piece. If his instrumental contributions weren't enough, Armstrong later went on to set the standard for jazz singing, as well, with his rich, gravely voice and fine musical sense.

Ebook's *Jazz Portraits* are unassuming electronic "books" about individual artists, consisting mostly of pages you leaf through, reading the text and pausing to view video clips of interviews with contemporaries and students of the featured musician, such as Dave Brubeck.

You can move from page to page by clicking advance and rewind arrows. Click on a Play icon to start a video clip or activate a control panel that lets you jump to any page in the book, set a bookmark, search for keywords, retrace your steps, or view an index of topics. Help is also available to guide you through the simple navigational features of the *Jazz Portraits* series.

Because of the simple book format, neither of these discs will dazzle you with multimedia effects. You're more likely to be floored by the great music and the fascinating observations of the musicians who comment on Basie and Armstrong. Keep in

Louis Armstrong's music is the focus of an outstanding jazz portrait from Ebooks.

mind that both musicians started in the 1920s and before, so even musicians who played with them in their later years are getting on in years (Dave Brubeck is in his mid-70s). Most of these comments come from jazz "contemporaries" only in a loose sense.

Still, Brubeck contributes some fascinating recollections of working with Armstrong. "He wasn't a great sight reader," recalls Brubeck, "but that only made what he did even better." Armstrong was able to produce wonderful music at will, says Brubeck, who describes a recording session in which Carmen Macrae asked Armstrong to sing harmony on a song just before taping started. Satchmo contributed some sublime vocal underpinnings to the song, with exactly the right notes, virtually on the spur of the moment.

Brubeck and other musicians assess what was special about Count Basie, too. Brubeck notes that when other great pianists sat in to replace Basie, the effects weren't the same, while trumpeter Doc Cheatham notes that Basie was one of the "great time keepers," who had a great sense of tempo and rhythm.

Jazz Portraits *feature major influences on this musical form, such as Count Basie and Louis Armstrong, portrayed in music, words, and video.*

Some pages also have clips of performances by Basie and Armstrong. You can view each of the bandleaders in scratchy, but interesting, old film clips that capture the magic of those live performances. Many names on the pages are highlighted in blue; click one of these and a pop-up window displays background information about the performer.

There's a music section, which presents 10 or 11 rare recordings (taken from radio broadcasts), along with notes on the performances. Basie is represented by 11 musical sections, including "Bag A' Bones," "Basie Boogie," and "Old Man River." Armstrong's classics are among the best known songs even outside the jazz world, and include "Muskrat Ramble," "Lucky Old Sun," "Panama," and "Chinatown." These selections can also be played on an audio CD player (skip track one, which contains only data). The rest of each disc consists of a text discography (only eight or nine recordings are listed for each artist) and a bibliography of books and articles about the musician.

Both Basie and Armstrong deserve more complete coverage, perhaps with annotated scores and more complete comments about each musical selection. However, we'll take these as a suitable tribute to a pair of influential artists who changed the way jazz was played forever.

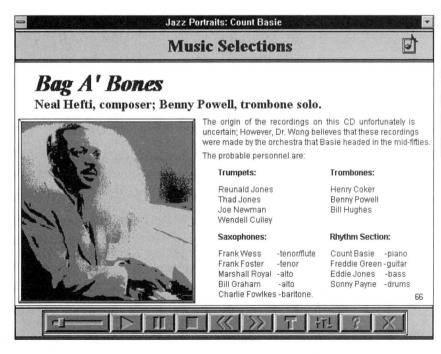

Although Count Basie is gone, his musical legacy lives on through an outstanding orchestra, and CD-ROMs that look at his seminal work.

Mega Movie Guide for Windows

Rating: ⊙⊙⊙1/2

Publisher Name: **Folio VIP Electronic Publishing**

Software Requirements: **MPC**

Suggested Retail Price: **$59.95**

This guide can help you select a good movie to watch, and it is the perfect tool to use before venturing out on a cold night to the video store and facing those walls and walls of titles you've never heard of before. You'll also find it a godsend when you check the cable guide and discover that there are 57 channels and nothing on (with apologies to The Boss).

Installation of *Mega Movie Guide* is clearly outlined and simple to perform.

There is a tutorial built right into the program, and it is suggested that the user go through it to become familiar with the way it works. Most of us like to watch a good movie when we have the time—but which one? We have all stood in the video store, or in the library, rapidly thumbing through a book that was available (even when the movie wasn't), or looked at the paper wondering and wishing there was some way to know if the film would suit our taste.

Finding the time to watch it is one thing, spending hours looking for it is another. This CD was created to take the work out of selecting a good movie. The *Guide* provides a comprehensive and current resource tool for selections. The format is a design utilizing search and retrieval capabilities with features such as browse, search, annotate, print, and export to an infobase. There is a System Menu that allows move, size, and close; a main menu for primary access to all features; a Reference window that enables the user to know exactly where they are in the program; a customizable Toolbelt for commonly used features; a Document window for text display; a vertical scroll bar, and a status line.

There are tons of movie information, movie clips, stills, and trivia on this disc for the true movie buff.

Simple searches are done by use of the Query button or from the main menu. The scope of search can be limited by the user, because the default is to search the entire program. For example, you may select to search a specific field, note, or group, and so on. Notes can be created by the user. The table of contents is available from the main menu.

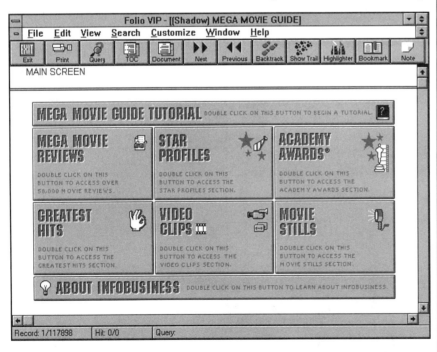

Mega Movie Guide has reviews, star profiles, academy awards, and other databases you can search for trivia and interesting nuggets.

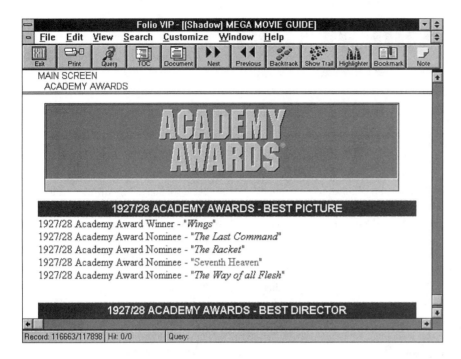

MAIN SCREEN
ACADEMY AWARDS

1927/28 ACADEMY AWARDS - BEST PICTURE

1927/28 Academy Award Winner - "*Wings*"
1927/28 Academy Award Nominee - "*The Last Command*"
1927/28 Academy Award Nominee - "*The Racket*"
1927/28 Academy Award Nominee - "Seventh Heaven"
1927/28 Academy Award Nominee - "*The Way of all Flesh*"

1927/28 ACADEMY AWARDS - BEST DIRECTOR

Record: 116663/117898   Hit: 0/0   Query:

Academy Award winning movies are profiled in the *Mega Movie Guide*.

You can use a mouse to navigate the menus, but the keyboard is also fully functional. Full view is the default, but it can be narrowed. Annotation works with features such as searchable highlighters and notes, bookmarks, groups, and all types of links. Printing produces WYSIWYG hard copies. Navigation uses arrow keys, control keys, and allows an array of techniques such as Backtrack, Show Trail, and so on. A quick key chart is included for the various methods.

This program is extremely powerful and comes with a well-written user's manual. Technical support is also available. In addition to its search capabilities, it is also a great customizable organizing tool. In much the same way as we use a marker to highlight textbooks, there is a Highlighter feature for creating personal notes. The user can use the predefined highlighters as well as create new ones.

The basic format is similar to Windows and easy to become adept at, assuming that you already know how to get around in

Windows. If you don't, it is all explained in the manual. I always respect a program that has various ways to learn to use it and options for keyboard or mouse. Within the user's manual, there is a quick start, a more detailed guide, an overview, and a glossary. In case there is a problem running the software, they have included a troubleshooting guide that most folks can understand and utilize.

The six main areas and the choices within are as follows. Mega Movie Reviews: year, rating, category, running time, review, main actors, director, expanded rating (a nice feature for parents), country, black-and-white or color, available on video, and type of movie. Star Profiles: a written review complete with green highlighting on the movies that the star has been in. Clicking the green slips you into the movie review so you can glance over it if you wish. Clicking the Backtrack icon returns you to the review that you were reading. Nice!

In another section, there are Academy Awards, beginning with 1927/28 and up to

1990, all categories are listed. Greatest Hits: beginning with the 1920s, per every decade up to current hits are listed in green highlight. Movie Clips: Now for the fun part! Double-click the one you want and enjoy! Movie Stills: produces a classic shot of some of the greats. I have to make note here, I loved this!

Mega Movie Guide is a wonderfully featured, intelligently done, and imminently entertaining program. At first, I thought it was going to be too complicated. I mean, I am the type of character who wonders "Why can't they just put all the William Hurt movies on the shelf all together for me?"

Though *Movie Select* and *Cinemania* (also reviewed in this chapter) are better movie guides from many standpoints, real movie lovers will want this one too. Every scrap of information, every obscure still, and every movie clip available probably won't satisfy the real fanatic, so *Mega Movie Guide* helps fill your hunger in a satisfying way.

Mega Rock Rap 'N Roll

Rating: ● ● ● 1/2

Publisher Name:
Paramount Interactive

Software Requirements:
MPC/Macintosh

Suggested Retail Price: **$59.95**

I'm outa here! *Mega Rock Rap 'N Roll* almost convinced your favorite computer author to switch careers. Of the hundreds of discs we looked at for this book, this is the only one that had me scrounging around for a patch cord to plug my Sound Blaster into that vintage Fender Bassman amp sitting in a corner of my office. Making music shouldn't be this easy—or this much fun! One more CD-ROM like this one, and I'm going to hock that last 486 I bought and buy a Marshall stack instead.

Mega Rock Rap 'N Roll is a combination Karaoke machine, mixer, sequencer, sampling synthesizer, and recording studio rolled into one CD. You can play 100 different musical backgrounds in ten different styles, adding hot licks and vocals from professionally recorded samples at the press of a key. You can distort and manipulate sounds, add your own sound effects and vocals (if you have a mic for your sound card), and then record them to audio tape or your hard disk for playback.

Don't let the garish graphics, hip title, or consonant droppin' manual throw you: this is a disc that any music lover under, say, 60,

who likes one of the represented musical styles will enjoy. Professional or serious amateur musicians will quickly exhaust the possibilities of the limited built-in sounds (after a few weeks, anyway), but everyone else will have a blast with this CD (available in both Windows and Macintosh formats) exploring and creating new music with an astonishing ease.

There are ten different music studios to work with, representing African, Big Band, Blues, Latin, Rap, Reggae, Rock, Soul, Street Jazz, and Techno Pop. About the only pop style missing is Country/Western Swing, but the others all lend themselves more to improvisation, anyway.

Each studio is functionally identical, but all are decked out with custom motifs appropriate to their particular milieu. The Big Band studio is all ebony black with brushed gold trim; Latin sessions are conducted against an adobe-meets-serape backdrop, while the Rap jams in a street studio decorated with pavement and spray paint.

When you enter the studio of your choice, you're presented with up to 10 song loop choices, arrayed in a stack along the left side of the window. Each of the original background tracks smacks of some very familiar music—and the titles reflect these influences. If you can't guess where the

Each music studio has a variety of controls that let you create your own musical recordings quickly.

inspiration comes from for "Stings Like A Beat," "Byrn The House," "Whip It Up," or "Main Sketches," you're no fan of The Police, Talking Heads, Devo, or Miles Davis.

Enjoy music-minus-one for multimedia with this 10 studio combo that lets you add vocals, instrumentals, and other effects to 100 built-in background loops.

It takes from 15 to 45 seconds to "load" a studio, because *Mega Rock* stores all its sound effects and background tracks in RAM for extra speed. There's no waiting for a slow CD-ROM drive as you work with a song, but if you have less than, say, 4MB available, the program compensates by loading fewer songs. In RAM-starved systems, there's no degradation of performance: you simply have less music to work with.

Assemble a medley of tracks by dragging any combination of song titles from the stack into the 10 "holes" in the Song-A-Lizer bar at the bottom of the screen. You can mix tunes in any order, repeat tunes, or include 10 copies of the same song. These tracks have been cleverly composed to blend together seamlessly end-to-end.

When you click the Start button, the tracks start to play in turn, ready for your manipulation. The ASDFG and ZXCVB rows on your keyboard each holds a little musical riff, played by an instrument appropriate to the studio you're working in. You'll find Albert Collins-icy guitar and Little Walter blues harp at your fingertips in the Blues studio, and lush Carlos Santana axe work hiding in the Latin wings.

The amazing part is how these little musical bits have been integrated so that they insinuate themselves into the music right on tempo, and in a logical place. (Or, maybe my sense of timing is *that good.*) Even fumble-fingered non-musicians will be able to kick back and create with this disc. It's like paint-by-numbers for music.

You can pump up the volume, whack away at two mouse kickers (which deliver sound effects that you specify with a single click), and bump one of eight vocal inserts. The top two rows of the keyboard produce sound effects you select with variable pitch: the farther right you move in the row, the higher the pitch. Other keys generate drum solos and various instrumental effects. A Key Map displays all the sounds available from your keyboard, but you can hide it once you've learned to drive your studio solo.

There's a microphone icon to click if you want to record your own vocals or sound effects through your sound card. When you're ready to record, you can mix your background tracks with the effects you add, and then save the session to your hard disk for playback later. You may also record to conventional tape using the output of your sound card.

Writing these books gives me little time to play out anymore, but I enjoy accompanying everyone from Lionel Hampton to Buckwheat Zydeco through the magic of audio CDs. *Mega Rock Rap N' Roll* is the perfect CD-ROM for frustrated musicians (and wanna-bes) like me who want to lay down some cool sounds with a keyboard, even if we don't happen to play piano.

Traditional Latin music sounds are incorporated into this *Mega Rock Rap N Roll* music studio.

Microsoft Cinemania '94

Rating: ●●●●

Publisher Name: **Microsoft**

Software Requirements: **MPC**

Suggested Retail Price: **$79.95**

This disc is a movie buff's dream! It combines reviews, biographies, filmographies, and summaries covering thousands of movies, actors, directors, and producers with priceless film clips. There's room here for everything from the obvious to the obscure—and much, much more.

Still photos and film clips bring classic films to life in *Microsoft Cinemania '94.*

How about:

• Leonard Maltin's capsule reviews (a sentence or two) of more than 19,000 movies from his *Movie and Video Guide 1994.* Films from the dawn of the industry to last week's pay-per-view showing are listed here.

• More than 1,200 insightful and detailed reviews from the always-superb Roger Ebert, excerpted from his *Video Companion 1994.*

• Brief reviews of 2,500 films from Pauline Kael's *5001 Nights at the Movies.*

• Baseline's detailed reviews of classic and recent films from *The Motion Picture Guide.*

You're interested in cast lists, biographies, and filmographies? There are nearly 4,000 of these extracted from Baseline's *Encyclopedia of Film* and Ephraim Katz's *Film Encyclopedia.*

Want more general information? Read from 850 articles from the Baseline and Katz texts, plus James Monaco's *How to Read a Film.* There's a complete listing of all Academy Awards nominees (not just winners!) since the very first Oscars in 1927.

Sprinkle in 20 lengthy film clips (from *Star Wars* to *Silence of the Lambs* and *Dances with Wolves*), almost 200 audio clips of dialog (many accompanied by still photos), dozens of musical selections, and a horde of stills and portraits, and *Cinemania '94* clearly represents a major movie lover's treat.

The Windows-based interface uses a remote-control like device to search and select topics at the press of a few buttons. Traditional menu-bar/buttons are also

available to access the Award List, Find Word search capabilities, History of recent accesses, Gallery of multimedia presentations, and a unique ListMaker. The latter lets you compile lists of movies arranged by genre, year, or other parameters, along with comments you type in. An excellent research tool! You can see some of the facts included in the figure below.

Most users will find the meat of the disc is in the movie reviews, which can be easily retrieved by clicking the Contents button at the bottom of the controller and typing a key word in the title. If more than one reviewer's comments are available, you can switch between them by clicking a labeled button. Many film titles, directors, and actors are highlighted in green, which means you can jump to their biographies or filmographies by clicking the highlighted word. Ratings (if applicable), format (black-and-white or color), and running times for each film are shown. A videocassette icon is shown if the film is available on videotape, and any awards may be found listed under the Blue ribbon icon, if displayed.

The consummate film buff's guide, with 19,000 capsule reviews, thousands of in-depth evaluations, and a sumptuous collection of film clips, music, dialog, photos, biographies, and filmographies.

Buttons are also available that enable you to copy a selected text screen to the Windows Clipboard (from which it can be pasted down into your word processing document or another application) or send it directly to your printer.

There's not a lot to complain about here. It would be nice to have more than 20 film clips, and we'd like to see every review Roger Ebert has available electronically (not just 1,200 key evaluations). But that's just nit-picking. After all, *Cinemania 94*'s strength is its comprehensive coverage that spans virtually every film you're likely to be interested in.

There are lots of motion-picture oriented CD-ROMs on the market, but this one should form the keystone of your collection. You may want to fill in here and there with some other review-oriented discs, but the largest potential gap in your information arsenal can be filled by *Cinemania '94* alone.

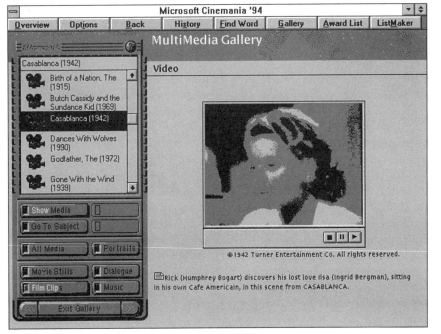

You can select from film clips taken from actual classic movies and view them on your computer screen, with full sound.

Microsoft Musical Instruments

Rating: ◉◉◉◉

Publisher Name: **Microsoft**

Software Requirements: **MPC**

Suggested Retail Price: **$79.95**

Microsoft Musical Instruments **looks at all types of music makers in detail.**

There may be no better way to acquire a direct knowledge of such a wide variety (over 200) of musical instruments than to buy and use *Microsoft Musical Instruments.* The program is one of the best multimedia titles ever produced, and one of the most popular. It combines numerous pictures of each instrument as well as some of its important components, with actual music played by the instrument. There is also a section on musical ensembles.

When you first run *Microsoft Musical Instruments,* a title screen comes up. There are a number of buttons at the top of the screen labeled Contents, Index, Back, Next, Random, Options, and Help. The best way to start is to click Contents, which moves you to the contents screen. Here you can select from Families of Instruments, Musical Ensembles, Instruments of the World, and A-Z of Instruments. By taking any of these paths, you can investigate the properties of musical instruments. If you pursue Families of Instruments, you can select from woodwinds, brass, strings, keyboards, and percussion. If you choose one of these, a screen with some of the instruments that fit that category pops up. Then, by clicking

either the instrument or the name of the instrument, you are taken to a screen showing either a single instrument or more likely another family screen, such as the saxophones. In the latter case, you can select a particular saxophone and arrive at an individual instrument screen.

Musical Ensembles takes a different approach. After selecting Musical Ensembles, a screen presents a number of different types of "band" available for you to study. They include orchestras, wind bands, steel bands, rock bands, and others. Clicking one of these areas of the screen sends you to another screen that may have sub-types of that type, such as Pop Band, Heavy-Metal

Band, and Rock and Roll Band, under rock bands. Typical instrument setups of each type are shown. The individual instruments can be clicked and you move to the instrument screen for that type of instrument.

Instruments of the World lets you view the instruments based on the region they come from or are used in. A map of the world split into nine sections appears after the Instruments of the World item is selected. By clicking one of these areas, a regional map comes up, with the various instruments of that region superimposed on the map. Again, if you click the instrument, you go to its instrument screen.

A-Z of Instruments is the path to take to check out all the instruments in the collection. Some really obscure instruments probably won't come up on any of the other screens. You can select the beginning letter of the instrument you are interested in or just page through the entire directory. Each page of the index has a small picture of each instrument and the name. By clicking the picture or the name, you go to the instrument screen.

An exceptionally strong multimedia educational tool covering over 200 musical instruments; this is a must-buy for anyone interested in music or musical instruments.

The instrument screen is obviously the heart of the CD-ROM. The icon that looks like a speaker beside the title is an audio icon; in this case, click it and you hear the proper pronunciation of the name of the instrument. A similar icon on the left center of the page plays a sample of the instrument. The quality of the samples is excellent and the length is not stingy, at least 15 seconds and in some cases, considerably longer. It's too bad you can't hear the sound clips; they are what defines this disc. The screen has a concise description of the instrument and its qualities. There are other icons that bring up

extra information about the instrument, like the Types and Facts icons at the bottom of the page. Anything in red can be clicked and a hypertext link will be traversed. Sometimes the red is a bit hard to distinguish; try clicking anything that strikes your fancy and a link may be activated.

The Random button at the top of the screen skips all forms of logical access to the instruments and just pulls them up randomly and continuously. It automatically plays the sound clip; for most clips, you have time to read the text of the screen before it goes to the next instrument. This is the most fun way to access the instruments; you never know what will come up next.

The Index button lets you access instruments alphabetically, but it also includes alternative spellings for the

instruments and aliases. It isn't completely redundant to A-Z of Instruments. The Next button moves you forward based on whatever logic you are currently using to access the instruments. The Back button backs you up to the screens you have previously seen. The Options button isn't too interesting, it is used mostly for printing out screens. The Help button provides help for using the application.

Microsoft Musical Instruments is a literacy disc; if you work with this for a while, you will become literate in the field of musical instruments, especially their sounds. It is painless; you will want to view the next screen, over and over again. About the only weakness in this product is that it isn't free. It's that strong. If you have any interest at all in musical instruments, buy it.

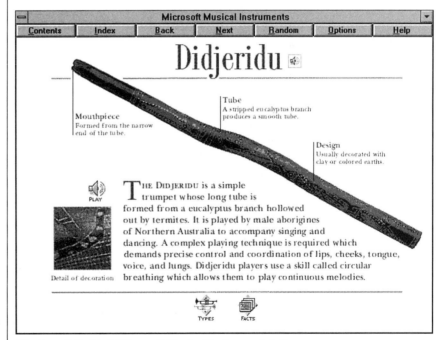

What's a didjeridu? *Microsoft Musical Instruments* **tells you.**

Microsoft Multimedia Beethoven: The Ninth Symphony

Rating:

Publisher Name: Microsoft

Software Requirements: MPC

Suggested Retail Price: $79.95

*M*ultimedia Beethoven: The Ninth Symphony is a combination music dictionary, music appreciation course, music history text, performance of the symphony, and game. The program was originally written for Macintosh, but we reviewed the PC version. *Multimedia Beethoven* is very simple to load into Windows and to use: the technology doesn't get in the way of the music.

The Table of Contents (the main menu) gives you a choice of Pocket Guide, Beethoven's World, The Art of Listening, A Close Reading, and The Ninth Game. When you are within any of these sections, you can click buttons to take you immediately back to the Table of Contents, a glossary, online help, or exit. Some sections have additional choices. Online help lets you move the mouse over a part of the screen, bringing up a window that briefly explains that part of the screen. By clicking the Glossary button from almost anywhere in the program, a list of letter ranges pops up. Click the letter range you want, and a list of musical terms comes up. Clicking the item of interest brings up a box with the definition of your term, and often also a button to click that will play something from CD (from the symphony) or from MIDI to illustrate the explanation. There are 133 musical terms, such as defiance

theme (specific to the 9th), diminution, tremolo, and trumpet.

The Pocket Guide lists each of the four movements of the Ninth Symphony and their major sections (Exposition, Joy Theme, Coda, to name a few). Point to one of the sections to highlight it, and then click. You are taken immediately to that section of the work. The music starts to play at that place, and the movement number and elapsed time into the movement appear in a box.

Beethoven's World is, in essence, a 124-page book about the life and times of Ludwig van Beethoven, and the conditions that influenced his music. You can click any of the nine chapters—Historical Background or Beethoven and Schiller, for instance—or you can click the arrows on the lower right corner to page forward and back through the entire book. The text is on the left side of the screen, and a picture is on the right, nearly always the same black-and-white sketch of the composer, although there are a few pictures of other people. Performing the Ninth Today gives, in part, the programmers' rationale for using a 1965 recording as the basis of this program; and More Reading is an annotated bibliography. An additional button at the bottom of the screen is Find. You can click it, and then type a word or phrase you'd like to find.

The Art of Listening is a 103-page music appreciation overview, that works the same as Beethoven's World. The only difference is the subject and the added sound clips. The five chapters are: Musical Architecture, Sonata Form Demystified, The Classical

The structure of Beethoven's Ninth Symphony is laid out for examination.

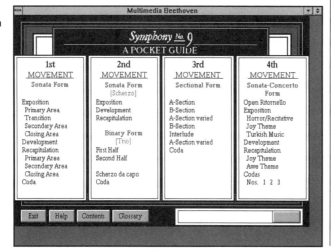

Orchestra, Anatomy of a Symphony, and The Text of Schiller's Ode. Musical Architecture, for example, describes such compositional techniques as repetition, variation, and contrast. There are often buttons in the text labelled Play Short-Term Contrast or Play Large-Scale Contrast. Most of the music clips are from the symphony (CD), but some examples are MIDI-generated.

Multimedia program teaching music appreciation, music history, and stylistic techniques using examples from and detailed analysis of Beethoven's Ninth Symphony.

A Close Reading is the meat of this program. Here you find 354 pages of running commentary that appears on-screen while you listen to the 68-minute *Ninth Symphony*. On each page the elapsed time appears, and you are given the choice of Play Through, which goes through the composition and text until you stop it, or Play Page, which just goes through a few seconds of music and then stops. The accompanying text explains what is happening in the music. Also on-screen is a box with the names of the sections within the particular movement you're in. Clicking one skips forward or back to it. About This Section is a button that, when clicked, brings up a short commentary about the entire section (for instance, the exposition of the first

Beethoven's Ninth Symphony is explored in this Microsoft product.

movement). When the "Ode to Joy" is played, another window pops up with the text—you can even toggle between the original German text and an English translation. At the bottom of the screen another button allows you to skip to another movement without backing out of this part of the program.

Finally, The Ninth Game is an unexpected surprise. It is extraordinarily well thought-out. You pick the number of players (1-4), type in their names, and then decide how many total points are necessary to win the game. Each game screen gives you a choice of three categories of questions: Listen Up! (dealing with musical concepts), Knowing the Score (about the 9th), and Life and Times. For each category you have a choice of point-values that determine how hard the questions are. This is the only place in the program where there is non-musical audio. Many of the questions require the player to click buttons to hear and compare musical examples. When you've chosen your answer, click in the appropriate box. Beethoven makes some comment in German (with a fairly bad accent) about your answer, and a note tells you whether

you are right or wrong. Ludwig's Reply also appears at the bottom, with a little more information. The graphics are amusing, too. Music lovers can choose easy questions and do fairly well; classical musicians can pick harder questions for a real challenge.

Multimedia Beethoven: The Ninth Symphony is an excellent program for both amateurs and serious musicians. Amateurs can learn about Beethoven's life and the basics of music appreciation; trained musicians can get into the nitty-gritty of the detailed musical analysis in A Close Reading. Everyone can enjoy The Ninth Game, which is cleverly designed. This program is very straightforward and easy to use, but it also lacks some of the niceties to which we have become accustomed in our high-tech times. There is no narration; Beethoven's World has no sound at all. Aside from the CD's symphony, there are a few MIDI-generated clips, and there are the verbal comments in the game. The use of color on-screen is almost nonexistent. These small quibbles notwithstanding, the program is well-balanced and useful for anyone wanting to learn more about classical music.

Midnight Movie Madness, with Gilbert Gottfried

Rating:

Publisher Name: **Multimedia PC Marketing Council**

Software Requirements: **MPC**

Suggested Retail Price: **$59.95**

*M*idnight Movie Madness, hosted by Gilbert Gottfried, is a scream! If you like Gottfried as a regular cable TV movie host, appreciated his performance in *Beverly Hills Cop* or as the parrot Iago in *Aladdin*, or simply tolerate his stand-up comedy act, you'll enjoy this disc.

There are more than 100 video clips, comedy, quizzes, trivia, sound, color, and just plain fun! Gottfried teamed up with other former National Lampoon editors to make this CD one that you will really have fun with. Installation was straightforward and easy. Gottfried comes on-screen in a trench coat standing in front of a vintage auto, in his normal crazy way, beginning a story about someone being in the trunk of the car. The stage is set, this is all for fun and laughs.

The main menu offers View, Options, and Help. The screen is in three parts for easy viewing. The control area is like a VCR for selecting Movies, Play, Stop, Back, or Next. On the other side, the movies play, and under that the title, stars, year, and so

on are shown. As you use the disc, Quiz and Trivia Options also appear.

This CD could be a lot of fun for a group of friends who are into old movies and trivia. Selecting the Movies icon brings up the Select Movie menu, which includes the following lists. Just reading the choices cracked me up.

Here are some zany examples: Category—Aliens, Big Monkeys, Celebrity Lowpoints, Do Not Go in the House, Frankenstein, Giant Beasts, Giant Tiny Props, Gimmicks, Loonies Who are Not Doctors, M. D., Mad Doctors, Men in Rubber Suits, Ray Harryhousen, Space—the Phony Frontier, Teens in Trouble, Tropical Terror, Vampires, and Werewolves.

Under Genres, you can choose from the following: Fantasy, Horror, Sci Fi, and Teen Horror. Actors are listed in alphabetical order (by first name, not last name) from Abel Salazar all the way to Zsa Zsa Gabor. Directors are similarly categorized, starting with Alex Nicol and ending with William Castle. You can also search by Decade, ranging from 1930 to 1970, or title.

Are you beginning to get the idea that this is serious theater material here? Did we

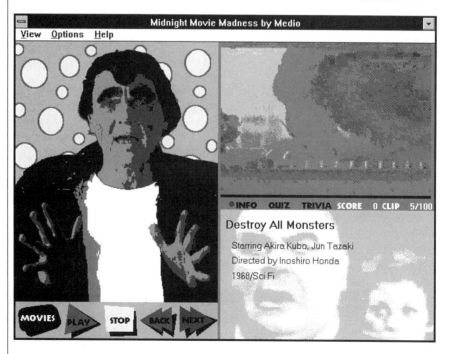

***Midnight Movie Madness* has information about some of the weirdest movies ever to grace cable television.**

really think this stuff was scary? I typed in some parameters at random, such as Aliens, Fantasy, Akira Kubo, Arnold Laven, 50s, and Amazing Colossal Man, and guess what? Gottfried wasn't fooled! I got an error message stating "No dice! Not even one movie fits all those conditions. You might try a simpler request. Or maybe it's time to get some more popcorn."

To be a little more realistic, I tried Space and the Phony Frontier, then All on all other categories. "Let them figure it out," I thought to myself. As the clip played, the stats were shown underneath. There are small radio buttons shown while the clip plays entitled: Info, Quiz, Trivia, and Score. I began to see that a person could use this program to bone-up on movie trivia. That's it—it's a study guide!

The first clip I got from my two choices was an exciting piece from *Flash Gordon.* Being basically lazy, I kept clicking Next as I watched the clips in varying lengths, then I noticed the facts at the bottom. I figure if I do this enough, I will become a world class gory movie genius! Something, I am sure, that every parent wishes their child will become. The quiz was funny. In one case, it showed a still, such as the one from *Cat Women,* where Gottfried's audio asked the pertinent question: "Why are these men shocked?"

When the Trivia Button was selected, there were even more in-depth, little-known sorts of Hollywood tid-bits that we Americans enjoy so much. Just in case you are up late and everyone is asleep, you can turn the sound off. At any time, all the screen info can be blown away by selecting full screen. The theater has come to the computer. Now all they have to do is figure out how to make hour-and-a-half movies and make hot-buttered, fat-free popcorn for us! This was an enjoyable break from sanity.

Midnight Movie Madness *may not be the most serious motion picture-oriented CD-ROM around, but it does hold some serious fun, whether you're a Gilbert Gottfried fan or not.*

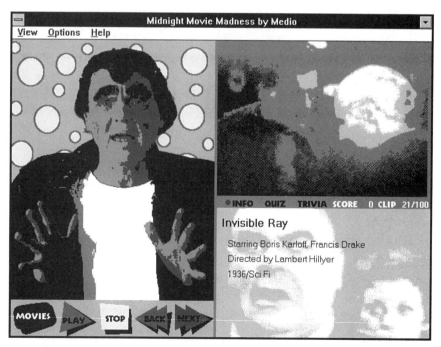

The Invisible Ray, and other classics of horror are all there for your review.

Movie Select

*M*ovie Select has carved out its own niche among the growing roster of movie review CD-ROMs available by providing some interesting expert system/fuzzy logic tools for choosing what movies to see from among 44,000 in its database.

If you really want all your movie bases covered, there are three CD-ROMs you absolutely must have. Microsoft's *Cinemania* is the only disc that combines Roger Ebert and Pauline Kael's analytical and entertaining reviews with a wealth of film clips, music, stills, and statistics. *Video Movie Guide*'s quirky content and coverage of offbeat movies make that disc an essential addition for lovers of the strange. The third must have is *Movie Select*, which does something the other two don't: it helps you narrow down your choices when agonizing over what movie to rent or watch on TV.

All the functions of this Microsoft Windows-based program branch from an art-deco main menu that is accessed with the click of a mouse on the appropriate icon/button. The movie recommendations section is the best part of this disc.

You tell *Movie Select* a little about your tastes in films by picking your all-time favorite movies from a list of virtually every motion picture ever made. (You can narrow your search to popular films or some other subcategory if you'd rather not scroll through the huge database.) Then, the expert system picks out some key themes, such as "triumph of the spirit," "good guys/bad guys," "love in jeopardy," or "grand scale," in the films you've chosen as favorites. It also looks at the genres—from comedy to drama. Then you're presented with a list of other films that incorporate some combination of those strengths, and are asked to choose the ones you really enjoyed.

Given that information, *Movie Select* pores through its database, and comes up with a list of highly recommended and recommended films that you might like. The results produced are fascinating.

I entered Charlie Chaplin's masterpiece, *City Lights*, *Casablanca*, and Akira Kurosawa's *Seven Samurai*, which are all personal favorites. *Movie Select* then asked me to choose from an interesting list of other films, including foreign movies like *8 1/2*, broad comedies like *Some Like It Hot*, *Being There*, the droll Peter Sellers vehicle, *Body Heat*, *Key Largo*, *Chinatown*, and *The Karate Kid*.

The final list of recommendations was broken down into categories and styles. *Movie Select* had decided that if I wanted to see an action/adventure film, I'd like *The*

Learn more about classic films through listings of actors, directors, and movies in *Movie Select*.

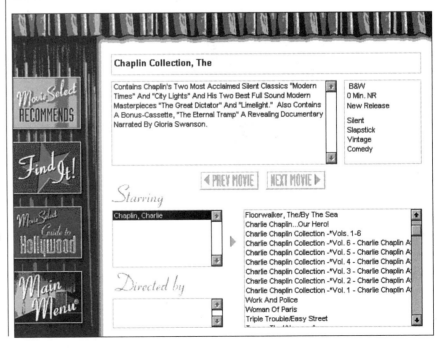

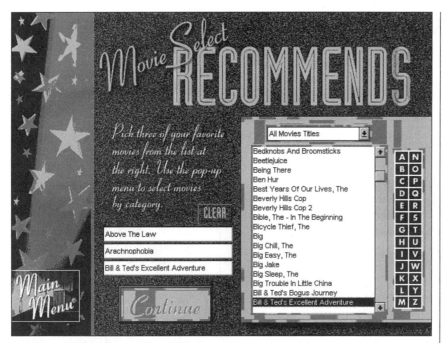

When you enter your favorite films into *Movie Select*, an artificial intelligence algorithm locates other films you should enjoy.

African Queen and *The Maltese Falcon* (an easy guess, because, like *Casablanca*, these are all Bogart films), as well as *The Thin Man* and *Chinatown* (a modern film noir in the same vein as *The Maltese Falcon*).

As comedy competition to *City Lights*, it offered flicks like *Moonstruck*, *The Philadelpha Story*, and *My Man Godfrey*. Foreign films included *The 400 Blows* and *El Norte*. Oddly, there were no recommendations for Westerns, even though Kurosawa films like *The Seven Samurai* are thinly-veiled Westerns and themselves inspired American oaters from *The Magnificent Seven* onward.

Movie Select's fuzzy logic gives you different films each time you run it, even if you choose the same favorites, so you have an endless stream of movie choices. Substituting *Repo Man*, *Risky Business*, and *This is Spinal Tap* (three more in my personal top-20) produced a new list of excellent films, although *The 400 Blows* and a bunch more Bogart films kept popping up,

leading me to wonder whether this expert system was keeping track of *all* my preferences during a session.

The verdict: *Movie Select*'s film recommendation system is an entertaining way to browse through all available movie titles to find some that you might not be familiar with that have qualities you enjoyed in other movies. If you're in the mood for a particular type of film, it will help you find one you like from among the thousands in that category.

This personalized approach is useful because, as you've probably noticed, most of us like quite a few films that never made any critic's top ten list. *Movie Select* thought I'd be interested in seeing *The Last Boy Scout*, a Bruce Willis-Damon Wayans film that I did enjoy immensely, even though the reviews were less than kind.

One caution: By default, two movie categories are not active—religion and adult films—and films in either genre will not appear in the recommended films list.

However, you can check off one or the other under *Movie Select*'s Preferences dialog box and such films then appear in the recommendations. While the one-line descriptions of the adult films are not explicit, they are not coy, either, so parents of younger children may want to monitor their kids' use of this disc.

In addition to the movie selection module, *Movie Select* has three other sections of less interest. In Select Find It!, you can search for movies by a favorite actor or director or search titles by a specific keyword. Another module, Hollywood Guide, has an alphabetical listing of films by actor, director, or title. Because the descriptions of each film are TV Guide-terse (a sentence or two, tops), you won't want to use this disc as a critical analysis tool. *Cinemania* is much better for that. You can use it to find films quickly, however.

The fourth module, Select Previews, provides digitized video clips from recent films, like *Indecent Proposal*, *Boomerang*, *Coneheads*, *Sliver*, and *Naked Gun 2 1/2*. These were all full-length theatrical trailers that were fun to watch. For some strange reason, every one of these preview films was a Paramount Pictures release. Paramount Interactive, of course, is the publisher of the CD-ROM, and Paramount also owns Que, the publisher of this book. Paramount doesn't own *me*, however, and you can rest assured that this disc wouldn't have made it to the top of my personal chart unless it was worthy.

Movie Select includes an expert system program that uses your own personal tastes to make recommendations of movies you'll enjoy with similar themes and strengths, from a database of 44,000 titles.

MusicBytes

*M*usicBytes is a set of multimedia music and sound effects clips on CD-ROM. There isn't anything special about that; there are many such products on the market. *MusicBytes* differs in two important ways, however. The first difference is that all the music is available in four different formats: MIDI, low-resolution (11kHz) WAVE files, high-resolution (22kHz) WAVE files, and CD-audio. The second difference is very important—top-flight, professional musicians were used in the composition and performance of the clips.

MusicBytes contains 27 original compositions, ranging in style from orchestral to rock, reggae to bluegrass, classical to funk, as well as many others. These are a cut above what you normally hear on such offerings; the musicians involved regularly play for artists and bands such as Pink Floyd, Steely Dan, Tom Petty, Natalie Cole, Liza Minnelli, Michael Jackson, Duran Duran, and many others. Some of the artists are session artists; some of them were actually regular members of bands such as Toto, Mr. Mister, and the Doobie Brothers. They have created the music we listen to on a daily basis; it's no surprise that this music is good.

All music and the over 100 sound effects also included on this CD-ROM are royalty-free. The only limitations are that you cannot develop a competing product with the samples on this disc and, if you wish to broadcast the music or sound effects, you must contact Prosonus for permission; no fee is involved. The music and sound effects are meant to be used in multimedia presentations. Clips of 5-, 15-, 30-, and 60-second duration (roughly) are available for all but one of the songs. The package includes a librarian that allows you to conveniently audition the songs/effects, catalog them, and copy selected files to your hard disk for easy inclusion in your presentation. The librarian supports multiple Prosonus CD-ROMs and plans include supporting similar products from competitors in the future. The files can also be accessed directly by other tools; use of the librarian is optional.

You might be wondering why four different formats are included for every song. The sound quality of each format differs. MIDI will usually be the lowest quality format, unless you have some sophisticated external synthesizers included as part of your system. If you're going to rely on your sound card, unless it supports wavetable synthesis, the quality of reproduction is not likely to be very good. However, MIDI files are very compact. If space is at a premium, and quality is not an issue (or you have the external synthesizers at hand), you may prefer to use MIDI files.

The next step up is 8-bit, 11kHz WAVE files. WAVE format is the Windows equivalent of audio CD, although the quality is not as good. The low-resolution 11kHz WAVE file is still quite a bit better than most sound cards, and will also be compatible with more multimedia

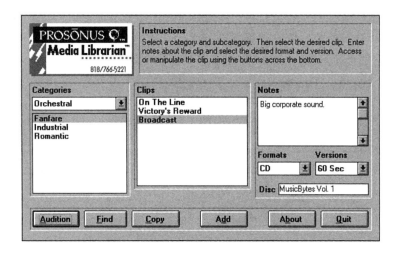

applications than will MIDI files. The sound quality is roughly comparable to that of a clock radio speaker. The disadvantage is that the file will be considerably bigger. A typical MIDI file might be 25,000 bytes; the same 11kHz Wave file might be 1,250,000 bytes—50 times larger. The high-resolution 8-bit, 22kHz WAVE file offers improved quality, roughly equivalent to a fairly good boom box, although the frequency range won't be quite as wide. It will be twice as big as an 11kHz file however, and roughly 100 times larger than the MIDI file. Many sound files of this size will fill up your hard disk fast.

Combining multiple audio formats and a wide variety of styles and performances by world renowned musicians license-free, **MusicBytes** *is a unique resource for the multimedia presentation designer.*

Finally, there is CD-audio. The quality of this format is far above WAVE files; it is as good as you can get, short of being in the studio when the clip is recorded. It isn't much different from WAVE files, other than it is digitized at a much higher frequency, and more bits are used for each sample. This makes CD-audio files enormous. As a result, there isn't much use transferring the music

to hard disk; it wouldn't be big enough to hold meaningful amounts of music. If you want to use CD-audio, you'll have to have the CD-ROM in the machine for your presentation.

If you're preparing multimedia presentations, there are a lot of sources for audio data. The combination of multiple supported formats and top quality music in a variety of styles from world renowned musicians makes *MusicBytes* unique, and perhaps indispensable.

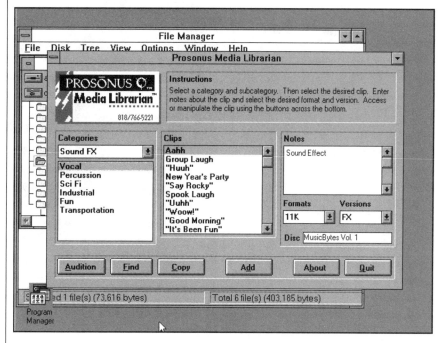

Everyone needs more sound effects, and *MusicBytes* Volume 1 is loaded with them.

A Music Lover's Multimedia Guide to Beethoven's 5th

Beethoven's well-known Fifth Symphony is explored from every possible angle.

N o, Microsoft doesn't have a lock on multimedia studies of classical music. Here's an excellent disc from InterActive Publishing. *A Music Lover's Multimedia Guide to Beethoven's 5th* is an educational program dealing primarily with *Beethoven's 5th Symphony*, the composer's life, and the instruments of the orchestra. Once you get into the multimedia program through Windows, you are given six menu choices: Beethoven's Biography, Listening to the 5th, The 5th's Structure, Musical Instruments, Games, and CD Player. Clicking CD Player informs you that you must exit the program and click another icon in order to play CDs. All the other choices are within the multimedia program.

At the bottom of the main menu screen there are several buttons that can be used throughout the program. These are Help, Main Menu, Glossary, Back, and Exit. The Help button has a surprise waiting: click it and you are given a narrated, guided tour of the program and all its various types of screens. Anytime later that you call up the Help screens, you get the appropriate part of this presentation.

Beethoven's Biography is a series of screens with text on the left and an appropriate image on the right, which together tell of Ludwig van Beethoven's life and precursors. In the text box is a button labelled Quote. Clicking this brings up a little window with a quote by or about the composer. At the bottom of the screen is a time line. A red arrow on the time line shows to what year the screen refers. You can click arrows at either end of the time line to move forward or back through time. Some years have several events; clicking one of these shows a short list in the text window, at the bottom of which you see something like "1 of 4." Click one item of

the list to see it, or click one of the directional arrows next to "1 of 4" to page through them all.

Listening to the 5th is the technical part of the program. The screen is divided roughly into thirds. On the left you see the number of the current movement and its major sections. Clicking one of these takes you immediately to that place in the symphony. In the middle of the screen is a brief (about a sentence) summary of what's happening in the first few bars of that section. Above this, the numbers tell you how far into the movement and how long that particular fragment is. For example, 0:00-0:05 would be the first 5 seconds of

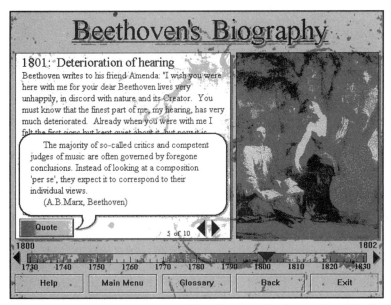

There's even a detailed biography of Beethoven as background on this disc.

that particular movement.

At the bottom of this middle window there is a box marked More. Clicking this gives you a full-screen, detailed summary of that entire section (exposition, development, etc.). Highlighted words are found in the glossary: click one to jump to the definition. Backing out of the More screen mentally, we come to the right side of the regular screen. This is where you control the music. A button with musical notes on it brings up a full-screen musical score. This fragment of the music is played by the orchestra, highlighting each bar as the music moves along. The Play Section button plays that page without the musical score, and Play All starts with that page and continues through the composition, simultaneously highlighting the name of that part of the movement on the left, and going through appropriate commentary on the center screen. There is also a Pause button.

The 5th's Structure is an index to the previous part of the program. Clicking this calls up one screen showing all four movements and listing their component sections. Clicking one of these takes you to

the appropriate page of Listening to the 5th.

Musical Instruments is a quick and easy introduction to the instruments of the orchestra. A chart of the orchestra appears, with each instrument listed in its place. The instruments are color-coded according to their family (strings, brass, etc.). Clicking any instrument brings up a photograph of someone playing the instrument and text describing it. The text can be paged forward or back using arrows. There is also a Range button that shows the range of the instrument on a piano keyboard; a Video button, which shows a few-second video with sound of that instrument being played alone; and a Section button, which takes you to a screen dealing with that instrument's family. The section screens work just like the individual instrument screens, with text and buttons for range and video. In addition, there are icons that allow you to jump to each of the instruments in that family. The sections can also be accessed directly from the main Musical Instruments screen by clicking one the of icons outside the orchestral chart.

Games gives you a choice of three games, after choosing number of players (1-2) and

novice or advanced level. At the novice level Play the Tune gives you eight color-coded piano keys. When you start the game, the computer depresses one key and that note sounds. Then you click the same key with your mouse. You get points for doing this successfully. Sounds easy, right? Then it plays two notes, and you follow, then three, and so on. By the time you get to about eight notes, it's pretty hard to remember what comes next. The advanced level has no colors—just plain piano keys. Match the Tune is a variation of a classic card game. There are 24 cards. Click two to turn them over. As each one turns in the novice level, you hear a sound clip and see the color, shape, and point value on the front of the card.

Multimedia analysis of Beethoven's 5th Symphony with additional information on the composer's life, as well as a glossary, an overview of orchestral instruments, and three music-based games.

If you are a fan of Beethoven, and are not burned out on the 5th, buy this disc. If, however, you've had enough of this particular symphony, you are not an ardent fan of the composer, or you are looking for a good general classical music tutorial, you would be happier with something else.

MusicMagic Songbook

Rating:

Publisher Name:
Midisoft Corporation

Software Requirements: MPC

Suggested Retail Price: $49.95

*M*usic Magic Songbook is a collection of songs in various styles that use your sound card or external MIDI devices to play MIDI music files (.mid). A bit of a primer on sound cards is in order. *Music Magic Songbook* tells you very quickly how good your sound card is (or isn't). Unless you bought your sound card very recently, or unless you bought a very good one, you may be disappointed in what you hear.

So, what is *Music Magic Songbook*? It is a combination of two separate products. It is a

songbook, with over 100 pieces of music in a number of musical genres. It is also has a MIDI player/arranger, called MusicMagic, that lets you explore the music in the soundbook and create or transcribe your own music.

As a bonus, it has an excellent description of the MIDI music standard and how it applies to your PC. It is a bit technical, but is much better than what probably came with your PC, Windows, or your sound card. Be warned: If your MIDI setup is incorrect, you may hear nothing or you may hear only a few of the instruments in the piece you are playing and you might not realize it, other than being generally discontent with the quality of many .mid files you hear.

The songbook contains songs in seven categories: Kids Tunes, Rock & Pop, Classical Ensemble, Classical Keyboard, Holiday, Jazz & Ragtime, and Around the World. There were a few quirks in how songs were assigned to categories; you will

find some folk songs in Kids Tunes and there is a Bach composition in Around the World, but for the most part the categories fit. The categories vary greatly in quality; perhaps little effort was put into some of the "non-serious" categories.

Kids Tunes contains 22 songs, including "Frere Jacques," "Pop Goes the Weasel," and "Twinkle, Twinkle, Little Star," as well as some folk songs, such as "Red River Valley" and "Scarborough Fair." Songs in this category are mostly weak. In "Scarborough Fair" for instance, track 12 in "Mixer view" (discussed later) sounds very out of place; it wipes out any perception of the melody. If you mute that track with MusicMagic, the song can be heard properly.

Rock & Pop also suffers, from both a lack of care and a complete lack of recognizable songs. Midisoft probably didn't want to pay royalties for songs still under copyright and so had a songwriter come up with some tunes "in the style of." This occurs frequently in music songbooks and is very disappointing. It is mitigated somewhat if these "style" tunes are well done. Of the twelve tunes present, "Brave New Tomorrow" and "Reflections" are fairly good, one or two others are fair, and the rest are poor. Sometimes it sounds like one or more instruments are out of tune with the rest. This can be fixed with MusicMagic, but you may not want to bother. These problems may be lessened by a better sound card or it may be just poor quality of the MIDI file. This section was very disappointing.

Classical Ensemble is much, much better. The twenty songs (generally excerpts of longer works) include Tchaikovsky's

MusicMagic Songbook presents lots of diffferent music for you to play and learn from.

Profiles of noted musicians and their work are highlighted in *MusicMagic Songbook.*

A mixed bag of MIDI music files, an excellent tutorial on setup of MIDI sound cards and an excellent MIDI player/arranger make this CD-ROM a good prospect for someone interested in computer-assisted music.

"Dance of the Sugar Plum Fairy," Vivaldi's "Spring" from *The Four Seasons,* and the second movement of Dvorak's *New World Symphony.* A text window is available on the songbook screen; for Classical Ensemble this window contains about three hundred words pertaining to the song, author, the time it was written in, etc. For instance, it notes that the melody for J.S. Bach's "Jesu, Joy of Man's Desiring" was "borrowed" from a hymn-writer, Johann Schop! This is a good section, done right and with care.

Classical Keyboard is also very good. There are 33 songs (generally excerpts of longer works) in this section, such as Schubert's *Marche Militaire,* Mozart's *Sonata in C Major,* and Pachelbel's *Gigue.* This section also has the 300-word commentary on the composition. This section, too, was done properly.

Jazz & Ragtime is a mix of "style" pieces ala Rock & Pop, as well as ragtime music written by Scott Joplin. Examples include "The Entertainer" and "Maple Leaf Rag," both by Joplin, and a "style" piece, "Ragtune."

The final section, Around the World, is fairly well done. There are 33 pieces in this section. A few pieces are traditional, such as "God Save the Queen" and Bach's "E Minor Bourree." Most are "style" pieces, with titles like "Boston Whaler," "Fiesta," and "Oktoberfest."

So, what is MusicMagic? It is a MIDI player/arranger, a tool that can turn passive listening into a visual experience, as you watch the score scroll by in perfect synchronization with the music. It can also lead to active participation, for you can go in and change the score. You can change individual notes, measures, or the whole score, change the way the instruments are mixed, use new instruments, mute existing instruments, change the tempo, and more.

The Mixer view gives you an individual mixer control for every instrument that is used by the piece. You can make an instrument the solo instrument by clicking the Solo button, or you can mute it using the Mute button, and there is a volume slider for each instrument as well. These are useful when you are studying or debugging a piece; you can block out some instruments to better appreciate others. A general volume control and a tempo control are also part of the mixer, as well as VCR style controls to move through and play the song. There is also a measure/beat/tick counter, so that you can identify sections precisely. The other screen that you might want to use if you are a perfectionist is the MIDI List.

MusicMagic Songbook is a mixed bag. It offers a wide variety of MIDI songs, which vary in quality from dreadful to excellent. Some songs have painfully obvious mistakes in them, although most songs are good or better. These songs give your sound card a workout, and will readily highlight its deficiencies. On the other hand, if you have a top-notch sound card, or a MIDI interface with an external synthesizer or synthesizers, you will hear some very impressive music. MusicMagic, a MIDI player/arranger, is an excellent tool for creating and manipulating MIDI songs. It has a reasonably good user interface and a full set of tools. The manual for the package is also a definite plus. It presents details on proper configuration of sound cards in a much clearer fashion than other sources. If you want to really experiment with music, you're going to need a tool like MusicMagic. Ignore the bad .mid files, treasure the good ones, and give MusicMagic a try.

So You Want to Be A Rock and Roll Star

Rating:

Publisher Name:
Interactive Records

Software Requirements:
Macintosh

Suggested Retail Price: **$59.95**

So You Want To be A Rock and Roll Star takes its name from The Byrds' hit song of the same name, and addresses the desires that bubble up in every garage band from Muscle Shoals to the Puget Sound. This disc won't replace a year at Julliard or a few months playing the Cavern Club, but it provides a lot of fun for musician wanna-bes as well as use-ta-bes, like me.

What you get on this disc are six great songs performed by "sound-alike" singers and musicians, in pretty good videos. Your selection includes the Patsy Cline weeper "Crazy," Otis Redding's posthumous monster-hit "Dock of the Bay," Wilson Pickett's tribute to "The Midnight Hour," Del Shannon's soaring "Runaway," the fabulous Ben E. King's "Stand By Me," and the Isley Brothers' challenge to John Lennon, "Twist and Shout."

Any of these can be played in full, accompanied by printed lyrics and visuals that range from pretty cool and appropriate to passable. You can also turn off the vocalist, guitarist, or keyboardist, in "music minus one" fashion so that you can sing or play along in those parts yourself. If ...Rock and Roll Star were nothing more than a karaoke machine, it would be pretty good.

However, hidden inside this disc is a patient guitar or keyboard teacher who can give you individualized lessons or explain how a given piece is played with some cogent analysis. The disc also offers some music theory lessons, and a Jargon menu you can use to look up any term discussed. You can view sheet music instead of the graphics as a song is played, or examine a color-coded chart of the chord progressions of any of the songs. There's also a digital tuning aid that will patiently sound any tone for as long as it takes to tune your guitar.

The CD audio-quality sound is great, even if the song selection is somewhat sparse. You can listen through your Mac's built-in speakers, some external speakers, or your stereo system if you've connected it to an appropriate input. Headphones plugged into the CD-ROM drive will also do in a pinch.

But don't feel cheated in getting only six

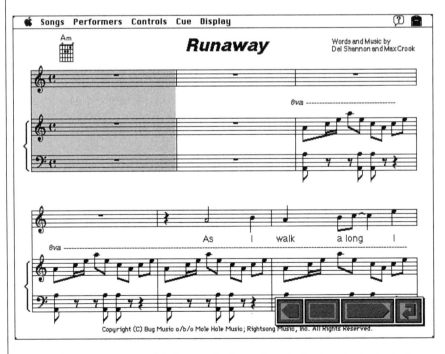

Your music teacher can explain how each piece of music is played using actual sheet music.

songs. Once you start digging and realize the wealth of information in the tutorials associated with each tune, you'll appreciate exactly what Interactive Records has done here. They've given you a loving, in-depth look at six classic songs, with a richness and reverence you couldn't expect if they'd attempted to cram a few dozen lesser works on this disc.

> *Rock karaoke, plus music lessons and some cogent analysis of six classic songs, make this a great disc for musician wanna-bes and rising stars.*

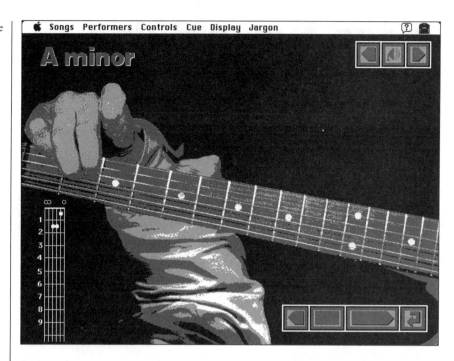

Both keyboard and guitar tutors are available to explain exactly how to play each song.

For those who don't like to read manuals, there's a fairly complete (if a little tedious) Guided Tour by the president of Interactive Records, who takes you through virtually every feature. Spend 15 minutes or so watching this segment, and you'll know everything you need to start using the disc. Try to ignore your host's enthusiasm, which seems to be aimed at inspiring awe in rank beginners. (More than once he emphasizes that "YOU can be the musician, YOU can be the Rock Star," when you use the "minus one" features. So what? There are a zillion audio discs and records that let you play along.)

I wish I'd owned ...*Rock and Roll Star* 25 years ago, when my own group, The Babylonian Disaster Squad, disintegrated. Heck, I wish my own son and namesake had listened to it a couple years ago. He moved

to Venice, California awhile back in search of a recording contract of his own. I didn't think he had a chance, at the time. But, have you heard of Robin Zander, lead singer of the group Cheap Trick? Well, today, my son is cleaning his house!

Video Movie Guide

Rating: ◉◉◉◉ 1/2

Publisher Name: Advanced Multimedia Solutions, Inc.

Software Requirements: MPC

Suggested Retail Price: $79.95

Chalk one up for ambiance. Okay, so the descriptions of individual films are sparse (rarely more than a paragraph or two) and some major stars rate only a few lines. Even so, if you love movies, you'll love this disc about movies available on video. It makes up in weirdness and fun what it lacks in depth. Are you ready for 1,300 pictures of the *boxes* videos come in?

I'll trade yet another lengthy treatise on *Citizen Kane* for the priceless glimpses at the offbeat and obscure films featured on *Video Movie Guide*. You'll find old movie serials and B-Westerns alongside television series episodes repackaged as "movies," and made-for-TV movies that later made it into the theaters. There are Japanese animated cartoons, direct-to-video releases never seen on television *or* in theaters, collections of cartoons, and comedy concerts.

If CD-ROMs were a game, *Video Movie Guide* would be Trivial Pursuit. Do you like Bela Lugosi? If so, you certainly already know about his classic films, like *Dracula* or *Murders in the Rue Morgue*. You're probably knowledgable about his weird excursions into comedy (*Abbot and Costello Meet Frankenstein*). You own a copy of the actor's "posthumous" film, the ever-awful *Plan 9 from Outer Space*, which listed him as the star even though Lugosi died months before filming began (and showed up only in clips taken from his silent movies). But, have you seen or heard of *Murder by Television*—filmed in 1935—with a pre-*Gone with the Wind* Hattie McDaniel?

That's the sort of stuff you can expect to uncover while dredging through the depths of *Video Movie Guide*.

Based on Mick Martin and Marsha Porter's Ballantine Books volume, this disc includes capsule reviews of 13,800 movies. These abbreviated commentaries list the key stars and credits for the films, but have none of the cogent analysis found in Roger Ebert or Pauline Kael's reviews on Microsoft's *Cinemania*. Of course, Ebert probably hasn't written much on films like *Aelita: Queen of Mars*, a strange 1924 Russian silent classic, in any case.

Martin and Porter wisely base their ratings (one Turkey to four stars) on how a film stacks up within a particular genre. While the best Westerns (*High Noon, Shane*) do stack up well against serious dramas (*Citizen Kane, The Pawnbroker*), the goals of most films within each category are so different that it's more fair to compare apples with apples and oranges with oranges. The authors even admit to changing their ratings from edition to edition as they reevaluate films they may have loved—or hated—the first time around.

Looking up T-rated (for Turkey) films can uncover some unappreciated gems in *Video Movie Guide*.

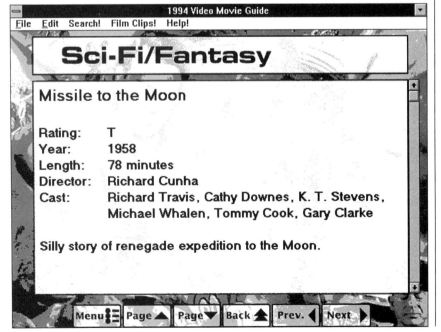

All the films covered are available on video, even though some of them may be dusty oldies you'll find in the video rental stores that are no longer available new.

Don't be put off by the quirky interface and the terse movie descriptions: this Windows-based disc is a wacky, off-the-wall treasure chest of virtually every well-known and obscure movie available on video—somewhere.

Clicking many of the words in the reviews whisks you off to another listing on the disc through the magic of hypertext links. There's weirdness to be found here, too, because many of the links seem to have been established by some automated process that establishes a connection without guaranteeing relevance.

For example, when you click the word Earth included in the phrase "Martian who invades Earth," (found in the review *Mars Needs Women*), the hypertext link brings up a review of an homage to the spirit of the collective farmer in Russia, a film entitled *Earth*. As you can see, you'll hit paydirt as often as dry holes when you browse through this disc, even if it is all fun.

If you want ambiance, check out the 35 minutes of movie trailers that previewed the actual films! There are 20-some great

trailers, displayed in a window draped to resemble a 1940s-1950s-era movie house. You can almost smell the popcorn as you view trailers for *Pride of the Yankees* or *Diary of Anne Frank*.

The Windows interface created for *Video Movie Guide* is as quirky as its content but no less non-standard than the art-deco face *Cinemania* displays to the world. A fixed-size 640 x 480 window (with appropriate movie-poster background) contains the main menu and six navigation buttons used to page through the text and move from screen to screen. The five main menu choices let you find a movie by title, genre, cast member, directory, or academy award winners. A pull-down menu also lets you enter just a keyword to search by.

The searching technique is as offbeat as you might expect. When you select the "search by title" strategy, an array of buttons with all the letters of the alphabet appears. Click the first letter of the title to narrow the search to a smaller range S-to-Sc, Sc to Se, Se-to-Sh. It's a little like trying to select one volume of an encyclopedia, and is quite clumsy, but somehow you expect quirks like this from *Video Movie Guide*.

Naturally, there's no consistency between the five search strategies. You can use the "encyclopedia" method to find film titles or cast members, but to locate an academy award winner you choose the decade and then the specific year to view. Searching by genre involves an intricate process of selecting the category of film (action/adventure, children/family, comedy, and so on) and then deciding whether you want to hunt by title or quality rating (on the turkey-to-stars scale).

Tip: search for Turkey films to unearth some truly memorable and deservedly obscure films. We'd entirely forgotten Ken Russell's 1975 disaster *Listzomania* until *Video Movie Guide* resurrected this musical for us. Naturally, the navigation methods this disc forces on you are tedious and illogical—all the better to encourage the

kind of aimless meandering that produces the best results.

If you love movies, you'll want to look long and hard for *Video Movie Guide*. It's not as slick or scholarly as *Cinemania*, and you'll need a sense of humor to appreciate the interface, but it's clearly the most fun you can have at the movies without leaving home.

The *Video Movie Guide* contains movie clips of such classics as *One Flew Over the Cuckoo's Nest*.

XPlora 1: Peter Gabriel's Secret World

Rating: ◎ ◎ ◎ ◎

Publisher Name: **MacPlay**

Software Requirements:
Macintosh

Suggested Retail Price: **$69.95**

Roughly 20 years ago, a journalist proclaimed, "I have seen the future of Rock n' Roll, and its name is Bruce Springsteen." Of course, the Boss thereupon got his picture on the cover of *Time* magazine, and the journalist became his manager. It was pretty big stuff at the time.

Today, a semi-journalist (me) presumes to state that I have seen the future of interactive musical entertainment, and its name is Peter Gabriel. I'm not kidding. (Peter, please contact my publisher as soon as you need a new manager.) If you have a Macintosh and more than a passing interest in music, purchase this CD-ROM now for a close-up look at ways in which music will be created and marketed in the future. You don't need to be a Peter Gabriel fanatic to appreciate this disc (I'm not). Anyone who enjoys art, rhythm, spiritual thinking, or myriad other avenues of creative expression, and isn't easily offended by mildly explicit images and language, will love *Xplora 1*.

I readily acknowledge to outraged Todd Rundgren fans that Todd virtually created electronic and interactive music as we know

it today, single-handed. However, on this disc, Gabriel draws on much more than the genius inside him, integrating the creativity found in diverse cultures and in other artists like himself. Rundgren projects outside the Utopia framework are very much solo efforts.

Here, Gabriel, a founding member of the group Genesis and now on his own as a solo artist since 1975, brings us a whole world of music and art to explore. He pulls off this technical and creative tour-de-force without once appearing self-important or self-involved. His passion and humor make this a wonderful treat for the eye, ear, and mind.

Xplora boasts an innovative, un-Mac-like interface that's difficult to describe, but effortless to use. The first time I ran this disc, the things I was seeing struck me as so weird that I went to the Monitors control panel to change my color depth and screen resolution to 256 colors and 640 x 480, and then restarted, just to make sure I wasn't experiencing some sort of conflict. However the Escher-like cloud background, divided at the top by a thick black bar is the real main screen. Peter pops up to get you started, and then appears throughout the disc in interviews and personal comments at appropriate times.

If you aren't a Peter Gabriel fan now, you will be after you see his amazing videos and hear the songs showcased on *Xplora1*.

As you wander through the disc in a decidedly non-linear fashion (it's virtually impossible to repeat a session even if you wanted to), you'll sample ten of Gabriel's best songs, their lyrics, and uncensored, full-length QuickTime videos. Choice titles include "Steam," "Eden," and "Digging in the Dirt." If, like everyone else in the world, you've seen the "Sledgehammer" video that propelled Gabriel to pop stardom in 1987, you'll know what to expect from these clips. All incorporate stunning creativity and totally original images unlike any other videos you've ever seen.

This stunning musical and artistic tour-de-force presents music, photographs, QuickTime full-length videos, and much more to stimulate your imagination and mind.

Keep in mind that all this blubbering praise is coming from someone who has never purchased a Peter Gabriel album nor attended one of his concerts. Indeed, as entertaining as it is, this disc should be given away free to anyone who will testify that they are not currently a Gabriel fan. He'd

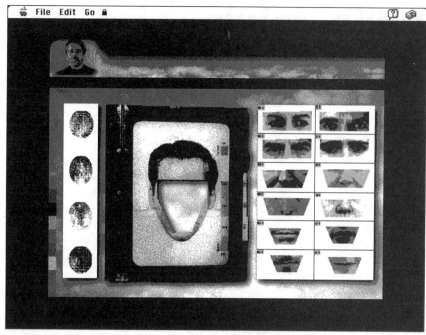

Peter Gabriel pops up in various guises to guide you through the disc.

sell a ton of albums after they took a look at this disc.

When you check in, you're given a briefcase to use to collect things, like backstage passes that give you access to videos in normally inaccessible parts of the disc. There's a full-motion video visit to Gabriel's Real World studios, where you can sit at the mixing board and re-do "Digging in the Dirt" with an inappropriately simple four-track mixing board, or sit in on a jam session.

The sheer quantity of things on this disc is amazing, too. You'll find a discography of all ten of Gabriel's albums, and information on two of the human rights organizations he supports.

Because I'm a huge fan of acts like Ofra Haza, Josefa Dahari, 3 Mustaphas 3, and Dissidenten, I really enjoyed the World Music section. This presents great samples from 40 different albums that you might never have the chance to hear otherwise, along with QuickTime clips from the World

of Music, Art, and Dance festival in San Francisco.

Even after hours and hours alone in the dark with this disc, I'm certain there's a lot more here to be enjoyed. If you have a Mac and are already a Gabriel fan, you undoubtedly own this disc. If you haven't discovered his music and art yet, do yourself a favor and explore the world along with him.

Billie Holiday

Rating:

Publisher Name: **Ebook, Inc**

Software Requirements:
MPC/Macintosh

Suggested Retail Price: **$29.95**

This CD is an absolute delight! If you don't know who Billie Holiday is, you owe yourself the treat of finding out. Do you like the blues? Jazz? Enjoy hearing a female sing from the soul until it has you captured under a spell? That's Billie Holiday! Just take a look at these lyrics from her tune "Fine and Mellow":

> My man don't love me
> He treats me oh so mean
> My man he don't love me
> He treats me awful mean
> He's the lowest man
> That I've ever seen

Billie Holiday, who lived from 1915 to 1959, was a black American singer... specifically, she was a jazz singer. She began singing in 1930 and earned a supreme position among modern jazz singers with her emotional impact and highly personal approach to a song. Her life was complicated by the drug addiction that eventually destroyed her career and hastened her death.

To learn more, get this CD and take yourself on a lovely trip of sound and education. The history is well collected and the matter is treated in an educational, historical keepsake format by Dr. Herbert Wong. Wong is among the most respected jazz historians, among his credits: he is the president of Palo Alto Jazz and technical advisor for the Smithsonian Institute of Jazz Oral History Program. Upon opening he appears and says to you "*Billie Holiday* is a multimedia record that contains actual recordings of her, along with a little background about the songs and what may have inspired creations."

Excerpt from Brubeck: "You know Billie Holiday to me was one of the great singers of all times.... The fact remains that after all the lurid stories of her star-crossed, self-destructive life, she did something no other woman has done in jazz. Today if you are using jazz and you're a woman, you sing some of Billie Holiday. There's no other way to do it. No vocalist is without her influence. All girl singers sing some of Billie, like all trumpet players play some of Louis. She wrote the text."

A rare treat in this section is a short clip—video and audio—with text of her appearing on TV in 1957 with The Count Basie All Stars.

This section is a veritable "trip down memory lane" with the people who were there and who were touched by her magic. So many greats have come and gone, and the concept of preservation in this manner is excellent. I hope Ebook does one on all our contributors, so we can pass it on to our next generation so that they can really experience how it was "in the good old days." Maybe if they use CD's like this, they won't laugh at us and our old fogey music!

Billie Holiday is an easy CD to install and use. If you are familiar with the Windows or Macintosh interfaces, just point and click and you will do fine. In some areas, there is a bottom bar that looks a lot like a tape recorder, with play, rewind, forward, etc. Occasionally there is a picture, put the cursor there and it changes into an icon of a white gloved hand; click, and the picture moves as the person speaks. Where the text is blue over black, click for a pop-out history or background of the person mentioned in the text. The combination of learning and enjoyment is done so well on *Billie Holiday*, and the ease of use makes it a very pleasant experience.

Jazz Singer Billie Holiday is featured, with her music, on this disc.

History of the Blues

From the opening bars of Muddy Waters wailing "Hoochie Coochie Man" to the final strains of urban blues at the close of this CD-ROM, you'll be grinning and tapping your foot along with the immortal musicians who make up its heart and soul. *History of the Blues* is as unpolished as some of the music it presents, but, like the blues itself, is filled with genuine human feelings.

Frankly, the blues deserve a better disc than this. But then, this review was written by a blues fanatic (since 1965) and musician who continues to play this music whenever he gets the chance. But, until Microsoft gets around to giving this genre the full treatment (as they did for Stravinsky or Beethoven), blues lovers should be happy to have *History of the Blues* available. Slick production techniques have never detracted from B.B. King's legacy, but neither did the lack of them damage the reputation of Robert Johnson.

History of the Blues is a music-filled presentation in slide-show format (that is, using only still photographs, rather than video clips). The disc leads you through four important topics of bluesology, using the words of Dr. Leonard Goines, a professor of music at Manhattan Community College, and himself a jazz, blues, and rock performer and recording artist.

The photos range from archival images of long-dead pioneers in the field to some fairly recent (mid-1970s, anyway) pictures of performers who are still with us. Each image is accompanied by descriptions supplied by a resonant-voiced narrator, who sounds enough like B. B. King to keep you in the proper mood for these presentations.

Scholarly, detailed, but not slick describes this disc devoted to the blues.

Both the Macintosh and DOS versions feature simple interfaces that provide only minimal options. You can pause a frame or repeat the music selection that accompanies it. Click the left or right arrow icon to advance to the next slide or return to a previous image. There's an Index icon that takes you to a list of all the topics and performers covered. If you select one of these, you see the frame or frames associated with that topic, and hear the music linked to the images. You may then return to the section of the presentation you were viewing when you accessed the Index, or jump to the portion featuring any of the Index entries.

Each of the four main sections (Roots, Twelve-Bar Blues, Classic Blues, City Blues) is spiced with actual musical selections, so you can hear B.B. King's expressive voice, or study the rolling left-hand figures of boogie-woogie piano playing, as popularized by Jimmy Yancey and others. Any disc devoted to blues music could do no less, but we wish there were more and longer musical pieces attached to each module. It would be wonderful to be able to click a button or two to activate additional sound excerpts or video clips.

In addition to the four-part presentation, *History of the Blues* includes a text teacher's guide, a discography that cites several key recordings for all the blues styles discussed, and biographies of key figures of the blues heritage. You find capsule descriptions of the life of well-known blues legends like B.B. King, Muddy Waters, and Robert Johnson, along with lesser-known figures, such as Blind Willie McTell, Chippie Hill, and Skip James.

Even after 30 years listening to blues, I learned some new things from this disc. And, lucky enough to meet and speak with some of the people profiled on this disc, including B.B. King, Paul Butterfield, and Rev. Gary Davis, I know they wouldn't be put off by the rough edges in this digital presentation. The blues deserves a whole raft of CD-ROMs, but until they arrive, the loving treatment of *History of the Blues* is well worth exploring. With any luck, you'll discover new and exciting music to explore on audio disc, or learn something interesting about old favorite performers.

Rating: ◉ ◉ ◉

Publisher Name: **Queue**

Software Requirements: **MPC/Macintosh**

Suggested Retail Price: **$49.95**

It's A Wonderful Life

Rating  1/2

Publisher: **Alpha and Omega**

System Requirements: **MPC**

Suggested Retail Price: **$39.95**

Frank Capra's *It's A Wonderful Life*, the perennial Christmas production most of us love to hate to love, is probably the consummate tear-jerker. Poor old George Bailey, the kindly small-town banker, beset, bedeviled, bankrupt; and, if that's not enough, blessed with a guardian angel, Clarence. Of course, Clarence is, well, a bit inept. He's been trying to earn his wings for a long time. George, presumably, would just like to earn enough to stay solvent but it's not to be. In a fit of depression he declares he wishes he'd never been born, a sentiment not unknown to lots of people at one time or another.

The story continues in the old familiar opened vein straight from whatever human organ supplies schmaltz. Clarence, the confusticated cherub, guides the hapless, bemused Bailey through the world as it would have been without one George. George eventually repents and all comes out right in the end; God's in His heaven, George is back in his life, George's friends and neighbors pitch in and the business is saved, and Clarence gets his wings, signaled by a tree ornament bell ringing without visible means of support, a bit like George Bailey at the start of the show.

So what's the point? There probably is no special point to this CD. It needs no more special reason for its existence than does a kitten. It was possible and practical to do. So Alpha and Omega did it. The movie is one of the oldest chestnuts on film, but it roasts well on CD-ROM, too. The flavor is all there and it's wholesome. If you love the old schmalzfest, it will always be no farther away than your CD-caddy. Even if you hate the movie, well, you can hate it at close range, anytime you like.

It's not that it had to be done, nor that it needed to be done, nor that, perhaps, anyone even wanted it done. It's that it *was* done; that they both were. The movie itself is one of those things designed to help you feel good and have a tiny little bit of faith that it's not always all in vain. The CD-ROM version puts that on your desktop.

It may not change your life. It certainly won't solve your problems in a miraculous instant. All it may or can do is what the movie was made to do, give you a peek into the fictive life of one character created to represent everyone who's ever been in trouble and who's been bailed out somehow.

Maybe that's enough.

It's A Wonderful Life still looks pretty good on the tiny viewing window.

The perennial Christmas chestnut re-roasted and served on CD-ROM. Plays well in Runtime Media Player in Windows, even on a single-speed drive. Why? Why not? Why are there kittens?

Jazz: An Interactive History

This first jazz history on CD-ROM is based on a Prentice Hall textbook, *Jazz: From Its Origins to the Present*, by Lewis Porter and Michael Ullman with Ed Hazell. Porter then supervised transforming the book into a wonderful interactive multimedia presentation. It can be used as is, or with a 100-page instructor's manual available free from the publisher.

There are 120 different samples of jazz, accompanied by video clips of jazz immortals like Louis Armstrong. Each piece is supplied as a MIDI file, which are actually played by the software, rather than reproduced mechanically like a recording. That means you can play the music back at a slower speed to study it in detail. Or, if you are a musician, you can sit at a keyboard or play drums or bass along with the tune.

This is great stuff! My own musical inclinations have always been along improvisational lines, since my own performing days date back to the days in the late-60s when a rock tune wasn't respected unless the band could play it for at least an hour, non-stop. Now that my professional days are over, I enjoy playing along with blues and jazz CDs, and this one is made for for folks like me.

Most of the examples include chord symbols, so that you can join in, too. This really gives new meaning to the term "interactive" CD! You'll enjoy wandering through the menus. The main screen gives you a choice of text, pictures, music, or information. Text, of course, is the complete contents of the book, arranged by chapters for study or browsing. When you encounter a photo, click it to pop up a large window for further study. Soon, you'll encounter actual clips of sheet music in the text. Click the speaker icon in the margin to hear them played, over and over, if you like. There's something you can't do with a printed textbook!

Studying all the chapters in this text will give you a good understanding of jazz and its history. The Picture Gallery lets you look through dozens of photos and video clips of jazz greats in action. After you've studied a given performer, you can go watch him or her play. The Music section lets you sort through all the song selections on the disc and play them in any order. Information is your guide to using the disc.

Many of the musical selections, totalling more than 60 minutes in length, can also be played on your CD audio player. Just be sure to skip Track 1, which contains data, unless your jazz tastes are much more advanced than mine. (If you're incurably curious, don't play this track too loudly: you could damage your speakers.)

Jazz: An Interactive History won't turn you into a jazz musician or a jazz lover, but if you are either of these two things, you'll prefer this enhanced, sound-filled version to the original book, and greatly enjoy your sonic exploration of this truly American art form.

Rating: ◉◉◉

Publisher Name:
Ebook/Compton's New Media

Software Requirements: MPC

Suggested Retail Price: $79.95

You can view photos of jazz greats by browsing through *Jazz: An Interactive History*.

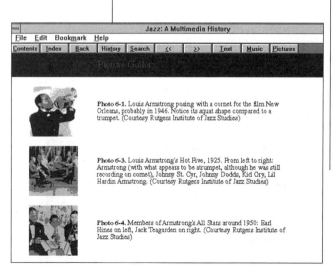

Jazz: A Multimedia History

File   Edit   Bookmark   Help

Contents | Index | Back | History | Search | << | >> | Text | Music | Pictures

Picture Gallery

Photo 6-1. Louis Armstrong posing with a cornet for the film New Orleans, probably in 1946. Notice its squat shape compared to a trumpet. (Courtesy Rutgers Institute of Jazz Studies)

Photo 6-3. Louis Armstrong's Hot Five, 1925. From left to right: Armstrong (with what appears to be a trumpet, although he was still recording on cornet), Johnny St. Cyr, Johnny Dodds, Kid Ory, Lil Hardin Armstrong. (Courtesy Rutgers Institute of Jazz Studies)

Photo 6-4. Members of Armstrong's All Stars around 1950: Earl Hines on left, Jack Teagarden on right. (Courtesy Rutgers Institute of Jazz Studies)

MCS CDMaster

Rating: ◎ ◎ ◎

Publisher Name: **Animotion Development Corporation**

Software Requirements: **MPC1**

Suggested Retail Price: **$49.95**

Animotion's logo includes the words "we do cool." "Cool" is a very good description for this CD-ROM title. As a combination CD-ROM player and CD-ROM cataloger, *MCS CDMaster* offers excellent graphics and full features in the form of two easy-to-use Windows applications.

Here's a computer CD to help you manage your audio CDs, through its tracking software and sophisticated stereo CD player worthy of any audiophile's rack.

By clicking the MCS CDMaster icon, a strikingly sharp CD player appears on-screen that looks and works (with mouse) just like

you would expect a home unit to work. Replete with "LED" lights, the music CD player's features include play, pause, multiple scanning speeds, skip, pause, stop, repeat, shuffle, volume control, elapsed time and remaining time monitoring functions, programmable play list, and even an eject button, if your CD-ROM player supports it.

If you like the same song or a couple of songs off a title, you can play it (or them) repeatedly. You can even save your tailored playlist to a file for future recall.

This package supports Windows multitasking—you can close the MCS CDPlayer and continue to listen to selections while working in other Windows or DOS applications.

MCS CDMaster in and of itself would be worth the purchase, however, Animotion also provides MCS TitleTrax, a dBASE-compatible software that allows you to easily input such information as your music CD's artist, title, the title of the selection, and date.

Once input, viewing the information is just as friendly. Font selections, available at the click of a mouse button, permit a change in font style and size. Information can then be displayed or withheld, so that you can make visible only the items that interest you.

Upon returning to MCS CDPlayer, you will notice that information that you have entered in MCS TitleTrax now appears in the Playlist Selection at the bottom of the CD Player. Change music CDs (to another title that was input into TitleTrax) and the playlist changes accordingly.

MCS TitleTrax allows sorting by items such as Compilation Artist, Compilation Title, Selection Artist, Selection Title, Recording Time, Recording Year, Track (or side) in both ascending or descending order. Reports can be printed with a Windows compatible printer.

MCS TitleTrax also allows database selection by media type—music CD, cassette tape, DAT tape, and even album (the round thing with a groove on each side found in the back of a closet). Especially convenient is the selection method, which allows you to pick one or any combination of media types to perform a search.

Also included on this CD is a sample of *MusicBytes* clip music from Prosonus. The thirteen music clips provide a wide range of music styles suitable for inserting in multimedia presentations and are, with certain restrictions (of course), license-free.

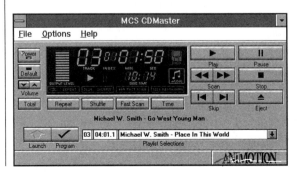

Control every audio CD function with this clever CD-ROM-based program.

Microsoft Multimedia Mozart: The Dissonant Quartet

As with the other Microsoft music-oriented CD-ROMs reviewed in this chapter, Multimedia Mozart explores the meaning and beauty of the music by showing us background material on the composer and world in which he lived. Winter explains how the elegance and grandeur of the 18th century built a foundation for Mozart's work, and the elegant concert halls and palaces that were a suitable stage for their performance.

You also discover the sublime details about musical instruments and how they create distinctive sounds. The violin, for example, appears to be a simple instrument, but actually is among the most complex of all instruments from an acoustic standpoint. Finally, you understand why instruments that are hundreds of years old are prized for their special qualities.

Then, you can view the entire score of the string quartet and examine the piece in detail. Winter explains the meaning of each phrase in terms that nonmusicians will marvel over, and professionals will absorb eagerly.

You can learn how to listen to quartet compositions, regarded in the 18th century as one of the highest forms of communication. You see how the four instruments blend together as separate voices in a wonderful song. If all this seems too serious and high-minded, you can take the Mozart challenge—a game for one to four players that tests how much you've learned about the Dissonant Quartet from this disc. The questions range from easy to difficult, to challenge the most knowledgeable music scholar.

Multimedia Mozart is a wonderful introduction to one of the finest composers and musical geniuses of all time.

I recommend this disc to anyone who's heard snippets of Mozart and would like to learn more. The quartet form makes an easy introduction to a complex musician's music. If you already love Mozart, you'll love this disc, too, because it gives even veteran music fans a deeper understanding of this work. Winter has wisely chosen an interesting piece that is not as overworked as some of Mozart's popular warhorses. It sounds as fresh and interesting to our ears as it must have on the day it was first performed.

Rating: ◉ ◉ ◉ ◉

Publisher Name: **Microsoft**

Software Requirements: **MPC**

Suggested Retail Price: **$79.95**

Learn about the cello and other instruments in a string quartet from *Microsoft's Multimedia Mozart: The Dissonant Quartet CD-ROM.*

The Instruments
The Cello

The cello is the bass member of the string family. (A double bass is the low bass member of that family.) The body of the modern cello varies in length from 73 to 80 cm.—more than twice the length of the violin. Because

Multimedia Music Book Series: Mozart

Rating:

Publisher Name: **Ebook, Inc.**

Software Requirements:
MPC/Macintosh

Suggested Retail Price: **$24.95**

By combining a good overview of Wolfgang Amadeus Mozart's background with some of his most well-known music, Ebook has produced a CD-ROM package that this author is quite pleased to have on his shelf.

Mozart is a slick combination of biographies, chronologies, graphics, essays, music trivia, and some of Mozart's best known and most beautiful music. This Windows-based application allows the user to select from several menu choices— Biographical Sketch, A Mozart Chronology, Aspects of Late 18th Century Life, Parameters of Classical Music, Music Forums in the Classical Period, The Music of Mozart, Mozart Trivia, Selected Bibliography, and Music Gallery.

Each of these sections contains clear, easy-to-read, and comparatively short articles. If you are looking for an overview of Mozart, this is certainly the place to look. There are a couple of features that make this an attractive package for younger learners— the text does not get weighed down in a lot of complicated terminology, and music definitions are defined through hot spots (pop-up definitions that appear by clicking highlighted words within the text). Perhaps a good definition of the text in this package is succinct and to the point.

The music selections on Mozart are comprised of Eine Kleine Nachtmusik, K.525 Allegro; Symphony No. 40 in G minor, K.550, Complete; Piano Concerto No. 21 in C major, K.467, Andante Elvira Madigan; Don Giovannni, K.527, Duet "la ci darem la mano"; Requiem, K.626 - Introit and Kyrie, which are performed by renown orchestras such as The Berlin Radio Symphony Orchestra.

One interesting feature is found in topic The Music of Mozart, where portions of the music are discussed and then played (at your choosing) as either melody or full orchestration. A fun item found on the title is a section called Mozart Trivia. This is a group of probably little known factoids disguised under trivia buttons.

Another particularly nice feature presented by Ebook is that this CD-ROM can be played in your music CD player. So, if you are looking for some good music, but don't want to turn your computer on, you don't need to purchase the same selections twice.

Learning how to jump around the menus and from area to area is very straightforward. With forward and reverse arrow keys at every topic item, it is easy to manipulate through the data. Who would want this title? Well, this author for one, and probably other adults with a sense of music appreciation.

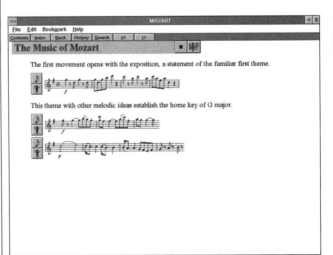

Take a close look at Mozart's music, life, and times.

Microsoft Multimedia Stravinsky

Microsoft has engaged scholar and pianist Robert Winter to prepare their fabulous line of multimedia discs highlighting important composers like Mozart, Beethoven and, in this disc, Igor Stravinsky. If they ever do one on Rachmaninov (who, in my opinion, would be a multimillionaire composer of movie soundtracks today), I'll be in heaven.

For now, this Stravinsky disc is lush and complete enough to please any lover of modern classical music. Make no mistake, Stravinsky was a pacesetter in his time, even though the story of him jumping for his life out a backstage window when the "Rite of Spring" was first performed in 1913 is untrue.

You'll learn that and much more about this pioneering ballet score from this great Microsoft disc. Multimedia has really been put to work here. You can learn about the instruments in the orchestra, see a detailed description of the ballet itself with musical accompaniment, and then read biographies of the composer and his collaborators.

The centerpiece is a complete performance of "Rite" itself, with musical notation that follows the score and comments that tell you exactly what is going on. You can watch as each theme unfolds and variations emerge like spring flowers. If you're musically literate, you can examine the score bar by bar, with help from Robert Winter. But you don't need to be a professional musician to appreciate this disc.

The interface into all this music is the typical friendly Microsoft face, with plentiful buttons to let you access chapters, sections, a glossary, or backtrack to retrace your steps. The controls are unobtrusive and let you do things like play through an entire passage, repeat a page of music, pause, or take a closer look at a secton. Winter's commentary is eye-opening.

When you're finished, take a break with The Rite Game, which tests you on musical topics about various passages in the piece. The better you answer tough questions, the faster you move through this game.

Rating: ◉ ◉ ◉ ◉

Publisher Name: **Microsoft**

Software Requirements: **MPC**

Suggested Retail Price: **$79.95**

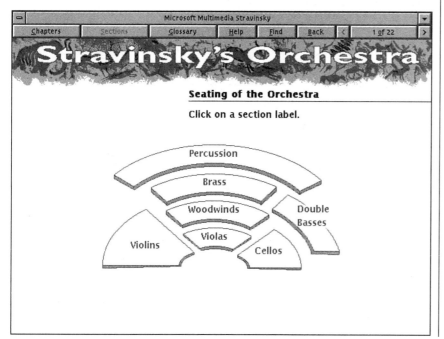

View the exact layout of Stravinsky's orchestra when Rite of Spring was performed for the first time in Paris, in 1913.

The Musical World of Professor Piccolo

Rating:

Publisher Name:
Opcode Interactive

Software Requirements: **MPC**

Suggested Retail Price: **$69.95**

*P*rofessor Piccolo takes you to Music Town, where he teaches you the basics of music and musical instruments, and how they all fit together to produce a particular sound. You can learn to read music, play musical games, or study music history. There are sections that cover musical instruments, telling you how different instruments fit into families, and how each covers a range of notes and type of music.

You can learn about music song forms, play a few musically-oriented games, and enroll in a music theory course at the Music School. Drop in for some tunes at the Rock Club, or visit the Symphony Hall for a major production. Everything is easy to understand, and immediately accessible with Professor Piccolo as your guide.

There are six different modules in Music Town. You can study the layout of the symphony orchestra and click each member to hear them play. "Peter and the Wolf" with a celebrity narrator won't teach you as much about music as this CD-ROM. You can study the symphonic form, and study Haydn's *Symphony #88* in great detail.

You can also learn musical terms and explore the history of key instruments in

The Library. Or, dash across the street to the church to learn about the history of religious music and its enormous impact on music of the present day. (If you don't believe that, listen to some gospel music some time, then compare it with country or blues!)

At the music school, you can take a comprehensive interactive music course, setting your own pace and using this disc instead of a textbook to find out how music is created and played. When you're done, you can drop in on the Jazz Club or Rock Club and hear groups perform great songs. You can learn about the history of each genre, and look at the structure of songs.

In the Arcade, you can play Musical Pursuit or other games. *Professor Piccolo* was designed by music teachers, so you know the information is good and well presented. This disc is suitable for beginning music students as well as those who just want to approach their favorite subject in a new and interesting way.

Professor Piccolo **invites you to Music Town, where you can learn about classical, jazz, and rock music from your personal tutor.**

PC Karaoke

Karaoke is one of those foreign afflictions, like fire ants, that burst upon our consciousness gradually, finally invading the shores of the United States and gradually taking over like some loathesome disease. Guess what? It's great fun! This disc and companion discs from Sirius can let you play with Karaoke in the privacy of your own home, without the expense of a major-league stereo machine.

The program itself is simple. You load it, it checks your CD-ROM drive, determines which of the many available discs you have inserted, and then presents you with a menu of song choices representing that disc. You then select the one you want to sing along with. You see the lyrics of the song on the screen of your computer, along with some innocuous graphics, and hear the basic tracks of the song—minus vocalist—through your Windows sound system. Hopefully, you'll have a microphone (one is supplied with the basic system, but not with the add-on discs) plugged into your sound card. Your voice is mixed in with the background tracks, and the whole thing is unleashed on the ears of an unsuspecting world.

When I first saw a *PC karaoke* display at Spring Comdex, 1993, I decided it's time to find a new country to live in. Then, I decided to investigate in person when my club had a midnight karaoke festival at a massive 100-person party in a hotel. It was great! I ended up hanging around for about four hours. I didn't sing, of course. I'm not allowed. After Vatican II proclaimed that all Catholics must sing hymns in church, just like Protestants, I was given a special dispensation by Rome. But I had a great time with the other participants, whether they had voices like asthmatic frogs, or a great baritone who put everybody away with his rendition of Duke of Earl.

You'll want to try *PC Karaoke*, too. Your own compact disc drive and speakers can do the job of an expensive karaoke machine with no further investment. Sirius provides many discs with a dozen or more song selections each. The classic oldies disc we tested had "Danny Boy," "My Wild Irish Rose," and "Over There." Other discs have rock songs, country and western tunes, or anything you might have a yen for. In fact, this is the only Japanese import you can name that only requires a single yen.

Rating: ◉◉◉

Publisher Name:
Sirius Publishing

Software Requirements: **MPC**

Suggested Retail Price: **$15.98**
(More than 30 different song discs available)

Each Sirius *PC Karaoke* disc has songs you can choose from from a menu like this one.

Sound Explorer

Rating: ◉ ◉ ◉

Publisher Name:
Midisoft Corporation

Software Requirements: **MPC**

Suggested Retail Price: **$29.95**

Midisoft's *Sound Explorer* is a collection of seven multimedia music programs, working samples that are not full versions. They are something more than demos, but less than the complete product. Think of each of these as "lite" versions of some interesting programs. The programs' samples cover MIDI music sequencing and notation software, digital audio recording and editing software, and several song collections.

One of the special features of this package is that you can link work that you are doing. For example: As you learn about a piece of music in Music Mentor, you can switch to an application like Recording Session that lets you view the music in the music notation. All the switching is available in the Midisoft *Sound Explorer*. The *Explorer* main screen stays available for launching other Midisoft products.

The modules include:

Midisoft MIDI KIT with Recording Session for Windows. Here is a great recording and editing program to play with! You get a MIDI adapter cable and a joystick connector extension to allow you to interface directly to all standard MIDI devices and instruments ranging from MIDI microphones to keyboards—to the PC!

The Midisoft Multimedia Music Library. Enjoy composers, be a composer, or edit compositions! You get garden variety Bach, Mozart, Joplin, and much much more. Comes with a booklet filled with info about the music and the artists. Interact or listen, just like all the others, help is also available if you need it.

Midisoft STUDIO for Windows. This module has business presentations, music education, performing for fun or profit...have your own studio and go for it! There is a clear and easy to understand menu named Studio Panel View, which provides detailed information on all tracks, as many as 32 in fact. It goes into detail in such areas as velocity, volume, and so on. The bottom part of the screen is familiar in that it looks like a regular tape deck, with a counter and a readout on the tempo.

There was a common thread to all of these samples: after a while, I found myself understanding and playing each different type of music with ease. I learned some very interesting facts and quips about music and composers. For example, did you know that Beethoven "Fur Elise" was a goof? It was really a song for a lady named Therese, but someone just heard it wrong and it has been mistakenly dedicated to Elise for years!

The beauty of the format and interface is that it is user friendly, familiar, and suits novice or pro. I can see these programs being utilized in education, business, or just for the fun of it. When I was a kid, there would have been no way to learn this much so easily and cheaply and enjoy it all at the same time. You can even call up something like "Silent Night" and have a little sing-a-long with the kids! You can all sit there and watch the dynamics, read about it, and feel very accomplished and so easily. For me, the only difficult part would be to choose which sample would be the best suited for my needs. Which is probably why Midisoft decided to put out this CD and let the buyer not only test drive, but really have a chance to use and create with the programs first. To sweeten the pot, there is a $20 offer included on future purchases. Nice deal, great idea and well done.

Sound Explorer gives you "light" versions of seven different Midisoft products.

Vivaldi: The Four Seasons

As good as Ebook's Mozart title is, *Vivaldi* is a step up, not so much because of content, but because of the extra effort seemingly put into the graphics and menu items. *Vivaldi* is a slick combination of presentations such as biographies, chronologies, graphics, and essays, merged with Vivaldi's *Four Seasons*.

Ebook's Vivaldi *is a good introduction to the composer's music, with excellent graphics.*

This Windows-based application is initially divided into four themes—Illustrative, Interpretive, Informational, and Themes. The text articles found principally under the Informational are further subdivided into categories like Biography, Historical Background, Music of the Baroque Era, The Violin, The Orchestra, The Four Seasons, Thematic Catalogues, and Glossary of Terms.

The sections are short, but easy to read. As with other musical discs from Ebook, this one isn't incumbered with jargon, and definitions are easy to find.

The music selections on *Vivaldi* are comprised of the digitally recorded *The Four Seasons*. One interesting feature is found in the topic Themes, where portions of the music are laid out in full score with the user option of selecting either melody or full orchestration.

An enhancement over *Mozart* is the extra graphics added to *Vivaldi*. Art of the period, portraits, and so on are merged throughout the text and are annotated at the click of a button on the graphic.

The Interpretive selection is a sort of Cliff Notes merged into screen graphics, which add commentary to the music as it is played. This is a particularly nice feature, adding greatly to the understanding of the flow of the music.

Another particularly nice feature presented by Ebook is that this CD-ROM can be played in your music CD player. So, if you are looking for some good music, but don't want to turn your computer on, you don't need to purchase the same selections twice.

Learning how to jump around the menus and from area to area is very straightforward. With forward and reverse arrow keys at every topic item, it is easy to manipulate through the data.

Who would want this title? With a host of information readily collected on one CD-ROM, it is an easy bet to speed your learning curve on Vivaldi. And as was previously mentioned, this title is well suited for parents who want their children to get to know the classical composers.

Rating: ◉ ◉ ◉

Publisher Name: **Ebook, Inc.**

Software Requirements: **MPC/Macintosh**

Suggested Retail Price: **$29.95**

Vivaldi's Four Seasons—Spring, Summer, Fall, and Winter, are the focus of this CD-ROM.

Additional CD-ROM Titles

Title: 600 Days to Coco's Island
Suggested Retail Price: $49.95
Publisher: Compton's NewMedia
Platform: MPC/Macintosh
Description: Movie of a sailing trip to a small island off Costa Rica.

Title: A German Requiem: The Greatest Choral Work of the Romantic Era
Suggested Retail Price: $66.00
Publisher: Time Warner Interactive Group
Platform: Macintosh
Description: A look at German choir singing.

Title: All my Hummingbirds Have Alibis, By Morton Sybotnik
Suggested Retail Price: $39.95
Publisher: Voyager
Platform: Macintosh
Description: Critically acclaimed for its score and graphics.

Title: Wolfgang Amadeus Mozart: The "Dissonant" Quartet
Suggested Retail Price: $59.95
Publisher: Voyager
Platform: Macintosh
Description: Original Macintosh version of the disc licensed by Microsoft for Windows.

Title: Antonin Dvorak: Symphony No. 9 "From the New World"
Suggested Retail Price: $79.95

Publisher: Voyager
Platform: Macintosh
Description: Detailed look at this popular symphonic work.

Title: Apple Pie Music: Music of American History, History of American Music
Suggested Retail Price: $95.00
Publisher: Lintronics
Platform: MPC
Description: Music and history joined to better understand the past. Over 400 songs plus photos and text to follow the development of all styles of music in America.

Title: Brahms "A German Requiem"
Suggested Retail Price: $66.00
Publisher: Warner NewMedia
Platform: Macintosh
Description: The 1868 work and notes on the work and the composer.

Title: Cinema Volta
Suggested Retail Price: $49.95
Publisher: Voyager
Platform: Macintosh
Description: Learn about the lives of the amazing electrical inventors of the 19th century. Includes a history of electronics and electricity.

Title: Classic Cartoons
Suggested Retail Price: $29.95
Publisher: Chestnut
Platform: MPC
Description: Public domain cartoons for your kids to enjoy, featuring Porky Pig and others.

Title: Composer Quest
Suggested Retail Price: $99.00
Publisher: Dr. T's Music Software
Platform: MPC
Description: Interactive music programs that teach about noted composers and their works.

Title: Cops & Robbers Films
Suggested Retail Price: $129.00
Publisher: ScanRom Publications
Platform: MPC
Description: Clips & sound bits from cops and robbers movies.

Title: Criterion Goes to the Movies
Suggested Retail Price: $24.95
Publisher: Voyager
Platform: Macintosh
Description: Reviews of thousands of classic films.

Title: Encyclopedia of Sound
Suggested Retail Price: $39.95
Publisher: Chestnut
Platform: MPC
Description: The Music Factory's encyclopedia of sound effects, clips, and utilities. Includes royalty-free full-length musical scores.

Title: Ephemeral Films, Volumes I & II
Suggested Retail Price: $29.95
Publisher: Voyager
Platform: Macintosh
Description: Reviews of films you never heard of, but will wish you had.

Title: Fractunes
Suggested Retail Price: $69.95
Publisher: Quanta
Platform: MPC
Description: Funny cartoons for kids.

Title: Franz Schubert: "The Trout"
Suggested Retail Price: $59.95
Publisher: Voyager
Platform: Macintosh
Description: This work was not finished, and Voyager takes a close look at it.

Title: Garbo CDROM
Suggested Retail Price: $24.95
Publisher: Walnut Creek
Platform: MPC
Description: The mysterious actress comes to life in film clips.

Title: Godzilla vs. Megalon
Suggested Retail Price: $29.95
Publisher: Chestnut
Platform: MPC
Description: Horrible Japanese special effects are a treasure if you know what to expect.

Title: Grooves
Suggested Retail Price: $149.00
Publisher: Sony
Platform: MPC/Macintosh
Description: Songs and more in this interactive disc.

Title: Hilarious Sports Bloopers
Suggested Retail Price: $29.95
Publisher: Chestnut
Platform: MPC
Description: See funny sports video clips without subscribing to any stupid magazine.

Title: History of American Musical Theater
Suggested Retail Price: $49.95
Publisher: Queue
Platform: MPC/Macintosh
Description: Hello, Dolly! I could have danced all night with this disc.

Title: History of Country Music
Suggested Retail Price: $49.95
Publisher: Queue
Platform: MPC/Macintosh
Description: Sound/slide show of country and western music, Texas swing, and bluegrass.

Title: History of Folk Music
Suggested Retail Price: $49.95
Publisher: Queue
Platform: MPC/Macintosh
Description: Woody Guthrie, Pete Seeger, and beyond.

Title: History of Popular Music
Suggested Retail Price: $49.95
Publisher: Queue
Platform: MPC/Macintosh
Description: Dave Barry says that popular music is by definition good, or else it wouldn't be popular, right?

Title: Hollywood at War
Suggested Retail Price: $149.00
Publisher: ScanRom
Platform: MPC
Description: War movie clips from World War II.

Title: Hollywood Movie Buff's Guide
Suggested Retail Price: $69.95
Publisher: ScanRom
Platform: MPC
Description: Comprehensive movie guide with reviews and statistics.

Title: Hollywood Trivia
Suggested Retail Price: $69.95
Publisher: ScanRom
Platform: MPC
Description: Movie Trivia for movie buffs.

Title: Hollywood's Newest Stars
Suggested Retail Price: $69.95
Publisher: ScanRom
Platform: MPC
Description: Pictures, biographies, and clips of new stars.

Title: Hollywood: Encyclopedia
Suggested Retail Price: $69.00
Publisher: ScanRom
Platform: MPC
Description: Hollywood facts and trivia.

Title: Hollywood: The Bizarre
Suggested Retail Price: $69.95
Publisher: ScanRom
Platform: MPC
Description: Bizarre movies and people from the city that invented weird.

Title: Horror & Science Fiction Movie Guide
Suggested Retail Price: $129.00
Publisher: ScanRom
Platform: MPC
Description: Complete listing of freaky movie categories.

Title: Hullabaloo Volume I: Rock's Classic Rock N'Roll
Suggested Retail Price: $29.98
Publisher: MPI Multimedia
Platform: MPC/Macintosh
Description: Visit with some of your favorites and watch them perform. Includes Chad & Jeremy, Jackie DeShannon, Paul Revere & The Raiders, Michael Landon, The Byrds, Sonny & Cher, and the Yardbirds. Michael Landon???

Title: Jazz Traditions
Suggested Retail Price: $49.95
Publisher: EBook
Platform: MPC/Macintosh
Description: Jazz classics and performers from the 1920s onward.

Title: Learn to Play Guitar
Suggested Retail Price: $49.95
Publisher: Cambrix
Platform: MPC

Description: Master chords and break out of your garage to a recording contract.

Title: Ludwig van Beethoven: Symphony No. 9
Suggested Retail Price: $79.95
Publisher: Voyager
Platform: Macintosh
Description: The original Macintosh version of the title Microsoft licensed for Windows.

Title: Microsoft Soundbits
Suggested Retail Price: $39.00
Publisher: Microsoft
Platform: MPC
Description: Soundbits from Hollywood's classic films.

Title: Microsoft Soundbits Hanna-Barbara Cartoons
Suggested Retail Price: $39.00
Publisher: Microsoft
Platform: MPC
Description: Cartoon voice clips from Huckleberry Hound and others.

Title: Microsoft Soundbits Sound Clips
Suggested Retail Price: $39.00
Publisher: Microsoft
Platform: MPC
Description: Musical sounds from around the world. (sax, didjeridoo, koto etc.).

Title: Modblaster
Suggested Retail Price: $69.95
Publisher: The Computer Niche
Platform: MPC
Description: Play, analyze, & manipulate the over 300 classical, jazz, & rock files in MOD format.

Title: Movies of the Thirties
Suggested Retail Price: $129.00
Publisher: ScanRom
Platform: MPC
Description: Listing and clips from the 1930s, just after talkies began to hit it big.

Title: Mozart
Suggested Retail Price: $29.95
Publisher: Voyager
Platform: Macintosh
Description: Essays, graphics, bio trivia, and music of Mozart.

Title: Mozart
Suggested Retail Price: $24.95
Publisher: Electronic Arts
Platform: MPC
Description: The Austrian composer is profiled yet again, but he deserves it.

Title: Mozart: The Magic Flute
Suggested Retail Price: $66.00
Publisher: Warner NewMedia
Platform: Macintosh
Description: Too many notes? We think not.

Title: Murmurs of Earth: The Voyager Interstellar Record
Suggested Retail Price: $59.99
Publisher: Time Warner Interactive Group
Platform: MPC/Macintosh
Description: Carl Sagan hoped to make billions and billions of dollars from this multimedia look at the space probe.

Title: Music Madness, Vol. 1/2
Suggested Retail Price: $99.00
Publisher: Wayzata Technology
Platform: Macintosh
Description: Create your own music, Over 640MB of sounds, tools and utilities.

Title: Prince Interactive
Suggested Retail Price: $59.95
Publisher: Compton's NewMedia
Platform: MPC/Macintosh
Description: One minute snippets of 15 classic Prince songs, along with new interpretations you can remix with a five-channel studio.

Title: Quicklaffs: Vol. 1 and 2
Suggested Retail Price: $39.95
Publisher: Gazelle Technologies, Inc.
Platform: Macintosh
Description: QuickTime movies of classic film comics from the '20s and '30s.

Title: Richard Strauss: Three Tone Poems
Suggested Retail Price: $59.95
Publisher: Voyager
Platform: Macintosh
Description: Another musical excursion from Voyager, for those with more modern tastes.

Title: Roger Ebert's Movie Home Companion
Suggested Retail Price: $79.95
Publisher: Quanta Press
Platform: MPC
Description: The only winner of Pulitzer Prize for movie critiques of over 1,300 movies.

Title: Salt of the Earth
Suggested Retail Price: $49.95
Publisher: Voyager
Platform: Macintosh
Description: Step back in time to the McCarthy era to explore the years of blacklisting, the beginnings of the women's movement, the labor movement, and the struggle of the minorities.

Title: So I've Heard Series Vol. I: Bach and Before
Suggested Retail Price: $24.95
Publisher: Voyager
Platform: Macintosh
Description: More looks at music from the Baroque Era (and before).

Title: So I've Heard Series Vol. II: The Classical Ideal
Suggested Retail Price: $24.95
Publisher: Voyager

Platform: Macintosh
Description: Learn about Mozart and others of the Classical Era.

Title: So I've Heard Series Vol. III: Beethoven & Beyond
Suggested Retail Price: $24.95
Publisher: Voyager
Platform: Macintosh
Description: Later classical period masterworks are examined.

Title: So I've Heard Series Vol. IV: Romantic Heights
Suggested Retail Price: $24.95
Publisher: Voyager
Platform: Macintosh
Description: Motivations and techniques of the Romantic composers are revealed in this disc.

Title: So I've Heard Series Vol. V: The Stravinsky Impact
Suggested Retail Price: $24.95
Publisher: Voyager
Platform: Macintosh
Description: From *Rite of Spring* to the *Soldier's Tale*, the impact of Stravinsky is explored in this disc.

Title: Sound Sensations
Suggested Retail Price: $39.95
Publisher: Chestnut Software
Platform: MPC
Description: Shareware collection of sound effects, music, voice, and more.

Title: Star Trek Collectibles
Suggested Retail Price: $79.95
Publisher: MCS Group
Platform: MPC
Description: Interactive guide for the Star Trek fan. Styled like an encyclopedia with easily accessed images and text for pleasure and reference.

Title: The Grammy Awards: A 34-Year Retrospect

Suggested Retail Price: $39.95
Publisher: Compton's NewMedia
Platform: MPC
Description: Award winning songs and their backgrounds.

Title: The History of Soul
Suggested Retail Price: $49.95
Publisher: Queue
Platform: MPC/Macintosh
Description: From Smoky Robinson to James Brown, they're all here in this soulful treatise.

Title: The Night of the Living Dead
Suggested Retail Price: $29.95
Publisher: Chestnut
Platform: MPC
Description: George Romero wishes he'd copyrighted his late-60s horror classic, filmed in Pittsburgh, PA.

Title: The Orchestra
Suggested Retail Price: $79.98
Publisher: Time-Warner
Platform: Macintosh
Description: The London Symphony Orchestra performs a Benjamin Britten symphony. Young Person's Guide with an Audio Notes program. Includes games of musical knowledge.

Title: The Orchestra: The Instruments Revealed
Suggested Retail Price: $79.98
Publisher: Warner NewMedia
Platform: Macintosh
Description: The London Symphony's "A Young Person's Guide to the Orchestra."

Title: The Residents FREAK SHOW
Suggested Retail Price: $69.95
Publisher: Voyager
Platform: Macintosh

Title: The String Quartet: The Essence of Music
Suggested Retail Price: $66.00

Publisher: Time Warner Interactive Group
Platform: Macintosh
Description: An examination of this essential musical form.

Title: The Three Stooges
Suggested Retail Price: $29.95
Publisher: Chestnut
Platform: MPC
Description: Women don't understand why guys find this trio so funny. Nyuk, nyuk.

Title: Videohound Multimedia
Suggested Retail Price: $79.95
Publisher: Visible Ink Software
Platform: MPC/Macintosh
Description: Over 50,000 reviews of movies. Easy search and access.

Title: Wild, Weird & Wacky
Suggested Retail Price: $79.95
Publisher: WPA Multimedia
Platform: Macintosh
Description: Over 250 of the strangest things ever recorded on film, which is saying a lot.

Title: World Beat
Suggested Retail Price: $59.95
Publisher: Medio Multimedia
Platform: MPC
Description: World Music on CD-ROM. This stuff is great—try it.

Title: You Can't Get There From Here
Suggested Retail Price: $29.95
Publisher: Voyager
Platform: Macintosh
Description: Original films from 1946-1950.

Chapter 9

Games

Games are the biggest money-makers in the CD-ROM industry, so you'll find a lot of effort put into developing flashy products that make the best use of your computer's sound and graphics capabilities. The list of top-sellers changes almost weekly, but some leading contenders at the time this book was written include pure arcade games like *Rebel Assault* (which nevertheless has many levels for varied action) and *Star Trek: 25th Anniversary*. You'll also find many different chess games, ranging from the animated, like *Battle Chess* and *Star Wars Chess*, to the lunatic, such as *Chess Maniac Five Billion and One*, from National Lampoon.

If you like virtual reality excitement, you'll enjoy games like *Lunicus*. In this epic, Earth scientists have repaired an ancient alien device, and find it contains videotapes of the Jurassic Era. Unfortunately, the device's owners have been alerted and are coming back to reclaim their property. The United Nations Moonbase Lunicus is the only hope for Earth's salvation...and you're in charge of the rescue! *The Journeyman Project* takes this type of game a step further with hours of QuickTime video featuring real human actors! The same technique is employed in *Conspiracy*, which stars Donald Sutherland as a sort of video help system.

Problem-solving games revolve around solving a murder, or otherwise figuring out the solution to a puzzle, by collecting clues.

Games of this ilk include *Who Killed Sam Rupert?*, *Sherlock Holmes: Consulting Detective* (one of the best, with multiple versions), and *The 7th Guest*. Most mysterious of all is *Myst*, which presents you with few clues and the eerie silence of an uninhabited island that is actually a gateway to hidden worlds.

You may enjoy simulations like *Gettysburg*, which reproduces the classic Civil War battle, or *SimCity*, which allows you to take charge of your own city and run it into the ground or to new heights, depending on the wisdom of your decisions.

Movies have been converted to CD-ROM games, too, ranging from George Lucas productions like *Indiana Jones* or *Rebel Assault* to *The Lawnmower Man*, which is based loosely on the film that was based even more loosely on the Stephen King story.

Games tend to be extraordinarily demanding on your hardware, and while most of those listed in this chapter purport to run on standard MPC or Macintosh configurations, some of them require special attention to memory usage. You may even have to prepare a special "boot" disk to run these programs. But these measures are usually worth it: the extra resources demanded by the very best games often translate into faster action, smoother animation, or better sound.

This chapter is one of the largest in the book, with more than 30 games reviewed. The quality level is better, too. We had to leave out reviews of games that are far better programs than programs that easily made the cut in less competitive categories. Explore these entertaining programs and have a little fun, for a change!

The 7th Guest

Rating:

Publisher Name:
Virgin Interactive Entertainment

Software Requirements:
MPC/Macintosh

Suggested Retail Price: **$99.95**

You heard it here first! *The 7th Guest* comes with the best free *audio* CD you are ever likely to get. Hidden on the second disc accompanying this hit game is a complete "soundtrack" album of the background music by famed composer George "The Fat Man" Alistair Sanger. The songs therein are as much fun as the game itself!

And that's saying quite a bit. *The 7th Guest* broke new ground in the interactive game field with its vivid, realistic 3D graphics, great sound, tough puzzles, and slick interface. Once you've played this game, you'll find its imitators pale more quickly than the ghosts that haunt the center stage.

You play the game in the role of the mysterious Ego, whose viewpoint is used to view the 3D, virtual-reality setting of the eerie Stauf mansion. Use the mouse to move through the various rooms, following cues from a floating skeleton hand that wafts about the screen to guide you.

Many of the rooms and settings contain puzzles to be solved. Each is preceded by a playlet acted out by the ghostly apparitions of six of the last guests to stay at the mansion. Then you are faced with the puzzle itself and a clue—or two. For example, in one room you find a cake decorated with miniature gravestones and skulls, and sliced up into cubes. You're asked to remove the cubes of cake so that each piece is the same shape and contains exactly

two of each type of decoration—plus one adorned with nothing but icing.

You can easily spend an hour or more working with the puzzle. Many are fairly simple maze-type challenges (once you've figured them out!): jump two squares forward, one back, three forward, one back, and so forth to spell out a word or phrase using the characters found on the spaces you land on. Because the clues are sparse (sometimes, you don't even know the goal of the puzzle), it takes some real thinking to figure out what to do. Ego and the owner of the mansion, Stauf, provide comments that can help or lead you astray.

If you get stumped, you can visit a book of clues in the Library, at the cost of some points. After the third visit to the book for

Just a kitchen? Think again—there's a puzzle to be solved here.

the same puzzle, the puzzle is solved for you automatically so that you can proceed to the next. Solving each puzzle unlocks one or more rooms in the mansion. When you finally complete the game, you'll find that all the rooms are unlocked the next time you play, and you can then work the puzzles in any order you choose.

State-of-the-art virtual reality 3D graphics and sound set the stage for this involving group of puzzles presented against the backdrop of a haunted mansion.

All the elements of *The 7th Guest* work together to evoke the proper mood. You might want to play this game alone, with the lights down low. Sanger's haunting music provides the appropriate backdrop as you roam through dimly lit halls and rooms. The disembodied voices add a discomforting presence. If that weren't enough, the tableaux acted out by the ghostly guests are chilling all by themselves.

Warning: The environment ranges from bawdy to grotesque, so this game is not recommended for those under 15. Puzzles are represented by a grisly throbbing brain, the game "cursor" is a floating human eyeball, and supernatural effects are preceded by macabre chattering teeth.

The game's "main menu" is actually a Ouija board/oracle called the Sphinx, which

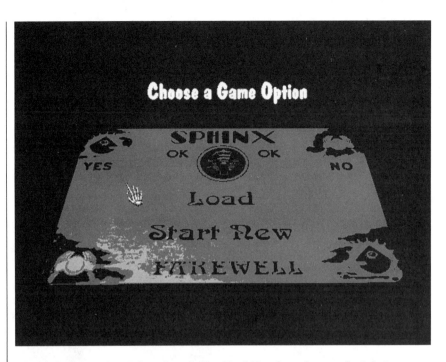

The 7th Guest mystery takes place in the Stauf Mansion, where eerie doings are commonplace.

handles major game functions such as loading and saving games, quitting, and so forth. You can save up to 10 versions of the scenario, using a name of your choice with up to 13 characters (clever number, eh?).

The 7th Guest places heavy demands on your hardware, so if you're running an IBM PC, don't take the MPC-1 rating lightly. You must have a sound card (the internal sound system in Macintoshes is fine) installed to play this game, and forget about trying to run the PC version under Microsoft Windows. Clear out some hard disk space before you install it: our copy put more than 5MB of files on the hard disk.

The chief weakness of this game is one that's common to all games of this genre: essentially, it's a puzzle you play through once, like a crossword. Once you solve it, there's not much point in playing it again, except to revisit the gorgeous graphics. In addition, the puzzles are by definition

inflexible. There's only one way to solve each puzzle, and if you can't figure that out, you're stuck (or must visit the book of clues).

The puzzles have been structured to challenge experienced players and newcomers alike, and do vary in difficulty. But, there are many players who will find most of the puzzles too hard, while others will find them too easy. All these "defects" are known to come with the territory. For your money, you'll get many hours of playing fun from *The 7th Guest*.

On the plus side, of course, are the stunning effects and feeling you get of complete immersion and involvement in the game's environment. Then, there's that audio CD. Even after you've solved all the puzzles in the game, you can play that over and over with the same enjoyment. When is Team Fat going to release a conventional album?

Beyond the Wall of Stars

Rating: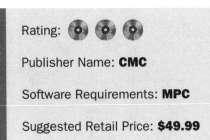

Publisher Name: **CMC**

Software Requirements: **MPC**

Suggested Retail Price: **$49.99**

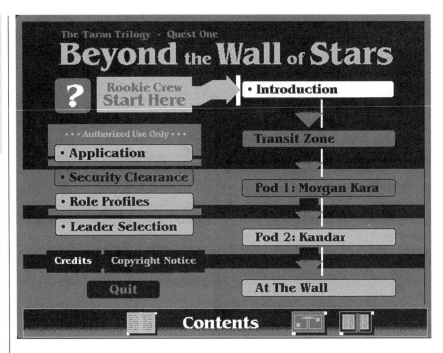

In *Beyond The Wall of Stars*, the young crew must travel to a distant planet on a mysterious mission.

Y ou're about to read a story unlike any you've ever read before." Thus begins the back-of-the-package description of *Beyond the Wall of Stars— Quest One of the Taran Trilogy*. In a very real sense, you are "reading" a story, for this program is "interactive fiction," which uses the capabilities of animation, graphics, sound, and text to tell its story. You control the actions of the characters, and you decide which path the characters take when faced with a decision. The author of this story is R.A. Montgomery, the creator of the Bantam Books book series "Choose Your Own Adventure," which has sold over 40 million copies and has been translated into 38 languages.

At the beginning of the scenario, you see an attractive starfield title screen with good quality introduction music (which stutters a bit when the CD is accessed, even on a 486/66 machine). Then follows the Table of Contents screen that enables you to jump to different sections of an adventure, after you've gained some experience with it.

The first step for a beginner should be to view the brief introduction on the game interface and the product support information, accessed from the table of contents. The game interface is fairly simple: you have icons at the bottom of the screen for

replaying a screen, leaving a bookmark (one only, although the bookmark screen leads you to think you can have multiple bookmarks), returning to the table of contents, and resuming the game. These and almost anything else you want to use are accessed by clicking them.

The program also contains a handful of hypertext links—highlighted text that you can click for more information about critical topics. When your tutorial is complete, you are asked to apply for membership to the crew. After you've entered a few details about yourself (which the program uses later), you get to make your first decision. The rest of the crew is deadlocked between

four potential leaders for the mission. You can study the dossiers of the crew (accessed by clicking each crew person's picture in a group portrait).

Information is available for the four potential mission leaders, as well as the rest of the crew. You should study this information carefully; it will be helpful to know the strengths and weaknesses of the crew as your mission proceeds. Once you've completed the study of the crew, you vote, again by clicking the image of the crew member you think can best lead the crew. This is your "puppet." While you aren't actually the leader, you make the decisions he/she executes. So much for free will!

There is a small amount of narration at the beginning, but most of the information is passed via pictures and text, with the audio being mostly music and sound effects. This program requires fairly good reading skills, and would be a crafty way to con a slow reader to improve his/her skills in the guise of playing a game. Non-readers or beginning readers won't be able to play, unless they have a person to read each screen to them.

A work of interactive fiction in which you can explore the ramifications of decisions you make as the member of a spaceship crew whose mission is to save their planet.

Beyond the Wall of Stars has a reasonably impressive number of branch points, but as you will find after exploring a number of alternative decisions, many of these points converge back into the same story line. This is to be expected; through the first 40 screens—not very far into the story at all— you can make five or more decisions. For five decisions, you have thirty-two different story lines. For each extra decision you make, the number of story lines doubles.

Many more independent story lines would overwhelm even a CD's information capacity. What is really going on is that there are a small number of true independent story lines. Each decision you make colors the story in a different way. In one, you find out a little about a kidnapped princess; in another, you meet a group of rebels. There are other lines, too, but eventually they come back to a small number of alternatives. The main plot(s) stay the same, but the details differ greatly, based on your decisions.

In the main, this program is interesting, but it does have its glitches. Some of the special effects are images over images. In some of these, the superimposed image doesn't know when to stop. A dust storm-like object passes over a picture of the desert, but doesn't stop when it reaches the edge of the picture. It flows into the border. Delays between screens can be a bit long, only a few seconds, but it seems like a lot because the feel is very much as if you are watching a movie. You must also be sure to deactivate any screen savers you have and set your screen resolution to 640 x 480 with exactly 256 colors. Early testing was plagued by

some serious problems due to using a 16-million color display; after a call to a very helpful tech support person, and upon switching to 256 color mode, these problems ceased.

On the plus side, the story lines observed were all interesting and engaging. Real pictures are mixed well with drawn graphics; in particular, the story is helped by using digitized pictures of the protagonists. Although any individual adventure is not very long (less than two hours), there are a large number of alternatives to explore, comprising many one to two hour adventures. Multimedia as presented in this disc is reminiscent of a silent movie, but you can see the potential it offers. All things considered, this disc would be best appreciated by late pre-teens, especially if they need help with their reading skills, hard-core science fiction fans, and those interested in how multimedia is beginning to be practiced. However, if you aren't in any of these categories, and the disc happens to be available to you, take a look. You might get pulled in.

Make the right choices to solve the problems posed in *Beyond the Wall of Stars*.

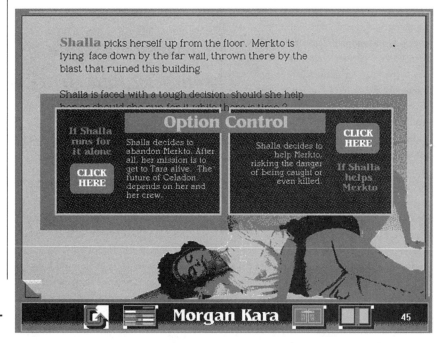

Castles II: Siege & Conquest

Rating: ⬤ ⬤ ⬤ ⬤

Publisher Name:
Interplay Productions

Software Requirements: **MPC**

Suggested Retail Price: **$75.00**

If you liked the original *Castles*, you'll love *Castles II: Siege & Conquest*. The game itself is much expanded, but the programmers have also added to the package a good number of reference materials dealing with castles historically. This is education the easy way! The accompanying booklet explains the game in detail, and is exceptionally well-written and easy to follow. It includes a tutorial for those wishing to begin play immediately, as well as detailed explanations of how to play, and a few helpful tips on strategy. Three separate reference cards summarize how to access various parts of the program and include a troubleshooting section, as well as the usual shortcut keyboard commands and helpful information concerning the game map and the action.

The object of the game is simply to be named King of the mythical country of Bretagne (modeled after 14th-century France). You, as one of five contenders for the throne, do this by gathering resources and conquering neighboring territories with your armies. You build castles to hold your land and to keep the peasants from revolting, and you strive to ensure the happiness of your people and the good will of the Pope. Your total points go up or down depending on how well you are doing. When you have at least 7,000 points, you petition the Pope to name you King. If you stay above 7,000 points for a given period of time, you are named King and you win.

When you start the game, you have a number of choices: difficulty level (there are four), plots on or off (this involves messengers from the other contenders and the Pope), music on or off, and placement of commodities.

After the introductory sequence, you reach the Directory. This, like much of the program, is point and click. A small box entitled Options allows you to turn off the music or speech. Along the top of the screen are four icons that can send you to the reference section, design book, tutorial, or to play a game.

Fascinating game of conquest and strategy set in the 14th century.

For the moment, let's skip the tutorial and have a look at what else *Castles II* has to offer. Clicking the reference icon gives you a choice in turn of 14 buttons with labels such as Intro to Castles, The Bailey, and Machicolations. These are short videos explaining and illustrating the listed topic. A click of the mouse starts the video. The full-screen video with narration is reminiscent of a BBC documentary; the British narrators are certainly a nice touch! Unfortunately, all this is a bit much for a poor 486/66 machine, resulting in slightly choppy sound and images that tend to "swim" and jump like old silent movies. Besides the videos, the reference section has a choice for Glossary. Clicking one of 24 choices brings up a pop-up window defining things like ballista and trebuchet.

The design book brings up a list of ten real-life castles and a View All button. The button takes you through all the information for all ten castles with video and narration. Or you can click the button for one of the castles and either choose one of the topics concerning it, such as history, construction, or a film, or click on View All, which in this case will go through all the information on this particular castle. You can also ask for hints on strategy.

The Directory's tutorial is a gem. This is, in fact, different from the tutorial in the manual; going through the multimedia tutorial is highly recommended, as it gives you a quick, audio-visual overview of the game. Click the mouse button on the Overview button within the tutorial module, and then sit back and watch. The tutorial explains the various parts of the game screen, and then goes through part of a sample game. Periodically you are given the choice of taking control or continuing the tutorial. Your choice depends on how daring (or how foolhardy) you are. Going through the entire tutorial will yield a number of valuable tips, and you can then take control at the end, in the midst of a good game.

The main game screen shows a map of the kingdom with its 36 territories. At the top of the screen are ratings points—how many you have and how many are available for use. These are divided into three categories: Administrative (for gathering commodities, dealing with the Black Market, and building castles), Military (recruiting infantry, archers, and knights, building siege engines of various types, attacking, policing the realm, and sending a saboteur), and Political (sending a scout, spy, diplomat, merchant, raising the happiness of the people, or calling a council).

Building a castle is an administrative task. You can either design your own or choose a design from the design book. Designing your own involves clicking pieces and then clicking where you'd like them to be placed on a close-up screen of your territory. After your design is finished, allocate the number of points you want to put toward the task, and let it go. No more tedious work assigning masons, carpenters, etc. like in the original *Castles*. You have more important things to do!

Most of your time is spent accomplishing tasks, and very little in battle. Before you attack a territory, you should send a scout there to see who owns it, what commodity is found there, and the like. When your attack is prepared and you decide to proceed, the game screen is replaced by the tactical combat screen, which is a close-up of the territory. The defender chooses his position first, and the attacker then places his men. If you are defending a castle, the Flat button collapses the castle walls so that you can easily see where you are placing your army (the walls are still there, just not visible). After you've placed your troops, give them orders.

Click one of yours and then on one of the enemy's, if you want to attack specific enemy units. You can also command your units to stand, melee (attack enemy troops, or if none are near, destroy the Keep or enemy siege engines), destroy (attacking the Keep or siege engines has priority over attacking people), or retreat. Click the Begin

button and the battle starts. It continues until one side or the other has won: all of one side is killed or retreats, or enough of the enemy occupies the castle Keep for a certain period of time, signifying the castle's surrender or defeat.

Periodically messengers arrive at your door with requests, threats, or offers. Choose your answer well, because you can easily turn a friend into an enemy, or alienate your people or the Pope!

If this sounds too complex, you can use the game options to tone down the action. The manual's tutorial suggests playing on the easy level, and turning plots (messengers) and tactical battles off. This last will relieve you of the work of placing and commanding your army. This is done for you, and you are told the final result.

Periodically throughout the game one of many video clips is shown. The manual tells us that these are from the films *Alexander Nevsky* and *The Private Lives of Henry VIII*. They add interest, but don't really mean much in terms of your game.

Overall, *Castles II: Siege & Conquest* is a very entertaining and educational game. It is certainly a great improvement over the original game, and the reference and design book sections are wonderful. The frustratingly uneven quality of the videos is, unfortunately, due to the limitations of today's PC technology.

Aside from this, the only bothersome aspect of the game is the tactical combat screen. Here, the tiny warriors are hard to follow and to differentiate, like so many ants moving and converging on one another. This is a tremendous game destined to delight *Castles* fans and new players alike. The basics are easy to learn, but the play can be made as complex as the most demanding player could ask.

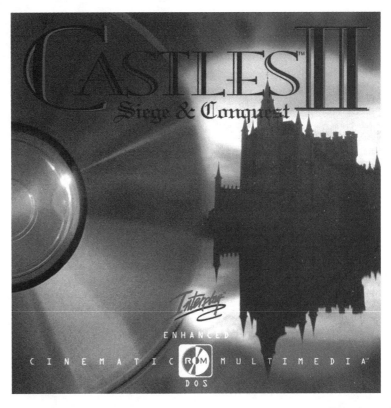

Battle Chess Enhanced CD-ROM

Rating:  1/2

Publisher Name: **Interplay**

Software Requirements:
MPC/Macintosh

Suggested Retail Price: **$54.95**

*B*attle Chess is one of many chess programs on the market for PCs. The main distinction that *Battle Chess* has over its competitors is its graphic depiction of animated combat when one piece captures another. Why is this important? For the most part, it isn't. *Battle Chess* has very slick animation, and by virtue of the large amount of space on the CD-ROM, a large amount of digitized audio. At one time, such displays of animation virtuosity were of themselves a reason to select a product. But animation for its own sake isn't enough anymore. The game of chess has been played for hundreds of years without animation, or computers for that matter. Where animation might be used effectively is in interactive tutorials. *Battle Chess* does have a tutorial, but the use of animation here, too, is less effective than it could be.

The MPC/Windows version of *Battle Chess* is very simple to install: you run a setup program stored in the MPCCHESS

directory of the Battle Chess CD-ROM. It asks a simple question or two and then installs the program. The installation of the DOS version of the program does not appear to be significantly different, other than the directory that the setup program is installed in is called CDCHESS.

To start *Battle Chess*, the Windows user clicks the Battle Chess icon, stored in the Games window. (They didn't selfishly create their own program group. Hallelujah!) Up comes the three-dimensional board. It is quite pretty to look at, the pieces are artistically designed. However, the first quibble is the color of the pieces. The

Battle Chess offers exciting battle scenes when a piece captures another.

"white" side is colored dark blue; the "black" side is colored red. These colors don't work well for fussy chess players who really like to see white and black pieces. There is no provision for changing colors of the pieces; if there were, the effect on the highly detailed

pieces would probably be ruinous.

The computer waits for you to move; by default, you are white and white always moves first. You move a piece by clicking the left mouse button on the square that the piece you want to move sits on, and then clicking the square you want it to move to. The piece slowly walks to the square you designated, accompanied by digitized audio walking sounds. The amount of time required for the piece to go to its place is a bit long, mostly because the program must read the animation routines each time from the CD-ROM. You can put them on your hard disk to speed things up, but they require 33MB of hard disk space. Most users won't want to do this, at least not permanently.

Some of the digitized walking sounds get downright annoying after a short time. However, you have control of several aspects of the animation and audio that let you go from full to none, with several options in between. You can also change to a two-dimensional board. The three-dimensional board is a bit hard to analyze for some players, at least at first, so this option is welcome. You lose the animation and sound, but you get a simple, attractive chessboard that is easy to play with. The program also plays very rapidly on the lower levels using a two-dimensional board.

The tutorial is one area where the rich animation of *Battle Chess* can be put to its best use. The tutorial begins well: Each type of chess piece comes out onto the board to tell you a little about its history and capabilities in the game of chess. However, the real power of the tutorial environment is not fully utilized. A few easily added features would greatly augment its effect. A specific example of this is that each chess piece describes how it is moved in the game of chess, both in words and by moving. However, the demonstration of its movement isn't complete for each piece, and the verbal description of the move might not be perfectly clear to a beginner. For instance, the rook describes how it moves by saying it moves parallel to the sides of the board. If your vocabulary is sufficiently broad, this is a clear description.

However, young children, who are perfectly capable of learning how to play chess, might not understand the word "parallel." The rook then explains that it can move forward, backward, and to each side, but mentions ranks and files in the same sentence; undefined, these terms can cause confusion. If the tutorial highlighted the squares that the rook could move to as it was describing its move, this confusion would be avoided. *Battle Chess* does come with a good tutorial pamphlet, which has these movement charts. By combining the information in the pamphlet with the tutorial, you get a clear idea of chess piece movement. However, the additions suggested would make the on-line tutorial much more robust. Given many users' distaste for reading information that comes with programs, this would be a worthwhile addition to the on-line tutorial.

Battle Chess is a good chess player, certainly a challenge for a novice or a casual player, but doesn't seem to be as strong as other recent chess programs. It has a number of features. Play difficulty can be set to nine different levels; it also has a time mode, where you can set the maximum time it will consider for a move (up to 10,000 minutes!), as well as a novice mode, where it can make blunders. You can force it to move at

any time, ask for a suggested move, take back up to sixty moves, set up the board any way you want it at any time (you can give yourself another queen in the middle of a lost game), and it supports modem play between humans. It also lacks features that many other programs have.

Battle Chess *is a chess program that, while not one of the state-of-the-art chess programs, is quite suitable for beginning players and is especially suited for those learning the game.*

For instance, *Battle Chess* does not provide a record of all the moves that have occurred in the current game, as most other programs do. To do this would require that the user know one of two commonly used chess notations. The on-line tutorial does not address either form of notation and the program does not use either form of notation in any obvious way, although one form of notation is taught in the tutorial pamphlet. This is another area where the on-line tutorial could be enhanced. An interactive chess notation teacher would be a valuable addition to the on-line tutorial. Once the user knows one of the notation schemes, the program can show him what its last move was, a feature missing from *Battle Chess.*

If you set the game to play at a high level, the time between turns can be quite long. When you come back to the board, you can easily forget the state of the board before the computer's move. Even if you are watching, the computer moves very quickly in non-animation mode; you can miss the move. A little line saying "Computer last move: P-QB4" would be helpful.

No program is going to do more than scratch the surface of chess for a beginner. A very useful addition to the tutorial pamphlet would be a moderate bibliography of beginner's chess literature. There are some wonderful chess books for the beginner available that really bring the game to life. A list of some of these, summarizing their approach to teaching the game of chess, would be a valuable enhancement to the tutorial pamphlet.

Battle Chess is a suitable program for a beginning chess player, or for a casual player who needs a tough, but not too tough, silicon opponent. If you know your way around a chess board, you'll probably want a program with more features. However, its on-line tutorial and pamphlet are quite good, and with a bit of modification could be awesome, due to its clever use of animation and sound.

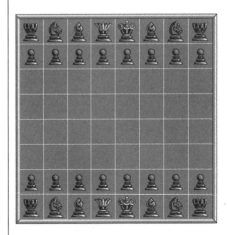

This lively setting makes an excellent venue for new chess players to learn the game.

Gabriel Knight: Sins of the Father

Rating: 1/2

Publisher Name: **Sierra On-Line**

Software Requirements: **MPC**

Suggested Retail Price: **$59.95**

*G*abriel Knight is another in a long line of interactive adventure games from Sierra On-Line. Sierra has been making adventure-type games for many years, and is probably the most recognized software company in the gaming industry. In Sierra's early years, their adventures included the popular *King's Quest*, *Space Quest*, and the infamous *Leisure Suit Larry*. All three of these series have been extremely successful and many sequels have been based on these characters. In the last few years, Sierra has been probing into new areas of interactive gaming, including the popular Quest for Glory series, which is a unique interactive role-playing game.

Unlike previous Sierra releases of CD-ROM versions of their floppy-based games, this one has much more added than just full dialogue. With *Gabriel Knight* they have added small multimedia movies that are shown at points in the game.

Gabriel Knight is an author who is researching material for his new book that deals with voodoo. In the story, voodoo has been a hot subject in New Orleans, where the game takes place. There has been a series of murders where voodoo paraphernalia has been left at the murder scene. Also tied to voodoo is a series of horrifying nightmares that Gabriel experiences whenever he falls asleep. Gabriel now spends most of his hours digging through his past trying to find out the cause of the nightmares.

The game uses the well-known standard Sierra interface with the disappearing menu bar at the top of the screen. Although similar to the other adventure interfaces, there are a few new icons that are added for *Gabriel Knight*. The interface is generally easy to use and makes using the keyboard almost unnecessary.

Much of the game is spent questioning other characters. There are many characters that need to be questioned and a nice feature of the game saves you a lot of note writing. Gabriel carries a miniature tape recorder that he uses to record every conversation that he has with people. He carries one tape for each person that he questions, so finding the information is relatively easy.

The graphics for the game have been done in the usual high quality for Sierra games. *Gabriel Knight* goes one step further by using 640 x 480 256 color for systems with video cards that are VESA compliant. The sound effects and music are also well done, and the recorded voice dialogue

If you pose the right questions, you may get the clues you need in *Gabriel Knight*.

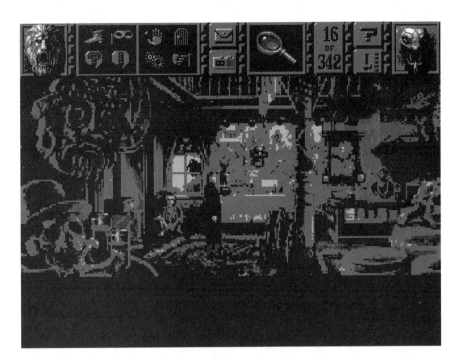

Futuristic police officer Gabriel Knight solves a crime—with your help—in this fast-paced game.

includes over 7,300 lines. The actors used to portray the voices of the characters bring some commonly known actors to the world of gaming. Some of the voices heard are Tim Curry as the voice of Gabriel Knight, Mark Hamil, Michael Dorn, Rocky Carroll, and Efrem Zimbalist Jr.

The CD comes with 657MB of data, which includes executables for both DOS 5.0+ and Windows 3.1+. The game requires at least a 386 with 4MB of RAM. The hard drive requirements of the game vary. The game can run entirely off the CD-ROM, but you can speed things up by installing part or all of the game files to your hard drive. If you choose the full install, the game will use about 33MB of storage. This makes the game run faster by storing the graphics and sound effects on the hard drive. The recorded voices continue to run from the CD.

Be sure to decide what level of hard drive installation you want to use before you begin in-depth playing and saving games.

During the course of this review, games were saved under the minimal install. The installation was re-run to do a complete installation to enable faster loading, and surprisingly the saved games were not compatible any more. This is not necessarily a bug in the game; recently some software companies have began to encode the data files for a particular installation. This is done to keep people from passing saved games from system to system. The exact reasoning behind this is not clear, just be aware of this peculiarity.

Dig through the past of Gabriel Knight to discover the keys to his terrifying nightmares.

The game does carry a label on the front of the box warning that the game contains adult subject matter and parental guidance is suggested. Although nothing worse than that can be seen on television, the game does contain visually graphic scenes and is not recommended for younger kids.

The weakness of the game is definitely the interrogation parts of the game. The questioning tended to be quite boring and it was relatively easy to miss relevant information. You are presented with different subject matter to ask each person, and it was usually necessary to ask a question 3 or 4 times before the important information was revealed. However, not all of the game is spent interrogating and the rest of the game is well done and exciting. If you are a fan of adventure games, this will definitely fulfill your expectations.

Gettysburg: Multimedia Battle Simulation

Rating:

Publisher Name:
Turner Interactive

Software Requirements: **MPC**

Suggested Retail Price: **$69.95**

The battle at Gettysburg is referred to as the bloodiest three days in the Civil War, and it can also be argued that it was the turning point in the Civil War. After this battle was won by the Union army, the fall of the Confederate army was imminent. What strategy should Robert E. Lee have used to win the battle? Well, in this battle simulation, you can play the role of the Union or Confederate general and try to re-write the history of the battle.

The opening sequence of the game is a historical review of the events that lead the Union and Confederate armies to meet in a bloodbath at Gettysburg. After the opening sequence, the game lets you choose all your

settings for the battle. If you have a curiosity in history, you will probably choose to sit back and watch for your first battle and set the computer to play both sides through a historical battle. The battle starts at 8am on July 1, 1863 with the arrival of the Confederate army in Gettysburg. Throughout the simulation, the troops follow the same steps that both sides took throughout the battle, and there is a narrative that explains the actions of both sides along with items of interest that take place during the battle.

In the historical battle, the goal of the Confederate army is to gain control of the

Baltimore Pike area. This is a main supply line for the Union army and Confederate control of this area would be devastating to the Union. You can play a game to reenact the events of the battle, or you can play a free game where you make all the decisions that could win or lose the battle against the computer.

When you decide to take control of the troops, there are a number of different options that you have at your disposal. In order to know what all the options are and how to operate the controls, there is fairly extensive on line help to guide you through your battles. You can command

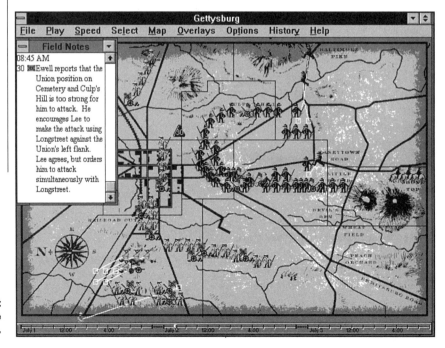

Gettysburg is a strategy game that provides rich background about the Civil War.

The Battle of Gettysburg was a strategic struggle during the American Civil War that is well-served by this involving game.

your troops to go on an offensive attack or you can retreat to one of the nearby hills and dig in for a defensive stand. After you make your command decisions, you have to deal with the challenges of getting the word to your troops. In the 1860s, there weren't radios or telephones, so getting word to the troops takes plenty of time. You also have to deal with the slow moving artillery, moving your cannons across a hill can take quite awhile.

The control interface is quite easy to use and has a lot of information available at the click of a mouse button. Troop movements are as simple as selecting the particular icons and then dragging the mouse along the desired path to their destination. Your cannons are slow moving, so you need to position them carefully within range of the target. Firing your cannons is quite simple, all you need to do is set the direction and the elevation and then select the type of load. You can use a solid shot to take out your enemies' artillery, or you can select a shot much like a shotgun to devastate approaching infantry.

Change the course of history by taking command of the Union or Confederate armies in this strategic battle simulator.

The disc comes with about 290MB of code, video clips, and sounds. There are quite a few video clips that you can view during the game. Some of them are taken from documentaries, but the majority of the clips on the CD come from Turner Pictures rendition of *Gettysburg*, which was a 1993 motion picture.

The installation process was simple and no problems were encountered. The game operates entirely off the CD for gameplay, and the only files placed on your hard drive are some .INI files and the Microsoft Video runtime programs. The program requires a system that is compliant with the MPC level 1 requirements. The program isn't very demanding on the system, so if your machine just meets the requirements of the program there shouldn't be any problem running the simulation.

If the CD has a weakness, it is in the video clips. They opted to use a larger display area for the video clip, in doing so they had to really reduce the frame rate. But other than the slow frame rate, the video clips were of good quality.

The program seemed to be quite well thought out and put together. The game should prove quite entertaining with the history of the battle and strategic play against the computer.

The Journeyman Project

Rating:

Publisher Name: **Presto Studios**

Software Requirements:
MPC/Macintosh

Suggested Retail Price: **$69.95**

*T*he *Journeyman Project* deserves all the hoopla surrounding it. This is one imaginative game, with an entertaining interface and lots of action—including several arcade-games-within-a-game that will challenge your reflexes.

The game takes place in the year 2318. The world is at peace. That's the good news. The bad news is that a rip in the fabric of time threatens to undo all this tranquility. Your goal is to discover the source of this disturbance and travel back in time as a member of the Temporal Protectorate. You work with space-age tools, viewing animated sequences and QuickTime videos shot with real professional actors (some of whom, like Graham Jarvis, you've actually heard of before).

The interface used for this game is quite novel. Apparently, you, as a crack Temporal Protectorate agent, wear a special pair of glasses (only one lens, actually) that has special viewing and tool options built into its "biotech interface." In addition to a view of the scene around you, your peripheral vision shows various messages, status displays, a pop-up message window, and other gadgets and information sources. Played in a darkened room with a stereo headset, *The Journeyman Project* can be quite intense. This has been a Macintosh hit for awhile, and now has become available in MPC format.

This is the next best thing to virtual reality. The photorealistic 3D worlds you explore embrace a branching storyline you can actually change depending on the decisions you make. There is no set order in which the goals must be accomplished and—amazingly enough—there is more

Earth in the far future is your homebase for battling temporal disturbances in *The Journeyman Project*.

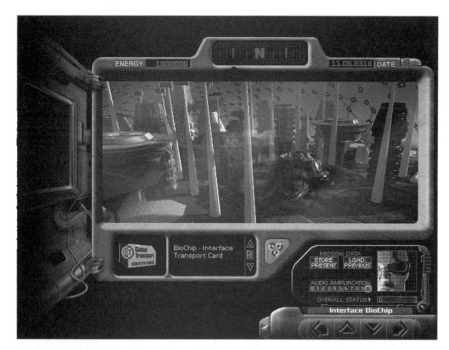

Arcade-games-within-the-game must be mastered if you are to locate the source of the temporal disturbance and save the universe in *The Journeyman Project*.

than one solution for each problem you face. Other games put you in the position of being a spectator, forced to play out the game in the way it was written, and no other.

I can only describe the pace of this game as leisurely. It's possible to play it without viewing the introduction or reading the instructions, because the biotech interface is that intuitive. However, you may spend an hour just getting to headquarters and receiving your assignment. The game begins with you walking up, donning your "glasses," and listening to a radio news report and morning nonsense chatter from a futuristic Rick Dees-clone. Then, you can wander around your apartment, checking it out, and seeing what a 24th-century toilet and shower stall look like. Once you find the front door to your apartment, you can stroll up and down the hallways for another

half hour or so, looking for the elevator. Press a few likely-looking doors, and you may get a recorded message from the apartment occupant.

The Journeyman Project *is an action-filled virtual-reality game of the future—and past—once you get past the opening sequences.*

Eventually, the elevator turns up and you descend to the first floor. There, you find a Global Transport module, learn how to use it, watch it zap an errant fly, and then it teleports you to Temporal Security headquarters. After you manage to gain access there (you need a passcode), you can find your way to a control panel where the game actually begins. Slow learners may take an hour to get this far, but experienced gamers will zip through the whole thing in five minutes. Still, that's a fairly lengthy preamble.

The wait was worth it. Without giving too much of the plot away, let me say you have a stunning—and tall—surprise waiting for you. *The Journeyman Project* is an excellent game that new and veteran gameplayers will enjoy. It's not difficult to learn, and has enough variations and twists to please every player.

Lunicus

Rating:  1/2

Publisher Name:
Paramount Interactive

Software Requirements:
Macintosh

Suggested Retail Price: $69.96

Here's another one of those games that lets you dawdle. If you care to, you can spend hours wandering around on lunar station Lunicus, eating, sleeping, and interacting with other crew members, without a clue as to what you should do next. However, once you figure out what to do, this is an action-packed arcade game with lots of excitement. Dawdle mode is fine for beginners, but expert gamesters will want to move through the boring parts to the action immediately. They won't be disappointed when they get to the good stuff.

The premise is simple. Planet Earth is in deep doo-doo. You're stationed with five other humans on a moonbase named Lunicus. The action starts in the year 2023, and paleontologists on Earth stumble across some ancient artifacts. Scientists manage to repair one of them, and are stunned to view video footage of the Jurassic period, which apparently is the real thing and not some product of Steven Spielberg and Industrial Light and Magic. However, home movies of T. Rex aren't the real focus here. The device summons the evil aliens who produced the artifact, and they proceed to conquer the

Earth and place it under the domination of the merciless Hive Queen and her mechanized army of bad guys.

If you read Orson Scott Card's award-winning SF novels *Ender's Game* and *Speaker for The Dead*, you know that *his* Hive Queen and her minions were only sorely misunderstood. No such luck in this game. These are really evil aliens who won't pack up and go home if you ask them nice. Some serious action is called for.

Luckily, this alien superscience manages to completely overlook United Nations moonbase Lunicus, located in a lowland area of Mare Imbrium. It is now many years later, and Lunicus is the only hope of the enslaved humans on Earth. The exact number of humans on Lunicus is unspecified, but the key players include Vladimir Molotov, commander of Lunicus these last three years, and endowed with a thick Russian accent. There's Dr. Sasha Serenskya, a tall, statuesque blonde who is the base doctor and seems to be somewhat of a flirt. Dr. Max Heisenstein is a Nobel-prize-winning scientist who "specializes" in chemistry, robotics, physics, and languages. Raife is a genetically-engineered human female who has been adapted for life in space, and now manages the base greenhouse. Terry McCallum is an engineer who monitors the power station of the base. There are also assorted guards and minions who perform lesser functions in the game.

Check out your fellow crew members of moonbase Lunicus before you travel to Earth to battle the Hive Queen.

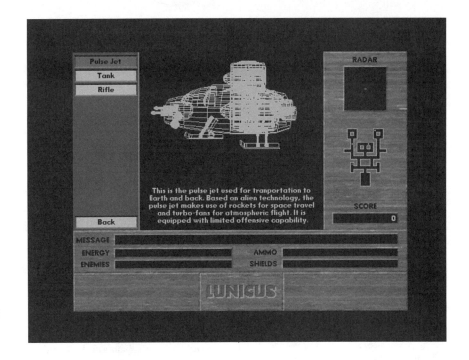

Your weaponry is awesome—but so is that of the evil Hive Queen which has taken over the planet Earth.

Who you are, and what your role is, can be discovered by playing the game.

One of the strong points of this game are the characters, who all have personalities, interesting backgrounds, strengths, and weaknesses. Dr. Heisenstein, for example, is a real old guy (having been born in 1984!), described as having hobbies that include "television trivia." The relationship between your character and Sasha is spiced with a little sexual tension: she flirts, but when you flirt back, you get the cold shoulder.

The early part of *Lunicus* is spent wandering around the moonbase, becoming familiar with its features (information panels, comm panels, and food panels all can be accessed), attending briefings, and trying to figure out what to do. Eventually, you may travel to Earth in your pulse jet and do battle with the aliens in Moscow, Tokyo, or Los Angeles. You'll fight such mechanized creatures as the Hypernode, Battlecruiser, Street Sweeper, Wasp, or awesome

arachnobot. Your weapons include a tank and rifle. You can locate grenade launchers and plasma cannons to add to your arsenal if you look carefully.

Lunicus **asks you to save Earth from the vicious Hive Queen, using only your wits and tons of programming built into this realistic 3D game.**

This is one of those virtual reality games that you roam through in 3D fashion. From time to time you encounter a coarse, 3D

model representing a person. You can move around or next to this model—called a Cyber Puppet—in realistic fashion. Stand face to face, and the screen dissolves to a 2D image of the person, with three or four conversational ice-breakers underneath, like "Uh, what should I do next?" or "What are you doing tonight after the briefing?" Click one of these and the character responds. You can learn a lot from the answers, but your range of questioning is severely limited.

There are more than 5000 movie sequences in this game, and the motion is fluid and believable. *Lunicus* is a rich game that deserves to be savored. Veteran gamesters will appreciate its fast action and attention to detail.

MegaRace

Rating:

Publisher Name:
The Software Toolworks

Software Requirements: **MPC**

Suggested Retail Price: **$69.95**

Welcome to *MegaRace*—where death is a short horizontal line on the monitor screen of life, according to Virtual World Broadcast Television host, Lance Boyle. This incredible game is a combination of *Grand Prix*, *Rebel Assault, Max Headroom*, and a dozen other breath-taking computer experiences. Next to this game, reality is only a pale imitation of life.

If I had to describe *MegaRace* in 25 words or less, 24 of them would be WOW. I was enraptured by the opening sequence, which is a combination of computer animation and full-screen, full-motion video that looks better than almost anything else I've seen on an IBM PC's screen. You're taken on a whirl-wind ride through a futuristic, Blade-Runner-style city to watch, along with other inhabitants of this world, the MegaRace TV show. Lance Boyle, played by a gifted character actor named Christian Erikson (he looks *very* familiar) who explains the show/game's concept so smoothly you forget you're watching what is, in essence, a tutorial. The sequence bounces back and forth between full-screen studio shots to television sets in viewer's apartments, to giant screens mounted throughout the city.

Then, it's time to choose your car and race track (ranging from NewSan in California to Factoryland and Terminal City). You get to watch your actual vehicle being manufactured, and then Lance turns you loose on your selected track. You can race underwater or in outer space using a vehicle, weapons, and armor that you specify. There are five venues in all, each with two to four individual race tracks.

You can race on "Uptown," an incredibly expensive, slick looking speedway created for the beautiful people and elegant nightlife. Or choose "Wasteland" or

Your host Lance Boyle prepares you for the race of your lifetime.

"Orbital Junkyard" if you like your racing gritty and hard. There's even a bonus track with mystery features, and no clues from the peanut gallery.

MegaRace is a stunning racing action game with 14 tracks in five environments, with plenty of 3D virtual reality action, sound, and effects.

The races themselves use fairly standard Grand Prix-type controls and moves: from your cockpit viewpoint, the track seems to rush toward you as you maneuver from side to side. You can speed up, slow down, and fire at obstructing cars to blast them out of your way. There are dozens of options that make the game more interesting and tough obstacles to overcome. For example, you might encounter radar jamming or a blinding zone that obscures your vision. Slippery stuff that makes you skid pops up unexpectedly. You must conserve your energy and collect new weapons and ammunition at every opportunity. There are rails to hold your car to the road and shields that offer temporary protection.

The sound and graphics make this an exciting game to play. I pump a simple Sound Blaster Pro through a stereo system to get ear-blasting effects and music. The full-motion video and animation is so realistic that, played in a dark room, this game can give you sweats. If you thought the images in *Rebel Assault* were realistic, this game makes the LucasArts effort appear primitive by comparison.

Unlike other games of this sophistication, *MegaRace* doesn't make you spend hours trying to figure out how to get it to run with your available hardware. You won't have to create a special boot disk or install some weird drivers to get it to run on your computer. In fact, I successfully managed to install and get the game running as a DOS task under Microsoft Windows, even though it is not a Windows application. The sound and video worked better outside of Windows, so that's how I ran it. The configuration program lets you choose the controller (keyboard, mouse, joystick, etc.)

and what kinds of memory to use (expanded memory, extended memory, etc.) if available.

Guess what? *MegaRace* doesn't even put 20MB of files on your hard disk so it can run faster. Only a few small files (a batch file to start the program, and a high scores data file) are needed. The game generates its amazing video images running directly from the CD-ROM. I have a speedy double-speed CD-ROM drive and 16MB of RAM in the machine I tested this game on, but the results were impressive nevertheless.

If you add excitement, graphics, sound, and ease of play to the simple installation, *MegaRace* has to qualify as one of the best games available for the IBM PC, and that's coming from someone who doesn't even like racing games in general.

Myst

Rating:

Publisher Name: **Broderbund**

Software Requirements:
MPC/Macintosh

Suggested Retail Price: **$59.95**

Nothing on the isle of Myst is what it seems, starting with this dock you discover on your arrival.

*M*yst is more than a game—it's a way of life. Players must explore a photorealistic, 3D world that gives new meaning to the term "virtual reality." As you arrive on the dock of the island-world, you know nothing of the enigma wrapped in an enigma that makes up this game. You're totally on your own to discover the purpose of the island, what happened to its inhabitants, and the location of various puzzles that you must solve in order to win the game. This is a particularly challenging game, because it's up to you to figure out the goal, the rules, and even who the other players are.

Depending on the kind of game you like, this is either the best game reviewed in this chapter, or the most infuriating.

The island of Myst is a gateway to numerous other seemingly disconnected ages of time, e.g. the Channelwood Age, Selenetic Age, and Stoneship Age, each accessible from a dentist-chair-from-Hell

that turns out to be a time travel machine— or something. These worlds were created by Atrus, who opened entrances to them by writing special books. Someone, perhaps one of Atrus' sons, is destroying the books. What is happening?

Well, don't expect the manual to tell you much. You get several booklets, each more cryptic than the last. You can start with the enclosure in the jewel box. It tells you how to move around in the game by clicking the mouse. Big help—you can figure that out yourself in about three seconds. There are also some notes on keyboard shortcuts. That's the extent of the aid you get in

solving the game, other than a few words of encouragement (it's *not* impossible, you're assured).

The supplied Journal of Myst is strictly a do-it-yourself affair: the first page asks you to imagine your mind as a blank slate and urges you to record every scrap of evidence you find, no matter how insignificant. There follows dozens of pages of blank, lined parchment, ready for your entries! You do get a separate booklet with tips for trouble-shooting installation problems. (If you think that because this is a Windows program, all your memory and driver troubles are over, think again. *Myst* works best when Windows has 10MB of RAM, and there are many video display drivers that must be updated to the latest versions.)

Your only real help are three scant clues in a hints booklet, and an offer to purchase the *Myst* Official Game Secrets book for $12.95 more. Don't bother with either unless you really get stuck—*Myst* is a meal best eaten alone.

The game is actually easy enough to play, provided you have lots of patience, plenty of time, and a modicum of ingenuity. You can move through the scenes by clicking with the mouse in the direction you want to go. There are vivid 3D graphics mixed in with a few animated sequences. You need to throw levers, press buttons, click on books, and read notes, looking for clues. There's a special Zip mode that can transport you rapidly through portions of the game you've already visited, but don't use it the first time through or you'll miss something for sure!

When using Zip, the cursor changes into a lightning bolt when it passes over some objects or areas of the screen. Click with the mouse to zip to those areas instantly. A few types of mechanical equipment operate more quickly in this mode—but we won't tell you which kind.

Brilliant graphics, challenging puzzles, and almost no help highlight this amazing computer adventure into worlds of the past—or future.

As in most adventures, you can pick up some objects and carry them with you. However, you can carry only one book page with you at a time. If you try to pick up another, the one you are already holding returns magically to its original location. So read carefully, and take notes in your Journal!

It's difficult to describe *Myst* in much detail without revealing secrets and tipping you off to the answers to puzzles that you'll enjoy solving on your own. Trust me when I say you'll find the graphics eerie, the music haunting, the sound effects chillingly realistic, and the puzzles extremely frustrating. Compared to *Myst*, a daunting game like *The 7th Guest* practically plays itself.

There's a mysterious starship that looks like something out of *Flash Gordon*, and dozens of other artifacts that you can explore. There's a planetarium, clock tower, underground tunnels, secret passageways, and much more. Your investigation starts out in the Library, where there are books to read and rooms to investigate. From there...well, I can say no more. Players of this game, however, just can't say enough about it.

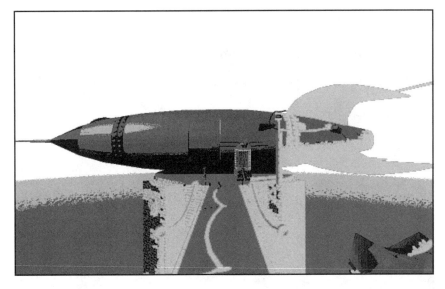

A starship? A weirdly shaped roadside diner? Nobody knows for sure in the land of Myst.

Rebel Assault

Rating:

Publisher Name:
LucasArts Entertainment Co.

Software Requirements: **MPC**

Suggested Retail Price: **$79.95**

For those of you who are too young to remember it (say, those 18 and younger), the *Star Wars* phenomenon of 1977 had a magnitude you'll never appreciate. In an age when movie special effects were still measured by those in *2001 A.D.*, a 1960s relic, the images, action, and characters in *Star Wars* blew audiences away in an unprecedented manner.

Scenes like this one appear lifted directly from the Star Wars movies *Rebel Assault* **is based on.**

Rebel Assault brings this same excitement to CD-ROM gaming, although, if you're not a veteran of the initial *Star Wars* onslaught, you might not understand exactly what all the fuss is about. After all, this is arcade fare similar to what you can get downtown at your favorite teen hangout. My carefully reasoned response to that gibe is, "IT'S ON YOUR OWN COMPUTER AT HOME, YOU MORON!" If nothing else, *Rebel Assault* is ample testimony to how far we've come in home and office computer hardware in the past five years.

Photorealistic graphics, which look enough like sequences from the actual films to fool casual fans, 3D movement, and CD-quality sound make this a riveting game. Your first stop is a training mission through Beggar's Canyon. Nobody is trying to shoot you, there are no hidden obstacles, just you

and the twisty-sharp turns of the Canyon itself. Piloting your T-16 Skyhopper is easy enough with the mouse: move left or right to bank left or right; move the mouse forward or back to bring your nose up or down. Well, that's what I thought, anyway.

After six consecutive missions that ended in a glorious blaze of fire (always in the exact same spot of the Canyon), I dug around in the junk cabinet and withdrew an old IBM joystick, which I plugged in to replace the Gravis GamePad on my six-year-old's 486/40. Enough of these new-fangled controllers. Real Jedi Knights don't use gamepads or mice.

Things went easier after that. If you're used to one particular controller, you can probably stick with that, but a joystick or other non-mouse is highly recommended.

Green Leader to Rookie One:
Are you ready?

Prepare for your training mission in *Rebel Assault*: **Darth Vader awaits at the end of the game.**

After the training mission, there are 15 levels of missions collected into groups of three or four degrees of difficulty, until the finale in the trench of the Death Star. At the end of each level, you get a passcode you should write down, because it's your only way of bypassing lower levels on repeated plays. There are Easy, Normal, and Hard modes to match the action to your own expertise.

Unless you're already familiar with LucasArts' earlier game in a similar vein, *X-Wing*, you'll want to start out at least the training mission in Easy mode. That joystick can be a little *too* responsive at times. You can always indulge your masochistic impulses later on.

Four channels of sound give you speech, music, sound effects, and background noise—simultaneously. Snippets of John Williams' original score make the game particularly stirring, and you'll hear realistic digitized speech commenting on your actions and giving you instructions.

Thrilling 3D, photorealistic action for arcade fans and lovers of the soon-to-be-revived **Star Wars** *series.*

Rebel Assault consumes a lot of resources, but has some built-in controls to adjust for your particular equipment configuration (you can specify a single speed, double-speed, or triple-speed CD-ROM drive, for example), and we had no trouble installing and running it on a Cyrix-based 486 with only 4MB of RAM (even after ignoring some of the installation instructions). Everything worked wonderfully, and it soon became the favorite game in the house, displacing *Doom* and *Hocus Pocus*.

Until virtual-reality helmets become a basic multimedia accessory, *Rebel Assault* will set a standard for 3D, nerve-wracking, shoot-em-up, fly-through games. If you enjoy that sort of thing, try out this game. If you don't, go back and play with your PhoneDisc database.

Sherlock Holmes, Consulting Detective, Volume 3

Rating:

Publisher Name:
ICOM Simulations, Inc.

Software Requirements:
MPC/Macintosh

Suggested Retail Price: $69.95

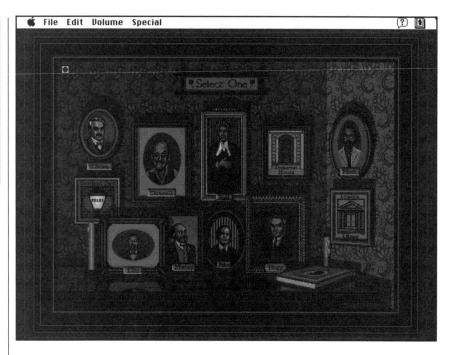

In *Sherlock Holmes, Consulting Detective, Volume 3,* you are present to guide Holmes as he investigates three of his most interesting cases: "The Solicitous Solicitor," "The Banker's Final Debt," and "The Thames Murders." In the first case, a solicitor has died of an apparent heart attack. Holmes, Watson, and you have been provided with a few mementos and some scandalous rumors. Is there a crime? If so, can you solve it? In "The Banker's Final Debt," a seemingly ordinary man, quiet and unassuming, is inexplicably murdered. What was the cause? "The Thames Murders" finds five bodies floating in the Thames one day. Were they isolated acts of passion or the acts of one savage murderer?

Through the use of a series of mini-movies, linked by your choices of who to question and what sites to visit, these cases come alive. The first part of the adventure introduces you to the game interface and some of Holmes' most trusted allies. By clicking various icons representing either the tools you can work with or the pictures of Holmes information sources, you get a brief description of that tool/person. You also get to see the first of many mini-movies, in which Holmes describes his relations with both the Baker Street Irregulars and the Baker Street Regulars. The movie controls are VCR-like and quite easy to master. Then you select which case you will tackle.

If you choose "The Solicitous Solicitor," you first see a mini-movie in which the Inspector discusses a possible poisoning case with Holmes. In this movie, a number of names and places are mentioned. You can have Holmes visit these people and places directly or send the Baker Street Irregulars to try to gather information. In order to solve the case quickly and efficiently, you should rely on the Irregulars to scout for you, but some places and people require you to go yourself.

Names and places of merit can be entered into your in-game notebook, but keep a pencil and paper handy during the movie. You must wait until the end of the movie to enter the names; it's too easy to forget when three or four names and a couple of places have been mentioned. You can pause the movie and rewind or fast-forward. If you forget a clue, you can go back in again and see the same movie, although this might not work forever; as the plot thickens, some characters may have other stories to tell.

In addition, you can have Holmes visit several offices in Scotland Yard, government offices, the London library, court, and other places that may help him solve his cases. You can also read the "London Times," either on the computer or a paper copy included as part of the package. A "London directory" and Watson's extensive files are also available for use in the case.

The movies themselves are interesting. Smooth video cannot be performed on more than a small area of the screen on PCs at the current time. These small windows are disappointing; however, if larger screen areas are used, the video becomes jerky. This program appears to take a different approach. It appears that each pixel of the small movie has been expanded into several.

A series of very well done mini-movies leads you through three fascinating Sherlock Holmes cases; your choices determine what movies you see and what information you get to help solve the case.

The video takes up about half of the screen and is smooth, but it is pixelated. Pixelation is a common special effect used in commercials; take tiny picture units and make them appear larger, giving the image a computer-generated look. This effect isn't over-done; it isn't at all hard to see even small details of the movie, but the images look a bit strange. Still, this is much better than having a perfect image that is a little larger than a postage stamp. It's a clever approach that works well. *Sherlock Holmes, Consulting Detective, Volume 3* also contains good quality audio. There are some good ideas in the way this program works that other adventure game designers could learn from.

The cases themselves are also chosen well. Some leads you are given are true and take you closer to a solution. Others send you away from the case; be willing to cease pursuing a line of inquiry that doesn't appear to be going anywhere. Sherlock Holmes mysteries are a passion for many mystery lovers. They will love this game. Most people like a good mystery. It will work for them, too. Only if mysteries leave you cold should you avoid this disc. Everyone else can have some fun with it.

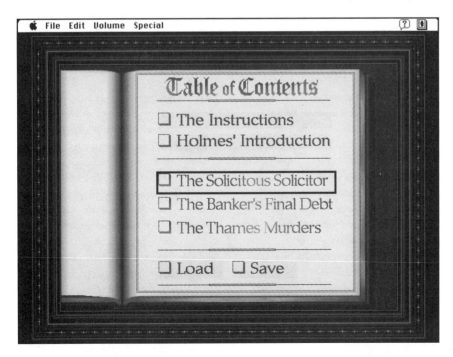

Test your sleuthing skills in three Holmes mysteries.

SimCity

Rating:

Publisher Name: **Maxis**

Software Requirements:
MPC/Macintosh

Suggested Retail Price: **$59.95**

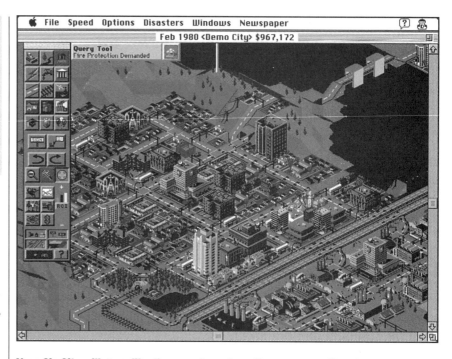

Your SimCity will grow like the one shown here if you manage its resources properly.

Interested in being your own city planner, with the power to subdivide land, create residential, commercial, or industrial areas, then supply police or fire protection? Welcome to SimCity!

The original Maxis *SimCity* has been one of the most addicting Macintosh games ever, and launched a whole genre of simulation games, ranging from *Civilization* to Maxis' own *SimAnt*, *SimFarm*, and *SimEarth*. There are even several third-party books written on how to play the game. We're happy to report that this new CD version from Interplay is more fun and entertaining than the floppy-disk-based original.

Build your own city from scratch, or work with one of the supplied scenarios to meddle in the affairs of a real-life city like Buenos Aires or Tokyo. Your town is populated to capacity with simulated citizens—Sims—who build houses, churches, stores, and factories, pay taxes, and can die off or move away if you muck things up too badly. But do a good job and your city grows and prospers.

Your tool kit is the floating palette at the left side of the screen. Just click an icon to turn the cursor into a lean, mean building

machine that can run electric lines, bulldoze trees or burnt-out tracts, create new residential, commercial, or industrial districts, or perhaps build an airport or nuclear power plant. As the city develops it is shown in the main window.

You need to create residential zones, which grow and prosper based on the amount of pollution (don't put them too near industrial zones!), traffic density, population density, access to roads, and available parks and utilities.

Commercial zones should be nearby, too, providing your Sims with places to work and shop. Industrial zones are for

heavy manufacturing. You need police and fire departments, stadiums, seaports, powerplants, and airports to keep your city thriving. But these amenities are expensive. Your city must grow large enough to support them.

Various pull-down menus let you control the speed of the game, activate or deactivate disasters, open or close informational windows, and view the scuttlebutt in the daily newspapers. A selection of windows provides graphs that track important growth and economic factors over time, or show the distribution of resources.

Managing a city is tougher than it looks. If you raise taxes too high, building will be stifled. Fail to allocate sufficient funds to police or fire protection, and crime, arson, and even unchecked grass fires can wreak havoc. Creating a successful SimCity requires a delicate balance of planned growth, attractive amenities, and shrewd taxation to cash in on voter pleasure with their working and living environment. It also helps to have a lot of time to waste making haste slowly. (I once let a *SimCity* scenario run 24 hours a day for three months on an old Mac Plus, fine-tuning my way to the multi-zillion dollar megamegalopolis level.)

Once a year, you receive a budget report detailing how you did. You can make corrections then, or let your current plan run a little longer to see if things improve (if trends are bad, they usually don't without deliberate effort).

The grandaddy of all simulation games is still a powerful contender, despite competition from stablemate SimCity 2000.

As you work with the program, you'll find a few ways to cheat, or at least reduce your overhead to acceptable levels. For example, any property abutted by at least one section of road or railway may be considered "connected" to the transit system, even though the road or track doesn't go anywhere. Or, you may discover that not building an airport is an admirable way to keep your fire department costs in check, because plane crashes are the most frequent cause of fires in SimCity.

The graphics in this version are welcome enough, but the animations and music, along with many of the voice-over effects, get old real fast. Fortunately, you can disable any and all of these from the Options menu. You can set the program to take you automatically to the site of any disaster or major event (saving you the trouble of hunting for it), and choose to try out your readiness by unleashing a disaster of your choice from a tempting list that includes fire, flood, air crash, tornado, earthquake, monster (your typical Tokyo-eating Godzilla clone), and nuclear meltdown. These can be disabled entirely through another option if you'd rather have a few years of peace and quiet.

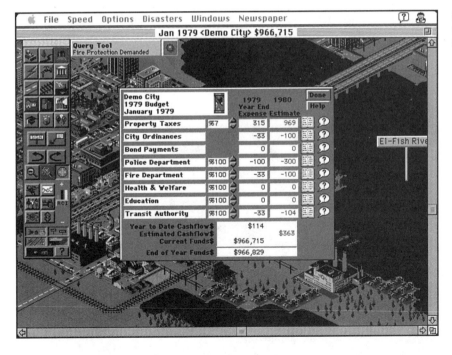

Once a year (or upon request) you can see a status report of how your city is doing.

Star Trek 25th Anniversary

Rating:

Publisher Name: **Interplay**

Software Requirements: **MPC**

Suggested Retail Price: **$59.95**

W hat should you expect from a game based on the most popular science fiction television series of all time? Good graphics, digitized sound from the original characters, good game play, and a feel of the original series would be nice. The graphics are good, but not excellent in *Star Trek 25th Anniversary,* but the other three elements are there.

The game starts with the introduction to "Star Trek" that preceded every episode,

only the programmers have added their names for those of the cast and crew. The first scenario is called "Demon World." You begin the scenario by practicing your combat skills against another Federation ship in mock combat. Once the war game is over, you, as Kirk, receive a message from Starfleet command. There's a problem on a planet. The Enterprise is to go and assist. Sound familiar?

You control the U.S.S. Enterprise and its crew in the game. There are two separate segments of the game: "On Board" and "Ground Mission." While you are on the Enterprise, you control the actions of Kirk, Spock, Scotty, Uhura, Sulu, and Chekov through commands that you give through Kirk. Each officer has his or her own set of actions that can be performed. Such things as arming weapons, raising shields, consulting Spock or the bridge computer, directing Scotty to prioritize damage

control, navigating and travel through space, going into orbit around a planet, and communicating with other ships and planets are available for you to perform, as well as other actions. Things aren't too bad until you get into combat. Then you have several things to do at once; it's pretty hectic. Ship-to-ship combat is fun, however, but it is also difficult.

Once you're on the ground, you will need some way to perform the various actions that a landing party would perform. By clicking the left mouse button, you cause Kirk to walk to the spot the mouse cursor was on. To do other things, you need to click the right mouse button. This activates the command interface, which causes an icon containing a figure to appear at an innocuous place on the screen.

As you move the mouse over it, various body parts or objects are highlighted. When the mouse cursor passes over the eyes, you

Classic Star Trek adventures make up this 25th anniversary disc.

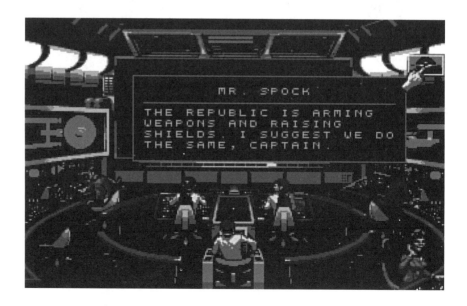

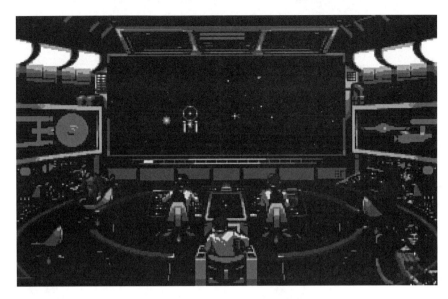

After 25 years, Captain Kirk is still boldly splitting infinitives as he commands his crew to go boldly where no chauvinist has gone before.

are able to invoke the "see" function. By then clicking the eye icon on what you want to look at, you can study it. The mouth works the same way if you want a character to talk. The right hand holds an object; clicking it means you want to use something. When the landing party first lands, the standard compliment of Star Trek items are available: phasers, med kit, tricorders, and communicator. Clicking the left hand allows a character to try to pick up an object. Clicking the Starfleet Insignia brings up the command option, which lets you save or load games, turn on or off sound effects and music, and quit.

Once on a planet, if you have Kirk talk to a character, you have a choice of what Kirk says. By judicious choice of words, you can get along a lot better. The manual makes it clear that violent behavior will not help you in your post-mission review with Starfleet (if you survive to complete your mission). You are to behave as a representative of Starfleet, as well as solve puzzles and aid others. If you earn commendation points for a mission, your crew will behave more efficiently on the next mission, reflecting both their increased experience and their increased confidence in you.

This is a game that really captures the feel of the series, whether you are battling the Klingons or Romulans in space or exploring a planet having an unusual problem with a landing party; it is especially effective because the voices of the original crew are all used.

The manual gives a fair amount of detail about ship's operations, combat, landing party equipment, and crew personalities. All the actors who were part of the original crew have lent their voices to this project. It isn't clear how many scenarios are part of the CD-ROM, but 47 total character voices are given in the credits. Most of these are minor characters, not recognizable from the original series, but there is one name that stands out. Harry Mudd is in one (or more) of the scenarios.

The graphics of the game are not stellar; selecting VGA graphics gives you 320 x 200 x 256 colors. EGA graphics give you 640 x 480 x 16 colors. However, the game has the feel of series: Once you're in the middle of a situation, you forget the graphics quality. Animation is smooth; at higher graphics resolution, that might have been lost, particularly on slower machines. This game is worthy of the original series; while it could be better technically, it is engaging. It's surprisingly fun to control Kirk; it gives a feeling of power. A devoted Trek fan or game fan will want this game.

The C.H.A.O.S. Continuum

Rating: 🔘 🔘 🔘 1/2

Publisher Name:
**Creative
Multimedia Corporation**

Software Requirements:
MPC/Macintosh

Suggested Retail Price: **$79.95**

*T*he *C.H.A.O.S. Continuum* is visually one of the best science fiction genre games out there yet for the MPC. Throughout the game the 3D graphics remain crisp and flow smoothly. Sound is also quite impressive, with a musical score that fits the atmosphere very well and some truly astounding sound effects.

The game is played from the unique point of a Time Probe, a droid that posses large information stores, various sensors, and a weapons system designed for defense. Nice attention was paid to making the player truly feel a part of their droid, and learning very well its strengths and weaknesses. The interface is simple to learn, a selection of buttons surrounding the main window through which you will actually see actions in the game take place.

Anyone skilled with a mouse should have no problems (though I found myself preferring the keyboard for actual movement within the game). I was pleasantly impressed to actually find that the game had a great plot. Though it does stick to the general guidelines of "super computer gone insane,"

it still approaches several points of that plot from refreshing new angles. In this case, the computer is C.H.A.O.S. (Cybernetic Holistic Autonomous Orbiting Server), and it is within the space station where it is housed that you will spend the larger portion of the game, though the story begins on Titan at the colony of New Eden.

The largest disappointment in the game was definitely the puzzles, most of them seem to have been thrown in at the last moment as distractions for the player; unfortunately, they can be very deadly distractions, and actually take away some of the feeling that the smoothly flowing storyline and graphics provide.

The game also claims "enhanced" playability, and while it is true that they have induced various random events throughout the game, you will find that the greatest pleasure from playing again is not in discovering a new game, but in sitting back and taking in the sights.

As a game for beginners, this would have to be a highly recommended, non-puzzle intensive challenge, with stunning effects. It's a worthwhile way to introduce a newcomer into the world of multimedia. Veteran gamers still may want to check it out, however, science fiction games are a rarity in this medium, and this is a worthwhile addition.

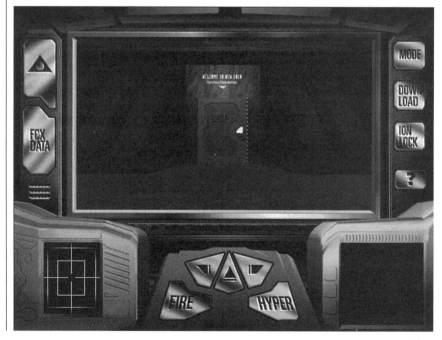

Chess Maniac 5,000,000,000 (and 1)

What the Lampoon loons have done to chess is a crime, but a Not Guilty by Reason of Insanity plea is entirely apropos. This should happen to every self-proclaimed "serious" classic pastime (and to a few of their aficionados). They've taken a serious game and made it into—well—a game; they've taken the pieces and moves and applied slapstick. And no cautious touches or well-considered brush strokes, either: they put it on with a long-napped roller and a spray gun! If there's a politically correct piece on this board it's only cannon fodder for the designers' consuming lust for ego-deflation.

Anyone who plays chess, however casually, will recognize the war college behind the game. But here, it's another facet of the college experience: the beer-bust cum bull-session approach. Chess players often threaten to "kick each other's behinds." On this board things get kicked, all right, but it's not always the gluteus that takes the hit.

Installation is not quite simple but it takes only a few moments. There are several configuration steps and a choice of partial or full installation. The difference is in drive space required (1.14MB for partial, 27MB for full) and speed of play. *Chess Maniac 5 billion (and 1)* will run directly from the CD-ROM in the partially installed version. The inherent slower performance of CD-ROM drives affects playing speed, but only a little. The vendor includes a card with step-by-step instructions and pointers to a batch of demo games.

The basic chess engine is Intelart's, and there is a straight version for the faint-hearted or incurably morose. It's the "bawdy" version where the fun lies, though. Here, the pieces are slightly different from the classic chessmen and odd things happen when you move pieces.

An animated chess with terminal mind warpage potential. Not for the incorrigibly strait-laced but may lace players into a strait jacket.

Start-up is attention-grabbing, to say the least. Heart patients or those with an aversion to apparent system damage, take note! The first time, you *will* get quite a start. After the production number, the Chess Maniac presents several choice screens that may or may not affect play and what you see on-screen.

The warpage persists throughout play. Your esteemed opponent throws distractions like confetti and cheats unabashedly. Comments, from snide to outright crude, spice up the game as various tries at cheating interrupt any semblance of concentration. Stop attempts at stealing pieces with a fast keystroke or they're gone forever, and when the shark cruises the board, someone's

Rating: 1/2

Publisher Name:
Spectrum Holobyte

Software Requirements: **MPC**

Suggested Retail Price: **$79.95**

chessman is going to disappear without that keystroke. Again, quickness counts. The distractions fly furiously and it takes a lot of concentration to play *and* dodge them. The Chess Maniac's spoken commentary adds its own few points to your blood pressure. He sounds like HAL, the *2001: A Space Odyssey* computer, but with an even snootier attitude.

Numerous menu choices permit configuring the game for screen attributes, move clocks, difficulty level, and how persistently the Chess Maniac cheats. Turning Cheat Mode off doesn't necessarily stop him completely.

This is real chess in bawdy mode. Make no mistake about that. The voice admonishes you for any illegal move and sends your piece back. You capture and lose pieces, the program recognizes en passant and castling, and the manual is a good basic explanation of the game. Of course, National Lampoon couldn't leave well enough alone so the explanations always have a few additions.

Overall, the game is tremendous fun. Its creators have taken silliness to a high art. It might be a good idea to have your psychologist's home phone number handy.

Comanche CD Maximum Overkill

Rating: ⊙ ⊙ ⊙ ⊙

Publisher Name:
Novalogic, Inc.

Software Requirements: **MPC**

Suggested Retail Price: **$74.95**

Probably the most noteworthy thing to be said about *Comanche Maximum Overkill* is "WOW!" The second noteworthy thing to be said about *Comanche* is "Read the Users Manual!" After that, hop in the Comanche and have yourself a blast (pun intended).

If you want good graphics, in fact very good graphics, and a challenging simulation, this is the CD-ROM title for you. From the detailed, full feature cockpit to the enemy that seems to come out of nowhere, to the strategy of trying to keep your helicopter in one piece, you will find your hands are full trying to successfully complete your mission. This is one of those instances where words prove difficult to adequately describe the action on the monitor.

The controls, although not complicated, are challenging (which is part of the fun of the game), and chances are it will take some time to master the nuances of manipulating the Comanche around the battlefield.

The great disclaimer to this article is that the author has not actually been in a Comanche to be able to provide a comparison. However, it is very safe to say that this simulation will provide many hours of challenging fun, and even if it isn't exactly

like the real thing (which it may well be), it really doesn't matter. *Comanche,* with its multiple views, various weaponry, and attacking challengers, is great sport.

Novalogic provides support for a host of joy sticks. This game was played using a standard over-the-counter type of joystick, and was very enjoyable. It is the author's suspicion that the game would be even more enhanced by using one of the "higher tech" joystick/yoke packages.

Indeed, this CD-ROM can make use of powerful hardware, if you have it. It is designed to work on an IBM 386, 486, or Pentium-compatible PC system and, either a normal joystick, joystick with throttle, ThrustMaster Flight Control System, CH

FlightStick, CH FlightStick Pro, or CH Flight Yoke. Other optional controls include ThrustMaster Weapons Control System (MkI, MkII), or foot pedals.

There is a very good chance that you will need a boot disk to start this application. It is, ummm, memory intensive. However, with a boot, this application performed flawlessly the several times it was run. The documentation that supports *Comanche* deserves an A+. Both the installation booklet and the users manual are comprehensive, detailed, and well thought out.

All in all, *Comanche* should bring many hours of fun simulations to those looking for a challenging helicopter battle game.

Conspiracy

Whew! In the past year, we've had direct-to-video movies from major studios, like *The Return of Jafar*, which bypassed theaters entirely. Now, we have game productions starring, of all people, major stars like Donald Sutherland, which jump directly from the software studios to your home PC. The advertising for *Conspiracy* makes a big deal of Sutherland's participation, so you are probably wondering how the star of Academy Award winners like *Klute* and *Ordinary People* fares on the small, er, tiny screen. Guess what? *Conspiracy* is a great adventure game, even though Sutherland himself plays only a minor role in the program as a sort of animated help file.

Conspiracy is an involving adventure game in which you play the role of a KGB agent—obviously taking place in the recent past, since the Soviet Union and KGB are no more. The end of the Cold War didn't put Tom Clancy out of business, and so this game just moves into the historical category without losing a step. Indeed, the crumbling decay of the disintegrating Soviet empire makes a great backdrop for this game, even if it's hard to feel threatened by this ex-superpower today.

Graphics for most of game play are simple, but as it is adventure game, that is to be expected. Several sequences within it have some video cuts of the final days of the Soviet Union, featuring actual documentary footage. There are other clips featuring Sutherland that are very nicely done also. These clips and this excellent actor really do add a special touch to the game.

Sound is also simply done, and there are a few sequences of speech within the game, but interactions between your character and computer-generated characters in the game are all textual.

Plot starts out with you being reassigned from the GRU to KGB Department P. Within this department you are quickly assigned to help root out corruption inside the KGB. Your job is made a bit more difficult by all the obstacles placed in your path. You must overcome each of these to find all the enemies of the Soviet state.

Challenging puzzles, some great video clips, and the charisma of Donald Sutherland (in a bit part) make this an interesting adventure game.

The puzzles in the game defiantly make it a joy to play, it is one of the more challenging adventure games I have seen for quite awhile. Many of the puzzles involve a time factor, which always seems believable. You are also very much aware of the passage of time, for you are not stuck in a static world. If within the game you are told a bar closes at 10:30, you can expect to be quickly thrown out when that time arrives.

Random encounters also add to the enjoyment of the game. Simply annoying passersby to picking up a prostitute are the range of actions allowed from these random events.

Hints are available from the ghost of the central character's father, played by Sutherland. Although having Sutherland pop up from time to time was interesting, these hints really are not very helpful, I mostly used them to figure out when I had really messed up and would have to go and do some backtracking.

Actions are easily mouse controlled, movement handled easy, and other actions able to be quickly accessed through an easy to pull up menu.

If you are a fan of adventure games, *Conspiracy* is definitely worth a look. Challenging puzzles are something that is growing harder and harder to find in today's gaming world, and *Conspiracy* is full of them.

Rating: ◉ ◉ ◉ ◉

Publisher Name:
Virgin Interactive Entertainment

Software Requirements: **MPC**

Suggested Retail Price: **$74.99**

Cowboy Casino

Rating: ⊙ ⊙ ⊙

Publisher Name: **IntelliPlay**

Software Requirements: **MPC**

Suggested Retail Price: **$39.95**

If you're ready to go back in time to the Old West for some fun poker action, then *Cowboy Casino* maybe for you. You start out in front of an Old West saloon with some full motion video of one of your opponents. Waiting for you inside are five wise-cracking card sharks from all walks of life. They range from a tough young cowboy to a goofy old prospector who brings his mule into the saloon for the card game.

The video in *Cowboy Casino* has the look of something from a 50s Western. It's complete with piano music and dancing girls in the background. You take your seat at the poker table and face the five other players. There is Miner on your left with his mule, Bandito next to him, followed by Cowboy, Gambler, and Dude. Each player has a unique personality that comes out as you play. The game has two different views you can choose from: facing the other players and overhead.

The game has full mouse support and you can choose your settings from the menus. The menus are designed to look like signs in the saloon. There are also a few icons in the game you can click with your mouse. One is a book on the table that belongs to the bartender. If you open the book you receive hints from the bartender

on odds and betting. Another icon is a pair of glasses that change the view from front to overhead. There is a speed selector so that you can speed the game up if you want.

From the menus you can set house rules. The house rules you can change are Maximum bet to Minimum bet, amount to ante, number of raises allowed, and the initial stakes. The menus all can be activated by the click of your mouse and are straightforward and easy to use.

You can choose to play any of four different poker games, including draw poker, 5 card stud, 7 card stud, and Texas hold'em. After you pick the game you want to play, the computer starts dealing the cards.

You don't have any way to choose your opponents in the game; you play against the same five players every time. After you get your cards it is time to place bets. The game

goes in order clockwise from the first person to deal. As the game goes and you place your bets, from time to time the other players come on-screen with remarks about you and your play. Some of the tough guys like Cowboy and Bandito insult you, and others like Dude and Gambler just comment about your play while Miner just likes to talk to his mule.

The game is fun to play poker against. However, the game is fairly easy to beat. As a player runs out of money, he drops out of the game. You don't hear anymore comments from that player for the rest of the game. Nor is there any way to set the level of play in the game. It would be nice to be able to set the play from easy to intermediate to pro. I would also like to see a way to turn off the video comments from the other players: it slows down the action and after an hour of poker you get tired of hearing them.

These unsavory characters are your poker opponents in Cowboy Casino.

Critical Path

Somewhere in the future, the third world war began as terrorist groups came into possession of nuclear and biological weapons. Over 90 percent of the population of Earth has either been killed or rendered insane by the chemical warfare. The small number of people that have survived thus far have begun to gather in safe areas. Today, a group of four decide to try to make it to a safe haven in their Apache helicopters. Unfortunately, along the way one of the helicopters experiences mechanical failure and the other is shot down by a missile.

The island where you crash is run by a psychotic General. You are lucky enough to make it to a control center of a small complex on the island, your partner (Kat) however is not so lucky. The two of you are able to communicate through a communication link, and it is up to you to provide backup and guidance to your partner as she makes her way through the booby-trapped complex.

The program was put together using high resolution backgrounds with live actors captured and superimposed onto the backgrounds. The interface used throughout the game is a shot of a control room. The control room has a video monitor that allows you to see views from Kat's video camera along with security cameras located around the complex. Also in the control room is a panel of buttons that activate some of the equipment around the complex (i.e. industrial cranes).

On the lower right is a detonator for various traps that have been laid around the complex. To activate the traps you need to decipher General Minh's log book, which contains the codes needed for the detonator. Finally you have your communications link

to Kat's headset and wristband. Through this link you can warn Kat of approaching danger and give her direction through dangerous areas by the using your security camera views.

The interface is quite easy to use and is fairly straightforward. The challenge throughout the game is to figure out the functions of all the buttons. You will kill Kat quite a few times just figuring out what is going on as they throw you right into the thick of things immediately after the introduction.

The program is designed to run under Microsoft Windows 3.1, the program runs in a 640 x 480 resolution and supports color depths to 24 bits. The video is shown using QuickTime for Windows. QuickTime is a format used by Apple Computer Inc., which means that the same CD is also compatible with Macs. The system requirements on the PC side are a 386DX-33MHz with 4MB RAM and a single-spin CD-ROM drive. However, the recommended system is a 486-25MHz with at least 8MB RAM and a double-spin CD. On the Mac platform, a

Rating: ⊙ ⊙ ⊙ 1/2

Publisher Name: **MediaVision**

Software Requirements: **MPC/Macintosh**

Suggested Retail Price: **$79.95**

25MHz 68030 processor with a 640 x 480 x 256 color monitor, 4MB RAM, and a single-spin CD are required. The program also requires the use of Mac System 7.X.

The disc comes with 228MB of data, which includes both executables for PCs and Macs. There are also a number of 24-bit bitmapped pictures that were used in the creation of the videos. The installation routine was quite smooth and you only needed to choose the desired color depth that you wanted the game to run under. The program used a maximum of 14.4MB of hard drive space installing the 24-bit color option.

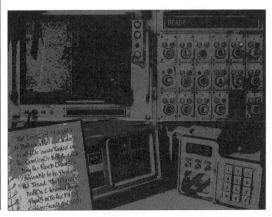

Your controls are all at hand as you maneuver through _Critical Path_'s screens.

Dragon's Lair

Rating: 1/2

Publisher Name: **ReadySoft**

Software Requirements: **MPC**

Suggested Retail Price: **$69.95**

Dirk is back and—finally—in the same spectacular presentation as the original arcade game. This CD-ROM game contains 627MB of graphics and sound that were taken from the original laser disc. As far as I remember, the CD contains all of the levels that were on the original arcade game, except the burning ropes and the falling platform. Most of the moves are still intact from the original game as well.

For those of you who are unfamiliar with the original *Dragon's Lair*, it was originally an arcade game that was released around 1983. In that day, it was the first of two or three arcade games that used the new laser disc technology. The laser disc-type arcade games never lasted all that long, mainly because at that time the laser technology was not reliable and the games were often out of order. But when running, these games were state of the art gaming. This type of game contains a series of prerecorded actions on a disc, and as you move through the level, you need to press a certain key sequence to complete the level. Should you make a wrong move, the program jumps to a death sequence on the disc.

The storyline behind *Dragon's Lair* is a heroic medieval knight (not in armor),

named Dirk, making his way through a castle filled with traps on his way to the dragon's lair. In the dragon's lair there is an evil fire-breathing dragon, named Singe, that is holding the beautiful princess Daphine.

Upon examining the graphics closely, one can see that they reduced the quality of the pictures from the original laser disc, but while playing the game or viewing from a slight distance it looks exactly like the real thing. All the sounds that you hear in the game are taken directly off of the laser disc as well. Dirk's movements can be controlled by using the keyboard or joystick.

Guide Dirk the Daring through the evil Singe's castle to save the beautiful princess Daphine from the Dragon's Lair.

The game play is quite smooth and the game runs at 12 frames per second. You would be surprised how closely the slow frame rate resembles the original game. The game uses a little space on your hard drive to store an optional data file that tells the game exactly how to load each scene for your machine. When you start the game, you have the option to synchronize each level with your machine. This takes about 30

minutes to 1 hour, but it may help smooth up the game on slower system. Basically this routine calculates how much of the scene needs to be preloaded into memory and how much can be read directly off the CD.

The only thing that they haven't gotten quite right is the randomness of the game. The game randomly selects a sequence of levels as you go through the game, but if you die on a scene you have to keep repeating the scene until you finish it or die. You get to continue the game if you want, but there is no save game option. The game sequence isn't as long as the arcade version, but you have to complete each level once to get through. Surprisingly, the game has the capability of giving you a mirror image of some scenes just like the original.

The requirements of the game is a 386 with 4MB of RAM and a single spin CD, although they highly recommend a 486 with 8MB RAM, local bus video, and a double-spin CD. The game ran great on my 486DX2-66.

Despite the fact the game could have been easily made even closer to the original arcade game, this game still brings the fun and excitement of the original arcade game.

Hardcase #1

*H*ardcase #1 is a CD-ROM comic book based on the exploits of Hardcase, a superhero from Malibu Comics' Ultraverse. As such, it will appeal to the older comic book buyer, particularly the collector who is looking for something more to accumulate. It's well-done, and Malibu will sell tons of this title to CD-ROM owning comics collectors, but in the larger scheme of things, look for CD-ROM comic books like this to become rarities and/or novelties fairly quickly.

Hardcase #1 *is an adult-oriented comic book on CD-ROM with vivid color, great narration, and an entertaining story.*

This is no animated comic for kids. The opening scenes feature quite a bit of gore, at least in comic terms, with dismembered body parts strewn about the landscape in the aftermath of a battle in which only Hardcase survives. The language is a little rough, too, although you won't hear any words that

Hardcase is a superhero with attitude, and a promising career ahead of him on CD-ROM.

aren't used on network television every day.

The story unfolds in time-honored comic strip panel form, with each frame revealed one at a time, along with multiple word balloons that are also spoken by some convincing actors. The sound effects and music that accompany the speech make this seem like an illustrated radio play, or perhaps one of those stories that Captain Kangaroo used to read to you in the morning. Many of the frames have some simple animation: a monster's hand squeezes the lifeless throat of a victim, a flashbulb goes off as a reporter photographs a death scene, etc.

The action follows Hardcase, who decides to retire to a movie acting career following the opening battle scene, but is called back to action when a bank is robbed near the movie set. He tests his convictions and powers in a confrontation that leads to a shocking decision. I won't spoil the ending,

Rating:

Publisher Name: **Malibu Comics**

Software Requirements: **MPC**

Suggested Retail Price: **$19.95**

but if you think he returns to his movie role, you're probably a prime candidate for this CD-ROM.

There's no real action required by the user. You just click a button and watch the CD-ROM display the story. You can repeat a scene, skip a scene, or start at any scene you like. There's also a "behind-the-scenes" look at the making of this CD, and a preview of other CD-ROMIX coming down the pike.

Indiana Jones, and the Fate of Atlantis

Rating: ◉ ◉ ◉ ◉

Publisher Name: **LucasArts**

Software Requirements: **MPC**

Suggested Retail Price: **$69.95**

Indiana Jones is back in action in this graphic adventure game based on the Indiana Jones movies by LucasFilms. There have been other Indiana Jones adventure games produced by LucasArts, but up until this one, the games have been based directly on the movies. But with this new adventure for Jones, LucasArts has probably made the best one yet.

In this adventure, Dr. Indiana Jones is trying to discover the secrets of Atlantis. Along your journey you visit many places in the world, from Iceland to Monte Carlo. As usual for Indiana Jones, he is trying to outwit the Nazis in the race to discover the power of Atlantis first. Standing in the way of Indy's goal is a wide variety of puzzles, including a wide variety of complex machines near Atlantis.

The game uses the same familiar interface that has been used in LucasArts games for some time. The interface makes the gameplay relatively smooth without the need to use the keyboard.

This game contains a very unique feature that is not found in the majority of adventure games. The game can be played in three different ways: using your wits, using your fists, or a team path. Depending on the path that you choose to play, there are a wide variety of different puzzles that need to be solved. And even the puzzles that are the same need to be approached differently. The path that you are to choose is suggested by the way you solve one of the first puzzles of the game. As clued by the types of paths, if you use your wits you can complete the game without having any fist fights. Whereas in the fists path, Indy prefers to take the direct approach and knock out his opponents. Finally, in the team path you have to switch roles between Indy and his partner Sophia to solve puzzles.

The disc comes with about 160MB of code and the game requires only 640K of memory. Hard drive space is only required to store a configuration file and to save games, therefore the entire game is run off the CD. For the relatively small amount of code, the graphics are quite well done and the full voice talkie contains almost 8000 lines of recorded text.

The one weakness with the game is the interrogation scenes. The majority of the outcomes depend on choosing the correct questions and answers. However, there is quite a large amount of dialogue that has absolutely no outcome on the game. This fact made it hard to determine whether the dialogue was just for fun or served a purpose. In fact, at the end of the game you need to choose the correct seven questions and answers to survive the game. If you make the wrong choice, you still prevent the Nazi agents from getting the power of Atlantis, but you still die.

Overall the game is well put together and the strengths heavily outweigh the weakness. The game will prove to be quite challenging to even the best of adventurers and will provide many hours of quality gaming.

Indiana Jones is an action adventure, based on the Steven Spielberg movie series.

Iron Helix

*I*ron Helix is a stunning new addition to the collection of sci-fi games on CD-ROM. And stunning graphics, game speed, and plot make it a very worthy addition indeed. The 3D virtual reality environment is chillingly realistic, and the graphics and soundtrack are of cinematic quality. This is a fast-paced, exciting, arcade-quality game.

The game's speed is incredible, with virtually zero loading time required from the CD-ROM between sequences. Indeed, I found it to be the fastest CD game I have ever played. No more click-and-wait, click-and-wait like you find in many games. If you blink, you'll miss something important in *Iron Helix*!

Spectrum Holobyte accomplished this feat in a simple way: All the action movement is confined to a very small window. It doesn't take many resources to keep this area constantly moving with split-second action, so the images you do see can move quickly and be portrayed with vivid realism. You'll wander through rusty and sooty chambers that remind you of a dark scene from *Aliens* or some other sci-fi melodrama, wondering whether you're in a game or some bad dream.

This mode does not hamper the game at all. Indeed, I found I much preferred the small window and the crisp graphics it allowed, along with the stunning speed, to the more conventional approaches

thus far used in the CD gaming industry. Some day, we'll all have quad speed (or faster) CD-ROM drives and more sophisticated video encoding schemes that will make this compromise unnecessary. Meanwhile, *Iron Helix* is as good as it gets.

> ## This arcade game's action is confined to a small window, but that adds to the excitement of its breath-taking speed and gorgeous graphics.

The plotline is also very nicely done. The ship, Jeremiah Obrian, loses its target lock during war games and decides to target the peaceful planet of Calliope. The crew members find themselves unable to stop the ship because they have a virus altering their DNA, and the ship computer's security access is based on DNA scanning. What a problem!

Rating: ◎ ◎ ◎ ◎

Publisher: **Spectrum Holobyte**

Software Requirements: **MPC**

Suggested Retail Price: **$79.95**

The first phase of the game is spent collecting DNA samples from about the Obrian, attempting to find some of a high enough rank to allow you access to the computers and most of the ship. While doing this, you must dodge the ship's Defender robot.

The second phase of the game requires you to destroy the Defender robot, and the third phase requires that you destroy the Obrian itself. As you can see, the challenges get more difficult and complicated as the game progresses.

The game's interface is extremely easy to use, easily accepting both mouse and keyboard commands. You won't have much trouble using it, since, with the small action window, much of the screen can be devoted to controls and informational windows.

If you like fast-paced arcade action, *Iron Helix* is definitely worth a serious look as your next CD gaming purchase. It has incredible graphics, speed, and game play that make it a product worthy of attention.

King's Quest VI: Heir Today, Gone Tomorrow

Rating: ⊙ ⊙ ⊙ 1/2

Publisher Name: **Sierra OnLine**

Software Requirements: **MPC**

Suggested Retail Price: **$49.95**

The King's Quest series by Sierra On-Line is one of the most popular adventure games. Recently Sierra began taking their normally floppy-based quests and putting them onto CD-ROMs. The CD contains the exact same game that comes with the floppy versions, with the addition of full voice recording throughout the game. You'll find both *King's Quest V* and *King's Quest VI* near the top of the CD-ROM best-seller lists. We looked at the latest edition to see how these venerable games hold up on disc.

In this latest episode in the King's Quest series, you play the role of Prince Alexander, who is in search of his lost love, Princess Cassima. After many years, Alexander finally learns how to find the far away world where Cassima lives. Upon arrival to the strange group of islands, Alexander finds that Cassima is being held captive by an evil prince and decides that he must help her. The islands contain many interesting and challenging puzzles to solve. Along the way, you encounter strange creatures, like the five gnomes that guard one of the islands.

The interface is completely mouse driven and no typing is involved. While easy to use, the interface tends to make certain puzzles easy by allowing clicking all over the screen until something works. The CD has all the dialogue recorded in voice, so there is also no reading necessary, although it does have an option to turn the dialog boxes on and not use the voices.

The CD comes with just over 500MB of data, which is mostly comprised of the recorded voices. The install routine was quite smooth and autodetects the proper hardware settings. You have the option during the install to do a large or small install. The small install uses the hard drive for only a configuration file and saved games, while the large option installs the graphics to the hard drive to help on slow CD-ROM drives.

The beginning of the game contains an opening movie that sets up the background of the story. The movie runs half screen and the graphics are quite well done, however the movie ran choppy and flickered in areas. The opening movie was the same as was distributed with the floppy-based version and was most likely designed to run on a hard drive rather than a CD.

The sound also left a lot to be desired. The sound throughout the game was generally of good quality; however, the method of mixing voice over the background music was poorly done. When there were voices to be played, the music would cut in and out between the dialogue.

Besides the few problems with the sound, the game is still quite challenging as an adventure game. If you have played other games in the King's Quest series, this game does measure up to the high level of game play found in the other releases.

King's Quest VI is the brainchild of Roberta Williams, one of the world's best-known game designers.

The Lawnmower Man

The Lawnmower Man was a decent Stephen King story, a mediocre motion picture (although many King fans liked it well enough), and now a fairly good game that leverages the interest in virtual reality to take you into a cyberworld that few games have dared venture into before (but which will be invaded by an alarming number of titles in the future—bet on it).

The disc is a hybrid disc for files that can run on either an IBM PC or a Macintosh, so if you have both computers, or have friends with the other platform, you can share. There are two kinds of movie files (one set for PCs and Macs) on this disc, captured directly from laser disc rather than lower-resolution videotape. Both Macs and PCs may drop frames to keep up with the audio track, so the faster your computer, the better these video clips will appear.

The hero is Jobe, a simpleton (that's the word the documentation uses) who normally spends his time cutting lawns and finds himself as a guinea pig for the evil Dr. Angelo (played by Remington Steele/Mrs. Doubtfire actor Pierce Brosnan, no less). He's given superhuman powers through the guise of a virtual reality system. Although the experiments were originally intended for peaceful purposes (yeah, sure!), Jobe's powers are soon sidetracked by an evil government agency that seeks to transform the lawnmower man into a destructive psychopath (and not even a postal employee) who attacks through the computer network.

This is an action game, pure and simple, with few puzzles to solve or much to do other than act as the scientist Dr. Angelo to battle either Cyberjobe, or Big Red, the killer lawnmowing machine, along with copies of other people Jobe has brought to his universe. You must rescue two other characters who have been placed in Cyberstasis spheres, and then escape from the virtual reality universe to win the game.

The speed of the game is very nice, as is the large picture, but unfortunately this means that some quality had to be sacrificed, and images are often indistinct and fuzzy. Action sequences and movie cuts from the movie of the same name will help to keep you entertained. The music, while nice, is really nothing to get excited about.

The controls are very simple and easy to master. I used the keyboard and had no problem getting into the action of the game.

The plotline you have to deal with is rather simple: you must stop a cyberspatial entity called Cyberjobe. This is to be accomplished through the completion of 12

Rating:

Publisher Name:
Multimedia Publishing Studio

Software Requirements:
MPC/Macintosh

Suggested Retail Price: **$41.95**

action sequences, each of which is a nice change of pace from the previous. There are activities like the Ledge of Darkness (jump from pillar to pillar to platform), Cyber Boogie (shoot virtual pulse lasers while flying through tunnels), crack a secret code, repeat Simon-like tunes on a virtual keyboard, or work your way through a circuit-board maze to freedom.

The Lord of the Rings

I n this fantasy role-playing game, you are immersed in the world of J.R.R. Tolkien. The characters, settings, and the plot of the game are taken from the three-volume set of books titled *The Lord of the Rings,* published in the 1950s. This CD-ROM is an enhanced version of the original floppy-disk-based version of *The Lord of the Rings,* which was released in 1990.

This is a Cinematic Multimedia production. The background music and some of the voices are standard digital audio that is synchronized to the graphical scenes.

Enter the world of J.R.R. Tolkien through *Lord of the Rings*, a new adventure game on CD-ROM.

This is the same type of multimedia production as used in *Battle Chess Enhanced* CD-ROM by Interplay.

If you are familiar with the original version, you will notice some changes and improvements in the game. With the CD technology, you get the normal enhancements of background music and voices, and with them there are enhancements in the user interface and mapping functions. The majority of the enhancements of the game are to make it easier to maneuver through the interface. Also added to the CD-ROM version of the game is a tutorial on the interface with a voice explanation of everything you need to know about the interface.

The game starts off with a few "movies" to set the background and story behind the game. The movies are generally well done; however, they have a relatively low frame rate that leads to a choppy look, and, even though the game only recommends a single spin CD-ROM and a 386SX, I experience some dropped frames on my double-spin CD and 486-66MHz.

The quest begins with the main character, Frodo, standing outside of his home ready to leave on his journey. Before he leaves, he needs to gather some of his friends to help him on the journey. Along the way you need to talk to people to get information and to recruit new help. The path you follow to fulfill your quest is somewhat vague, and it is entirely up to you to choose your path.

The game interface is an overhead view and movement is best controlled by a mouse; however, even with the mouse moving around, the map can be quite a challenge. There are quite a few openings that are only as wide as the characters, and hitting the holes exactly can be quite tricky.

The disc comes with 223MB of data on the disc (not including the musical tracks) and the program installs the main game files on your hard disk, which occupies 3.4MB. The system requirements of the CD are a 386SX, 530K base memory, 1MB EMS, and a CD-ROM with a 150kps transfer rate.

The major weakness of the game is the poor control in the interface. I found myself having to click through three or four menus and sub-menus to get to my final selection. When making the game they probably wanted to maintain the look of the original game, but they could have made the interface easier to maneuver.

On the positive side, the game is more than a role-playing game. There is a challenging quest to complete, with only portions of the game where the luck of the dice comes into play in battle.

Mad Dog McCree

*M*ad Dog McCree is a perfect example of making a silk purse out of a sow's ear. Working within the IBM PC's hardware limitations, American Laser Games has managed to come up with a full-motion video arcade-style shooting game that really works—and works well. Only a tedious amount of repetitive action keeps this one from being a four-star game—but I'm sure the vendors laugh all the way to the bank every time the best-seller lists are published.

You've shown up at Tombstone at a bad time. Mad Dog McCree and his gang of cut-throats have locked the sheriff up in jail, and have taken the mayor and his daughter prisoner at their hideout. A crusty Gabby Hayes look-alike asks you to help out with your six-shooter. You can take some target practice with bottles at the corral (it's not really the OK Corral, it's more so-so), or head straight to the saloon, bank, or jail for a confrontation with the outlaws.

You're equipped with a pistol that can be reloaded by placing it in your holster and pressing the right mouse button (try to do this before your showdowns), and a surrogate hand that is superimposed on the video screen. The number of lives you have is indicated by a set of white hats, and a helpful undertaker pops up in a video clip to remind you of how many lives you have left.

When the gun-cursor is positioned over your target, press the left mouse button to shoot. You have to get the bad guy before he shoots you or you lose a life. You also forfeit a life if you maim or kill an innocent bystander (they, like Gabby Hayes look-alikes, hideouts, and impotent sheriffs, were mandatory in the old West).

The installation program lets you choose from an MPC1 or MPC2 configuration, depending on the video capabilities and CD-ROM speed of your system. The help screens describe the exact equipment you need to "qualify" for each level of performance. The MPC2 setup provides larger, faster, more colorful video displays.

If you've never seen video on a PC before, you'll think *Mad Dog McCree* has a tiny screen, with low resolution, jerky video. If you're used to postage-stamp-sized video images, on the other hand, you'll marvel at how large, clear, and smooth the video is. You get more than a quarter-screen of pretty good video with this game.

I was more impressed with the smoothness of the transitions from one outcome to another. For example, in the opening sequence, if you shoot the bad guys who dart into the picture, they fall down and die. If you miss, they either shoot you or run off. Because each outcome requires different video, you'd expect to see some jumpiness when the picture switches from one to the other in subsequent playings. But the image looked as smooth whether I plugged the bad guys or let them get away. I couldn't spot a transition.

Rating:

Publisher Name: **American Laser Games**

Software Requirements: **MPC**

Suggested Retail Price: **$79.95**

The game didn't vary much each time I played it. When Gabby Hayes speaks to you, you must shoot two outlaws (in the same sequence). If you march off to the saloon, you must kill a bushwhacker every time, and then go into the bar and knock off One-Eye and his cohorts to get the keys to free the sheriff and go after Mad Dog. The villains and required killings were the same each time. It would have been nice to have some tree-huggers in a protest demonstration, or perhaps a clutch of attorneys to mow down for a change of pace.

However, this is otherwise an excellent game that you'll find highly entertaining—for awhile.

You got the drop on him—now fire!

Maniac Mansion 2: Day of the Tentacle

Rating:

Publisher Name: **LucasArts**

Software Requirements: **MPC**

Suggested Retail Price: **$69.95**

This sequel to Maniac Mansion is just as much fun.

The world is at risk of being taken over by "tentacles" and it is up to you to save the world from the rule of the evil tentacles. In this full "talkie" enhanced CD-ROM version, you play the role of three different people who are trying to save the world from being taken over by evil tentacles. This is a sequel to *Maniac Mansion,* which was released about 5 years ago, and this original game is included as a bonus.

The trouble begins for the three heroes when a tentacle drinks some toxic waste and becomes extremely evil. This is quite a unique adventure game, where you control three different characters. The only catch is that one of the characters (Hoagie) is in the past, Laverne is in the future, and Bernard is in the present. Each of the three characters has a number of different obstacles to overcome to save the world. Unfortunately, there are some things that cannot be done with items found in the time frame of the character. No problem, the three characters can communicate and pass inanimate objects back and forth through the Chron-o-John (time machine made from a portable toilet) that will enable everyone to complete their tasks.

The interface is probably the best adventure gaming interface ever designed. To do tasks, you construct simple sentences with the actions on the left side of the screen and inventory items on the right, along with the items that appear in the main screen. The sentences are constructed by selecting each object for the sentence with the mouse; in addition, the actions can be selected with keyboard commands. This enables very fast construction of actions with the use of the keyboard and mouse.

The disc comes with 280MB of code and an additional 16MB of demos for other LucasArts games. The game requires a 386 with 2MB EMS, and will run under DOS or Windows. Hard drive space is only required to store a configuration file and to save games, therefore the entire game is run off of the CD. This is the reason that a double-spin CD-ROM is recommended.

There are no obvious weaknesses in the game, it is probably one of the best-designed adventure CD-ROM based games. For the avid adventurer, this disc will provide a good challenge and will give many hours of gameplay. The puzzles are often tricky and require very creative thinking, but they are not impossible to solve.

Sam & Max: Hit the Road

It's the toughest case in the history of the world, at least for Sam and Max, free-lance police. In this full talkie, enhanced CD-ROM version, you guide Sam and Max through the case of the missing Bigfoot.

The graphics in the game are done with cartoon-type pictures and really add a lot to the effect of the game. The CD is another in the line of LucasArts full Talkie CD-ROM games. All the dialogue has been recorded and put on the disc. This means that there is no reading to do during the game. The voices used for the game are a highlight in the game and add many extra laughs that would not been encountered by reading the dialog boxes.

Someone has kidnapped Bigfoot, and it's up to Sam and Max to track them down in this slapstick-style comedy adventure game.

Through the game you control Sam and Max by using LucasArts' brand new point and click interface. The new interface is completely mouse driven and generally allows easy manipulation of the actions you want to take. With the new interface, the graphics now take a full screen view with easy access to the inventory in the lower left corner of the screen.

The game contains many puzzles that are quite challenging to solve; you definitely need to think creatively to solve the puzzles. A real nice feature added to the game helps relieve the common frustrations in the game. At any point in the game, you can play a game like "Car Bomb," which is very much like the old Battleship game, or you could just play something mindless like helping Max smash road signs. After the stress release, you can resume your adventure with a completely new outlook.

The disc comes with 210MB of code and the game requires a 386-33Mhz with 4MB. Hard drive space is only required to store a configuration file and to save games; therefore, the entire game is run off the CD. This is the reason that a double-spin CD-ROM is recommended. The disc also comes with audio tracks on the CD that are the complete musical themes that are heard in different parts of the game.

The only real weakness of the game is the interface. This is the first game made by LucasArts with their new interface. Although there were no problems with the interface, the old interface was a much better interface for game play. Aside from this, the game is solidly put together and the puzzles are often tricky and require very creative thinking, but are not completely impossible to solve.

Rating: 3 1/2

Publisher Name: **LucasArts**

Software Requirements: **MPC**

Suggested Retail Price: **$69.95**

"Soiled Office Space Available" and "Vehicles Will Be Stolen" tell Sam and Max that they're investigating a rough neighborhood.

Star Wars Chess

Rating:

Publisher Name:
The Software Toolworks

Software Requirements: **MPC**

Suggested Retail Price: **$79.95**

Serious chess players dream about a match-up with Gary Kasparov. Amateurs like me imagine vanquishing Darth Vader. If you're more interested in putting a little action into a slow-moving game than improving your international rating, *Star Wars Chess* may be just what you are looking for. A sort of *Battle Chess* for the TV generation, it features 72 different entertaining animations that bring your chess board to life with all your favorite characters from *Star Wars*.

Think of this as either a very slow arcade game, or a rather speedy version of chess. The characters do move around in interesting ways, from the lumbering of Chewbacca to the stiff gait of the robot C3PO to the smooth glide of R2D2. Pieces don't just capture each other, they zap opposing players with rayguns or light sabers. C3PO pops in with stunningly clever sayings at appropriate times. You can play against another human or the computer, with levels of play from Beginner to Expert.

You may laugh at some of the matchups. Chewbacca is an appropriate enough knight, and C3PO stodgy enough to serve as a bishop. R2D2 makes a logical pawn, and Yoda a servicable rook. Brother and sister Luke Skywalker and Leia Organa are King and Queen for the Rebel forces. However, their counterparts on the side of the Empire are Darth Vader (Queen [?]) and the Emperor (King). Yoda's fellow rooks are giant, AT-ST Walkers, and the Empire pawns are towering Storm Troopers.

There are digitized sound effects from the movie, a stirring soundtrack, and lots of other action. As a chess program, this one uses the same logic as *Chessmaster 3000*, so it can be a formidable opponent if you set it for more difficult levels. You may take back and replay moves and set up the board in any arrangement you like to re-create classic games from the past (or your own pitiful experience). There is a Mentor icon you can click to receive hints.

Chessmaster 3000— with Star Wars characters and animation added to confuse good players and entertain poor ones.

As with many chess programs, you can switch sides whenever you like, so if the situation seems too dire (even with hints), just change to the opposing side and enjoy the situation. I've never understood the interest in animated chess programs. It makes as much sense as installing a 24-second clock on the baseball field, and could be potentially more distracting than helpful. (Do you really want to play chess while John Williams' score plays in the background?) However, those who like *Star Wars*, or who need some help to avoid falling asleep at the chessboard, will love this program.

Fight the Evil Empire with animated characters from Star Wars in this chess program.

Who Killed Sam Rupert, Virtual Murder 1

Who Killed Sam Rupert is an interactive, multimedia murder mystery in which you have the opportunity to act as detective in solving the murder of Sam Rupert, a restaurant owner known for his famous wines. This game gives you the opportunity to collect clues, observe live-action video questioning of suspects by your assistant (Lucy Fairwell), evaluate forensics results, perform follow-up questioning of suspects, even check alibis, and eventually request a warrant for the arrest of your prime suspect.

A murder mystery with a gritty adult plot, Who Killed Sam Rupert? uses music, vivid graphics, and the pressure of a ticking clock to challenge your mind and nerves.

The answer to the question that the title poses is certainly not a giveaway. If you do a poor job of note taking, or don't pay attention to the clues, you will find yourself looking very bad during the press confer-

ence. Even if you make it past the press conference (which determines whether or not you can perform any additional questioning or request a warrant), you still have to request a warrant by choosing the appropriate suspect, alibi, method, etc. Incorrect warrant choices, of course, result in incorrect arrests, and innocent suspects will be vindicated.

The multimedia effects make this an entertaining package. The music adds an aura of mystery and live action videos give you an opportunity to observe the reactions of the suspects to the questions. Picture generation, though, at the crime scene is a bit slow.

As you might expect from a murder investigation, the milieu is gritty and best suited for adults or mature teens. If this were a movie, it would easily earn an R rating: Sam Rupert has been cheating on his wife for a number of years, the language used includes the use of at least one very strong four letter word, one suspect's sexual orientation is described using a derogatory term, and yet another suspect and his (female) roommate sleep together.

Nothing unusual here, of course, but perhaps not something you care to expose your pre-teenager to in a game setting, just yet. Parents may be caught offguard because the author, Shannon Gilligan, has produced mysteries for children, including *Our Secret Gang* about fifth and sixth graders who form their own detective agency.

Like many games of this type, *Sam Rupert* has only one plot and one solution, and once solved there is not much need to

revisit it. An interesting twist would have been to change some of the clues, alibis, etc., so that multiple plots and solutions where provided with the game. We downgraded this disc a bit because you really aren't given many alternatives or choices beyond the few built into the game itself. A *lot* more can be done with this format than this disc shows.

Interestingly enough, time, a valuable commodity during the game that gets eaten in chunks by interviews and the investigation, can also be your friend at the end. If you arrest the wrong suspect at the end of the game, you are allowed to go back and choose again if time permits.

Who Killed Sam Rupert? is a good opportunity to search for clues and piece together the pieces of a murder mystery puzzle, if you can overlook the unsavory character development. As a combination of *Murder, She Wrote* and *NYPD Blue*, this disc will please mystery fans for as long as they are able to stretch out the meager plotlines and alternatives.

Rating: 1/2

Publisher Name: **Creative Multimedia Corporation**

Software Requirements: **MPC**

Suggested Retail Price: **$39.99**

Wolfpack

Rating:  1/2

Publisher Name: **NovaLogic**

Software Requirements: **MPC**

Suggested Retail Price: **$39.95**

Depending on what you want from a WWII tactical naval combat simulator, *Wolfpack* may either please or disappoint you. If you prefer realistic outcomes to flashy graphics, you will like *Wolfpack*. Arcade fans won't be too impressed by this game, though, although the very high quality opening sequence may lead you to first think otherwise. The game graphics are quite adequate to give you the feel of actually being in the sub or destroyer.

In *Wolfpack*, you take command of either a German wolfpack (group of attack submarines) or an Allied convoy. If playing the German side, your goal is to sink the Allied tankers and transports, while avoiding their protecting destroyers. Playing the Allied side reverses the goal: you must protect the convoy, while ideally sinking the subs in the wolfpack.

Most scenarios involve multiple ships for both sides; there are several ways to change your command focus to the ship you are interested in; one of them should suit your tastes. One important thing to note, however, is that when you leave a ship, it does *not* automatically return to computer control. It continues whatever you last ordered it to do,

mindlessly. The result can range from beneficial, if you were, say, maneuvering deep to escape the scenario once your sub had fired all its torpedoes, to catastrophic, if you were diving rapidly and forgot to go back to the sub before it destroyed itself by hitting bottom or being crushed.

Wolfpack contains an impressive amount of detail. It supports Adlib and CMS sound boards and compatibles; a Pro Audio Studio 16 card on the test machine worked well with the Adlib selection. Sound adds to the realism, although it may slow things down on machines with slower processors. *Wolfpack* can also use the built-in speaker in your computer, with little loss of realism. The user interface is controllable by mouse, joystick, or keyboard, but the documentation strongly recommends use of a mouse. The major controls that you are familiar with from WWII naval movies are at your command. There is a detailed damage model for each ship you control, covering damage to nine systems, such as the forward torpedo tubes, the periscope and flooding for subs and the rudders, depth charges, and 'on fire' for the destroyers. This damage screen is really needed for the subs: you must immediately surface when flooding, for example. This knowledge is somewhat less important for surface ships; you won't need to monitor it so often when controlling them.

The controls the captain can access are diverse and true to the time period in which the battle is being fought. For instance, in 1942 and after, a sub captain has access to METOX or NAXOS, which warn him when Allied ships have painted him with their radar. METOX is an early system;

NAXOS becomes available once the Allied forces switch to centimeric radar systems in 1944. This example shows how the game designers have sweated the details. The Allied destroyers have the good old depth charges and deck guns we've seen in so many movies, but after 1940, they also have the nasty "hedgehogs"—forward firing spigot mortars—that explode on contact with the sub. Hedgehogs fire in front of the destroyer, while the depth charges fire behind it. Used properly, either is deadly.

Wolfpack seems to have included enough of the elements of submarine warfare so that you can accurately simulate sub/convoy engagements for a wide variety of situations.

One weakness that seems glaring: Although you are nominally the captain, you actually are doing the work, setting the course and speed, targeting and firing the torpedoes, etc. However, when it comes to diving, this is inadequate. You can set the sub to dive slowly or quickly, but you can't specify a particular depth (other than periscope depth or surface). It's easy to put one sub into a dive and then shift to another sub. Soon you are informed that the diving sub has hit the bottom or was crushed, or somehow met a bad fate by diving too deep. It would be helpful for a captain to be able to specify a depth to dive to. Other than that, there is little that begs to be changed in this game.

Additional CD-ROM Titles

Title: Adventures in Heaven
Suggested Retail Price: $39.95
Publisher: Most Significant Bits
Platform: MPC
Description: Hundreds of shareware adventure games for all ages, featuring an easy to use menu shell.

Title: Aegis: Guardian of the Fleet
Suggested Retail Price: $69.95
Publisher: Time Warner Interactive Group
Platform: MPC
Description: World War II sea battle simulator for experienced game players.

Title: Armored Fist
Suggested Retail Price: $69.95
Publisher: NovaLogic
Platform: MPC
Description: 3D tank simulation game lets you choose to control the U.S. or Soviet tanks, set the strategy, and plan your missions.

Title: B-17 Flying Fortress
Suggested Retail Price: $49.95
Publisher: Microprose
Platform: MPC
Description: WWII flight simulator as you command your own bomber on critical missions to save the Allies.

Title: Backroad Racers
Suggested Retail Price: $49.95
Publisher: Revell
Platform: MPC

Description: Another model assembly guide and auto racing game in the European Racers mold.

Title: Beneath A Steel Sky
Suggested Retail Price: $74.99
Publisher: Trilobyte
Platform: MPC
Description: Arcade game of the future, with lots of exciting action.

Title: Blue Force
Suggested Retail Price: $89.95
Publisher: Tsunami Press
Platform: MPC
Description: Become a motorcycle cop in this role-playing game.

Title: Bridge Deluxe with Omar Sharif
Suggested Retail Price: $49.95
Publisher: Interplay/MacPlay
Platform: MPC/Macintosh
Description: Learn from the undisputed best bridge player ever to portray Dr. Zhivago.

Title: Buzz Aldrin's Race Into Space
Suggested Retail Price: $69.95
Publisher: Interplay/MacPlay
Platform: MPC/Macintosh
Description: The second man on the moon guides you in your own chase to outer space.

Title: Capstone Game Collection
Suggested Retail Price: $79.95
Publisher: Capstone Entertainment
Platform: MPC

Description: Hundreds of shareware games for you to try before you buy.

Title: Castle of Dr. Brain
Suggested Retail Price: $69.95
Publisher: Sierra Online
Platform: MPC
Description: Can you defeat the evil doctor, or will you become his next victim?

Title: CD Game Pack
Suggested Retail Price: $79.95
Publisher: Software Toolworks
Platform: MPC
Description: Another game collection for IBM PCs.

Title: CD Game Pack II
Suggested Retail Price: $99.95.
Publisher: Software Toolworks
Platform: MPC
Description: The second edition of this games collection has more games and a higher price tag.

Title: CD-Fun House
Suggested Retail Price: $39.95
Publisher: Wayzata Technologies
Platform: MPC/Macintosh
Description: Over 1000 games for IBM PC and Macs, including casino and parlor classics.

Title: CD-ROM Software Jukebox
Suggested Retail Price: $49.95
Publisher: Selectware
Platform: MPC

Description: Just games, but you're bound to find some you like in this mammoth collection.

Title: Chessmaster 3000
Suggested Retail Price: $79.00
Publisher: Resource International
Platform: MPC
Description: Learn chess from one of the most highly rated computer tutors.

Title: City in Trouble Year 2000, London or Paris version
Suggested Retail Price: $89.00
Publisher: Aditus Inc.
Platform: MPC
Description: Visit the chosen capital as an American spy to stop an evil drug lord.

Title: Classic Board Games
Suggested Retail Price: $49.00
Publisher: Merit Software
Platform: MPC
Description: Electronic versions of the classic games including chess, Othello, and others.

Title: Conan the Cimmerian
Suggested Retail Price: $29.95
Publisher: Virgin
Platform: MPC
Description: If you like Conan, you'll be back quicker than your opponents can say, "Hasta la vista, Baby!" in this action-filled role-playing game.

Title: Cosmic Osmo
Suggested Retail Price: $79.95
Publisher: Broderbund
Platform: MPC/Macintosh
Description: Help Osmo find his way home.

Title: Curse of Enchantia
Suggested Retail Price: $42.99
Publisher: Virgin
Platform: MPC

Description: Role playing game for Dungeons and Dragons graduates.

Title: CyberRace
Suggested Retail Price: $69.95
Publisher: Sony
Platform: MPC
Description: Possibly a great game, but we couldn't get our copy to work.

Title: Dagger of Amon-Ra
Suggested Retail Price: :$59.95
Publisher: Sierra
Platform: MPC
Description: This science fiction/puzzle game will test your wits, and patience.

Title: Dare, Bluff or Die
Suggested Retail Price: $59.00
Publisher: Motherlode
Platform: MPC
Description: A role playing history of the West, and not to be confused with the Madonna documentary film.

Title: Dark Sun
Suggested Retail Price: $65.00
Publisher: Strategic Simulations
Platform: MPC
Description: This role-playing adventure game lets you create your own characters and stories.

Title: DarkSeed
Suggested Retail Price: $39.95
Publisher: Cyberdreams
Platform: MPC/Macintosh
Description: Another science fiction game that pits you against futuristic foes in a quest to preserve humankind.

Title: Deathstar Arcade Battles
Suggested Retail Price: $29.95
Publisher: Chestnut
Platform: MPC
Description: There are zillions of space war shareware games, and most of them are on this disc.

Title: Dracula Unleashed
Suggested Retail Price: $49.95
Publisher: Viacom
Platform: MPC
Description: Best-selling version of the Bram Stoker horror classic, with great graphics.

Title: Dune
Suggested Retail Price: $99.99
Publisher: Virgin
Platform: MPC
Description: Frank Herbert's mind-numbing epic novel comes to CD-ROM. Do battle with sandworms, and don't eat too much spice.

Title: EcoQuest
Suggested Retail Price: $69.95
Publisher: Sierra Online
Platform: MPC
Description: Save the ecology and your planet with this game.

Title: Educational Gameland
Suggested Retail Price: $39.95
Publisher: Pacific HiTech
Platform: MPC
Description: Free and shareware: try-before-you-buy software.

Title: ESPN Sunday Night NFL
Suggested Retail Price: $69.95
Publisher: Sony
Platform: MPC
Description: Football fun for the pigskin fanatic.

Title: Eternam
Suggested Retail Price: $59.95
Publisher: Interactive
Platform: MPC
Description: Virtual reality in a game to reclaim a fun park.

Title: Evasive Action
Suggested Retail Price: $59.95
Publisher: Software Toolworks

Platform: MPC
Description: Avoid getting hit, but strike first.

Title: Fantasy Fiefdom: Medieval England
Suggested Retail Price: $89.95
Publisher: Software Sorcery
Platform: MPC
Description: Castles, sorcerers, and more.

Title: F-15 III
Suggested Retail Price: $59.95
Publisher: Microprose
Platform: MPC
Description: Fly jet fighters in this Top Gun simulator.

Title: Firefighter!
Suggested Retail Price: $49.95
Publisher: Macmillan
Platform: MPC/Macintosh
Description: Put out fires without getting burned in this action game.

Title: Flying Nightmares
Suggested Retail Price: $49.95
Publisher: DoMark
Platform: Macintosh
Description: A flight simulator with an evil twist.

Title: Gahan Wilson's Haunted House
Suggested Retail Price: $59.95
Publisher: Byron Preiss Multimedia Company, Inc.
Platform: MPC/Macintosh
Description: Acclaimed cartoon artist Gahan Wilson's funhouse.

Title: Great Naval Battles
Suggested Retail Price: $69.95
Publisher: Strategic Simulations
Platform: MPC
Description: Command the naval task force in World War II.

Title: Gunship 2000
Suggested Retail Price: $49.95
Publisher: Microprose
Platform: MPC
Description: Helicopter war in this arcade classic.

Title: Hell Cab
Suggested Retail Price: $99.99
Publisher: Time Warner Interactive Group
Platform: MPC/Macintosh
Description: Take Raul's tour of New York City and end up venturing through time to the Roman coliseum.

Title: Hot Lines
Suggested Retail Price: $49.95
Publisher: EBook
Platform: MPC/Macintosh
Description: Simple graphics game; not sure why they put it on CD-ROM.

Title: Inca
Suggested Retail Price: $59.95
Publisher: Sierra Online
Platform: MPC
Description: Puzzle solving game.

Title: Isaac Asimov's The Ultimate Robot
Suggested Retail Price: $79.95
Publisher: Microsoft
Platform: Macintosh
Description: Robot games from the master of cybernetic fiction.

Title: Jet Pack
Suggested Retail Price: $69.95
Publisher: Microprose
Platform: MPC
Description: F-117 & F-15 fighter games.

Title: Jones in the Fast Lane
Suggested Retail Price: $69.95
Publisher: Sierra Online
Platform: MPC
Description: Another arcade game.

Title: Jump Raven
Suggested Retail Price: $45.95
Publisher: CyberFlix
Platform: MPC/Macintosh
Description: New futuristic game with your team fighting against evil through fast arcade action.

Title: Jutland
Suggested Retail Price: $89.95
Publisher: Software Sorcery
Platform: MPC
Description: Game of strategy for those of us with a naval inclination.

Title: Kids Collection
Suggested Retail Price: $19.95
Publisher: Capstone
Platform: MPC
Description: Three floppy disk-based games put on CD-ROM: Adventures with Fievel in An American Tale, Trolls, and a Rock-A-Doodle coloring book.

Title: King's Quest V
Suggested Retail Price: $59.95
Publisher: Sierra Online
Platform: MPC
Description: Puzzle solving game, an earlier version of the game reviewed elsewhere in this chapter.

Title: Klotski
Suggested Retail Price: $19.95
Publisher: Quanta
Platform: MPC
Description: Move blocks around, using Reverse Polish Notation.

Title: Labyrinth of Time
Suggested Retail Price: $69.95
Publisher: Electronic Arts
Platform: MPC
Description: Puzzle solving adventure game.

Title: Lands of Lore
Suggested Retail Price: $74.99
Publisher: Westwood
Platform: MPC
Description: New adventure game with puzzles, featuring the voice of Patrick Stewart.

Title: Legend of Kyrandia
Suggested Retail Price: $59.95
Publisher: Virgin
Platform: MPC
Description: A great new puzzle solving adventure game.

Title: Leisure Suit Larry
Suggested Retail Price: $59.95
Publisher: Sierra
Platform: MPC
Description: Solve puzzles to get Larry a date. Larry gets cruder and more explicit with each release, but his adventures keep selling.

Title: Loom
Suggested Retail Price: $99.95
Publisher: LucasArts
Platform: MPC
Description: Fantasy adventure for the whole family. A classic CD-ROM that is still available.

Title: Lost Treasures of Infocom
Suggested Retail Price: $59.99
Publisher: Activision/Infocom
Platform: MPC/Macintosh
Description: Games from Infocom that you'll enjoy.

Title: Maniac Sports
Suggested Retail Price: $49.95
Publisher: Software Toolworks
Platform: MPC/Macintosh
Description: A collection of varied sports-oriented games.

Title: Mechwarrior II: The Clans
Suggested Retail Price: $79.95
Publisher: Activision
Platform: MPC
Description: Action arcade game with mechanized robotic fighters and weapons.

Title: Microsoft Multimedia Golf
Suggested Retail Price: $65.00
Publisher: Microsoft
Platform: MPC
Description: Links game with more courses and better graphics.

Title: Might & Magic: World of Xeen
Suggested Retail Price: $59.95
Publisher: New World Computing
Platform: MPC
Description: Interactive adventure using multimedia sorcery.

Title: Monopoly Deluxe
Suggested Retail Price: $74.99
Publisher: Virgin
Platform: MPC
Description: The board classic, somehow padded out to fill a CD-ROM with extra graphics and stuff.

Title: Mosaic Magic
Suggested Retail Price: $29.95
Publisher: EBook
Platform: MPC/Macintosh
Description: Fun games you won't get tiled of.

Title: Multimedia Trivia
Suggested Retail Price: $59.95
Publisher: Electronic Arts
Platform: MPC/Macintosh
Description: Test your knowledge of useless information.

Title: Murder Makes Strange Deadfellows
Suggested Retail Price: $59.95
Publisher: AimTech
Platform: MPC

Description: Solve the murder mystery, if you can.

Title: MVPs Game Jamboree
Suggested Retail Price: $29.95
Publisher: Chestnut
Platform: MPC
Description: Nine of MVP's best, plus FREE!, their latest game.

Title: No. 11 Downing Street
Suggested Retail Price: $69.95
Publisher: Silicon Alley
Platform: MPC
Description: From The Adventures of Ninja Nanny and Sherlock, an interactive mystery game.

Title: Out Of This World
Suggested Retail Price: $59.95
Publisher: Interplay/MacPlay
Platform: MPC/Macintosh
Description: Outer space arcade game.

Title: Pacific Islands
Suggested Retail Price: $49.95
Publisher: Readysoft
Platform: MPC
Description: You command a 1995 tank platoon in the Pacific.

Title: Pentomino
Suggested Retail Price: $19.95
Publisher: Quanta
Platform: MPC
Description: The classic board game, brought to CD-ROM.

Title: Quantum Gate
Suggested Retail Price: $79.95
Publisher: HyperBole Studios
Platform: MPC/Macintosh
Description: Futuristic sci-fi adventure game.

Title: Rags to Riches
Suggested Retail Price: $59.95
Publisher: Interplay/MacPlay

Platform: MPC/Macintosh
Description: For richer or for poorer, but richer's a lot better.

Title: Return of the Phantom
Suggested Retail Price: $49.95
Publisher: MicroProse
Platform: MPC
Description: Role playing game built around the infamous Phantom.

Title: Return to the Moon
Suggested Retail Price: $49.95
Publisher: Lunar Eclipse
Platform: MPC
Description: Sci-fi adventure game.

Title: Return to Zork
Suggested Retail Price: $79.95
Publisher: Activision/Infocom
Platform: MPC/Macintosh
Description: The ancient classic has updated graphics and a new interface.

Title: Scrabble Deluxe
Suggested Retail Price: $49.99
Publisher: Virgin
Platform: MPC
Description: The board game on CD-ROM.

Title: Secret of Monkey Island
Suggested Retail Price: :$59.95
Publisher: LucasArts
Platform: MPC
Description: Puzzle solving adventure..an oldie but still goodie.

Title: Secret Weapons of the Luftwaffe
Suggested Retail Price: $99.95
Publisher: LucasArts
Platform: MPC
Description: Combat flight simulator with World War II aircraft.

Title: Shuttle: The Space Flight Simulator
Suggested Retail Price: $39.99
Publisher: Virgin

Platform: MPC
Description: You'll have a blast with this challenger.

Title: Soft Kill
Suggested Retail Price: $39.95
Publisher: Xiphias
Platform: MPC/Macintosh
Description: Techno-thrill on U.S. infrastructure and the defense system.

Title: Software Jukebox: All American Sports
Suggested Retail Price: $49.95
Publisher: SelectWare Technologies, Inc.
Platform: MPC
Description: Sports games of all types.

Title: Software Jukebox: Arcade
Suggested Retail Price: $49.95
Publisher: SelectWare Technologies, Inc.
Platform: MPC
Description: Lots of arcade action on the games packed onto this disc.

Title: Solitaire
Suggested Retail Price: $49.95
Publisher: Interplay/MacPlay
Platform: MPC/Macintosh
Description: Dozens of different solitaire variations, including Klondike.

Title: Space Quest IV
Suggested Retail Price: $59.95
Publisher: Sierra Online
Platform: MPC
Description: Interactive game for those who liked King's Quest.

Title: Spellcasting Party Pack
Suggested Retail Price: $49.95
Publisher: Accolade
Platform: MPC
Description: Interactive puzzle solving game for the D&D crowd.

Title: Spirit of Excalibur
Suggested Retail Price: $39.95
Publisher: Virgin
Platform: MPC
Description: Puzzle with Arthurian overtones.

Title: Sport's Best
Suggested Retail Price: $29.95
Publisher: InterActive Publishing
Platform: MPC
Description: Multilingual disc of games including tennis, paragliding and kickboxing.

Title: Star Trek: Judgment Rites
Suggested Retail Price: $59.95
Publisher: Interplay/MacPlay
Platform: MPC/Macintosh
Description: Another Star Trek game.

Title: Stellar 7
Suggested Retail Price: $59.00
Publisher: Sierra
Platform: MPC
Description: Sci-fi flight combat on the surface of an alien planet.

Title: Stonekeep
Suggested Retail Price: $79.95
Publisher: Interplay/MacPlay
Platform: MPC/Macintosh
Description: Castles and wizards fill this role playing game.

Title: Strike Commander Dix
Suggested Retail Price: $69.95
Publisher: Origin
Platform: MPC
Description: Combat flight game.

Title: Supersonic
Suggested Retail Price: $79.95
Publisher: Interactive
Platform: MPC/Macintosh
Description: Simulations and games with military aircraft.

Title: Tetris Gold
Suggested Retail Price: $49.95
Publisher: Spectrum
Platform: MPC
Description: The classic Russian game and others in this game pack.

Title: The Arcade
Suggested Retail Price: $39.95
Publisher: Compton's New Media
Platform: MPC
Description: Arcade games in many different guises.

Title: The Case of the Cautious Condor
Suggested Retail Price: $59.95
Publisher: AimTech
Platform: MPC
Description: Solve the mystery to win this game.

Title: The Games Collection
Suggested Retail Price: $59.00
Publisher: American Databankers
Platform: MPC
Description: Most recent collection of the best shareware games on the market.

Title: The Lost Vikings
Suggested Retail Price: $39.95
Publisher: Interplay/MacPlay
Platform: MPC/Macintosh
Description: Find the lost tribe of Norsemen.

Title: The Magic Death: Virtual Murder 2
Suggested Retail Price: $49.99
Publisher: Creative Multimedia
Platform: MPC
Description: Individual or party mystery game, the sequel to Who Killed Sam Rupert?

Title: The Terror of the Deep
Suggested Retail Price: $59.95
Publisher: ReadySoft, Inc.
Platform: MPC/Macintosh

Description: Role playing, animated fight scenes, 3D sequences in the ocean.

Title: The Wiz-Pak 6-Pak
Suggested Retail Price: $29.95
Publisher: Wizardware Multimedia
Platform: MPC
Description: Nearly 200 educational games for the entire family.

Title: The XIth Hour
Suggested Retail Price: $99.99
Publisher: Virgin
Platform: MPC/Macintosh
Description: A reporter returns to the Stauf mansion to solve the mystery.

Title: Tony LaRussa Baseball
Suggested Retail Price: $69.95
Publisher: Strategic Simulations
Platform: MPC
Description: Manage your own baseball team with Tony's help.

Title: Total Distortion
Suggested Retail Price: $99.95
Publisher: Pop Rocket, Inc.
Platform: MPC/Macintosh
Description: Music video adventure game.

Title: Trump Castle 3
Suggested Retail Price: $59.95
Publisher: Capstone
Platform: MPC
Description: Create your own casino characters to play the games.

Title: Ultima I - VI bundle Pack
Suggested Retail Price: $69.95
Publisher: Origin
Platform: MPC
Description: Interactive series of games in the Ultima role-playing series.

Title: Video Cube: Space
Suggested Retail Price: $49.95
Publisher: Aris Multimedia

Platform: MPC
Description: A Rubik-like puzzle with unscramble photos from NASA.

Title: Virtual Tarot
Suggested Retail Price: $49.95
Publisher: Virtual Media Works
Platform: Macintosh
Description: Tell fortunes with cards.

Title: Wing Commander
Suggested Retail Price: $39.95
Publisher: Origin
Platform: MPC
Description: Sci-fi combat flight simulator.

Title: World Circuit
Suggested Retail Price: $49.95
Publisher: Microprose
Platform: MPC
Description: Formula I racing game.

Title: Wrath of the Gods
Suggested Retail Price: $49.95
Publisher: Maxis
Platform: MPC/Macintosh
Description: A new role-playing game based on ancient times.

Chapter 10

General Interest

The General Interest category includes everything and anything, from looks at our National Parks to discs devoted to U.S. and foreign travel. You'll find CDs on parenting, and others that collect information on Yoga or wines of the world.

There are more than 30 discs reviewed in detail in this chapter, and listings of many more. Many are devoted to health topics, such as the *Mayo Clinic Family Health Book* or *The Family Doctor*. *Fitness Partner*, a disc that lets you create your own workout program, also fits into this category.

If you're interested in puttering around the home, you'll want to investigate *Home Design* or *Complete House*, which let you design your own residence (and give you plenty of ideas on how to do it). There are discs on gardening and cooking, too, for you homebodies.

Those who'd rather get away from it all can look over reviews of discs like *California Travel*, *Dream Vacations: Hawaiian Style*, or *Everywhere USA*. A disc called *National Parks of America* is your guidebook to every national recreation area in the country—those close to home and far afield. When you're ready to go, a CD-ROM called *Travel Planner* can help you vacation smoothly.

Sports fans will love *Total Baseball*, *Sporting News' Pro Football Guide*, or the ultimate sports CD: *Sports Illustrated's 1994 Almanac*. All three have plenty of records and statistics. If sports aren't your thing, you can learn more about the Earth and surrounding planets with CD-ROMs like *In the Company of Whales*, *Beyond Planet Earth*, or *Oceans Below*.

Beyond Planet Earth

Rating:

Publisher Name:
The Discovery Channel

Software Requirements: **MPC**

Suggested Retail Price: **$49.95**

Wouldn't you know that one of the best sources for real-world documentaries in the universe would produce one of the best CD-ROMs about the universe? The Discovery Channel's *Beyond Planet Earth* takes you on an interactive journey to Mars and beyond, with videos, text, and interviews with space experts on our solar system and space exploration.

All eyes turned heavenward the summer of 1994 with the collision of a comet with the planet Jupiter, so this compilation of information is especially timely. That's doubly so since we recently observed the 25th anniversary of the first walk by human beings on the surface of the moon. One of those pre-Michael Jackson moonwalkers, Buzz Aldrin, Ph.D., serves as a technical expert for this disc.

This Windows-based program has an interface similar to the one in the other Discovery Channel

CD reviewed in this chapter, *In the Company of Whales.* The main menu screen offers a choice of four ways to access the 50 minutes of video, 200 space photographs, and comprehensive reference material on the disc. You can choose from The Planetary Theater, The Solar Gallery, Space Experts, and Mission to Mars.

The centerpiece of the disc is The Planetary Theater, which includes actual Discovery Channel programs, like the complete 15-minute documentary, *Tales from Other Worlds.* There are also clips from *Fate of the Dinosaurs* (were dinos killed by a collision with a comet?), *The New Solar System*, *Star Cycle*, and *The Electric Sun.* As each video plays, the script is displayed in a scrolling window to the left of the small video window, so that you can read along—or ahead.

The Solar Gallery contains photographs and text, along with video clips on eight different topics. You can learn about

journeys to the planets, the "rocky" inner worlds of our solar system, or explore the gas giants Jupiter and Saturn. You learn about moons, meteors, comets, asteroids, and other bodies in our solar system.

The Space Experts module is your opportunity to interview four noted scientists about their views on eight different topics. I couldn't resist asking Buzz Aldrin what his favorite celestial body was. After all, he's one of only a handful of human beings who has actually visited another body other than planet Earth. Guess what? Dr. Aldrin's

The Discovery Channel takes you beyond our planet with videos, pictures, sound, and interactive interviews with experts.

Go Beyond Planet Earth and explore our solar system.

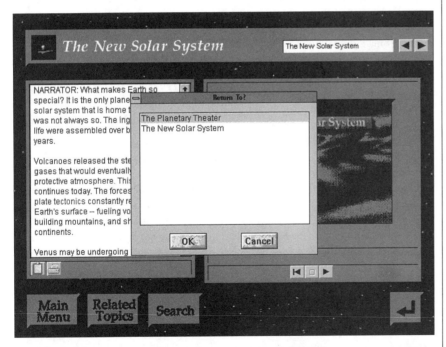

Choose from many different movies and mini-documentaries, displayed on a small screen next to the script.

fave planet is Mars, which he once thought might be visited during his lifetime.

Even if the journey takes longer than Dr. Aldrin once expected, you can experience it now through the final section of the disc: Mission To Mars.

There are four different views in this module, told in pictures, videos, and text. They include About Mars (a comprehensive description of the planet), Previous Missions (listings of all the unmanned missions to date), Future Missions (planned unmanned missions scheduled before the year 2000), and First Steps (how humans may visit Mars). Although President Bush set a target date of 2019 for the first U.S. landing on the red planet, many experts today think that date is optimistic. In this section you learn why, exactly what's involved in the trip, and how much it could cost.

There are hypertext glossary entries scattered throughout *Beyond Planet Earth*, so if you encounter a term you don't understand, you can look it up on the spot. Text from any section can be copied to the Clipboard, and then pasted into other applications for use in research papers (attributed quotes only!). You can also search for information on related topics.

You also find experiments and activities for kids in the user's guide, and additional resources for further study, such as books, lists of space-interest organizations, and addresses of government agencies that deal with space. How do you pack for space? What musical compositions have been inspired by the heavens? Do meteorites shower everyday? Believe it or not, it's fairly simple to collect samples from rainwater immediately after a major meteor shower: they'll be the particles in the water that can be attracted by a magnet!

Beyond Planet Earth shows how documentaries like those shown on The Discovery Channel can be brought to life through interactive computer features. This is one general interest CD-ROM that will be of interest to the whole family.

The Family Doctor, 3rd Edition

Rating: ◉ ◉ ◉ 1/2

Publisher Name:
Creative Multimedia

Software Requirements:
MPC/Macintosh

Suggested Retail Price: $79.99

Here's a fresh perspective for you. *The Family Doctor* was reviewed for us by one of the sharpest PC users we know, who happens to be a wheelchair-riding multiple sclerosis patient who's seen more doctors and gathered more medical information than he ever wanted. He attacked this disc, his first-ever home medical guide, with a healthy dose of skepticism.

The report is that *The Family Doctor* stands up well. While not as impressive as the *Mayo Clinic Family Health Book*, also reviewed in this chapter, it offers a wealth of valuable information. Buy the Mayo disc first for its superior illustrations, videos, and narration, and then consider this one for your collection for additional information, particularly on rare diseases. The disc has been improved from previous versions with the addition of a new section on first aid and emergency care, brand-new information on rare diseases, and some updated video clips.

This CD is a home medical guide by the author of the syndicated column of the same name, Dr. Allan Bruckheim, M.D., FAAFP. Dr. Bruckheim has been advising lay people on medical matters for awhile and it shows. The information is current and much more complete than you would have thought

likely in a general-audience health guide.

The amount of raw information on this CD is astonishing. Dr. Bruckheim and Creative Multimedia have managed to include some 2,300 frequently asked questions, 300 color illustrations, a prescription drug guide with 1,600 entries and pictures of many of the pill forms, a nice human anatomy guide with video and sound, a database on rare disorders, an animated first aid guide, a resource list, and a strong search program. You can print out all the files for future reference.

Almost every selection provides pointers to more information and it's worth the extra drag and clicks to check it. Many of the articles list bibliographies for further research.

The CD installed easily in Windows, requiring only the usual Windows Run SETUP procedure. The Mac version only requires installing QuickTime (if it hasn't already been installed on your system). The disc is a little slow starting up but no worse than any CD with a large interface program. The interface might feel slightly odd to Windows users. Pull-down menus work after the Macintosh fashion, click, drag the highlight bar to your selection, and then release the mouse button. The menus don't stay down in the typical Windows manner. Mac users will find this and the HyperCard interface in their version comforting.

At startup, a nice opening screen appears with a quick-select guide to the left, supplementing the text buttons on the main screen. On the main screen, buttons for the nine key program functions nestle on the right (this button bar is movable on the Mac version). The main areas include:

Questions & Answers—This is the main body of the CD. It contains some 2,300 of

the medical questions Dr. Bruckheim has addressed in his tenure as a syndicated medical columnist. Many of the articles include pointers to other information on the CD, usually available by a simple drag and click. Everything on this disc seems to be linked to everything else that might be apropos. The structure of the database guides you from the more general ideas or questions to specific issues, virtually painlessly.

The Family Doctor *is your one-stop-shopping resource for family health information, with solid information on drugs, anatomy, diseases, and first aid.*

Rare Disorders—This is one of the more intriguing sections. There are diseases explained here that may affect only a few dozen people. (One had only 40 reported cases.) The articles explain the conditions as fully as practical in a popular work and include many of the other conditions that might mimic one of the truly rare ones. Bibliographic pointers to medical literature enable further research.

Prescription Drug Guide—1,600 commonly prescribed medicines are listed by generic name. You can find them by trade name using the Search and Browse system. Many of the listings are accompanied by pictures of the pill forms under the Additional Information pull-downs. The listings include how prescribed and supplied, how to take them, side effects, and conditions they are usually prescribed to treat. It's not the *Physician's Desk Reference*, but it's not as hard to use or understand, either.

Basic First Aid—This is just what it says, a solid guide to handling medical emergencies for the layman. It covers treating minor to life-threatening situations, with solid advice on everything from cuts and bruises to heart attacks, drowning, electrical shock, and poisoning.

Resources—Listings of associations and foundations related to medical concerns, a listing of educational and Support groups, and a collection of health-related booklets. This is a good source of places to look for informational and support groups related to specific conditions.

Illustrations—This contains some 300 files of informational illustrations of Anatomy, Body Processes, the appearances of various Diseases and Injuries, Medical Procedures, and Health & Social Issues. The illustrations are clear and informative, well labeled, and good quality. They provide a helpful adjunct to the textual information, putting a "face" on the data.

Anatomy of the Human Body—Beauty really is only skin deep. If you find the human body fascinating, this section only reinforces that interest. All the body's major systems are shown with their organ placement. The movies that accompany each major system division show them well, often in live action. You can choose from three magnification levels and as the cursor touches an item, a right button click (or a double-click on a Mac) activates a sound file that gives the correct pronunciation and more detailed information for that anatomical term. Even more detailed illustrations are available in the Illustrations menu by selecting that section's Human Anatomy division. Few of these are as good as those provided in the Mayo Clinic disc, but the layperson will still find them illuminating.

Search & Browse—Here's *The Family*

Doctor's power plant. You can search for a specific term, drug, organ, or program item or any combination thereof with Boolean (AND/OR) operators available at a click-and-drag. Try "allergy" and "penicillin" and you'll get a listing of 30 articles covering these two items in combination in,

apparently, descending relationship to penicillin allergy, from anaphylactic shock reaction to penicillin to general information on allergies and including a list of illustrations of various allergic reactions.

While not our first choice as a home health guide, *The Family Doctor* is packed with solid information, comforting guidance, and tons of reference material.

The Family Doctor provides personal, in-depth medical information.

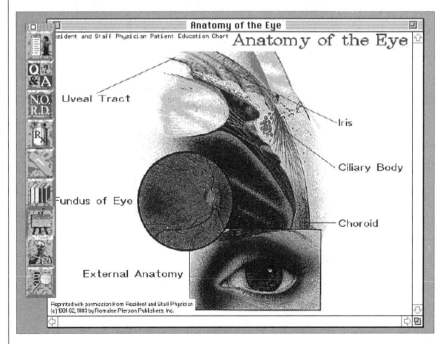

Detailed anatomical illustrations add depth to *The Family Doctor*.

Fitness Partner

Rating:

Publisher Name:
Computer Directions

Software Requirements: **MPC**

Suggested Retail Price: **$49.95**

On the surface, *Fitness Partner* seems like one of those solutions in search of a problem. Are you really in the mood to do aerobics in front of a tiny image that occupies only a fraction of your small computer display, perhaps triggering a hard disk crash with all the jumping about? Does it make sense to trade Jane Fonda and that 27-inch color TV in the family room—for this?

In truth, the trade is far from equal, but not like you might expect. *Fitness Partner* is theoretically superior to any single workout video—but is it so in practice? A quick glance at your groaning shelf of exercise tapes will provide an important clue. You may need a dozen different aerobic videos to provide the kind of variety and flexibility that is built into this single CD-ROM product. It's not a video show that you buy to watch and, perhaps, work out with (you'd be surprised how often these tapes are viewed from the comfort of a couch or recliner). *Fitness Partner* is a Microsoft Windows-based application on CD-ROM that can help improve your fitness, and live healthier while (if necessary) losing weight. This disc's approach has some advantages, and disadvantages as well.

On the one hand, one fitness nut who

looked at this product couldn't imagine who would pay $50 for it when you can get several tapes from the "Buns of Steel" series or any other set of workout videos for that. She also couldn't find any value in the exercises that were shown even if she didn't have tapes and live instructors as an option.

The vendor, on the other hand, asks you to forget about the tiny on-screen image for a minute. They feel that skeptics will fixate on that with the same zeal that they scoffed at the idea of converting a computer into a $2,000 fax machine with an add-in board two years ago. Instead, imagine having the ability to design a different, custom exercise

This surprisingly effective exercise tool lets you design your own aerobics routine, from brief to grueling, using personal information to tailor the workouts to your needs.

routine for each day of the week, tailored for your own height, weight, sex, and needs.

You can program each session to fit your own schedule. If you have 30 minutes on Mondays, Wednesdays, and Fridays, but only 15 minutes on Tuesdays and Thursdays, you can build a full session, complete with

warmup, vigorous excercise, and cool-down period to fit each time slot. With a videotape, you may be punching buttons more often than a Bowl Game fanatic on New Years Day.

Fitness Partner is easy to install in your Windows-based PC (it also works with the now-defunct VIS CD-ROM player system). The interface is a standard Windows configuration, using buttons and dialog boxes, menus, and scrollable lists that you can manipulate easily with a mouse.

The first time you use *Fitness Partner*, you need to enter your name, age (which determines an optimal pulse rate to achieve while you exercise), and gender (used to determine the intial number of repetitions and speed of the exercises) into the dialog boxes that appear. Then, specify your current fitness level, either beginner, intermediate, or advanced. The program offers parameters to help you choose the correct level. For example, you'd click the intermediate check box if you exercise one or two times a week, and advanced if you already exercise daily.

After that, you need to tell *Fitness Partner* your primary goal, either to lose weight or tone muscles. It then creates a recommended workout for each day of the week. At first, all seven will be identical. You can use the Design module to change these basic programs to customized versions that better fit your needs. Indeed, you can select specific exercises from a list box that includes elbow circles, head presses, heel lifts, knee bends, lunges, and all manner of standard moves. Adjust the number of reps or time spent with the exercise, and vary the speed of each set. Up to 10 different exercises can be selected for the warm-up section of a session, another 20 specified for the workout portion, and a final group of up to 10 for the cool-down section.

In fact, up to nine different users can enter personal information into the program and schedule their own workouts. An advanced Profile module allows entering body measurements, weight, and both short- and long-term goals. The measurements and weight information can be used to track your progress as you use the program.

Okay, we're back to that tiny image again. Guess what? You don't have to look at the screen 100 percent of the time. Because you've selected the moves and routines yourself, you don't need a large screen image to try and figure out what to do next. The instructor, an actual aerobics expert rather than a movie star, prompts you vocally to get ready for each successive exercise. You'll find that an occasional glance at the screen, even with the small image, is all you need to keep going. Of course, you can't listen to your own music (instead of the built-in sound track) if you're listening to the instructor. Following the instructor visually just isn't an option with this tiny image.

One of the reasons you own so many exercise tapes is that you got bored with the old ones. *Fitness Partner* should keep your interest while saving you the time formerly spent trotting off to the gym, aerobics class, or video rental store. However, if you get bored with a video, you can easily get bored with this CD-ROM, as well.

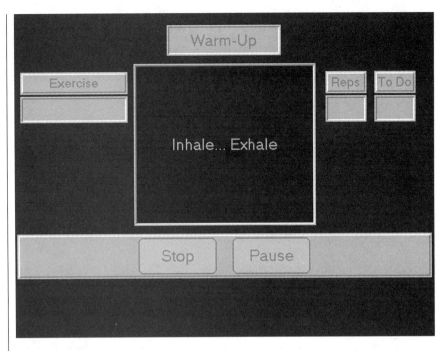

On-screen prompts help you maintain a steady pace during your customized workout.

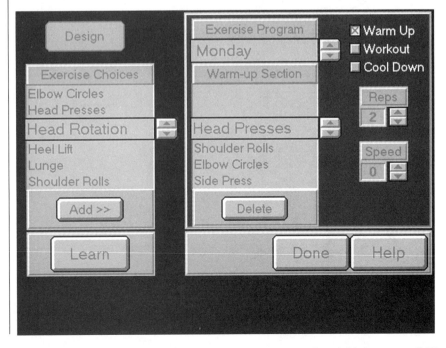

You can design your own workouts using *Fitness Partner*.

Home Design: Gold Edition for Windows

Rating: 💿 💿 💿

Publisher Name:
Expert Software, Inc.

Software Requirements: **MPC**

Suggested Retail Price: **$49.95**

You wouldn't let a stranger pick out your clothes—so why leave the design of your home to someone else? That's the idea behind *Home Design: Gold Edition for Windows*, a CD-ROM that includes a specialized drawing program for building your own home plans, along with 25 popular designs for you to rework and tweak.

Certainly, drawing up actual blueprints for a house calls for an architect or trained designer, but this disc can help you draft rough drawings to use as a basis for finished designs. *Home Design* is a superior alternative to sketching out a layout on paper with a pencil, or, worse, trying to convey your ideas with words alone. The disc can also be used to create a floorplan of your existing home, so that you can experiment with redecorating ideas.

Home Design uses drag-and-drop drawing of the sort pioneered by Shapeware's Visio. You create a home plan by drawing the outlines of walls using standard drawing tools.

Box, oval, line, and freehand tools are available from a button bar at the top of the working window at all times (unless you've hidden them). Several other clever utensils, such as a wall tool (which creates wall outlines) and a door tool (it draws the door and marks its swing arc with a dotted line automatically!) help speed many tasks.

Specify line thickness, pattern fills, and choose a text font from any typestyle installed in your Windows system. You can set the drawing to any scale you want, and can work with or without grid guides. View your plan using four different levels of zoom. *Home Design* is really a full-featured home design tool, lacking only some of the more sophisticated features, fine detail in shapes, and variety of shapes offered with Visio.

Eight "libraries" of shapes—baths, beds, den, dining room, kitchens, living room, office, and symbols—can be loaded into a separate window. The designer can then drag individual furniture and accessory shapes to the home plan and position, size, or rotate them as required. As with "real" drawing programs, several shapes can be grouped together, locked in place, or placed in front of or behind other shapes. Individual shapes are treated as independent objects that can be moved and manipulated as required.

If that's all *Home Design* provided, it would be a useful CD-ROM on its own. Many other features have been thrown in to make this a comprehensive home planning tool. You can insert objects from other Windows applications into your drawings to dress them up. These include Visio 2.0 drawings (so you can incorporate shapes developed with that program into your plans), QuickTime for Windows movies, PowerPoint presentations, Excel spread-

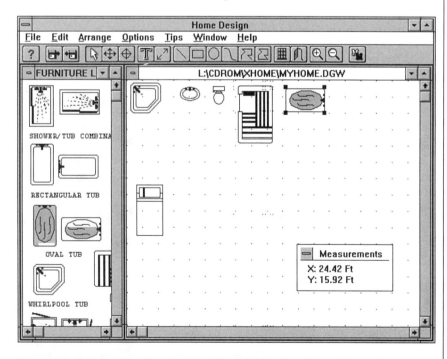

You can design your own home using a library of furniture items that can be dragged onto your plan.

Home decorating ideas, arranged by rooms of the house, are supplied with full-color pictures and voice narration.

sheets, Word for Windows documents, and dozens of other objects. If you have a sound card and microphone, you can record WAV files and embed them in your design—so a home plan really can speak to the architect!

Because *Home Design* supports Windows' Object Linking and Embedding (OLE) feature, components that you import from other applications can be "linked," (i.e., automatically updated in your home design document whenever you change them in the original application), or "embedded" (permanently installed in your design, independent of the original file, but still editable using the tools of the creator application).

If you find OLE confusing, there's a good discussion of the concept in the *Home Design* manual, which will get you up and embedding with the best of them in a few minutes. It even helps you decide when to link and when to embed. A glossary and visual glossary (for when you may not know what it's called, but you know what it looks

like) are also included.

A separate costing program is also available on this CD-ROM. It can be used to help calculate the costs of financing, building, or decorating your home. There are calculators to figure amortization tables for fixed and adjustable rate mortgages, and places where you can type in the average building costs for your area.

Home Design doesn't leave you on your own when it comes to coming up with ideas. A pop-up "media library" window offers a gallery of videos, slides, and drawings showing sample home plans, room by room designs (kitchens, baths, etc.), examples of room accessories (flooring, doors and windows, wallpaper, lighting, draperies, etc.), and design ideas for decorating, kitchen planning, furniture, and other aspects. If you want background music as you work, the CD includes light songs in ten different styles (from blues to New Age).

In the main menu bar, a pull-down Tips menu offers ideas for saving energy, efficient

design, solar energy, and using natural gas. If that weren't enough, the disc is furnished with an excellent 98-page Design and Decorating Guide that addresses the aesthetic and practical issues you need to consider. It takes you through basic planning concepts, and then moves into site considerations, lifestyle factors (do you want a family room or a formal dining room?), and decorating concepts (including color theory). You'll learn how to arrange for balance and beauty, and use window and floor coverings to make a room look larger, cozier, or more formal.

Checklists and planning sheets are available for each room of the house, along with sample floorplans. This book alone is worth a few bucks, and the ideas it explains integrate seamlessly with the design module.

Home Design: Gold Edition for Windows is like a subscription to a bride's magazine. You'll need it only for a short period of time (unless you design homes for yourself every year), but during that span it'll prove invaluable. It's well worth the $49.95 just for the fun of mapping out your next home yourself. Inveterate dreamers will also enjoy this disc, because they can go through the exercise of designing their ideal home over and over without spending a nickel on an architect.

Home Design *is a complete home design planning aid, with drag-and-drop drawing program, costing module, sample plans, and multimedia idea library in an easy-to-use format.*

In the Company of Whales

Rating:

Publisher Name:
The Discovery Channel

Software Requirements: **MPC**

Suggested Retail Price: **$49.95**

Pretend the Discovery Channel had scheduled a 45-minute documentary on whales over your local cable TV system. Now, picture being able to watch various segments of this show—with exclusive, never-seen-before footage—in any order you wanted. Then, after you were finished, imagine being able to ask questions of the four scientists who consulted on the production.

Now, get yourself a study guide with charts and illustrations showing the anatomy of whales and the answers to some age-old questions, such as what are those rows of "ridges" on the underside of baleen whales (they let the whale "expand" to process more water containing its food!). Add in a generous helping of whale sounds and action video clips. The sum total is an impressive presentation by any standard.

You can't expect to receive an interactive television program through your cable television system anytime soon, but a single CD-ROM from The Discovery Channel, *In the Company of Whales,* offers all this, and more. From the stirring music that accompanies the introductory sequence to Enterprise captain Patrick Stewart's literate narration, *In The Company of Whales* is a jewel that nature lovers and cetacean watchers of all ages will enjoy.

This disc takes advantage of the ages-old fascination humans have for whales, from Jonah's "great fish" through Moby Dick and Shamu. Their huge size, intriguing intelligence, and reverse "fish-out-of-water" classification have made whales the center of extensive research, even though they are, as a class, difficult to study and often misunderstood. *In the Company of Whales* helps clear up much of the misunderstanding.

Like many multimedia discs, this one "likes" standard 256-color 640 x 480 display screens best, but accepts other configurations with few glitches. After I clicked OK on a warning dialog box noting that the program ran best with plain-vanilla video, it proceeded to center its 640 x 480 screen on my 1024 x 1024, 16.7 million color display. I noticed a few odd color effects during dissolves from one image to another, and the small video pane displays action sequences in a box that isn't centered within the allocated frame area.

Though Microsoft Windows-based, this disc has nary a pull-down menu in sight: all features are accessed through a custom interface that's attractive and intuitive. For example, the main screen is a full-color picture of the fluke of a diving whale with six 3D buttons resting on its "surface." Four of the buttons take you to the key modules of the disc: At a Glance, Whales in Motion, The World of Whales, and Ask the Experts.

The At a Glance section is a narrated,

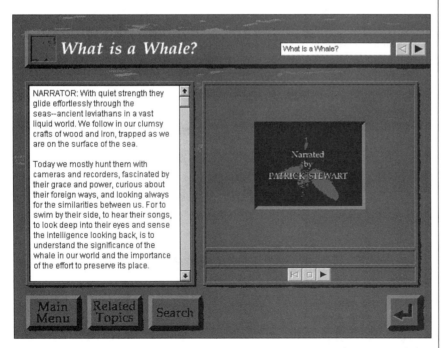

What is a Whale? is one of the minidocumentaries on this Discovery Channel disc.

guided tour of the program that tells you everything you need to know to navigate *In the Company of Whales*. A few minutes reviewing the information presented here will help you enjoy the disc that much more.

Whales in Motion is the gateway to all the video presentations on the disc. These include *What is a Whale?* a 14-minute minidocumentary narrated by Patrick Stewart. Billed as the "feature presentation" of the disc, it can be viewed in its entirety, or in stand-alone segments of a minute or two, with titles like Water Ballet, Significance of the Whale, or Whales in Their Habitat. After viewing the entire presentation, you can return to a favorite segment for review, over and over. This is better than an index counter on a VCR!

Other videos include *The Migrating Gray Whale*, *The Songs of the Humpbacks*, *What is Echolocation?*, *Meet the Whales*, *Body Language*, and *A Right Whale's Life*. Each is viewed using a video "engine" that shows the image in a small window (about 180 x 120 pixels) with play, stop, and restart buttons underneath. A title bar above the video window shows the title of the current presentation, with arrow buttons that can be used to switch to another video from the collection.

A superb presentation on whales, with minidocumentaries, short video clips, pictures, and text that can be accessed in an endless variety of interesting ways.

At the left side of the screen is a written transcript of the narration in a scrolling box,

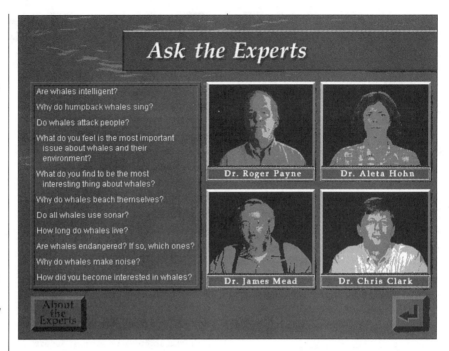

Ask the Experts is your chance to grill noted scientists on a selection of whale-oriented topics.

so that you can review the spoken sound track as it's being read (or skip ahead, if you like). Many of the words are highlighted in blue; click one and a pop-up glossary appears with a definition.

Four buttons at the bottom of the screen take you back to the main menu screen, the previous menu, or bring up dialog boxes that can be used to search for particular words among the available presentations or topics related to the current video. Using these buttons, you can jump around within the program to other videos, or view still photos and text on associated material.

The World of Whales has nine comprehensive sections, with titles like How Whales Evolved, Whale Senses, and Common Questions. Each section is accompanied by still photos and captions, articles, and/or brief videos that address the topic.

Ask the Experts is a lot of fun, because you get to interview four top cetologists, posing any of 11 tricky questions to the

scientist(s) of your choice. Queries include, "Are whales intelligent?" and "Why do whales make noise?" The researchers don't always agree on the answers, so it's interesting to try out the same question on all four to see if there's a consensus, or to discover where they disagree.

The small users guide packed in the CD jewel box finds room for some suggestions for follow-up, hands-on activities, a bibliography, and a list of other resources, such as recordings of whale songs.

Even though we still have many "educational" CD-ROMs that are nothing more than digitized film strips, discs like *In the Company of Whales* demonstrate just how well computerized multimedia can be applied to fascinating subjects. This disc takes good advantage of the computer's capabilities to show you things you never suspected about the Earth's largest-ever creatures.

Mayo Clinic Family Health Book

Rating:

Publisher Name:
IVI Publishing

Software Requirements:
MPC/Macintosh

Suggested Retail Price: $69.95

Four million patients can't be wrong! The throngs who flock to the Mayo Clinic's three locations from all over the world gain access to what may be the best 1,100 physicians and researchers ever assembled by one institution. Now you can take advantage of this wisdom in your own home through the Clinic's comprehensive family health guide on CD-ROM.

Like Mayo Clinic's companion *Total Heart* offering, this CD shouldn't be used to replace a timely visit to your family doctor. But within its hundreds of pages of hypertext-linked information, you'll find clues that alert you to medical emergencies that should be attended to by a professional, comforting descriptions of treatments and their followup, and a rich vein of basic medical and health lore.

Navigating the easy-to-use Microsoft Windows or Macintosh interface, you find more than 50 video clips and animations that shed light on complex health topics with well-narrated mini-presentations. The 400-plus full-color, still illustrations can be accessed almost instantly by clicking icons embedded in the text. Over an hour of

audio narration adds extended verbal captions to the photos, charts, and drawings.

The Family Health Book is, indeed, organized like a conventional bound book, in five parts. Parts I, II, and III (Lifecycles, the World Around Us, and Keeping Fit) address normal human growth and development, the changes to expect, strategies for avoiding illness, and dealing with habits or emergencies that can threaten your health. Parts IV and V (Human Disease and Disorders and Modern Medical Care) mainly concern disease, diagnosis, treatment, and preventive care. The handy appendixes include explanations of lab tests, an index of generic and brand-name drugs, conversion charts for weights, and a comprehensive medical dictionary.

If you are comfortable working with your Windows or Mac system's interface, you'll feel right at home with *The Family Health Book*. Main sections can be accessed by clicking one of the topic buttons at the right side of the screen, but you can also use pull-down menus, which duplicate the section listing. An array of icons at the bottom of the screen transport you to a table of contents or a Notes window you can use to type in comments or transcripts of information you read or hear (there is no built-in copy or save procedure). A handy Trail icon lets you jump immediately to any previous screen you've viewed in the current session by choosing from a listing of page

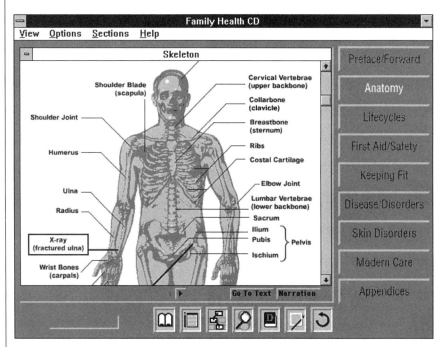

Click any portion of an illustration to see a close-up anatomical view with spoken narration.

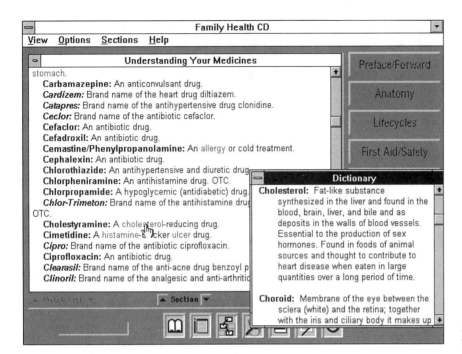

A pop-up dictionary provides definitions of unfamiliar terms.

This comprehensive family health guide will provide first aid guidance in emergencies, educate you to better care for the health of you and your loved ones, and prompt you to see a physician in those times when professional help is needed.

and topic references. There's also a Search button that triggers full-text searches of the entire book, based on keywords you type in and qualifying parameters such as AND and OR.

The medical dictionary can also be reviewed at the click of another icon, the Go Back icon, which is the quickest way to retrace your steps as you browse through this CD. As you can see, moving through *The Family Health Book* is both fast and intuitive.

To further encourage you to pursue information in the order and format that best pleases you, each page of text is liberally sprinkled with highlighting and icons that represent cross-references, accompanying charts, and relevant videos, animations, or sound clips.

Presented in clear language for the intelligent—or curious—layperson, *Mayo Clinic Family Health Book* belongs in the CD-ROM library of every health-conscious computer user. The only weakness is the

lack of a provision for copying or printing passages for reference.

National Parks of America—David Muench Photographer

Rating: ◉ ◉ ◉ 1/2

Publisher Name:
Multicom Publishing Inc.

Software Requirements:
MPC/Macintosh

Suggested Retail Price: $49.95

*N*ational Parks of America is a simple disc in concept. It takes a set of pictures of the national parks and links them with multimedia to provide you with an armchair tour of any park you want. The major parks, like the Grand Canyon, Yosemite, Yellowstone, Canyon de Chelley, and others also have audio narration of their slides, videos, and a season-by-season climate animation. Some text is available, providing driving directions, points of interest, and the mailing address of the park. There is also a function called Travel Plan that lets you select national parks based on criteria you input.

You can click the program's title slide to move to the main menu slide, which shows the United States broken up into seven regions. You first select the region you are interested in. This brings up another map that contains that region split into states. You can then click the state you are interested in, and bring up a map of it. This map shows the national parks in that state, along with major roads that lead to them; these maps are very nicely done. By clicking the name of the park (clicking the outline of the park will not work), you bring up a park-level screen. The less-visited parks have icons for text, printing, and slides. The major parks have included icons for a video of the park and climate information via an animation. There is also a set of icons to let you return to various screens directly; you can go back to the main menu from the park level if you wish.

Choose the slide show, and for the smaller parks you hear a MIDI music track and see the first of several slides of the park you have chosen. For the larger parks, instead of music, a narrator gives a brief commentary on the slide. The slides are about quarter-screen size, but if you want them to be full-sized, just click the picture itself or on the slide icon again. As you move from slide to slide, you'll notice that response time is a bit slow. Faster CD-ROM drives will not suffer from this.

The Travel Plan function allows you to select criteria like regions and/or states, as well as topics of interest for vacationers, such as backpacking, boating, handicap access, and pet access, as well as others. Once you click the search button, all the parks that fit

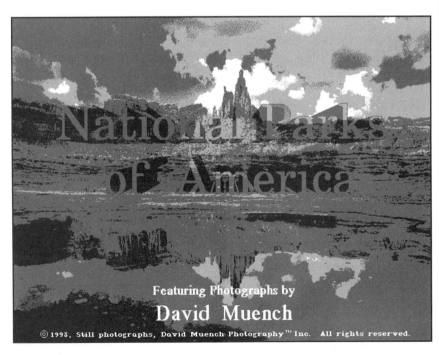

National Parks of America

Featuring Photographs by
David Muench

David Muench's photos of our national parks are wonderful to look at.

the criteria you have specified are listed. Then you can preview them individually.

If you aren't fond of the click-it method of selecting what parks you are interested in, you can bypass it all and search the data by using panel-based menus. This method has two additional advantages. When you've selected a park you are interested in, a list of slides with a brief note about each comes up. You can also select a list of all parks that have videos associated with them.

The photography is beautiful; America is graced with gorgeous national parks and David Muench is talented enough to take full advantage of their splendor. The program interface is simple, functional, and well thought out. The MIDI music included with the disc is all top caliber, apparently chosen so that even modest sound cards sound good when playing it. It is a very impressive work.

A well-done package with beautiful photos of the national parks; there are some potential installation problems with complex systems and less-than-perfect quality videos; it would be a valuable source for future vacation planning.

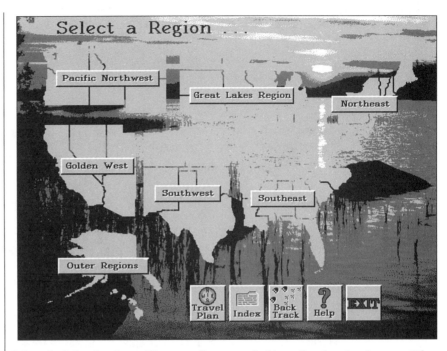

Arizona's rich natural wonders are well-represented by national parks shown on this disc.

There are a few weak points in this package. As part of the installation, the program warns you that it will modify your AUTOEXEC.BAT file to work with the QuickTime video package it has installed. Specifically, it wants to change your path statement to add the directory (c:\qtw\bin) that has these programs in it. If you have an AUTOEXEC.BAT file that uses multiple configurations, it isn't smart enough to know how to change it properly. There are other situations that could also cause this part of the installation to fail, such as a path length too long for DOS to handle. If you don't see a short video before the title screen and you don't hear narration as part of the first few screens and the videos don't work, it is this step that has failed. If you're a computer guru, you should be able to fix up things yourself. If not, you'll have to write for technical support; there didn't appear to be an appropriate phone number as part of the package.

The videos are not of very good quality and are very small. You do have a zoom button that shows you a bigger version of the video, but it's not very good quality. They give you a rough feel for the park however, and represent positive additions to the package. The pictures are not directly usable outside of the CD-ROM program. The format of the pictures is not a standard IBM .PIC format, even though they have that file extension. You can use a screen capture program to grab the images, but purchase of this disc does not entitle you the use of these pictures in other works. There is a phone number you can call should you wish to license these photos; there will almost certainly be a fee involved.

To sum up, this is a beautifully done product with a few warts. If the quality of the videos isn't important to you and you don't have a very complex PC setup that causes installation problems with the package, the photos are worth seeing.

Space & Astronomy

Rating:

Publisher Name:
Walnut Creek CDROM

Software Requirements: **None**

Suggested Retail Price: **$39.95**

A re you an astronomy buff? Want to get your hands on 1,080 image files, over 5,000 text files, and software related to astronomy and space? Then get a copy of *Space & Astronomy*, Walnut Creek CDROM's compilation of all sorts of information concerning the things that go on outside our planet Earth.

Space & Astronomy is compatible with DOS, Windows, and Mac, but also is compatible with and has viewing programs for the Amiga, Atari ST, DEC Stations 3100 and 5000, Next, OS/2, Silicon Graphics Iris, Sun SPARC, and X11-based computers. Some of these computers have higher resolutions than your average PC or Mac, and some of the images on the disc are more suited for their capabilities. One GIF-format image was 3300 x 2560 and couldn't be easily viewed on a PC, although images this big are uncommon. Most are 1280 x 1024 in 256 colors or less and are displayable on most recent PCs and Macs.

Space & Astronomy is a data archive of all sorts of information relevant to space and astronomy. Most all of the data falls into three categories: images, programs, and text.

Among the image directories present are artistic, astronaut, earth, eclipse, galactic, Kennedy Space Center, planetary, satellite, rocket, and space shuttle images. Most of these photos are presented as they were taken; there isn't much in false color, so this disc won't be as interesting to those who are looking for those artificially enhanced pictures that are so common in many popular science magazines. Most pictures

Space and Astronomy is filled with exciting NASA photographs.

Space and Astronmy has photos of extravehicular activities (EVAs) like this one.

taken of Earth and from Earth are in full color, and some pictures, particularly those of the annular eclipse of a few years ago, are fantastically colorful. Photos taken from space are usually grayscale, but are striking nonetheless, and there are a number of very colorful pictures of the planets on the disc.

A huge selection of good images, soft-ware/shareware, and textual information makes this disc a "must buy" for any-one interested in space and astronomy.

As far as programs go, there are general astronomy programs, satellite tracking programs, various simulation programs, a weather tracking program, a neural net demonstration program from NASA, and file viewers for all the platforms mentioned above. There are over 110 separate files on the disc related to programs. Most DOS/Windows programs are in zipped format, and they are by far the most common programs on the disc. Many of these programs are shareware, and a user is expected to send a fee to the author if they use the program after a trial period.

The amount of text on the disc is mind-boggling. There are complete archives of some sources of information. For instance, the Jet Propulsion Labs press releases from 6/62 to 3/92 are available. There are also large collections of data available on asteroids (the taxonomy of asteroids has several files devoted to it), astronauts (you can find out if your alma mater has ever graduated an astronaut with the information present in one file!), astronomical calendars, NASA Daily News from 11/92 to 8/93, fact

sheets from various sources, copies of the Jet Propulsion Labs biweekly UNIVERSE publication, the Space Digests from USENET, space station info, and more.

The strength of this disc quite frankly is in its data. It has no formal interface, although there are text and graphics viewers available on disc, you may use your own, if you have them. All that data is also a weakness. Some data just isn't very interesting to the average person; other data is hard to understand; some files are actually raw data with no obvious key available. There are only a few of these, however, and those in a position to use such data may feel that it is worth the price of the disc alone, even if most of us don't even know what it is.

Each category of material on this disc, graphics, software, and text, would probably be enough on its own for an astronomy buff to buy this disc. The combination of all three adds up to an incredible value that shouldn't be passed up by those interested in this field.

Sports Illustrated 1994 Multimedia Sports Almanac

Rating:

Publisher Name:
StarPress Multimedia

Software Requirements:
MPC/Macintosh

Suggested Retail Price: **$59.95**

*S*ports Illustrated has never done anything halfway. What other magazine gives you a telephone shaped like a gym shoe, or a blooper video just for subscribing? Has *Scientific American* ever offered anything like that? Or a great CD-ROM like this one—which brings multimedia sports thrills from the year 1993 on a disc that can run equally well on IBM PCs *and* Macintoshes?

This disc has so much on it, *SI* had to fill the front and back covers of the box it comes in with photos, text, and bullet points, and then augment that with another two pages of description in a foldout cover. We're talking about at least 30 minutes of reading material before you get this disc out of the box! So, throw away your back issues of *Sports Illustrated*. Everything you need is right here on the disc.

You could spend days just checking out all the graphical menus, which have more branches than a banyan tree. The main menu alone forces you to choose between Pro Football, Pro Basketball, Baseball,

College Football, College Basketball, Other Sports, *Sports Illustrated* Magazine, a Q&A trivia game, Year in Review, and a library of photos, videos, and articles. That's just the top menu level.

If you manage to navigate down a level, say to Pro Basketball, you find more choices: Teams, Players, the 1992-1993 Season, The Record Book, the Basketball Year in Review, and other topics. Other Sports covered include figure skating, hockey, track and field, boxing, swimming—virtually everything but bowling, which everyone knows is more of a mental exercise, like

chess, than an actual sport.

Each module brims over with videos, articles, matchless *Sports Illustrated* photography, and a rousing rock music soundtrack. I found this disc pretty thrilling, and I'm one of those people who likes to go to a movie during the Super Bowl because the theaters are virtually empty.

The interface may sound cluttered from my description, but it's actually first-rate, being neither Macintosh- nor Windows-like. You simply click a major sport icon to delve into coverage of that sport from preseason to championship game(s). Access the Search

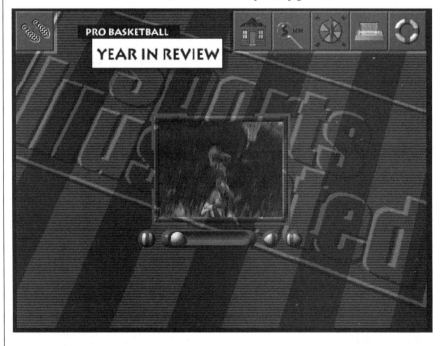

The tiny video screen can scarcely contain all the action in this Sports Illustrated Year in Review.

Sports Illustrated presents an incredible amount of sports action on one disc.

button at any time to find out information about a specific player or team. Click Print to get a hard copy of charts, articles, or lists. Choose the Library article to search for specific articles, photos, or videos.

The videos look like something you'd see on an HBO sports special (that's where they actually came from). You hear the crowds roar and the bones crunch as bodies collide. You watch as Michael Jordan leads the Chicago Bulls to their third straight NBA title. There's even a play-by-play look at Buffalo's record-setting comeback against the Houston Oilers—and their later demolition at the hands of the Dallas Cowboys in the Super Bowl.

The Record Book is logically organized by sport, event, and stat to make it easy to look up milestones and settle bets. This CD-ROM is an almanac in every sense of the word. Best of all, this disc is a bargain, considering what it contains. It has a sug-gested list price of $59.95 (at a time when some second-rate CD-ROM games command $79.95 price tags), and I've seen it in stores for less than $35.00.

I'm not much of a sports spectator unless one of my local teams is involved, so I found this disc to be a fascinating way to catch up on only the best and most interesting moments of the recent seasons. If you're truly a multisport fan (the term comes from fanatic), you'll like *Sport Illustrated's 1994 Multimedia Sports Almanac* even more.

Sports Illustrated *does a bang-up job of providing thrilling videos, articles, and information from the 1993 season in this first-rate multimedia disc that runs on both IBM PC and Macintosh systems.*

Yoga!—A Multimedia Guide to Yoga

Rating:

Publisher Name:
Quanta Press Inc./Krea Technology

Software Requirements: **MPC**

Suggested Retail Price: **$69.95**

In the Eastern tradition, a person wishing to practice yoga seeks out a guru who can carefully guide him/her in beginning the process. One section of *Yoga!—A Multimedia Guide to Yoga* suggests that Western tradition does not necessarily require this, as the abundance of books in our culture reduces the need for such instruction, although it is recommended that personal instruction be exploited when available.

Books are probably not an adequate method of learning a discipline as rich and involved as yoga is. Multimedia CD-ROM instruction, however, is considerably more powerful when used properly than learning from a book. For yoga is best learned by demonstration: photographs and text descriptions do not do it justice. This CD-ROM goes much further than one might expect from its rather humble packaging toward introducing a beginning student to yoga.

Before the main menu appears, a disclaimer comes up recommending that a potential student consult with a doctor before undertaking the yogic exercises the disc describes. It also strongly recommends that a practitioner stop when any pain is felt. Yoga overdone can be dangerous and damaging. You should not ignore these warnings!

Yoga instructors modify the injunction against pain slightly, urging their students to go to the point of pain, but in these situations, they are there to monitor the student. It's fairly obvious to an instructor when a student exceeds the safe limits of a posture, and he/she is there to intervene. When you're learning by yourself, avoid taking an exercise to a painful level!

The expert yogic consultant for this disc is Mr. M. M. Gore, a guru with 16 years of experience at one of India's finest yoga institutes. From the organization of the material on this disc, Mr. Gore is obviously an expert teacher. The computer interface is also well thought out; icons are appropriately labeled with text or a descriptive picture in clear fashion. Yoga postures are demonstrated by mannequin animation; much of the animation interface is completely analogous to VCR controls. The first time you see the mannequin in an

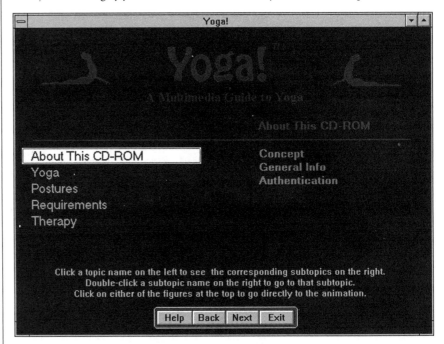

Yoga! **And more than you wanted to know about this discipline are included in this comprehensive disc.**

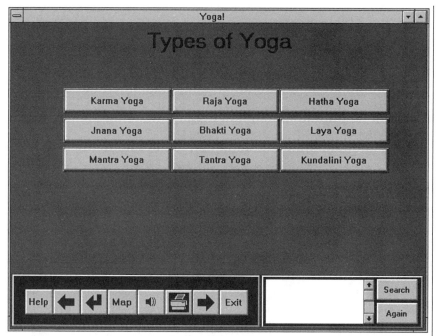

Choose your Yoga discipline here and begin your studies.

introductory screen, you may snicker; it doesn't look like it is going to be a very effective teacher. But appearances deceive; it does work.

The main menu provides five main categories that have sub-categories. These are About the CD-ROM, Yoga, Postures, Requirements, and Therapy. The first category, About the CD-ROM, describes why Krea Technology chose yoga as its first CD-ROM offering, as well as describing salient features of the program interface, who the program is meant for (just about everybody), and describes the credentials of Mr. M. M. Gore. This information is presented both as text and as narration. The use of narration is very effective; the effect is very much as though you had your own guru talking to you. In particular, you get correct pronunciations (and spellings, via the text) of the numerous Sanskrit words that are a part of yoga; their pronunciations are not obvious.

The next section, Yoga, defines what yoga is, presents the history and origin of yoga, describes the many types of yoga (only Hatha Yoga is taught by this disc), and the components of yoga (e.g., pranayama—breath control, and samadhi—self realization). Although the amount of information presented is not large, it is rich; you will get the impression you have been told more than what you really have been.

A first-rate product that covers yoga in a thoughtful and comprehensive way, with animation of 20 important postures of Hatha Yoga.

The Postures section is the meat of the disc. A brief description of what is meant by the term posture (asana) is given, and a few terms are given to describe the aspects of postures (static and/or dynamic). The postures themselves are presented on an odd, but very effective animation screen. On the left side of most of the screen is the animation window. On the right is the Introduction window, where text concerning the posture is presented.

The Steps section is synchronized with the animation. Since the speed of the animation can be user-controlled, this is a neat trick. The Benefits section describes those problems for which the posture is useful, while the Cautions section describes when it is to be avoided (pregnancy, for instance). The Breathing section is crucial; many of the positions do not realize their full potential unless the student breathes properly as he/she develops the position. Repetitions advises how often to repeat the posture.

The Requirements section details things like when to exercise, what to eat, what to wear, and how long to wait after eating before exercising. It also discusses whether a teacher is needed. This disc is probably sufficient to introduce an interested person to yoga, but those wanting to progress should try to find a teacher. Some of the other forms of yoga are considered dangerous for self-exploration by novices; if you wish to branch out from Hatha Yoga, please find an instructor.

The final section concerns Therapy, what conditions yoga might be useful in assisting. Yoga is in no way a substitute for proper medical care, but represents directed forms of exercise that might be useful in remedying some physical problems. This section also contains those conditions for which a posture is counter-productive. Again, heed these warnings.

The modest packaging of the disc might lead you into thinking this was an unprofessional product. It is not; the information presented is first rate. The disc teaches you what an instructor would teach you in your first few sessions in a class.

BodyWorks

Rating:

Publisher Name:
Software Marketing Corporation

Software Requirements:**MPC**

Suggested Retail Price: **$69.95**

Okay, so *BodyWorks* won't get you through medical school. It is, however, a remarkably detailed look inside the human body, with sound, colorful graphics, QuickTime movies, and amazing 3D views you can rotate to any angle. If you've always wondered how to pronounce "zygomatic arch," or just want to know where it is, this CD-ROM is the best place to start.

Compared to other medically-oriented discs, like *Mayo Clinic Family Health Book*, this one is intended primarily as an anatomy reference. It does have a health section with information on common illnesses, first aid, nutrition, and other topics, but the Mayo entry is much more detailed in those areas. This one comes out on top in the amount of specific anatomical information you can access, and the novel ways in which the data can be retrieved. It certainly beats those cut-rate reprints of the classic *Gray's Anatomy*, which has all the bones in the wrong places. (I'm still recovering from the human race's loss of two chromosomes since my high school days.)

For example, this disc lets you search for medical terms that you haven't the foggiest idea of how to spell by using phonetic entries or reasonably close guesses. There are magnified and animated cutaway drawings that show the underlying structure, and enough Latin to please any medical jargon freak. If you actually want or need to learn all these structures, there are built-in lesson plans and quizzes to help build and test your knowledge.

The main window of *BodyWorks* (which is fixed at a 640 x 480 resolution, even when your Windows configuration is set for 800 x 600 or some other configuration) devotes most of its area to the graphics display. Along the top of the pane are icons that can summon each of the main categories, divided into skeletal, nervous, muscular, cardiovascular, respiratory, digestive, sensory, circulatory, endocrine, and lymphatic systems. Genitourinary, Health and Fitness, and Living buttons are also

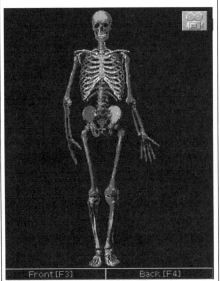

***BodyWorks* is a comprehensive tour of the human body, with videos, animations, and 3D models.**

there for quick access.

At the right are buttons listing various subtopics for the current category, with explanatory text in a scrolling list below. Click a button once to generate an arrow that points to the associated body part in the main panel. Double-click to jump to a more detailed image and accompanying text. Many words and phrases in the text are highlighted to indicate there are hypertext links to definitions of new terms or other related articles. Icons for pictures, movies, or 3D views pop up when those options are available.

Many body parts are illustrated with 3D views. These are not photographs or drawings, but, rather, actual 3D mathematical models that can be viewed using the integrated rendering program. You can look at a wire-frame model, a rough, angular version, or a smoothed-out, fully-shaded rendering. Then, use the controls to rotate the model for viewing on any axis, from any angle.

BodyWorks *will be of keen interest to science students and those with a deep fascination in the detailed anatomical information it provides.*

California Travel

California Travel is an excellent tool for previewing and roaming around, so to speak. If you are planning a trip, studying America, or just curious, you will find this quite helpful. The main screen consists of six sections: Urban Southern California; Central Coast; San Francisco Bay Area; Southern California Desert; The Sierras; and North From San Francisco.

At the top of the main screen, there are four choices: File, with the subheadings Open, Print Topic, and Print Setup. I was particularly attracted to the ability to print from the text within the program, thinking of many uses for students. Second is Edit, which allows for Copy to the Clipboard. You can also choose to Annotate from Edit, which is really great if you have been there and want to make personal notations, organize your trip, or just make a note for yourself for later reference. Third, there is a definable Bookmark that you can create; and fourth, there is Help. I must say that the Help feature was not much help, in that it merely listed the Viewer and version number.

The program is fairly self-explanatory and supports basic point-and-click navigation throughout. When a "movie" is available, there is a film icon at the bottom of the current screen. That is when Lee Foster steps in and gives his information-packed tour. I enjoyed hearing his personal recommendations of restaurants, hotels, museums, historical points of note, and much more. His love of California was evident and was presented in a congenial manner.

In one film clip he said that he was standing at Sweeny Ridge, south of San Francisco, the point where, in 1769, the bay was discovered. Did you know that for 200 years, ships had passed that bay covered by landscape and that it took a man on horseback to discover it? I didn't either!

To explain how each region is handled, let's take a look at the Urban Southern area. Simply clicking the rectangle brings up another screen, which has choices of major cities such as San Diego, San Diego North, Orange County, Los Angeles, and Beverly Hills. At the bottom of this screen, there is a film icon and a map icon. The map can be minimized and left open if you like to see it while you browse.

The program includes a Photo Gallery that allows searching through the contents index by title or subject. Pictures can be cascaded and there is an online Catalog of other Ebook CD-ROM productions, with a short statement of their philosophy. Anywhere in the program where there is text, there is also the familiar green highlighting, showing that there is an explanation underneath. Clicking the green words produces a pop-out with more information. Any text can be copied and pasted. Writing a California report would be a cinch with this program! Beats the heck out of scribbling on note cards if you ask me!

There are 800 miles of coast in California, and it is a diverse and interesting state to learn about. If your dad had time, and he was really smart, he might take you on the tour the way Lee Foster, the electronic travel guide, does it on this CD. He is visible and audible in the four "movies" that play as he tells an enchanting story. There are people in this world who have a gift for teaching in a way that makes the learning enjoyable. Foster has this gift and I found myself wishing I could have known him when I was a kid in school.

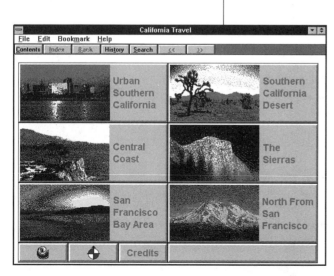

Visit the Golden State through this disc, with a collection of pictures and information.

Rating: ⊙ ⊙ ⊙ 1/2

Publisher Name: **Ebook, Inc.**

Software Requirements: **MPC/Macintosh**

Suggested Retail Price: **$29.95**

Chestnut's "The Complete Bookshop"

Rating:

Publisher Name: **Chestnut**

Software Requirements: **MPC**

Suggested Retail Price: **$29.95**

Wellllll...not quite a complete bookshop. They don't have the entire Library of Congress on there. That's what I would call complete but, then, I'm a voracious reader. Neither Chestnut nor anyone else could produce a general interest literature CD that I would call complete.

Hundreds of public domain works of literature on a single disc, ready for viewing.

Consider that praising with faint damnation. This isn't a bad collection as far as it goes, and it goes pretty far. I hope Chestnut will continue to develop it and fill up more disc space on future editions. It's up to 205MB so far, and there are more public domain and shareware electronic text works being released almost daily.

Just a few of the directories cover Alcohol and Brewing, including mixing guides, Cooking, Computing, the Compuchef program, Great Literature, Health and Nutrition, How-To, Poetry, etc., etc., etc. There's a set of archive and miscellaneous utilities at hand as well.

In the Great Literature directory (Greatlit) one finds the *Aeneid*, *Aesop's Fables* in a couple of versions, Shakespeare in text and learning programs, *The Rosicrucian Mysteries*(!), and a great lot more, much of which I sampled by simply opening the .TXT files with a word processor and reading away. Failing that, a little effort to copy to hard-disc and unarchive frees up those files for reading.

In the Misc directory you find things like *The Great Wisdom of the Ages*, organized as an electronic book with 81 categories; *There and Back Again*, a cute basic trainer for orienteering in the woods or the city; readings on Cyber-crime; a basic legal information file, and more.

If or when I ever find a literature CD that's full, I may never get away from my computer again. This one has kept me peering through my bifocals for many hours so far.

Most of the programmed files I tried worked fine right off the CD drive, although those that require writing files obviously wouldn't. You have to copy those to HD, unpack, and run. Those worked too, though. Your mileage may vary, of course. Shareware authors can't test on every platform in the world but most try to keep it simple enough to cover most configurations.

Using the disc is easy: log in to your CD-Drive, type "go," and follow the directions. It might have made more sense to have the READ ME instructions first on the menu instead of the View Program Listings, but you don't have to read first to check out the listings. It will help, though, to read those instructions when it comes time to unpack things, especially if, like me, you're not a DOS guru.

It would be impossible to catalog the entire disc. Suffice it to say that anyone will undoubtedly find something of interest, most probably many things. Looks like a winner to me, at least until that Library of Congress CD comes out.

Complete House

You probably don't live in too many homes that you own yourself in a lifetime, and a house represents the biggest investment most of us ever make—so why leave all the planning to strangers?

If you can use your Windows computer, you can design your own home using the tools provided on *Complete House*, by Deep River Publishing. It includes a multimedia guide to designing a home, as well as a separate computer aided design (CAD) program with the drawing tools you need to put your ideas down on paper (or screen).

Six sections greet you when you load the program. This Windows-based product has a helpful Getting Started section that introduces you to the disc and its contents.

The House Design module looks at a three-way relationship you may never have thought about before: the home, the homeowner, and the environment. You learn about design principles, how to determine your needs, various construction principles, and styles of houses.

In the Kitchen and Bath Design module, you learn about how to design a functional kitchen or bath, and view award-winning rooms so that you can select your own layouts and features. There's also a Magazine of Designs, which shows designs for many different houses by leading architects and building firms. There are text and audio comments that help you understand how these designs came about.

Rating: 💿 💿 💿

Publisher Name:
Deep River Publishing

Software Requirements: **MPC**

Suggested Retail Price: **$39.95**

A Resources list provides a bibliography, glossary, environmental resources, and other data you'll find useful.

Complete House *is a home design toolkit with instructional material and a complete drawing program.*

The final module is the CAD/FP program itself. This is a quite complete drawing program with all the tools you need to draw floor plans, drop in furniture and fixtures from a library of shapes, and add text. There are 20 sample floor plans you can use. Print out your plan when finished.

Complete House is a great CD-ROM for those who want to design their own home. It's not as slick and filled with multimedia options as Expert Software's *Home Design* (also reviewed in this chapter), but you might find the CAD/FP program a little easier to use. (Me, I prefer Visio Home.)

Complete House

The major sections of **Complete House** are listed below.
Double click on a centered icon to flip to the beginning of the section.
Click on a map icon in the lower right corner of a box to see a map of section topics.

Getting Started | House Design | Kitchen & Bath Design
Magazine of Designs | CAD/FP | Resources

The *Complete House* gives you the tools to design and build your own house—at least, on paper.

Consumer Information

The collected works of the U.S. Government Printing Office! Well, not quite, but those TV ads about Consumer Information from PO Box 100, Pueblo, CO imply there is a lot of consumer information to be had there. There is, and most—if not all—of it is on this CD-ROM. Although government publications are free, you can save a lot of money from not having to write in for the information they advertise on television.

Quanta Press appears to have collected all the pamphlets the U.S. Government Consumer Information Service supplies and put them in one place, your desktop computer. Looking through the titles gives you the impression this thing is HUGE! There are CDs with more raw data. There are CDs with more pictures. There are CDs with fancier output. But how many CDs put the whole government's Consumer Information collection at your fingertips? Well, so far, one: This one.

From Business through Family through Health through Military Benefits to Travel, there are informational files in dozens of subcategories, complete with graphs, pictures, charts, and sound files; roughly 117 megabytes in all. If you mailed away for all the information on this CD, that would add up to a lot of stamps; and there's no telling what the local postman might have to say about the load. You'd undoubtedly end up on someone's list of Subversive Consumers, out to overthrow the government through mail overload.

Installation of both DOS and Windows interfaces is quick and efficient. Both work well and quickly. The DOS version admits of two sub-versions, Pueblo and Puebhi. Puebhi is the high resolution version for the graphic files. Pueblo (the pun is, presumably, intended) only yields 320 x 240 graphics. Sound files are apparently raw audio tracks and do not play through the sound card unless you have an audio connector cable from the CD drive to the sound card.

The Windows interface shines. It is well laid out, easy to read, and easy to use. You can browse the title list or graphics captions list. Unlike some Windows interfaces, clicking the maximize button really does make the display fill the screen, at least in 640 x 480 Windows mode. If you have some idea of just what you are looking for, the Search function is fast and powerful. You can search Titles or Captions with some pretty vague criteria and it will land you in a category close to the goal. Very impressive. It probably can be fooled—any search engine can—but several attempts, choosing purposely vague phrases, always got into the right general area.

The DOS interface supports mouse operation, but it is a little dull, not at all as pretty as the Windows version, but it works as well. The Windows interface is a bit of a spoiler but the DOS version will get you the information just as surely.

Overall, *Consumer Information* is a slick package that fills a niche few probably thought even to look at. The U.S. Government produces a lot of information annually and, while some may be better than others, it is arguably the biggest single source of consumer information in the world. Some of the information is simplistic, to be sure, but whatever the need, this compilation provides, at the least, a starting point for research.

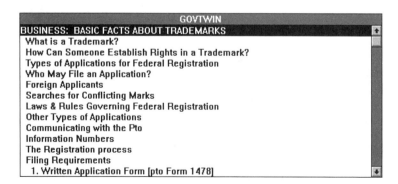

Consumer information you order from that famous Pueblo, Colorado PO Box is all here on this disc.

Dream Vacations—Hawaiian Style

Dream Vacations—Hawaiian Style is a CD-ROM that makes an excellent investment for anyone planning a vacation in this Pacific paradise. You can learn enough from this disc to save five or ten times its cost in misspent vacation dollars.

The heart of the CD is a narrated tour of each of the six tourist-accessible major islands in the 132-island chain, which can help you decide which are best-suited for your lifestyle. Do you want highly developed Oahu, with its slick, tourist-oriented beaches, shows, and museums? Or, would you prefer to wander around the quiet, uncrowded island of Molokai? You can tour each island in turn and make an informed decision before you sign up for one of those package tours.

You'll also find a cookbook filled with tempting island recipes, a listing of events planned for the current year, a directory that can be searched for topics like restaurants,

surfing, or tennis, and a travel planner that helps you decide what to wear and how to get there.

Dream Vacations—Hawaii Style is not aimed at armchair travelers, and provides an unsatisfying replacement for actually visiting the Aloha State. The narration is clipped and hurried, reminding you of nothing more than one of those real estate shows on television designed to lure the homebound to an open house. Lines like, "If romance, tropical rainforests, and secluded sandy beaches are what you're looking for, you can be sure you'll find it on the garden island of Kauai," could be used to sell condos with a little judicious editing. Even so, the Chamber of Commerce-style presentation tells you everything you need to know to plan for an in-person visit.

The information is available through an interface that mimics a map of the island chain. You can click each of the eight largest islands to switch to a section devoted to

Rating: 2 1/2

Publisher Name:
Advanced Software

Software Requirements: **MPC**

Suggested Retail Price: **$49.95**

important tourist information about each, spiced with more than 200 gorgeous, but post-card-bland photographs.

A slide show introduction to each island's main attractions is supplemented by scrollable listings of important sights, major beaches, tips for getting around, and descriptions of popular activities, from biking to parasailing. Lodging, restaurants, and shopping opportunities are also covered. This disc makes it easy to compare and contrast all these features among each of the major islands.

The main menu "map" also includes a hula dancer icon, your gateway to a general introduction to Hawaii, and a lobster, which leads to a cookbook of five dozen entree, desert, and cocktail recipes. If Lomi Lomi Salmon isn't enough to lure you to the islands, you can check out the Events Calendar or search for specific topics of interest with the Island Directory.

A map of the Hawaiian Islands serves as your main menu for this dream vacation.

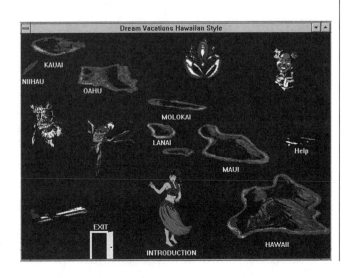

ESPN Baseball by Intelliplay

Rating: ⊙ ⊙ ⊙ 1/2

Publisher Name: **Intelliplay**

Software Requirements: **MPC**

Suggested Retail Price: **$59.95**

Do you want to become the next Hank Aaron? You better have some God-given talent. But if you just want to improve your hitting, whether you're a lowly hitter or if you can whack them out of the park like Hammerin' Hank, then Ron Fraser and Intelliplay have the CD-ROM for you: *ESPN Baseball by Intelliplay*

The brains behind the disc is Ron Fraser. Fraser was the baseball coach at the University of Miami (Florida) for over 30 years and was head baseball coach for the United States in the 1992 Olympic Games. At the time of his retirement, Fraser was the winningest active college coach, with 1,271 wins. His accomplishments include NCAA coach of the year three times, two national championships, and 139 players sent from his teams into baseball's professional ranks. That's pretty impressive by any score.

ESPN Baseball is as easy to use as your VCR. Just click a topic you would like more information about and a video will be shown explaining in-depth anything you could possibly want to know about the topic. And, like a VCR, it has rewind and pause buttons so that you can go back and repeat anything you may have missed. With the amount of information Coach Fraser

put into this CD-ROM, that is a very useful tool! All you need is a camcorder to record your own batting stance for comparison with the clips on this disc.

There are several sections that can be called up with a simple click on an icon. For example, there's Ask The Coach. When you click this button in the content selection panel, you are presented a list of "interview" type questions that you can pose to Ron Fraser for detailed answers.

Or, try out What's The Call. When you click this selection you are presented with a list of "live" game situations that test your knowledge and interpretation of the rules and conduct of the game. To play a video of the situation, just double-click that selection in the list. If there is a fun part of this software this is it, although I must warn you that playing it can be addictive.

This software is based solely on video running through Windows. And it takes some pretty serious hardware to get it moving along at a useful pace, well beyond the minimum MPC-1 equipment that it will theoretically run on. Recommended is a 486DX33(or faster) processor, 8MB of RAM, accelerated local bus SVGA video with 1MB of RAM set to

display at least 65,000 colors, and a CD-ROM drive with a minimum 300K per second transfer rate. As an added bonus, *ESPN Baseball* places 5MB of files onto that precious hard disk space that no-one seems to have enough of anymore. That's major league hardware, but then, this disc has great graphics that are quite a bit above the "lowest common denominator" standards of MPC-1.

If you buy this software for entertainment purposes, you might be sadly disappointed, as it is geared more towards the serious ball player who really wants to improve hitting skills. Besides the Ask the Coach and the What's the Call features, this software can be a very dry, technical reference on hitting a moving round object with a piece of stick. On the other hand, if you are serious about improving your hitting, you may never find a more in-depth reference on the subject, and having that information in a video style format just adds to the usefulness of that information and this software.

Ron Frasier is your hitting coach in this ESPN-sponsored educational disc.

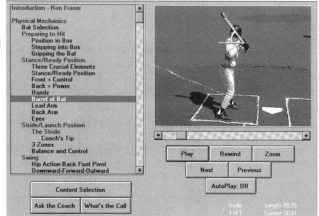

Everywhere USA Travel Guide

If you have Microsoft Windows and two weeks off, all you need to schedule an enjoyable vacation in the United States are these discs and a little cash. No matter where you live or what you like to do, you'll find attractions right in your backyard and within your budget on *Everywhere USA Travel Guide.*

This is a colorful two-disc set (at a bargain price!) with thousands of color pictures, full motion video, and audio covering every state in the union, including rural areas and metropolitan hotspots. One disc is devoted to the Eastern United States, while the other deals with the Western states.

Since I was planning a visit to Indianapolis to drop in on Que Corporation after I finished this book, I decided to see just what there is to do in the state capital of the Hoosier State. I turned *Everywhere USA*'s search engine loose on Indianapolis. Oops. Okay, so this city isn't exactly a major tourist destination. Most of the things I came up with involved the Indianapolis 500 and the Colts football team. So, let's broaden the search a little to include all towns within 50 miles of Indianapolis.

That worked out

Everywhere USA is your travel guide to Indiana or interesting places around the country.

much better. It turned out that the James Dean Gallery is located nearby, commemorating not the sausage king, but the dead actor. The program also turned up the Benjamin Harrison home, an interesting Children's Museum, and a first rate living historical exhibit—Connor Prairie—that is a town inhabited by actors impersonating real pioneers.

Most sites listed come with a photograph or two, information on costs, time it will take to visit the attraction, contact information, and a locator map. You can print out the data to take with you, too.

You find information on art, music, theater, cultural centers, museums, aquariums, zoos, nature activities, science centers, gardens, national parks, historic sites, reenactments, sports, theme parks, festivals, state fairs, and more. Well, not in Indiana, of course (which must be the largest major state without a large theme park; we have four of the largest in the world in Ohio, according to this disc).

You can view activities through a list,

Visitors take a buggy ride down a country road at Amish Acres. Courtesy of Amish Acres.

Rating: ◉ ◉ ◉

Publisher Name:
Deep River Publishing

Software Requirements: **MPC**

Suggested Retail Price: **$49.95**

slide show, or thumbnail mode that provides little glimpses of the photos available for viewing. The Custom search panel lets you type in criteria such as Children's Activities, Free Admission, Dining, Handicapped Access, Camping, Beaches, Tours, Hiking, etc.

Better than a bound travel guide, **Everywhere USA** *helps you find places to go and things to do at a bargain price.*

This is a good disc that has limited applications only if you think to use it only once a year when you travel. Clever folks will want to play with *Everywhere USA Travel Guide* all year long as an armchair tourguide and an enjoyable way to browse through the attractions in our country. Because you get two full discs for $49.95 (or less), this is a wonderful bargain, too.

The Exotic Garden

Rating:

Publisher Name:
VT Productions, Inc.

Software Requirements: **MPC**

Suggested Retail Price: **$49.95**

Indoor gardeners, have we got a disc for you! Primarily aimed for indoor cultivation of tropical, subtropical, and popular ornamental plants, *The Exotic Garden* can help you choose and care for your plants. Many different species are presented in full-color photographs, accompanied by descriptions of how to care for and propagate the plants.

The Exotic Garden *is the indoor gardener's online guide to ornamental and tropical plants, with 500 gorgeous photographs.*

This Microsoft Windows-based program is as easy to navigate as an urban windowbox. You can view text on selected topics in a small window, moving from topic to topic with arrow buttons. There's a History list that you can use to jump back and forth among previous topics. View pictures "embedded" in the text by clicking a camera icon.

The text describes each plant's native habitat, helping you to create a similar growing environment in your home. It also offers advice on choosing plants, placement to help them thrive, and care. The picture library allows you to make a quick visual decision from high quality still frames. If you don't know plants, but you know what you like, this route can help you select attractive plants quickly.

You may also search by keywords to look for particular types of plants. For example, if you want to find all the plants that flower in the spring, you can search for that keyword. Locate plants suitable for beginner gardeners by searching for "beginner." If you like to keep your home or apartment a bit on the cool side, scan for "cool" to locate compatible flora. Compound searches can locate listings using multiple keywords.

There's a short movie, Why Plants Flower, which uses high speed time-lapse photography to deliver a brief lesson about the lifecycle of the plant and the importance of the bloom. You learn all about the importance of bees in pollinating plants, although the film doesn't explain how to introduce bees into an indoor garden.

The A-Z guide is alphabetically indexed by family, genus, or common name, and each plant listing has all you need to know to care for the plant. It includes troubleshooting tips and methods of propagation.

There's not a lot of video, sound, or graphics in this disc, apart from the short movie and 500 color photos. However, indoor gardeners will welcome this addition to their information library. Computerized searches ease the quest for data, and once you've spent some time with this disc, it can be much faster than leafing through a book (pun unintentional, but I left it in, anyway).

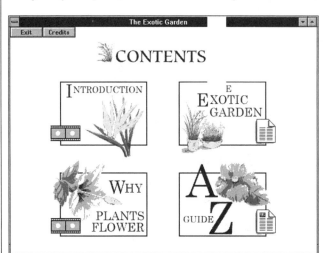

Exotic Garden **presents lots of information you can use to select and care for your indoor plants.**

The 1993 Guiness Multimedia Disc of Records

World records aren't just facts, figures, and statistics, as you'll discover from the *1993 Guiness Multimedia Disc of Records*. It contains remarkable statistics along with video clips, photos, illustrations, voice-overs, and sound effects that take you behind the scenes to view the fascinating world of record setters.

> ## *The fascinating world of record-setters is arrayed for your browsing pleasure in this multimedia disc with sound, videos, and photos in addition to endless scrolling lists of facts and figures.*

I discovered just how engaging this world can be when I conducted a series of interviews at the home of Parke G. Thompson, an Akron, Ohio attorney, who is listed in the current Guiness Book of World Records as the most-travelled human being in history. Parke's travels have taken

him to virtually every place on the face of the Earth—including inaccessible sites like the South Pole, which don't exactly welcome tourists. I gained some valuable insights into what it takes to do something that no human being has done before. These are very special people.

You'll find a host of special people on this disc, which contains 3,600 new and updated world records, hypertext links that let you search related entries quickly, and a new Random Record Explorer that pops up interesting facts at random, and makes browsing easy and pleasurable. There are videos showing the Beatles' first trip to the United States, Jesse Owens at the 1936 Olympics, and glimpses of the massive Normandy invasion. You see the Apollo 11 moon landing, views of Saturn from the Voyager spacecraft, and rare glimpses of the fastest mammal on Earth in action.

You'll find records on fruit and vegetable oddities, presidential elections, human speed records, weather "worstest"

Rating:

Publisher Name:
Grolier Electronic Publishing

Software Requirements:
Macintosh

Suggested Retail Price: **$59.95**

and "mostest" standards, as well as obscure sports records.

The chief defect is a somewhat clunky interface that depends heavily on scrolling lists. The program's main window is a smallish 512 x 342 pixels—obviously meant to fit onto the tiny 9-inch screen of the least-common-denominator Classic-style Macintoshes. Still, the feats and exploits that get people listed in this collection are compelling enough that if you like that sort of thing, you'll want this disc anyway.

Elvis Presley joins the Army in a video clip on the record-setting King in the *Guiness Multimedia Disc of Records*.

JFK Assassination: A Visual Investigation

Rating:

Publisher Name: **Medio**

Software Requirements: **MPC**

Suggested Retail Price: **$59.95**

Where were you when John F. Kennedy was assassinated? I was sitting in a high school biology class when our principal made the first announcement. *JFK Assassination: A Visual Investigation* is the latest product keying in on public fascination with the killing to hit the market in the 30 years since November 22, 1963.

Virtually every adult person alive then remembers exactly where they were and what they were doing at that horrible moment. This disc helps bring back those memories for those who want to explore a moment in history. Others will like this disc for the new information it contains.

New information? Yes, some of the data on this disc will be new, at least to you. For example, there were 12 different home movies made of the assassination, but only the most vivid one—the Zapruder film—has been widely seen by the public. Four other home movies of the event are provided on this disc.

Conspiracy buffs, of course, will delight in the examinations of bullet trajectories.

(There's one graphic that clearly shows at least one bullet coming from a building other than the Texas Book Depository. Now that it has been conclusively proven that Elvis is, in fact, alive, the JFK assassination is the only real conspiracy the fanatics can focus on.)

This Windows-based disc is easy to navigate. The main menu screen offers an audiovisual introduction, an overview of the event, a tour around Dealey Plaza, films and photos, a careful analysis, and tons of text about the assassination. The text includes the Warren Commission Report, an assassination factbook, and *Crossfire: The Plot That Killed Kennedy*, by Jim Marrs.

You can access any of this information by clicking the buttons with your mouse. Most will zero right in on the home movies (I know I did). It soon became obvious why these movies haven't been widely seen. They were taken from vantage points not as good as that Abraham Zapruder had, and don't show the actual shooting as clearly (or at all). Moreover, taken as a whole, these movies can be misleading (at least, I think they're misleading). One thing that struck me was that in many of them, immediately after the shooting the crowds all seem to turn toward and then run toward the grassy knoll—the one that government investigations have told us harbored no assassins. Nobody seems to be looking up at the Texas Book Depository. Could it be that Oliver Stone was...right?

Many of the videos can be viewed in normal or slow motion, and sometimes in full screen and full screen slow motion so that you can examine the footage in detail. This is a well-done disc, with lots of excellent information and analysis.

If you thought the JFK assassi-nation had been looked at from every possible angle, you haven't seen this multimedia disc from Medio.

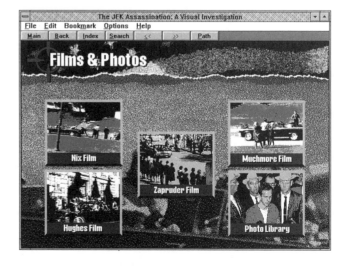

The Lifestyles of The Rich & Famous Cookbook by Robin Leach

*L*ifestyles of the Rich and Famous Cookbook takes you into the homes and kitchens of celebrities who adore good food and are gifted entertainers. This program is done in the well-known glamorous and exciting Robin Leach style. If you like that sort of thing (and millions of people who watch Robin's show *do*), you'll appreciate this disc.

In grand style, Leach and friends show us what it takes to make an extravagant, fun, and successful party. Interestingly enough, in one of the QuickTime for Windows movies, we are shown many ways that the invitations are created, they tell us the party starts when our guests get it in their hands.

There are recipes, audio, video, and photographs to guide and entertain. One line I loved was "success is excess." Price seems to be the very last priority, something we can all relate to, right? Everyone who is interested in fine party food and a little dazzle in their entertainment can learn from this program.

It is recommended that we begin with the online manual, which is selected from the Help menu. The program allows for copy, paste, and annotate, making it nicely customizable for each user's needs and personal input. The Help makes good sense, is easy to use, and is all-familiar, something we are always pleased to see. From the Cookbook Menu Bar, you can access the main menu, Index, Table of Contents, goto, go back, history, recipes, movies, biographies, and cooking tips. At some points there will be Additional Text (Captions), and clicking either the pointer or hand cursor points produces a pop-out with more information.

Let's look at one of the recipes under the heading (which also names the host) "Congratulations Elizabeth and Larry." I will click Chocolate Tulips and hope that I can finish my work here before dashing out to the gas station for a candy bar before I finish. Leach enters via audio as the text is displayed. "Who are Elizabeth and Larry," I am wondering as he tells us it is the wedding of Elizabeth Taylor and Larry Fortensky at Michael Jackson's estate, in the gazebo. Only 165 people were invited to this wedding of the decade, complete with gold trimmed dishes and champagne. The recipe for Chocolate Tulips includes normal ingredients such as eggs, milk, flour, heavy cream, and butter. Instructions for putting it all together are easy to understand and make me hungry!

Most of the recipes also provide photos including table and decorations, packaging being an important part of enjoyment.

In looking for and through the recipes, there is an option to use the radio button, the menu text, or the index. At the bottom of the screen displaying recipes, there is a button to click that says "event," so that you can see more about the actual party that the particular recipe was from. There is always more and more information; you can go as far into it as you wish. I like that, throughout the program, I was able to get around in more than one way, find my way back, and learn, hear, or see more if I had an interest.

Rating: 1/2

Publisher Name:
Compton's NewMedia

Software Requirements:**MPC**

Suggested Retail Price:**$39.95**

The movies were really entertaining, and if you ever wanted to know the story of Ivana Trump, there is an interview for your perusal. Of course, there is a section of her favorite Czech recipes. She glazes over the deserts saying that they are all terrible for the waistline. Did she have to remind me? It might be fun to see which rich and famous person you relate to and delve into their story and visit their party, see their photos, and try one out for yourself.

Robin Leach fans will love this look inside the lives of the rich and famous, learning how they eat (or is that dine?) and party.

Mayo Clinic: The Total Heart

Rating:

Publisher Name: **IVI Publishing**

Software Requirements:
MPC/Macintosh

Suggested Retail Price: **$59.95**

If you think a little knowledge is a dangerous thing, try ignorance sometime. Learning about the care and treatment of the human heart through this outstanding Mayo Clinic offering is the first step toward preventing and curing cardio-vascular disease—which accounted for roughly one million deaths in the United States last year.

Doctors and researchers at the world-famous Minnesota institution have teamed with multimedia experts to spice up the hundreds of pages of text in this learning tool, with four-dozen video clips and animations, 150 full-color illustrations, and an hour of audio narration.

Eleven different sections are accessible from the main screen, using a standard Microsoft Windows or Macintosh interface. These include Anatomy, Normal Heart, Heart Disease, Reducing Risk, Heart Tests, Treatments, Issues in Cardiology, Drug Directory, and Emergency procedures. You can find the information about a specific topic by clicking the button associated with one of these sections, browsing through the table of contents, or using the Search facility (which can scan for multiple keywords using AND/OR parameters).

This multimedia approach simplifies a complex subject. Instead of telling you what sounds a doctor listens for through a stethoscope, this CD-ROM shows you. You can watch the flow of blood through the heart, see how heart valves operate, and study coronary-artery bypass surgery up close.

Heart health is examined from both preventive and treatment stand-points. You learn what factors increase the chance of a heart attack or stroke, and how to tip the odds in your favor. Those already suffering from heart disease will appreciate the Drug Directory, which serves as a sort of mini-Physicians' Desk Reference, listing common drugs by type, generic and brand names, along with effects, possible side-effects, and conflicts.

With its impeccable Mayo Clinic credentials, this CD is obviously the last word on cardiac health for the layperson in terms of accuracy, completeness, and presentation. Only a few flaws mar this otherwise excellent disc. The narration accompanying many of the still illustrations is clearly superfluous, consisting of an announcer reading a single line of caption text (that appears on the screen simulta-neously). The user interface of the Windows version departs somewhat from the industry standard (you can't resize or move scrollable windows, for example). Most serious is the lack of any capability for copying graphics and text for permanent reference.

A complete guide to cardiovascular health through the Mayo Clinic experts' engaging hypertext explanations, vivid video, animation, and sound clips.

Anatomy: The Heart Muscle

◀ ▶ Go to Text Narration

You'll learn about anatomy and heart disease in Mayo Clinic's *The Total Heart*.

Oceans Below

Have you ever had the urge to place yourself under tons of dark, murky water, with your life dependent on the proper functioning of a complicated mechanical device and the contents of a heavy steel tank strapped to your back? If so, you probably don't think of SCUBA (self-contained underwater breathing apparatus) diving in the same terms I do. Of course, the opportunities for underwater sightseeing are much more limited if you happen to live near Lake Erie, as I do, instead of, say, near the crystal-clear waters off some Florida coral reef.

However, no matter where you live, you can experience the exotic undersea world that teems with dazzlingly colored fish and amazing underwater formations through *Oceans Below,* a multimedia diving CD-ROM from The Software Toolworks. This is another one of those simulator programs that the programmer, Amazing Media, does so well (see reviews of *Capitol Hill* and *Space Shuttle* in Chapter 6). Only this time, you don't get to take along a Personal Digital Assistant (PDA)—it would get wet. Instead, you go through a rigorous training program in preparation for your visits beneath the sea. You learn about underwater safety, and how all the equipment works (or should work) to keep you breathing.

Then, you can explore 17 different dive sites through 200 video segments and 125 photographs that detail all manner of underwater animal and plant life. There are plane and ship wrecks to scavenge through. You can even learn about history by finding the 68 sunken treasures hidden among the diving locations.

This Windows-based program is extraordinarily easy to use once you get past the installation program (which insists on installing QuickTime for Windows, even if you already have it, and then tells you to reboot your computer even if you don't need to). Beautiful graphics serve as picture-frames around icons you can use to access the various functions. The Help icon (a life preserver!) offers advice on how to use the program. You can learn about diving equipment and the dive environment by clicking the Dive Info icon (an image of the flag used to mark the position of a diver). There's a world map that lets you explore primo worldwide dive locations. More detailed Regional Maps let you zero in on an individual place. Specific spots are indicated by large bubbles on the map. There's also a Treasure Chest icon that opens to list all the treasures you've collected on your dives.

Before you dive, you'll want to view an informational video about the dive area,

check over a sea life chart to see what kind of creatures you can expect in this area, and then begin your dive. You join a dive master for safety, and receive one final briefing before you go under. Then, you descend and explore the underwater world by clicking in various directions with your mouse. Vivid graphics show you the sights up close. You can click an animal, plant, or other object of information to receive more information about it. Look out for buried treasure, too.

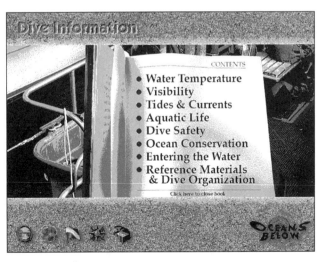

Lots of information about your dive can be reviewed before you go *Oceans Below.*

Parenting—Prenatal to Preschool

Rating:  1/2

Publisher Name:
Creative Multimedia Corporation

Software Requirements:
MPC/Macintosh

Suggested Retail Price: **$69.95**

*P*arenting—Prenatal to Preschool is a compilation of books, images, and sound clips that should be of use to both parents and parents-to-be. If you want to pore through a lot of information in a hurry, or want a fairly comprehensive reference guide on a single CD-ROM, this disc is a good place to start, despite an unimpressive interface.

As a tool for those interested in the development of prenatal to preschool children, this CD-ROM should be a nice addition to the library.

The disc is comprised of the complete text of *Your Child: A Medical Guide, The New Parent's Q&A Book, The Ultimate Baby Name Book, The Complete Pregnancy & Baby Book, The Miracle of Birth,* and *The Couple's Guide to Fertility.* This CD-ROM title should be able to answer many common and perhaps uncommon questions raised by young or expecting parents. Even old hands at child-rearing should find something new and interesting in these books.

Included on the CD are some 400 images, including drawings and sketches. The images are straightforward and intended to be educational, covering a broad range of topics including fetal development and parental interaction. Also packaged with the disc are sound bites such as those made by young children denoting speech patterns typically associated with various age groups.

The CD-ROM's format consists of drop-down-style menus that allow you to click the various selections. The information has been collected in a convenient fashion and learning your way around should not be terribly difficult. A convenient search feature allows you to isolate a word or combination of words to quickly locate the available CD-ROM information on the subject word or

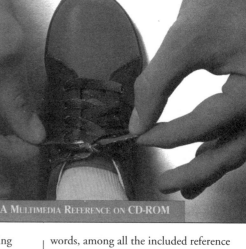

words, among all the included reference works.

Designed to be a tool for the new parent, in which a lot of information on one particular subject is collected and readily available, this CD-ROM certainly meets that goal. As a part of this title, you will find medical advice and emergency first aid, along with a host of information providing organizations and ways to reach them.

However, you'll probably want another CD-ROM as a supplement to this one, such as the *Mayo Clinic's Family Health Book* or *The Family Doctor,* but then, a complete library has never been this easy to compile or use.

Pixel Garden

For the serious backyard gardener, one who is enchanted by the beauty of flowers, this disc is a joy. *Pixel Garden* provides an online database of 522 outdoor ornamental plants common in the United States, developed by a trio of professional horticulturalists.

Located by botanical or common name on the index, each plant has a vivid photo (there are 560 pictures in all) plus information on its uses and needs. Plant Search allows the user to let the computer find the plant that will work for you for each individual location in your garden. Search criteria include hardiness (USDA Hardiness Zone ratings—the average annual minimum temperature in which the plants can live), light condition, environment, height, color, plant type, and flowering period.

The user simply specifies one or more characteristics and the computer shows the possibilities. It's possible to enter multiple parameters (i.e., both red and yellow for flower color), and the program is smart enough to locate species that come in several varieties that meet your specifications.

If you have a special use for your plant (e.g., to control erosion, provide food for wildlife, etc.) or want a species that will thrive under difficult conditions (draught, low fertility soil, heavy air pollution), the search function can help out there, too.

A great database of outdoor plant information you can use to fill those problem spots in your yard with blooming flora.

With Random Walk, you set the pace through the beauty of nature. For those who dream of English gardens, this walk is a wonder, but you'll find yourself stopping often to learn more about these lovely plants.

Rating:

Publisher Name:
Quanta Press, Inc.

Software Requirements: **MPC**

Suggested Retail Price: **$59.95**

The interface is easy to use. You can highlight names on the index, or use a word wheel to quickly find a particular plant from the alphabetical list. With the latter tool, as you type the first few characters of a plant's name, the highlight bar is repositioned closer to the plant you're searching for. Up/down arrows and PgUp/PgDn keys can also be used to quickly move around in the list.

This disc quickly became the favorite of our family gardener, a notorious non-computer user who can crank out a letter in Microsoft Word and changes CD-ROMs on behalf of our four-year-old, but otherwise has little interest in things cybernetic. She saw a demonstration of this disc, said, "Whoa, I can use this!" and promptly settled in for a long session of hunting for plants that could survive in that woodsy patch on the East side of our property line. If *Pixel Garden* can turn her into a computer user, it will work for anyone.

While the program shows 522 plants, it seems to miss a number of popular favorites that I needed information on. And if it gave data on soil, planting, and upkeep, this disc would be close to perfect.

Outdoor plants is the focus of *Pixel Garden*, which lists growing information for many different species.

Sporting News Multimedia Pro Football Guide

Rating:

Publisher Name:
Compton's New Media

Software Requirements: **MPC**

Suggested Retail Price: **$39.95**

Baseball/Football cards are on their way out! The age of multimedia is here, and Compton's New Media/ *The Sporting News* has found an awesome replacement for those old ragged cards. The guide is an exciting reference that puts a world of football facts, figures, and hundreds of hard-hitting video clips at your fingertips.

From the guide's main menu, you can select one of seven informative journeys. A statistics path displays statistics for all major football categories.

The Hall of Fame path lets you find information about any member of the hall of fame. It consists of two screens, the member list screen and the member information screen. And if available, a video clip of the selected member is available from the member information. You can relive the excitement of Jim Brown ripping through one tackler after the next on his way towards the end zone.

The Weeks in Review path lets you explore all the games of the 1992 season week by week. Go to week one and you can relive the Colts punishing Bernie Kosar of the Browns for 11 excruciating sacks. Watch the video and see Bernie go down! (If you can stand it!)

If you would like to test your knowledge of football facts, the Trivia path should be the one taken. Play by yourself or against a friend and watch as your correct answers lead you closer and closer to that goal line. Answer wrong a few times too often and you might just end up with that dreaded safety.

The Players and Coaches path lets you find information about a player or coach. Click the all players button and a list of all NFL players from 1970 through the 1992 season is shown. Click a particular player and up pops a player information screen filled with pictures, notes, and video clips (if available) of a particular player.

The Highlights path lets you explore video highlights from games in the 1992 season. Go to week 11 and watch as Steve Young picks apart the Saints to come back in the fourth quarter and lead his team to victory.

The Teams path lets you explore information about a particular team in the NFL. It consists of two screens, the Team List screen and the Team Information screen. You can access current and historical records, including player rosters, statistics, and game results.

The guide recommends that the user have at least an MPC-level 1 machine. That is fine if you would like to see the pictures and read the statistics, but if you really want to relive the 1992 season and watch the players in action, a move to an MPC-level 2 machine is highly recommended.

The interface for the Guide is well thought out and very easy to use. Just click a button to go down your selected path, or double-click a name to see more information and pictures on that particular player.

Sporting News Football. Better than trading cards, this disc provides stats, highlights, and videos from the NFL.

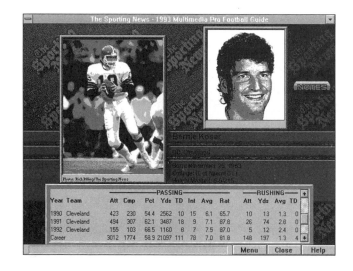

Total Baseball

If your home (or mind) is full of baseball memorabilia, this package will be a welcome addition to the clutter. Supplemented by more than 600 photographs and 20 sound clips, *Total Baseball* contains enough articles and statistics (some 2,300 pages worth) to satisfy even the most diehard baseball fanatic, and may help bring order to your interest in this all-American pastime.

The drop-down menus and search methods, although a bit cumbersome, open the door to articles that are exceptionally well written, detailed, and fluid. While perusing *Total Baseball,* the reader finds topical information sorted under a host of categories such as The History, The 100 Greatest Players, Streaks and Feats, Tragedies and Shortened Careers, Scandals and Controversies, and many more.

Those looking to take advantage of a CD-ROM for its sound features will enjoy the sound clips, 20 in all, which include bites from Goose Goslin's 1935 World Series winning hit, Don Larson's 1956 World Series perfect no-hit game, and Hank Aaron's 1974 715th home run.

Of particular interest was Red Barber's 1939 re-creation of a spring training game between the Cincinnati Reds and the New York Yankees. Red, several hundred miles away from the game, re-created it solely from a ticker tape feed. This sound clip from *Total Baseball,* in which the ticker tape can be heard in the background, gives the listener an excellent opportunity to experience the skills that made Red Barber an announcer extraordinaire for so many years.

Apparently taken in large part (if not total) from the book by the same name, you could easily find yourself absorbed for several hours on this CD-ROM reading the stories alone. However, in addition to the text, there are around 600 wonderfully clear photos that make you appreciate both a high resolution monitor and the ease of CD-ROM access. Take a look, for instance, at Matty Alou when you have the opportunity.

As rich as the early years of baseball, and as current as, oh, just a couple seasons ago. Total Baseball *is an exciting source of text, video, and sound clips detailing major events and personalities that have made this such an enduring sport.*

Rating:

Publisher Name:
Creative Multimedia Corporation

Software Requirements:
MPC/Macintosh

Suggested Retail Price: **$69.99**

The downsides to the *Total Baseball* CD-ROM, if there are any, lie in the occasional misspelled or grammatically incorrect word, and the fact that each year's edition actually covers events only through the previous season.

Photo Credit: National Baseball Library

Cy Young

Travel Planner—Gold Edition for Windows

Rating: **1/2**

Publisher Name:
Expert Software, Inc.

Software Requirements: MPC

Suggested Retail Price: $49.95

Now boarding at Gate 10, a nifty travel planner for Windows by Expert Software. Replete with road maps, facts about cities and towns, slide shows, and full motion video presentations about a host of locations, merged with easy-to-use features make this CD-ROM package both entertaining and useful.

The Travel Planner (Gold) by Expert Software sports an introductory screen showing the United States. Title bars, menu bars, tool bars, and status bars provide all the access and information that you will need to manipulate *Travel Planner's* database of information.

Setting your itinerary is as simple as inputing your starting location and destination and determining whether you want to get there by the shortest route or the fastest route. Preferences are even available for Highways, Primary, Secondary, and Toll Roads. As a travel planner, this package is very well thought out. Printing out the itinerary is equally as easy with a Windows configured printer.

Travel Planner *is a good, basic guide to planning travel around the United States.*

Also available are some nicely done video presentations, both full motion and slide,

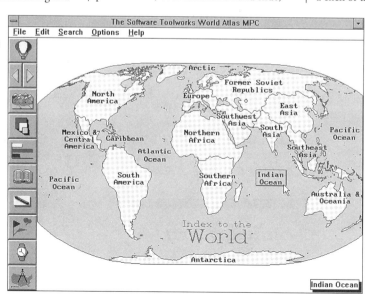

of various states, cities, and regions. The controls closely resemble those of a VCR (without, however, those nasty little program features so often prevalent with your home VCR). The multimedia features allow you to control and change the background music (which is a very nice touch).

The maps can be customized to show items such as capitals, major cities, secondary roads, and even airports. Street level detail of cities is not provided, but a good deal of information about cities *is* provided.

Some 750 points of interest can be displayed along with corresponding phone numbers. Detailed listings of national car rental agencies, major hotels and their respective toll-free numbers are available at a click of the mouse.

Also provided are emergency credit card numbers for lost or stolen cards. Leg by leg trip descriptions can be provided by choosing the appropriate icon.

The instruction manual, as often appears to be the case with Expert Software's publications, is well thought out and can be a valuable guide to the CD-ROM purchaser. It bears repeating that this software is well conceived and should be a nice addition to your reference collection.

World Religions

If you're looking for a basic comparative reference work on faiths of the world, this disc may suit your needs very well. *World Religions* contains summary descriptions of major world religions. The author notes that the contents "have been used as supplementary materials" for a three-term class taught at a community college.

The title is reasonably easy to maneuver around, and contains, for the most part, short paragraphical descriptions of its topics. The work contained within the title could not be classified as exhaustive, nor does the author claim it to be. There are some complete documents contained on the CD. *The Humanist Manifestos* I and II are contained within the title, for example.

The religions summarized include Shamanism, Egyptian Religion, Mesopotamian Religion, Indo-European Religion, Vedic Religion, Hinduism, Buddhism, Jainism, Sikhism, Chinese Religion, Shinto, Zoroastrianism, Judaism, Christianity, Islam, and Humanism.

This simple text reference to world religions makes a good reference guide, but has no multimedia features.

Rating: **1/2**

Publisher Name:
Quanta Press, Inc.

Software Requirements: **MPC**

Suggested Retail Price: **$69.95**

Topics include items such as Reality, Society, Self, Ritual, Time, References, Symbols, Founders, Geography, Scriptures, Beliefs, and History. Some of the topics, such as Challenges, occur adjacent to a more select group of religions. Additional summary information occurs as subtopics to some of fore noted topics.

The CD-ROM contains pop-up word definitions and graphics. Throughout the text, there are highlighted words, which when clicked, provide additional information.

There are no audio or multimedia effects with this title. It is nothing more than a database of summary information of the major religions of the world.

For those interested in summary information of a host of religions, *World Religions* should provide an adequate reference source. It's really little more than a textbook, or collection of textbooks on disc, with added searching capabilities.

World Religions gives you an overview of many different world religions.

Additional CD-ROM Titles

Title: 600 Days to Coco's Island
Suggested Retail Price: $49.95
Publisher: Compton's New Media
Platform: MPC/Macintosh
Description: Movie of a sailing trip to a small island off Costa Rica.

Title: 7 Natural Wonders
Suggested Retail Price: $49.90
Publisher: StarCore
Platform: MPC/Macintosh
Description: Natural wonders of the world in picture and text, from Mount Everest to the Great Barrier Reef.

Title: Antique Toys
Suggested Retail Price: $59.95
Publisher: Gazelle Technologies
Platform: MPC/Macintosh
Description: Toys and dolls catalogued and described for the collector or enthusiast.

Title: A Million Laughs
Suggested Retail Price: $39.95
Publisher: InterActive
Platform: MPC/Macintosh
Description: Jokes and gags that everyone will enjoy.

Title: A World Alive
Suggested Retail Price: $49.95
Publisher: Voyager
Platform: Macintosh
Description: James Earl Jones discusses the animals of the St. Louis Zoo.

Title: About Cows
Suggested Retail Price: $29.95
Publisher: Quanta
Platform: MPC/Macintosh
Description: Lighthearted history, trivia & nostalgia about our favorite farm animal.

Title: Amazing Universe
Suggested Retail Price: $79.95
Publisher: Hopkins Technology
Platform: MPC/Macintosh
Description: Visual program on astronomy.

Title: American Street Rods
Suggested Retail Price: $99.95
Publisher: John O'Connor Publishing
Platform: MPC/Macintosh
Description: 100 photos plus descriptions of classic American hot rods.

Title: Americans In Space
Suggested Retail Price: $59.95
Publisher: Multicom
Platform: MPC/Macintosh
Description: From Alan B. Shepherd to the Space Shuttle; all the Americans who have traveled in space are listed here.

Title: Angkor Wat
Suggested Retail Price: $19.90
Publisher: StarCore
Platform: MPC/Macintosh
Description: The ancient temple in Southeast Asia is explored in detail, with a tour of the largest religious monument in the world, grander than anything left by Greece or Rome.

Title: Astonishing Asia
Suggested Retail Price: $15.90
Publisher: StarCore
Platform: MPC/Macintosh
Description: Even veteran travelers will be surprised at the treasures of Asia shown here, in 30 minutes of video and 600 color photographs.

Title: Astrology Source
Suggested Retail Price: $59.95
Publisher: Multicom
Platform: MPC/Macintosh
Description: If you believe your life is controlled by the planets and stars, you'll want this disc.

Title: Aquatic Art
Suggested Retail Price: $99.95
Publisher: Gazelle
Platform: MPC/Macintosh
Description: Photos and commentary on the marine life of Hawaii and the Caribbean

Title: Automap Road Atlas
Suggested Retail Price: $99.95
Publisher: Broderbund
Platform: MPC
Description: An atlas of the highways and byways f the United States.

Title: Automobile Registry '94
Suggested Retail Price: $59.95
Publisher: Aces Research
Platform: MPC/Macintosh
Description: View the autos and review the data on over 50 makers and 200 models from around the globe.

Title: Baseball's Greatest Hits
Suggested Retail Price: $79.95
Publisher: Voyager
Platform: Macintosh
Description: Legendary moments in baseball history using QuickTime video clips.

Title: Better Homes & Gardens Guide to Gardening
Suggested Retail Price: $59.95
Publisher: Multicom
Platform: MPC/Macintosh
Description: Tips on raising plants and vegetables in your home garden.

Title: Better Homes & Gardens Healthy Cooking CD Cookbook
Suggested Retail Price: $59.95
Publisher: Multicom
Platform: MPC/Macintosh
Description: Serving up healthy meals that are low in fat, high in nutrients.

Title: Bible Library
Suggested Retail Price: $89.95
Publisher: Sony
Platform: MPC
Description: A treasury of facts and stories about the Bible.

Title: Brazil: An Exotic Journey
Suggested Retail Price: $69.95
Publisher: 3D-ROM Multimedia
Platform: MPC/Macintosh
Description: Learn about all the regions of this country through slides, animation, and movies.

Title: Bridge Deluxe with Omar Sharif
Suggested Retail Price: $49.95
Publisher: Interplay/MacPlay
Platform: MPC/Macintosh
Description: Tips from the best bridge player to ever portray Dr. Zhivago.

Title: Britain At Its Best
Suggested Retail Price: $24.95

Publisher: Compton's NewMedia
Platform: MPC
Description: A travel guide to Great Britain and the British Isles.

Title: Card Shop Plus!
Suggested Retail Price: $39.95
Publisher: Software Toolworks
Platform: MPC
Description: Learn about cards from this CD-ROM.

Title: Cars, Cars, Cars
Suggested Retail Price: $79.98
Publisher: MPI Multimedia
Platform: MPC/Macintosh
Description: In-depth study of the automobile using animated graphics, photos, and sound.

Title: CD-ROM Premiere
Suggested Retail Price: $7.99
Publisher: Time-Warner
Platform: MPC/Macintosh
Description: Sample a collection of interactive programs from Time-Warner's best.

Title: CD-ROM Software Jukebox Arcade
Suggested Retail Price: $49.95
Publisher: Selectware
Platform: MPC
Description: A collection of arcade style games for the IBM PC.

Title: CD-ROM Software Jukebox Sports
Suggested Retail Price: $49.95
Publisher: Selectware
Platform: MPC
Description: Sports-oriented games for the IBM PC.

Title: Chartres Cathedral
Suggested Retail Price: $19.90
Publisher: StarCore
Platform: MPC/Macintosh

Description: A tour of the famed French cathedral, with stories of Druids and Vikings, and how this great edifice survived.

Title: Comic Book Confidential
Suggested Retail Price: $29.95
Publisher: Voyager
Platform: Macintosh
Description: Catalog of comic books for both the reader and the collector.

Title: Compton's Multimedia Golf Guide California/Hawaii Edition
Suggested Retail Price: $39.95
Publisher: Compton's NewMedia
Platform: MPC
Description: Where to golf in the Golden State and Aloha State.

Title: Cookbook USA
Suggested Retail Price: $50.00
Publisher: J & D Distributing
Platform: MPC/Macintosh
Description: Easy search and access to over a million recipes, which can be printed out to index cards or standard sheets, or saved to separate files.

Title: Crossword Cracker
Suggested Retail Price: $79.00
Publisher: Nimbus Information Systems
Platform: MPC
Description: Finally finish that crossword through structural searches or words.

Title: Deal-A-Meal Interactive
Suggested Retail Price: $69.95
Publisher: GoodTime Software
Platform: MPC
Description: Richard Simmons video directs you through his plan.

Title: Digital Gourmet
Suggested Retail Price: $145.00
Publisher: TeleTypesetting
Platform: MPC/Macintosh
Description: Another cookbook-on-disc.

Title: Digital Tours: The World of Flight
Suggested Retail Price: $59.95
Suggested Retail Price: $AVE-ON
Platform: MPC
Description: 700 quality photos plus text on aviation and space subjects.

Title: Digital Tours: The World of Trains
Suggested Retail Price: $59.95
Suggested Retail Price: $AVE-ON
Platform: MPC
Description: For the train enthusiast, over 700 high resolution photos.

Title: ESPN Golf
Suggested Retail Price: $39.95
Publisher: IntelliPlay
Platform: MPC/Macintosh
Description: Golfing tips from the cable sports network.

Title: ESPN Sports Shorts
Suggested Retail Price: $39.95
Publisher: Moon Valley
Platform: MPC
Description: Short clips about a broad variety of sports.

Title: Exotic Japan
Suggested Retail Price: $59.95
Publisher: Voyager
Platform: Macintosh
Description: Learn about Japanese customs and history from this CD-ROM.

Title: Experience Hawaii
Suggested Retail Price: $79.99
Publisher: Advanced Software
Platform: MPC
Description: Plan your dream vacation to the Aloha State.

Title: Exploring Ancient Architecture
Suggested Retail Price: $59.95
Publisher: Medio Multimedia
Platform: MPC

Description: Tour inside well-known ancient architecture from the Neolithic, Egyptian, Greek, and Roman time period.

Title: FDR: History Maker
Suggested Retail Price: $54.95
Publisher: Computer Vistas
Platform: MPC
Description: Delve into the life of Franklin D. Roosevelt through pictures, video, narration and text.

Title: Food AnalystPLUS
Suggested Retail Price: $199.00
Publisher: Hopkins Technology
Platform: MPC
Description: Menu planning, nutrition, dietary information, and weight loss.

Title: From Alice to Ocean
Suggested Retail Price: $69.00
Publisher: Claris Clear Choice
Platform: MPC/Macintosh
Description: PhotoCD with pictures of a journey across the Australian continent.

Title: Funny
Suggested Retail Price: $39.99
Publisher: Time Warner Interactive Group
Platform: MPC/Macintosh
Description: Jokes, joke, punch lines, and more.

Title: Gardening
Suggested Retail Price: $39.95
Publisher: Chestnut
Platform: MPC
Description: The guide every home gardener needs for planning and landscaping your yard.

Title: Great Barrier Reef
Suggested Retail Price: $15.90
Publisher: StarCore
Platform: MPC/Macintosh
Description: Enjoy the beauty of this South Pacific marvel.

Title: Greg LeMond's Bicycle Adventure
Suggested Retail Price: $79.95
Publisher: Eden Interactive
Platform: MPC/Macintosh
Description: Skill training tips from this Tour de France winner.

Title: Guide to Special Interest Videos
Suggested Retail Price: $79.95
Publisher: Quanta
Platform: MPC/Macintosh
Description: Find those specialized videos for your hobby or other interest.

Title: Ham Radio & Scanner Companion
Suggested Retail Price: $19.95
Publisher: John O'Connor Publishing
Platform: MPC
Description: Shareware collection of applications and programs for enthusiasts.

Title: Ham Radio
Suggested Retail Price: $39.95
Publisher: Chestnut
Platform: MPC
Description: Complete display of info, programs, and data on amateur radio.

Title: Hobby Corner: Nature Hobbies Vol. 1
Suggested Retail Price: $59.95
Suggested Retail Price: $AVE-ON
Platform: MPC
Description: Complete guide to 5 nature hobbies for all ages

Title: Home Medical Advisor Pro
Suggested Retail Price: $69.95
Publisher: Pixel Perfect
Platform: MPC
Description: Your home doctor. Take two aspirins and use this CD in the morning.

Title: How Baseball Works
Suggested Retail Price: $69.95
Publisher: Byron Preiss Multimedia
Platform: MPC/Macintosh

Description: Learn the ins and outs of America's favorite professional sport.

Title: Inca Ruins
Suggested Retail Price: $19.90
Publisher: StarCore
Platform: MPC/Macintosh
Description: Explore the remnants of this South American Indian culture.

Title: Indian Monsoon
Suggested Retail Price: $15.90
Publisher: StarCore
Platform: MPC/Macintosh
Description: See the devastation wrought by this terrible force of nature.

Title: Information USA
Suggested Retail Price: $69.95
Publisher: Infobusiness
Platform: MPC
Description: Lots of information in this CD-ROM almanac.

Title: John Schumacher's New Prague Hotel Cookbook
Suggested Retail Price: $29.95
Publisher: Quanta
Platform: MPC/Macintosh
Description: High class food from a high class chef.

Title: Kathy Smith's Fat Burning System
Suggested Retail Price: $69.95
Publisher: Xiphias
Platform: MPC/Macintosh
Description: Follow along with Kathy Smith in designing your own workout program.

Title: Key Action Traveler
Suggested Retail Price: $39.95
Publisher: Softkey
Platform: MPC
Description: Travel guide to the United States on disc.

Title: Key HomeDesigner
Suggested Retail Price: $39.95
Publisher: Softkey
Platform: MPC
Description: Design your own home with this program.

Title: Leonardo the Inventor
Suggested Retail Price: $49.95
Publisher: InterActive
Platform: MPC/Macintosh
Description: The inventive side of Leonardo da Vinci, the definitive Renaissance Man.

Title: Let's Go: 1993 Budget Guide to U.S.A.
Suggested Retail Price: $24.95
Publisher: Compton's NewMedia
Platform: MPC
Description: Cheap travel in the US.

Title: Let's Visit Mexico/South America/ Spain
Suggested Retail Price: $49.95
Publisher: Queue
Platform: MPC/Macintosh
Description: More tours of popular countries through interactive slide shows.

Title: Lifesaver 2.0
Suggested Retail Price: $149.00
Publisher: Educorp
Platform: Macintosh
Description: Interactive first aid study with animated video. Perfect to use for a refresher course.

Title: London
Suggested Retail Price: $59.00
Publisher: Sony
Platform: MPC/Macintosh
Description: All the best sights in London, with videos, sound, and more.

Title: Master the Markets
Suggested Retail Price: $29.95

Publisher: Compton's NewMedia
Platform: MPC
Description: Your personal stock market guide.

Title: Microsoft Complete Baseball
Suggested Retail Price: $79.95
Publisher: Microsoft
Platform: MPC/Macintosh
Description: Microsoft's guide to our national pastime.

Title: Mount Everest
Suggested Retail Price: $15.90
Publisher: StarCore
Platform: MPC/Macintosh
Description: The tallest mountain on Earth in pictures and text.

Title: National Parks of America
Suggested Retail Price: $59.95
Publisher: Multicom
Platform: MPC/Macintosh
Description: Explore the natural beauty of Federally owned lands.

Title: National Parks
Suggested Retail Price: $59.95
Publisher: Cambrix
Platform: MPC
Description: From Old Faithful to the Grand Canyon.

Title: New Basics Electronic Cookbook
Suggested Retail Price: $69.96
Publisher: Xiphias
Platform: MPC
Description: Another electronic cookbook with some tasty tips and recipes.

Title: Ocean Life: Hawaiian Islands
Suggested Retail Price: $49.95
Publisher: Sumeria Inc.
Platform: MPC/Macintosh
Description: Exotic fish and plants in the waters surrounding the Hawaiian Islands.

Title: Our Earth
Suggested Retail Price: $99.95
Publisher: National Geographic
Platform: Macintosh
Description: Natural wonders of the Earth as seen by National Geographic photographers

Title: Our Solar System
Suggested Retail Price: $39.95
Publisher: Chestnut
Platform: MPC
Description: Photos taken around the world of the galaxies. Programs, star locators, data and simulations from NASA, Washington, and more.

Title: Outdoor World's Fly Fishing #1 | CD-RO

Suggested Retail Price: $49.95
Publisher: EE Multimedia Productions Inc.
Platform: MPC
Description: Learn how to catch flies, or catch fish with flies. Or maybe they mean lures. You fishermen will understand this technical stuff.

Title: Panama Canal
Suggested Retail Price: $19.90
Publisher: StarCore
Platform: MPC/Macintosh
Description: There's more than malaria and Ruben Blades in Panama, and this disc proves it. You'll learn about the 40-year struggle to cross 30 miles of Isthmus.

Title: PharmAssist CD-ROM
Suggested Retail Price: $69.95
Publisher: Software Marketing
Platform: MPC
Description: Easily accessed information on the prescription and non-prescription medications in today's market. Also includes an interactive family health guide

Title: PlanIt Adrenalin Personal Information Manager
Suggested Retail Price: $59.95
Publisher: Media Vision
Platform: MPC
Description: Personal planning calendar for the busy executive.

Title: Sante'
Suggested Retail Price: $59.95
Publisher: Hopkins Technology
Platform: MPC
Description: Complete dietary health package with recipes, diet, and exercise programs.

Title: Scouting Report
Suggested Retail Price: $79.95
Publisher: Quanta
Platform: MPC
Description: Scouting statistics used in major league baseball.

Title: Short Attention Span Theater: Dating and Mating
Suggested Retail Price: $49.95
Publisher: Time Warner Interactive Group
Platform: MPC/Macintosh
Description: Guide to life for the terminally weird.

Title: Short Attention Span Theater: It's All Relative
Suggested Retail Price: $49.95
Publisher: Time Warner Interactive Group
Platform: MPC/Macintosh
Description: Humor is relative on this disc from the cable TV series.

Title: Space Series: Apollo
Suggested Retail Price: $69.95
Publisher: Quanta
Platform: MPC/Macintosh
Description: Learn about the space missions that put men on the moon, and brought all of them back, too.

Title: Stories of Murder, Mystery, Magic, Terror and More
Suggested Retail Price: $37.95
Publisher: World Library
Platform: MPC
Description: Scary stories for adults.

Title: Tao of Cow
Suggested Retail Price: $29.95
Publisher: Quanta
Platform: MPC/Macintosh
Description: More cow lore. Honest.

Title: Team NFL: 1993
Suggested Retail Price: $29.95
Publisher: Optimum Resources
Platform: MPC/Macintosh
Description: NFL statistics from the recent football season.

Title: The Amazon Rainforest
Suggested Retail Price: $15.90
Publisher: StarCore
Platform: MPC/Macintosh
Description: Learn about the unexplored regions of South America. See spotted jaguars and multi-colored toucans.

Title: The American Sign Language Dictionary
Suggested Retail Price: $69.95
Publisher: HarperReference
Platform: MPC/Macintosh
Description: 2,500 of the most common language signs used in the U.S. Includes electronic text search, finger spelling, and an optional audio. Foreign language lexicons also available.

Title: The Blue Whale
Suggested Retail Price: $15.90
Publisher: StarCore
Platform: MPC/Macintosh
Description: This mammal isn't called blue because it can hold its breath. Learn the real facts from this CD-ROM.

Title: The Book of Lists #3
Suggested Retail Price: $39.95
Publisher: VT Productions
Platform: MPC/Macintosh
Description: Trivia arranged in list form for easy reading in the bathroom, subway, car pool, etc.

Title: The Egyptian Pyramids
Suggested Retail Price: $19.90
Publisher: StarCore
Platform: MPC/Macintosh
Description: Fascinating look at one of the great man-made wonders of the ancient world.

Title: The Great Wall
Suggested Retail Price: $19.90
Publisher: StarCore
Platform: MPC/Macintosh
Description: See the only man-made object that can be discerned from outer space, in a slide show with narration and music.

Title: The Herbalist
Suggested Retail Price: $99.95
Publisher: Hopkins Technology
Platform: MPC
Description: Complete study of herbal medicine. Includes easily accessed photos, text, herb music, and verse.

Title: The Madness of Roland
Suggested Retail Price: $59.95
Publisher: Hyberbole Studios
Platform: Macintosh
Description: Story of Roland (Orlando), Arthur's mad knight.

Title: The Outdoor Athlete
Suggested Retail Price: $39.95
Publisher: Johnson Books
Platform: Macintosh
Description: Fitness program for outdoorsy types.

Title: The Plant Doctor
Suggested Retail Price: $79.95
Publisher: Quanta
Platform: MPC
Description: When your green thumb turns black, load this disc.

Title: The Sierra Club Electronic Guides
Suggested Retail Price: $24.95 each
Publisher: InterOptica
Platform: MPC/Macintosh
Description: Choose from Mt. Everest, The Blue Whale, The Amazon Rainforest, The Great Barrier Reef, The Grand Canyon, Indian Monsoon, and The Wildebeest Migration. Explore each marvel through visuals and text.

Title: Space 90
Suggested Retail Price: $110.00
Publisher: EBSCO Subscription Services
Platform: MPC
Description: Database of all space launches, attempts, and planned missions from the very beginning to the present.

Title: The Taj Mahal
Suggested Retail Price: $19.90
Publisher: StarCore
Platform: MPC/Macintosh
Description: Built as a wedding gift, this Indian wonder remains one of the most beautiful structures in the world.

Title: Terrorist Group Profiles
Suggested Retail Price: $79.95
Publisher: Quanta Press Inc.
Platform: MPC/Macintosh
Description: All the details on those terrorist groups. Find your favorite and enlist. Does Interpol have this disc?

Title: The Trans-Siberian Railway
Suggested Retail Price: $19.90
Publisher: StarCore
Platform: MPC/Macintosh
Description: See the broad expanses of Siberia from the comfort of the world's longest railway, at 5,900 miles! With maps, pictures, and text.

Title: The View from Earth
Suggested Retail Price: $79.98
Publisher: Time Warner Interactive Group
Platform: MPC/Macintosh
Description: Looks at the planet Earth.

Title: UFO
Suggested Retail Price: $59.95
Publisher: Software Marketing
Platform: MPC
Description: This singular program explores the evidence of extraterrestrial happening, including 500 documented sightings.

Title: Under the Sun: Digital Days Calendar
Suggested Retail Price: $34.95
Publisher: Johnson Books
Platform: Macintosh
Description: Daily calendar with important events.

Title: Venice
Suggested Retail Price: $19.90
Publisher: StarCore
Platform: MPC/Macintosh
Description: Quick! Before it sinks! View this Italian city filled with art treasures and steeped in history and sewage. Interactive text links animations, illustrations, maps, and photos.

Title: Vital Signs: The Good Health Resource
Suggested Retail Price: $95.00
Publisher: Software Mart, Inc.
Platform: MPC/Macintosh
Description: Intended for families and individuals as a source and guide on daily life safety.

Title: Washington D.C. At Its Best
Suggested Retail Price: $24.95

Publisher: Compton's NewMedia
Platform: MPC
Description: "Guided tour" museums, sites, hotel and restaurant reviews

Title: Whales & Dolphins
Suggested Retail Price: $69.00
Publisher: Sony
Platform: MPC
Description: A look at either the second most intelligent or most intelligent species on Earth, depending on who's doing the rating.

Title: Wildebeest Migration
Suggested Retail Price: $15.90
Publisher: StarCore
Platform: MPC/Macintosh
Description: Watch them wildebeest run, as 1.5 million of these animals travel 1,000 miles across the Serengeti plain.

Title: Wines of the World
Suggested Retail Price: $59.95
Publisher: Multicom
Platform: MPC/Macintosh
Description: An assertive little disc, with plenty of nose and a fruity aftertaste, plus lots of facts about potables.

Title: World Tour: America Alive, Europe Alive, Asia Alive
Suggested Retail Price: $99.00 each
Publisher: MediAlive
Platform: MPC
Description: Advice on seeing these continents while they are still living, a plan I heartily agree with.

Title: Wyatt Earp's Old West
Suggested Retail Price: $49.95
Publisher: Amazing Media
Platform: MPC/Macintosh
Description: Travel west for an interactive visit with the legend. Experience this time period with hundreds of photos.

Title: ZCI Encyclopedia of Western Lawmen & Outlaws
Suggested Retail Price: $49.95
Publisher: ZCI Publishing
Platform: MPC/Macintosh
Description: Bad guys, good guys, and Indians clash in the Old West.

Title: ZCI World Encyclopedia of 20th Century Murder
Suggested Retail Price: $49.95
Publisher: ZCI Publishing
Platform: MPC/Macintosh
Description: All the best murders are in here, if you like that sort of thing.

Title: ZCI World Encyclopedia of Assassination
Suggested Retail Price: $49.95
Publisher: ZCI Publishing
Platform: MPC/Macintosh
Description: Nothing like a few good assassinations to brighten up your day, in this fact-filled disc of killings from Julius Caesar to Anwar Sadat—and beyond.

Chapter 11

Graphics

CD-ROMs make a great medium for graphics applications and their files because of the sheer amount of material that can be contained on a single disc. Back in the bad old days, I collected clip art on 1.44MB floppy disks, and eventually accumulated a few hundred of these that took up several drawers in my media closet. Today, I have two discs of clip art that came with CorelDRAW! 5 with about 22,000 images that are the equivalent of more than 700 floppies! And that's only the *core* of my clip art collection.

So, graphics CDs for the IBM and PC are heavily concentrated in clip art for desktop publishing. You'll find EPS, PICT, and TIFF files available from a number of sources at reasonable prices. Don't forget to check out shareware discs, which may have public domain images scanned from government publications, old books, or other sources.

Some top-selling discs in this category include Pixar 128, which has 128 different photographic quality textures, and can be used by Pixar Typestry, Adobe Photoshop, or other graphics applications. There is also Click Art from T/Maker. This clip-art pioneer offers a wide variety of discs for the Macintosh and PC, including Animals and Nature (150 images), Artistry and Borders (375 varieties), and Sports and Games (180 action-packed pictures).

Metro Imagebase offers 2000 high quality images, covering everything from business to borders on its disc, equally divided between 1000 EPS and 1000 TIFF images. Or, you might want to check out Architectural Photofile. Available from Loggia, this disc has has bridges, churches, housing, industry, transit, and more.

In addition to image discs, you find in this chapter graphics tools like Pixar Showplace, a 3D imaging program, and Do It On Your Desktop, a handy multimedia program. Examine some of the other discs reviewed, and see how CD-ROMs can take the strain off your bulging hard disc by keeping image files handy—but on the shelf and out of the way. Kodak PhotoCDs are also available from a variety of vendors (especially Corel) with high resolution photographs—each large enough to fill up six high density floppy disks!

Aris Entertainment's Worldview

Rating:  1/2

Publisher Name:
Aris Entertainment

Software Requirements: **MPC**

Suggested Retail Price: **$39.95**

Got your seatbelt fastened? A-OK. 5-4-3. Sure you want to go on this mission? Oops, too late. Liftoff! MediaClips is going to the moon and a little bit beyond. What's that itinerary again? Lessee...Mercury, Venus, Earth, Mars, Jupiter...wait a minute, you missed Mars! Well, we'll catch it on the way back.

OK, it's not THAT good, but it isn't bad either. This is Aris' clip collection of 100 space photos, apparently gathered from the declassified shots the U.S. government makes available. NASA Apollo, space shuttle, and other missions are represented as well as the some of the Naval Observatory's more dramatic photos. There are photos from the Voyager and Pioneer missions and some Earth Resources Technology Satellite pictures. It's definitely a trip. Does NASA take American Express?

The collection covers from Earth to the farthest reaches of the universe, including pictures of cities from space, natural features of Earth, one quasar thought to be at the edge of the known universe, and most of the planets (they did miss Mars, though) and, of course, shots of the moon, the sun, and astronauts on the moon. Throw in a few nebulae here and there and

you've got a pretty good collection of stock space photographs.

I'm still trying to find the moon in the "moonrise" clip though. It's supposed to show the moon just above Earth's horizon. Sorry, no moon there but that was the only glitch I could find.

The pictures are clear and mostly sharp. Any that aren't are more due to the nature of shooting photographs from or in space or through telescopes than to any lack on Aris' part. I wouldn't think NASA, etc. likely to release their flubs. Since I grew up through the space program, I wasn't as impressed as I might have been, but it's nice to have a collection of those historical pictures at hand

on the desk. They bring back those do-you-remember-what-you-were-doing-when kinds of thoughts.

This is the most informative of the Aris discs I've checked. It even includes little things like one mission when the crew was to locate and photograph the Henderson Islands in the South Pacific for a possible emergency shuttle landing site. They were to do that using the best available survey maps of the area...which were published in the 19th century. The information is complete, though it looks like they either used Government-supplied captions directly or paraphrased them. The language has that taint of "Government-ese."

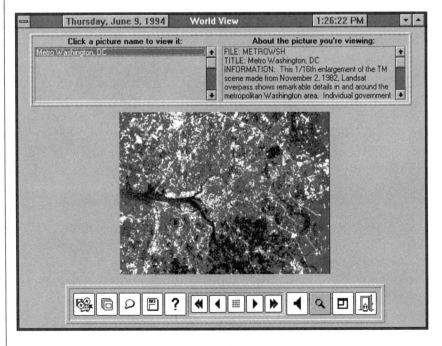

Worldview shows the Earth from a birds'-eye view.

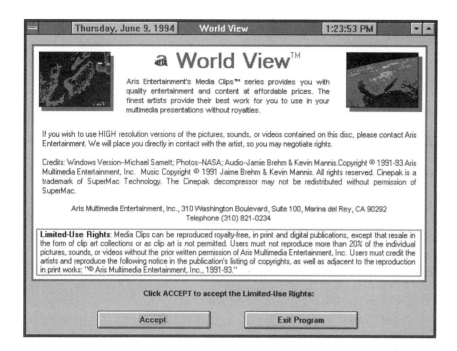

Worldview has clips of the world you can use in your own publications.

The search engine works well. It'll search by keyword, file name, general description, and even by color name. While one or two searches turned up pictures that didn't quite seem to fit, I always found the keyword I typed into the search dialog box somewhere in the information box text (even to the point, though, of finding Marshall Space Center for a search keyed on "mars"). You get a list of all the picture files that contain the word so you do have to look manually a little. Of course, the more specific the criterion, the more accurate the find. File name or specific searches worked best for me, usually yielding only one or two pictures I was looking for.

This disc includes 25 video clips in Video for Windows and MPEG. They range from JFK's announcement of "putting a man on the moon before the decade is out" to shuttle launches, NASA animations, the obligatory astronauts floating around the ship, and the Apollo moon landing. Even one of the Mercury launches is in there. I

Space age images from NASA files give you pictures (and sound) you can use in your presentations and publications.

couldn't tell if it was Shepard or Glenn, though.

As with all their MediaClips products, Aris addresses the buyer's probable wish to do more than just view the images. They supply all 100 files in 8-bit, 320 x 240 and 640 x 480 .BMP and .PCX formats, 24-bit TIFF for use in high-res paint programs, and their audio in both .WAV and .VOC formats. They also extend on-the-box permission to reproduce up to 20 percent of the images, sounds, or videos royalty-free in print or digital publications so long as the artists and Aris Entertainment's copyright are duly credited.

Anyone wanting higher-resolution copies of pictures, movies, or sounds can contact Aris Entertainment, who will then put them in touch with the artists so they can negotiate rights, etc.

Famous Faces

Rating:

Publisher Name:
Jasmine Multimedia Publishing

Software Requirements:
Windows 3.1

Suggested Retail Price: **$39.95**

*F*amous Faces is a good demonstration of what the state-of-the-art video on PCs is capable of. It hints at what it will be able to do in the future. Sad to say, video is still so demanding of PC resources and disk space that *Famous Faces* is somewhat disappointing. What they are trying to do is right on target, though.

Installation of Famous Faces is very simple. You type "D:\setup" (assuming D is your CD-ROM) in the Windows Program Manager "Run" window. It asks you to confirm the drive letter of your CD-ROM, and then installs the needed software almost instantly. Its icon is stored in your Games program group.

By double-clicking the Famous Faces icon, you enter the program. A title screen comes up; single-click it to move to the program. The main menu presents icons for six categories of famous people to select from: Politics, Arts, Sports, Science, Business, and Religion. Clicking one of these brings up the famous people for that group. The first icon is Politics. Clicking it brings up a list of 62 famous people, in two pages. Famous people such as American presidents, British royalty, and European and Asian leaders make the

list. Clicking the name of the person you wish to see brings up the movie interface. A small 160 x 120 section of the window is devoted to the video.

You can click an icon to start/stop the movie, show a short quote/biography of the famous person, go back to the names list for the current category, or go back to the main menu. You can also click forward or back arrows to access the next famous person, or you can click an icon to quit.

Unfortunately, the limitations of the six categories cause some people to be placed in categories that, while they might be the best fit, are still clumsy. For instance, Sacco and Vanzetti and George Patton are in the

Politics section. That is the best of the six sections for them, but a broader range of categories would have helped. Amelia Earhart and Charles Lindbergh are in the Sports section; Lindbergh is also in the Science section. Al Capone shows up in Business! Again, this is the best choice, except perhaps for Politics, but a bit unfortunate.

One disappointing thing you find is that after you exit Politics, the other five categories contain far fewer individuals. The Arts category has 18, Sports has 5 (besides Lindbergh and Earhart are Mohammed Ali, Joe Lewis, and Babe Ruth), Science has 8 (Lindbergh, the

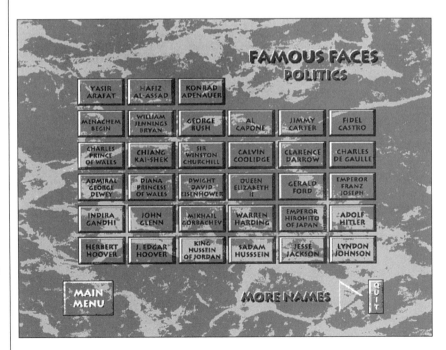

Choose *Famous Faces* in various categories, such as such well-known politicians as Menachem Begin, John Glenn, and Al Capone...Al Capone?

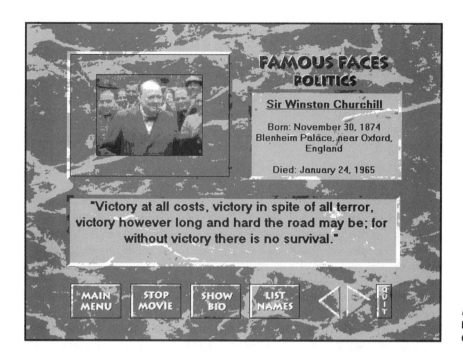

Famous Faces **includes pictures of historical figures like Sir Winston Churchill.**

Wright Brothers, Madame Curie, Einstein, Edison, Bell, John Glenn, and Jonas Salk), Business has 6 (Capone, Carnegie, Disney, Edison, Ford, and J.P. Morgan) and Religion has 8 (Mahatma Gandhi, Billy Graham, Jesse Jackson, Pope John XXIII, Ayatollah Khomeini, Martin Luther King, Jr. and Pope Pius XII).

In each of these five categories, you could make the case for at least double the number of individuals. The CD-ROM seems to have space for it; a directory listing showed less than 300MB used. Sound clips are also used very sparsely. Although his speeches were hateful, you can better understand how Hitler led his country into war with his bombastic and impressive speaking talents. It was sad to see that a clip of him speaking was not included. Other notable people who inexplicably lacked sound clips were Winston Churchill, Walt Disney, Jimmy Carter, Alexander Graham Bell, and Thomas Edison. Among the few who had sound clips were Richard Nixon, Martin Luther King, Jr., J. Edgar Hoover, and Orson Welles.

An excellent concept that is weakened by the current limitations inherent in multimedia video; much more attractive to those who can make use of their freely reusable video clips of over 100 famous people.

Actually, although this disc had room for more entries, this technology will really blossom when many hundreds of famous people, in full screen video and with sound clips, can be accessed in this way. For while saddled with the limits of the technology of today, this disc shows where multimedia is going. The program's interface and conceptualization are perfect; what is needed are much faster CPUs and video cards, and much larger storage media to really do what *Famous Faces* set out to do. As a pioneer effort, it is well worth seeing (although not necessarily buying).

Jasmine Multimedia sells a number of discs with similar concepts, such as *Science in Motion, Sports in Motion, Amazing Moves* (stunts), and *Best of Stock Video.* In these products, and in this one as well, you can extract the video clips and use them freely in your own multimedia presentations. Those with an interest in such projects may find this disc much more valuable; it is highly recommended to them. Jasmine Multimedia is pushing the envelope with these offerings. Hopefully, they will be around when technological innovation can allow them to field the next generation of multimedia video software.

A Guide to Multimedia/Media Library Volume 1

Rating:

Publisher Name:
Ask Me Multimedia

Software Requirements: **MPC**

Suggested Retail Price: **$29.95**

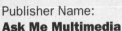

This review covers two products, *A Guide to Multimedia* and *Media Library Volume 1*, both products from Ask Me Multimedia. *A Guide to Multimedia* is both a multimedia tutorial and a product demonstration disc. The product being demonstrated is SST Lite (Super Show & Tell), a somewhat crippled version of their SST multimedia package. SST Lite can only create presentations of ten slides or less, cannot create stand-alone disc presentations, and cannot create interactive presentations. In all other respects, however, it has complete functionality. *Media Library Volume 1* contains videos, animations, morphs, sounds, music, backgrounds, and various other things that can be used in SST multimedia presentations.

A Guide to Multimedia has a number of multimedia presentations. All were created with SST. Some are tutorials explaining multimedia technology and how to create effective multimedia presentations. Others are examples of what users have actually done with SST. One of the demos was done by an 11-year-old girl. The tutorials give good background information about

multimedia applications, and provide many excellent tips about what to do and not to do with multimedia. There is both an art and a science of how to present information effectively in a multimedia format; this disc introduces you to the science of multimedia presentation. The art is up to you.

A Guide to Multimedia includes a limited number of support files; certainly enough to experiment with, but not a full tool kit. The formats for sound, video, animation, music, etc. are not specific to SST, so you can take .WAV sound and .MID music files and use them in your presentations, .BMP, .GIF, .PCX, and other image files, .FLC and .AVI animation

files, and other common PC formats.

There are over 100 royalty-free clips of this sort in the package, which are supposed to be optimized for use with SST, but using external files caused no obvious difficulties. For customized files, you have to create them using other tools; SST has no capability to record .WAV files, for instance, nor does it have a drawing package with any power (it can do boxes, lines, and ovals, but isn't at all powerful). The same holds true for music, animation, morphing, and video. You can buy these files, however, and Ask Me Multimedia hopes you will buy their *Media Library Volume 1*.

You can preview images in windows like this.

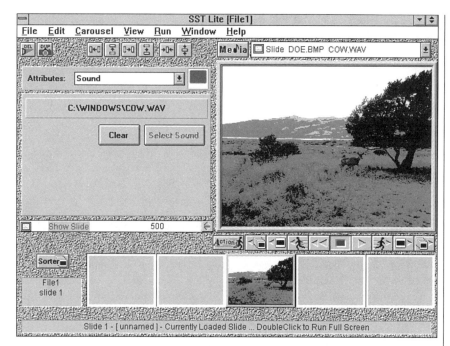

The slide show you assemble is shown in full screen mode.

read off the hard disk. Be sure to have plenty of memory, though.

SST has all sorts of other bells and whistles; many types of fade-in and fade-out, definable hot spots where you can click to affect the path the presentation takes (this does not work in SST Lite), fine control of timing of events, animated text, slide sorting, and others. It's hard to say whether this would be an adequate tool for professional work, but it's definitely a product to be looked at. For a non-professional looking to experiment with multimedia, it is certainly suitable. SST has a retail price of $149.95; you'll need it for any extensive work. SST Lite is much cheaper, and would allow you to try it before you buy it. Both *A Guide to Multimedia* and *Media Library Volume 1* are well done, and well worth a look.

Media Library Volume 1 contains 100 scenic photos for slide backgrounds in 8- and 24-bit color .BMP format, 100 wallpaper-type slide backgrounds, 80 original MIDI music compositions (from 10 seconds to 3 minutes long), 75 sliding bullets and 3D buttons for interactive presentations, 50 .WAV sound effects and celebrity impressions, 50 .FLC animations, 21 .AVI video clips, 10 .AVI morph clips, and one full length music video.

The photos and wallpaper designs are beautiful and the MIDI music is excellent (it is intended for use as bridging between slides, so some pieces are quite short). The .WAV files are not as impressive, although it is quite easy to get all sorts of .WAV files from bulletin boards, CD-ROM collections, etc. The animations aren't very impressive either, with some notable exceptions. The .AVI files suffer from the current PC lack of capability to do full screen or even quarter screen video; your video window isn't much bigger than a large postage stamp. Unless you need a specific person or event in your multimedia (your boss, Winston Churchill,

the first footprint on the moon, etc.), try to substitute animation, if possible, until PC capabilities improve. It won't be long now.

The performance of SST Lite itself was for the most part, quite impressive. The package for *A Guide to Multimedia* claims that you can create a multimedia presentation in 60 minutes or less. You can, but you'll only scratch the surface at first. It will take awhile to get the hang of everything. The user interface is fairly logical, although not everything is obvious. As your mouse cursor passes over items, a status line on the bottom of the screen gives a one line description of what the item does.

You can easily splice together text, a background image, sound and a superimposed video, or animation on a slide. Be careful about putting sound together with a soundless video or animation. They will slow each other down, even on a 80486/66 MHz machine. You can probably minimize this effect if you specify that the video is to be loaded into memory, rather than being

A CD-ROM based demonstration version of a multimedia presentation creation package, SST, with the first volume of CD-ROM-based support files for it, show surprising capabilities for presentations combining graphics, sound, animation, video, and special effects.

Allegro InPrint Art Library

Rating:

Publisher Name:
Allegro New Media

Software Requirements:
MPC/Macintosh

Suggested Retail Price: $59.95

*A*llegro's *InPrint Art Library* is a series of CD-ROMs that each have 100 or more professional-quality TIFF files that can be imported into any IBM PC or Macintosh image editor that supports that bit-mapped file format. A single disc works in both Macs and PCs, so businesses that have both platforms can easily get double-duty out of this series.

Allegro offers collections of TIFF files for both PC and Macintosh with graphic photos, textures, and scenic images covered.

The discs we received for review included Scenic Photos, Graphic Textures, and Graphic Photos. The photo discs include a great browser that lets you preview images and search for pictures by category, and an "interactive multimedia personal graphics tutor," with creative usage tips.

The images on these discs are all full color or grayscale images. You are free to use them as you wish, but only when incorporating them into a new document, desktop publication, or presentation. That is, you can't distribute or sell these files as is, say, for your own clip art collection.

There are lots of good images on these discs. The Scenic Photos disc includes landscapes, still lifes, doorways, textures, architecture, waterbodies, and miscellaneous categories. You find church doors, iron gates, rippling waters, roof tops, ferns and lilies, Grand Canyon scenes, and famous works of sculpture.

The Graphic Photos disc is divided into categories like celebrations, picture frames, globes, hands, music, plaques, sculpture, sports, trophies, and miscellaneous. You'll discover some great baby pictures, American flags, a neon clock, various sports paraphernalia, all sorts of musical instruments, and, if you have some need for them, a good assortment of photos of trophies!

The Graphic Textures range from abstract to realistic. You'll find tie-dye swirls, fireworks, and brushed gold, along with jelly beans, confetti, denim, and various shades of granite or other rocks.

With 100 TIFF files per disc, these collections all work out to 50 cents or less per image. The pictures are all professional quality, so you'll find them highly usable in your desktop publications or presentations.

This shot of Old World rooftops is one of the images included in the Allegro *InPrint* **series of CD-ROM clip art.**

Allegro InPrint Art Library Volume 1: Cartoon Idioms

Cartoon Idioms is a selection of cartoon clip-art that illustrates 101 common diomatic phrases, useful for placing in company newsletters and other desktop publications. Each picture is available in both 24-bit color and 8-bit grayscale versions and is stored in the Tagged Image File Format (TIFF), a file format that most graphics applications can use. A typical color drawing prints out to 6-inch by 6-inch at 200 dots per inch and requires almost a megabyte of storage.

The CD contains no other support files, just the images, but the instructional flier contains specific information on how to properly load and use the images with many popular Mac, Windows, and DOS applications, such as Microsoft Word, WordPerfect, PageMaker, QuarkXPress, CorelDRAW!, Photostyler, and Photoshop. A number of basic hints and tips are also included in the flier, as well as thumbnail images of the color versions of each drawing. The tips will be very valuable to someone just starting out in the sometimes confusing world of graphic file importation.

Using the drawings was quite straightforward, even without the instructions in the flier. Please note: The thumbnail prints in the flier don't begin to do the pictures justice; each thumbnail print is only 1.25-inch by 1.25-inch, too small to appreciate each drawing. The artwork is very good; the artist is especially talented in using a 24-bit color palette. The color selection in many of the drawings is quite beautiful; most drawings also contain uncolored portions that accentuate the colors that are present.

Looking at the grayscale versions of these pictures is far less interesting. The artist who drew these pictures is talented, but his clever use of color makes this work stand out.

If you need this type of clip art, then by all means, buy this disc; otherwise, you might want to try to get a friendly dealer to let you browse the collection before you buy.

The organizing idea of the collection is a pictorial representation of 101 common idiomatic expressions, like "Face the Music," "Get A Grip," and "Cat Got Your Tongue." The coupling of these expressions with the drawings seems not to work very well in most cases. Humor seems to be the intent of the added captions, but they usually miss the mark. In many cases, it seems like you are looking at the result of a cartoon contest, where readers write funny captions for a captionless drawing. In a real-world contest, most of these captions would not be winners. The flier does suggest that the user

Rating: ◉ ◉ 1/2

Publisher Name:
Allegro New Media, Inc.

Software Requirements:
Windows 3.0 or later, or Mac

Suggested Retail Price: **$59.95**

feel free to white out these captions if desired, and describes how to do this. In many cases, a user can supply a much more humorous caption than the idiomatic expression that goes with the drawing. Some of the drawings, stripped of their captions, are not funny at all, but represent excellent examples of clip art.

One word of warning. A few of these cartoons are a bit risqué, and several are not politically correct or are in slightly poor taste. One or two seem just plain ugly. On the plus side, a number are genuinely funny, and many have useful potential as clip art when stripped of their captions and word balloons. There are no usage fees for these drawings beyond the price of the disc, but the images can only be used by the owner of the disc as a design element of a print or multimedia project. In other words, others can't take these images and repackage them as part of a different collection, but you can spice up a document or newsletter with them as much as you wish.

Aris Entertainment's Animal Kingdom

Rating:

Publisher Name:
Aris Entertainment

Software Requirements: **MPC**

Suggested Retail Price: **$39.95**

They're animals, I tell you, all animals! And they are. This clip-art disc from Aris' MediaClips series takes you all around the world for a good overview of four-legged, winged, and two-legged (with a bit of knuckle-walking) creatures. You get apes, lizards, penguins, lions and tigers and bears, (Oh, my!) and a lot more.

In 100 pictures, it's obviously not an exhaustive collection; there are a lot more animals than that. But it's not meant to be a zoology text. It's a collection of clips for someone who might want to produce some kind of work where some wildlife pictures might fit. These would fit in very nicely.

The pictures are all high-quality, many taken by professional wildlife photographers, researchers, and possibly some very good amateurs. I didn't find one that wouldn't be usable. The collection is restricted to land animals and birds, although some live near water and swim or wade to hunt.

We were particularly impressed with the informational text this time. There's enough that you get a decent understanding of each animal's habitat, habits, and location. Aris throws in some occasional nice details that qualify as quirky bits to pique the interest.

This CD would work as nicely as a supplement for the kids' term paper research at the elementary to middle school level as it does as a clip collection. It's certainly not an encyclopedia of ethology, but it is a lot more informative than some of Aris' other offerings. Because I've criticized the poverty of information on other Aris CDs, this one is a nice change that I hope indicates a trend.

The slide show would make one heck of a screen saver and any of the pictures would be nice wallpaper. In fact, Aris could do us and themselves a favor by developing such a function for use with their CDs.

As with all their MediaClips products, Aris addresses the buyer's probable wish to do more than just view the images. They supply all 100 files in 8-bit 320 x 240 and 640 x 480 .BMP and .PCX formats, 24-bit TIFF for use in high-res paint programs, and their audio in both .WAV and .VOC formats. They also extend on-the-box permission to reproduce up to 20 percent of the images sounds or videos royalty-free in print or digital publications so long as the artists and Aris Entertainment's copyright are duly credited.

Anyone wanting higher-resolution copies of pictures, movies, or sounds can contact Aris Entertainment, who will then put them in touch with the artists so they can negotiate rights.

What this collection will do is leave you wanting more, a characteristic that shouldn't hurt Aris' sales a bit.

This tiger can be copied to your own publication as clip art.

Aris Entertainment's Jets & Props

If you like coffee table books, you'll love this CD set. If you like such images in readily usable formats, you'll like it even more. All around, *Jets & Props* is a mini-air show for the desktop, an impressive item for airplane fanciers of any age from the budding aeronautical engineer to the average Joe who occasionally looks up and wonders what that plane might look like close up.

A guided tour of modern aircraft, a two-disc set of 200 excellent pictures and audio.

Jets & Props is a two-disc collection of 200 airplane photos that, while it may not knock your socks off, will let you know what the most common modern (and some not-so-modern) aircraft look like. Jet aircraft are on one disc, propeller-driven on the other. The images are good quality, viewable in either 320 x 240 small format (about 2" x 2" on a 14" monitor) or large format 640 x 480 (about 6" x 6"). There's detail enough for the aficionado and broad overview enough for the younger set. The kids will probably love the 25 PACO-format movies on each disc.

While the thumbnails are small, after just one or two run-throughs, they are clear enough to allow you to pick out a desired image pretty easily. Switching images in the large-size display does require clicking the next image and enlarge buttons in sequence, but it soon becomes second nature.

I would like it better if the Notes of Interest were a little more detailed. The short descriptions provided with each image are barely adequate to whet the information junkie's appetite. And, after all, isn't information what the typical CD buyer is after? That's not to say that there isn't a lot of data on the discs (pictures and animated imagery just love memory), but more textual information would add just a touch of

education to the typical youngster (or even middle-aged youngster's) fascination with airplanes.

Rating: ◉ ◉ 1/2

Publisher Name:
Aris Entertainment

Software Requirements:
MPC/Macintosh

Suggested Retail Price: **$39.95**

Jets & Props has information about airplanes of all types.

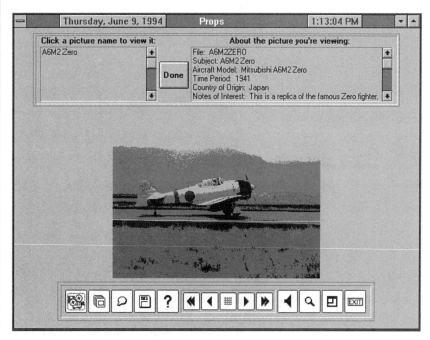

Artist In Residence: Fresco

Rating:

Publisher Name: **Xaos Tools**

Software Requirements:
Macintosh

Suggested Retail Price: **$79.95**

*F*resco is the first of Xaos (pronounced Chaos) Tools' Artist in Residence series. It contains 80 background images that can be used for illustrations or graphic designs. The textures are offered in three formats, strictly for Macintosh consumption:

- 9 x 12-inch, 300 dpi, 24-bit, maximum quality compress PICT files. Each of these consume 30MB on your hard disk; they're obviously suitable for heavy-duty imaging applications.

- 9 x 12-inch, 72 dpi, 24-bit PICT files. You can use these for small documents (no more than three inches in its longest dimension) or as "for position only" placeholders in documents. Replace these lower-resolution versions with the real thing at output time.

- 640 x 480, 8-bit (256 color) PICT files. These are of sufficient quality for display on computer or video screens.

Fresco *offers 80 creative textures at low- to high-resolutions for inclusion in your Photoshop or desktop publishing/presentation documents.*

An included browser lets you preview each of the textures, using QuickTime as the display engine. QuickTime can display each of the textures as a slide show that you can control yourself by clicking on the controls with the mouse button. Each screen of textures displays thumbnail versions of 16 different surfaces, ordered so the subtle textures are presented in the earlier screens, progressing to the more dramatic versions. If you want more detail than these swatches offer, you can also page through full-screen showings of the complete images, one texture at a time.

All the textures on this disc were created by internationally recognized painter George Lawson. They are much more interesting and beautiful than standard textures captured by scanning ordinary objects and surfaces. Lawson's textures have names like Agate and Current, and run the gamut from nature subjects to surfaces found only in the imagination.

Xaos Tools is the developer of Paint Alchemy, an add-on program for Adobe Photoshop that provides virtually limitless effects through the Plug-In menu of Photoshop or compatible programs like PixelPaint Professional 3 or Fractal Design Painter. *Fresco* adds new effects to your arsenal, and will be appreciated by any graphics professional looking for new images.

Clip-Art Cornucopeia CDROM

Clip-Art Cornucopeia comes with an extensive image collection. This CD-ROM contains 5,050 black-and-white clip-art images, amassing a total of 408MB. Ranging in subject from cartoon animals and wild west caricatures to space craft and school scenes, these clip-art images are perfect for any desktop publishing program that supports .PCX or .WPG files.

There are 5,000 royalty-free public domain clip-art images on one disc, ready for your desktop publications and WordPerfect documents.

The dual Windows Paintbrush and WordPerfect Graphics formats make the images extremely portable. The images were drawn from the .WPG clip art originally published on GEnie's WordPerfect Round Table during 1989-1993. All but a small portion of the 5,050 separate images in this collection have come from public domain sources. There are a few groups that were created by the round table's system operators, but by far the majority have come from the United States and state government publications and old books with expired copyrights. The images are the result of five years of intensive research through many hours spent in public and university libraries.

These clip-art images have been divided into 95 different categories. A few of the main categories include holidays, animals, nature items, scenery of places, instruments, literary images, cultural images, and birthday greetings. The main categories have been split into many different sub categories.

For example, if you wanted to browse through the holiday images, you would find the major holidays in subdirectories. The subdirectories include holidays such as Christmas, Easter, Thanksgiving, and St. Valentine's Day. Under these subdirectories you find quite a few clip-art images of each major holiday—not just one, but many to choose from. The animal clip-art images range from insects, horses, dogs, and cats to bears, dinosaurs, and many more.

The nature items like flowers, trees, clouds, suns, moons, and rain are also included. The images range from literary images such as Shakespeare, or can be a myth such as Sherlock Holmes. Fairy tale images for the children are also included. In addition, also with this CD-ROM are birthday greetings that almost have

Have you ever suspected your computer of doing this to you when you weren't looking?

Rating:

Publisher Name:
Walnut Creek CDROM

Software Requirement: **MPC**

Suggested Retail Price: **$29.95**

all the most common names to use. The scenery clip-art images are the best to view. It will take you hours just to go through these clip-art images.

Clip-Art Corncucopeia is a very handy tool to have, if you love to put images in any of your letters, reports, or any other desktop publications or WordPerfect documents. You can create your own post cards, birthday cards, signs, or banners with these images. This CD-ROM is thoroughly indexed and includes an easy-to-use file browser. The View program displays directories on the disc, and entering with one keystroke can bring you to the subdirectories. Then everything can be viewed from there. Only .PCX files can be viewed from this viewer, but the .WPG versions are identical.

Included with this disc is PKUNZIP, which can be used to unzip the graphics right onto your hard drive to use. One drawback of the extensive file collection of this CD-ROM is that just about all these images are of the past, but they are cute and quaint. A point to make for future CD-ROMs for clip-art images would be to include colored graphics and more modern clip art.

Clip Art Goliath

Rating: 1/2

Publisher Name:
Chestnut CD-ROM

Software Requirement: **MPC**

Suggested Retail Price: **$19.95**

This venerable CD-ROM includes 11,000 clip-art images consuming 150MB, many of very good quality, and you've probably seen this disc bundled or available separately at very low cost. We've found it at computer shows for as little as $7.50—just a few cents per image.

These are all black-and-white (non-grayscale) bitmapped images, generally in .PCX and TIFF format, with a few WordPerfect Graphics (.WPG) and other formats thrown in. You don't get any scalable outline drawings in Encapsulated PostScript (EPS), Adobe Illustrator (AI), or CorelDRAW! (CDR) formats. These are scanned-in images of paper hardcopies, plain and simple. The majority of them are done well enough that you'll be proud to place them in your desktop publications.

However, there are a few "gotchas" to be aware of.

First, the 11,743 files on the disc include many duplicates. Most images are provided in both .PCX and TIFF formats. Because virtually every image-capable application being sold today can use both .PCX and TIFF, there's not much reason to include both formats. We didn't check every

subdirectory to see if every file is duplicated, but it's probably safe to guess that there are roughly 4,000–5,000 unique images on this disc.

That would still be quite a lot, since many commercial clip-art collections on floppy disk provide you with only a few hundred unique images. Unfortunately, the quality of the images on *Clip Art Goliath* varies over a broad spectrum. All are bitmapped images, so the quality depends not only on the expertise of the artist, but the resolution at which they were scanned. You can't scale bitmapped images to a larger size easily without the individual pixels in the drawing becoming objectionably large (producing the infamous "jaggie" effect).

Many of the images have acceptable resolution—96 dpi and up. For example, we found a very nice giraffe image measuring 576 x 720 pixels that would reproduce extremely well. Other pictures, though, were coarse, low resolution disasters that were barely discernible as images when viewed up close. They'd be useful only for those putting together very basic documents using, say, a 9-pin dot matrix printer that couldn't

Turkey pictures can come in handy around Thanksgiving time.

do justice to the better images on this disc.

Probably one-third of the images in *Clip Art Goliath* can be termed very good; another third are acceptable, and the final third low resolution filler material.

This is strictly a disc of images, although there is a menu program that lets you browse through the names of the files on the disc, as well as several utility programs for viewing the images. Other utilities convert .PCX to TIFF files and back again, and perform various DOS tricks (such as displaying directories of file names side-by-side). We used U-Lead's ImagePals to produce a catalog of thumbnail images (Collage Complete for Windows will also work) that we could browse through.

Lots of duplicates, but lots of good quality .PCX and TIFF clip art on this 11,000-image disc of pictures, utilities, and more.

It's not too difficult to sort through the chaff to get to the wheat, and at the prices this disc is sold for, it's hard to beat. You'll probably need three or four clip-art discs in your collection, and you won't be ashamed to have this one available to fill in the gaps.

Corel Professional Photos CD-ROM

Corel Systems now markets a series of CD-ROMs in Kodak PhotoCD format, each with 100 royalty-free images (you can use them for just about anything except assembling your own clip-art collection), which you can use for ads, brochures, presentations, and multimedia applications.

Corel offers more than 140 PhotoCD-compatible CD-ROMs with 100 royalty-free images in a broad range of categories.

So far, Corel has 140 different titles available, covering everything from sunrises and sunsets to predators, waterfowl, butterflies, auto racing, bridges, and people. There are specialized discs, like Doors of San Francisco or Skiing in Switzerland, and those devoted to any destination you can think of, from rural Africa to Turkey. You find discs in this collection on Old Singapore, another on Cactus Flowers, and a pair of them with nothing but pictures of New Zealand. Commonly sold through mail order sources for as little as $29.95, these discs make a great addition to your imaging library.

The same disc works with either a PC or Macintosh, and includes CorelMOSAIC, Corel's visual file management tool that can be used to catalog not only PhotoCD files but PICTs, GIFs, TIFFs, Quicktime Movies, and Fonts. *Note:* This standalone version cannot be used with CorelDRAW! files. (Corel wants you to have a copy of CorelDRAW! in order to use its proprietary files.)

CorelMOSAIC shows small bitmapped representations, or thumbnails, of your files, so that you can browse through them visually rather than by file names—which usually don't tell you a lot about the image the file contains. Even Macintoshes, which allow "icon previews" of certain types of images, are better served by this tool.

You may use CorelMOSAIC to store graphics files from different drives and directories in collections called "libraries." Any files added to a library include pointers to their actual locations on disc, so you can find them quickly, and a single library can contain images that reside in many different places. Images can also be compressed and stored within the library file itself. There is a limit of about 1000 images per library.

CorelMOSAIC can update your libraries when you modify the preview image, notes, keywords, or the original image itself. The program can update automatically, or at your direction. The program can also be used to convert files from one format to another.

Rating: ● ● ●

Publisher Name: **Corel Systems**

Software Requirements:
MPC/Macintosh

Suggested Retail Price: **$49.95**

CorelMosaic lets you view images from libraries it stores on your hard disk.

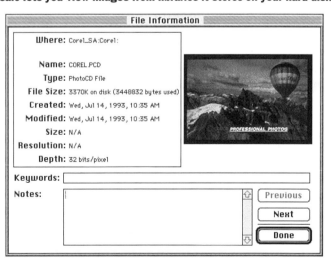

Do It On Your Desktop! CD

Rating:

Publisher Name:
Moon Valley Software

Software Requirements: **MPC**

Suggested Retail Price: **$39.95**

*D*o *It On Your Desktop!* will graphically enhance the Windows Program Manager shell in several ways. The program includes the Systometer that tells you a lot more about your computer setup than Microsoft Windows does. It has what they call a Mousometer. The Mousometer tracks the distance that your mouse moves across the desktop, while the *Do It On Your Desktop!* is active and Windows is running. It can be tracked in feet, yards, miles, meters, and kilometers.

The Keyometer tracks the amount of keystrokes, characters, or words per minute that are typed. With the resource meter, you can track computer uses in a couple of different areas, like system, GDI, and user resources. The Systometer includes a Time and Date display also. The Rameter is a memory meter. The memory meter display shows the amount of free memory that is available for windows.

The CPU meter tracks the CPU activity of your system as you use Windows and Windows programs, the meter mimics a heart monitor. The Diskometer displays the kilobyte and percent of free space available

on one or all of your hard disk drives. Also with the Diskometer, if you double-click the amount of free space on the meter, it will bring up the File Manager. This is a very handy feature.

You may display all of the meters at once or pick and choose the ones you want, also picking how many columns you want to display at one time is an option. Also you may opt to have the Systometer always visible regardless of what other windows programs you are running.

The Program Manager Enhancements include an Application finder, which will display all of your Windows applications in alphabetical order so you can find that one program you don't know where you put. You may arrange the Group Icons in a different way, all the icons can go to the left, right, top, or bottom, and they will also be arranged in alphabetical order like Windows

should have done.

Instead of having the boring name "Program Manager" at the top of your Windows screen, you can put your name or whatever you want to put there. The option for Look & Feel consists of changing the title bars, dialog boxes, and window borders. The title bar can be changed with styles like foot prints, geometrical shapes, etc. and finally the fonts of the title bars can be changed. The text can be given a 3D effect with raised letters and can be moved from left to right to center, the text can also be reversed.

Windows can now have custom frames, with options that include patterns, icons, or custom made frames to personalize your Windows. The best part of the Look & Feel is the Exploding windows option, Windows programs disappear and reappear in either a circular, rectangular, or rotating effect.

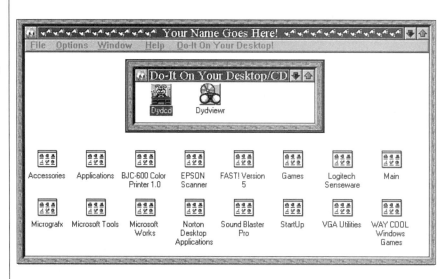

Create your own presentations with *Do It On Your Desktop*.

Fractal Frenzy

Lee H. Skinner, a New Mexico artist, had an epiphany of his own when he received an issue of *Scientific American* that featured the Mandelbrot set of fractal images on the cover. He was dumbfounded and flabbergasted that such richly decorative beauty could be generated by such a simple mathematical algorithm.

He has created this CD-ROM with more than 2000 fractal images in 1024 x 768 and 640 x 480 resolution and 256 colors. You can view the images with any IBM PC or Macintosh, by using the included viewer programs or your own image editor, such as Adobe Photoshop.

More than 2,000 startling images make Fractal Frenzy a joy to explore.

There's not much to this disc but the fractal images themselves. The main viewer is a primitive character-based browser that lets you explore each of the subdirectories on the disc. Highlight the name of one of the GIF-format files, press Enter, and the image is displayed on the screen. The 640 x 480 versions of the images can be used in your own desktop publications, as backgrounds, textures, or for other effects, without paying

royalties. The higher-res versions can be licensed for a small fee.

There are also viewers provided for Amigas, NeXT, and Sun Sparcstations equipped with CD-ROM drives. All the images were generated using the freeware program Fractint. Groups of images are also provided in low-res thumbnail format so that you can preview the pictures without loading them one by one into a viewer.

If you don't know what fractals are, the best place to start is imagine an aerial view of a coastline. From a high altitude, the coastline has many inlets, bays, and peninsulas. If you zoom in to a closer view, you'll find that smaller sections of coastline resemble the larger view, with their own smaller inlets, bays, and peninsulas. Fractals work the same way, with each little piece of

Rating:

Publisher Name:
Walnut Creek CDROM

Software Requirements:
MPC/Macintosh

Suggested Retail Price: **$29.95**

the image composed of smaller versions of the main shape, no matter how much you zoom in.

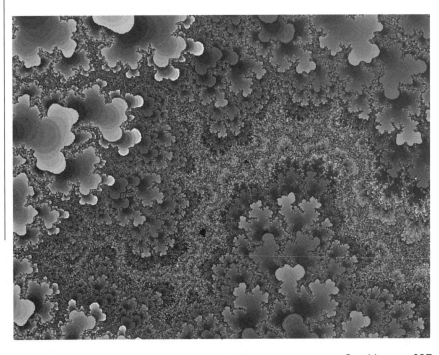

Images like this one fill *Fractal Frenzy*, and can be viewed on IBM PC, Macintosh, Amiga, and systems based on other platforms.

Kodak PhotoCD Access

Rating:

Publisher Name:
Eastman Kodak Company

Software Requirements:
MPC/Macintosh

Suggested Retail Price: **$39.95**

If you work with images and don't know about PhotoCD yet, you're in for a treat. Kodak's PhotoCD technology is a godsend for anyone who wants to store and use high resolution color images (plus other graphics, text, and sound), and this CD-ROM of sample images and software to access them makes an excellent preview for what's in store.

The disc itself is a picture of simplicity. It includes the PhotoCD Access software as an application, plus a group of PhotoCD image files stored in multiple resolutions. When you load Access, you can view a contact sheet of thumbnail images of each picture on the PhotoCD disc, view individual photos at full screen size, or perform simple manipulations like rotating, flipping, or mirroring the images. If you want to use the images in another application, Access lets you export them as PICT files (for the Macintosh), TIFF files (for use with PCs or Macs), or as Encapsulated PostScript, Level 2 files (without an embedded preview image).

What are PhotoCD images? The PhotoCD format is a special CD-ROM format that can be easily read by most XA-compatible drives (virtually all drives being sold today). Consumers can have their own photos placed on PhotoCDs for about $20 for a 24-exposure roll by their photofinisher. The PhotoCD can be viewed on your television by using a PhotoCD player that doubles as an audio CD player. Or, you can use the PhotoCD in your CD-ROM drive and computer.

Up to about 100 images can be stored on a single PhotoCD disc, at five different resolutions: 128 x 192 pixels, 256 x 384 pixels, 512 x 768 pixels, 1024 x 1536 pixels, and 2048 x 3072 pixels. You may choose a resolution suitable for your particular application: low res for screen display, higher res for desktop publishing or professional output. PhotoCD technology makes high resolution scanning available to the average person, your photofinisher must make the investment in the equipment, not you. Moreover, PhotoCDs make a great "shoebox" since the discs are less likely to be lost than color negatives or slides, and you can always have digital prints made from them by your photofinisher.

PhotoCD discs can also store other forms of graphics and sound, but at present the most common use is for pictures only. There are many professional applications for PhotoCD images, too. Clip-art discs have already appeared on the market. This disc can be your introduction to an exciting new technology. Note that many photo collections on PhotoCD are supplied with this Access software, so you may not have to purchase it separately.

Kodak's *PhotoCD Access* software lets you view low-resolution versions of images stored in three different formats on a PhotoCD disc.

Multimedia Kaleidosonics

N ow, here's a disc that defies categorization, and isn't even that easy to describe. I'll take a crack at doing both. If I told you that *Multimedia Kaleidosonics* is a computerized kaleidoscope with musical accompaniment, you'd form a picture in your mind that is wholly inadequate. Forget about the simple mirrored patterns of the child's toy, and think instead about a continuous series of 3D views, constantly changing and swirling with a New Age and light/fake jazz fusion soundtrack. That's *Multimedia Kaleidosonics*.

What programmer John W. Ratcliff has done is assemble a collection of high-speed graphics routines, and combine them with 48 minutes of original music composed and performed by Rob Wallace, along with some images of space, seashores, or mountains. You may choose one of these environments and then sit back and watch the show.

Swirling multimedia effects and sound make this disc a hypnotic attention-getter for those who like to play with graphics.

In its most basic mode, you don't have to do anything with *Multimedia Kaleidosonics* except watch it work its magic. When you get bored watching all the images squirm around on your screen, you'll notice that most of the keys on the keyboard (the alpha keys from A-Z, plus the function keys, for starters) have some effect on the renderings

you're viewing. You can place random two-dimensional moving or static objects on-screen by pressing some keys. Others add 3D objects that move and spin. Still other keys modify the textures applied to the objects (there are 20 different surfaces, from brick to fractals), or change the background picture. The effects are quite unpredictable, like those generated by a kaleidoscope.

My only tip-off that this wasn't a true Windows program came when Kaleidosonics at first refused to run, claiming there wasn't enough memory available. Since I had about 24MB of true RAM, and 87 percent of my system resources free, that meant I had a DOS program on my hands that couldn't get enough free DOS memory to load. The program worked fine (under Windows or otherwise) when I switched to another computer that allowed DOS programs 550K to work with.

Rating: ●●●

Publisher: **Masque Publishing**

Software Requirements: **MPC**

Suggested Retail Price: **$49.95**

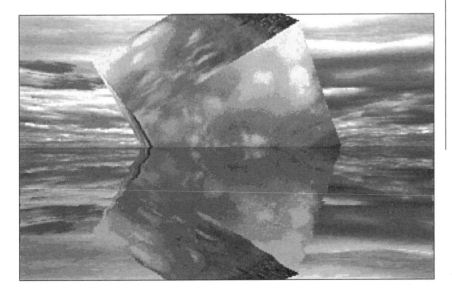

You might lose your bearings looking at abstract images like this one produced by *Multimedia Kaleidosonics*.

Multimedia Works

Rating:  1/2

Publisher Name:
Lenel Systems, International

Software Requirements: **MPC**

Suggested Retail Price: **$59.95**

If you are looking for a combination multimedia package, *Multimedia Works* by Lenel Systems, International should make you a very happy camper. The ability to add sound, stills, and movies to presentations will become more important as desktop presentations, CD-ROM drives, and other computerized capabilities become more pervasive. This disc gives you a head start into multimedia production with some solid tools and an excellent, easy-to-use interface.

Complete with a multimedia show builder, a multimedia player, a multimedia embedding application, and a Windows for Workgroups multimedia mailing feature, *Multimedia Works* affords you the opportunity to use your computer to make a presentation with a multiplicity of combination sounds, animations, and multimedia clips.

The Multimedia Show Builder allows the user to synchronize and arrange the sequence of various audio, animations, and videos. With the ease of point-and-click, the presenter can arrange or adjust the order in which the multimedia presentation is made.

Audio input can be timed with animations, video presentations can be sequenced to run immediately or after a specified pause. In fact, there appear to be few limitations to the arranging possibilities that make this a very nice package. With the background feature, you have the opportunity to place a color, or even a company logo, as the background setting to the multimedia presentation.

To play a show, simply run the show builder, and then click the Play option under Display, or hit F9.

The Multimedia Player plays audio, video, graphics, and animations, (from both digital and analog sources) in an equally friendly manner. Again the operator simply chooses the file he or she wants to run and clicks the mouse (or drags from the Windows File Manager), and the software selects the appropriate medium to run the application. Multiple files can be run sequentially as well.

This disc offers a full-featured multimedia tool kit for creating your own shows with sound, videos, and graphics.

Multimedia-Enabling Server permits the embedding of multimedia into other Windows-based applications using methods such as OLE (Object Linking and Embedding), command-line interface, and DDE (Dynamic Data Exchange). OLE (pronounced OLAY) lets you create objects, including videos, and insert them physically into other files, including word processing or desktop presentation documents. DDE lets you insert data created with another application and update its display inside other documents any time the original data file is modified.

Both these features are handy in the development of presentations that use, for instance, Windows-based word processors, such that after reading some portion of text, a multimedia presentation can be brought up from within the word processing application.

Multimedia Mail is available for those users using a Windows for Workgroups network. This feature permits the sending and reading of a multimedia message between networked computers. Note, however, the documentation is specific in that it is only available for networks using Windows for Workgroups. Still, there are a lot of users of this peer-to-peer network who will appreciate this feature.

Included with the CD-ROM are a host of sound bites, animations, and multimedia clips you can choose for your presentation. These can add a bit of spice to enliven the dullest show.

This package, with its ease of use, clear menus, and multiplicity of features, is sure to be a good package for both the beginner interested in multimedia and those with more sophisticated skills looking for a means to create their own multimedia presentation.

Pixar 128

ixar 128 is nothing more than a CD-ROM filled with 128 different textures that you can use with your image editor to produce great graphics images. You need an application that supports applying bitmapped files, like these, to an image as a texture, but everything from Adobe Photoshop to Fractal Design Painter can do that.

The files on this disc are in two formats: 512 x 512 pixel, 24-bit (16.7 million color) TIFF files, and 128 x 128 pixel, 8-bit (256-color) TIFF files. They include various wood, brick, metal, "siding," fabric, ground, skin, stone, roof, and floor textures. So what's so hard about putting together a disc like this, anyway? Just grab yourself a camera, take 128 different shots (not even four 36-exposure, 35mm rolls of film), and spend a day capturing them with a desktop scanner. Pretty easy, right?

Wrong. These textures are all completely *tileable*. That means their patterns are arranged in such a way that when you repeat a given image by placing it side-by-side with another copy, the edges merge perfectly to form a continuous, seamless image. That's relatively simple to do with random patterns and textures, such as rough concrete. It's not exceedingly difficult with patterns that repeat already, such as stripes or regular polka dots. But what do you do with things like paperclips or distinctive wood grains?

Pixar has taken the time to cunningly arrange their patterns to tile perfectly, no matter how simple or complex the subject matter. You can combine these to fill any area up to 4000 x 4000 pixels, or 13.3 x 13.3 inches at 300 dpi. A Photoshop-compatible Plug-In for both IBM PC and

Macintosh are included, so you can use Photoshop, Fractal Design Painter, PixelPaint Professional, PhotoStyler, or other programs to apply these textures.

This disc contains 128 useful textures that can be seamlessly tiled using your IBM PC or Macintosh image editing program.

The TIFF files on this CD-ROM can be used by any PC or Macintosh machine, as well as UNIX systems equipped with a CD-ROM drive. You get 15 different brick textures, 13 fabrics in tweeds, canvas, lace, and velvet swatches, a modest collection of fence, floor, and roofing textures, along with a good selection of animal skins. More than two dozen wood textures, from Australian rosewood to figured birdseye maple, are on the disc. You find dozens of ground and stone motifs, from street asphalt to red granite. Wall textures, louvered metals, and miscellaneous items like nails or iridescent ribbon fill out the collection.

Rating: ● ● ●

Publisher Name: **Pixar**

Software Requirements: **MPC/Macintosh**

Suggested Retail Price: **$99.00**

Pixar 128 has 128 different graphics textures to include in your images created with Photoshop or a compatible program.

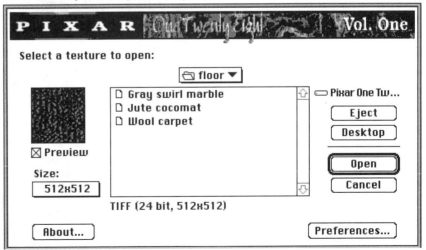

Pixar Showplace

Rating:

Publisher Name: **Pixar**

Software Requirements:
Macintosh

Suggested Retail Price:**$299.00**

Pixar Showplace has 3D ClipObject clip art that you can use to create scenes for output as PICT, TIFF, or EPS files.

Creating realistic 3D images can be time-consuming to create, even with sophisticated software. *Pixar Showplace* lets you create 3D scenes by importing predesigned "ClipObjects" from a library. You then coat them with some eye-catching surface appearances ("looks") and arrange the objects as you want within the scene. Then, save the image to your disk.

Pixar Showplace uses the same MacRenderMan technology used to create the magic ballroom scene in *Beauty and the Beast,* and to create effects for the cyborg in *Terminator 2* as well as dinosaurs in *Jurassic Park.* With this disc, you get 125 different ClipObjects. They run the gamut from basic shapes like cones, spheres, and cubes to furniture, trees, fruit, and other objects. You can generate stairs, unearthly terrains, and fireworks using plug-ins built into the program. The shape of any object can be modified easily.

Showplace provides 60 different "looks" ranging from wood grains to shiny metals and burnished gold tones. The disc also

includes Glimpse, an editing tool you can use to create your own texture maps from PICT and TIFF files. With Glimpse, you can produce looks from any of the textures on the *Pixar 128* disc, also reviewed in this chapter. Or, you can modify how existing textures appear on your objects.

The final step is to adjust the angle of view of the "camera" used to create your snapshot of the image. You can move the camera around in 3D space, and then snap a preview image. When you're finished creating a scene, it can be exported as a PICT, TIFF, or EPS file, and then used in your image editor, desktop publishing program, or presentation software.

Pixar Showplace and its sample ClipObject provide a novel sort of 3D clipart that you'll want to consider for your Macintosh imaging.

Showplace in wireframe mode shows only the outline of the object.

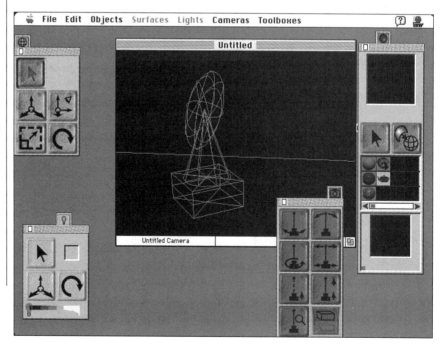

Additional CD-ROM Titles

Title: Amazing Moves: The Best in Bizarre Stunts & Feats
Suggested Retail Price: $99.95
Publisher: Jasmine Multimedia
Platform: MPC/Macintosh
Description: A compilation of clips, available for use royalty-free, of bizarre happenings involving humans and animals.

Title: Amazing Universe
Suggested Retail Price: $79.95
Publisher: Hopkins Technology
Platform: MPC/Macintosh
Description: Crisp images from space of the galaxies and more.

Title: America Remembered
Suggested Retail Price: $199.00
Publisher: Boraventures
Platform: MPC
Description: 500 images recorded from postcards of America.

Title: America
Suggested Retail Price: $69.95
Publisher: MediaRights
Platform: MPC/Macintosh
Description: Browse through 160 professional quality photos of America and Americans.

Title: Americana
Suggested Retail Price: $29.95
Publisher: Aris Entertainment
Platform: MPC/Macintosh
Description: The photography of Roger Goldingay's travels across America. A self-running slide show with 100 photos.

Title: Business Backgrounds
Suggested Retail Price: $39.95
Publisher: Aris Entertainment
Platform: MPC/Macintosh
Description: Clip art for backgrounds of your slide presentations.

Title: Calculated Beauty
Suggested Retail Price: $44.00
Publisher: Rocky Mountain Digital Peeks
Platform: Macintosh
Description: Fractal images as clip art.

Title: China Scenes
Suggested Retail Price: $79.00
Publisher: Golden Shine Books
Platform: MPC
Description: Photos of the people and locations of China for your desktop projects.

Title: ClickArt
Suggested Retail Price: $199.95
Publisher: T/Maker
Platform: MPC/Macintosh
Description: Largest and most professional collection of clip art for your desktop publishing projects, with several thousand images, and many different collections available.

Title: Clipart Heaven
Suggested Retail Price: $39.95
Publisher: Southeast Data Products
Platform: MPC
Description: Thousands of clipart images.

Title: Comstock Desktop Photography Vol. 1/2/3
Suggested Retail Price: $89.00-$199
Publisher: Comstock
Platform: MPC/Macintosh
Description: This large photography stock house has thousands of images you can use free for most purposes, or for a special licensing fee for advertising, products, or other big-ticket applications.

Title: Corel Artshow 3
Suggested Retail Price: $49.00
Publisher: Corel
Platform: MPC
Description: Winning images in Corel's annual Corel Draw illustration contest.

Title: Deep Voyage
Suggested Retail Price: $39.95
Publisher: Aris Entertainment
Platform: MPC/Macintosh
Description: Undersea images for your desktop publishing projects.

Title: Desktop Magic
Suggested Retail Price: $49.95
Publisher: Wizardware Multimedia
Platform: MPC
Description: Multimedia tool for business users.

Title: Don's Dingbats
Suggested Retail Price: $59.95
Publisher: Quanta
Platform: MPC
Description: Odds and ends and ornaments for desktop publishing.

Title: Earth Air Fire Water
Suggested Retail Price: $69.95
Publisher: MediaRights
Platform: MPC/Macintosh
Description: These clip art images are elementary, my dear Watson.

Title: Encyclopedia of Clipart
Suggested Retail Price: $69.95
Publisher: The Florida Lions Den
Platform: MPC
Description: 85 categories of clipart.

Title: Fantazia Fonts and Sounds
Suggested Retail Price: $49.95
Publisher: Fantazia Concepts
Platform: MPC
Description: WAV files and fonts you can use in your presentations.

Title: Font Elegance
Suggested Retail Price: $49.99
Publisher: Fantazia Concepts
Platform: MPC
Description: Stylize your documents to catch their attention. Some 3,000-plus fonts for easy use and access.

Title: Fontek Background & Borders
Suggested Retail Price: $349.00
Publisher: Letraset USA
Platform: MPC
Description: Six collections available on one CD-ROM. Borders, shapes, patterns, textures, and scenes in both high and low resolution.

Title: Fractal Ecstasy
Suggested Retail Price: $49.95
Publisher: Cambrix
Platform: MPC
Description: Thousands of fractal images for your projects as backgrounds or textures.

Title: Fresh Arte
Suggested Retail Price: $99.95
Publisher: Quanta
Platform: MPC/Macintosh

Description: New clip art you'll want for your desktop publishing.

Title: Full Bloom
Suggested Retail Price: $39.95
Publisher: Aris Entertainment
Platform: MPC/Macintosh
Description: Flower photos for desktop publishing.

Title: GIFs Galore
Suggested Retail Price: $39.95
Publisher: Walnut Creek
Platform: MPC/Macintosh
Description: Images numbering 5,000 on all subjects in full color.

Title: Incredible 2000 Image Pak
Suggested Retail Price: $79.95
Publisher: T/Maker
Platform: MPC/Macintosh
Description: Value-priced set of 2000 clip art images in EPS and other formats.

Title: Island Designs
Suggested Retail Price: $39.95
Publisher: Aris Entertainment
Platform: MPC/Macintosh
Description: South Pacific images for desktop publishing.

Title: Kodak Arrange-It
Suggested Retail Price: $279.95
Publisher: Kodak
Platform: Macintosh
Description: Software for cataloging and arranging your PhotoCD images.

Title: Kodak Create-It
Suggested Retail Price: $169.95
Publisher: Kodak
Platform: Macintosh
Description: Create your own presentations using PhotoCD images.

Title: Mediasource: Corporate/Industrial
Suggested Retail Price: $59.95
Publisher: Applied Optical Media Corp.

Platform: MPC
Description: Lots of images in corporate or industrial settings.

Title: Mediasource: General Topics Vol. 1 and 2
Suggested Retail Price: $59.95
Publisher: Applied Optical Media Corp.
Platform: MPC
Description: General subjects clip art.

Title: Mediasource: Historical
Suggested Retail Price: $59.95
Publisher: Applied Optical Media Corp.
Platform: MPC/Macintosh
Description: Clip art with historical themes.

Title: Mediasource: Lifestyles
Suggested Retail Price: $59.95
Publisher: Applied Optical Media Corp.
Platform: MPC
Description: Clipart picturing active lifestyles, sports, etc.

Title: Mediasource: Medicine & Health Care
Suggested Retail Price: $59.95
Publisher: Applied Optical Media Corp.
Platform: MPC

Title: Mediasource: Sights & Sounds
Suggested Retail Price: $19.95
Publisher: Applied Optical Media Corp.
Platform: MPC/Macintosh
Description: Music and sounds clip art.

Title: Mediasource: Natural Sciences
Suggested Retail Price: $59.95
Publisher: Applied Optical Media Corp.
Platform: MPC/Macintosh
Description: Nature and science-based clipart.

Title: Money, Money, Money!
Suggested Retail Price: $39.95
Publisher: Aris Entertainment
Platform: MPC/Macintosh

Description: Finally! Financial clip art! Scrooge McDuck would love this one.

Title: New York, NY
Suggested Retail Price: $29.95
Publisher: Aris
Platform: MPC/Macintosh
Description: Roger Goldingay discovers New York City. Royalty-free photos to enhance any presentation.

Title: Ocean Imagery
Suggested Retail Price: $79.95
Publisher: Gazelle Technologies, Inc.
Platform: MPC/Macintosh
Description: Collection of photos covering water sports, ocean views, and landscapes.

Title: Ocean Magic
Suggested Retail Price: $79.95
Publisher: Gazelle Technologies, Inc.
Platform: MPC/Macintosh
Description: Underwater images as clipart.

Title: People At Leisure
Suggested Retail Price: $129.95
Publisher: Gazelle Technologies, Inc.
Platform: MPC/Macintosh
Description: Over 200 high-quality photos of sporting and water activities, health and fitness, babies, kids, seniors, etc.

Title: Perfect Presentations ClipMedia 3
Suggested Retail Price: $195.00
Publisher: Macromedia
Platform: MPC/Macintosh
Description: Clip art categories of Nature, Americana, Environment, Video Backgrounds, and more.

Title: Pop and Politics
Suggested Retail Price: $79.95
Publisher: TechScan
Platform: MPC/Macintosh
Description: World renowned musical and political figures at work and relaxing.

Title: Presentation Magic
Suggested Retail Price: $49.95
Publisher: Wizardware Multimedia
Platform: MPC
Description: More tools for your multimedia presentations.

Title: Publique Art
Suggested Retail Price: $99.00
Publisher: Quanta Press
Platform: MPC/Macintosh
Description: Over 2500 clipart images.

Title: Scenic and Architecture
Suggested Retail Price: $49.95
Publisher: CD-ROM Galleries
Platform: Macintosh
Description: Scenic photos and buildings for your desktop publications.

Title: Scenic and Nature II
Suggested Retail Price: $49.95
Publisher: CD-ROM Galleries
Platform: Macintosh
Description: More scenic photos and nature.

Title: Swimsuit, V.1
Suggested Retail Price: $129.95
Publisher: Gazelle Technologies, Inc.
Platform: MPC/Macintosh
Description: Over 200 models in swimwear.

Title: The Balthis Collection
Suggested Retail Price: $39.95
Publisher: Dana Publishing
Platform: MPC/Macintosh
Description: Clipart photography from the famed photographer.

Title: The Clipart Warehouse
Suggested Retail Price: $39.95
Publisher: Chestnut
Platform: MPC
Description: 10,000 clips of everything imaginable.

Title: The TOTO Textures Collection
Suggested Retail Price: $189.00
Publisher: Toto Computer Graphics
Platform: Macintosh
Description: Textures for your graphics projects and presentations.

Title: Too Many Typefonts
Suggested Retail Price: $29.95
Publisher: Chestnut Software
Platform: MPC
Description: Large collection of shareware & freeware fonts.

Title: Travel Adventure
Suggested Retail Price: $39.95
Publisher: Walnut Creek
Platform: MPC
Description: Travel pictures you can use as clip art in your publications.

Title: Tropical Rainforest
Suggested Retail Price: $39.95
Publisher: Aris Entertainment
Platform: MPC/Macintosh
Description: Amazon images of animal and plant life, and scenics, for desktop publications.

Title: Type Fest
Suggested Retail Price: $69.95
Publisher: EBook
Platform: MPC/Macintosh
Description: Hundreds of fonts for your documents.

Title: Type Treasury
Suggested Retail Price: $69.00
Publisher: Bitstream Inc.
Platform: Macintosh
Description: More fonts.

Title: Type Treats
Suggested Retail Price: $90.00
Publisher: Raynbow Software
Platform: MPC/Macintosh
Description: Still more fonts.

Title: Typecase
Suggested Retail Price: $49.95
Publisher: SWFTE International Ltd.
Platform: MPC
Description: An excellent collection of fonts, supplied with one of the best browser/installers ever.

Title: Typecase II
Suggested Retail Price: $49.95
Publisher: SWFTE International Ltd.
Platform: MPC
Description: A second collection of fonts in TrueType format.

Title: Visual Concepts Vol. 1: Backgrounds
Suggested Retail Price: $49.95
Publisher: Northern Lights Software
Platform: MPC/Macintosh
Description: Royalty-free high quality backdrops.

Title: Wild Places
Suggested Retail Price: $39.95
Publisher: Aris Entertainment
Platform: MPC/Macintosh
Description: Wilds of nature in clip art form.

Title: Wildlife Babies
Suggested Retail Price: $29.98
Publisher: Corel
Platform: MPC/Macintosh
Description: Royalty Free, over 100 animal young for screen savers or stock photos.

Title: Wild, Wacky and Weird
Suggested Retail Price: $79.98, MPI Multimedia
Platform: MPC/Macintosh
Description: Strange moving images, sound, and photos for entertainment for in-house purposes.

Title: Wrapture Reels One: Animated Textures
Suggested Retail Price: $179.95

Publisher: Form & Function
Platform: Macintosh
Description: Textures for your presentations—and they move!

Title: Wraptures One
Suggested Retail Price: $95.00
Publisher: Form & Function
Platform: Macintosh
Description: More textures for presentations.

Title: Wraptures Two
Suggested Retail Price: $129.00
Publisher: Form & Function
Platform: Macintosh
Description: Another textures collection for graphics applications.

Title: Zen and the Art of Resource Editing
Suggested Retail Price: $15.00
Publisher: BMUG, Inc.
Platform: Macintosh
Description: Seemingly unlimited source of icons, patterns, sound, fonts and more. Learn to do tweaking with ResEdit and other hip things to your next desktop project.

Chapter 12

Shareware

Shareware discs have to be among the best bargains among any CD-ROMs you can buy. Most have from hundreds to thousands of ready-to-run applications, fonts, utilities, clip art, and other files. Many are public domain or freeware, while others are shareware that you can try out for a specified period of time. If you continue using the product after you've evaluated it, you should send a small registration fee to the author, usually $5 to $30.

These discs sell for very low prices because the cost to produce them is virtually nil. Anyone and everyone can collect programs from a wide variety of sources—including other shareware CD-ROMs—and distribute them. Because it can cost less than $1 to produce a CD-ROM with no fancy packaging, the vendor can sell them to a distributor for $5, who can then peddle them to consumers like yourself for $10, or arrange for retail sale at $19.95 or less.

Everyone benefits. You get to try out great software for almost nothing. Authors love having their work widely disseminated. Disc vendors have an inexpensive product to sell. Drive vendors see all that extra software as another reason you should buy their drive.

Shareware CD-ROMs fall into several neat categories. First, there are collections of many different categories of programs, all on a single disc. In the Mac world, one of the best is *Shareware Breakthrough*. This is one of the best shareware discs on the market. The vendor doesn't just throw shareware at you and leave you hanging. The disc is furnished with a snazzy shell that lets you browse through the offerings, read about the files in the categories that most interest you, and then launch and run programs for a test drive.

In the PC world, some of the best discs are those flying under the NightOwl banner, a whole series of great discs from Walnut Creek (one of the more professional shareware disc vendors around), and Quantum Axcess's line.

Other shareware discs zero in on a specific type of program, utility, or file. These include *Too Many Typefonts*, *QRZ Ham Radio*, *Hobbes OS/2*, and *Project Gutenberg*. There are discs of clip art, those full of games, and some dedicated to Microsoft Windows, UNIX, or other operating systems. The Association of Shareware Professionals also puts out a disc showcasing its members' wares.

Shareware discs are sometimes hard to find, because there aren't the same distribution channels found for discs with "retail" products on them. Check out smaller computer stores, Hamfests, and computer flea markets. There's a computer swap meet at a local Tadmore Shrine temple near me every month and recently the tables seem to be dominated by folks selling CD-ROMs at very low prices. Probably half of these are shareware discs, with many of the rest being "unbundled" OEM versions of commercial discs.

Read over the reviews and listings in this chapter, and then go find yourself some shareware CDs. And remember, if you like a program on the disc and want to continue using it, be sure and send the author the modest registration fee asked.

CICA for Windows

The Center for Innovative Computing Applications, eh? Well, they're innovative in one way, at least, giving you an impressive 613MB worth of Windows programs on a single CD-ROM. This disc consists entirely of Windows freeware and shareware, with bug fixes, patches, and quite a lot of Microsoft's development information thrown in. Also included are discussions recorded from various on line forums. Too bad they couldn't have included a better browser to sort out all these files.

There are icon files, mouse drivers and cursor modifiers, games, image viewers and manipulators, screen savers and modules, typing tutors, macros for word processors, sounds, pictures, compilers, program development information, collections of Windows journals and other publications, utilities, and who knows what all else. Walnut Creek must just say, "Include 'em all! Let our customers sort 'em out!" If you like shareware and run Windows, you'll like that attitude and like this CD.

Virtually everything available in shareware and freeware for Microsoft Windows as of November, 1993 is included on this disc, packed to the brim with 600MB of high-quality applications, utilities, and text files.

Walnut Creek has collected virtually everything available for Windows at the time this disc was published, in November, 1993. There is enough here to keep the most dyed-in-the-wool Windows junkie happy for a very long time. Just looking over and evaluating the more than 3,000 files crammed onto this CD could keep one busy.

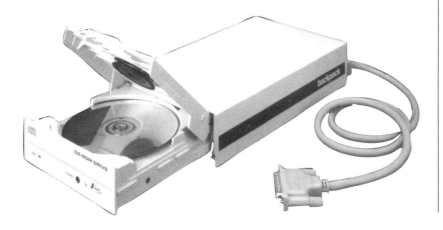

```
┌─────────────────────────────────────────────────────────────────────┐
│ ─              Gander - N:\dirs.txt                          ▼ ▲      │
├─────────────────────────────────────────────────────────────────────┤
│ File  Edit  Display  Search  Filters  Help                           │
├─────────────────────────────────────────────────────────────────────┤
│ \win3\access            MS Access utilities                        ▲ │
│ \win3\demo              Demo Windows Files                          █ │
│ \win3\desktop           Desktop Apps, Screen, Image, and BitMap Files│
│ \win3\drivers\printer   Printer Drivers for Windows                  │
│ \win3\drivers\video     Video Files, Drivers for Windows             │
│ \win3\excel             Excel spreadsheet utilities                  │
│ \win3\fonts             Windows Font Files                           │
│ \win3\fonts\atm         Windows ATM Font Files                       │
│ \win3\fonts\truetype    TrueType Font Files                          │
│ \win3\games             Windows Games                                │
│ \win3\icons             Windows Icon Files                           │
│ \win3\misc              Miscellaneous Windows Files                  │
│ \win3\nt                Windows NT Files                             │
│ \win3\pagemkr           Pagemaker files                              │
│ \win3\patches           Patches and bug fixes                       │
│ \win3\patches\symantec  Patches and bug fixes                       │
│ \win3\pdoxwin           Paradox for Windows Files                    │
│ \win3\programr          Windows Programming Files                    │
│ \win3\programr\bcpp      Borland C++ Windows Programming             │
│ \win3\programr\listings  Program Listings from Publications          │
│ \win3\programr\tp        Turbo Pascal Programming Files              │
│ \win3\programr\vbasic    VisualBasic (VB) Files                      │
│ \win3\programr\vbasic\vblib  VisualBasic (VB) Files                  │
│ \win3\sdl               MS (SDL) Supplemental Development Libraries  │
│ \win3\sounds            Windows Sound Files and Utilities            │
│ \win3\toolbook          Asymetrix ToolBook Applications              │
│ \win3\util              Windows Utilities Files                      │
│ \win3\winsock           Windows Sockets                              │
│ \win3\winword           MicroSoft Word for Windows (WfW)             │
│ \win3\wpwin             WordPerfect for Windows Files                │
│ \win3\wrk               MicroSoft Windows 3.1 Resource Kit (WRK)   ▼ │
└─────────────────────────────────────────────────────────────────────┘
```

CICA comes with only a primitive browser program that displays only the file names on the disc.

There are 350 great games, ranging from classics like AFORCE to new gems such as Warheads for Windows. Desktop publishers will bask in the glow of 200 high quality fonts, in both TrueType and Adobe Type 1 formats. Thousands of icons are available for the inveterate customizer, along with diagnostics software, backup/restore programs, and data conversion utilities.

There's a section of the disc dedicated to electronic bulletin board system (BBS) operators, who are likely to be heavy users of this disc.

The interface is bare-bones skeletal but works just fine for the experienced shareware explorer (less experienced hands will find it extremely frustrating). Just load the disc, log to your CD-ROM drive, type go, and watch as the installation program sets up a CICA directory on your hard disk. From then on, all that's necessary is to run VIEW.EXE from File Manager.

VIEW is not a Windows-based program (which seems odd for a disc of Windows shareware), but it works just fine. Obviously, at 600MB-plus of useful material, the vendor has devoted all available space to software and and related files, and very little to the interface itself.

To use VIEW, choose a subdirectory from the list presented and select the individual program you want to examine more closely by using the cursor arrow keys. Then press Return. That brings up a dialog box that lets you specify the subdirectory you want your files unzipped (decompressed) to. The README files contain good instructions for installing the files you extract to run under Windows.

Because you're pretty much on your own in exploring this disc, the arrangement of the files is crucial. Fortunately, the directory structure appears pretty well thought out. It's not arranged in neat aisles like a

department store with all the screen savers here and all the GIF files there, but, with the effort of taking a note or two, finding things isn't difficult. There are very few duplications; most of this is all new, interesting shareware fodder to appease your hunger to try out new software.

Don't be surprised if Walnut Creek publishes another edition of Windows shareware sometime soon. There was a file in CICA's \win3 directory labeled "last100uploads." Somebody out there is writing a lot of Windows applications and utilities! Incidentally, Walnut Creek notes that this CD was made with the permission but not the endorsement of CICA and that no public funds were used in producing it.

Until the next edition comes out, this disc will reign as the CD-ROM to top for Windows shareware in terms of quality and quantity.

QRZ Ham Radio CD-ROM
for DOS and Windows

Rating:

Publisher Name:
Walnut Creek CDROM

Software Requirements: MPC

Suggested Retail Price:
$39.95

Shareware or not, there's lots of good things on this disc for any amateur radio operator. This 500MB-plus CD-ROM contains a Ham Radio Callbook that occupies almost half the disc and is the main appeal. The Callbook covers the U.S. and with this version added the Canadian call signs so that you can also search the VE calls.

The disc runs under UNIX, DOS, or Microsoft Windows. The Windows mode appears to be the mode of choice and much effort and thought have gone into the excellent menu-driven interface. The search and retrieval of calls and associated data are fast. The output can be in comma-delimited format for use with other databases, address label format for printing address labels, and full information format, which contains the call letters of the Ham operator, first and last name, address, date of license issuance, and date of birth, plus, in some cases, a previous call sign.

The DOS interface is command-line driven (a menu interface for use with DOS

would be a good addition in future releases). Using the Callbook or the rest of the CD does not require any installation or setup. It runs directly from DOS by typing QRZ at the DOS prompt or from Windows by typing QRZWIN.EXE. Included is an icon if you want to create your own program item in Windows. The Callbook allows searching by call letters, the call suffix, or name, street, state, and Zip.

Apart from the Callbook, a directory called (\win3) has various hypertext files that are accessible in Windows from the Windows help file menu. These hypertext files allow access to many of the other text files on the disc. Some of the text files accessible in this manner are files on rules, topics about antennas, and technical and

modification information on various models of radios, scanners, and transceivers. (Also included are a number of FCC exam questions regarding the Novice, Technician, General, Advanced, and Extra Class licenses.)

There are quite a few text files that are not in hypertext format yet, such as the indexes of past QST and QEX articles and other Ham Radio journals.

Along with the Ham Radio programs, there is a multitude of other Ham Radio related information such as packet radio. An assortment of Sound Blaster compatible (.WAV) file recordings of popular digital data transmissions such as RTTY, Packet, and AMTOR. These files allow you to verify the operation of nearly any TNC data receiving terminal.

You can keep and access ham log files using the great Windows program included on the *QRZ* disc.

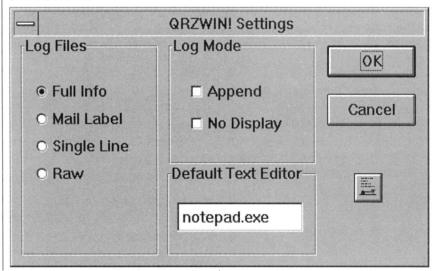

This shareware/ freeware/public domain disc includes useful information for ham operators looking for a callbook and associated programs of interest to radio amateurs.

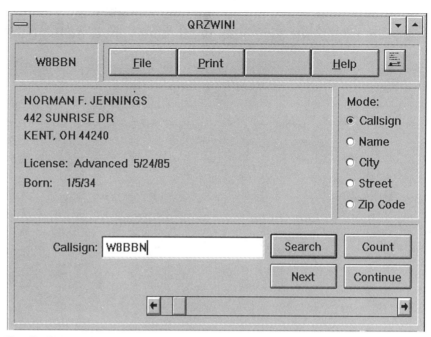

Ham Radio operators will love the Callbook included in *QRZ*.

A file called CDF.EXE in the main directory locates files on the CD. However, it requires a SET statement in your AUTOEXEC.BAT file in order to know where to find the program.

Most of the information contained on the disc is in a multitude of subdirectories, and most have a file called 00_index.txt that briefly describes the files in the related directory. This CD-ROM should be in the library of any Ham operator that uses a callbook or needs to print mailing labels for clubs, hamfests, and so on. Considering all the information on this CD-ROM, it is a very desirable tool for any Ham Radio Operator or anyone else interested in Ham Radio.

Shareware Breakthrough

Rating: ⊙ ⊙ ⊙ ⊙

Publisher Name:
Beachware

Software Requirements:
Macintosh

Suggested Retail Price:
$12.95

*S*hareware Breakthrough collects virtually all the best shareware available for the Macintosh, almost 600MB of it in 12,000 files on a single CD-ROM. You'll find exciting games, cogent educational programs, useful DPT software, dazzling multimedia, essential utilities, and applications that will enhance your productivity.

Access to all this is easy, thanks to a powerful Browser program that lets you page through all the software on the disc, read descriptions of the files, and run many of the programs.

We're glad this disc is so good, because shareware discs for the Macintosh have always been relatively rare, compared to their PC counterparts, mostly because of the much smaller installed base of Macintosh systems. Indeed, the amount of shareware produced for Macs is significantly smaller, although if you know where to look—CompuServe and America Online are good sources—there is plenty to be found.

The smaller number of available Macs, dearth of local bulletin board services (BBSs) serving the Mac community, and reduced

numbers of shareware authors seeking to serve this tiny market are all to blame. I spoke in several panels at the leading shareware seminar for vendors the last two years, and found few Mac mavens in attendance. Because there are virtually no millionaire Mac shareware authors (but lots of them in the PC world), Macintosh shareware offerings tend to come from smaller (usually one-person) operations and are more limited in scope.

> *All the best Macintosh shareware is here on this disc, including 300 games, hundreds of fonts, and valuable business/ productivity boosters.*

But that doesn't mean there isn't some good stuff here. First, the Browser helps you find files that might interest you, offering descriptions, file size, version, shareware info, artwork, or font samples. You may then use this shell to copy your favorite files and folders to your hard drive, or launch programs directly from the CD-ROM. The Browser has Mark buttons that can be used

to collect sets of files for copying.

Most of the files on this disc are shareware, requiring a registration fee if you continue to use the program. Others are in the public domain and can be used however you like, without sending in any fees. A few are categorized as freeware, which means you can use the current version at no charge. Freeware programs are sometimes upgraded to shareware, or even commercial status. Red Ryder, an early telecommunications program, is now sold commercially as White Knight.

While most of the programs are applications you can launch by double-clicking them, there are also fonts, desk accessories, system extensions, INITs, and CDEVs, and a collection of HyperCard stacks (you must have HyperCard or HyperCard Player installed to run them).

Here are some of the fields and icons that appear in the Browser:

Shareware Info. This field contains the author and his or her suggested shareware fee when applicable. We tried to gather this info from every program and file, but there are over 12,000 files on this disc and a few were probably missed.

Program Icon. This is the icon for the current program or file. If you click this icon, the program automatically launches, if you are viewing a program. If you are looking at a file, such as an Excel spreadsheet, and you click the icon, it will try to open the file with Excel. Note that the Browser may ask you where on your hard drive Excel is located if you try to open an Excel sheet.

Program/File List. This is an alphabetical listing by section of all the programs or files

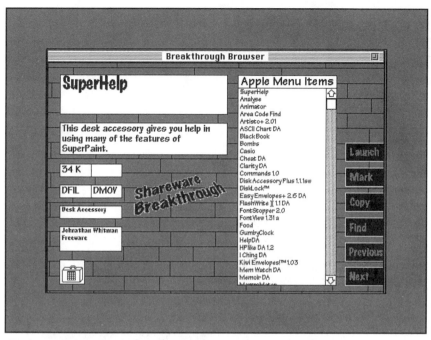

Shareware Breakthrough has virtually all the best Macintosh shareware in a single package.

Attax is one of the many games on the Shareware Breakthrough disc.

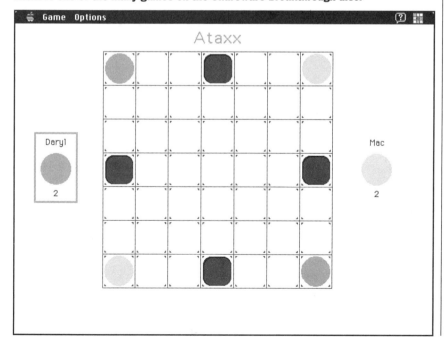

in the current section. Click a file name to view more specific information about the file. Choose a different listing by selecting a new category from the Section menu. Notice that the sequence of each item in Browser may not correspond to the alphabetical listing for some of the sections. This is because some sections are organized by subsection instead of alphabetical order. For example, if you go to the MacPaint Clipart section and start pressing the Next button, you will notice that the file names are not in alphabetical order. This is because they are grouped into related subsections such as Animals, People, Borders, and so on. This organization is similar to the folders found in the Finder.

Look at all you get on this disc:

More than 300 games, organized into adventure, arcade, card, strategy, board, and other categories; four dozen practical jokes; 350 educational programs for primary through college students; hundreds of fonts (almost 600 TrueType and Type 1 varieties); some 1,300 Encapsulated PostScript graphics, 150 GIFs, 300 PICT, and Startup Screens; and a collection of 1,200 low-resolution MacPaint files.

Business users will find 250 or more personal and business productivity programs from calculators to spreadsheets and databases. Another 250 files are utility programs that can check for viruses, act as handy desk accessories, or modify your system as extensions. HyperCard programmers will find XCMDs and XFCNS (extended commands and functions) they can merge into their own stacks. Finally, there are QuickTime movies you can view and enjoy.

This is virtually the only Macintosh shareware disc you need—for now. Shareware changes monthly with updates, upgrades, bug fixes, maintenance releases, and new products. Plan on purchasing the next edition of this disc every six months or so, and you'll stay on top of the burgeoning Macintosh shareware arena.

Way Cool Games for Windows

Rating: ◉ ◉ ◉ ◉

Publisher Name:
Quantum Axcess

Software Requirements: **MPC**

Suggested Retail Price:
$19.95

Quantum Axcess is setting new standards of quality for shareware discs like *Way Cool Games for Windows*. Instead of giving you nothing more than a disc full of programs with, perhaps, a browser to let you search through file names and descriptions, Quantum Axcess is integrating their offering with slick launcher/shells you can use to search through, read about, and then try out key programs.

That's a great benefit for busy shareware browsers. We handed this disc to a six-year-old tester with the instructions, "Play as many games as you can without bothering us; if you can't figure out how to play it, go on to something else." Two hours later he reported back that this disc is Way Cool, indeed.

The *Way Cool* CD is a Games for Windows CD. It has over 300 programs, such as card games, arcade games, desktop games, and puzzle games. Because you can play most of the games right from the CD, you don't have to take up a lot of your hard drive space. It also has a sound-enabled browser. The CD installs easily and only takes about 2MB on the hard drive.

When the shell program first opens, you see and hear an elevator; this will be the only time you're pestered to register the programs on the CD. On the main menu you are asked "Would you like to play a game?" There are six buttons; five will take you to selected games under categories such as cards, arcade, puzzles.

Way Cool Games for Windows *has hundreds of great games for the Microsoft graphical user interface.*

For each game highlighted on the scrolling list, the right side of the screen gives you information on that particular game, including the name of the author, the price, and a brief description of the program.

You also have the option of running the program from the CD or installing it to your hard drive. If you choose Install, you will be asked where to install the game and reminded to register it. Way Cool will then install the game and place the game's icon in the Way Cool Windows Games Group in the Program Manager.

The interface for *Way Cool Games for Windows* looks like an elevator!

This disc will entertain and intrigue you for hours. There are 38 different card games for you to learn and enjoy, including Black Jack, Poker, Cribbage, Bridge, and Solitaire. There are also 78 arcade games to test your skills, including Tetris type games, Missile Attack, space games, and one that asks you to find Elvis in space. You find 35 desktop games that infect your screen with crawling worms, swimming fish, ghosts, and a cat that chases your mouse. There are running horses, a gun fight, and you can even have your very own Windows Lava Lamp.

The puzzle games include Concentration-type games, Mahjongg, crosswords, Word Hunt, sliding puzzles, and jigsaw puzzles that you can add your own bitmaps to. They have also included other games like I.Q. tests, Periodic Tables, Skiing, and Planetariums.

There just are too many things to list. Most of the games are sound card compatible, and some do require a 256 color video graphics card. The CD also includes a compressed zip file for each one of the games. The *Way Cool Games for Windows* CD will be a fine addition to anybody's Windows and CD Collection.

The programs on this CD are shareware, public domain, or freeware. With the shareware games, you are free to play the games for a limited time. Then, if you are satisfied and continue using a game, you are required to pay and register individual games with their respective authors. Other games are public domain and freeware, which you are free to use as long as you want with no registration fee.

When you reach your floor, you can select from many different categories of games, and launch them directly from this browser.

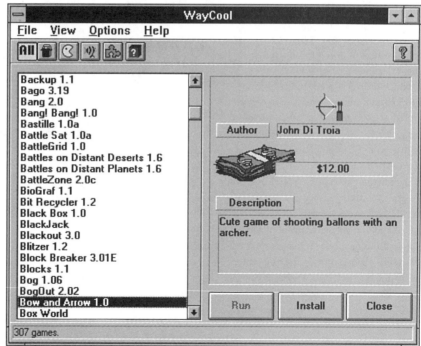

The ASP Advantage

*T*he *ASP Advantage* (ASP stands for Association of Shareware Professionals) CD is one more addition to the large group of CDs offering shareware. It is, however, unique in several ways.

First, it's endorsed by the largest group representing authors of commercial shareware products. That means, every product meets ASP standards, which can be important for you, the shareware user. ASP doesn't endorse the distribution of "crippleware," which is a software product with a major function disabled. ASP shareware is a full version of the product. The only thing missing is the registration fee and your unfettered conscience if you decide to continue using it.

ASP has other firm standards that it applies to its members. While you may not like every product on this disc, you can be assured that none of it is a waste of your time. There's no junk here, even if the selection isn't as broad as you might like.

On the plus side, the menu systems (which can be run from both DOS and Windows) are very easy to use, and are the nicest I have seen for easy selection of files. Such things as a text search command, tag option, and very detailed file descriptions make for instant ease of use.

> *An easy-to-use menu system in this shareware disc offers simple access to a wide selection of quality shareware.*

The area where you stand to be the most disappointed is definitely in selection. While the CD covers a wide range of interests from philosophy to action games, you will find your selection always somewhat limited. Of course, because this disc represents only output from ASP members, you wouldn't expect to find everything under the sun here, anyway. Quality level is above average, though, on just about all the programs available.

If you are a fan of the ASP's work, this is a must have. And if you are about to buy your first shareware CD, you could make a worse choice. Given the modest cost of shareware discs in general, it doesn't hurt to have several of these around, even if some of their contents overlap. The ASP disc is updated periodically, so you always can look forward to a new one in a few months.

GamePack CD

You can pay big bucks to download the very best IBM PC-based shareware games from an information service like CompuServe or America Online. Many of these games are over a megabyte in size. You can also download them from a local electronic bulletin board system (BBS) and pay little or nothing for your connect time. However, your computer may be tied up for a couple hours while your modem tediously transfers the file to your computer.

GamePack CD *has 40 of the best VGA-based games for IBM PCs in one package with a handy browser/installer program included.*

Save yourself some trouble and pick up this CD-ROM, *GamePack CD: 40 Best VGA Games.* If these aren't the 40 best shareware games available for the IBM PC, I don't know what are. You'll find the nationwide sensation DOOM (and recent Ziff-Davis shareware of the year winner) on the disc, along with other "virtual reality" 3D games like Castle Wolfenstein and Blake Stone. Popular "Duke Nukem"-style shoot 'em ups like Halloween Harry, Monster Bash, and old Duke himself (including the latest version) are also here.

Popular adventure titles like Jill of the Jungle, Jetpack, and Commander Keen: Goodbye Galaxy share disc space with first-rate educational programs (Word Rescue, Math Rescue) and computer implementations of board game classics, such as Chinese Checkers, Cyrus Chess, and PC-Gammon.

Trust me, these are all great games. I own registered versions of six of these (that is, I liked them well enough to send actual cash money—several hundred dollars worth, overall—to the vendor to register and receive additional episodes), and have played most of the others. Still, I liked being able to find a few new gems in once place and readily installable from the CD-ROM.

A shell program installs itself on your hard disk in the directory of your choice, and gives you a list of all the programs on the CD. You can view a brief (and inadequate) description of a highlighted game by pressing F1, print the manual with a touch of F2, generate a registration form with F3, and view information about shareware in general and Gold Medallion Software in particular with two more function keys.

The shell program can also install any of the games to your hard disk, or remove one if you decide not to keep it. Any game can

be played (almost) directly from the menu by pressing Enter when the game is highlighted. The game is copied to your hard disk and launched immediately.

Don't underestimate the convenience of having this CD-ROM. I had already downloaded Raptor from a BBS, but ended up with a multimegabyte file that was inconvenient to transfer to another computer (it wouldn't fit on a single floppy, even in compressed form, and who can remember all the PKZIP commands required to split a file and rejoin it, anyway?). I just took the CD-ROM to the other computer and installed Raptor using that system's CD-ROM drive. Great!

Rating: ◎ ◎ ◎

Publisher Name:
Gold Medallion Software

Software Requirements: **MPC**

Suggested Retail Price:
$19.95

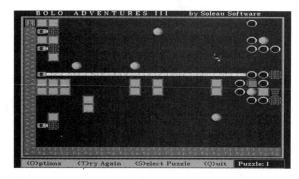

Bolo Adventure is one of 40 VGA games included on this CD-ROM.

Giga Games

Rating:

Publisher Name:
Walnut CreekCD-ROM

Software Requirements: **MPC**

Suggested Retail Price:
$19.95

Games are one type of shareware that has enjoyed stunning success in recent years. The reason for that have been some very savvy moves by shareware authors, and the wider distribution of shareware games on CD-ROMs like this one. Simply put, one disc like *Giga Games* can get hundreds of great offerings into the hands of millions of potential buyers, many of whom don't have access to a modem or a local BBS to download from, or, perhaps, the time and inclination to do so.

And be warned: Many of the games on this disc will tempt you into registration. Unlike utilities or applications, which give you little tangible material for your registration other than a clear conscience, a printed manual, and access to technical support and upgrades, games that are registered with the shareware vendor often are gateways to many new levels or episodes of the game. If you like what you see on *Giga Games*, you'll want to register and get more!

Giga Games is a relatively new addition to the ranks of shareware CDs. This one, perhaps rather obviously, is filled with games. The selection is very impressive; I found myself quite happily looking through the vast selection available on this CD. All gaming categories are very nicely covered.

A vast selection of shareware is available for the game aficionado.

The menu system is rather obtuse, you will find yourself glaring at it rather frequently. Though subjects are logically divided up, I really wished I had a tag option, or that I at least was not dropped to DOS everytime I got a program off of the CD.

Much of the nice selection, is, however, some rather lousy shareware. You will have to look for the quality items, but they are in there for the finding. The very best of current shareware games, as well as the worst, are all on here. However, you'll find that the quality of commercial games also varies widely (although the price doesn't seem to), and here, at least, you can try before you buy.

If you are a diehard gamer, this one is definitely worth checking out. The vast selection may just be enough to sate your gaming appetite for a while. And for anyone else just wanting to check out the world of shareware games, this definitely allows you a broad spectrum to base your opinions on.

Walnut Creek CDROM

HOBBES OS/2

I once expressed the concept of rarity in this manner, saying that a certain thing "was scarcer than OS/2 shareware." That was a long time ago. Now OS/2 has taken its place as a viable (and hard to crash!) operating system of particular interest to those who need rock-solid multitasking environments. There's enough of an installed base to encourage the development of innovative shareware, freeware, and public domain software for OS/2 systems. Apparently, there's something approaching a gigabyte of this stuff available, and most of it is on the *HOBBES OS/2* CD-ROM.

This CD-ROM contains the OS/2 archives from the Internet site at FTP-OS2.CDROM.COM. OS/2's main weakness (lack of device drivers) is cured with the purchase of this one CD-ROM. It is definitely a must have for any serious OS/2 aficionado, as it not only has device drivers but also a whopping 3,000 OS/2-related files, which fill up the 650MB CD-ROM.

HOBBES comes with an easy-to-use archive browser called, appropriately enough, View, which is a gem in the rough. Run View to browse an archive, and then click on the files you want. If it is a compressed file, View sends you to a decompression screen where you can choose where you want to decompress files. After you select the directory, just hit Enter and View automatically decompresses the files to that directory. If it is a text file you are looking for, View has a built-in text viewer. Just click the file you want to read and view puts it automatically on-screen.

HOBBES has BBS support included. It is ready to go online if your BBS uses one of these popular file formats: RBBS, PCBoard, Opus, Spitfire, Wildcat, or Maximus. I tried it on a TBBS platform with a PCBoard file base and it was a breeze to install.

> ## This disc has the most comprehensive selection of shareware and freeware for the OS/2 operating system.

My favorite demo on the disc is a communications program called Livewire. Livewire 2.1 is an excellent terminal program for OS/2. It is easy to set up, and you can select from either a Qmodem or a Procomm command format. If you have any aspirations of going online with OS/2, you should definitely give this product a trial run.

Some of the programs run right off the hard disk. Why waste valuable hard disk space when *HOBBES* comes with 120MB of preinstalled software ready to run? Directly from the CD-ROM, you can run Emacs 19.22, EMX 0.8H, Ghostscript 2.6.1, and TeX.

If you are a game player, *HOBBES* is loaded with them. After playing Wizards of War and Minesweeper, I settled into my childhood favorite, Asteroids. All the games were easy to install with the View program decompressing them for you automatically.

The CD-ROM is just packed with files. Among the 3,000 files you can find: Shell replacements, 5,000+ icons, system utilities, backup programs, networking utilities, and Gnu and UNIX utilities including the GCC and EMX C compiler. There are also many sound drivers, printer drivers, and serial port drivers.

There are text files on a variety of subjects including OS/2 programming, system-supported hardware, and user documentation, including IBM's Red Books and the latest OS/2 Frequently Asked Question List. This disc has the most comprehensive selection of shareware and freeware for the OS/2 operating system.

If you are currently running OS/2 or are planning to run it, this is a definite must have. You could save on the price alone by not having to call long distance to download those elusive OS/2 device drivers. And the files on this disc are safe to use, as they have been virus scanned.

Rating: ● ● ● ●

Publisher Name:
Walnut Creek CD-ROM

Software Requirements:
OS/2 x.x

Suggested Retail Price:
$19.95

InfoMagic "Standards"

Rating: 1/2

Publisher Name:
Infomagic

Software Requirements: **MPC**

Suggested Retail Price:
$19.95

InfoMagic publishes information in job lots. For example, this disc contains just under 600MB of national and international communications standards and documentation. Everything from ANSI to Zmodem is on here somewhere.

There is the CCITT Bluebook, 1988, with its 1992 revisions, the Network Resource Guide, Internet Requests For Comment (RFC's) in HyperText, ISO standards, DOS tools for handling .TAR and .ZIP files, and more and more and more. Just about every standard that affects computer communications is stored on this disc. InfoMagic updates the information every six months. The only missing piece is IEEE standards, apparently because IEEE

did not permit publication in CD-ROM form.

What does it all mean? Well, if you want to know what the rules are, they're here. If you want to know how "the NET" came to be, here are the standards and a lot of the discussion that went into their creation and adoption. Looking at it from just a historical point of view, *"Standards"* shows just how much can be accomplished when like-minded folks decide they want to do something and decide to cooperate in doing it.

Just what anyone who wants to know about standards needs as a permanent reference.

The "Net" began when a couple of computer system operators wondered if they could connect their systems together to share data and communicate. The Defense Advanced Research Projects Agency later got into the act after interconnection was proven practical. They wanted to ensure communications in an emergency and so funded the development of a distributed data network that could function even if some links were disabled by a disaster. The idea caught on among universities, businesses, and so on and the network grew into what it is now.

Nobody's quite sure just what or how big the "Net" is now. The last guesstimate I remember reading is that, worldwide, more than one million systems and more than seven million users are connected directly. Many more connect through part-time links through bulletin board systems, personal e-mail connections, and so on.

All of that depends on standards so that computers can "talk" to each other. All of those standards, the ones that are most widespread, are on this CD.

This disc runs in DOS but includes a Windows interface for Internet RFCs in HyperText format. The directory structure is logically laid out and easy to figure out, although very large. The file Fullindx.txt can take a long time to work through.

There are a few glitches. For example: Volume 8 of the CCITT Bluebook files is in "troff" format, a UNIX print formatting tool; but it is still readable enough. About 14MB of the information is zipped, but tools are available in the DOS directory to decompress them.

All the other files are formatted with DOS's CR-LF end-of-line treatment, but UNIX users have the LS_LR files to enable reading on their systems that handle end-of-line with LF only.

This CD is just the thing for serious Internet "surfers," system administrators, or the user who just wants to know how things work. It's big, complete, and more interesting than you might at first think. It's a good way to get an idea what the "man behind the curtain" is doing, a view behind the scenes. If the "Information Superhighway" ever gets built, these standards are the roadbed.

Night Owl's Shareware #11

S ome CD-ROM users have a big problem with shareware collections. Handing them one is like turning a six-year-old loose in the local candy store with a credit card. Somebody's going to end up bankrupt!

On one hand, shareware treasuries like *Night Owl's Shareware #11* are great! You can play around for days trying utilities, games, financial programs, scientific programs, and various toys.

On the other hand, shareware treasuries put lots of wear and tear on your conscience. Your basic honest (broke) citizen ends up deleting all those neat programs because there's no way he or she can afford all those registration fees. Of course, he or she also ends up missing them.

Night Owl has flown down and seized 648MB and dropped it here for us to play with. There are programs for just about everything you could want from ASP (Association of Shareware Professionals) miscellany to word processing. In between are business packages, computer drafting software, modem utilities, and a lot else.

There are nearly 5,000 individual files on this disc. If this is Night Owl's usual style, we can hardly wait for Edition 12, which, I hear, is due out almost any day now. I may never finish playing.

For the typical DOS neophyte, using this disc is almost embarrassingly easy: insert disc, run RUN_ME, follow the directions, and trip happily away through this cyber-candy store. It works equally well in all its three modes. From DOS you can choose

either straight-up keyboard interface or a nice front-end graphical user interface that allows choosing programs with a mouse. From Microsoft Windows, it works just like any other Windows program, with point-and-click ease. The menus are self-explanatory and everything works.

The viewing functions are particularly nice. You can read the Read-me's, peruse the DOCs, and, if you're into that sort of thing, look over the EXEs. That allows you to get a good overview of each selection before bothering to copy it to your computer's hard disk.

When you want to try something, tag the file name by pressing the designated key, invoke the UNZIP function, and the interface software quietly unpacks the files into its own working directory on your hard disk. You can try the program from there or, if it's a Windows program, install it and run

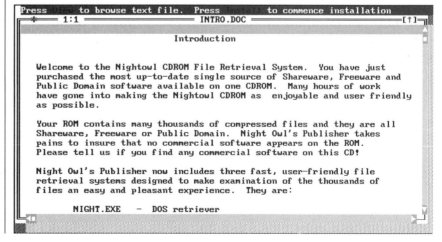

Rating: ◎ ◎ ◎

Publisher Name:
Night Owl Software

Software Requirements: DOS

Suggested Retail Price:
$19.95

it under Windows. In most cases, though a few of the Windows programs include Uninstall, deleting a program you don't want to keep is your problem.

My final opinion? This CD is nice, but it's dangerous. (You can get lost in there playing!) It's like having your own private applications programmer, but it doesn't take as long until your applications are ready.

Night Owl discs always contain the best in recent shareware, with no duplications between editions.

```
Press    to browse text file.  Press         to commence installation
╺═══ 1:1 ═══                  INTRO.DOC                      ═══[↑]═╸
                          Introduction

     Welcome to the Nightowl CDROM File Retrieval System.  You have just
     purchased the most up-to-date single source of Shareware, Freeware and
     Public Domain software available on one CDROM.  Many hours of work
     have gone into making the Nightowl CDROM as  enjoyable and user friendly
     as possible.

     Your ROM contains many thousands of compressed files and they are all
     Shareware, Freeware or Public Domain.  Night Owl's Publisher takes
     pains to insure that no commercial software appears on the ROM.
     Please tell us if you find any commercial software on this CD!

     Night Owl's Publisher now includes three fast, user-friendly file
     retrieval systems designed to make examination of the thousands of
     files an easy and pleasant experience.  They are:

          NIGHT.EXE   -  DOS retriever
```

Night Owl 12

Rating:

Publisher Name:
Night Owl Publisher, Inc.

Software Requirements: **MPC**

Suggested Retail Price:
$19.95

Night Owl 12 is all new, and filled with great shareware.

Yes... it's happened, just like they said it would. Night Owl Publisher, Inc. (maybe that should be Ink... as in RED ink on my bank statement) has laid yet another mine on Disc Drive specifically designed, I'm sure, so shareware authors can crack my armor on the way to my wallet. After all, even modest $10 to $25 fees can mount when you have so many good programs on one disc.

So, if you already have *Night Owl 11*, the question is: what's different between *Night Owl 11* and *Night Owl 12*?

Steve Smith at Night Owl, in a phone conversation, claimed there are no duplicates between any issues of Night Owl Shareware CDs. Similarities of file names are due to new revisions of existing programs. I see no reason whatever to disbelieve him. White said they take pride in that. They should.

Another difference is in their retrieval interface program. You can now switch between different issues by selecting "Change CD" under the Category Menu pull-down. It's no longer necessary to keep separate directories on your hard drive for each issue of Night Owl shareware. This

works for issues 10, 11, 12, and future releases.

One important thing that isn't different is Night Owl's interface. You can actually use a Night Owl shareware CD without feeling like you're flailing through a jungle of directories and file names like Indiana Jones hunting a pre-Columbian artifact. Issue 12 retains 11's triple-threat interface, normal DOS key banger, DOS-based GUI with mouse support, and full-functioned Windows point-and-click. The screens are bright, easy to read (for people with normal vision, anyway), and the directory structure makes sense.

The Windows interface, though, is still tough to read, at least for those with less than perfect vision. One nice difference I noticed is that *Night Owl 11* would sometimes mysteriously lock up or fail to find files, then, equally mysteriously, work fine after restarting the interface program. This CD has yet to do that to me. A question remains: Is that because Night Owl found and corrected a problem or because I

did some janitorial work on my system and lots of things run better?

The next question on my agenda was: What's different on the new disc? Reading through the two CDs' directories; I did notice different file names, different descriptions, and one additional directory, but to compare the two 600+ MB CDs manually would probably have left me blind and crazy. I compared the two, and the results showed that *Night Owl 11* has 4,796 files and 648,928,885 bytes and that Night Owl 12 has 3,991 files and 621,351,570 bytes.

Overall, *Night Owl 12* seems to continue their product line nicely. There is a lot of shareware being written. New releases seem to pop up daily and Night Owl seems to catch and cage them in good order, releasing a new CD about every four to six months. Night Owl 13 is due out in July or August, according to Steve Smith.

Walnut Creek's "Project Gutenberg"

P roject Gutenberg Etext is a plan, a vision, if you will, a vision to make information available to all, and freely. Begun at Illinois Benedectine University, Project Gutenberg was designed to place as much literature into electronic form, with as wide a distribution as possible. More than 150 titles have been converted and the project continues, predominantly with volunteers typing in texts as they become available in the public domain or by permission. Project Gutenberg's goal is to have 10,000 of the most used English-language books converted to electronic text by 2001.

Walnut Creek has collected the Project Gutenberg archives and placed them onto CD-ROM media, allowing persons lacking access to the Internet archives to benefit from the project.

The CD comprises about 100MB of information, having some 150 titles in directly readable ASCII text format and .ZIP files. Each title is stored in both formats. The directory structure is divided into

Project Gutenberg's produce for 1990, 91, 92, 93, and 94, the Cleveland Freenet collection of historical documents, some informational directories, and one of the papers from the International Philosophical Preprint Exchange. The latter's files are in PostScript and other formats in some cases. Abstracts are text files.

Here you can find *Anne of Green Gables*, *The Wizard of Oz*, *Through the Looking Glass*, the *John Carter of Mars*, and *Tarzan novels* by Burroughs, the Constitution, the Bill of Rights, The Mayflower Compact, and many, many more classic works of English and American literature. You can read them directly from the CD or import them into a word processing program for easier reading or printing. Copying the .ZIP files to the hard drive keeps the text readily available for commentary or research without unduly occupying precious storage space.

The interface on this disc isn't at all fancy, just a straight DOS viewer. The directory structure is less than intuitive.

Rating:

Publisher Name:
Walnut Creek CD-ROM

Software Requirements:
MS-DOS, CD-ROM Drive

Suggested Retail Price: $29.95

Apparently Walnut Creek simply transferred the Project Gutenberg files directly and copied those as is, without alphabetizing or otherwise altering the ordering. Project Gutenberg specifies their files are to be transmitted without alteration. So that might explain the apparent lack of organization. It doesn't detract greatly from the value of the collection, but it does force the user to search a bit when looking for a particular work.

Once you have found a text, you must decide which version to read. Some of them appear in several different versions, depending upon how recently they were entered. The Project Gutenberg folks don't hide anything. Earlier versions may contain errors of transcription or formatting, and they leave those versions for anyone to read. It's worth reading the informational and disclaimer files to see how they work and how best to use the files.

This is a nice addition to your bookshelf. It isn't especially pretty, but it's a useful and usable collection of classic and popular literature. There's even a King James Version Bible and a couple of Internet "bibles."

```
                        \etext93\
──────────────────────────────────────────
Directory etext93
==================
2sqrt10.txt    The Square Root of 2                   Feb 1993
2sqrt10.zip
32pri10.txt    The 32nd Mersenne Prime, by David Slowinski   Jun 1993
32pri10.zip
alad10.txt     Aladdin and the Lamp                  Mar 1993
alad10.zip
badge10.txt    Red Badge of Courage, by Stephen Crane   Jul 1993
badge10.zip
blexp10.txt    Norman Coombs' "Black Experience in America"   May 1993
blexp10.zip
civil10.txt    Civil Disobedience, by Henry David Thoreau   Jun 1993
civil10.zip
clinton.txt    Clinton's Inaugural Address           Jan 1993
dcart10.txt    A Discourse on Method, by Rene Descartes   Mar 1993
dcart10.zip
ee610.txt      Etext of the number "e"               Apr 1993
ee610.zip
gmars10.txt    The Gods of Mars, e10 by Edgar Rice Burroughs   May 1993
gmars10.zip
gmars11.txt    The Gods of Mars, e11 by Edgar Rice Burroughs   May 1993

<Enter>-Select File  <S>-Search  <R>-Rev. Search  <ESC>-Main Menu  <?>-Help
```

The *Project Gutenberg* disc includes several hundred megabytes of plain text files of public domain classic literature.

SIMTEL MS-DOS CD-ROM

Rating:

Publisher Name: Walnut Creek CD-ROM

Software Requirements: MPC

Suggested Retail Price: $19.95

If you have ever found yourself digging through BBS's file bases for the perfect utility to suit your current problem, this disc is for you. This CD is packed with over 9,000 MS-DOS programs that do just about anything imaginable. The programs on this CD are taken from the Simtel Internet site (ftp.cdrom.com). The Simtel archive contains many programs for many different operating systems and computers. This CD-ROM contains the entire MS-DOS archive at Simtel.

Upon putting the CD in the drive, you instantly gain access to every program on the disc. There is no installation required to browse through the CD, and when you come across a program that you want to use, you are able to decompress the files to any location on writeable media. The disc is arranged in categories of programs. Some categories are general, pertaining to hardware (i.e. Printers), while others are for specific programs (i.e. third-party AutoCad programs).

The content of the disc is primarily shareware and freeware programs, containing technical documents, utilities, programming tools, source code, communication programs, and printing utilities. The programs on the disc are, in most cases, the latest version available as of the publishing of the disc (October 1993). The disc also includes many utilities that date back to the mid-to-late 80s, which means that there are many utilities for your older computers.

An excellent library of utilities that will do just about every-thing from A to Z.

If this disc has a weakness, it is the interface for browsing through the disc. The interface is a simple DOS-based viewing program with very limited searching capabilities. The searches are limited to forward-only searching. The database of files on the disc is very simple as well, giving short one-line descriptions for each program.

One of the unique features of the disc are two types of files added to the disc. They are NCD's TREEINFO.NCD and 4DOS's DESCRIPT.ION. NCD (Norton Change Directory) is a popular directory changing and tree-viewing utility that is found in Norton Utilities by Symantic software. 4DOS is a shareware COMMAND.COM replacement that is also found in the recent releases of the Norton Utilities as NDOS. The DESCRIPT.ION file gives extended description for the DIR command in 4DOS. The disc also includes built-in support for the popular BBS packages, enabling sysops to put the disc on-line easily.

While the majority of people will not have any use for every file on this disc, the disc makes a nice library to search through should you come across an odd job, and will definitely save you time. This is also an ideal disc for sysops that are looking for a wide variety of programs to add their BBS's file archives.

SIMTEL MSDOS CDROM

Over 9000 MSDOS programs from the Simtel Internet Archive

Walnut Creek CDROM

Additional CD-ROM Titles

Title: 1st Canadian Shareware Disc
Suggested Retail Price: $80.95
Publisher: BetaCorp Technologies
Platform: MPC
Description: Ten categories of shareware from Canadian authors, eh?

Title: ADA CD-ROM
Suggested Retail Price: $39.95
Publisher: Walnut Creek
Platform: MPC/Macintosh
Description: Source code, utilities, and documentation for this Department of Defense-favored language.

Title: Audio 1
Suggested Retail Price: $24.95
Publisher: Knowledge Media
Platform: MPC
Description: Over 400 MB of audio & graphic shareware and freeware.

Title: C User Group
Suggested Retail Price: $49.95
Publisher: Walnut Creek
Platform: MPC
Description: Lots of programming stuff for UNIX and other C programmers.

Title: CD-ROM Paradise
Suggested Retail Price: $29.95
Publisher: CD ROM Paradise
Platform: MPC
Description: Over 500MB of shareware for IBM PCs.

Title: Disc to the Future—Programmers' Reference
Suggested Retail Price: $129.00
Publisher: Wayzata Technologies
Platform: MPC/Macintosh
Description: Source code & utilities for the PC programmer.

Title: Educational Gameland
Suggested Retail Price: $39.95
Publisher: Pacific Hitech Inc.
Platform: MPC
Description: Free & shareware kids' games.

Title: Ham Radio & Scanner Companion
Suggested Retail Price: $19.95
Publisher: John O'Connor Publishing
Platform: MPC
Description: Shareware collection of application and programs for enthusiasts.

Title: Internet Info
Suggested Retail Price: $39.95
Publisher: Walnut Creek
Platform: MPC/Macintosh
Description: Information about Usenet groups, FTPs, telenet, and more.

Title: ISLO's Select Shareware
Suggested Retail Price: $99.00
Publisher: Islo Tech
Platform: MPC
Description: Shareware collection of excellent utilities, applications, and fonts.

Title: JEM Disc
Suggested Retail Price: $36.95
Publisher: Jewel Distributing
Platform: MPC
Description: Shareware specifically configured for BBSs.

Title: Libris Britania
Suggested Retail Price: $69.95
Publisher: Walnut Creek
Platform: MPC/Macintosh
Description: A British shareware collection, wot?

Title: Mega A/V 1
Suggested Retail Price: $69.00
Publisher: Profit Press
Platform: MPC
Description: Over 600MB of sound and graphic shareware.

Title: Mega CD-ROM 1
Suggested Retail Price: $19.00
Publisher: Profit Press
Platform: MPC
Description: Over 8,000 virus-scanned files of shareware.

Title: Mega CD-ROM 2
Suggested Retail Price: $29.00
Publisher: Profit Press
Platform: MPC
Description: Over 7,000 virus-scanned files, different from volume one.

Title: Mega Media
Suggested Retail Price: $34.95
Publisher: Knowledge media
Platform: MPC
Description: Graphics, sound, and video library.

Title: Mega Win & OS/2 Shareware
Suggested Retail Price: $79.00
Publisher: Walnut Creek
Platform: MPC/Macintosh
Description: Over 600MB of virus scanned shareware for Windows and OS/2.

Title: Motherlode CD-ROM shareware for Windows
Suggested Retail Price: $50.00
Publisher: Motherlode Publications
Platform: MPC
Description: Mother of all shareware discs.

Title: Multimedia Mac Shareware
Suggested Retail Price: $80.00
Publisher: BetaCorp Technology
Platform: Macintosh
Description: Over 2,500 Macintosh shareware titles.

Title: Night Owl's V.7
Suggested Retail Price: $59.00
Publisher: Night Owl Publishing
Platform: MPC
Description: Another collection of shareware from Night Owl, one of the premiere shareware publishers.

Title: Night Owl's V.9
Suggested Retail Price: $59.00
Publisher: Night Owl Publishing
Platform: MPC
Description: Large collection of BBS ready shareware, in subdirectories for quick installation on your board.

Title: Nova CD-ROM
Suggested Retail Price: $39.95
Publisher: Walnut Creek

Platform: MPC/Macintosh
Description: Games, sounds, fonts, and more.

Title: Programmers Mega pack
Suggested Retail Price: $59.95
Publisher: Beta Corp
Platform: MPC
Description: Library of C, Pascal, ASM source code and utilities.

Title: PSL Monthly CD
Suggested Retail Price: $19.95
Publisher: PSL
Platform: MPC
Description: A monthy shareware disc from the Public Software Library.

Title: SDN 1 Plus
Suggested Retail Price: $29.00
Publisher: Profit press
Platform: MPC
Description: 600MB of virus scanned files.

Title: Selectware Software Jukebox
Suggested Retail Price: $49.00
Publisher: SelectWare
Platform: MPC
Description: Lots of games and other programs.

Title: Shareware Extravanganza 4 Disc Set
Suggested Retail Price: $99.00
Publisher: The Ultimate Shareware Company
Platform: MPC
Description: Wow! Over two gigabytes of shareware, including 25,000 Windows programs!

Title: Shareware Gold II
Suggested Retail Price: $79.00
Publisher: Quanta Press
Platform: MPC
Description: Golden oldies? No, new shareware offerings for the IBM PC.

Title: Shareware Grab Bag Vol. 3
Suggested Retail Price: $99.00
Publisher: ALDE Publishing
Platform: MPC
Description: Another good shareware library, with odds and ends, just like its title suggests.

Title: Shareware Heaven
Suggested Retail Price: $49.95
Publisher: Southeast Data Products
Platform: MPC
Description: BBS ready shareware.

Title: Shareware Overload
Suggested Retail Price: $29.95
Publisher: Chestnut Software
Platform: MPC
Description: Over 600MB of zipped shareware for the IBM PC covering utilities, fonts, and more.

Title: Shareware Studio Vol. 1
Suggested Retail Price: $29.95
Publisher: Data Express
Platform: MPC
Description: First in a new series of shareware discs for the IBM PC.

Title: Shareware Studio Vol. 2
Suggested Retail Price: $39.95
Publisher: Data express
Platform: MPC
Description: A large and diverse shareware library.

Title: Simtel 20
Suggested Retail Price: $24.95
Publisher: Walnut Creek CD-ROM
Platform: MPC/Macintosh
Description: More than 9,000 utilities, tools, and source code for programmers.

Title: Software Du Jour
Suggested Retail Price: $49.95
Publisher: ALDE Publishing
Platform: MPC

Description: 500 selections to show you what you can find through shareware.

Title: Software Vault Collection I
Suggested Retail Price: $99.95
Publisher: Ameican Databankers
Platform: MPC
Description: First in a new series of shareware collections.

Title: Sound Sensations
Suggested Retail Price: $39.95
Publisher: Chestnut Software
Platform: MPC
Description: Shareware collection of sound effects, music, voice, and more.

Title: Source Code
Suggested Retail Price: $39.95
Publisher: Walnut Creek
Platform: MPC/Macintosh
Description: Software routines for the programmer, in many languages, ready to use and reuse.

Title: Super Blue
Suggested Retail Price: $149.00
Publisher: ALDE Publishing
Platform: MPC
Description: All IBM PC software in the library of the New York Amateur Computer Club.

Title: Technotools
Suggested Retail Price: $29.95
Publisher: Chestnut Software
Platform: MPC
Description: Shareware collection of tools and utilities for the IBM PC.

Title: The Original Shareware
Suggested Retail Price: $99.95
Publisher: PC Componet, Inc.
Platform: MPC
Description: Over 8,000 files

Title: The Gold Collection
Suggested Retail Price: $79.00
Publisher: American Databankers
Platform: MPC
Description: Fifty categories hold thousands of the best and newest shareware from around the world.

Title: Wayzata's Best of Shareware
Suggested Retail Price: $59.00
Publisher: Wayzata Technology
Platform: MPC/Macintosh
Description: Over 1,000 shareware programs for the IBM PC and Macintosh.

Title: Windoware
Suggested Retail Price: $29.95
Publisher: Chestnut Software
Platform: MPC
Description: A broad range of Windows games, fonts, and utilities shareware.

Title: Windows Shareware Gold
Suggested Retail Price: $99.00
Publisher: Digital Publishing Company
Platform: MPC
Description: Another great Windows shareware collection.

Title: World of Games—Shareware
Suggested Retail Price: $99.00
Publisher: PC-SIG Inc.
Platform: MPC
Description: Gaming shareware for the IBM PC.

Title: World of Windows—Shareware
Suggested Retail Price: $99.00
Publisher: PC-SIG Inc.
Platform: MPC
Description: Tons of Microsoft Windows shareware games, utilities, and applications.

Part III
Resource Listing

PART III

Resource Listing

3G Graphics
206/774-3518 Gen.
800/456-0234 Sales

A. M. Best Company
908/439-2200 Gen.
908/439-3296 FAX

Activision for Kids
310/473-9200 Gen.
310/820-6131 FAX

Advanced Multimedia Company
914/734-9171 Gen.
914/734 4053 FAX

Advanced Software
408/733-0745 Gen.
408/733-2325 FAX

Advantage Plus Dist., Inc.
813/885-1478 Gen.
919/362-8294 FAX

ALDE Publishing
612/934-4239 Gen.
612/835-3401 FAX

Allegro New Media, Inc.
201/808-1992 Gen.
201/808-2645 FAX

Amazing Media
415/453-0686 Gen.
415/453-9024 Sales

American Bible Society
212/408-1494 Gen.
800/322-4253 Sales
212/408-1512 FAX

American Library Association
312/944-6780 Gen.
800/545-2433 Sales

American Mathematical Society
401/455-4000 Gen.
401/331-3842 FAX

American Theological Library Assoc.
708/869-7788 Gen.
708/869-8513 FAX

Animotion Development Corporation
205/591-5715 Gen.
205/591-5716 FAX

Applied Optical Media Corporation
215/429-3701 Gen.
610/429-3810 FAX

Apriori Software Corporation
708/830-6844 Gen.
708/830-6844 FAX

Aris Entertainment
310/821-0234 Gen.
310/821-6463 FAX

Arizona Macintosh Users' Group
602/553-8966 Gen.
602/553-8771 FAX

Aristotle Industries
202/543-8345 Gen.
202/543-6407 FAX

Asiatronics Limited
212/986-2540 Gen.
212/986-2193 FAX

Ask Me Multimedia
612/531-0603 Gen.
612/531-0645 FAX

Astronomical Data Center
301/286-6953 Gen.

AVCA
512/472-4995 Gen.
510/472-4996 FAX

Autologic, Inc.
805/498-9611 Gen.
805/499-1167 FAX

Aware, Inc.
617/577-1700 Gen.
617/577-1710 FAX

Baseline
212/254-8235 Gen.
212/529-3330 FAX

Beacham Publishing
202/234-0877 Gen.

Beachware
619/558-6000 Gen.

Betacorp Technologies, Inc.
905/564-2424 Gen.
905/564-6655 FAX

Biosis
215/587-4800 Gen.
800/523-4806 Sales
215/587-2016 FAX

Bliss Interactive Technologies Group, Inc.
512/338-2458 Gen.
512/444-2849 FAX

Blue Mountain Software, Inc.
206/457-0024 Gen.

Bob Judd Productions
603/433-2329 Gen.
603/433-7008 FAX

BodyCello
619/578-6969 Gen.
800/922-3556 Sales
619/536-2397 FAX

Boraventures Publishing
212/219-9111 Gen.
212/219-0829 FAX

Bowker Electronic Publishing
908/ 464-6800 Gen.

BPI Communications
212/764-7300 Gen.
212/536-5347 Sales
212/536-5215 FAX

Broderbund
800/521-6263 Sales

BTG, Inc.
703/556-6518 Gen.
703/761-6237 Gen.
703/556-9290 FAX

Burcau Development, Inc.
201/808-2700 Gen.

201/808-2676 FAX

Bureau of Electronic Publishing
201/808-2700 Gen.
800/828-4766 Sales
201/808-2676 FAX

Bureau of Statistics
202/623-7988 Gen.

Byron Preiss Multimedia Co., Inc.
212/645-9870 Gen.
212/645-9874 FAX

C.A.R.
314/454-3535 Gen.
800/288-7585 Sales
314/454-0105 FAX

CACI, Inc.
703/876-2065 Gen.
800/752-5215 Sales
703/841-3709 FAX

CAD Information Systems, Inc.
303/440-4363 Gen.
303/440-5309 FAX

California Data Solutions
619/584-2200 Gen.
619/584-2211 FAX

Cambium Development
914/472-6246 Gen.
914/472-6729 FAX

Candlelight Publishing
800/677-3045 Gen.
801/373-2499 FAX

Capital Disk Interactive
202/965-7800 Gen.
202/965-7815 FAX

Carole Marsh Family CD-Roms
404/577-5085 Gen.

800/536-2438 Sales
404/577-4881 FAX

CD/LAW, Inc.
603/446-7979 Gen.
800/675-1717 Sales
603/446-7965 FAX

CD-ROM, Inc.
303/526-7600 Gen.
303/526-7395 FAX

Chestnut CD-ROM
617/494-5330 Gen.
617/494-6094 FAX

CMC
503/241-4351 Gen.
800/854-9126 Sales
503/241-4370 FAX

Commerce Clearing House, Inc.
708/940-4600 Gen.
708/940-0942 FAX

Commodore Business Machines, Inc.
610/666-7950 Gen.

Compact Publishing, Inc.
202/244-4770 Gen.
800/964-1518 Sales
202/244-6363 FAX

Company of Science & Art
206/628-4526 Gen.
401/274-7517 FAX

Compton's NewMedia
619/929-2500 Gen.
619/929-2555 FAX

Computer Directions
209/435-5777 Gen.
209/435-3131 FAX

Comstock, Inc.
212/353-8600 Gen.
212/353-3383 FAX

Conexus, Inc.
619/268-3358 Gen.
619/268-3409 FAX

Congressional Information Service, Inc.
301/654-1550 Gen.
800/638-8380 Sales
301/654-4033 FAX

Context Systems, Inc.
215/675-5000 Gen.
215/675-2899 FAX

Corel Corporation
613/728-3733 Gen.
800/772-6735 Sales
613/761-9176 FAX

Creative Multimedia Corp.
503/241-4351 Gen.
503/241-4370 FAX

Crystal Dynamics, Inc.
415/473-3400 Gen.
415/473-3410 FAX

Dartnell
800/621-5463 Gen.
312/561-3801 FAX

Davidson & Associates, Inc.
310/793-0600 Gen.
800/556-6141 Sales
310/793-0601 FAX

Deep River Publishing
207/871-1684 Gen.
207/871-1683 FAX

DeLorme Mapping Systems
207/865-4171 Gen.
207/865-9291 FAX

DesignWare, Inc.
617/924-6715 Gen.
800/536-2596 Sales

617/924-1699 FAX

DIALOG Information Services, Inc.
415/858-3785 Gen.
800/334-2564 Sales
415/494-0475 FAX

DigiDesign
502/895-0565 Gen.
415/327-0777 FAX

Digital Directory Assistance, Inc.
301/657-8548 Gen.
617/639-2900 Sales
301/652-7810 FAX

Digital Photograhic Imaging, Inc.
616/676-3347 Gen.
800/779-3325 Sales

Digital Publishing Co.
612/531-9811 Gen.
800/279-6099 Sales
612/595-0802 FAX

Digital Wisdom, Inc.
804/758-0670 Gen.
800/800-8560 Sales
804/758-4512 FAX

Digital Zone
206/623-3456 Gen.
206/454-3922 FAX

Discis Knowledge Research, Inc.
416/250-6537 Gen.
416/250-6540 FAX

Discovery Home Entertainment
301/986-1999 Gen.

Discovery Systems
614/761-2000 Gen.
614/766-3146 FAX

Disney Productions
818/841-3326 Gen.

800/688-1520 Sales
818/846-0454 FAX

Dr. T.'s Music Software
617/455-1454 Gen.
617/455-1460 FAX

Dynamix, Inc.
503/343-0772 Gen.
503/344-1754 FAX

DynEd International
415/578-8067 Gen.
800/765-4375 Sales
415/578-8069 FAX

Ebook, Inc.
510/429-1331 Gen.
510/429-1394 FAX

Eagle Eye Publishers, Inc.
703/242-4201 Gen.
703/242-4204 FAX

EarthInfo, Inc.
303/938-1788 Gen.
303/938-8183 FAX

Eastman Kodak Company
716/724-4000 Gen.
800/235-6325 Sales

EBSCO Publishing
508/535-8500 Gen.
508/535-8545 FAX

The EDGE Interactive Software
818/304-4771 Gen.

Educorp
619/536-9999 Gen.
800/843-9497 Sales
619/536-2345 FAX

Eduquest
404/238-3184 Gen.

EE Multimedia Productions
801/973-0081 Gen.
800/826-6810 Sales
801/973-0184 FAX

Electronic Arts
415/571-7171 Gen.

Electronic Edge
718/343-6621 Gen.
516/775-1316 FAX

Electronica
408/475-2750 Gen.
408/479-8992 FAX

Ellis Enterprises, Inc.
405/749-0273 Gen.
800/729-9500 Sales
405/751-5168 FAX

Environmental Systems Research Institute
909/793-2853 Gen.
909/793-5953 FAX

Expert Software
503/646-2286 Gen.
503/644-9779 FAX

Falcon Software
603/764-5788 Gen.
603/764-9051 FAX.

Fantazia Concepts
800/951-0877 Gen.
216/951-9241 FAX

Farallon Computing
415/596-9100 Gen.
415/596-9020 FAX

Fathom Pictures, Inc.
415/289-2500 Gen.
415/331-3390 FAX

Faulkner Technical Reports, Inc.
609/662-2070 Gen.
800/843-0460 Sales
609/662-3380 FAX

First Byte
310/793-0610 Gen.
310/793-0601 FAX

Folio VIP Electronic Publishing
801/375-3700 Gen.
801/344-3787 FAX

Free Spirit Software
317/878-5342 Gen.
317/878-4751

Future Technologies
702/733-2022 Gen.
800/551-3926 Sales
702/733-1737 FAX

Future Trends Software
214/224-3288 Gen.
214/224-3328 FAX

Gale Research, Inc.
313/961-2242 Gen.
800/877-4253 Sales
313/961-6083 FAX

Gazelle Technologies, Inc.
619/536-9999 Gen.
619/536-2345 FAX

Geographic Data Technology, Inc.
603/795-2183 Gen.
800/331-7881 Sales
603/795-4289 FAX

Gold Disk, Inc.
408/982-0200 Gen.
408/982-0289 FAX

Grolier Electronic Publishing
203/797-3530 Gen.
800/285-4534 Sales
203/797-3835 FAX

Group 1 Software
800/368-5806 Sales
301/731-0360 FAX

Groupware
206/472-1400 Gen.
206/473-1634 FAX

H. W. Wilson Company
718/588-8400 Gen.
800/367-6770 Sales
718/538-2716 FAX

Haines & Company
216/494-9111 Gen.
216/494-0226 FAX

Hammerhead Publications
305/426-8114 Gen.
305/426-9801 FAX

Harris Design
212/864-8872 Gen.

Healthcare Information Services, Inc.
916/648-8075 Gen.
800/468-1128 Sales
916/648-8078 FAX

HeartBeat Software Solutions
213/404-7083 Gen.
213/802-1435 FAX

Herner and Company
703/558-8200 Gen.
703/558-4979 FAX

Hewlett-Packard Co.
415/691-5805 Gen.

Highlighted Data, Inc.
203/516-9211 Gen.
203/516-9216 FAX

Holbrook & Kellogg, Inc.
703/506-0600 Gen.
703/506-1948 FAX

Hopkins Technology
612/931-9376 Gen.
612/931-9377 FAX

Horizons Technology, Inc.
800/828-3808 Sales
619/292-7321 FAX

HSC Software
310/392-8441 Gen.
310/392-6015 FAX

Humongous Entertainment, Inc.
206/485-7988 Gen.
206/485-1212 Sales
206/486-9494 FAX

Hyperbole Studios
206/451-7751 Gen.
206/451-7844 FAX

HyperGlot Software Co., Inc.
615/558-8270 Gen.
615/588-6569 FAX

HyperLaw, Inc.
212/787-2812 Gen.
800/825-6521 Sales
212/496-4138 FAX

Ibis Communications, Inc.
410/290-9082 Gen.
410/290-6589 FAX

IBM Corp.
914/642-3000 Gen.
914/426-2255 Sales
800/242-6349 FAX

ICP
317/251-7727 Gen.
317/251-7813 FAX

IGW Canada, Inc.
403/247-9506 Gen.
403/247-9915 FAX

Image Club Graphics, Inc.
403/262-8008 Gen.
403/261-7013 FAX

InfoBusiness, Inc.
801/221-1100 Gen.
800/657-5300 Sales
801/221-1194 FAX

Information Access Company
415/591-2333 Gen.
800/227-8431 Sales

Information Resources, Inc.
213/376-8081 Gen.

Information Sources
510/525-6220 Gen.
800/433-6107 Sales
510/525-1568 FAX

Information Update
214/422-2171 Gen.

Innovative Advertising & Design
802/879-1164 Gen.
800/255-0562 Sales
802/878-1768 FAX

Innovative Media Corp.
217/544-4614 Gen.
217/544-4731 FAX

Instant Replay Corporation
801/634-7648 Gen.
801/634-1054 FAX

Intel Corporation
408/765-8080 Gen.

Intelex Corp.
706/782-7844 Gen.
706/782-4489 FAX

Intellimedia Sports, Inc.
800/269-2101 Gen.

Intelliplay
800/269-2101 Sales

InterActive Publishing Corp.
914/426-0400 Gen.
914/426-2606 FAX

InterArc
703/264-9786 Gen.
800/833-3627 Sales
703/318-7319 FAX

Interactive Audio
415/285-0778 Gen.

Intermedia Interactive Software
215/387-0448 Gen.
215/387-3049 FAX.

Interplay Productions
714/553-6655 Gen.
714/252-2820 FAX

IT Makers
408/274-8669 Gen.

IVI, Inc.
612/686-0079 Gen.

J. D. Express
516/563-0617 Gen.
516/563-0618 FAX

Jane's Information Group
703/683-3700 Gen.
703/836-1593 FAX

Jasmine Multimedia Publishing
818/780-3344 Gen.
800/798-7535 Sales
818/780-8705 FAX

Jet Propulsion Laboratory
818/306-6130 Gen.
818/306-6929 FAX

Johnston & Company
801/756-1111 Gen.

Josten Learning Corporation
619/587-0087 Gen.
800/548-8372 Sales

Journal Graphics
303/831-6400 Gen.
303/831-8901 FAX

Kar Technologies
619/340-5900 Gen.

Killer Tracks
213/957-4455 Gen.
800/877-0078 Sales
213/957-4470 FAX

Knowledge Access International
415/969-0606 Gen.

Knowledge Adventure
818/542-4200 Gen.
818/542-4205 FAX

Knowledge Engineering
404/364-2001 Gen.
800/548-7947 Sales

Knowledge Garden, Inc.
516/246-5400 Gen.

Knowledge Media
916/872-3826 Gen.
800/78CDROM Sales
916/872-3826 FAX

Laser Plot, Inc.
508/757-2831 Gen.
800/888-0888 Sales

Laser Resources, Inc.
310/324-4444 Gen.
800/535-2737 Sales
310/324-9999 FAX

LaserTrak Corporation
303/530-2711 Gen.

The Learning Team
914/273-2226 Gen.
914/273-2227 FAX

Legi-Tech
916/447-1886 Gen.
916/447-1109 FAX

The Library Corporation
304/229-0100 Gen.
800/852-4911 Sales
304/229-0295 FAX

Library Line
212/889-3819 Gen.

Library of Congress
202/707-6100 Gen.
202/707-1334 FAX

Lightbinders, Inc.
415/621-5746 Gen.
800/43CDROM Sales
415/621-5898 FAX

Little, Brown, and Company
617/859-5549 Gen.
800/289-6299 Sales
617/859-0629 FAX

Lotus Development Corp.
617/577-8500 Gen.
800/554-5501 Sales

LucasArts
415/721-3300 Gen.
415/721-3344 FAX

Lunar Eclipse Software
703/759-0700 Gen.
703/841-9503 FAX

Macmillan New Media
617/225-9023 Gen.
617/868-7738 FAX

Macmillan Publishing Company
800/257-5755 Gen.

MacroMedia, Inc.
415/252-2000 Gen.
800/288-4797 Sales
415/626-0554 FAX

Mainstream America
717/562-0650 Gen.
717/562-0657 FAX

Marine Information Systems, Inc.
619/223-8947 Gen.
619/223-8942 FAX

Marketplace Information, Corp.
617/894-1661 Gen.
617/894-1656 FAX

Marshall Cavendish
516/826-4200 Gen.
800/821-9881 Sales
516/785-8133 FAX

Masque Publishing
303/290-9853 Gen.

Matthew Bender & Co.
800/223-1940 Gen.
518/487-3584 FAX

Maxis
510/254-9700 Gen.
510/253-3736 FAX

Maxmedia Distributing, Inc.
407/877-3807 Gen.
407/877-3834 FAX

MCA Inc.
818/777-1747
818/777-7180 FAX

McGraw-Hill, Inc.
212/337-5916 Gen.
800/722-4726 Sales
212/337-4092 FAX

MECC
800/685-6322 Gen.
612/569-1551 FAX

Mecklermedia
203/226-6967 Gen.
800/632-5537 Sales
203/454-5840 FAX

Media Clip-Art, Inc.
609/795-5993 Gen.
609/667-5690 FAX

MediaVision
510/770-8600 Gen.
510/623-5749 FAX

Medical Economics Data
201/358-7500 Gen.
800/526-4870 Sales
201/573-4956 FAX

Medical Publishing Group
617/893-3800 Gen.
800/342-1338 FAX

Melissa Data Company
714/492-7000 Gen.
714/492-7086 FAX

Meridian Data, Inc.
408/438-3100 Gen.
408/438-6816 FAX

Merit Software
214/385-2353 Gen.
214/385-6205 FAX

Metromail Corporation
708/620-3191 Gen.
708/620-3014 FAX

Micro Mart
908/985-0002 Gen.
908/297-7399 FAX

MicroPatent
203/495-6900 Gen.
203/495-6909 FAX

Microsoft Corporation
206/882-8080 Gen.
800/426-9400 Sales
206/936-7329 FAX

Microsource
800/528-1415 Gen.
602/968-0177

Microware Systems Corporation
515/224-1929 Gen.
515/224-1352 FAX

Midisoft Corporation
800/PRO-MIDI Sales

Mind Training Systems, Inc.
313/445-7811 Gen.

Mitchell International
800/854-7030 Gen.
619/530-4677 FAX

ModelVision, Inc.
205/461-0878 Gen.
205/461-0879 FAX

Moon Valley Software
602/863-3668 Gen.

MPI Multimedia
708/460-0555 Gen.
708/460-0187 FAX

Mr. CD-ROM
407/877-3807 Gen.
407/877-3834 FAX

Multi-Ad Services, Inc.
309/692-1530 Gen.
800/447-1950 Sales
309/692-5444 FAX

Multicom Publishing Inc.
206/622-5530 Gen.
206/622-4380 FAX

The Multimedia Publishing Studio
404/877-1615 Gen.
800/995-9999 Sales
404/877-1330 FAX

NASA
818/354-8751 Gen.

National Biomedical Research Foundation
202/687-2121 Gen.
202/687-1662 FAX

National Bioscience
612/550-2012 Gen.
800/747-4362 Sales
800/369-5118 FAX

National Council on Family Relations
612/781-9331 Gen.

National Educational Training Group
708/369-3000 Gen.
800/323-0377 Sales
708/983-4541 FAX

National Geophysical Data Center
303/497-6826 Gen.
303/497-6513 FAX

National Information Services Corporation
410/243-0797 Gen.
410/243-0982 FAX

NEC Home Electronics, Computer Products
312/860-9500 Gen.

NewsBank/Readex
203/966-1100 Gen.
800/223-4739 Sales
203/966-6254 FAX

Newsweek Interactive
800/634-6850 Gen.

Nielsen Marketing Research
312/489-6300 Gen.
312/498-7662 FAX

Nightengale Conant
312/647-0300 Gen.
800/323-5552 Sales

Northern Telecom
615/734-4000 Gen.

Novalogic, Inc.
818/774-0812 Gen.
818/774-9528 FAX

Now What Software
415/885-1689 Gen.

NTC Publishing Group
708/679-5500 Gen.
800/323-4900 Sales
708/679-2494 FAX

Oasis Publishing
800/377-5297 Gen.

OCLC Forest Press
614/764-6000 Gen.
800/848-5878 Sales
614/764-0161 FAX

Omni Graphics
305/525-9422 Gen.

One Mile Up
703/642-1177 Gen.
800/258-5280 Sales
703/642-9088 FAX

Online Computer Systems, Inc.
301/428-3700 Gen.
800/922-9204 FAX

Opcode Systems, Inc.
415/856-3333 Gen.
415/856-3332 FAX

Optic Solutions
817/543-0098 Gen.

Optical Media International
408/376-3511 Gen.
800/347-2664 Sales
408/376-3519 FAX

Orange Cherry New Media
914/764-4104 Gen.
800/672-6002 Sales
914/764-0104 FAX

OSHA
801/487-0267 ext.228 Gen.
202/219-6091 Gen.

Oxford University Press
212/679-7300 Gen.
212/725-2972 FAX

Pacific Hitech, Inc.
801/278-2042 Gen.
801/278-2666 FAX

Paragon Publishing Systems
603/471-0077 Gen.
603/471-0501 FAX

Paramount Interactive
415/812-8200 Gen.
415/813-8055 FAX

Park Place Productions
619/929-2010 Gen.
619/929-2020 FAX

Passport Designs, Inc.
415/726-0280 Gen.

PC CompoNet, Inc.
310/943-9878 Gen.
310/947-1131 FAX

Penton Overseas, Inc.
619/431-0060 Gen.
800/748-5804 Sales
619/431-8110 FAX

Philips Interactive Media Systems
310/473-4136 Gen.
310/479-5937 FAX

**Philips Professional Publishing
International**
303/440-0669 Gen.
303/443-8242 FAX

Photos On Disk
916/933-5554 Gen. and FAX

The Pier Exchange
716/875-4931 Gen.
800/438-9734 Sales
716/875-4931 FAX

Pixar
510/236-4000 Gen.
510/236-0388 FAX.

Pop Rocket, Inc.
415/731-9112 Gen.
415/731-1710 FAX

Power User
814/864-4666 Gen.
800/424-0234 Sales
814/864-3993 FAX

Prentice Hall
212/373-8830 Gen.
212/373-8642 FAX

Presto Studios, Inc.
619/689-4895 Gen.
619/689-8397 FAX

Pro CD, Inc.
617/631-9200 Gen.
617/631-9299 FAX

Prosonus
818/766-5221 Gen.
800/999-6191 Sales
818/766-6098 FAX

Q Systems Research Corporation
212/941-1440 Gen.
212/941-7960 FAX

Quality Learning Systems
416/492-3838 Gen.

Quanta Press, Inc.
612/379-3956
612/623-4570 FAX

Quanta Press Inc./Krea Technology
612/379-3956 Gen.

Quantum Leap Technologies, Inc.
305/446-4141 Gen.
800/762-2877 Sales
305/446-4074 FAX

Queue
203/335-0906 Gen.
800/232-2224 Sales
203/336-2481 FAX

R&R Development Corporation
212/929-2206 Gen.

Random House, Inc.
212/751-2600 Gen.

Reactor, Inc.
312/573-0800 Gen.
312/573-0891 FAX

ReadySoft, Inc.
905/475-4801 Gen.
905/764-8867 FAX

Reed Reference Publishing
908/771-8676 Gen.
800/521-8110 Sales
908/665-3528 FAX

Reference Press
512/454-7778 Gen.

Research Publications, Inc.
203/397-2600 Gen.
800/444-0799 Sales
203/397-3893 FAX

Revell-Monogram, Inc.
708/966-3500 Gen.
203/397-3893 FAX

ROM Publishers, Inc.
402/476-6234 Gen.

Roth Publishing, Inc.
516/466-3676 Gen.
800/899-7684 Sales
516/829-7746 FAX

S & S Enterprises/ Just Software
708/257-7616 Gen.
800/766-3472 Sales
708/257-9678 FAX.

Salem Press, Inc.
201/871-8668 Gen.
800/221-1592 Sales

San Francisco Canyon Co.
415/398-9957 Gen.
415/398-5998 FAX

Sanctuary Woods Multimedia Corporation
415/578-6340 Gen.
415/578-6344 FAX

Save-On Software
717/822-9767 Gen.
800/962-6107 Sales

ScanRom Publications
516/295-2237 Gen.
212/809-5570 Gen.
516/295-2240 FAX

Science for Kids
910/945-9000 Gen.
910/945-2500 FAX

Sega of America
415/508-2800 Gen.

SelectWare Technologies, Inc.
313/477-7340 Gen.
800/342-3366 Sales
313/477-6488 FAX

Semaphore Corporation
408/688-9200 Gen.
408/688-9200 FAX

Sierra On-Line, Inc.
209/683-4468 Gen.
209/649-0340 FAX

Silicon Alley
415/921-0409 Gen.
415/921-2834 FAX

SilverPlatter Information Inc.
617/769-2599 Gen.
800/343-0064 Sales
617/769-8763 FAX

Simon & Schuster
212/698-7000 Gen.
800/223-2336 Sales
212/698-7007 FAX

Sirius Publishing, Inc.
602/951-3288 Gen.
602/951-3884 FAX

Slater Hall Information Products
202/393-2666 Gen.
202/638-2248 FAX

Soft-Wright
303/329-6388 Gen.
303/329-0901 FAX

SoftLine Information, Inc.
203/968-8878 Gen.
203/968-2370 FAX

Software Marketing Corporation
602/893-3377 Gen.
602/893-2042 FAX

Software Mart, Inc.
512/346-7887 Gen.

Software Sorcery
619/452-9901 Gen.
619/452-5079 FAX

Software Toolworks
415/883-3000 Gen.
415/883-0367 FAX

Sonic Images Productions, Inc.
202/333-1063 Gen.

Sound Ideas
905/886-5000 Gen.
905/886-6800 FAX

Spectrum Holobyte
510/522-3584 Gen.
510/522-2138 FAX

Spinnaker Software
617/494-1200 Gen.
617/494-1219 FAX

St. Martin's Press
212/674-5151 Gen.
212/777-6359 FAX

Staff Directories, Ltd.
703/739-0900 Gen.

Strategic Simulations Corporation
408/737-6800 Gen.
408/737-6814 FAX

Sumeria, Inc.
415/904-0800 Gen.
415/904-0888 FAX

Sun Microsystems, Inc.
415/960-1300 Gen.
800/346-7111 Sales

SunShine
512/453-2334 Gen.

SunSoft, Inc.
415/960-1300 Gen.
800/227-9227 Sales
415/336-6218

SuperMac Technology
408/541-6100 Gen.
408/541-6150 FAX.

Syracuse Language Systems
315/478-6729 Gen.
315/478-6902 FAX

T/Maker Company
415/962-0195 Gen.
415/962-0201 FAX.

Tadpole Productions
703/471-7453 Gen.
703/471-1126 FAX

Takin Care of Business, Inc.
800/925-5304 Gen.
714/680-8876 FAX.

Tandy Corp.
817/390-2195 Gen.

Tax Analysts
703/533-4400 Gen.
800/955-3444 Sales
703/533-4444 FAX

TEC Systems
414/336-5715 Gen.
414/337-1585 FAX

Tech Pubs Hal, Inc.
201/507-0030 Gen.
201/507-0192 FAX

Telecentral
317/328-9917 Gen.
800/799-9917 Sales
317/293-3856 FAX

Texas Caviar, Inc.
512/346-7887 Gen.
512/346-1393 FAX

The Discovery Channel
301/986-1999 Gen.
301/986-4827 FAX

Time Warner Interactive Group
818/955-9999 Gen.
818/973-4552 FAX

Titus Software Corporation
818/709-3692 Gen.
818/709-6537 FAX

Totem Graphics
206/352-1851 Gen.

Trans World Intertainment
916/246-0738 Gen.
800/578-1545 Sales
916/246-2608 FAX

TTI
310/641-4622 Gen.
800/366-0136 Sales
310/641-4626 FAX

Turtle Beach Systems
717/843-6919 Gen.

U.S. Bureau of the Census
301/763-4100 Gen.
301/763-4794 FAX

U.S. Dept. of Commerce
202/377-2000 Gen.
202/454-5840 FAX

U.S. Geological Survey
703/648-4460 Gen.

U.S. Patent & Trademark Office
703/308-0322 Gen.
703/308-0493 FAX

Viacom New Media
708/520-4440 Gen.
708/459-7456 FAX

Virtual Gallery Corporation
713/621-9933 Gen.
713/621-9934 FAX

Virtual Reality Laboratories, Inc.
805/545-8515 Gen.

Visible Ink Software
800/735-4686 Gen.
313/961-6083 FAX

Vortex Interactive
619/929-8144 Gen.
619/929-8021 FAX

Voyager Company
914/591-5500 Gen.
800/446-2001 Sales
914/591-6484 FAX

VT Productions, Inc.
408/464-1554 Gen.

Walnut Creek CDROM
510/947-5996 Gen.
800/786-9907 Sales
510/674-0821 FAX

Wayzata Technology, Inc.
218/326-0597 Gen.
800/735-7321 Sales
218/326-0598 FAX

West Publishing Company
612/228-2500 Gen.
800/328-0109 Sales

Westwind Media
717/937-3000 Gen.
800/937-8555 Sales
717/937-3200 FAX

Whitestar Mageware
505/988-8989 Gen.
505/988-1642 FAX

Wilson Learning Corporation
612/944-2880 Gen.

Wings for Learning/Sunburst
914/747-3310 Gen.
800/321-7511 Sales
914/747-4109 FAX

Wizard Ware
800/548-7969 Gen.

Wolftone MultiMedia Publishing Co.
404/992-7500 Gen.

World Library, Inc.
714/748-7197 Gen.
800/443-0238 Sales
714/756-9511 FAX

Xiphias
310/841-2790 Gen.
310/841-2559 FAX

Xaos Tools
415/487-7000 Gen.

Ziff Communications Company
212/503-4400 Gen.
212/503-4414 FAX

Index

G

U

V